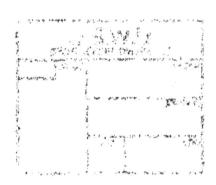

Bluetooth™ Profiles
The Definitive Guide

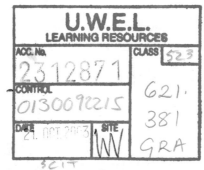

Dean A. Gratton

Prentice Hall PTR
Upper Saddle River, New Jersey 07458
www.phptr.com

ISBN 0-13-009221-5

9 780130 092212

95999

Library of Congress Cataloging-in-Publication Data

A CIP catalog record of this book can be obtained from the Library of Congress

Production Supervisor: Wil Mara
Publisher: Bernard M. Goodwin
Cover Design: Talar Boorujy
Cover Design Director: Jerry Votta
Editorial Assistant: Michelle Vincenti
Marketing Manager: Dan DePasquale
Buyer: Maura Zaldivar

© 2003 Pearson Education, Inc.
Publishing as Prentice Hall Professional Technical Rerefence
Upper Saddle River, New Jersey 07458

Prentice Hall books are widely used by corporations and government agencies for training, marketing, and resale.

For information regarding corporate and government bulk discounts, please contact Corporate and Government Sales, at 1-(800)-382-3419, or corpsales@pearsontechgroup.com.

Other company and product names mentioned herein are the trademarks or registered trademarks of their respective owners.

Printed in the United States of America
10 9 8 7 6 5 4 3 2 1

ISBN 0-13-009221-5

Pearson Education LTD.
Pearson Education Australia PTY, Limited
Pearson Education Singapore, Pte. Ltd.
Pearson Education North Asia Ltd.
Pearson Education Canada, Ltd.
Pearson Educación de Mexico, S.A. de C.V.
Pearson Education—Japan
Pearson Education Malaysia, Pte. Ltd.

To Sarah, my wife, my lover, my best friend: forever by my side.
To Tony, my father, who won't understand a bloody word!
To Sid and Joyce, my grandparents, for their support and guidance.
And finally, to Henry John Camden: this is just the beginning.

About Prentice Hall Professional Technical Reference

With origins reaching back to the industry's first computer science publishing program in the 1960s, Prentice Hall Professional Technical Reference (PH PTR) has developed into the leading provider of technical books in the world today. Formally launched as its own imprint in 1986, our editors now publish over 200 books annually, authored by leaders in the fields of computing, engineering, and business.

Our roots are firmly planted in the soil that gave rise to the technological revolution. Our bookshelf contains many of the industry's computing and engineering classics: Kernighan and Ritchie's *C Programming Language,* Nemeth's *UNIX System Administration Handbook,* Horstmann's *Core Java,* and Johnson's *High-Speed Digital Design.*

PH PTR acknowledges its auspicious beginnings while it looks to the future for inspiration. We continue to evolve and break new ground in publishing by providing today's professionals with tomorrow's solutions.

PRENTICE
HALL
PTR

Contents

Part 2—The Profiles in Depth

Foreword

This is a welcome book. Profiles have been one of the most ignored and least understood aspects of the whole Bluetooth specification. Within that is a very great concern, for profiles are what will ultimately make the Bluetooth specification either successful or one of the biggest failures within the wireless community. Unless everyone can be made aware of profiles and their effects—both developers and ultimately customers—then Bluetooth technology will not live up to its promise.

Behind that statement is Bluetooth's biggest problem—its promise. The Bluetooth specification started life as a pretty modest idea: its goal was to replace cable—in particular, the cable between a mobile phone and a laptop PC. Along the way, that concept has struck a chord with developers throughout every sector of electronics design. From games to refrigerators, planes to cars, everyone can see a brave new world free of the apron strings of pieces of wire. But the very diversity of applications brings a dangerous sting in its tail. If a single standard can solve so many diverse problems, how can we ensure compatibility? As we contemplate the benefits that wireless applications can bring, new scenarios come to mind. Traditionally, a keyboard would only connect to a PC; yet once it is wirelessly enabled, why shouldn't it connect to my phone to allow me to type text messages? Why shouldn't my phone talk to my rental car to tell it my favourite seat position and radio preferences? They may sound implausible, but prototypes of both are already working. And many more new connection paradigms will be presented and tested as Bluetooth hardware becomes more freely available.

As time progresses and more devices gain the ability to talk to each other, the concept of the Bluetooth specification becomes a Babel of interoperability issues. No manufacturer will have the foresight to perceive every combination in which their product could participate. Left to a free market, the customer experience would quickly degrade as users discovered that some products worked with others, but that each individual product had a different compatibility matrix. To make the increasingly complex edifice workable, it became apparent that some form of guideline needed to be established to cover the essentials of each major application area, but that these also needed to ensure they did not cramp creativity. A way had to be found that provided flexibility yet ensured a base level of user experience. A similar problem had already been identified and solved within DECT, which introduced a Generic Access Profile to make handsets from different manufacturers compatible. Bluetooth developers have learned from that experience and introduced Bluetooth profiles.

That is what this book explores. As I read through the initial proofs, I was drawn back to the full specification. It has grown steadily over the past year and that growth emphasises just how important profiles have become. It reminded me of the old Monty Python sketch where John Cleese is being interviewed as a Shakespearean Actor. On being questioned about the leading parts, he categorises their relative importance by the number of words spoken. If the same gauge were taken to Bluetooth, it would tell an interesting story. The hardware and radio is fully defined in approximately one hundred pages. The stack takes a further thousand, but the profiles are already way past that and growing on a daily basis. Yet despite their superiority in page count, they are largely ignored. Within the Bluetooth community, the talk is of items like RF sensitivity or HCI transport, but rarely of profiles. Many misunderstand them and seem to write them off as a simple API without realising their true worth. Profiles are the key to Bluetooth interoperability. Any Bluetooth designer who does not fully understand them develops products with immense risk, because without them we are throwing away the foundation of user experience.

I hope that the pages that follow will help to bring the profiles to life and instill their real importance into the reader. They are not just a final hoop to be jumped through to gain an approval certificate, but the bedrock upon which "real" Bluetooth applications are built. If customers are to respect the Bluetooth brand, they will expect products to work out of the box. If they don't, customers will shun the technology. First, customers will return products back to stores; then, customers will reject Bluetooth technology altogether. We have a duty to make it work and that means understanding and implementing profiles.

As with all books of this kind, what you will learn is only the beginning. I hope it will inspire you. As you read these pages, more working groups are developing additional profiles that further extend the bounds of Bluetooth's potential. As a reader who I assume is already interested in developing Bluetooth applications, I'd recommend you review and participate in the profile creation process.

I share Dean's enthusiasm—Bluetooth technology may never be the universal panacea that the marketing machine claims it to be, but properly implemented it can solve a remarkable number of problems and create a surprising number of new usage models.

This is a valuable volume on that route. Each reader who leaves it with a better under-standing of profiles will ultimately find that they are adding to the customer experience and by so doing helping the global success of the Bluetooth specification.

Nick Hunn
Managing Director
TDK Systems Europe

Preface

There must be something in the Belgium air, for it seems to inspire many people to write. My own experience of authoring a book began with an idea I conceived whilst slowly sipping a cool Trappist beer in the Triangel restaurant at the end of the wonderful Cogels Osylei in Antwerp. I was considering the Bluetooth Profiles specification and its effective implementation into the "grand scheme of things," when my eyes where drawn to Anneke, the landlady, as she placed several glasses of beer before expectant customers. Their contented reactions made me realise that effective profile implementation begins first and foremost with the customer or end-user. Building an understanding of user expectations from a union of observation and existing knowledge is the key to understanding the true value of profile development, both now and in the future.

My early career as a software engineer, developing software for the amusement industry, taught me the importance of creating the right *user experience.* For the user, the Bluetooth experience should be a wonderful and almost seamless transition from having cables to having no cables. *For all intents and purposes,* the user should be unaware that a Bluetooth enabled application sits beneath the wireless communication tools at their disposal.

I look upon the profile specification as being the veins within a leaf. They provide support and structure, but without their surrounding matter they have no purpose and no reason to exist. A comprehensive understanding of the user experience is fundamental to the development of future Bluetooth Profiles and this philosophy forms the foundation for the entire book. In essence, I hope to provide all developers and researchers with the necessary understanding to find their own answers to the questions raised by the prospect of a world without wires.

I have worked within the Bluetooth industry for a number of years and have witnessed first hand the various implementations that are currently available from numerous vendors. The English novelist Aldous Huxley once said "Consistency is contrary to nature, contrary to life. The only completely consistent people are dead." This quote has particular meaning for the book. The old ways are slowly slipping away and, as voyagers and explorers in this exciting new arena, we have an opportunity to cross new boundaries and shape the technological world of the future. *Bluetooth Profiles* will enable you to gain an holistic understanding of the technology from both a developmental and consumer perspective; as such, it should give you the scope and insight to become a key contributor to the future of wireless communications.

Acknowledgements

If you are reading this, then I have actually done it: I have managed to write my first book. This undertaking has certainly been enjoyable, although there were times when the realisation of my editorial deadline loomed large and seemed a heavy weight to bear. First and foremost I must thank Bernard Goodwin for giving me the opportunity to have my work published.

In writing this book, I have had a considerable amount of support and encouragement from numerous people in the wireless industry along with friends and family: I thank them all for their support.

In illustrating these profiles, I have sought input from a number of leading organisations that have already invested in and developed these products. I would like to both acknowledge and thank each of them for their support. A special thanks to Nick Hunn of TDK Systems Europe (www.tdksys.com) for not only writing the foreword to this book, but for ultimately introducing me to Bluetooth technology and for providing me with both technical support and product-related material.

Special thanks also to Tom Siep of the Bluetooth Special Interest Group (www.bluetooth.com), Willy Sagefalk of Axis Communications (www.axis.com), Plantronics (www.plantronics.com), Troy Holtby of 3Com Corporation (www.3com.com), Steve Beckers and Mirella Kimpen of Alcatel Microelectronics (www.alcatelmicroelectronics.com) and Jennifer Bray of Cambridge Silicon Radio (www.csr.com) for providing me with both technical support and product related material.

xvii

Finally, I want to thank my good friend Pierre Tanner of Little Back Room Designs (www.lbrd-photography.co.uk) for your talent in making me look particularly dashing in the *About the Author* section.   .

Introduction

We have all heard the stories and read the headlines: Bluetooth technology is set to become *the* revolutionary communications tool that will affect all our lives in one form or another. It will simplify the operation and installation of both new and existing products. Despite numerous vendors providing a vast range of exciting wireless merchandise, its functionality will be, for the most part, invisible and seamless. After all, Bluetooth's greatest gift will inevitably be its user-transparency. It will become an invisible friend that no-one sees yet whose presence will undoubtedly impact upon the lives of us all, leaving us wondering how we ever managed without it.

This book does not aim to provide you with a history of Bluetooth technology, nor does it explain why it was created. Instead, it embodies the firm belief that it is already here. *Bluetooth Profiles* is primarily intended for engineers who are about to embark upon developing new profiles, as well as those wishing to understand, in greater depth, the Bluetooth Profiles specification. However, its functionality goes far deeper than that. From a marketing point of view, the book aims to illustrate the importance of the user perspective within profile development. In essence, it will enable you to get a sense of what needs to be established from a consumer-oriented stance. There are a number of commercial models of the Bluetooth specification in action that reinforce the importance of the user. This, above all else, is crucial when considering the development of products that may well become 'life-changing' in their on-shelf significance.

The creation of the current specification is an acknowledgement of the dedication of a large community, which has committed both its time and effort to produce a new wireless philosophy. This introduction provides you with an overview of what you can expect to find within the book, summarising its structure and allowing it to be used as a useful reference.

In Part I, *Building On Solid Foundations,* we take a macro-view of the Bluetooth protocol stack and establish a basic understanding of its various dependent peripherals. An assumption is made here about the reader; it is assumed that you already have a Bluetooth protocol stack and that you are now ready to provide working applications. *Bluetooth Profiles* will help you overcome the deep-seated question of 'how do I do it?' With this in mind, we take a look at the currently available development kits and explore their contribution to the development process. The book by no means makes any recommendations or provides any bias, but merely offers you, the developer, a series of examples on which to base your own decision. Finally, this section discusses the value of *Interoperability.* The knowledge that vendorA will seamlessly interoperate with vendorB fills the user with confidence and promotes future utilisation. The Bluetooth Profiles specification acknowledges the need for applications and end-user functionality to have common characteristics. Users will be able to interact with many vendors' products knowing that these characteristics will be an integral part of the final product.

The *Profiles In Depth* section explores how each profile might be perceived by the user. It is particularly concerned with what the user's experience should be and what the dependencies are in each instance. Each profile chapter then summarises the contents into an easily digestible format aimed at both the intermediate and advanced developer; these may also be used as quick reference chapters. You will notice when reading through the section that the dependencies are shared between many profiles and that, consequently, the chapters have some duplication. This is entirely intentional and from a tutorial perspective has great value, as it will allow you to learn about each profile on an individual basis, without the constant need to flick between chapters for relevant information. I hope that this format will make your journey of discovery more enjoyable and will further demonstrate the simplistic nature of the profile composites. Without a doubt, it is an extremely important section of the book; the philosophy throughout is all about getting this user experience absolutely right. The user should be, for the most part, totally unaware of the technology that sits beneath such applications and devices, taking completely for granted that the product will do 'exactly what it says on the box'.

Our last section, Part III, *The New Profiles* considers the newer profiles that are emerging from the Bluetooth Working Groups. Here, the book emphasises the notion that each company or developer has the power to create a profile; of course this is, as always, subject to the approval of the Bluetooth *Special Interest Group* (SIG). There is great potential for us all to create innumerable diverse applications, limited only by our imaginations. This book will, I hope, encourage you to 'spread your wings' and let your imagination take flight. Perhaps the greatest message the book has to impart, or perhaps reinforce, is the knowledge that it takes a team of dedicated, imaginative software and hardware engineers to bring about better and more creative wireless products: always with the end user in mind. As part of this team, you have an amazing opportunity to become an integral contributor to the future success and diversity of Bluetooth.

Part 1

BUILDING ON SOLID FOUNDATIONS

With the enormous potential for Bluetooth applications we start the book with an appraisal of the Specification of the Bluetooth System: Core. The part title *Building On Solid Foundations,* relates particularly to the components that make up the Bluetooth protocol stack, as this forms the foundation from which all profiles are conceived. In Chapter 1, we explore broadly the structure of the stack, providing emphasis on profile development and the specific components that are required to realise your application. We further explore the purpose of the profiles and consider what they ultimately achieve.

Numerous stack and development kit vendors offer bespoke and tailored packages to help overcome the initial hurdle faced when embarking upon the development of Bluetooth enabled products. We reflect upon how an *Application Programming Interface* (API) is realised from the various protocols, which underlie a large part of both the stack and the kits' functionality. In our discussion of available stacks, we also consider the benefit of using third parties in helping create your Bluetooth application and ultimately advancing its route to market.

1

My Bluetooth Application

1.1 INTRODUCTION

Bluetooth Profiles is concerned primarily with the development of Bluetooth specific applications, which in turn encompass the requirements as defined by the Specification of the Bluetooth System: Profiles, v1.1. Bluetooth applications in their infancy were injected into public view and subject to immediate expectations. For Bluetooth technology to become a viable wireless solution, we had to move from the wonder and mini-celebrations[1] that were invoked when we all initially created our first successful connections. At various stages of development, numerous emotions were experienced. We were able to progress from creating our first connection to performing a file transfer over an emulated serial port, using a legacy application; then came synchronisation and so on. Yet, in our peripheral vision, we gained a glimpse of the sales and marketing team constantly pressing us with numerous questions—when will it be ready?, when will it jump through this hoop?, and when will it perform that triple-summersault? In essence, we were not developing Bluetooth applications fast enough. Indeed, the Bluetooth marketing machine began chugging away long before the first products were anywhere near release, resulting

---

[1]The author recalls on one occasion (not wanting to imply that it happened that often), but as a consultant software engineer, accompanied by a firmware and a hardware engineer, we all realised that our first Bluetooth connection and subsequent file transfer was successful and consequently celebrated by opening a bottle of champagne.

in a seemingly endless wait for the promised revolution to arrive. An enormous amount of frustration was inevitable for all concerned, as issues of core functionality were thrashed out in the boardrooms of manufacturers around the globe. This resulted in the underlying tone of Bluetooth promotion resting, to a greater extent, upon the software and hardware embodiment of the products rather than on the users' experience of utilising Bluetooth technology. Increasingly, however, these experiential elements are being viewed as a primary route for achieving critical mass and, as a result, the public is finally beginning to open up to the possibilities of a wireless world.

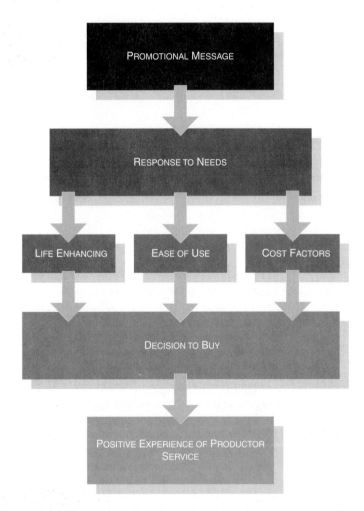

Figure 1-1   The psychological elements of the buying process that hold particular value to future Bluetooth developers. The process is cyclical, where positive feedback re-enters the promotional message.

Figure 1-1 illustrates the psychological elements of the buying process that hold particular value to future Bluetooth developers; here, we can view the progression from a positive buyer experience to a new promotional message as a cycle of user-oriented market growth. Indeed, if we gain nothing else from reviewing the Bluetooth market, we should, at the very least, reinforce within ourselves the importance, from a development perspective, of seriously applying real-world usage potential to future Bluetooth products.

The promotional drive of Bluetooth technology, to date, has naturally taken the traditional routes of press, collateral and event opportunities through conferences and, of course, the ever-popular Unplugfests; but the best promotion of potential Bluetooth applications will, without a doubt, emerge through the users themselves. Consumer enthusiasm toward the freedom afforded by the adoption of Bluetooth-enabled electronics will inevitably become highly contagious. At home and in the office, as with any technology, it will continue to evolve. The future will almost certainly see it become an accepted part of everyday life.

1.2   WHAT ARE BLUETOOTH PROFILES?

Time and time again, developers, sales, marketing and users often wonder and ask what are the Bluetooth Profiles? Profiles enable end-user functionality by defining user and behaviour characteristics. They have many defining objectives, one of which is to achieve a level of interoperability between manufacturers. In defining their functionality, certain expectations are made of the underlying Bluetooth protocol stack. Each profile defines what features of the stack are required and how they are subsequently used. In Figure 1-2, we illustrate the dependencies of all the profiles within the current specification as a hierarchal organisation. In Figure 1-3, we illustrate the components that make up a typical Bluetooth protocol stack.

As an application developer, you will embody the functionality within your Bluetooth specific application and utilise the underlying capabilities of a Bluetooth protocol stack through an *Application Programming Interface* (API). All profiles define a set of user interface expectations and these will surface through your applications to the user. The user will become familiar with the terminology and should experience a commonality of features between the various manufacturers' products. This is evident in the common terminology mandated by the Profiles as to what should be described to the user. In one such example, a user is prompted to enter a *Bluetooth Passkey*, which will be common to all products whether embedded (mobile phones, wireless modems and so on) or used in a Microsoft Windows or Linux operating system environment.

The Profiles define a minimum set of characteristics that should be inherent in all products. Manufacturers should avoid a re-education of the 'user-population' by adhering to the philosophy that users have already developed a relationship with the technology that surrounds them on a daily basis. The purpose of any new technology should be that of support rather than suppression.

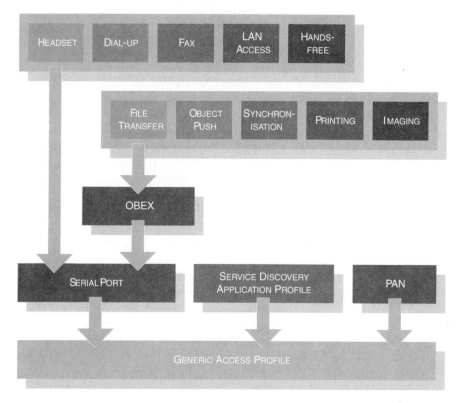

Figure 1-2   An hierarchal organisation of the current profiles, illustrating the dependent profiles.

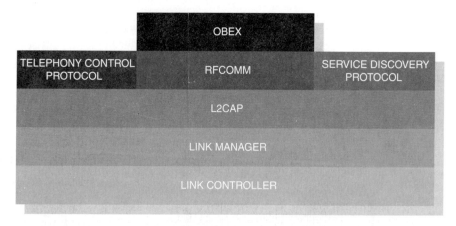

Figure 1-3   A typical structure forming the components that make up a Bluetooth protocol stack.

1.3   DEVELOPING BLUETOOTH APPLICATIONS

Numerous Bluetooth products have already emerged onto the marketplace. Yet this is just the beginning of the 'market stream,' as both the variety of applications and rate of release are expected to grow considerably over the next few years. The products form the end-function for the user; they are the embodiment of hardware, software, manufacturing, production, sweat and tears. As such, they come in many guises: integrated or stand-alone applications on a Microsoft or Linux operating system. Alongside these, we have witnessed the release of products that are embedded: mobile phones, *Personal Digital Assistants* (PDAs) and cordless handsets.

With the prospect of undertaking the development of a new product, the engineer can draw upon various development suites that aid in the creation of both hardware and software. Much of the groundwork has already been covered, making it unnecessary to 're-invent the wheel'.

Bluetooth development kits themselves offer various levels of support—from a low- or high-level perspective. Each kit is designed to offer various benefits to the developer, obviously depending upon what you need to achieve. The primary, generic purpose of all development kits is to provide a supported core tool for the development of your new and unique Bluetooth application, aiding in your development life-cycle and certainly making life easier by allowing you rapid realisation of your product expectations. In addition to this generic primary benefit, each kit will 'sing its own praises' by reinforcing a number of product-specific value-added traits such as free developer seminars, access to knowledge base directories, technical training or round the clock support.

A general premise is that *Host Controller Interface* (HCI) or *Link Manager* (LM) commands are entered through a common window, which affords the developer the ability to observe a variety of operational data simultaneously. Typically, this is the minimum expectation of a development suite. Common viewable operations include protocol monitoring through the stack layers, message exchanges and the transmission and monitoring of individual commands or events, typically at the higher-layers, such as *L2CAP*, *RFCOMM* and *SDP*. Through this observation portal, the developer is also equipped with

Table 1-1   Key features that form Cambridge Silicon Radio's Casira development system.

FEATURES
Fully Bluetooth Compliant to v1.1
Various interfaces for RS232, USB, PCM and Synchronous Serial
Drivers to support USB and UART
A BlueCore Software Development Kit
Flash tools for easy upgrading of firmware

Figure 1-4   The Casira development system from Cambridge Silicon Radio.
(Courtesy of Cambridge Silicon Radio.)

a powerful tool for code debugging and editing. Another key benefit to the kits is their in-
nate teaching ability in that the kits provide an immediate professional development environment for those new to Bluetooth Profiles and wishing to understand the Bluetooth
protocol in greater depth. It also demonstrates how each layer of the stack interacts with
each other. By studying the readily available source code within any Bluetooth development kit, you instantly arm yourself with the confidence of a proven application template
on which to evolve your individual knowledge and abilities.

Your development kit may come complete with a full Bluetooth protocol stack,
which will be reconfigurable for different interfaces between the Bluetooth host and host
controller; there will be more about this later on in this chapter. All kits are linked to a

Table 1-2   Key features that form Alcatel Microelectronics MTC-60180 development
system.

FEATURES
Fully Bluetooth v1.1 qualified
Various interfaces for UART, PCM and GCI
BlueRF compatible
Integrated software on embedded flash up to HCI
Easy transition from Flash to ROM for a more cost-effective solution

particular manufacturer's device and, as such, there may well be some company-specific constraints surrounding the APIs needed to design an application. This does not alter the fact that, by using a development kit, much of the work has already been accomplished on your behalf. From a marketing perspective, any organisation planning to provide a Bluetooth development kit would be naïve not to consider any promotional opportunities attached to such an offering.

1.4   UNDERSTANDING THE BLUETOOTH PROTOCOL STACK

Many companies have invested considerable effort in developing Bluetooth protocol stack solutions, which can be purchased off the shelf or tailored for a particular project, where minimum development effort is required; numerous companies have also offered *Open Source*[2] solutions. With a solid foundation in a *Software Development Kit* (SDK), developers can realise their specific applications with greater speed and economic efficiency. Solutions can be tailored for Microsoft Windows or Linux-based operating systems as well as embedded platforms. In the following sections, we analyse in some more detail the relationship of the Profile and Protocol and further understand the interaction between the host and host controller.

Figure 1-5   The MTC-60180 development system from Alcatel Microelectronics. (Courtesy of Alcatel Microelectronics.)

---

[2]Open Source is the availability of source code to an application where other developers can improve and modify it to meet their own development expectations.

1.4.1 The Profile and the Protocol

In our earlier discussion, we touched upon the purpose and objectives that the Profiles serve. In development terms, the creation of an end-function, is dependent upon the realisation of a Profile specification using the underlying protocol. The Profile addresses the characterisations by stipulating what it expects from the Bluetooth protocol stack. How that application manifests itself to the outside world is also prescribed by the requirement defined in the Profile. With an SDK, a developer may utilise the features of a Bluetooth protocol stack by addressing core functionality through an API. As a company wishing to develop Bluetooth applications, an API may have already been tailored to meet with your specific requirements. In Figure 1-6, we further illustrate the structure of the stack where an API has been imposed upon the key components, in turn exposing core functionality to the application developer.

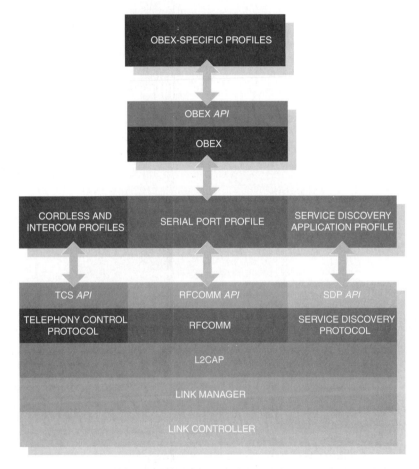

Figure 1-6 The Bluetooth protocol stack exposes APIs throughout, where application developers utilise these interfaces to realise end-user functionality.

Using Figure 1-6 as our example illustration, APIs such as that illustrated in Table 1-3 and Table 1-4 can be used to control and manipulate core functionality at the heart of the Bluetooth protocol stack.

In Table 1-3 an application may use these APIs in order to quickly establish an RFCOMM connection to its peer device; whereas Table 1-4 illustrates some possible APIs that may be used to learn of the services of devices that are in radio range.

1.4.2 Understanding the Bluetooth Host

The Bluetooth *Host* is the set of protocol higher-layers provided to manipulate and control the *Host Controller*; we provide this illustration in Figure 1-7. This interface is controlled through the HCI and most Bluetooth development kits are exposed at this level. Conceptually, the HCI is not a layer, but forms the *Hardware Abstract Layer* (HAL), where any company's host controller can be plugged into the host and work together transparently; the host can be considered hardware independent.

The HCI has been constructed to facilitate many transport layers to include *Universal Serial Bus* (USB), *Universal Asynchronous Receiver/Transmitter* (UART) and RS232. This provides diversity in the availability of development kits where the various applications may differ. In one such example, a USB interface may be provided for the host controller to interact with the host, where a USB dongle is inserted into a notebook device, which houses the host. A connection is established over the USB interface and the host can manipulate and control the host controller that exists on the USB dongle.

1.4.3 Understanding the Bluetooth Host Controller

The Bluetooth *Host Controller* is the set of protocol lower-layers provided to manipulate and control the *radio unit;* we provide this illustration in Figure 1-8. The Host Controller

Table 1-3 Some typical APIs that would be used to open and close an RFCOMM connection as well as transmit and receive data over the connection.

API	DESCRIPTION
RFCOMM_OpenConnection	An API function that would be used to open or create a communications link with the peer device.
RFCOMM_CloseConnection	An API function that would be used to close or disconnect a communications link with the peer device.
RFCOMM_TxData	An API function that would be used to transmit data to the peer device.
RFCOMM_RxData	An API function that would be used to receive data from the peer device.

Table 1-4   Some typical APIs that would be used to retrieve service information
from a remote device.

API	DESCRIPTION
SDP_ErrorResponse	An API function, which is used to signal an incorrectly formatted request from the client.
SDP_ServiceSearchRequest SDP_ServiceSearchResponse	These APIs are used in combination to instigate a search request to identify corresponding records held within a server.
SDP_ServiceAttributeRequest SDP_ServiceAttributeResponse	These APIs are used in combination to retrieve specific attribute record information from a server.
SDP_ServiceSearchAttributeRequest SDP_ServiceSearchAttributeResponse	Finally, these APIs are used in combination to encompass both the functionality of the SDP_ServiceSearchRequest and SDP_ServiceAttributeRequest. This functionality attempts to reduce the SDP traffic when seeking specific services.

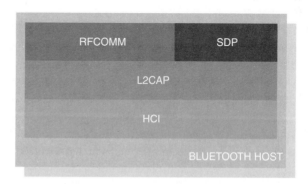

Figure 1-7   An implementation of a host, which forms part of the higher-
layers of the Bluetooth protocol stack.

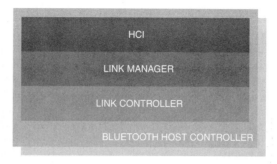

Figure 1-8   An implementation of a host controller, which forms part of the
lower-layers of the Bluetooth protocol stack.

is controlled through the HCI, which in turn is responsible for link management and the
over the air-interface.

1.5   INTEROPERABILITY

The Bluetooth *Special Interest Group* (SIG) is astutely sensitive to the prominence of interoperability within the marketplace. Accordingly, all specifications are subject to inten-
sive qualification prior to a licence for use being granted. Events such as Unplugfests hold
great value, as they allow manufacturers to test the interoperability of their individual
products with each other. From a marketing perspective, achieving ease of interoperability is paramount for any manufacturer's product to succeed in the marketplace. A key tool
of the Profiles is to provide a base frame structure that transcends all branding and ultimately provides the interoperability that, as developers, we depend upon in order to see
our product evolve from sketchpad to shelf. The only way to ensure compatibility is to actually test against a range of reference devices. To this end, a number of test labs and tools
have emerged, all pledging to make interoperability issues vanish from any proposed
product specification. In the following section we discuss, in part, the qualification
process, which leads to a fully qualified and compliant Bluetooth product.

1.6   QUALIFICATION

Bluetooth Qualification, as its name suggests relates to the requirement that all Bluetooth
products are developed in accordance with the current set of Bluetooth Specifications, as
required by the Bluetooth Adopters agreement. The base establishment of the rules and
procedures surrounding the qualification of a product is called the *Bluetooth Qualification
Programme* (BQP). All guidelines and practices of the BPQ are formalised by the *Bluetooth Qualification Review Board* (BQRB), which in turn, is chartered by the Bluetooth

Table 1-5   The steps undertaken as outlined by the qualification guidelines.

QUALIFICATION
The applicant forms an agreement with the Bluetooth SIG to become a Member.
The Member sources information relating to relevant test specifications; test case reference lists; test case mapping table; a program reference document and ICS/IXIT Proforma.
The Member appoints a Bluetooth Qualification Body (BQB) to assist them in the qualification process.
The Member's material is submitted for the Compliance Folder to the BQB.
Prepare and submit an application for each Bluetooth product to the BQB.
The Member performs all test cases by an accredited *Bluetooth Qualification Test Facility* (BQTF), where test reports are submitted to the compliance folder.

SIG via the *Programme Directive* (PD). Promoters of the Bluetooth SIG will select delegates to join the BQRB when required to do so. The process of qualification has been devised with the developer in mind and holds strong the mission of protecting rather than of stifling its natural evolution.

In general, product qualification can be accomplished using the following steps, as laid out within the current qualification guidelines; this is also summarised in Table 1-5. In Figure 1-9, we illustrate the hierarchal delegation of the qualification programme.

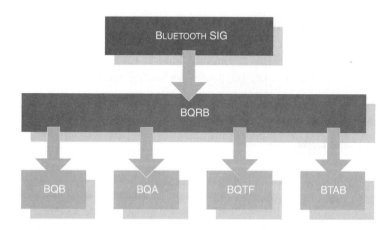

Figure 1-9   The authoritative delegation for the Bluetooth Qualification
            Programme.

1.7 SUMMARY

- Bluetooth Profiles define a set of common characteristics at the user interface level.
- Profiles help establish commonality between products and establish commonality for the user's experience.
- The Profiles also encourage interoperability with all manufacturers.
- Many development kits are available to help application developers' realise their products much more quickly.
- Some development kits are provided with SDKs, which further alleviate the need to re-invent the wheel.
- The specifications make a clear distinction between the host and host controller.
- The host forms part of the higher-layers, whereas the host controller forms part of the lower-layer structure.
- When products are developed, they must be qualified to ascertain their conformance against the Bluetooth specifications.
- Products that are qualified are certified as compliant.

Part 2

THE PROFILES IN DEPTH

In this section, we enter the heart and principal purpose of the book. We explore in some detail the application potential and offer numerous examples of usage models. We also consider the user interface characteristics of each profile and review the profile dependencies provided within the specification.

The implementation of a profile ultimately provides an end-user function and encourages a common theme for interoperability. There are thirteen profiles in the current v1.1 specification; each profile presented in this section can be reviewed independently as a self-contained pocket reference for the reader. As such, there is no need to cross-reference other chapters.

Each chapter is laid out in a structured way to introduce a profile from a conceptual point-of-view and to stimulate the growth of further ideas. An exploratory presentation is made of typical user expectations, focusing primarily upon how a user might perceive the end-functionality of a given profile with illustrative examples.

Please note that some content is shared by the 'Lifting the Lid' sections of the various profile chapters in Part Two. This is entirely deliberate on the part of the author; the structure is intended to allow the reader to gain a comprehensive understanding of each profile on an individual basis, without the need for continual cross-referencing. It also illustrates the simplicity of application development as the same dependencies can be seen at work within a variety of profiles.

2

The Generic
Access Profile

2.1 INTRODUCTION

The *Generic Access Profile* establishes a level of basic functionality, abstracted from the core protocol components. In Figure 2-1, we illustrate the components that make up the core protocol, where at the upper-edge of the illustrated components, implementers would establish function primitives in the form of an *Application Programming Interface* (API). This exposed API would then allow implementers to realise their profile requirements. In turn, this ultimately would allow them to construct Bluetooth applications.

Furthermore, providing this basic set of rules and procedures it then becomes sufficient to realise that the behaviour of such devices is governed with simple rules that relate to their connectivity, discoverability and common characteristics at the user interface level, with some additional emphasis provided for security. These rules and procedures are used to establish commonality between products, which will ultimately achieve a cohesive user experience.

All *foundation profiles*[1] have their basis in the Generic Access Profile. That said, this profile outlines a set of comprehensive requirements that may be used in the *govern-*

---

[1]The reference to *foundation profiles* refers to the initial set of proposed profiles that form the Specification of the Bluetooth System: Profiles, v1.1. It is used to distinguish it from the new profiles that are being proposed and may form part of a future release of the specification.

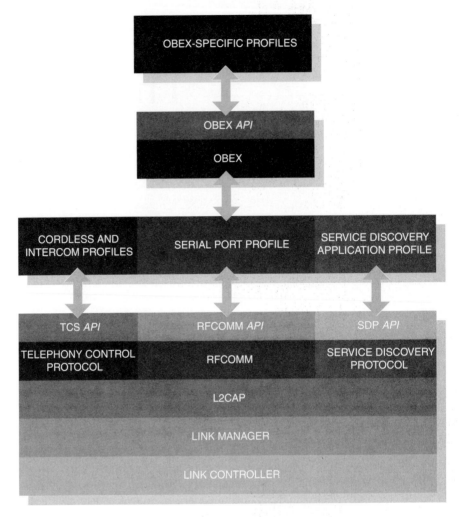

Figure 2-1   The range of layers covered by the Generic Access Profile.

ing profile;[2] for instance, if a feature in the Generic Access Profile is described as optional, it may be determined that a feature should be mandatory in the governing profile. This chapter aims to build upon your understanding of this fundamental profile and allow you to strengthen your knowledge of the features which make up both it and its governing profiles.

---

[2]The reference to *governing profile* is used to distinguish the requirements of the Generic Access Profile and that of another profile. The governing profile will sometimes require other features that may be mandatory, whereas the corresponding feature in the Generic Access Profile may be optional.

Table 2-1   The list of requirements (and symbols) used to denote the inclusion
or exclusion of specific features within a profile.

REQUIREMENT	SYMBOL	DESCRIPTION
Mandatory	M	A feature that must be supported by a profile.
Optional	O	A feature that may be used by a profile.
Conditional	C	A feature that may be used by a profile, if other capabilities are provided.
Excluded	X	A feature that, although possibly supported by the device, will not be used by the profile.
Not Applicable	N/A	A feature that is not applicable for the operation of that profile.

2.2   DEFINING PROFILE REQUIREMENTS

In providing a comprehensive understanding of profile implementation, it is important to emphasise certain key features. These features are often denoted with degrees of adoption and are described as *mandatory, optional, conditional, excluded* and *not applicable*. Table 2-1 condenses the categorisation of these key features and offers clarification to their meaning, as they will be referred to during the course of this book.

2.3   PROFILE PRINCIPLES

In our introduction, we touched upon the notion that a set of rules and procedures exist to help govern the operation of Bluetooth-enabled devices, which support the Generic Access Profile. The profile further provides clarification with regards to the dependencies as shown in our earlier illustration and especially describes how each component realises such functionality. Essentially, what is achieved here is a clear definition of the requirements on the core components that make up the Bluetooth protocol stack; we will discuss this in more detail later on.

In general, *DeviceA* represents the initiating party and *DeviceB* represents the accepting party. The terms are often used interchangeably, when describing specific operations in various contexts and are provided here for reference. The Generic Access Profile describes procedures for two devices that wish to discover and connect to the services on offer, although participating devices are not necessarily restricted to this two-way communication. In Figure 2-2, we demonstrate that the central notebook is capable of connecting to many devices that are in radio range, where these devices can offer a variety of services. In the example shown, the PDA may then independently wish to connect to the printer.

The operations of DeviceA and DeviceB are used to facilitate the general procedures as previously outlined, although we have touched upon deviations that may occur in

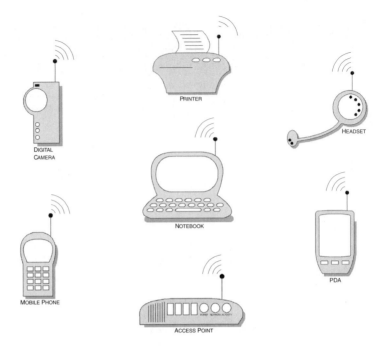

Figure 2-2   The Generic Access Profile provides a comprehensive set of procedures for DeviceA (the Notebook in this example) that wishes
to connect to and make use of the services provided by DeviceB
(let us say the PDA). However, the PDA may independently initiate a connection to another Bluetooth-enabled device.

other profiles. DeviceB may operate several profiles (or services) and, as such, the implementation of DeviceB may differ to accommodate these variations. In simple terms, the
Generic Access Profile provides the foundation upon which other profiles can be based.

This profile does not mandate the operation of a master-slave switch; this is specifically addressed by the needs of the governing profile. It is DeviceB that usually determines whether or not it has a need to become master and in one such example, DeviceB
may already be the master of an existing piconet and therefore may insist that it remains
master of that relationship. Alternatively, DeviceA may decide that a role-switch is not
permitted and choose to remain master as well. In either case, the device may decide not
to continue and fail the link establishment altogether.

It is advisable that the role-switch is performed immediately after the physical-link
is established, where the connection request parameters[3] determine whether or not a role-
switch can be performed. It is the governing profile that will ultimately determine whether
or not master-slave switching is mandatory. In another example, a master-slave switch is

---

[3]The flexibility of the Bluetooth protocol stack, in particular the various HCI and LMP commands available,
allow various methods of creating a successful ACL connection. The text refers to one particular example of a
connection set-up.

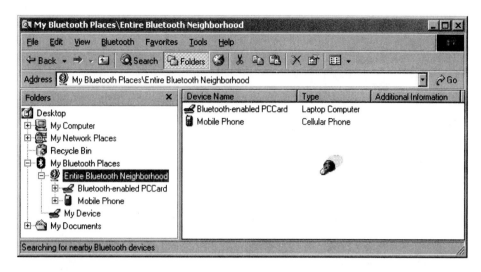

Figure 2-3 The screen shot shows the results of a device discovery procedure where the list of expected parameters are named according
to the general rules provided within the Generic Access Profile.
(Courtesy of TDK Systems Europe.)

mandatory if the LAN Access Profile is configured for multi-user mode; see the *LAN Access Profile*, Chapter 10 for more information.

2.4   USER EXPECTATIONS

The Generic Access Profile provides generic capabilities for the user who, in turn, will be capable of connecting to any device and determining the services available to him or her. This generic capability should be inherent within different manufacturers' products and as such interoperate regardless. This seamless and transparent operation makes Bluetooth technology the success it is today.

What allows this operation to be successful is the common set of rules and procedures that govern the generic behaviour of Bluetooth-enabled devices. These can also be extended to naming conventions used at the user interface level, where the user wishes to discover available devices in radio range. The user will inevitably come across several parameters that are used to uniquely identify a device and its services.

The following sections provide the common naming conventions that the user will come across at the user interface level. In the later sections, discoverability, connectability and pairing procedures are also explored.

2.4.1   Bluetooth Parameters

As we have already discussed, the user will come across several names, which are used to identify the device. On discovering the capabilities of a device, the user will learn of its name and its class, as well as its unique Bluetooth address. In Figure 2-3 and Figure 2-4,

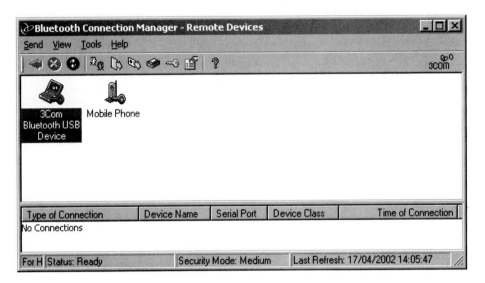

Figure 2-4   The screen shot shows the results of a device discovery procedure where the list of expected parameters are named according
to the general rules provided within the Generic Access Profile
(the 3Com Bluetooth Connection Manager has discovered another 3Com device and a mobile phone is also shown).

the parameters are disclosed to the inquiring device when the user performs a device discovery operation.

2.4.1.1 Bluetooth Device Address.   The *Bluetooth Device Address* parameter
uniquely identifies the Bluetooth device and is often referred to as BD_ADDR at the baseband level. For every Bluetooth device, there will be a unique address assigned to it. It is
based upon the *Media Access Control* (MAC) address notation, which is already used to
uniquely identify a computer that is connected to a *Local Area Network* (LAN). The
BD_ADDR is retrieved during an inquiry or device discovery procedure and is described
as the *Bluetooth Device Address* at the user interface level as previously shown in Figure
2-3 and Figure 2-4.

We show in Table 2-2, the HCI_Read_BD_ADDR command, which is used to request the device address from the local device and the Command_Complete event is
used to acknowledge completion of the request. In the return parameters, the success of
the command is determined by the Status parameter and the BD_ADDR parameter will
contain the address of the local device.

At the baseband level, BD_ADDR is represented as 48-bits; however, the user will
see a 12 byte hexadecimal notation, where this representation may be subsectioned for an
easy read. The presentation of this number will have the *most-significant byte* (MSB) and
least-significant byte (LSB) shown from left-to-right.

Table 2-2   The command and event used in combination to retrieve the local Bluetooth Address.

COMMAND	PARAMETERS
HCI_Read_BD_ADDR	Status BD_ADDR
EVENT	**PARAMETERS**
Command_Complete	Num_HCI_Command_Packets Command_OpCode Return_Parameters

2.4.1.2   Bluetooth Device Name.   When performing a device discovery procedure, a user-friendly name is also retrieved and presented to the user, as we have seen in Figure 2-3 and Figure 2-4. The unique Bluetooth address is not a sufficient description to determine what the device is capable of and, as such, a user-friendly name can be provided to aid identification. On the user interface level, this parameter is referred to as the *Bluetooth Device Name*.

Table 2-3   The command and events used in combination to retrieve the user-friendly name from the remote device.

COMMAND	PARAMETERS
HCI_Remote_Name_Request	BD_ADDR Page_Scan_Repetition_Mode Page_Scan_Mode Clock_Offset
EVENT	**PARAMETERS**
Command_Status	Status Num_HCI_Command_Packets Command_OpCode
Remote_Name_Complete	Status BD_ADDR Remote_Name

Table 2-4   The PDUs available within LMP that are responsible for retrieving the Bluetooth
                Device Name.

PDU	PARAMETER
LMP_name_req	Name Offset
LMP_name_res	Name Offset
	Length
	Fragment

We show in Table 2-3, the HCI_Remote_Name_Request command, which is used to request the user-friendly name from the remote device and the Remote_Name_ Complete event is used to acknowledge completion of the request.

The following *Link Manager Protocol* (LMP) *Protocol Data Units* (PDUs), in Table 2-4, detail the LMP commands that are used to retrieve the user-friendly description. The Bluetooth Device Name can be up to 248-bytes in length, although not all bytes have to be used. There may be restrictions in what can be displayed at the user interface level and generally only the first 20 bytes can be shown. What can be displayed will typically be determined by the restriction of the user interface of the device itself and thus may be implementation-specific. Such environments may include an embedded cordless handset or a mobile phone, which has a limited display.

The LMP_name_req command is sent indicating which fragment to expect. The response is then received with the LMP_name_res command, where the parameters determine the length of the name and the fragment, since the Bluetooth Device Name can be fragmented over several DM1[4] packets.

2.4.1.2.1 Name Discovery.   The *Name Discovery* procedure obtains the Bluetooth Device Name, as we have previously discussed, where the provision of this feature is optional. The retrieval process at the user interface level is described as the *Bluetooth Device Name Discovery* and is usually performed during a *limited* or *general device discovery* procedure. This process encompasses the idle mode procedures that are typical for the Generic Access Profile.

2.4.1.3 Bluetooth Passkey.   Before two devices can have a relationship, there has to be an element of trust. The *Bluetooth Passkey* is used to build that trusted relationship prior to performing authentication. In Figure 2-5, the user is prompted to enter a Bluetooth Passkey to commence the process of establishing the trusted relationship.

We show in Table 2-5, the HCI_PIN_Code_Request_Reply command, which is used to respond to a PIN_Code_Request event, where it specifies the passkey to use for the current connection. This is typically generated during an HCI_Create_Connection or through the HCI_Authentication_Requested commands.

---

[4]The *Data Medium* (DM) Bluetooth packet type is capable of achieving a high reliability rate.

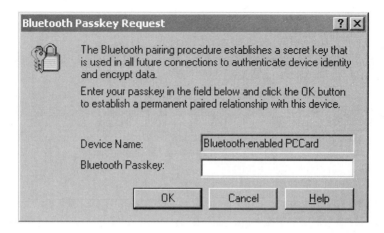

Figure 2-5 The screen shot shows a user being prompted to enter a Bluetooth Passkey before two devices can have a trusted relationship. (Courtesy of TDK Systems Europe.)

The Bluetooth Passkey is often referred to as the *Personal Identification Number* (PIN) and is described as PIN_{UI} for user interface representation and PIN_{BB} for baseband level representation. However, the user will only see the term Bluetooth Passkey when connecting to DeviceB, as previously shown in Figure 2-5.

The passkey or PIN is then used in the pairing procedure and is further used to generate a common link key; there will be more about this later (see Section 2.5.4, *Pairing*). In Figure 2-6, we illustrate the user being prompted when an invalid passkey has been entered; in some instances, the user may be prompted again to enter a valid passkey.

Consideration should also be given to devices that do not have a user interface but must still utilise a Bluetooth Passkey. In these instances, it is possible that this passkey

Table 2-5 The command and event that are used in combination to retrieve the local Bluetooth Address.

COMMAND	PARAMETERS
HCI_PIN_Code_Request_Reply	BD_ADDR
	PIN_Code_Length
	PIN_Code
EVENT	**PARAMETERS**
Command_Complete	Num_HCI_Command_Packets
	Command_OpCode
	Return_Parameters

Figure 2-6 The screen shot shows a user being prompted when the incorrect Bluetooth Passkey was entered. (Courtesy of TDK Systems Europe.)

can be stored within the device itself and should only take the form of decimal digits. Remember, the inquiring device (DeviceA) should also be capable of supporting the entry of decimal digits. A Bluetooth headset may require the user to authenticate with the device and, as such, enter a valid passkey. In such instances, manufacturers have either supplied the user with a Bluetooth Passkey card or have made it part of the unique serial number.

Whether the passkey is stored or entered in by the user a transformation has to occur from PIN_{UI} to PIN_{BB} to allow the generation of the link key for the pairing procedure, as we previously touched upon. This is achieved through mapping alphanumeric characters, which are entered on the user interface level to the UTF-8[5] format for the appropriate baseband representation. The user interface level is also capable of managing a range of alphanumeric characters, which include decimal and alphabetic. The PIN_{BB} is 128-bits in length or 16-bytes, although not all bytes have to be used and, as such, the PIN_{UI} may be less than the maximum 16-bytes available.

2.4.1.4 Bluetooth Device Class. When performing a device discovery, a *Bluetooth Device Class* is retrieved to specifically identify the type of device and the type of services that it is capable of supporting. Within an FHS[6] packet, a *Class of Device* (CoD)

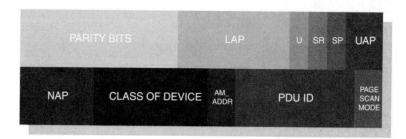

Figure 2-7 The structure of the FHS packet used only for reference to illustrate the position of the CoD structure.

---

[5]Unicode is a fixed-width standard for which 8-bit or 16-bit encoding can be used. The UTF-8 format is used to encode English characters that occupy one byte, whereas Asian or Arabic characters occupy two bytes.
[6]An FHS packet is a control packet used to reveal the BD_ADDR, clock offsets and the CoD. It is used during page and inquiry responses.

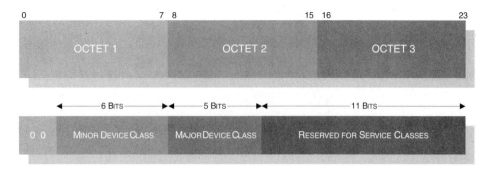

Figure 2-8 The structure of the class of device, illustrating the Minor Device, Major Device and Service Class fields and their respective lengths.

field is used to provide sufficient information with regard to the service, major and minor class groupings; Figure 2-7 shows the placement of the CoD field within the FHS packet.

The CoD field is further sectioned into 3-bytes (or 24-bits) as shown in Figure 2-8. In the illustration, we can uniquely identify the *Service*, *Major* and *Minor* device class grouping, where in the following sections we will look more closely at the parameters which make up this field.

Table 2-6 The Service Class categorisation.

23	22	21	20	19	18	17	16	15	14	13	SERVICE CLASS
23	22	21	20	19	18	17	16	15	14	13	Bit # of CoD
0	0	0	0	0	0	0	0	0	0	1	Limited Discovery
0	0	0	0	0	0	0	0	0	1	0	Reserved
0	0	0	0	0	0	0	0	1	0	0	Reserved
0	0	0	0	0	0	0	1	0	0	0	Positioning (Localisation)
0	0	0	0	0	0	1	0	0	0	0	Networking
0	0	0	0	0	1	0	0	0	0	0	Rendering (Printing, Speakers)
0	0	0	0	1	0	0	0	0	0	0	Capture (Scanner, Microphone)
0	0	0	1	0	0	0	0	0	0	0	Object Transfer
0	0	1	0	0	0	0	0	0	0	0	Audio
0	1	0	0	0	0	0	0	0	0	0	Telephony
1	0	0	0	0	0	0	0	0	0	0	Information

Table 2-7   The range of Major Device Classes available to Bluetooth-enabled devices.

MAJOR DEVICE CLASS					
12	11	10	9	8	Bit # of CoD
0	0	0	0	0	Miscellaneous
0	0	0	0	1	Computer: Desktops, Laptops and PDAs
0	0	0	1	0	Phone: Mobiles, Cordless, Payphones and Modems
0	0	0	1	1	LAN and Network Access Point
0	0	1	0	0	Audio: Headsets, Speakers and Stereos
0	0	1	0	1	Peripherals: Mouse, Joysticks and Keyboards
0	0	1	1	0	Imaging: Printing, Scanner, Camera and Displays
1	1	1	1	1	Unclassified, device code has not been assigned

The Service class is the highest form of categorising a Bluetooth device. In Table 2-6, we show the service class definitions that are currently available.

Table 2-7 identifies the Major class grouping. This represents another level of granularity for the definition of a Bluetooth device.

Taking the granularity to the next level, the following tables identify further groupings when the Major Device class is not suitable, although the correct interpretation is given for the Major Device class context. In Table 2-8, we illustrate the available groupings for the *Computer Major Class*.

Table 2-8   The Minor Device Class set for the Major Device Class grouping for Computer.

MINOR DEVICE CLASS					
7	6	5	4	3	2	Bit # of CoD
0	0	0	0	0	0	Unclassified, device code has not been assigned
0	0	0	0	0	1	Desktop Workstation
0	0	0	0	1	0	Server-class Computer
0	0	0	0	1	1	Notebook
0	0	0	1	0	0	Handheld PDA or PC
0	0	0	1	0	1	Palm-sized PDA or PC
0	0	0	1	1	0	Wearable Computer (watch sized)

Table 2-9   The Minor Device Class set for the Major Device Class grouping for Phone.

						MINOR DEVICE CLASS
7	6	5	4	3	2	Bit # of CoD
0	0	0	0	0	0	Unclassified, device code has not been assigned
0	0	0	0	0	1	Mobile Phone
0	0	0	0	1	0	Cordless
0	0	0	0	1	1	Smart Phone
0	0	0	1	0	0	Wired Modem or Voice Gateway
0	0	0	1	0	1	Common ISDN Access

In Table 2-9, we illustrate the available groupings for the *Phone Major Class*. In Table 2-10, we illustrate the available groupings for the *Access Point Major Class*. Table 2-10 shows the loading on the access point, which occupies bits 5, 6 and 7 of the minor device field; the lower 3-bits of the field are reserved.

In Table 2-11, we illustrate the available groupings for the *Audio/Video Major Class*. In Table 2-12, we illustrate the available groupings for the *Peripheral Major Class*. The field is sectioned, where the upper two bits, 7 and 6 are used to specify the Keyboard, Mouse and a Combo device. The lower four bits can then be used in combination for multifunctional devices; this is shown in Table 2-13.

Table 2-10   The 3-bit upper area of the minor device class that depicts the utilisation of an Access Point.

			MINOR DEVICE CLASS
7	6	5	Bit # of CoD
0	0	0	Fully Available
0	0	1	1 to 17% Utilised
0	1	0	17 to 33% Utilised
0	1	1	33 to 50% Utilised
1	0	0	50 to 67% Utilised
1	0	1	67 to 83% Utilised
1	1	0	83 to 99% Utilised
1	1	1	No Service Available

Table 2-11   The Minor Device Class set for the Major Device Class grouping for Audio/Video.

7	6	5	4	3	2	**MINOR DEVICE CLASS**
						Bit # of CoD
0	0	0	0	0	0	Unclassified, device code has not been assigned
0	0	0	0	0	1	Device conforms to the Headset Profile
0	0	0	0	1	0	Hands-free
0	0	0	0	1	1	Reserved
0	0	0	1	0	0	Microphone
0	0	0	1	0	1	Loud Speaker
0	0	0	1	1	0	Head Phones
0	0	0	1	1	1	Portable Audio
0	0	1	0	0	0	Car Audio
0	0	1	0	0	1	Set-top Box
0	0	1	0	1	0	HiFi Audio Device
0	0	1	0	1	1	VCR
0	0	1	1	0	0	Video Camera
0	0	1	1	0	1	Camcorder
0	0	1	1	1	0	Video Monitor
0	0	1	1	1	1	Video Display and Loud Speaker
0	1	0	0	0	0	Video Conferencing
0	1	0	0	0	1	Reserved
0	1	0	0	1	0	Gaming/Toy

In our final look at the class grouping, Table 2-14 illustrates the available groupings for the *Imaging Major Class*. The field is also sectioned, where the upper four bits, 7, 6, 5 and 4 are used to specify the Display, Camera, Scanner and a Printer device.

The lower two bits can then be used in combination for multifunctional devices; this is shown in Table 2-15.

The following commands, as shown in Table 2-16 and Table 2-17, are used in combination to identify and set the device categorisation as we previously discussed. The

Table 2-12   The 2-bit upper area of the minor device class that depicts the categorisation of a peripheral.

MINOR DEVICE CLASS		
7	**6**	**Bit # of CoD**
0	1	Keyboard
1	0	Pointing Device
1	1	Combo Keyboard/Pointing Device

Table 2-13   The 4-bit lower area of the minor device class that depicts the categorisation of a multifunctional peripheral device.

MINOR DEVICE CLASS				
5	**4**	**3**	**2**	**Bit # of CoD**
0	0	0	0	Uncategorised
0	0	0	1	Joystick
0	0	1	0	Gamepad
0	0	1	1	Remote Control
0	1	0	0	Sensing Device

Table 2-14   The 4-bit upper area of the minor device class that depicts the categorisation of an imaging device.

MINOR DEVICE CLASS				
7	**6**	**5**	**4**	**Bit # of CoD**
0	0	0	1	Display
0	0	1	0	Camera
0	1	0	0	Scanner
1	0	0	0	Pinter

Table 2-15   The 2-bit lower area of the minor device class that depicts the categorisation of a multifunctional imaging device.

		MINOR DEVICE CLASS
3	**2**	**Bit # of CoD**
0	0	Uncategorised
x	x	Reserved

HCI_Read_Class_of_Device parameter is used to retrieve the capabilities of the local device, which in turn informs other devices of its capabilities. A Command_Complete event is used to acknowledge a successful operation.

The HCI_Write_Class_of_Device parameter is used to set the capabilities for the local device, which in turn informs other devices of its capabilities. A Command_Complete event is used to acknowledge a successful operation.

2.5   MODES

The following sections now discuss modes of operation for discoverability, connectability, pairing and security. Each mode of operation determines the behaviour of a device and, as such, the governing profile may determine if these features are mandatory or optional.

For some discoverability procedures, such as time available for discovery or inquiry scan substates, a time constraint may be applied to that operation. Table 2-18 provides a list of timers available to the Generic Access Profile. The notation $T_{GAP}^{(xxx)}$ is used to identify the timer for a specific operation, where *xxx* identifies the timer reference within the table; the values provided are only recommendations.

Table 2-16   The command and event used in combination to retrieve the Bluetooth Device Class.

COMMAND	PARAMETERS
HCI_Read_Class_of_Device	Status
	Class_of_Device
EVENT	**PARAMETERS**
Command_Complete	Num_HCI_Command_Packets
	Command_OpCode
	Return_Parameters

Table 2-17 The command and event used in combination to set the Bluetooth Device Class.

COMMAND	PARAMETERS
HCI_Write_Class_of_Device	Status
EVENT	**PARAMETERS**
Command_Complete	Num_HCI_Command_Packets Command_OpCode Return_Parameters

2.5.1 Discoverability

The mode of discoverability determines whether or not a device can be discovered for use with any other device. There are several modes of operation for discoverability and these will be discussed in the following sections. A device will only operate in one mode at any one time and can be discoverable if set in the limited or general discoverability mode. Once made discoverable, a device will only be available for at least $T_{GAP}^{(103)}$.

The initial procedure required for discovering the availability of a device is an *inquiry* and, as such, if a device is configured for non-discoverability it will not respond to an inquiry, although, other baseband activities may take precedence where the device is unable to respond. The term *silent device* is used to describe a device that fails to respond as per the reasons previously outlined. In Figure 2-9 and Figure 2-10, we can see two different implementations performing an inquiry, where a list of devices that have been found are then shown.

Table 2-18 The available Generic Access Profile timers.

TIMER	VALUE	DESCRIPTION
$T_{GAP}^{(100)}$	*10.24 s*	To be used during inquiry and device discovery for the normal time span that a device performs an inquiry.
$T_{GAP}^{(101)}$	*10.625 ms*	The minimum time that a discoverable device enters the inquiry scan substate for at least $T_{GAP}^{(101)}$ and every $T_{GAP}^{(102)}$ thereafter.
$T_{GAP}^{(102)}$	*2.56 s*	This determines the maximum time between repeated inquiry scans, where $T_{INQUIRY\_SCAN}$ defines the maximum interval period at *2.56s*.
$T_{GAP}^{(103)}$	*30.72 s*	The minimum time allowed for a device to be in a discoverable mode.
$T_{GAP}^{(104)}$	*1 min*	The maximum time allowed for a device to be in limited discoverable mode.

Figure 2-9   The screen shot shows DeviceA performing a device discovery,
where the initial procedure initiated is a discovery of devices in
radio range (the 3Com Bluetooth Connection Manager is shown
performing a device discovery).

A device will enter the *inquiry substate* to discover devices in radio range, where
the Bluetooth Device Address, clocks and our other set of parameters, as we discussed
earlier, are retrieved. A device that wishes to be discovered will enter the *inquiry scan
substate* to allow it to respond to the inquiring device. Variations of the *Inquiry Access
Code*[7] (IAC) are used for operating the different modes. The *Limited Inquiry Access Code*
(LIAC) is agreed between two devices for providing limited discoverability, whereas the
General Inquiry Access Code (GIAC) is used for all devices; these two variations are discussed in more detail in the following sections.

Using the `HCI_Inquiry` command, we will place the device into an *inquiry
mode*, where it is capable of discovering other Bluetooth-enabled devices in radio range.
The IAC is generated from the *Lower Address Part*[8] (LAP) parameter, which can be seen
in Table 2-19. The `Inquiry_Length` parameter is used to determine how long the procedure should take, after which the procedure is halted. Finally, the `Num_Responses`
parameter contains the number of devices that have responded during the inquiry mode
procedure. As each device is found, an `Inquiry_Result` event is generated, providing
an immediate notification to the host of the discovered device(s); however, it is recommended that a device should be reported once, since it may have been discovered in a previous inquiry (see Table 2-20).

---

[7]The IAC is packaged into an ID packet, which is specifically used for paging, inquiry and response procedures.
The ID packet has a fixed length of 68-bits and is generally robust.
[8]The LAP is one third of the Bluetooth Device Address; `BD_ADDR` also has two further parts: the *Upper Address Part* (UAP) and the *Non-significant Address Part* (NAP).

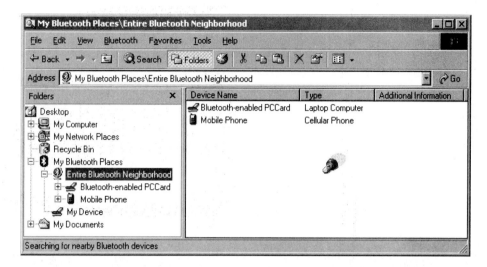

Figure 2-10   The screen shot shows DeviceA performing a device discovery,
where the initial procedure initiated is an inquiry of devices in
radio range. (Courtesy of TDK Systems Europe.)

In Table 2-21, we provide a further HCI command that is used to place a device into
a *Periodic Inquiry Mode*, where at definable periods an inquiry will take place. The two
additional parameters `Max_Period_Length` and `Min_Period_Length` are used to
determine the period between consecutive inquiries. The `Inquiry_Length` parameter
still determines the total period in an inquiry.

Table 2-22 shows the `HCI_Write_Scan_Enable` command that is used to
place a device into a *page scan mode*, an *inquiry scan mode* or both modes depending on
the `Scan_Enable` parameter. When the command has been completed, a `Command_`
`Complete` event is then generated. This, in turn, allows a device to respond to an inquiry
during a discovery procedure.

Table 2-23 shows the `HCI_Read_Scan_Enable` command that is used to learn
of the mode of the device as per the `HCI_Write_Scan_Enable` setting.

2.5.1.1   Non-Discoverable.   This mode inhibits a device from being discovered
and at the user interface level is described as *non-discoverable* or in a *non-discoverable
mode*. As such, the device will never enter the *inquiry response state*. Its use within this

Table 2-19   The LAP value is used to determine the type of inquiry.

LAP	DESCRIPTION
0x9E8B33	General or Unlimited Inquiry Access Code (GIAC)
0x9E8B00	Limited or Dedicated Inquiry Access Code (LIAC)

Table 2-20   The command and event used in combination to instigate an inquiry procedure.

COMMAND	PARAMETERS
HCI_Inquiry	LAP
	Inquiry_Length
	Num_Responses
EVENT	**PARAMETERS**
Command_Complete	Num_HCI_Command_Packets
	Command_OpCode
	Return_Parameters
Inquiry_Result	Num_Responses
	BD_ADDR[n]
	Page_Scan_Repetition_Mode[n]
	Page_Scan_Period_Mode[n]
	Page_Scan_Mode[n]
	Class_Of_Device[n]
	Clock_Offset[n]
Inquiry_Complete	Status

profile is optional, although it becomes mandatory if the limited discovery mode is supported.

    2.5.1.2   Limited Discoverable.   This mode provides limited discoverability and, at the user interface level, is described as *discoverable* or in a *discoverable mode*. Again, its use within this profile is optional, but the governing profile may dictate otherwise.

    When a device is placed in the limited discoverable mode, it sets bit 13 in the service class field as shown in Table 2-24. The table provides a comparative perspective with regards to its placement with other settings, which we discussed in an earlier section.

    Limited discoverability provides flexibility with regard to making specific events temporarily available, where the mode should not be available for more than $T_{GAP}^{(104)}$. The procedure for the LIAC is provided by two scanning methods: *parallel* or *sequential*, but only one is used.

    In the parallel scanning method, the device will enter the inquiry scan state once in $T_{GAP}^{(102)}$ and perform the inquiry scan for the GIAC or LIAC at least $T_{GAP}^{(101)}$. Similarly, the sequential scanning method for the device will enter the inquiry scan state once in

Table 2-21 The command and event used in combination to place a device into a periodic inquiry state.

COMMAND	PARAMETERS
HCI_Periodic_Inquiry_Mode	LAP
	Inquiry_Length
	Num_Responses
	Min_Period_Length
	Max_Period_Length
EVENT	**PARAMETERS**
Command_Complete	Num_HCI_Command_Packets
	Command_OpCode
	Return_Parameters
Inquiry_Result	Num_Responses
	BD_ADDR[n]
	Page_Scan_Repetition_Mode[n]
	Page_Scan_Period_Mode[n]
	Page_Scan_Mode[n]
	Class_Of_Device[n]
	Clock_Offset[n]
Inquiry_Complete	Status

Table 2-22 The command and event used in combination to place the device into a page scan mode, an inquiry scan mode or both modes.

COMMAND	PARAMETERS
HCI_Write_Scan_Enable	Scan_Enable
EVENT	**PARAMETERS**
Command_Complete	Num_HCI_Command_Packets
	Command_OpCode
	Return_Parameters

Table 2-23   The command and event used in combination to learn of the status of the
`Scan_Enable` state.

COMMAND	PARAMETERS
`HCI_Read_Scan_Enable`	`Scan_Enable`
EVENT	**PARAMETERS**

`Command_Complete`	`Num_HCI_Command_Packets`
	
	`Command_OpCode`
	
	`Return_Parameters`

$T_{GAP}^{(102)}$. However, it will scan for the GIAC for at least $T_{GAP}^{(101)}$, and enter the inquiry scan state more frequently than once in $T_{GAP}^{(102)}$, but scan for the LIAC for at least $T_{GAP}^{(101)}$. Precedence is provided for the inquiry response state when an inquiry message is received so that the message can be appropriately actioned.

The following sections now further clarify the limited inquiry and device discovery procedures for DeviceA, whereas the behaviour of DeviceB has been presented in previous sections. Here, we want to look specifically at the behaviour of DeviceA when the device is in an idle state.

2.5.1.2.1 Limited Inquiry.   The *limited inquiry* procedure obtains the BD_ADDR, clock,[9] CoD and the current status of the page scan mode. At the user interface level, the term *Bluetooth Device Inquiry* is used to describe the process, as previously shown in Figure 2-9. As a minimum, one inquiry procedure is mandatory where bonding is made available; otherwise the availability of the limited inquiry method is optional.

Table 2-24   A small section of the major service classes that are set in the Service Classes
section of the class of device field.

23	22	21	20	19	18	17	16	15	14	13	SERVICE CLASS Bit # of CoD
0	0	0	0	0	0	0	0	0	0	1	Limited Discoverable Mode

...

| 0 | 1 | 0 | 0 | 0 | 0 | 0 | 0 | 0 | 0 | 0 | *Networking* |
| 0 | 0 | 0 | 0 | 0 | 0 | 1 | 0 | 0 | 0 | 0 | *Telephony* |

---

[9]The acceptor responds with its own native clock setting, which allows both devices to synchronise their communication.

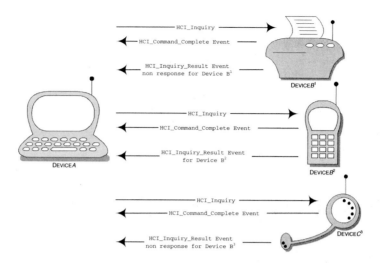

Figure 2-11   The sequence of events that occur when DeviceA wishes to
learn more about the devices in radio range. In the illustration
provided DeviceB[1] is configured for non-discoverable mode
and DeviceB[3] is configured for general discoverability and, as
such, neither produces an inquiry response.

Figure 2-11 describes a sequence of events that occur when DeviceA wishes to
learn of other devices in radio range. DeviceA uses the LIAC to perform the inquiry and
will remain in the inquiry state for at least $T_{GAP}^{(100)}$, see Table 2-18. In the illustration provided, DeviceB[2] responds, whereas the other two devices have been configured for *non-
discoverability* and *general discoverability*. Devices that have been configured for limited
discoverability will only respond to the LIAC and, as such, are only available for a limited
period of time or for specific events. Inquiring devices have the option to use GIAC or
LIAC, since many circumstances may limit the response of the acceptor. Timing restrictions are applied to this operation, where the inquiry has to be completed within the time
available to the acceptor during the limited discoverability ($T_{GAP}^{(103)}$).

2.5.1.2.2   Limited Device Discovery.   The *limited device discovery* procedure obtains the same set of parameters initially retrieved by the limited inquiry. However, the limited device discovery procedure also requests the Bluetooth Device Name, although it can
be obtained at a later stage during connection establishment. At the user interface level, the
term *Bluetooth Device Discovery* is used to describe the process and in Figure 2-12, we can
see the user has specifically selected the type of devices he or she wishes to see.

The `HCI_Set_Event_Filter` command is used to specifically filter out other
devices during an inquiry. The command can be configured to allow only new devices to
respond to a device with a certain CoD and a device with a specific `BD_ADDR` should
only respond.

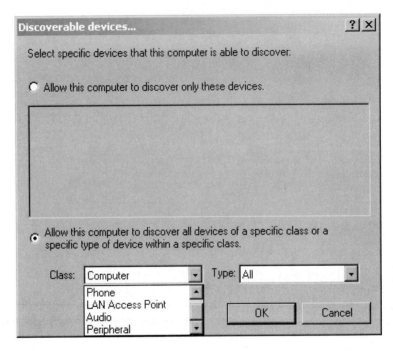

Figure 2-12   Here we can see a user configuring his or her Bluetooth device to
                  discovery specific devices. (Courtesy of TDK Systems Europe.)

In Table 2-25 we illustrate the HCI_Set_Event_Filter command that is used by the host to select different event filters. As a default, the Auto_Accept_Flag is off and, as such, no filters have been defined; this flag is formed as part of the Filter_Condition_Type parameter. As part of the Filter_Condition_Type, Inquiry_Result event filter parameters, a device may be configured for all new devices to respond to an inquiry process or a device should respond with a specific CoD or BD_ADDR. A Command_Complete event is generated informing the host that the filter has been created, where an Inquiry_Result event is then generated informing the host of the results. However, the Filter_Condition_Type, Connection_Setup filter parameters enable connections from all devices or allows connections from a specific device with a CoD or a BD_ADDR. In this instance, a Connection_Request event is generated if any of these conditions are met.

In Table 2-25, we also see the parameters that make up our Inquiry_Result event filter and the Connection_Request event, which are generated as a result of defining the Filter_Condition_Type parameter. The host controller informs the host as soon as the *inquiry response* is received from the remote device.

2.5.1.3   General Discoverable.   Like the limited discoverable mode, the user interface describes this option as *discoverable* or in a *discoverable mode*. This mode is generally open and available with no specific conditions attached. Its use within this profile is optional, but again the governing profile may dictate otherwise.

Table 2-25 The command and event that are used in combination to create a specific inquiry result filter.

COMMAND	PARAMETERS
HCI_Set_Event_Filter	Filter_Type
	Filter_Condition_Type
	Condition
EVENT	**PARAMETERS**
Command_Complete	Num_HCI_Command_Packets
	Command_OpCode
	Return_Parameters
Inquiry_Result	Num_Responses
	BD_ADDR[n]
	Page_Scan_Repetition_Mode[n]
	Page_Scan_Period_Mode[n]
	Page_Scan_Mode[n]
	Class_Of_Device[n]
	Clock_Offset[n]
Connection_Request	BS_ADDR
	Class_Of_Device
	Link_Type

The device responds to the general inquiry using the GIAC, but never responds to a LIAC when configured for general discoverable mode. Whilst in this mode, a device will enter the inquiry scan state more frequently than once in $T_{GAP}^{(102)}$ and will scan for the GIAC for at least $T_{GAP}^{(101)}$.

The following sections now further clarify the general inquiry and device discovery procedures for DeviceA. The behaviour of DeviceB has been presented in previous sections. Here, we want to look specifically at the behaviour of DeviceA when the device is in an idle state, that is, awaiting interaction in this particular mode of operation.

2.5.1.3.1 General Inquiry. The *general inquiry* procedure obtains the BD_ADDR, clock, CoD and the page scan mode of the discovered devices. Devices that have been configured for limited discovery will also respond when issued a GIAC. At the

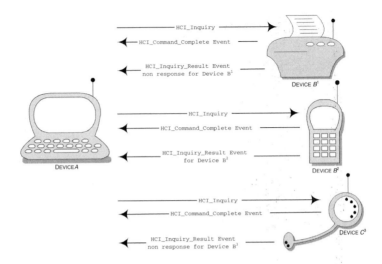

Figure 2-13 The sequence of events that occur when DeviceA wishes to learn more about the devices in radio range. In the illustration provided, DeviceB[1] is configured for non-discoverable mode and, as such, does not produce an inquiry response.

user interface level, the term *Bluetooth Device Inquiry* is used to describe the process in hand, see Figure 2-9. As a minimum, one inquiry procedure is mandatory, where bonding is made available—otherwise the availability of the general inquiry method is optional.

Figure 2-13 provides a sequence of events that occur when DeviceA wishes to learn of other devices in radio range. DeviceA uses the GIAC to perform the inquiry, where it will remain in the inquiry state for at least $T_{GAP}^{(100)}$, see Table 2-18.

2.5.1.3.2 General Device Discovery. The *general device discovery* procedure obtains the same set of parameters initially retrieved by the general inquiry. However, the general device discovery procedure also requests the Bluetooth Device Name, although it can be obtained at a later stage during connection establishment. At the user interface level, the term *Bluetooth Device Discovery* is used to describe the process.

The process for which a device discovery occurs begins with a general inquiry, but the acceptor must be in a position where it can respond to this inquiry.

2.5.2 Connectability

The mode of connectability determines whether or not DeviceA can be connected to any other device in radio range. There are several modes of operation for connectability and these will be discussed in the following sections.

In a connectable mode, the device will respond to paging, whereas a device that is configured as non-connectable will provide no response. Earlier, in Section 2.3, *Profile Principles*, we introduced the configurations available to DeviceA and DeviceB. Here we also learned that DeviceA would supply page trains and DeviceB would sit in the page scan state awaiting its *Device Access Code* (DAC).

2.5.2.1   Non-Connectable.   When a device is configured for non-connectable mode, it will never enter the page scan state and, at the user interface level, it is described as *non-connectable* or in a *non-connectable mode*; its use within this profile is optional.

2.5.2.2   Connectable.   A device configured for connectable mode will enter the page scan state awaiting its own DAC and its use within this profile is mandatory. At the user interface level, it is described as *connectable* or in a *connectable mode*.

2.5.3   Bonding

The bonding and pairing processes are often used synonymously, which both seem to also encompass the authentication process. The bonding procedure can be described as a user's intent to pair, where the pairing process refers to the generation of link keys; we discuss the specific architecture of pairing in more detail in the following section. A user who wishes to connect to a remote device initiates the bonding process with his or her intent, where higher-layer procedures may be involved. More specifically, the user performs device and service discovery procedures to learn of the devices in radio range. The term bonding is used when the paging device itself chooses to initiate the pairing process. The devices that have been discovered are in a bondable state, where the user can now choose to pair with the remote device. In Figure 2-14, we show a user initiating the pairing process by selecting the pair menu option; when a user has reached this stage, it is this intent that describes the user as bonding. At the user interface level, the term *Bluetooth Bonding* is used to describe this process.

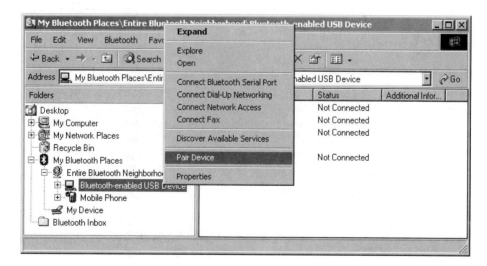

Figure 2-14   The user has discovered the devices in radio range and now can choose to pair with the remote device. (Courtesy of TDK Systems Europe.)

Figure 2-15   The remote device is informed of the user's intent to pair. Both
                   users are then presented a dialog box to enter their Bluetooth
                   passkeys. (Courtesy of TDK Systems Europe.)

The device needs to know the DAC of the remote device it intends to bond with,
which can be achieved through a device discovery. For both devices to take part in the
bonding process, DeviceB should be capable of being discovered either with the general
or limited discoverability modes, where the initiator then proceeds to initiate authentication. Dedicated bonding is used when the explicit generation and exchange of a link key is
required, whereas general bonding, where the generation of the link key is provided under
certain conditions and further initialisation is required from the higher-layers.

With the user's intent, the remote device is also informed that a device wishes to
connect to it, as we can see in Figure 2-15. If this is an unauthorised access, the user can
choose to ignore this request and the initiating party will be unable to connect.

Nonetheless, if the user does know or is waiting for this connection he or she can
double-click the Bluetooth icon on the taskbar to be prompted to enter the corresponding
Bluetooth Passkey. Similarly, the user on the initiating part is also prompted to enter the
Bluetooth Passkey for the remote device, as we have illustrated in Figure 2-16. Essentially, the two Bluetooth passkeys are entered simultaneously, where the generation of the
link keys are then performed.

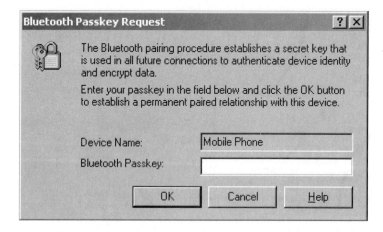

Figure 2-16   Both devices are simultaneously prompted to enter their
                   passkeys to authenticate. (Courtesy of TDK Systems Europe.)

2.5.4 Pairing

We introduced the Bluetooth Passkey in Section 2.4.1.3 and described the purpose of the key, where it was used to establish a trusted relationship between DeviceA and DeviceB. There are two instances that describe the process of bonding and authentication. In the first instance, the user may initiate the bonding process with the sole purpose of creating this trusted relationship. In the second instance, the user is perceived to authenticate using the passkey. The pairing process refers to the provision of the Bluetooth passkey and the link key generation procedure; authentication is then performed.

This procedure is referred to as the LMP Pairing procedure and begins when these two devices do not already share a common link key. Figure 2-17 provides a sequence of events that occur during the pairing process. To achieve this, both devices create an *initialisation key*, based upon the Bluetooth passkey (or PIN), a random number and the Bluetooth Device Address (BD_ADDR), see Section 2.4.1.1, *Bluetooth Device Address*.

When the initialisation key is created, the link key can then be generated. The link key is then subsequently used for mutual authentication, thus allowing the devices to communicate with each other and form that trusted relationship. The two devices now share a common link key and are now referred to as *bonded*. Looking at the LMP commands that start this process, we note that DeviceA sends the LMP_in_rand command. DeviceB then responds with the LMP_accepted command. Both devices then proceed to calculate the initialisation key based upon the parameters provided earlier.

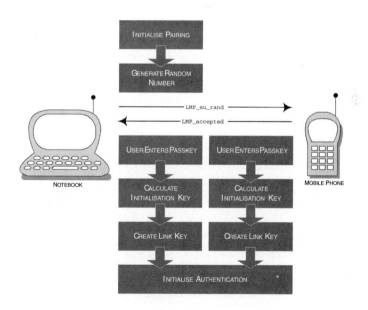

Figure 2-17 The sequence of events for the pairing process, also referred to as LMP Pairing, which leads up to the generation of the link key.

A combination key or a unit key is then specifically used to determine the generation of the link key, where a set of rules govern the selection process. Table 2-26 shows the LMP commands used when pairing occurs between DeviceA and DeviceB, and also shows the `LMP_comp_key` and `LMP_unit_key`, which are used when selecting a combination or unit key method, respectively.

In concluding this section, if a device is considered to be *pairable* then it is capable of pairing and is therefore in a *pairable state*. However, a device that does not accept pairing is deemed to be in a *non-pairable state* and therefore does not perform pairing, see Section 2.5.4.1, *Pairable* and 2.5.4.2, *Non-Pairable*.

2.5.4.1   Pairable.   At the user interface level, the user is presented with the configuration for the device as *bondable mode* or simply *bondable*. Its use within this profile is optional, although becomes mandatory if the bonding procedure is supported. When in a *pairable* state, DeviceB should respond when it receives an `LMP_in_rand`, with `LMP_accepted` or with `LMP_in_rand` if the device has a fixed passkey.

2.5.4.2   Non-Pairable.   At the user interface level, the user is presented with the configuration for the device as *non-bondable mode* or simply *non-bondable*. Its use within this profile is optional, but the governing profile may dictate otherwise. When in the *non-pairable* state, DeviceB should respond when it receives an `LMP_in_rand`, with `LMP_not_accepted`, where the reason parameter should indicate *pairing not allowed* (`0x18`), see Appendix A.

2.5.5   Security

Bluetooth technology is capable of offering several security modes, which we will discuss in more detail later. Firstly, the introduction of security within Bluetooth technology has become a necessity, since the availability of diverse and ad-hoc connectivity would increase the risk of unwanted intrusion within the environment it was exposed to. Once devices have authenticated, encryption may be used for the actual transfer of data, thus

Table 2-26   The range of LMP PDUs available for two units when pairing.

PDU	PARAMETER
`LMP_in_rand`	Random Number
`LMP_au_rand`	Random Number
`LMP_res`	Authentication Response
`LMP_comp_key`	Random Number
`LMP_unit_key`	Key

providing greater confidentiality in the data exchanged. In the immediate section to fol-low, we explore the authentication process in the Generic Access Profile context.

2.5.5.1   Authentication.   The term *Bluetooth Authentication* is used at the user interface level and is performed when the devices share a common link key or initialisa-tion key.[10] You may remember in our earlier discussion that pairing occurs prior to the au-thentication process, which is the process of obtaining the passkey and generating the initialisation key. This process is, of course, subject to the configuration of the pairable mode, where the device can be configured not to engage in pairing.

The authentication process encompasses LMP Authentication, but LMP Pairing must have been performed prior to this event. As for the LMP Authentication procedure, this is primarily based on a challenge-response scheme. Here, the verifier or DeviceA sends the `LMP_au_rand` command, containing a random number to the claimant or De-viceB; the random number forms the challenge aspect of this scheme. The response, forming the final part of this scheme, is sent to the verifier using the `LMP_sres` com-mand, which contains the result of the operation. If the operation is what the verifier ex-pected then it considers the claimant as authenticated.

The LMP Pairing procedure occurs when there is no link key and, as such, if an `LMP_au_rand` is sent to the claimant it will respond with `LMP_not_accepted` offer-ing the reason as *key missing* (`0x06`), see Appendix A. If a key has been previously asso-ciated with the claimant, then the claimant proceeds to calculate the response and provides the verifier with a response through `LMP_sres`. However, if the calculated re-sponse is incorrect the verifier can terminate the connection with the command `LMP_de-tach`, offering the reason as *authentication failure* (`0x05`), see Appendix A; Table 2-27, summarises the LMP commands used during authentication and Figure 2-18 provides a sequence of events that occur during the LMP Authentication procedure.

2.5.5.2   Encryption.   This section is provided to supplement the notion of en-cryption introduced previously. To summarise, the process of encryption commences when at least one device has been authenticated. DeviceA (or master) takes the initiative and needs to determine whether to include encryption for point-to-point or broadcast communication. If DeviceB (or slave) is agreeable to the parameters offered by the mas-

Table 2-27   The range of LMP PDUs available for authentication.

PDU	PARAMETER
`LMP_au_rand`	Random Number
`LMP_sres`	Authentication Response
`LMP_detach`	Reason

---

[10]These keys are sometimes referred to as the secret key.

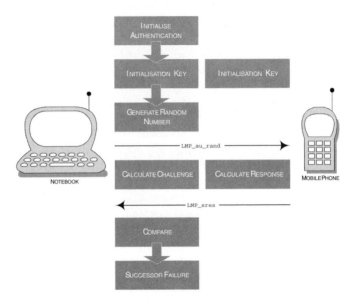

Figure 2-18   The sequence of events for LMP Authentication, which follow the LMP Pairing sequence.

ter, the master proceeds to communicate further detailed information about the encryption parameters.

The actual process is invoked when the two parties agree to use encryption and then L2CAP communication terminates, where the master then sends the `LMP_encryption_mode_req` command. If this is acceptable to the slave, it too terminates all L2CAP communication and responds with the `LMP_accepted` command. The next step in this process actually determines the size of the *encryption key* and it is the master that sends the `LMP_encryption_key_size_req` command, where it offers an initial recommendation of the key size to use. The slave, in turn, then offers its own recommendation, where it informs the master what it thinks it might be capable of. Both master and slave will repeat this process until they reach an agreement; however, if neither party reaches a decision, then the `LMP_not_accepted` command is sent, offering the reason as *unsupported parameter value* (0x20), see Appendix A.

Upon accepting the key size, the `LMP_accepted` command is issued and the encryption procedure then takes place by issuing the `LMP_start_encryption_req` commnd with a random number, which is used to calculate the encryption key. Table 2-28 summarises the available commands for the encryption process.

The following sections now look at the various security level modes available for devices wishing to authenticate, although a device wishing to initiate authentication against another device must be at least in Security Modes 1 or 2.

2.5.5.3   Non-Secure (Security Mode 1).   At this level, a device will not initiate an authentication process—specifically, the following LMP commands are never issued:

Table 2-28 The range of LMP PDUs available for encryption.

PDU	PARAMETER
LMP_encryption_mode_req	Encryption Mode
LMP_encryption_key_size_req	Key Size
LMP_start_encryption_req	Random Number
LMP_stop_encryption_req	*None*

LMP_in_rand, LMP_au_rand and LMP_encryption_mode_req. Authentication is optional for devices that offer this level of security.

2.5.5.4 Service Level Enforced Security (Security Mode 2). The *Service Level Enforced Security* tends to be moderated through the specific channel or application, providing flexibility for various applications that may be executed concurrently. As such, no security enforcement is made until the channel establishment process has been completed or at least initiated; see Section 2.6.2, *Channel Establishment*.

Security Mode 2 is mandatory if more than one other security mode is available, excluding support for Security Mode 1.

The requirements of the security process in this mode are categorised as authorisation: determining whether DeviceA is permitted to access the services available through DeviceB; authentication: performed by verifying the device by means of a Bluetooth passkey; and encryption: securing the data on the physical link.

2.5.5.5 Link Level Enforced Security (Secruity Mode 3). The *Link Level Enforced Security* is the highest available security method available to a Bluetooth-enabled device, although providing limited discoverability and non-connectable modes offer additional security where limited or unwanted access is required.

Security Mode 3 is mandatory if more than one other security mode is available, excluding support for Security Mode 1.

The paging device issues the LMP_host_connection_req command since it is interested in establishing a relationship with DeviceB. However, prior to completing the connection establishment of the two devices, the LMP Pairing, LMP Authentication and encryption procedures are all executed, ensuring that all security measures have been put in place. Failure to meet with these requirements will result in the LMP_not_accepted command being issued offering the reason of *authentication failure* (0x05), see Appendix A, and the connection terminating.

When the devices have agreed and reached a point where no further security measures are required, both parties then issue the LMP_setup_complete command and the initial data packet can then be transmitted. Table 2-29 summarises the available commands for connection establishment.

Table 2-29   The available LMP PDUs available for connection establishment.

PDU	PARAMETER
LMP_host_connection_req	*None*
LMP_setup_complete	*None*

2.6   ESTABLISHMENT PROCEDURES

Prior to an establishment procedure, it is assumed that an inquiry and device discovery have already been performed making available to DeviceA the various establishment parameters.[11] We now look more closely at the availability of HCI commands that are used to create an ACL connection with the remote device. Table 2-30 shows the parameters that make up the HCI_Create_Connection command, which is used to create an ACL connection with the remote device. The BD_ADDR parameter contains the specific address of the intended device.

The Packet_Type parameter will determine what packet types will be used during the LM level connection. The information available in the Page_Scan_Repetition_ Mode and Page_Scan_Mode parameters have been previously determined during the inquiry process. One other important parameter to note is the Allow_Role_Switch. This determines whether the initiating device (DeviceA) permits the master-slave switch.

The host is issued the HCI_Create_Connection command, where the host controller then informs the host of its current status, with the Command_Status event. When the connection is successfully created between the two devices, both host controllers issue a Connection_Complete event acknowledging that the connection was successful. A unique identifier is assigned for that connection using the Connection_ Handle parameter.

2.6.1   Link Establishment

The link establishment process creates a *physical* link between DeviceA and DeviceB and is a mandatory feature for both devices. The link establishment procedures are, to a large extent, managed at the LMP level. At the user interface level, this process is described as *Bluetooth Link Establishment*.

2.6.2   Channel Establishment

The channel establishment process creates a *logical* link between DeviceA and DeviceB and is an optional feature for DeviceA and a mandatory feature for DeviceB. The channel establishment procedure is managed by the L2CAP entity where, at the user interface level, this process is described as *Bluetooth Channel Establishment*.

---

[11]Parameters, such as the Bluetooth Device Address, Device Name, CoD, clock and page scan mode are all used to determine whether to carry out an establishment procedure.

Table 2-30 The command and events used in combination to create a connection with a remote device.

COMMAND	PARAMETERS
HCI_Create_Connection	BD_ADDR
	Packet_Type
	Page_Scan_Repetition_Mode
	Page_Scan_Mode
	Clock_Offset
	Allow_Role_Switch
EVENT	**PARAMETERS**
Command_Status	Status
	Num_HCI_Command_Packets
	Command_OpCode
Connection_Complete	Status
	Connection_Handle
	BD_ADDR
	Link_Type
	Encryption_Mode

The channel establishment process commences when the link establishment process has been completed. In an acknowledgment, DeviceA sends the channel establishment request L2CAP_ConnectReq, where security procedures may be invoked after the channel establishment. This process is completed when DeviceB responds with L2CAP_ConnectRsp.

2.6.3   Connection Establishment

The connection establishment process creates a link between the two applications that reside on DeviceA and DeviceB. At the user interface level, this process is described as *Bluetooth Connection Establishment*.

The connection establishment process commences when the channel establishment procedures have been completed. The specific protocol engaged between these two applications remains application-specific. It is possible for parameters of initialisation and configuration to be exchanged during this phase.

2.7 SUMMARY

- All profiles are fundamental to the Generic Access Profile.
- A governing profile may change the basic requirements of the Generic Access Profile to accommodate its needs.
- Rules are set out to determine the behaviour of discoverability, connectability and common characteristics at the user interface level.
- Features within this profile are set out as mandatory, optional, conditional, excluded or not applicable. These may be superseded by the governing profile.
- The Generic Access Profile extends its influence to the Bluetooth protocol layers, such as LMP, RFCOMM and L2CAP.
- The Generic Access Profile has many configurations and roles, where different modes of operation prescribe a specific context.
- This profile does not mandate specific master-slave roles, as these are left to the discretion of the governing profile.
- There are several Bluetooth parameters available at the user interface level, each of which describe a particular element.
- Many of the procedures undertaken at the user interface level are described appropriately to reflect their respective behaviour, such as limited inquiry, general inquiry, connectable, non-discoverable and pairable.
- Pairing is the process of acquiring a Bluetooth Passkey and the generation of an initialisation key.
- Bonding encompasses the procedures, which lead up to two devices being bonded.
- When two devices have a trusted relationship, they are described as bonded.
- Authentication is performed after the pairing process.
- Authentication is based upon a challenge-response scheme.
- Encryption occurs when both devices have been authenticated.
- Encryption is used to protect data transmission.
- There are three levels of security modes available: 1, 2 and 3.
- Establishment procedures offer granularity in the connection process.
- The link establishment process is used to create the physical channel.
- The channel establishment process is used to create the logical channel.
- The connection establishment process is used at the application level.
- Multiple connections can occur between devices.

3

Service Discovery
Application Profile

3.1 INTRODUCTION

The *Generic Access Profile*, Chapter 2, offered us a foundation on which we can base our
governing profiles. It established generic behaviour for devices during discoverability,
connectability and provided common characteristics at the user interface level, through
the use of rules and procedures.

In a similar manner, the *Service Discovery Application Profile* (SDAP) provides us
with a foundation on which we can establish user-level clarity with the discovered services of Bluetooth-enabled devices that are in radio range. The SDAP establishes a level
of basic functionality, abstracted from the *Service Discovery Protocol* (SDP). Like the
Generic Object Exchange Profile, Chapter 11, it achieves this by establishing a common
set of procedural primitives. The service discovery application establishes its high-level
functionality from the primitives offered to us by the SDP; there will be more about SDP
later on in this chapter. Figure 3-1 offers a representation of a Bluetooth-enabled device in
an environment where potentially all the devices surrounding it will respond to a service
discovery. The notebook adopts the role of a *Local Device*, where the *Remote Devices,*
that is, a printer, access point PDA, mobile phone and so on, surrounding it may respond
to a service discovery.

You may recall from the *Generic Access Profile*, Chapter 2, that an inquiry and device
discovery would initially be performed to learn of the devices that are in radio range.

Figure 3-1   The various applications available to a Bluetooth-enabled device.
The SDAP provides a model for which we can coordinate the
collection of these services into a user-friendly manageable form.

Initiating a service discovery could be achieved by selecting the discovered device, where
the local device would then perform a service discovery; in Figure 3-2, we illustrate the result of performing a service discovery. The illustration shows only one particular example,
where a Bluetooth-enabled device has provided us with a list of services that it is capable of
supporting. You will also notice that the SDAP has organised the collection and presentation of the services discovered, also indicating its current connection status. The user can
now select the device and choose to connect to the many services on offer, subject to any authentication requirements imposed by the governing profile.

In Figure 3-3, we can now see that the user can either double-click[1] or right-click
the service icon to begin the process of connecting and using its services.

Essentially, SDAP in combination with SDP provides the basic primitive functionality to allow a local device to discover services of remote devices that are in radio range.
If we refer back to our earlier illustrations in Figure 3-1 and Figure 3-2, we witness the

---

[1]The double-click and right-click operations refer to a mouse that is connected to your local device (in this example, a PC or notebook computer running a Microsoft Windows operating system) and where both operations
trigger the two methods of enabling. It is noted that this operation may vary from device to device and as such
the number of buttons may vary on a mouse and indeed no mouse may be connected. The example just draws
your attention to how it may be possible and acknowledges that implementations may differ.

Figure 3-2   A local device has performed a service discovery and has learned
of the available services that the remote device has to offer. The
service discovery application has coordinated the presentation of
the services into a selectable form, where the user can choose
the service he or she wishes to use. (Courtesy of TDK Systems
Europe.)

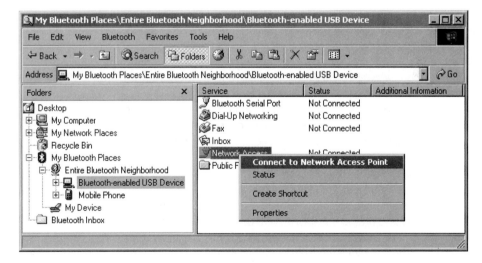

Figure 3-3   A local device has performed a service discovery and has learned
of the available services that the remote device has to offer. The
user now has the opportunity to connect to the device and make
use of its services. (Courtesy of TDK Systems Europe.)

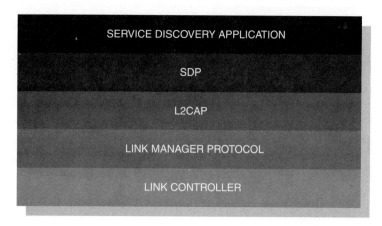

Figure 3-4   The various components that form the building blocks of the
SDAP. In similar usage models, the SDP function primitives are
exposed at the SDP upper-edge, where applications have a transparent interface to the underlying mode of transport.

availability of a remote device responding to the local device offering its available services. In later sections, we will examine in more detail how SDAP uses its underlying
protocol to transport the service information to the local device.

3.2   PROFILE PRINCIPLES

The SDAP provides two new roles: a *Local Device* and a *Remote Device*. The local device is capable of requesting service information from the remote device to learn of the
capabilities that it is able to provide.

In Figure 3-4, we can see the components that make up the SDAP and it is these
building blocks that are required to realise a compliant profile. In our introduction, we
touched upon the notion that a set of features and procedures exist to help govern the operation of Bluetooth-enabled devices, which support the SDAP. The profile also provides
clarification with regards to the dependencies as shown in Figure 3-5 and especially describes how each component realises such functionality. Essentially, what is achieved
here is a clear definition of the requirements of the core components that make up the
Bluetooth protocol stack; we will discuss this in more detail later on.

There are no fixed master-slave roles, this allows either device to be free to initiate or
terminate a connection, although typically the local device will initiate the primary connection, where inquiry and device discovery procedures have been previously undertaken.

In Table 3-1 clarification is provided with regards to the roles used within the context
of this profile. In general, *DeviceA* represents the initiating party and *DeviceB* represents
the accepting party. The terms are often used interchangeably, when describing specific
operations in various contexts and are provided here for reference.

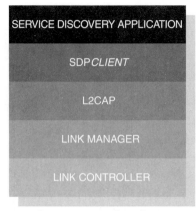
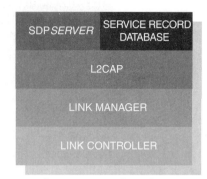

Figure 3-5   The core components of the Bluetooth protocol stack are shown. This illustrates how the components of the SDAP are integrated.

Table 3-1   The list of behavioural characteristics that are typical for this profile.

CONFIGURATION	ROLE	DESCRIPTION
DeviceA	Local	The local device initiates the service discovery procedures with the remote device to learn of the services it is capable of supporting.
	Client	In the client-server model, the local device acts as the client who in turn requests from the server the data that is pertinent to its service request.
	Initiator	This configuration describes the device that instigates the original connection or the device that wishes to initiate communication over an existing link.
DeviceB	Remote	The remote device accepts incoming connections from the local device, which in turn will be provided with the list of services it requests.
	Server	In the client-server model, the remote device is described as the device that serves the client by offering the information it has requested.
	Acceptor	This configuration describes the process of the device accepting the initiated communication from DeviceA.

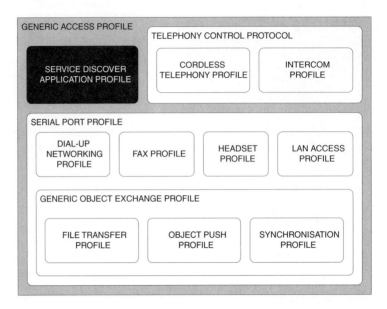

Figure 3-6   The dependent components of the Bluetooth protocol stack that
makes up the SDAP. The areas that are shaded are relevant.

3.3   LIFTING THE LID

3.3.1   Dependencies

In the following sections, we take an opportunity to explore in greater depth the dependencies that make up this profile. In Figure 3-6, we provide a conceptual illustration representing the dependencies that make up the SDAP; the areas that are shaded are relevant
to this profile. As you can see, the profile depends upon the basic functionality offered to
us by the *Generic Access Profile*, Chapter 2 and the components of the Bluetooth protocol
stack. We will now discuss in turn the basic requirements of these dependent components
and any deviations that may occur from the basic functionality originally offered to us.

3.3.1.1   The Service Discovery Protocol.   We touched upon the fact that SDAP
relies upon SDP as its underlying transport. Our focus here is to describe the processes
used to obtain service information and to establish how the underlying Bluetooth transport is facilitated in achieving this.

SDP has been designed to sit above the L2CAP component of the Bluetooth protocol stack, as shown in our earlier illustrations. In our first look at understanding this protocol, we will examine its architecture in more detail and then consider specific aspects of
integration over L2CAP. In later sections, we will also discuss how SDP *Protocol Data
Units* (PDUs) such as SDP_ServiceSearchRequest, SDP_ServiceSearchRe-
sponse and so on are used to realise function primitives.

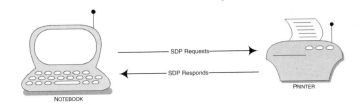

Figure 3-7   In this example, the client (notebook) and the server (printer) use
the response-request paradigm to exchange information about the
one service being offered.

3.3.1.1.1   The Client-Server Model.   In Figure 3-5, we illustrated the components
that made up our local and remote device protocol stack. In the illustration, you may have
noticed that an SDP *Client* and SDP *Server* are depicted. In this context, they interact with
each other, where the client requests and the server responds; we illustrate this concept in
Figure 3-7.

In the example, the client requests the services from the remote device, where it informs the client that it has one service available. Devices are capable of supporting many
services and, as such, we can see in Figure 3-8 that the client requests information about
the services that the remote device can support and the SDP server provides a response
with multiple services attached.

The SDP client and the local device communicate with the SDP server of the remote device. Accompanying the SDP server, a *Service Discovery Database* (SDDB) is
used to store information about the services that the remote device is capable of providing. The database is made up of a series of *Service Records*, which we will discuss in
more detail later on. These service records contain detailed information, which enables
the local device to know how to use the service on offer. Supplementing this core capability, the owner of the remote device may select how the client should use a service.

In Figure 3-9, the user is capable of configuring the service to use authentication or
encryption. When a local device then uses this particular service, as in the example provided, we can see the user being prompted to select changes for the File Transfer service.
The user will have to undertake authentication and encryption procedures before using
that particular service.

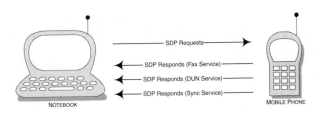

Figure 3-8   In this example, the client (notebook) and the server (mobile phone)
use the response-request paradigm to exchange information about
the many services being offered.

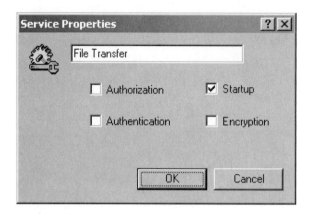

Figure 3-9 Service Records are created for the services that a device is capable of providing. Supplementing these core capabilities, information relating to the requirements of Authorisation, Authentication and Encryption are also stored.

3.3.1.1.2 Identifying Services.   *Service Attributes* are used to describe the characteristics of a service that should be sufficient for a local device to use. They essentially comprise two units: an *AttributeID* and an *AttributeValue,* as we can see in Figure 3-10. The `AttributeID` is a 16-bit unsigned integer, which is used to uniquely identify the service attribute. In Table 3-2, we provide a list of common service attributes and their associated `AttributeID` values that are commonly used throughout this book. The `AttributeValue` is a variable length parameter, where its contents are dependent upon the `AttributeID`.

The `AttributeValue` is constructed using *data elements*. The SDP interprets the `AttributeValue` to determine its content, where its structure is made up of a *header* and a *data* field. In Figure 3-11, we can also see that the `Header` is further divided into two sections, containing information, which relates to the `Type` and `Size` descriptors. The `Type` descriptor is made up of 5-bits and is placed at the most significant section of the `Header` byte where it is used to help identify the structure of the following data elements; for example, with an `AttributeID` of `ServiceClassIDList`, what follows is a *Universally Unique Identifier* (UUID). However, with an `AttributeID` of `ServiceName`, a Text string would follow. In Table 3-3, we can see the number of available types that can be used.

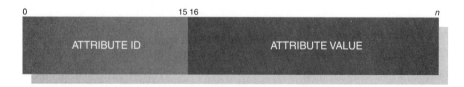

Figure 3-10   The structure of a service attribute.

Table 3-2   The SDP provides a set of unique attributes, which are used to provide sufficient
information for a local device to determine what services are available.

ATTRIBUTE	DESCRIPTION
ServiceRecordHandle	
	This attribute has an ID of 0x0000 and is used to uniquely identify a service record. We discuss this in more detail later on in Section 3.3.1.1.3, *The Service Discovery Record*.
ServiceClassIDList	
	This attribute has a unique ID of 0x0001 and is used to provide a sequence of data elements, which represent the service class that the record supports. For example, a Cordless Telephony Service would contain a UIUD of *Cordless Telephony* and a more generic definition UUID of *Generic Telephony*.
ProtocolDescriptorList	
	This attribute has a unique ID of 0x0004 and is used to describe the underlying protocols that are used to fulfill the service. Using our earlier example, the Cordless Telephony Service depends upon *TCS-BIN-CORDLESS* and *L2CAP*. This attribute would contain UUID information relating to the protocols used. Other such combinations include RFCOMM and L2CAP.
BluetoothProtocolProfileDescriptorList	
	This attribute has a unique ID of 0x0009 and is used to describe the governing profile. Continuing our example, a UUID for *Cordless Telephony* would be used to uniquely identify the profile.
LanguageBasedAttributeIDList	
	This attribute is used to provide user-level description at the user interface, where a choice of languages is available. It has a unique AttributeID of 0x0006, where further offsets are used to provide specific detail about the service being provided.

(continued)

Table 3-2   *Continued*

ATTRIBUTE	DESCRIPTION
ServiceName	
	This attribute is used to provide a user-friendly name of the service being provided by the remote device. It has an AttributeIDOffset of 0x0000 based upon the attribute LanguageBasedAttributeIDList.
ServiceDescription	
	In supplementing the ServiceName, this attribute further provides a description of the service. It has an AttributeIDOffset of 0x0001 based upon the attribute LanguageBasedAttributeIDList.
ProviderName	
	This attribute is used to describe the manufacturer who, in turn, will be providing the service. It has an AttributeIDOffset of 0x0002 based upon the attribute LanguageBasedAttributeIDList.
ExternalNetwork	
	This attribute is used to describe the externally connected telephone network that the Cordless Telephony is connected to; it has an AttributeID of 0x0301.
AudioFeedbackSupport	
	This attribute is used to denote whether audio support should be provided for the Dial-up Networking and Fax Profiles; it has an AttributeID of 0x0305.
RemoteAudioVolumeControl	
	This attribute is used to denote whether a remote volume setting on a headset can be supported; it has an AttributeID of 0x0302.

0   4 5   7

TYPE   SIZE

◄————————— 5 Bits —————————►◄——— 3 Bits ———►

Figure 3-11   The header is divided into two sections.

In Table 3-4, we identify the `Size` descriptor, which occupies the remaining 3-bits of the `Header` byte; this descriptor is contained in the least-significant section. It is used to describe the size of the data represented by the `Type` descriptor.

Let us pause for a moment and summarise what has been previously outlined. A service is constructed with a series of `ServiceAttributes`. These attributes are capable of uniquely identifying to a local device what service is being supported by the remote device. In its construction, a series of data elements are used to describe the format of the `ServiceAttribute`, where an `AttributeID` and `AttributeValue` are used. In Table 3-2, we identified a list of common attributes that are often referred to in this book. The `AttributeValue` is further used to describe the format contained within the data element. In Figure 3-12, we illustrate the encoding of the `ServiceClassIDList` for Cordless Telephony.

In the illustration, we can see that the `AttributeID` contains the `Service-ClassIDList` reference of `0x0001`, see Table 3-2. The `AttributeValue` is constructed to contain two UUID values, which represent Cordless Telephony (`0x1109`) and Generic Telephony (`0x1204`). With this type of encoding, the construction becomes twofold: in the first instance, we describe that a data sequence follows, by using the `Type` descriptor 6, see Table 3-3.

Secondly, our `Size` descriptor indicates 5; see Table 3-4, which illustrates that the following 1-byte contains the size of the entire data sequence. In the illustration, we also note that our `Length` is 6-bytes. The encoding of the remaining data sequence now indicates a `Type` descriptor of 3, which denotes UUID and the `Size` descriptor indicates that the next 2-bytes contain the actual UUID value.

With a collection of `ServiceAttributes`, a *Service Record* is constructed; this record essentially conveys to a local device *all* the information it needs to know about using the service. Figure 3-13 provides a conceptual structure of a service record. In the following section, we discuss in some more detail the use of service records and how service browsing is achieved.

3.3.1.1.3 The Service Discovery Record.   In our earlier introduction we provided an illustration, which demonstrated that a device was capable of supporting multiple services, see Figure 3-2. A service record is maintained for each service the device is capable of supporting and, as such, a *Service Record Handle* is created to uniquely identify a service record.

Table 3-3   The list of available `Type` descriptors that form the most-significant section of the
`Header`.

TYPE	DESCRIPTION
0	Null.
1	An unsigned integer.
2	A signed 2's complement integer.
3	A Universally Unique Identifier (UUID).
4	A text string.
5	Boolean (`TRUE` or `FALSE`).
6	A *sequence* of data elements.
7	A data element alternative: a sequence of data elements, where one must be chosen.
8	A Uniform Resource Locator (URL).

A minimum of two attributes are required to make a service record, these are `Ser-viceRecordHandle` and `ServiceClassIDList`, where the latter attribute must contain at least one UUID; Table 3-5 provides a list of `AttributeIDs`, which ultimately would identify the service for the Cordless Telephony Profile.

The `ServiceRecordHandle` is a 32-bit unsigned integer and is stored on the remote device SDP server. You may recall from Figure 3-5 and our earlier discussion on the

Table 3-4   The list of available `Size` descriptors that form the least-significant section of the
`Header`.

SIZE	DESCRIPTION
0	1 Byte (or zero if a Null `Type` descriptor).
1	2 Bytes.
2	4 Bytes.
3	8 Bytes.
4	16 Bytes.
5	This value denotes that the following 1 Byte contains the size.
6	This value denotes that the following 2 Bytes contain the size.
7	This value denotes that the following 4 Bytes contain the size.

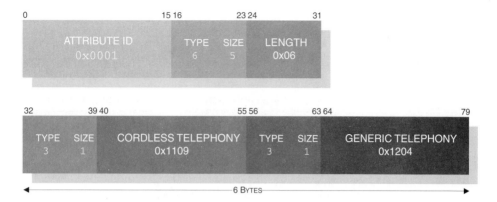

Figure 3-12 The encoding of the `ServiceClassIDList` for the Cordless Telephony service.

client-server model where the local device maintains an SDP client and the remote device manages the SDP server. The SDP server communicates with the *Service Record Database*, as to the available services it can offer the local device.

3.3.1.1.4 Browsing Services. When performing a service discovery of a remote device, the client undertakes a series of procedures to learn of the services it supports. *Browsing* is used to refer to the mechanism that is employed when you seek an *unknown* or *general*

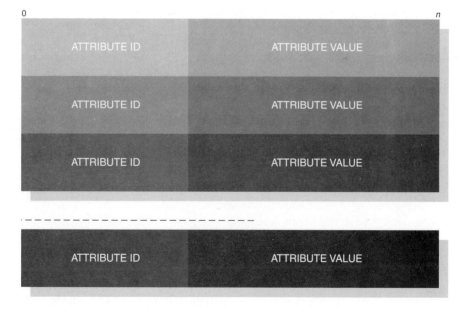

Figure 3-13 A service record is used to describe the variable collection of `ServiceAttributes`. This is sufficient information for a local device to understand the remote device capabilities.

Table 3-5 The list of `AttributeIDs` that make up a service record for the Cordless Telephony Profile.

ATTRIBUTE	DESCRIPTION
`ServiceRecordHandle`	With an `AttributeID` of `0x0000`, this uniquely identifies this service record within the SDP server.

`ServiceClassIDList`
 	
`ServiceClass0`
 	
`ServiceClass1`
	With an `AttributeID` of `0x0001`, the following `ServiceClass0` would contain the UUID for the *Cordless Telephony* (`0x1109`). The `ServiceClass1 AttributeValue` would identify *Generic Telephony* (`0x1204`).

`ProtocolDescriptorList`
 	
`Protocol0`
 	
`Protocol1`
	With an `AttributeID` of `0x0004`, the following `Protocol0` would contain a UUID for the protocol *L2CAP* (`0x0100`), whereas in `Protocol1` a UUID would contain the protocol identifier for *TCS-BIN-CORDLESS* (`0x0005`).

`BluetoothProfile-`
`DescriptorList`
 	
`Profile0`
 	
`ParameterFor0`
	With an `AttributeID` of `0x0009`, the following `Profile0` would identify the UUID for the *Cordless Telphony* service class and has a value of `0x1109`. The `ParameterFor0` accommodates the version number supported by this profile.

`ServiceName`	With a base `AttributeID` of `0x0006`, this attribute has an offset of `0x0000`. It is a configurable item and has the `AttributeValue` of a Text string.
`ExternalNetwork`	With an `AttributeID` of `0x0301`, this attribute identifies the external network the Cordless Telephony currently supports.

service is sought. In our earlier discussion, we provided several `AttributeIDs` that are used to construct a service record. A generic `AttributeID`, which is common to all services is the `BrowseGroupList` attribute, this has a unique value of `0x0005`. As with any `AttributeID`, the associated `AttributeValue` can be constructed with a data sequence. In this particular instance, the `AttributeValue` relates to the group to which the service belongs.

With the intent to search for services on a remote device, the local device constructs a *Search Pattern*, which is a list of UUIDs. UUIDs are 128-bit values, which have been shortened for use within Bluetooth applications. The shortcut has been provided by first establishing a *Bluetooth Base UUID*, which is shown in Table 3-6.

Table 3-6   The Bluetooth Base UUID that is used as a default reference from which all other UUIDs are generated.

BLUETOOTH BASE UUID
00000000-0000-1000-8000-00805F9B34FB

The UUIDs that have been presented so far are aliases and take the form of what is referred to as a 16- or 32-bit UUID; in turn, they all should refer to the 128-bit notation. These UUIDs have been assigned and can be referenced in the Bluetooth Special Interest Group, Bluetooth Assigned Numbers, v1.1, February 2001. For a search pattern to be successful, it needs to be converted to the 128-bit notation, since all searches will be compared at this range. In Table 3-7, we illustrate the arithmetic operation, which performs the conversion from the 16-bit and 32-bit representation into the full 128-bit notation.

3.3.1.1.5   The Service Discovery Protocol Data Unit.   Earlier, we touched upon the fact that a set of function primitives is established to realise true functionality within SDAP. In an attempt to expand our understanding of the companionship of the profile and protocol, we will begin by looking more closely at how the Service Discovery Protocol is used. Furthermore, we will explore the underlying mechanism that is exposed to the Service Discovery Application Profile, which in turn provides it with its primitive functionality.

A set of abstractions is used to provide and forms the basis of the core functionality. The SDP employs the use of a series of PDUs. The local device retrieves specific information with regards to the services available on the remote device, using a combination request and response PDU.

The profile relies upon the protocol for the request and response functionality and, in turn, the protocol then further relies on its underlying transport mechanism to facilitate the transport of the PDUs. To achieve this, the protocol makes use of the services provided by L2CAP, where the connection-orientated transport service is made available. The L2CAP component then subsequently uses an Asynchronus-Connectionless (ACL) link to take the PDUs over the air.

In Table 3-8, the combination request and response PDUs that are available within the protocol are illustrated, although you must bear in mind that the illustration provided does not represent an *Application Programming Interface* (API). Higher-level functionality or a user application would be employed to extract the relevant data from the PDU,

Table 3-7   The arithmetic operation, which is used to covert 16-bit and 32-bit UUIDs to the full 128-bit UUID notation.

16-Bit AND 32-Bit TO 128-Bit CONVERSION
$128_{Bits} = 16_{Bits} * 2^{96} + \text{Bluetooth Base UUID}$
$128_{Bits} = 32_{Bits} * 2^{96} + \text{Bluetooth Base UUID}$

Table 3-8   The SDP provides simple request-response PDU paradigm used to retrieve information about the specific services of the remote device.

FUNCTION	DESCRIPTION
SDP_ErrorResponse	This response PDU is generated, when the SDP receives a request from the client, when it is incorrectly formatted.
SDP_ServiceSearchRequest SDP_ServiceSearchResponse	This combination request-response PDU is used to instigate a search request using the ServiceSearchPattern parameter to identify corresponding records held within the server. The response provides a series of parameters, some of which describe the TotalServiceRecordCount and a ServiceRecordHandleList contains a list of the records found.
SDP_ServiceAttributeRequest SDP_ServiceAttributeResponse	This combination request-response PDU retrieves specific attribute record information from the server, whereas the previous function retrieved all records that match a particular pattern. A range of parameters is provided in the response, where the ServiceRecordHandle identifies the specific record and the AttributeIDList provides the list of attributes retrieved.
SDP_ServiceSearchAttributeRequest SDP_ServiceSearchAttributeResponse	Finally, this combination request-response PDU encompasses both the functionality of the SDP_ServiceSearchRequest and SDP_ServiceAttributeRequest. This functionality attempts to reduce the SDP traffic when seeking specific services.

where it would interpret the data and formulate the appropriate response. As such, the local and remote devices, which form the communicating parties, each have their own user application to fulfill their respective functional expectations.

The SDAP is conceptually positioned above the SDP in a user application on the local device, where it is referred to as the `SrvDscApp` (or Service Discovery Application). Here, it not only relies upon the protocol, it also embraces the use of a client (*SDP* client) and a management component; elsewhere in this book, this is commonly referred to as a *Management Entity*[2] (ME) for consistency. This component forms the basis on which discovery effort is coordinated, providing instructions for some certain operational modes, such as an inquiry or a paging state. The placement and existence of such a module remains implementation-specific. The remote device coordinates requests from the local device with the use of an SDP server and a service record database, which contains service records relevant to the services available.

In essence, the profile allows you as a developer to realise an API, which utilises the inherent protocol. The SDAP is therefore capable of providing this primitive functionality through the use of the SDP. We discuss the application perspective in more detail in Section 3.3.1.2, *SDP in the Service Discovery Application Profile.*

This itself is the minimum functionality you would expect from the profile, but should not be seen as an inadequacy, since it does not restrict the growth of other implementation-specific APIs. Coincidentally, in Part III, *The New Profiles*, the *ESDP: An Overview*, Chapter 18, we discuss the *Extended Service Discovery Profile* (ESDP) and how it fits within the SDAP context.

The SDP PDUs are used to instruct the server to undertake browsing procedures and to retrieve service record information about its services. As we previously discussed, the client and server operate a request and response paradigm. The SDAP will construct PDUs containing information relating to the `AttributeID` and `AttributeValues` in turn instructing the server to carry out its operation. Each PDU has a unique value, which are shown in Table 3-9.

In Figure 3-14, we illustrate the structure of a SDP PDU; this is applicable to all `SDP_ErrorResponse` PDUs. However, a *Continuation State* parameter is added to the remaining PDUs, since an SDP PDU response may be too large to fit into a single response. The server indicates that the client has only received a partial response and the client re-issues the original request with the `ContinuationState` copied into the new request to retrieve the remainder of the response.

The `ContinuationState` is of a variable length and is constructed of two further parameters. The *Info Length* parameter is the first byte used to indicate the size of *Continuation Information* parameter. When the request is re-issued, the server is first informed of the size of the `ContinuationInformation`, which instructs it where it had segmented the original response. The `InfoLength` parameter is set to zero to indicate that the response was completed in one transaction. We can see the structure of the PDU with the `ContinuationState` parameter as shown in Figure 3-15. You will also

---

[2]The SDAP actually refers to the equivalent entity as a *Bluetooth Module Controller*, but essentially the ME supports the same mechanisms.

Table 3-9   The list of values that are used to identify the PDU.

VALUE	PDU
0x00	Reserved.
0x01	SDP_ErrorResponse
0x02	SDP_ServiceSearchRequest
0x03	SDP_ServiceSearchResponse
0x04	SDP_ServiceAttributeRequest
0x05	SDP_ServiceAttributeResponse
0x06	SDP_ServiceSearchAttributeRequest
0x07	SDP_ServiceSearchAttributeRequest

notice from our illustrations that a `TransactionID` parameter and a `Parameter-Length` are also shown. The former parameter is a 16-bit unsigned integer used to identify the request PDU and is selected at random by the client, but it must be different to any other pending request. The `TransactionID` in the response PDU will be used to match the associated request. The `ParameterLength` is a 16-bit unsigned integer and is used to accurately describe the entire length of the PDU.

During normal operation the client and server exchange information with a request-response operation. However, if an incorrectly formatted request is sent to the server, it will respond with `SDP_ErrorResponse`. In Table 3-10, we can see the PDU format with its set of parameters.

The `ErrorInfo` parameter is implementation-specific, whereas the `ErrorCode` parameter attempts to provide a reason for the failure. In Table 3-11, we can see the list of errors that are used to describe the reason for failure.

3.3.1.1.5.1 SERVICE SEARCH REQUEST AND RESPONSE. Earlier, we touched upon the fact that a search pattern is created to seek services from the remote device. In the

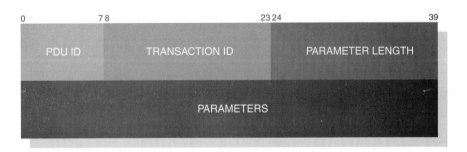

Figure 3-14   The structure of the SDP PDU.

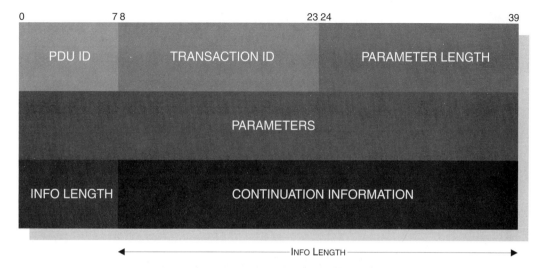

Figure 3-15   The structure of the SDP PDU with the `Continuation-State` parameter.

`SDP_ServiceSearchRequest` PDU, the `ServiceSearchPattern` contains the data element sequence, which will contain a series of UUIDs. In Table 3-12, we identify the request-response PDUs with their set of parameters. The `MaximumServiceRecordCount` parameter is a 16-bit unsigned integer that specifies the maximum number of services that should be returned. The `ContinuationState` parameter is constructed of a 1-byte `InfoLength` parameter used to describe the size of the `ContinuationInformation` parameter. The latter parameter here would contain n-bytes of information, which relates to a previous uncompleted response. The `ContinuationInformation` parameter must not be greater than the maximum of 16-bytes. If no partial response has been provided then the first part of the `ContinuationState` parameter is set to zero, indicating that there was no previous partial response.

The `SDP_ServiceSearchResponse` is returned containing a list of `ServiceRecordHandles`, which have been selected based upon the search pattern criteria. The `TotalServicesRecordCount` is an unsigned integer, which stores the number of services obtained and should never exceed the `MaximumServiceRecordCount`; the `TotalServicesRecordCount` will be zero if none were found. The `ContinuationState` parameter is constructed of a 1-byte `InfoLength` parameter used to describe the size of the `ContinuationInformation` parameter, where a

Table 3-10   The `SDP_ErrorResponse` that is used to indicate an error in the request packet.

RESPONSE	PARAMETERS
SDP_ErrorResponse	ErrorCode
	ErrorInfo

Table 3-11   A range of `ErrorCodes` that is used to identify why a request failed.

ERROR	DESCRIPTION
0x0000	Reserved.
0x0001	Unsupported SDP Version.
0x0002	Invalid `ServiceRecordHandle`.
0x0003	Invalid Request Syntax.
0x0004	Invalid PDU Size.
0x0005	Invalid `ContinuationState`.
0x0006	Insufficient Resources.

maximum size of 16-bytes is possible. If no partial response has been provided, then the first part of the `ContinuationState` parameter is set to zero, indicating that the response was completed.

3.3.1.1.5.2 SERVICE ATTRIBUTE REQUEST AND RESPONSE.   This combination of request-response PDUs will allow a specific service to be retrieved from the server. In the `SDP_ServiceAttributeRequest` PDU, the `ServiceRecordHandle`, which is a 32-bit unsigned integer, contains the identity of the service to be retrieved; this handle was previously retrieved using the `SDP_ServiceSearchRequest` PDU. In Table 3-13, we identify the request-response PDUs with their set of parameters. The `MaximumAttributeByteCount` parameter is a 16-bit unsigned integer that specifies the maxi-

Table 3-12   The request-response combination used to retrieve a specific search pattern containing a list of UUIDs.

REQUEST	PARAMETERS
`SDP_ServiceSearchRequest`	`ServiceSearchPattern`
	`MaximumServiceRecordCount`
	`ContinuationState`
RESPONSE	**PARAMETERS**
`SDP_ServiceSearchResponse`	`TotalServiceRecordCount`
	`CurrentServiceRecordCount`
	`ServiceRecordHandleList`
	`ContinuationState`

Table 3-13   The request-response combination used to retrieve a specific search pattern
containing a list of UUIDs.

REQUEST	PARAMETERS
SDP_ServiceAttributeRequest	ServiceRecordHandle
	MaximumAttributeByteCount
	AttributeIDList
	ContinuationState
RESPONSE	**PARAMETERS**
SDP_ServiceAttributeResponse	AttributeListByteCount
	AttributeList
	ContinuationState

mum number of bytes that should be returned. The `AttributeIDList` contains a data
element sequence, where the actual size varies; this is used to identify the attributes that
are being sought from the remote server. The `ContinuationState` parameter is constructed of a 1-byte `InfoLength` parameter used to describe the size of the `Continu-`
`ationInformation` parameter. The latter parameter here would contain *n*-bytes of
information, which relate to a previous uncompleted response. The `ContinuationIn-`
`formation` parameter must not be greater than the maximum of 16-bytes. If no partial
response has been provided, then the first part of the `ContinuationState` parameter
is set to zero, indicating that there was no previous partial response.

   This particular request-response PDU minimises the amount of PDU traffic over the air-
interface, since a specific service record is being retrieved. The response is generated when
a service record being requested has been found. The `AttributeListByteCount`
holds the total number of bytes that are contained in the `AttributeList` parameter. The
`AttributeListByteCount` must never be larger than the `MaximumAttribute-`
`ByteCount` parameter. The `AttributeList` contains a data element sequence of the
service that was retrieved by the server. The `ContinuationState` parameter is constructed of a 1-byte `InfoLength` parameter used to describe the size of the `Continua-`
`tionInformation` parameter, where a maximum size of 16-bytes is possible. If no
partial response has been provided, then the first part of the `ContinuationState` parameter is set to zero, indicating that the response was completed.

   3.3.1.1.5.3 SERVICE SEAR CH ATTRIBUTE REQUEST AND RESPONSE.   This combina-
tion of request-response PDUs combines the functionality offered to us in our previous
PDUs. In the `SDP_ServiceSearchAttributeRequest` PDU, the `Service-`
`SearchPattern` contains the data element sequence, which will contain a series of
UUIDs. In Table 3-14 we identify the request-response PDUs with their set of parameters.
The `MaximumAttributeByteCount` parameter is a 16-bit unsigned integer that

Table 3-14   The request-response combination that is used to retrieve a specific search
pattern containing a list of UUIDs and returns a list of `AttributeIDs` and
`AttributeValues`.

REQUEST	PARAMETERS
SDP_ServiceSearchAttributeRequest	ServiceSearchPattern
	MaximumAttributeByteCount
	AttributeIDList
	ContinuationState
RESPONSE	**PARAMETERS**
SDP_ServiceSearchAttributeResponse	AttributeListByteCount
	AttributeLists
	ContinuationState

specifies the maximum number of bytes that should be returned. The `AttributeID-
List` contains a data element sequence, where the actual size varies; this is used to
identify the attributes that are being sought from the remote server. The `Continua-
tionState` parameter is constructed of a 1-byte `InfoLength` parameter used to de-
scribe the size of the `ContinuationInformation` parameter. The latter parameter
here would contain *n*-bytes of information, which relates to a previous uncompleted response. The `ContinuationInformation` parameter must not be greater than the
maximum of 16-bytes. If no partial response has been provided, then the first part of the
`ContinuationState` parameter is set to zero, indicating that there was no previous
partial response.

The response is generated when a service record being requested has been found.
The `AttributeListByteCount` holds the total number of bytes that are contained in
the `AttributeList` parameter. The `AttributeListByteCount` must never be
larger than the `MaximumAttributeByteCount` parameter. The `AttributeLists`
contains a data element sequence of the service that was retrieved by the server. The
`ContinuationState` parameter is constructed of a 1-byte `InfoLength` parameter
used to describe the size of the `ContinuationInformation` parameter, where a
maximum size of 16-bytes is possible. If no partial response has been provided, then the
first part of the `ContinuationState` parameter is set to zero, indicating that the response was completed.

3.3.1.2   SDP in the Service Discovery Application Profile.   In Section 3.3.1.1,
The Service Discovery Protocol we learned about how request and response messages are
created to provide us with basic functionality. We then went on to discuss how we could
create an API and expose it to our application, where genuine functionality could be realised. We also learned that the SDP component would parse incoming request and re-

sponse packets, where an action can be decided based upon the encoded data. In this section, we now consider the objectives of SDP in the *profile* and its expectations. In establishing our operations and its primitive functionality, the profile discusses mandatory features that it expects from the protocol and provides guidance with regards to how a service discovery application might achieve these objectives.

In our earlier discussion, we touched upon the application convention that is used with an application embodying service discovery capabilities. We discussed that an application residing on a client would be named `SrvDscApp` (Service Discovery Application). The `SrvDscApp` uses the SDP client to instigate request and to subsequently receive response PDUs to learn of the services available. The remote device must support an SDP server, where responses are sent back to the local device. These dependencies are illustrated in Table 3-15.

The `SrvDscApp` would undertake a series of actions to retrieve the services from the remote device. A remote device may be in one of three states when the local device commences its search; these are described in Table 3-16. These states are not restricted to a one-to-one communication link. A device discovery may return the availability of numerous devices that are in radio range and it is assumed that the ME, as previously discussed, is capable of instructing the lower-layers to enter inquiry and page scan substates. The `SrvDscApp` may undertake service retrieval from one device at a time, where it first establishes a connection to collect the service information. When all service information has been retrieved, the `SrvDscApp` will terminate its current connection and establish a new connection with the next device, although if the device is currently connected then the `SrvDscApp` may choose not to terminate its connection.

In Figure 3-16, we illustrate the possible sequence of events that occur between the local and remote device. The illustration does not show any authentication processes, since the user of the remote device determines the provision of authentication and pairing, and therefore its use is optional.

You may recall from our earlier discussion in Section 3.3.1.1.1, *The Client-Server Model*, that the user of a remote device can choose to mandate the authentication and encryption requirements. The inquiry and pairing procedure may not necessarily be undertaken since the device may be *trusted* or *already* connected.

The idiosyncrasies of a `SrvDscApp` remain implementation-specific, but its core capabilities to retrieve service information are mandated. We now take an opportunity to reflect on function primitives, which may in turn be a suitable framework for a developer to start looking at an implementation of the SDAP. In describing these primitives, it is assumed that these will have access to the PDUs and its underlying functionality, which we

Table 3-15   As a minimum, the local device must support the use of a client application and the remote device must support the use of a server.

FEATURE	LOCAL	REMOTE
SDP Client	M	O
SDP Server	O	M

Table 3-16 The remote device will be in one of these states. The `SrvDscApp` must be capable of managing the appropriate sequence of events to retrieve service information from the remote device.

STATE	DESCRIPTION
Unknown	The remote device has not been discovered and the user would need to perform an inquiry and device discovery procedures to learn of the availability of the device in radio range.
Trusted	A device in this state would indicate that a previous connection had occurred, but it is no longer connected. As a result of this previous connection the devices maintain a trusted relationship, that is both devices have paired.
Connected	The local and remote devices have an active connection.

previously discussed. In Table 3-17, we outline the mandatory (M) and excluded (X) PDUs that are required to implement such primitives. Our discussion refers to the operation of a local and remote device and how interaction is achieved between them.

In Table 3-18, we illustrate suggested, although not necessarily compulsory, since implementations will differ from manufacturer to manufacturer, function primitives, which in turn encompass a complete sequence to retrieve a service. An actual function content is con-

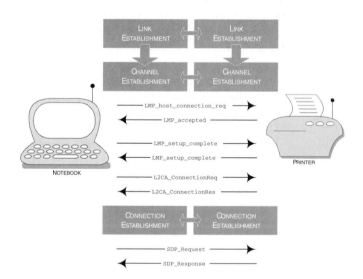

Figure 3-16 The sequence of events that occur when an SDP session is established. Authentication may be required between the local and remote device, but it is not shown here.

Table 3-17   A `SrvDscApp` must have access to the core capabilities of the SDP.

PDU	LOCAL	REMOTE
SDP_ErrorResponse	X	M
SDP_ServiceSearchRequest	M	X
SDP_ServiceSearchResponse	X	M
SDP_ServiceAttributeRequest	M	X
SDP_ServiceAttributeResponse	X	M
SDP_ServiceSearchAttributeRequest	M	X
SDP_ServiceSearchAttributeResponse	X	M

structed at the discretion of the developer. You may wish to incorporate activities such as inquiry and page scan substates, where you can at least obtain the availability of devices within radio range. Alternatively, you may wish to keep it simple and restrict to simply acquiring service information. It is important to understand what is discussed here is not cast in stone and as a developer any API that you create is at your discretion.

3.3.1.3   L2CAP.   The L2CAP layer provides transparency for the upper layers of the stack from the layers typically found within the host controller. L2CAP payloads are passed to the *Host Controller Interface*[3] (HCI), which is then subsequently passed onto the *Link Manager Protocol* (LMP). The range of upper layers, which include RFCOMM, SDP and *Telephony Control Protocol Specification* (TCS) all make use of the capabilities offered to us by L2CAP. Its primary role is to provide *protocol multiplexing*, allowing numerous simultaneous connections to be made, and also providing the ability for *segmentation* and *reassembly*. This refers to the ability to manage large payloads in the application, which may need to be fragmented into smaller payloads for the lower-layers to manage; these are then transmitted over the air-interface. Finally, the L2CAP layer exchanges *Quality of Service* (QoS) information, ensuring that sufficient resources are available and that both Bluetooth devices are attaining the best service.

In Table 3-19, we summarise the broad capabilities that are expected from L2CAP and in the table you will notice features are marked with *M* (Mandatory), *O* (Optional), *X* (Excluded), *C* (Conditional) and *N/A* (Not Applicable), these determine what is expected from the L2CAP layer.

3.3.1.3.1   Channel Types.   In Table 3-19, we have identified that *Connection-orientated Channels* are mandatory, whereas *Connectionless Channels* are excluded; this

---

[3]L2CAP payloads are passed directly onto LMP when implemented on a hostless system.

Table 3-18   An `SrvDscApp` must have access to the core capabilities of the SDP.

PRIMITIVE	DESCRIPTION
OpenSearch	This primitive may be used to first establish a connection with a remote device where at least a communications pathway exists over the air-interface for service information to be exchanged.
CloseSearch	Conversely, this function would be used to terminate a connection with the remote device once sufficient service information has been obtained.
ServiceSearch	This type of primitive may be used to encompass multiple searches on many remote devices. An `OpenSearch` may have been performed prior to a `ServiceSearch`, where a list of known devices had been retrieved beforehand. The `ServiceSearch` primitive encapsulates the searching of all the devices found based upon a search pattern.
ServiceBrowse	Again, using the `OpenSearch` to establish the availability of remote devices, the `ServiceBrowse` primitive would be used to collect specific search information based upon a `BrowseGroup`.
EnumerateSearch	A search can be performed on the basis of a Class of Device (CoD) identification. This primitive encompasses some form of filtering where specific devices based on the CoD are filtered.

type of channel is aimed at broadcasting, where all devices may be targeted. L2CAP uses PDUs to transport connection, signalling and configuration options, which will be discussed in a moment. The higher-layers of the Bluetooth protocol stack will instigate a connection with L2CAP using the `L2CA_ConnectReq` request packet, where the corresponding result is contained within the `L2CA_ConnectRsp` response packet. An `L2CA_ConnectRspNeg` negative response packet is used to denote a response, where the connection with the remote device was unsuccessful. Since our profile resides above L2CAP and employs its services, we are only concerned with the upper protocol layer of L2CAP. This higher functionality is offered to us through a series of L2CAP events and is denoted through the prefix `L2CA_`; see Table 3-20.

When creating an L2CAP connection between two devices, a *Protocol/Service Multiplexor* (PSM) value is used to denote the higher-layer protocol that is using the connection; Table 3-21 identifies these values and the corresponding protocol they represent. The value of `0x0001` (SDP) is used for this profile.

Table 3-19 The illustration shows specific procedures that this profile depends upon to re-alise its compliant implementation.

PROCEDURE	LOCAL	REMOTE
Connection-Orientated Channel	M	M
Connectionless Channel	X	X
Connection Establishment	M	C
Configuration	M	M
Connection Termination	M	C
Echo	M	M
Command Rejection	M	M
Maximum Transmission Unit	M	M
Flush Timeout	M	M
Quality of Service	O	O

3.3.1.3.2 Signalling.   When establishing communication with a remote device, a *signalling channel* is created and reserved for use during connection, disconnection and configuration of subsequent L2CAP connections. A *channel* is used to describe the communication and data flow that exists between L2CAP entities and Table 3-22 illustrates the range of *Channel Identifies* (CIDs) that are used to identify the channel type. As we can see in Table 3-19, *Connection Establishment* and *Termination* is mandatory in the local device, although the remote device may be capable of initiating and terminating a connection to the local device. The `L2CA_DisconnectReq` re-

Table 3-20 The range of prototypes used to illustrate how L2CAP is architected and how interaction between higher- and lower-layers is achieved. For this discussion, our concern here is with the higher-layer.

PROTOTYPE	DESCRIPTION
`L2CA_`	This prefix prototype is used to denote the higher-layer interaction, typically used by RFCOMM, SDP and TCS.
`L2CAP_`	This prefix is used to denote peer-to-peer signalling interaction of L2CAP entities.
`LP_`	Finally, this prefix denotes lower-layer interaction, where L2CAP interfaces with the LMP layer.

Table 3-21   The PSM values that are used to identify the higher-layer protocol.

PSM	DESCRIPTION
0x0001	SDP
0x0003	RFCOMM
0x0005	TCS-BIN
0x0007	TCS-BIN-CORDLESS

quest packet is used to terminate the connection with the remote device and a `L2CA_DisconnectRsp` response packet is used to ascertain the result of the termination; although all disconnection requests must be completed successfully. The support of *Configuration* is shown as mandatory and we will discuss these specific options in more detail in the following section. Finally, *Echo* and *Command Rejection* are both mandatory for a compliant SDAP.

3.3.1.3.3 Configuration Options.   In establishing a connection with the remote device, the channel is subject to configuration and the higher-layer prototype `L2CA_ConfigReq` request packet is used to carry configuration requests. Its associated response is contained within the `L2CA_ConfigRsp` packet; an `L2CA_ConfigRspNeg` packet is used to denote a negative response during configuration, where for example the suggested *Maximum Transmission Unit* (MTU) is too large. In Table 3-19, we have identified that the MTU and *Flush Timeout* parameters are mandatory, whereas the QoS is optional.

The default MTU setting for the signalling channel is 48 bytes, whereas other channels may be capable of transferring larger payloads; essentially the MTU determines the size of payloads that are capable of being exchanged between two devices. During configuration, the local device will inform the remote device that it is potentially capable of accepting larger payloads. If the remote device is unwilling to accept a larger MTU, then the local device is informed with the response contained within the `L2CA_ConfigRspNeg` packet.

Table 3-22   The CIDs used to represent the logical channel.

CID	DESCRIPTION
0x0000	Null
0x0001	Signalling Channel
0x0002	Connectionless Reception Channel
0x0003 to 0x003F	Reserved
0x0040 to 0xFFFF	Dynamically Allocated

When L2CA_ request and response packets are being exchanged, the Flush Time-out parameter is used to determine how long the local device is prepared to continue to transmit an L2CAP fragment before it gives up; the packet is subsequently flushed or in other words discarded. The suggested Flush Timeout value is sent during the L2CA_ConfigReq request packet. However, if no value is set, then the default value is used. The SDAP uses the default value of 0xFFFF.

As we have already mentioned, the QoS configuration is optional, but if it is used during an L2CA_ConfigReq request, then the *best effort* service is established as a default; the available services that are supported for an L2CAP channel are shown in Table 3-23. However, if the QoS service is set at *Guaranteed,* then parameters such as *Token Rate*, *Token Bucket*, *Peak Bandwidth*, *Latency* and *Delay Variation*, are used to determine an acceptable guaranteed service, where the L2CA_ConnectRspNeg, will indicate that these values are unacceptable. These parameters are then subject to further negotiation.

3.3.1.4   Link Manager.   The *Link Manager* (LM) layer sits between the HCI and the *Link Controller* (LC), although on a hostless system the LM will have direct interaction with L2CAP. It accepts commands from HCI and translates them into operations for the LC, where ACL and *Synchronous Connection-Orientated* (SCO) links are created and established. It is during this stage of ACL and SCO establishment that a master-slave switch would be performed as governed by the requirements of this profile. The LM is also responsible for placing the device into a low-power mode, which includes *hold*, *sniff* and *park*.

In providing *general* error management, devices that operate mandatory procedures during interoperability, must either acknowledge their support or provide a suitable reason informing the initiator why the procedure failed. The LMP_Detach PDU is used to inform the device of the error that occurred; typically the reason *unsupported LMP feature* (0x1A) is reported, see Appendix A.

Table 3-23   The range of service definitions that are used during QoS.

SERVICE	DESCRIPTION
No Traffic	This indicates that the channel will not be sending any traffic and, as such, any parameters can be ignored.
Best Effort	This default value attempts to achieve a minimum service with the remote device, where no guarantees are offered.
Guaranteed	With this service definition, we indicate that we wish to achieve the maximum bandwidth permitted, of course subject to the nature of a wireless environment.

In our following discussion, we take an opportunity to explore the dependencies that make up the SDAP, where we provide a narrative of the capabilities that are expected at this level. Table 3-24 identifies the capabilities that are required from this layer and in the following subsections we discuss the specific procedures in more detail.

3.3.1.4.1   Capabilities.   Table 3-24 summarises the broad capabilities that are expected from the LM and in the table you will notice procedures are marked with *M* (Mandatory), *O* (Optional), *X* (Excluded), *C* (Conditional) and *N/A* (Not Applicable); this will determine what is expected from the procedures at the LM. What has been included in the table is a set of deviations that the profile requires, which is above the common set of procedures expected at LM.

Authentication and encryption in this profile is not necessarily mandated. However, if the remote device imposes such restrictions on the local device, it is expected that both devices will provide support. If a device does not support such a procedure, then the error behaviour as previously outlined must be adhered.

3.3.1.4.1.1   AUTHENTICATION.   *Authentication* is used when DeviceA and DeviceB share a common link key or initialisation key, which is typically obtained during the pairing process. You may remember from our earlier chapter that the pairing process requires a user to enter a Bluetooth Passkey.

The authentication process encompasses LMP Authentication procedures, but all LMP Pairing procedures must have been performed prior to this event. As for the LMP Authentication procedure, this is primarily based on a challenge-response scheme. Here, the verifier or DeviceA sends the `LMP_au_rand` command, containing a random number to the claimant or DeviceB; the random number forms the challenge aspect of this scheme. The response, forming the final part of this scheme, is sent to the verifier using the `LMP_sres` command, which contains the result of the operation. If the operation is what the verifier expected, then it considers the claimant as authenticated.

The LMP Pairing procedure occurs when there is no link key and, as such, if an `LMP_au_rand` is sent to the claimant it will respond with `LMP_not_accepted` offering the reason as *key missing* (0x06), see Appendix A. If a key has been previously associated with the claimant, then the claimant proceeds to calculate the response and provides the verifier with a response through `LMP_sres`. However, if the calculated response is incorrect the verifier can terminate the connection with the command `LMP_detach`, offering the reason as *authentication failure* (0x05), see Appendix A; Table 3-25 summarises the LMP commands used during authentication.

Table 3-24   The summary of procedures, which are deviations from the standard procedures that are typically inherent at this level.

PROCEDURES	LOCAL	REMOTE
Authentication	C	C
Encryption	C	C

Table 3-25   The range of LMP PDUs available for authentication.

PDU	PARAMETER
LMP_au_rand	RandomNumber
LMP_sres	AuthenticationResponse
LMP_detach	Reason

3.3.1.4.1.2 ENCRYPTION.   The process of encryption commences when at least one device has authenticated. DeviceA (or client) takes the initiative and needs to determine whether to include encryption for point-to-point or broadcast communication. If DeviceB (or server) is agreeable to the parameters offered by the master, the master proceeds to communicate further detailed information about the encryption parameters.

The actual process is invoked when the two parties agree to use encryption and then L2CAP communication terminates, where the master then sends the LMP_encryption_mode_req command. If this is acceptable to the slave, it too terminates all L2CAP communication and responds with the LMP_accepted command. The next step in this process actually determines the size of the *encryption key* and it is the master that sends the LMP_encryption_key_size_req command, where it offers an initial recommendation of the key size to use. The slave, in turn, then offers its own recommendation, where it informs the master what it thinks it might be capable of. Both master and slave will repeat this process until they reach an agreement, however, if neither party reaches a decision then the LMP_not_accepted command is sent, offering the reason as *unsupported parameter value* (0x20), see Appendix A.

Upon accepting the key size the LMP_accepted command is issued and the encryption procedure then takes place by issuing the LMP_start_encryption_req command with a random number, which is used to calculate the encryption key. Table 3-26 summarises the available commands for the encryption process.

3.3.1.5   Link Controller (LC).   The LC layer is the lowest layer depicted in the dependencies of this profile and is responsible for a large number of core capabilities. It

Table 3-26   The range of LMP PDUs available for encryption.

PDU	PARAMETER
LMP_encryption_mode_req	EncryptionMode
LMP_encryption_key_size_req	KeySize
LMP_start_encryption_req	RandomNumber
LMP_stop_encryption_req	*None*

manages air-to-interface transactions and determines the fundamental timing of ACL and SCO data packet transmission and reception, as well as coordinating effort at its upper-edge with the LM. It also encompasses the management of the various packet types and the various inquiries and paging procedures that are available. In turn, the following sub-sections provide clarity with regards to the capabilities that are a requirement at the LC level for the SDAP. In our understanding of the dependencies, we begin by examining in more detail the supported capabilities and a small discussion is offered for each, where support is deemed as mandatory. If you are a developer providing profile-specific applications, then it is unlikely that you will engage in a large part of this component, although in some audio-related applications direct access may be required, where a faster transport mechanism can be supported. Nevertheless, many manufacturers have architected an audio-specific API for intelligible access to this component.

3.3.1.5.1   Capabilities.   Table 3-27 summarises the broad capabilities that are expected from the LC and in the table you will notice features are marked appropriately; this will determine what is expected from the features at the LC.

3.3.1.5.1.1   INQUIRY AND INQUIRY SCAN.   An inquiry procedure is used to learn of the other devices in radio range, where the *Bluetooth Device Address* (BD_ADDR) and clock offsets are obtained; it is DeviceA that will enter an *inquiry substate* to perform this procedure. A device that wishes to be discovered (DeviceB) will enter an *inquiry scan substate*, where the device will respond with an *inquiry response*. In this state, DeviceB is waiting to receive an *Inquiry Access Code* (IAC). From an application perspective, these modes of operation are discussed in more detail in the *Generic Access Profile*, Chapter 2. It is here that specific rules are determined with regards to the behaviour of such devices and how long these devices can operate in such modes. When devices have been discovered, this information is passed over to the SDAP, which manages the specific attributes that make up that device.

Table 3-27   The summary of capabilities that are required for the LC to enable a compliant SDAP.

PROCEDURES	LOCAL	REMOTE
Inquiry	M	X
Inquiry Scan	X	M
Paging	M	X
Page Scan	X	M
Inter-piconet	O	O
Packet Types	M	M

What is being established here, as a dependency, is that the Bluetooth protocol stack must encompass and support such behavioural procedures for this profile to be considered compliant.

3.3.1.5.1.2 PAGING AND PAGING SCAN. The *inquiry substate* and *inquiry scan substate* procedures are the initial methods used to learn of other devices in radio range; to this extent, the device has discovered sufficient information to gain a connection with the remote device. This is achieved when DeviceA has the intent to create a connection with DeviceB; DeviceA is now placed into a *paging substate*, where it will periodically transmit the *Device Access Code* (DAC). The DAC is used to target the device directly and the clock offset is used to gain an idea of the clock cycle of DeviceB. These parameters were originally obtained during our inquiry procedures. If DeviceB wishes to be connected, then it will enter a *page scan substate* and will respond accordingly to DeviceA. An inquiry procedure may be avoided if the BD_ADDR is already known, although a connection may take a little longer if the clock offset is not known.

3.3.1.5.1.3 INTER-PICONET. Inter-piconet capabilities describe the process that allows the master to manage multiple connections from slave devices. During a connection, other users may temporarily witness degradation in the service that is being provided; however, the master must be capable of accepting new participants in the piconet.

3.3.1.5.1.4 PACKET TYPES. There are numerous packet types available and Table 3-28 identifies the most often used packets for profile support. There are also a number of

Table 3-28 The summary of packet types that are required for the LC to enable a compliant SDAP.

PACKET TYPE	LOCAL	REMOTE
DM1	M	M
DH1	M	M
DM3	M	M
DH3	M	M
DM5	M	M
DH5	M	M
HV1	X	X
HV2	X	X
HV3	X	X
DV	X	X

common packet types that are used for general purpose transport; for example, the ID packet is used for inquiry procedures and a POLL packet would be sent by DeviceA to determine if a slave is active on a channel.

The DM1 packet type is used to transmit control data over any connection, but may be used to transport a genuine payload. HV1, HV2 and HV3 are various SCO packet types to carry audio-specific data, where a DV packet can combine ACL and SCO specific data; their support in this profile is reflected in Table 3-28. Various ACL packet types are also available, in fact seven types including the DM1 type are attributed to carrying user-specific data; these include DH1, DM3, DH3, DM5, DH5 and AUX1; similarly, Table 3-28 summarises their support in this profile.

3.4   SUMMARY

- Service Discovery is used when learning about the services or capabilities that remote devices are capable of supporting.
- It is assumed that an inquiry and a device discovery procedure have already been performed.
- Performing a device discovery allows you to learn of the devices in radio range, whereas a service discovery provides you with a list of services that can be supported by that device.
- A local and remote device is used to represent the partying devices: a local device initiates a service discovery and a remote device responds.
- A client and server model is used to represent the operating model when requesting and responding to PDUs.
- A series of PDUs exist to illustrate the operations required to perform a specific function.
- The SrvDscApp is used to realise functionality at the user-interface level.
- The SrvDscApp utilises an API, which in turn performs the necessary operations, which may provide device discovery procedures as well as service discovery procedures.
- SDAP relies on the SDP as its underlying mode of transport.
- SDP is structured to provide you with response-request scheme, working with a client-server model.
- Unique AttributeIDs and AttributeValues are used to describe to a local device what the services are.
- A user may make use of services by initiate a connection with the device.

4

The Cordless
Telephony Profile

4.1 INTRODUCTION

The *Cordless Telephony Profile* provides the usage models described as the *3-in-1 phone*. These new usage models accommodate general wireless telephony enabling Bluetooth solutions within the home or office environment. Bluetooth-enabled cordless handsets and multimedia PCs are all part of the 3-in-1 phone usage model allowing these devices to access a fixed telephone network, such as a *Public Switched Telephone Network* (PSTN) or an *Integrated Services Digital Network* (ISDN). It also extends the functionality already offered within a mobile phone, where short-range communication can be supported allowing the mobile phone to access similar fixed telephone networks; Figure 4-1 and Figure 4-2 illustrate the usage models supported by this profile.

4.1.1 Comparing Cordless Telephony with the Headset Profile

The *Cordless Telephony* and *Intercom Profiles* both depend upon the TCS; the Bluetooth *Telephone Control Protocol Specification* or the *TCS-Binary* (TCS-BIN), further shortened to TCS. This is discussed in some more detail in Section 4.5.1.3, *The Telephony Control Protocol*. In Figure 4-3, we compare the stack components that make up both the Cordless Telephony and Headset application types, where the Bluetooth protocol stack

Figure 4-1 A Bluetooth-enabled gateway is capable of supporting a connection from a cordless handset and a mobile phone.

architecture can be compared and examined in more detail. As we previously mentioned, the Cordless Telephony Profile is based upon TCS and, as we can see from our illustration, the Headset Profile is dependent upon the implementation provided by RFCOMM. This provides the Headset with the *AT Command Control* and is implemented as the name suggests, through a series of AT Commands, which enable and control signalling.

In our new usage scenarios as illustrated in Figure 4-1 and Figure 4-2, all interacting devices make use of a base station or as the profile describes it *a gateway*; we will look at this role in more detail later. We can see that a headset device can equally lend itself to the role of a cordless handset, where audio transfer is made between the base station and the headset, in the same way it occurs for the cordless handset. However, it would require the headset to be compliant with the Cordless Telephony Profile (Figure 4-3), that is, have an implementation that encompasses TCS; moreover, a dual implementation of the AT Command Control and the Cordless Telephony may be considered, allowing the user to switch between usage scenarios. The implementation of this switch may be transparent, allowing the user to seamlessly move from one environment to another.

Figure 4-2 A Bluetooth-enabled gateway is also capable of supporting a multimedia-enabled notebook or PC.

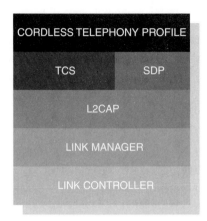 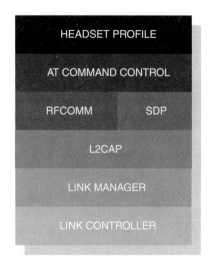

Figure 4-3   The Cordless Telephony and Headset Profile protocol components are placed side-by-side to illustrate the differences in stack architecture.

4.2   USAGE MODELS

This section of the chapter now considers both existing and future usage models through scenarios that may be typical for the Cordless Telephony Profile. We begin by exploring the existing models, where, the 3-in-1 phone models is explored in further detail; in our future usage models section, we consider other scenarios where the Cordless Telephony Profile may benefit from other profile overlap as discussed in our earlier section.

4.2.1   Existing Usage Models

The scenarios provided in Figure 4-1 and Figure 4-2 represent our existing usage models. In the illustration a *mobile phone*, *cordless handset* and a *multimedia notebook* are shown. The same illustration also shows a *gateway* (GW), which may be connected to an external network such as a PSTN and an ISDN network. The GW also assumes responsibility for call set-up in both incoming and outgoing communication. It is possible for the gateway to accept multiple[1] connections from *terminals* (TLs); terminals represent the devices that support the Cordless Telephony Profile and include mobile phones, cordless headsets and multimedia PCs or notebooks as previously described.

---

[1]Specifically, the number of active connections permitted would be seven. This is due to the number of concurrent connections that can be maintained by one master device. The AM_ADDR represents the slave member address and is used to identify active participants; this is currently restricted to 3 bits, although slaves that become disconnected or parked give up this address.

In an attempt to understand the existing usage models, we begin first by considering the extended functionality provided by a mobile phone. This dual capability falls within the remit provided by a cordless handset, since the mobile phone will have the capability of connecting to the gateway to allow it to connect to the external network, thus avoiding the *Global System for Mobile communications* (GSM) Network. This, in turn, provides cheaper calls. The Cordless Handset usage model is simply the case of removing the need for cables. In many residential and office environments, we already witness the cordless handset model. Here, we are making the crossover to the Bluetooth model, which in turn, provides us with greater diversity for the applications we choose to develop.

In our last scenario, the multimedia notebook has the capability through a Bluetooth dongle[2] or an integrated Bluetooth system[3] of connecting to a gateway and providing it with speech through the built-in or externally connected speakers; outgoing communication is achieved through a microphone.

The gateway device is already capable of supporting up to seven users and, as such, its behaviour is very much like an access point, where multiple connections can be made to just the one unit. In an office environment, this could be extended such that roaming from one gateway to another may also be supported.

4.2.2   Future Usage Models

With an immediate continuation of the multimedia notebook scenario, we can easily identify the ability of a headset being used. Similarly, a headset supporting the Cordless Telephony Profile can be connected wirelessly to the gateway. In existing office environments, headsets are used with local[4] base-stations; as such, headsets provide the user the flexibility to move around and free their hands.

In the home environment, the availability of cordless handsets and a gateway can be extended to the home PC user, where an Internet connection can be established though the gateway. Of course, this would require that the Dial-up Networking Profile accommodates and integrates the Cordless Telephony Profile. Alternatively, the gateway could provide the ability as a *LAN Access Point* (LAP), see *The LAN Access Profile*, Chapter 10 or as a *Network Access Point* (NAP), see the *PAN: An Overview*, Chapter 16, to allow seamless connections to be achieved with your *Internet Service Provider* (ISP).

In our previous section, we mentioned the ability for a user to roam from one gateway device to another in an office environment. A more concrete example is that of a telephone receptionist. Often, a receptionist's role is not just to answer telephone calls; they may also help with office administration. With a Bluetooth-enabled headset that supports

---

[2]A Bluetooth dongle is a device that extends the capability of a PC or notebook; it bestows the wireless ability to connect to other Bluetooth-enabled devices. PCMCIA or USB adaptors are typical products that have emerged on the market and support many of the profiles covered within this book.

[3]Some larger PC and notebook manufacturers have begun to supply PCs and notebooks with Bluetooth wireless connectivity as an integrated part of the unit. As we see the popularity of Bluetooth technology increase, more and more manufacturers will choose to incorporate a Bluetooth solution into their products.

[4]The term local base-station in this context refers to a corded-handset on an individual's desk. In some cases, the user will choose a corded headset to provide them with hands-free capability.

the Cordless Telephony Profile, they can receive and make outing calls while they are attending to their administrative duties. With the limited functionality provided with the few buttons on the device, manufacturers may choose to develop a wireless button-operated device whose role would be to extend the functionality of the headset. This Bluetooth *Headset-pad* would allow the user to transfer calls between extensions and have a range of dialling options.

4.3   PROFILE PRINCIPLES

The Cordless Telephony Profile provides two new roles: a *Gateway* (GW) and a *Terminal* (TL). The GW device is used as an endpoint, where it interfaces to the outside world over such technologies as PSTN or ISDN. It is capable of managing multiple connections from terminal devices, where speech and data services are provided to a cordless handset, mobile phone or multimedia PCs. In Figure 4-4, we can see how Cordless Telephony components are integrated with the existing Bluetooth protocol stack.

    The profile defines a set of protocols and procedures, which are required to realise the profile implementation. Several feature definitions are provided enabling capabilities such as *Calling Line Identification Presentation* (CLIP), *Connection Management* and *Dual Tone Multiple Frequency* (DTMF); we will discuss more about these and other features later.

    The GW must remain master of the piconet and all TLs must perform the master-slave switch, see Section 4.5.1.6.3, *Master-Slave Switch*, when configured for multi-terminal mode. Authentication and encryption are mandatory and should be used between

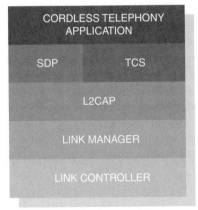
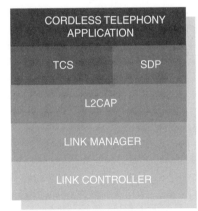

BLUETOOTH-ENABLED GATEWAY DEVICE   BLUETOOTH-ENABLED TERMINAL DEVICE

Figure 4-4   The core components of the Bluetooth protocol stack are shown and illustrate how the components of the Cordless Telephony Profile are integrated.

Table 4-1   The list of behavioural characteristics that are typical for this profile.

CONFIGURATION	ROLE	DESCRIPTION
DeviceA	TL	A device acting as a terminal, which may take the form of a mobile phone or cordless handset. In this particular context, the device is described as initiating the connection with the accepting device.
	Initiator	This configuration describes the device that instigates the original connection or the device that wishes to initiate communication over an existing link.
DeviceB	GW	A device that behaves as a gateway, where it manages incoming and outgoing external communication. It is also the party that accepts incoming connections from the terminal. The gateway may also instigate a connection with a terminal, where the terminal will take on the role of acceptor.
	Acceptor	This configuration describes the process of the device accepting the initiated communication from DeviceA.

TLs and the GW—as such, the procedures as described for authentication and encryption in the *Generic Access Profile*, Chapter 2 must be followed.

In Table 4-1, clarification is provided with regard to the roles used within the context of this profile. In general, *DeviceA* represents the initiating party and *DeviceB* represents the accepting party. The terms are often used interchangeably, when describing specific operations in various contexts. They are provided here for reference.

The Cordless Telephony Profile does operate master-slave switching and either the GW or TL may initiate the connection. As such, the initiating party is referred to as DeviceA or the initiator. DeviceB is the acceptor. Any device in this party may initiate a connection, but the GW must remain the master if it is configured for multi-terminal support.

4.4   USER EXPECTATIONS

The Cordless Telephony Profile is dependent upon the underlying profiles, where *Connection Establishment* procedures are applicable and are illustrated in the *Generic Access Profile*, Chapter 2. The connection establishment procedures encompass the availability

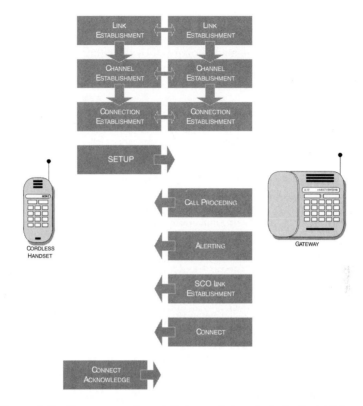

Figure 4-5   The sequence of events that occur during a typical call establishment.

of an initialised and configured L2CAP connection. If the device is in Park[5] Mode, then the device is unparked prior to any creation of a *Synchronous Connection Orientated (SCO)* connection; if no previous session exists, then one is created and the device may request parked status. Therefore, it is assumed that the GW and TL devices have previously performed an inquiry, discovery and any authentication and encryption.

With multi-terminal support enabled, the gateway is capable of supporting up to seven devices. With multiple devices connected, this establishes a *Wireless User Group* (WUG). Only three active voice communication links can be active, which is due to the limitations of bandwidth imposed by the nature of SCO.

An incoming call from the external network will generate an audible alert, notifying the user of an incoming connection; CLIP is used to identify the incoming caller. The user may now accept or reject the call by operating the buttons available on the cordless

---

[5]This mode provides low-power usage and, as such, little activity of the slave, but it remains synchronised with the channel, see our later discussion in Section 4.5.1.6.4, *Supporting Park Mode*. It is recommended that park mode be supported for this profile so that TLs and possibly GWs may conserve battery consumption.

handset. With a multimedia notebook, specific software for the cordless telephony application may be used to accept or reject the caller by operating a menu-driven user interface.

A user may initiate an outgoing call by operating the buttons available on the cordless handset. If a TL loses a connection with the GW, as a result of moving out of radio range, then the GW will attempt to re-establish the original connection by regularly paging the TL device.

4.5 LIFTING THE LID

4.5.1 Dependencies

We have previously explored both existing and future usage models, but we now take an opportunity to consider the dependencies that make up this particular profile in greater depth. In Figure 4-6, we provide a conceptual illustration representing the dependencies that make up the Cordless Telephony Profile; the areas that are shaded are relevant to this profile. As you can see, the profile depends upon the basic functionality offered to us by the *Generic Access Profile*, Chapter 2, the *Service Discovery Application Profile*, Chapter 3 and the *Telephony Control Protocol*. The basic functionality, along with any variations occuring within it, are now discussed as we take a closer look at the basic requirements of the dependent components.

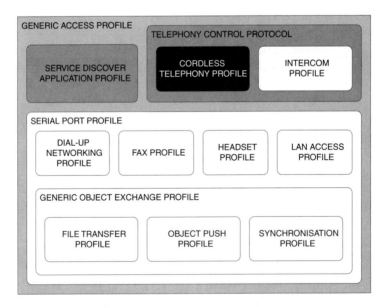

Figure 4-6   The dependent components of the Bluetooth protocol stack that make up the Cordless Telephony Profile. The areas that are shaded are relevant to this profile.

4.5.1.1 Generic Access. The capabilities of the Cordless Telephony Profile are provided by the *Generic Access Profile,* Chapter 2. Earlier we learned that a level of basic functionality is achieved through establishing a set of rules and procedures. These specifically relate to a device's connectivity, discoverability and common characteristics at the user interface level, with some additional emphasis provided for security. By establishing a commonality between products through these rules and procedures, we are able to provide achieve a cohesive user experience. This section now takes an opportunity to reflect upon the behavioural aspects of Bluetooth-enabled devices as outlined by the Generic Access Profile.

In Table 4-2, the basic set of procedures is illustrated identifying functional expectations, which in turn govern operation. These procedures help determine the context that the device would operate in—for example, a device may wish to be discoverable for a period of time or it may require a level of security that differs from one device to another depending upon the services it is capable of offering.

In Table 4-3, we consider the specific set of operations that are required for this profile. In the table, you will notice features are marked with *M* (Mandatory), *O* (Optional), *X* (Excluded), *C* (Conditional) and *N/A* (Not Applicable); this will determine what is expected from the features of the Generic Access Profile.

Table 4-4 identifies the security requirements for this profile. You will also notice that these features are marked in a similar fashion to the previous table. Remember that Security Mode 1, is a non-secure mode where Bluetooth-enabled devices will never initiate any security procedures; whereas, Security Modes 2 and 3, initiate different levels of

Table 4-2 The core set of procedures as required by most profiles.

PROCEDURES	DESCRIPTION
Discoverability Mode	This mode prescribes the overall discoverability of a device, allowing it to be placed into a non-discoverable, limited or general discoverable mode. The mode would allow devices to become generally available to other users or it can be restricted to personal use.
Connectability Mode	When determining a baseband connectable state, this mode is used to place a device into a connectable or non-connectable mode.
Pairing	Pairable and non-pairable modes are used to realise the security aspects when operating or intending to use a device. A device may require authentication and, as such, the user would be required to enter a Bluetooth Passkey. The pairing procedure starts the link key generation process, which in turn allows authentication to take place.

Table 4-3   The illustration shows specific modes of operation that this profile depends upon to realise its compliant implementation.

MODES	TL	GW
Non-discoverable	N/A	M
Limited Discoverable	N/A	O
General Discoverable	N/A	M
Non-connectable	N/A	X
Connectable	N/A	M
Non-pairable	M	M
Pairable	O	M

security procedures at various stages of connection establishment. In this instance, the profile mandates that support should be provided for at least Security Mode 2 or 3.

In our final consideration of the basic rules and procedures required from the Generic Access Profile, the idle mode procedures outline behavioural characteristics when DeviceA chooses to initiate them against DeviceB. The procedures listed in Table 4-5 provide a clear indication of how a device should operate when performing such an activity.

In summary, we can conclude that there are a specific set of events associated with a procedure. For an in-depth look at how procedure is conducted, refer back to the *Generic Access Profile,* Chapter 2.

The mechanisms for providing device discoverability are the provision of a well structured FHS packet, which is shown in Figure 4-7. This packet is used to identify the remote device, where information such as *Bluetooth Device Address* (BD_ADDR) and clock offsets is determined. You may also notice from this packet that the *Class of Device* (CoD) field is also provided. This information is relayed to the user interface, which in

Table 4-4   The illustration shows specific security procedures that this profile depends upon to realise its compliant implementation.

PROCEDURE	TL	GW
Authentication	M	M
Security Mode 1	X	X
Security Mode 2	C	C
Security Mode 3	C	C

Table 4-5 The illustration shows specific behavioural procedures that this profile depends upon to realise its compliant implementation.

PROCEDURE	TL	GW
General Inquiry	M	N/A
Limited Inquiry	O	N/A
Name Discovery	O	N/A
Device Discovery	O	N/A
Bonding	M	M

turn provides common characteristics about discovered devices. The class of device is used during the discovery mechanism to learn more about the type of device and what it may be capable of providing. This structure of information is depicted in Figure 4-8 and is made up of 3-bytes (or 24-bits as shown). The following sections now consider the Cordless Telephony attributes, which will ultimately make use of the *Service*, *Major* and *Minor Device Class* fields.

4.5.1.1.1 Service Class. This high-level form of defining a Bluetooth device identifies where in the Service Class field the Cordless Telephony Profile resides; see Table 4-6, which shows the category of service. In this instance, the category of service falls within *Telephony*.

4.5.1.1.2 Major Device Class. This high-level form of defining a Bluetooth device identifies where in the Major Device Class the Cordless Telephony Profile resides; see Table 4-7, which shows the major class grouping. Here, the category falls within phone, since a cordless handset or mobile phone may be used.

4.5.1.1.3 Minor Device Class. The Minor Device Class in this profile is used to convey further context for the setting within the major class grouping, see Table 4-8.

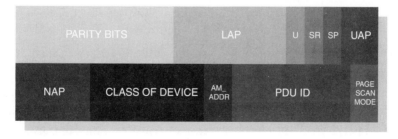

Figure 4-7 The structure of the FHS packet used only for reference to illustrate the position of the Class of Device structure.

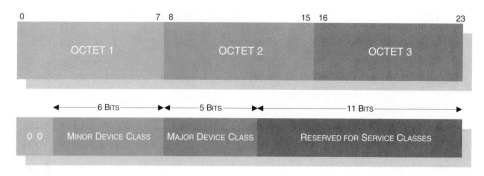

Figure 4-8   The structure of the class of device, illustrating the Minor Device, Major Device and Service Class fields and their respective
lengths.

Here, the bit may be set appropriately for *Cordless* to denote the type of device available
to the user.

4.5.1.2   Service Discovery.   In the *Service Discovery Application Profile*, Chapter 3, we introduced the characteristics of the mechanisms used to retrieve service information from a remote device. Typically, a client will initiate inquiry and discovery
procedures as outlined in our previous section, to learn of the devices in radio range. A
client would then make use of an application, which would embody the functionality of
the underlying *Service Discovery Protocol* (SDP). The *Service Discovery Application*
(SrvDscApp) uses an *SDP Client* to instigate a request to the remote device where the
SDP Server will respond; as such, the TL and GW must employ the use of an SDP client
and server, respectively, as illustrated in Table 4-9.

   Protocol Data Units (PDUs) are used to instruct the SDP server to undertake
browsing procedures and to retrieve service record information; you may recall that these
PDUs carry payloads about requests containing AttributeIDs and Attribute-
Values describing what exactly is being sought. As we previously discussed, the client
and server operate a request and response paradigm. SDAP will construct PDUs containing information relating to the AttributeID and AttributeValues, in turn instructing the server to carry out its operation. The various request and response PDUs that
are required are shown in Table 4-10, where features indicated are described.

Table 4-6   The Service Class categorisation for the Cordless Telephony Profile.

											SERVICE CLASS
23	22	21	20	19	18	17	16	15	14	13	Bit # of CoD
0	1	0	0	0	0	0	0	0	0	0	Telephony

Table 4-7   The Major Device Class for the Cordless Telephony Profile.

MAJOR DEVICE CLASS					
12	11	10	9	8	Bit # of CoD
0	0	0	1	0	Phone

Table 4-8   The Minor Device Class for the Cordless Telephony Profile.

MINOR DEVICE CLASS						
7	6	5	4	3	2	Bit # of CoD
0	0	0	0	1	0	Cordless

Table 4-9   As a minimum, the local device must support the use of a client application and the remote device must support the use of a server.

FEATURE	TL	GW
SDP Client	M	X
SDP Server	X	M

Table 4-10   The list of PDUs that are required for the operation of the Cordless Telephony Profile.

PDU	TL	GW
SDP_ErrorResponse	X	M
SDP_ServiceSearchRequest	M	X
SDP_ServiceSearchResponse	X	M
SDP_ServiceAttributeRequest	M	X
SDP_ServiceAttributeResponse	X	M
SDP_ServiceSearchAttributeRequest	O	X
SDP_ServiceSearchAttributeRequest	X	O

A service record is maintained for each service a device is capable of supporting and, as such, a *Service Record Handle* is created to uniquely identify this. The `ServiceRecordHandle` is a 32-bit unsigned integer and is stored on the SDP server. The service record shown in Table 4-11 identifies a GW device and provides a list of `AttributeIDs`, which ultimately would identify the service for the Cordless Telephony

Table 4-11   The list of mandatory and configurable items that make up this profile's service discovery record.

ATTRIBUTE	DESCRIPTION
ServiceRecordHandle	With an `AttributeID` of `0x0000`, this uniquely identifies this service record within the SDP server on the GW device.
ServiceClassIDList ServiceClass0 ServiceClass1	With an `AttributeID` of `0x0001`, the following `ServiceClass0` would contain the `UUID` for the *Cordless Telephony* and the `ServiceClass1` would identify the *Generic Telephony* service classes. Their respective `UUID` values are summarised in Table 4-12.
ProtocolDescriptorList Protocol0 Protocol1	With an `AttributeID` of `0x0004`, the following `Protocol0` would contain a `UUID` for the protocol *L2CAP*, whereas in `Protocol1` a `UUID` would contain the protocol identifier for *TCS-BIN-CORDLESS*. Their respective `UUID` values are summarised in Table 4-13.
BluetoothProfile- DescriptorList Profile0 ParameterFor0	With an `AttributeID` of `0x0009`, the following `Profile0` would identify the `UUID` for *Cordless Telephony* service class, which is summarised in Table 4-12. The `ParameterFor0` accommodates the version number supported by this profile.
ServiceName	With a base `AttributeID` of `0x0006`, this attribute has an offset of `0x0000`. It is a configurable item and has an `AttributeValue` of a `Text` string, where its default setting is *Cordless Telephony*.
ExternalNetwork	With an `AttributeID` of `0x0301`, this attribute identifies what external network the Cordless Telephony device currently supports. Table 4-14 summarises the type of networks available.

Profile. A minimum of two `AttributeIDs` are required to make a service record—these are `ServiceRecordHandle` and a `ServiceClassIDList`, which must contain at least one `UUID`.

When browsing for services on the remote device, a local device constructs a search pattern using a *Universally Unique Identifier* (UUID). A UUID is a 128-bit value, which has been shortened for use within Bluetooth. The shortcut has been provided by first establishing a *Bluetooth Base UUID*, which we discussed in the *Service Discovery Application Profile*, Chapter 3.

The UUIDs that have been presented so far in this chapter are aliases and take the form of what is referred to as a 16-bit UUID or a 32-bit UUID, but in turn they all should refer to the 128-bit notation. These UUIDs have been assigned and can be referenced in the Bluetooth Special Interest Group, Bluetooth Assigned Numbers, v1.1, February 2001. For the search pattern to be successful, they all need to be converted to the 128-bit notation, since they will all be compared at this range. An arithmetic conversion algorithm is used to construct the 128-bit value.

Table 4-12 summarises the service class UUIDs used to identify the particular profile in use; this also correlates with the identification of the device during a device discovery procedure, as previously outlined in our earlier Section 4.5.1.1, *Generic Access*.

As part of the service record, the dependent underlying protocols are also identified. The local device retrieves this information, where it can fully understand the exact requirements needed to fulfil the service. The Cordless Telephony Profile is dependent on the protocols as shown in Table 4-13; the table also shows their associated UUID values.

The Cordless Telephony GW device is capable of supporting several externally connected networks, which are summarised in Table 4-14. The `AttributeValue` that would follow is an 8-bit unsigned integer used to uniquely identify the particular network; these values are also shown.

4.5.1.3   The Telephony Control Protocol.   This section provides a more detailed introduction to the TCS protocol. The *Cordless Telephony* and *Intercom Profiles* both depend upon the implementation of the TCS. In Figure 4-9, we illustrate the placement of the TCS component and how it is architected and moulded into the Bluetooth protocol stack. We can also see how the *AT Command Control* is also incorporated within the same architecture, which we touched upon earlier. More specifically, the TCS is imple-

Table 4-12   The list of service classes that match a corresponding profile. This correlates with our previous Generic Access section.

CLASSES	UUID
CordlessTelephony	0x1109
GenericTelephony	0x1204

Table 4-13   The list of protocols that are used in this profile; their associated UUID values are also shown.

PROTOCOL	UUID
TCS-BIN-CORDLESS	0x0005
L2CAP	0x0100

mented over L2CAP, where other implementations, such as the Headset Profile, use the services provided by RFCOMM.

With the provision of telephony applications coordinating the user interface characteristics, the TCS component is left to manage the audio communication effort and direct appropriate Asynchronous Connectionless (ACL) communication through the Bluetooth protocol stack, where numerous internal interfaces are identified. The TCS component has further entities within its architecture, which have been especially created to manage and coordinate activities of speech and data communication, which we will now describe in more detail.

4.5.1.3.1   Inter-operating Devices.   In this section, we consider the operation of devices that interact using the TCS protocol and also examine how the various Bluetooth protocol layers interact. In our earlier discussion, we introduced the various usage models available to a user and, as such, the operation of these devices follow simple procedures.

TCS has both a single- and multiple-point available. In the former configuration, a *single-point* method is used to direct a call to a specific Bluetooth-enabled device whilst our latter configuration supports a *multiple-point* method to direct a potential call to numerous devices. The single-point configuration is mapped to a connection-orientated L2CAP channel, whereas a multiple-point method is mapped to a connectionless L2CAP channel.

Table 4-14   The list of externally connected networks that may be connected to a GW device.

NETWORK	VALUE
PSTN	0x01
ISDN	0x02
GSM	0x03
CDMA	0x04
Analogue Cellular	0x05
Packet Switched	0x06
Other	0x07

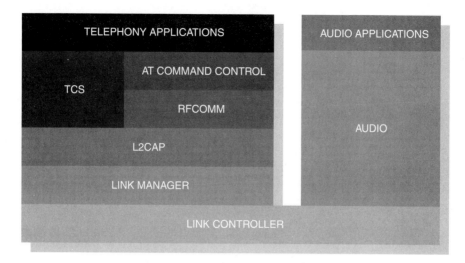

Figure 4-9   The complete architecture of the audio and telephony control
illustrates how audio is integrated and managed within the
Bluetooth protocol stack.

In Figure 4-10 and Figure 4-11 we provide a conceptual representation of Bluetooth-enabled devices interoperating using the TCS protocol. Figure 4-10 illustrates the single-point method, where a call request is used to notify the mobile phone of an incoming call and subsequently, the phone establishes the speech or data channel. In Figure 4-11, we illustrate the multiple-point method where in this particular instance, all devices are notified of the call request. We show that Cordless Handset *B* accepts the incoming call, where by a single-point signalling channel is created; both devices then establish a speech or data channel.

With the ability to manage single- and multiple-point communication between Bluetooth-enabled devices, a TCS architecture must reflect the capability to inherently coordinate simultaneous communication between peer devices. Each instantiation of a TCS component would be uniquely identified through the *Channel Identifier* (CID) of an

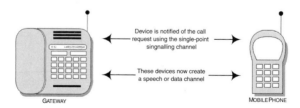

Figure 4-10   A Bluetooth-enabled gateway notifies the mobile phone of the
call request, where a speech or data channel is subsequently
created.

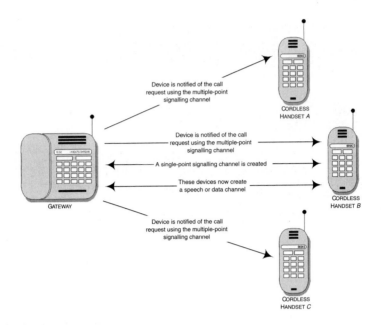

Figure 4-11   A Bluetooth-enabled gateway notifies the cordless handsets that
are in radio range of the call request. Cordless Handset *B*, accepts the incoming call and creates a single-point signalling
channel, then it creates a speech or data channel.

L2CAP connection. This would allow communication to be directed accordingly for connected devices.

   In Figure 4-12, we illustrate the conceptual architecture that is proposed for a TCS
implementation. In it you will notice the entities that characterise the TCS component.
The *Call Control* (CC), *Group Management* (GM), *Connectionless* (CL) and *Protocol
Discrimination* entities have their own responsibilities in providing a telephony service;
these are now identified in Table 4-15.

   In our earlier discussion, we touched upon the fact that the Cordless Telephony and
Intercom Profiles rely upon TCS to provide a telephony service. Our focus here is to describe the processes used to provide such a service and to establish how the underlying
Bluetooth transport is facilitated in achieving this. In doing so, the reader will come to understand how the various types of scenarios are supported.

   TCS has been designed to sit above the L2CAP component of the Bluetooth protocol stack. In our first look at understanding this protocol, we will examine how the TCS
protocol is used to transport data between peer devices.

   4.5.1.3.2   TCS Messaging Format and Coding.   In Figure 4-13 we illustrate what
is referred to as a TCS *signalling message*. In other protocols to be introduced in later

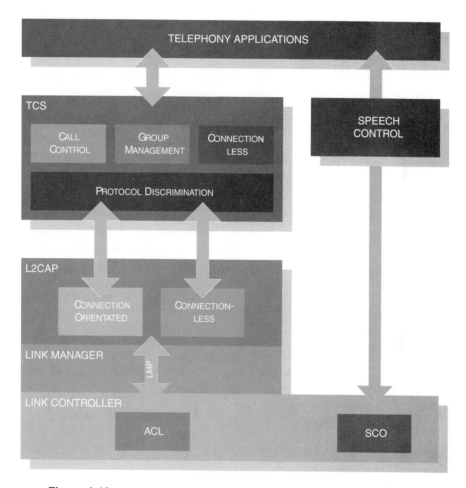

Figure 4-12   A conceptual illustration identifying the structure of the TCS component.

chapters, varying terms are used to refer to the *packet*[6] used to transport a *payload*.[7] The signalling message has been adapted from the *International Telecommunications Union* (ITU) Telecommunications division, Q.391 Digital Subscriber Signalling System No. 1 (DSS 1) and ISDN User Network Interface Layer 3 Specification for Basic Call Control.

The structure of the message packet is constructed using two octets, which comprise a *Message Type*, *Protocol Discriminator* and an *Information* field. The `Message Type` field is used to describe the function or purpose of the message. It occupies the first 5-bits

---

[6]The generic term packet is used to describe the nature of a structure that is used to encode data.

[7]A payload refers to encoded data that is transported between devices. It will contain information that the peer device will act upon.

Table 4-15   The TCS protocol can be further broken down, where identifiable entities are used to coordinate and manage related activities.

ENTITY	RESPONSIBILITY
Connectionless	This entity is used to coordinate non-speech related activities. Where data may be passed between Bluetooth-enabled devices without the need for a speech call to be established.
Call Control	This entity coordinates and interfaces the connection and disconnection of speech and data calls between Bluetooth-enabled devices.
Group Management	When groups of devices are interacting, this entity manages the group effort as well as looking after such activities as paging and security. This particular entity is also responsible for coordinating effort between WUGs.
Protocol Discrimination	The protocol discrimination entity is responsible for correctly routing traffic between the entities that are responsible for it.

of the first octet. In our earlier discussion, we identified three core entities that are used to manage the various functions within TCS. As such, the Message Type values are depicted in accordance with the respective entity in Table 4-16 for Call Control, Table 4-17 for Group Management and finally Table 4-18 for Connectionless.

The various Message Type groups, that is CC, GM and CL, are identified with the Protocol Discriminator field, which is illustrated in Table 4-19. This is used to convey the local device's intention to the remote peer device.

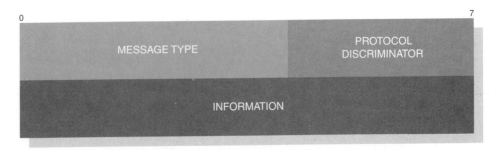

Figure 4-13   The structure of the signalling messaging as used within the Cordless Telephony Profile.

Table 4-16 The `Message Type` field for Call Control messages used within TCS.

4	3	2	1	0	MESSAGE TYPE (CC)
					Bit # of Message Type field for Call Control
0	0	0	0	0	ALERTING
0	0	0	0	1	CALL PROCEEDING
0	0	0	1	0	CONNECT
0	0	0	1	1	CONNECT ACKNOWLEDGE
0	0	1	0	0	PROGRESS
0	0	1	0	1	SETUP
0	0	1	1	0	SETUP ACKNOWLEDGE
0	0	1	1	1	DISCONNECT
0	1	0	0	0	RELEASE
0	1	0	0	1	RELEASE COMPLETE
0	1	0	1	0	INFORMATION
1	0	0	0	0	START DTMF
1	0	0	0	1	START DTMF ACKNOWLEDGE
1	0	0	1	0	START DTMF REJECT
1	0		1	1	STOP DTMF
1	0	1	0	0	STOP DTMF ACKNOWLEDGE

The final field of the signalling message is the `Information` field; it contains data relevant to the type of function, which is specific to the `Message Type` field. The `Information` field is further categorised into three informational elements, which are constructed using 1-byte, 2-byte or of a variable length field. In Figure 4-14, we illustrate the construction of a 1-byte `Information` field, whereas Figure 4-15 illustrates a 2-byte construction.

In Figure 4-16, we can see the construction of a variable `Information` field, where the `Length` field indicates the total length of the data to follow in the `Contents` field. In all our illustrations of the `Information` field, a `Flag` field is used to denote the category of information being carried. If the `Flag` field is set to 1, then this would indicate that a fixed 1- or 2-byte `Information` field follows, whereas a `Flag` field set to 0, would indicate that a variable `Information` field follows.

Table 4-17   The `Message Type` field for Group Management messages used within TCS.

					MESSAGE TYPE (GM)
4	**3**	**2**	**1**	**0**	**Bit # of Message Type field for Group Management**
0	0	0	0	0	INFO SUGGEST
0	0	0	0	1	INFO ACCEPT
0	0	0	1	0	LISTEN REQUEST
0	0	0	1	1	LISTEN ACCEPT
0	0	1	0	0	LISTEN SUGGEST
0	0	1	0	1	LISTEN REJECT
0	0	1	1	0	ACCESS RIGHTS REQUEST
0	0	1	1	1	ACCESS RIGHTS ACCEPT
0	1	0	0	0	ACCESS RIGHTS REJECT

Table 4-18   The `Message Type` field for Connectionless messages used within TCS.

					MESSAGE TYPE (CL)
4	**3**	**2**	**1**	**0**	**Bit # of Message Type field for Connectionless**
0	0	0	0	0	CL INFO

Table 4-19   The `Protocol Discriminator` field and its usage within TCS.

			PROTOCOL DISCRIMINATOR
7	**6**	**5**	**Bit # of Protocol Discriminator field**
0	0	0	Call Control
0	0	1	Group Management
0	1	0	Connectionless

Figure 4-14   A 1-byte Information field used in the Signalling Message.

Table 4-20 illustrates the various information element codings available for the `Identifier` field. Recall that the `Flag` field denotes 1-byte, 2-byte or a variable length, which are also indicated in the table.

The `Contents` field transports data relevant to the current activity, as indicated in Table 4-20. In the following sections, we provide two examples of how coding is achieved in the `Information` field. Our first example, Figure 4-17 illustrates the structure of the *Call Class* coding.

For the call class structure, the `Flag` field would be set to 1, indicating that it is a 1- or 2-byte `Information` field. The `Identifier` field would be set to the value, as indicated in Table 4-20. The values available to the `Contents` field, which constitutes the call class specific data, would have the values identified in Table 4-21 available to it.

In our second example, the *Destination CID* coding is used to locate the established L2CAP channel with the remote peer device. You may recall that a Bluetooth-enabled device may communicate and connect to a number of devices. As such, the CID of the L2CAP channel is used to uniquely identify and route the traffic accordingly.

For the destination CID structure, the `Flag` field would be set to 0, indicating that it is a variable length `Information` field. The `Identifier` field would be set to the value as indicated in Table 4-20 and the destination CID specific data, would contain the destination CID of the active connection. In Figure 4-18, the `Length` field would be set to 2, since the destination CID is constructed using 2-bytes.

During the exchange of signalling messaging, a message will be ignored if a `Protocol Discriminator` field is present or if the message is too short or unrecognised. When a message is delivered unexpectedly, the TCS component will not be in an appropriate state to receive such a message then this too will be ignored.

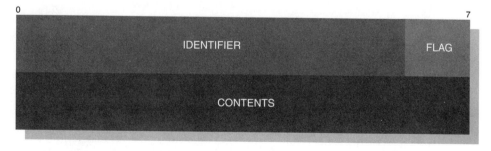

Figure 4-15   A 2-byte `Information` field used in the Signalling Message.

Table 4-20   The available codings for the `Identifier` field.

							CONTENTS
6	**5**	**4**	**3**	**2**	**1**	**0**	**Bit # of Contents field**
0	1	0	0	0	0	1	Sending Complete (Single Byte)
1	0	0	0	0	0	0	Call Class (Double Byte)
1	0	0	0	0	0	1	Cause (Double Byte)
1	0	0	0	0	1	0	Progress Indicator (Double Byte)
1	0	0	0	0	1	1	Signal (Double Byte)
1	0	0	0	1	0	0	Keypad Facility (Double Byte)
1	0	0	0	1	0	1	SCO Handle (Double Byte)
0	0	0	0	0	0	0	Clock Offset (Variable)
0	0	0	0	0	0	1	Configuration Data (Variable)
0	0	0	0	0	1	0	Bearer Capability (Variable)
0	0	0	0	0	1	1	Destination CID (Variable)
0	0	0	0	1	0	0	Calling Party Number (Variable)
0	0	0	0	1	0	1	Called Party Number (Variable)
0	0	0	0	1	1	0	Audio Control (Variable)
0	0	0	0	1	1	1	Company Specific (Variable)

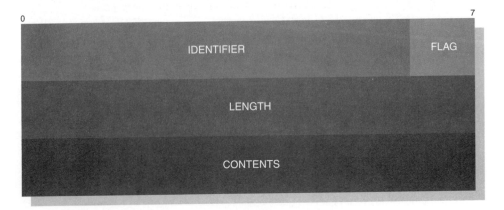

Figure 4-16   A variable length `Information` field used in the Signalling Message.

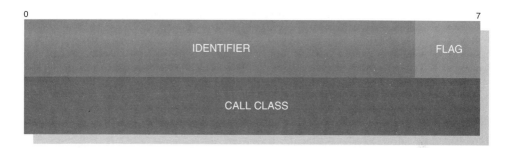

Figure 4-17   A 2-byte `Information` field, which in this example contains data relevant to the call class.

Table 4-21   The Call Class values that form part of the `Contents` field.

CALL CLASS		
1	**0**	**Bit # of Call Class forming the Contents field**
0	0	External Call
0	1	Intercom Call
1	0	Service Call
1	1	Emergency Call

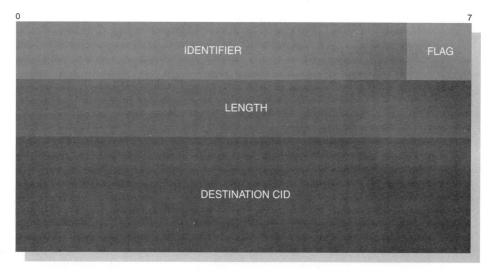

Figure 4-18   A variable-length `Information` field, which in this example contains data relevant to the destination CID.

4.5.1.4   TCS in the Cordless Telephony Profile.   In Section 4.5.1.3, *The Telephony Control Protocol,* we leaned about how signalling messages are created and subsequently constructed to provide us with a telephony service. It showed us how we could construct a series of signalling messages which, in turn, are used to achieve an end-function. In this section, we now consider the objectives and expectations of TCS in the *profile*.

4.5.1.4.1   Call Control.   In Table 4-15 we identified the responsibilities of the CC entity. Its primary responsibility is to coordinate the connection and disconnection of speech and data calls between the TL and GW. In Table 4-22, we illustrate the set of Call Control procedures that are required to achieve a compliant Cordless Telephony Profile.

4.5.1.4.2   Supplementary Service.   In Table 4-23, we illustrate the set of Supplementary Services that can be made available internally or externally.

4.5.1.4.3   Group Management.   In Table 4-15 we identified the responsibilities of the GM entity. Its primary responsibility is to manage group effort between the TL and GW and to coordinate effort for WUGs. In Table 4-24, we illustrate the set of Group Management procedures that are required to achieve a compliant Cordless Telephony Profile.

Table 4-22   The illustration shows specific Call Control procedures that this profile depends upon to realise its compliant implementation.

PROCEDURE	TL	GW
Call Class	M	M
Call Request	M	M
Overlap Sending	M	M
Call Proceeding	M	M
Call Confirmation	M	M
Call Connection	M	M
Non-selected User Clearing	M	M
In-band Ring Tones and Announcements	M	M
Failure of Call Establishment	M	M
Call Clearing	M	M
Call Information	M	M

Table 4-23 The illustration shows specific Supplementary Services that this profile depends upon to realise its compliant implementation.

PROCEDURE	TL	GW
DTMF Signalling	M	M
Caller Line Identity	M	M
Register Call	M	M

4.5.1.5 L2CAP. The L2CAP layer provides transparency for the upper layers of the stack from the layers typically found within the host controller. L2CAP payloads are passed to the *Host Controller Interface*[8] (HCI), which is then subsequently passed onto the *Link Manager Protocol* (LMP). The range of upper layers, which include RFCOMM, SDP and TCS all make use of the capabilities offered to us by L2CAP. Its primary role is to provide *protocol multiplexing*, allowing numerous simultaneous connections to be made and also providing the ability for *segmentation* and *reassembly*. This refers to the ability to manage large payloads in the application, which may need to be fragmented into smaller payloads for the lower layers to manage; these are then transmitted over the air-interface. Finally, the L2CAP layer exchanges *Quality of Service* (QoS) information, ensuring that sufficient resources are available and that both Bluetooth devices are attaining the best service.

In Table 4-25, we summarise the broad capabilities that are expected from L2CAP and in the table you will notice features are marked with *M* (Mandatory), *O* (Optional), *X* (Excluded), *C* (Conditional) and *N/A* (Not Applicable); these determine what is expected from the L2CAP layer.

4.5.1.5.1 Channel Types. In Table 4-25, we identify that both the *Connection-orientated* and *Connectionless Channels* are mandatory; the connectionless channel is

Table 4-24 The illustration shows specific Group Management procedures that this profile depends upon to realise its compliant implementation.

PROCEDURE	TL	GW
Obtain Access Rights	M	M
Configuration Distribution	M	M
Periodic Key Update	M	M
Faster Inter-member Access	M	M

---

[8]L2CAP payloads are passed directly onto LMP when implemented on a hostless system.

Table 4-25   The illustration shows specific procedures that this profile depends upon to realise its compliant implementation.

PROCEDURE	TL	GW
Connection-orientated Channel	M	M
Connectionless Channel	M	M
Connection Establishment	M	C
Configuration	M	M
Connection Termination	M	C
Echo	M	M
Command Rejection	M	M
Maximum Transmission Unit	M	M
Flush Timeout	M	M
Quality of Service	O	O

aimed at broadcasting, where only the GW will support this feature. L2CAP uses PDUs to transport connection, signalling and configuration options, which will be discussed shortly. The higher layers of the Bluetooth protocol stack will instigate a connection with L2CAP using the `L2CA_ConnectReq` request packet, where the corresponding result is contained within the `L2CA_ConnectRsp` response packet. An `L2CA_ConnectRsp-Neg` negative response packet is used to denote a response, where the connection with the remote device was unsuccessful. Since our profile resides above L2CAP and employs its services, we are only concerned with the upper protocol layer of L2CAP. This higher functionality is offered to us through a series of L2CAP events and is denoted through the prefix `L2CA_`; see Table 4-26.

When creating an L2CAP connection between two devices, a *Protocol/Service Multiplexor* (PSM) value is used to denote the higher-layer protocol that is using the connection; Table 4-27 identifies these values and the corresponding protocol they represent. The value of `0x0007` (TCS-BIN-CORDLESS) is used for this profile.

4.5.1.5.2   Signalling.   When establishing communication with a remote device, a *signalling channel* is created and reserved for use during connection, disconnection and configuration of subsequent L2CAP connections. A *channel* is used to describe the communication and data flow that exists between L2CAP entities and Table 4-28 illustrates the range of that are used to identify the channel type. As we can see in Table 4-25, *Connection Establishment* and *Termination* is mandatory in the local device, although the remote device may be capable of initiating and terminating a connection to the local device.

Table 4-26 The range of prototypes used to illustrate how L2CAP is architected and how interaction between higher and lower layers is achieved. For this discussion, our concern here is with the higher-layer.

PROTOTYPE	DESCRIPTION
L2CA_	This prefix prototype is used to denote the higher-layer interaction, typically used by RFCOMM, SDP and TCS.
L2CAP_	This prefix is used to denote peer-to-peer signalling interaction of L2CAP entities.
LP_	Finally, this prefix denotes lower-layer interaction, where L2CAP interfaces with the LMP layer.

The L2CA_DisconnectReq request packet is used to terminate the connection with the remote device and an L2CA_DisconnectRsp response packet is used to ascertain the result of the termination, although all disconnection requests must be completed successfully. The support of *Configuration* is shown as mandatory and we will discuss these specific options in more detail in the following section. Finally, *Echo* and *Command Rejection* are both mandatory for a compliant Cordless Telephony Profile.

4.5.1.5.3 Configuration Options. In establishing a connection with the remote device, the channel is subject to configuration and the higher-layer prototype L2CA_ ConfigReq request packet is used to carry configuration requests. Its associated response is contained within the L2CA_ConfigRsp packet; an L2CA_ConfigRspNeg packet is used to denote a negative response during configuration, where the suggested *Maximum Transmission Unit* (MTU) is too large. In Table 4-25, we identify that the MTU and *Flush Timeout* parameters are mandatory, whereas the QoS is optional.

The default MTU setting for the signalling channel is 48 bytes, whereas other channels may be capable of transferring larger payloads; essentially the MTU determines the size of payloads that are capable of being exchanged between two devices. The Cordless Telephony Profile requires that a minimum MTU of 171-bytes should be established to

Table 4-27 The PSM values that are used to identify the higher-layer protocol.

PSM	DESCRIPTION
0x0001	SDP
0x0003	RFCOMM
0x0005	TCS-BIN
0x0007	TCS-BIN-CORDLESS

Table 4-28   The CIDs that are used to represent the logical channel.

CID	DESCRIPTION
0x0000	Null
0x0001	Signalling Channel
0x0002	Connectionless Reception Channel
0x0003 to 0x003F	Reserved
0x0040 to 0xFFFF	Dynamically Allocated

allow support for multiple TLs. During configuration, the local device will inform the remote device that it is potentially capable of accepting larger payloads. If the remote device is unwilling to accept a larger MTU, then the local device is informed with the response contained within the L2CA_ConfigRspNeg packet.

When L2CA_ request and response packets are being exchanged, the Flush Timeout parameter is used to determine how long the local device is prepared to continue to transmit an L2CAP fragment before it gives up; the packet is subsequently flushed (or in other words discarded). The suggested Flush Timeout value is sent during the L2CA_ConfigReq request packet. However, if no value is set, then the default value is used. The Cordless Telephony Profile uses the default value of 0xFFFF.

As we have already mentioned, the QoS configuration is optional. If it is used during an L2CA_ConfigReq request, then the *best effort* service is established as a default. The available services that are supported for an L2CAP channel are shown in Table 4-29.

Table 4-29   The range of service definitions that are used during QoS.

SERVICE	DESCRIPTION
No Traffic	This indicates that the channel will not be sending any traffic and, as such, any parameters can be ignored.
Best Effort	This default value attempts to achieve a minimum service with the remote device, where no guarantees are offered.
Guaranteed	With this service definition, we indicate that we wish to achieve the maximum bandwidth permitted—this is, of course, subject to the nature of a wireless environment.

However, if the QoS service is set at *Guaranteed,* then parameters such *Token Rate, Token Bucket, Peak Bandwidth, Latency* and *Delay Variation,* are used to determine an acceptable guaranteed service, where the `L2CA_ConnectRspNeg`, will indicate that these values are unacceptable. These parameters are then subject to further negotiation.

4.5.1.6   Link Manager.   The *Link Manager* (LM) layer sits between the HCI and the *Link Controller* (LC), although on a hostless system the LM will have direct interaction with L2CAP. It accepts commands from HCI and translates them into operations for the LC, where ACL and SCO links are created and established. It is during this stage of ACL and SCO establishment that a master-slave switch would be performed as governed by the requirements of this profile. The LM is also responsible for placing the device into a low-power mode, which includes *hold, sniff* and *park.*

In providing *general* error management, devices that operate mandatory procedures during interoperability, must either acknowledge their support or provide a suitable reason for failure. The `LMP_Detach` PDU is used to inform the device of the error that occurred; typically, the reason *unsupported LMP feature* (`0x1A`) is reported, see Appendix A.

In the following discussion, we take an opportunity to explore the dependencies that make up the Cordless Telephony Profile where we provide a narrative of the capabilities that are expected at this level. In Table 4-30, we identify the capabilities that are required from this layer and in the following subsections discuss the specific procedures in more detail.

4.5.1.6.1   Capabilities.   Table 4-30 summarises the broad capabilities that are expected from the LM. In the table, you will notice procedures are marked accordingly; this will determine what is expected from the procedures at the LM. What has been included in the table is a set of deviations that the profile requires, which is above the common set of procedures expected at LM.

Table 4-30   The mandatory requirements that are required for a compliant Cordless Telephony Profile. As the table shows, support for encryption and SCO links for this profile are now mandatory.

PROCEDURES	SUPPORT
Encryption	M
Master-slave Switch	M
Park Mode	M
SCO Links	M

4.5.1.6.2 Encryption. Encryption is mandatory for this profile and, as such, a summary of the activities that occur during this process is now provided; more detailed information can be found in the *Generic Access Profile*, Chapter 2. Once both devices have agreed to undertake encryption, which occurs after the authentication process, DeviceA (or master) takes the initiative and needs to determine whether to include encryption for point-to-point or broadcast communication. If DeviceB (or slave) is agreeable to the parameters offered by the master, the master proceeds to communicate further detailed information about the encryption parameters.

As previously mentioned, the actual process is invoked when the two parties agree to use encryption, where subsequent L2CAP communication terminates. The master then sends the `LMP_encryption_mode_req` command. If this is acceptable to the slave, it too terminates all L2CAP communication and responds with the `LMP_accepted` command. The next step in this process actually determines the size of the *encryption key* and it is the master that sends the `LMP_encryption_key_size_req` command, where it offers an initial recommendation of the key size to use. For this profile to be compliant, the initial recommendation offered is five octets. The slave, in turn, then offers its own recommendation, where it informs the master what it thinks it might be capable of—nevertheless, the minimum recommended size must be initially offered. Both master and slave will repeat this process until they reach an agreement; however, if neither party reaches a decision, then the `LMP_not_accepted` command is sent, offering the reason as *unsupported parameter value* (0x20), see Appendix A.

Upon accepting the key size, the `LMP_accepted` command is issued and the encryption procedure then takes place by issuing the `LMP_start_encryption_req` command with a random number, which is used to calculate the encryption key. Table 4-31 summarises the available commands for the encryption process.

4.5.1.6.3 Master-Slave Switch. The master-slave switch operation is required[9] when the GW is configured for multi-terminal[10] support. The failure of a TL to perform this operation prohibits the successful connection to a GW. Figure 4-19 provides an illustration

Table 4-31 The range of LMP PDUs available for encryption.

PDU	PARAMETER
`LMP_encryption_mode_req`	Encryption Mode
`LMP_encryption_key_size_req`	Key Size
`LMP_start_encryption_req`	Random Number
`LMP_stop_encryption_req`	*None*

---

[9]A GW supporting multi-terminal connections must remain the master of the piconet.
[10]The TL may refuse the request to become the slave if it needs to remain the master.

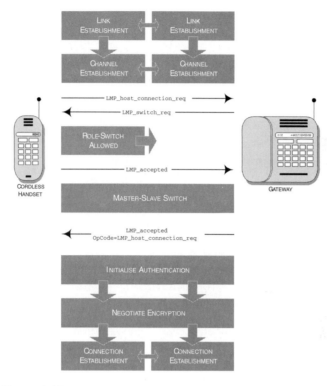

Figure 4-19   The events that take place during a master-slave switch.

of the events that occur when the TL successfully performs the master-slave switch request[11].

Table 4-32 provides the HCI command and event combination that are used to perform the master-slave switch operation between the TL and GW. This table represents one such method of performing a switch, where other HCI commands, such as the HCI_Create_Connection command, specify the same request as part of their parameter set-up. In this instance, the Allow_Role_Switch parameter is used during the connection establishment to determine if a switch can be performed by the local device, that is, the device initiating the connection (DeviceA). The remote device (DeviceB) is duly notified with its corresponding HCI command, Accept_Connection_Request of whether it can be supported.

Table 4-33 provides the two LMP general response messages, which are mandatory for this profile. During an LMP_accepted operation, the response contains the OpCode of the operation that was successful; whereas the response from the LMP_not_accepted provides the OpCode of the operation that was not successful. Accompanying

---

[11]The Bluetooth protocol stack provides the flexibility of issuing a master-slave switch at any time during a Bluetooth connection establishment; Figure 4-19 provides one such example.

Table 4-32   The command and two-stage event notification that are used in combination to perform the master-slave switch.

COMMAND	PARAMETERS
HCI_Switch_Role	BD_ADDR
	Role
EVENT	**PARAMETERS**
Command_Status	Status
	Num_HCI_Command_Packets
	Command_OpCode
Role_Change	Status
	BD_ADDR
	New_Role

this OpCode, a *reason* or error code is provided to help to determine why the operation failed; a full list of LMP reasons can be found in Appendix A.

There general response messages are used in combination with the following LMP role-switch specific messages, which are shown in Table 4-34. We will now explore the behaviour of both these devices when performing the master-slave switch operation. You may remember from our earlier discussion that both the TL and GW are capable of initiating a connection.

When DeviceB (or slave) initiates a master-slave switch, it terminates the final ACL packet and stops any further L2CAP transmissions. It then sends LMP_slot_offset command immediately followed by the LMP_switch_req command. Similarly, if the master accepts the master-slave switch, it terminates all L2CAP transmissions and then issues an LMP_accepted command, if the transaction is a success. However, if the operation is rejected, then an LMP_not_accepted command is provided as the response, with a specific reason for its failure. Furthermore, when the operation has been completed, despite its success or failure, L2CAP communication is resumed.

Table 4-33   The general response messages used within LMP.

PDU	PARAMETERS
LMP_accepted	OpCode
LMP_not_accepted	OpCode
	Reason

Table 4-34   The PDUs available within LMP that are responsible for managing the role-
switch behaviour.

PDU	PARAMETERS
`LMP_switch_req`	`Switch instant`

`LMP_slot_offset`	`Slot Offset`
	
	`BD_ADDR`

When DeviceA (or master) initiates a master-slave switch, it terminates the final
ACL packet and stops any further L2CAP transmissions before sending an `LMP_`
`switch_req`. Similarly, if the slave accepts the master-slave switch, it terminates all
L2CAP transmissions and then issues an `LMP_slot_offset` command immediately
followed by an `LMP_accepted` command. However, if the operation is rejected, then
an `LMP_not_accepted` is provided as the response, with a specific reason for its fail-
ure. Furthermore, when the operation has been completed, despite its success or failure,
L2CAP communication is resumed.

4.5.1.6.4 Supporting Park Mode.   The recommended power saving mode for this
profile is *Park Mode* and is indicated as mandatory in the summary of capabilities as
shown in Table 4-30. When a device participates in this mode, it will relinquish its *Active Member Address* (`AM_ADDR`) and then is assigned two new addresses, as shown in
Table 4-35.

In its effort to reduce power consumption, the device will no longer participate in a
piconet or be addressed by the master. During periodical intervals, the device will listen
for broadcasts to allow it to become an active member of the piconet again. In Table 4-36,
we identify the HCI commands that are used to place a device into this mode. Placing a
device into park mode will modify the behaviour of the LM, where the `Connection_`
`Handle` parameter of an ACL link identifies the specific connection that has to be placed

Table 4-35   When a device is placed into park mode, it releases its current `AM_ADDR` and is
assigned two new addresses as shown.

ADDRESS	DESCRIPTION
`PM_ADDR`	The *Parked Member Address* is an 8-bit value identifying the parked slave and is also used to unpark the slave in a master-initiated unpark procedure.
`AR_ADDR`	The *Access Request Address* is an 8-bit value identifying the parked slave and is also used to unpark the slave in a slave-initiated unpark procedure.

Table 4-36 The command and two-stage event notification that are used in combination to place the device into park mode.

COMMAND	PARAMETERS
HCI_Park_Mode	Connection_Handle
	Beacon_Max_Interval
	Beacon_Min_Interval

EVENT	PARAMETERS
Command_Status	Status
	Num_HCI_Command_Packets
	Command_OpCode
Mode_Change	Status
	Connection_Handle
	Current_Mode
	Interval

into this mode. The `Beacon_Min_Interval` and `Beacon_Max_Interval` parameters inform the device when to periodically listen for broadcasts. It is noted that no active SCO connections are permitted during the operation of park mode; if one exists then an error *Command Disallowed* will be returned by the `Command_Status` event, see *Appendix B* for a list of HCI errors and reasons.

When a device wishes to exit park mode, then the HCI command, as identified in Table 4-37, is used to bring the device back into active mode. The `Connection_Handle` parameter of an ACL connection is used to identify the specific connection that wishes to be returned to active mode.

General response messages, as previously illustrated, are used in combination with the following LMP park mode specific messages; these are summarised in Table 4-33.

During the operation of park mode, the master may request that the slave enter the low-power saving mode. All communication at the L2CAP level is finalised and the LM then issues the `LMP_park_req` PDU. Similarly, the slave finalises its communication at L2CAP and responds with the `LMP_accepted` PDU. When both devices have agreed to engage park mode, the slave relinquishes its AM_ADDR. However, if the slave rejects park mode, it will respond with `LMP_not_accepted` and communication will recommence. The slave may also request that it enter park mode, where similar actions are carried out during this procedure.

Table 4-37   The command and two-stage event notification that are used in combination to place the device into active mode.

COMMAND	PARAMETERS
HCI_Exit_Park_Mode	Connection_Handle
EVENT	**PARAMETERS**
Command_Status	Status Num_HCI_Command_Packets Command_OpCode
Mode_Change	Status Connection_Handle Current_Mode Interval

Table 4-38   The PDUs available within LMP that are responsible for managing the parking behaviour.

PDU	PARAMETERS
LMP_park_req	PM_ADDR AR_ADDR Access_Schemes ...
LMP_unpark_PM_ADDR_req	AM_ADDR PM_ADDR Timing_Control_Flags ...
LMP_unpark_BD_ADDR_req	AM_ADDR BD_ADDR Timing_Control_Flags ...

Table 4-39 The command and events that are used in combination to create a SCO connection. The host controller first sends the `Command_Status` event, but when the connection has been established, the `Connection_Complete` event is generated on both devices.

COMMAND	PARAMETERS
HCI_Add_SCO_Connection	Connection_Handle
	Packet_Type
EVENT	**PARAMETERS**
Command_Status	Status
	Num_HCI_Command_Packets
	Command_OpCode
Connection_Complete	Status
	Connection_Handle
	BD_ADDR
	Link_Type
	Encryption_Mode

4.5.1.6.5 SCO Links. A SCO link is set-up using the `HCI_Add_SCO_Connection` command (see Table 4-39), where a series of `Voice_Setting` parameters are used to denote the type of SCO channel and the audio coding schemes. The `Voice_Setting` parameters are written using the `HCI_Write_Voice_Setting` command and are shown in Table 4-40.

It assumed that the partying devices have an existing ACL communications link, where pairing, authentication and encryption have already taken place. The ACL

Table 4-40 The command and events that are used in combination to write the voice setting parameters for a SCO link.

COMMAND	PARAMETERS
HCI_Write_Voice_Setting	Voice_Setting
EVENT	**PARAMETERS**
Command_Complete	Num_HCI_Command_Packets
	Command_OpCode
	Return_Parameters

Connection_Handle parameter is used, in part, to then create our SCO connection using the HCI_Add_SCO_Connection command. Although the host controller generates a Command_Status event, it does not indicate that the SCO connection has been created. The host controller for both devices uses the Connection_Complete event to notify both hosts whether the SCO connection has been successful or not, where the new Connection_Handle and Link_Type identify the new connection. You may also wish to note that the Packet_Type parameter is used to specify the type of high quality voice transmission, where HV1, HV2 or HV3 can be requested over the SCO link.

The Voice_Setting parameters are shown in more detail in Table 4-41, the parameter makes use of two bytes, but only the first ten bits are useful. The HCI_Write_Voice_Setting command also returns a Status of whether the command succeeded or not. The Voice_Setting parameters define the behaviour of all SCO connections that are active between partying devices.

4.5.1.7   Link Controller.   The LC layer is the lowest layer depicted in the dependencies of this profile and is responsible for a large number of core capabilities. It manages air to interface transactions and determines the fundamental timing of ACL and

Table 4-41   The Voice_Setting parameters that are used to define the behaviour of all active SCO connections.

										PARAMETERS
9	8	7	6	5	4	3	2	1	0	Bit # of Voice Setting Parameters
0	0	0	0	0	0	0	0	0	0	Linear
0	0	0	0	0	0	0	0	0	1	μ-Law Baseband Coding
0	0	0	0	0	0	0	0	1	0	A-Law Baseband Coding
0	0	0	0	0	0	0	0	0	0	1's Complement
0	0	0	0	0	0	0	1	0	0	2's Complement
0	0	0	0	0	0	1	0	0	0	Sign-magnitude
0	0	0	0	0	0	0	0	0	0	8-bit Input for Linear PCM
0	0	0	0	0	1	0	0	0	0	16-bit Input for Linear PCM
0	0	x	x	x	0	0	0	0	0	Used for denoting the PCM Bit Offset
0	0	0	0	0	0	0	0	0	0	CVSD air-coding format
0	1	0	0	0	0	0	0	0	0	μ-Law air-coding format
1	0	0	0	0	0	0	0	0	0	A-Law air coding format

SCO data packet transmission and reception, as well as coordinating effort at its upper-edge with the LM. It also encompasses the management of the various packet types and the various inquiry and paging procedures that are available. The following subsections now consider the capabilities that are a requirement at the LC level for the Cordless Telephony Profile. In our understanding of the dependencies, we begin by further examining the supported capabilities. If you are a developer providing profile-specific applications, then it is unlikely that you will engage in a large part of this component, although in some audio-related applications direct access may be required, where a faster transport mechanism can be supported. Nevertheless, many manufacturers have architected an audio-specific Application Programming Interface (API) for intelligible access to this component.

4.5.1.7.1 Capabilities.   Table 4-42 summarises the broad capabilities that are expected from the LC and in the table you will notice features are marked with *M* (Mandatory), *O* (Optional), *X* (Excluded), *C* (Conditional) and *N/A* (Not Applicable); this will determine what is expected from the features at the LC.

4.5.1.7.1.1 INQUIRY AND INQUIRY SCAN.   An inquiry procedure is used to learn of the other devices in radio range, where the BD_ADDR and clock offsets are obtained; it is DeviceA that will enter an *inquiry substate* to perform this procedure. A device that wishes to be discovered (DeviceB) will enter an *inquiry scan substate*, where the device will respond with an *inquiry response*. In this state, DeviceB is waiting to receive an *Inquiry Access Code* (IAC). From an application perspective, these modes of operation are discussed in more detail in the *Generic Access Profile*, Chapter 2. It is here that specific rules are determined with regard to device behaviour and duration of operation in such modes. When devices have been discovered, this information is passed over to the *Service Discovery Application Profile*, Chapter 3, which manages the specific attributes that make

Table 4-42   The summary of capabilities that are required for the LC to enable a compliant Cordless Telephony Profile.

PROCEDURES	DEVICEA	DEVICEB
Inquiry	M	X
Inquiry Scan	X	M
Paging	M	X
Page Scan	X	M
Inter-piconet	O	O
Packet Types	M	M
Voice Codecs	M	M

up that device. What is being established here, as a dependency, is that the Bluetooth protocol stack must encompass and support such behavioural procedures for this profile to be considered compliant.

4.5.1.7.1.2 PAGING AND PAGING SCAN. The *inquiry substate* and *inquiry scan substate* procedures are the initial methods used to learn of other devices in radio range; to this extent, the device has discovered sufficient information to gain a connection with the remote device. This is achieved when DeviceA has the intent to create a connection with DeviceB; DeviceA is now placed into a *paging substate*, where it will periodically transmit the *Device Access Code* (DAC). The DAC is used to target the device directly and the clock offset is used to gain an idea of the clock cycle of DeviceB. These parameters were originally obtained during our inquiry procedures. If DeviceB wishes to be connected, then it will enter a *page scan substate* and will respond accordingly to DeviceA. An inquiry procedure may be avoided if the BD_ADDR is already known, although a connection may take a little longer if the clock offset is not known.

4.5.1.7.1.3 INTER-PICONET. Inter-piconet capabilities describe the process that allows the master to manage multiple connections from slave devices. During a connection, other users may temporarily witness degradation in the service being provided; however, the master must be capable of accepting new piconet participants.

Table 4-43 The summary of packet types that are required for the LC to enable a compliant Cordless Telephony Profile.

PACKET TYPE	TL	GW
DM1	M	M
DH1	M	M
DM3	M	M
DH3	M	M
DM5	M	M
DH5	M	M
HV1	M	M
HV2	M	M
HV3	M	M
DV	X	X

Table 4-44   The summary of voice codec schemes available for voice-related profiles.

VOICE CODEC	TL	GW
CVSD	M	M
A-Law	M	M
μ-Law	M	M

4.5.1.7.1.4   PACKET TYPES.   There are numerous packets types available and Table 4-43 identifies those most frequently used for profile support. There are also a number of *common* packet types that are used for general purpose transport; for example, the ID packet is used for inquiry procedures and a POLL packet would be sent by DeviceA to determine if a slave is active on a channel.

The DM1 packet type is used to transmit control data over any connection, but may also be used to transport a genuine payload. HV1, HV2 and HV3 are various SCO packet types to carry audio-specific data, where a DV packet can combine ACL and SCO specific data; their support in this profile is reflected in Table 4-43. Various ACL packet types are also available. In fact, seven types including the DM1 type are attributed to carrying user-specific data. These include DH1, DM3, DH3, DM5, DH5 and AUX1. Similarly, Table 4-43 summarises their support in this profile.

4.5.1.7.1.5   VOICE CODECS.   Table 4-44 summarises voice codec support in this profile. Voice coding schemes are used to provide compression and to overcome potential errors in data transmission. *Continuous Variable Slope Delta* (CVSD) provides the second scheme, which is particularly efficient for voice communication; it also tolerates potential errors in the audio data. The *Pulse Code Modulation* (PCM) has two types of logarithmic compression; these are A-law and μ-law, where either compression technique can be applied on the voice channels over the air-interface.

4.6   SUMMARY

- The Cordless Telephony Profile provides usage scenarios that form the 3-in-1 phone concept.
- The Cordless Telephony Profile and Intercom Profile are very similar in nature, where both profiles depend on the TCS.
- The TCS is a specific component that manages and coordinates incoming and outgoing calls; it resides above L2CAP in the Bluetooth protocol stack architecture.
- A cordless handset is used, which has been specifically Bluetooth-enabled; a mobile phone may also behave as a cordless handset.
- A multimedia PC may also have functionality that enables it to provide cordless telephony-like capabilities though the use of external or internal speakers and a microphone.

- Park Mode is recommended for any TL, since this will ultimately conserve battery life.
- In multi-terminal support, the GW is capable of managing up to seven connections from different TLs.
- When a GW is configured for multi-terminal support, it must remain master of the piconet.
- The GW can support only three active SCO channels. This limitation is imposed due to the bandwidth reserving nature of SCO.
- There are elements of crossover with the Intercom Profile. Intercom calls are supported between TLs.
- A headset may be used to replace the cordless handset, but it must support the Cordless Telephony Profile.

5

The Intercom Profile

5.1 INTRODUCTION

In a continuation from the *Cordless Telephony Profile*, Chapter 4, the *Intercom Profile* provides the usage model, where two *terminals* (TLs) may communicate with one another, fulfilling a direct communication link. This new usage model accommodates general wireless telephony, enabling Bluetooth solutions within the home or office environment. Bluetooth-enabled cordless handsets and multimedia PCs are all capable of supporting intercom functionality. This also extends the functionality already offered within a mobile phone, where short-range communication can be supported, allowing the mobile phone to access another mobile phone or cordless handset; Figure 5-1 and Figure 5-2 illustrate the usage models supported by this profile.

The Intercom Profile is supported by devices that form part of the 3-in-1 usage model, as described in the Cordless Telephony Profile. Essentially, where a direct speech link is required, the Intercom profile is used to establish that direct one-to-one connection. This profile, as with the Cordless Telephony Profile, is dependent upon the TCS implementation. The Bluetooth *Telephone Control Protocol Specification* or the *TCS-Binary* (TCS-BIN), further shortened to TCS, is discussed in detail in our previous chapter.

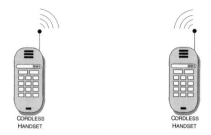

Figure 5-1   A one-to-one intercom connection is sustained by two cordless
handsets in this illustration.

5.2   USAGE MODELS

This section considers our existing usage model through scenarios that may be typical for the
Intercom Profile. The scenario provided in Figure 5-1 and Figure 5-2 represent our existing
usage model. In the illustrations, a *mobile phone* or *cordless handset* is shown. The role of the
cordless handset is to establish a one-to-one communications link with another cordless handset. With this capability inherent in a cordless handset, it falls within the category described
as the 3-in-1 usage scenario, which we introduced in the Cordless Telephony Profile. The Intercom usage model prescribes short-range communication typically found in a small office
environment and can equally be mapped onto other similar environments, where such examples include a door entry system and an intercom system for the care of patients in a hospital.

5.3   PROFILE PRINCIPLES

The Intercom Profile does not necessarily define any new roles, although participating devices that support this profile are generally described as a *Terminal* (TL), where such devices may be a *cordless handset*, *mobile phone* or a *multimedia PC*. In Figure 5-3, we can

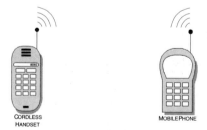

Figure 5-2   A one-to-one intercom connection is also sustained by a cordless
handset and a mobile phone that supports the Intercom Profile.

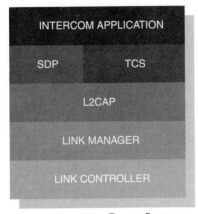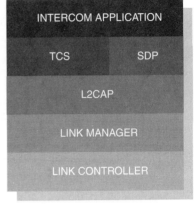

Figure 5-3   The core components of the Bluetooth protocol stack are shown,
illustrating how the components of the Intercom Profile are
integrated.

see how the Intercom components are integrated within the existing Bluetooth protocol
stack.

The profile defines a set of protocols and procedures that are required to realise the
profile implementation. Several feature definitions are provided that enable *Call Information*, *Intercom Call* and *On Hook* capabilities. We will discuss these and other features
later.

There are no fixed master-slave roles. This allows either device free to initiate
and/or terminate a connection. The user may determine whether authentication and/or encryption should be used between the two devices; however, if it is used, then the procedures as described for authentication and encryption in the *Generic Access Profile*,
Chapter 2 must be adhered to.

In Table 5-1, clarification is provided with regard to the roles used within the context of this profile. In general, *DeviceA* represents the initiating party and *DeviceB* represents the accepting party. The terms are often used interchangeably when describing
specific operations in various contexts and are provided here for reference.

5.4   USER EXPECTATIONS

The Intercom Profile is dependent upon the underlying profiles, where *Connection Establishment* procedures are applicable and are illustrated in the *Generic Access Profile*,
Chapter 2. The connection establishment procedures encompass the availability of an initialised and configured L2CAP connection. If the device is in park mode, then it is unparked prior to any creation of a Synchronous Connection-Orientated (SCO) connection;
if no previous session exists, then one is created and the device may request parked status.

Table 5-1   The list of behavioural characteristics that are typical for this profile.

CONFIGURATION	ROLE	DESCRIPTION
DeviceA	TL	A device acting as a terminal, which may take the form of a mobile phone or cordless handset. In this particular context, the device is described as initiating the connection with the accepting device.
	Initiator	This configuration describes the device that instigates the original connection or the device that wishes to initiate communication over an existing link.
DeviceB	TL	A device acting as a terminal, which may take the form of a mobile phone or cordless handset. In this particular context, the device is described as accepting the connection with the initiating device.
	Acceptor	This configuration describes the process of the device accepting the initiated communication from DeviceA.

Therefore, it is assumed that the TL devices have previously performed an inquiry, discovery and any authentication and/or encryption.

An incoming call from another TL will generate an audible alert, notifying the user of an incoming connection; *Calling Line Identification Presentation* (CLIP) may be used to identify the incoming caller if the TL supports it. The user may now accept or reject the call by operating the buttons available on the cordless handset. With a multimedia PC, specific software for the intercom application may be used to accept or reject the caller by operating a menu-driven user interface.

A user may initiate an outgoing call by operating the buttons available on the cordless handset. If a TL loses the connection with its peer, as a result of moving out of radio range, then the TL will attempt to re-establish the original connection by regularly paging the TL device.

5.5   LIFTING THE LID

5.5.1   Dependencies

Now that we have explored various aspects of existing usage models and their respective user expectations, let's take an opportunity to explore in greater depth the dependencies that make up this profile. In Figure 5-5, we provide a conceptual illustration representing

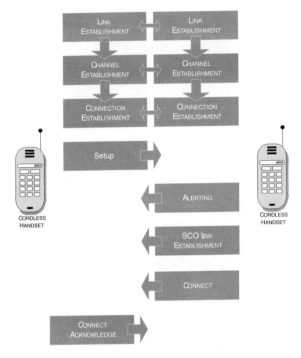

Figure 5-4   The sequence of events that occur during call establishment.

the dependencies that make up the Intercom Profile; the areas that are shaded are relevant to this profile. As you can see, the profile depends upon the basic functionality offered to us by the *Generic Access Profile*, Chapter 2, the *Service Discovery Application Profile*, Chapter 3 and the *Telephony Control Protocol*. We will now discuss, in turn, the basic requirements of these dependent components and any deviations that may occur from the basic functionality originally offered to us.

5.5.1.1   Generic Access.

The Intercom Profile is one of the profiles that relies upon the capabilities provided by the *Generic Access Profile,* Chapter 2. You may recall that a level of basic functionality is achieved through establishing a set of rules and procedures. These specifically relate to a device's connectivity, discoverability and common characteristics at the user interface level, with some additional emphasis provided for security. Furthermore, it is these rules and procedures that are used to establish commonality between products, which will ultimately achieve a cohesive user experience.

In Table 5-2, the basic set of procedures is illustrated identifying functional expectations, which in turn govern its operation. These procedures help determine the context that the device would operate in; for example, a device may wish to be discoverable for a

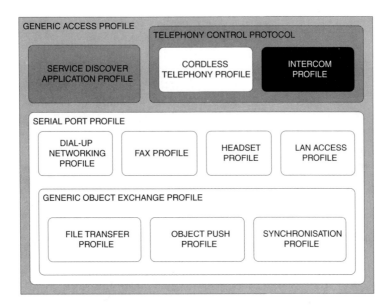

Figure 5-5 The dependent components of the Bluetooth protocol stack that make up the Intercom Profile. The areas that are shaded are relevant to this profile.

Table 5-2 The core set of procedures as required by most profiles.

PROCEDURES	DESCRIPTION
Discoverability Mode	This mode prescribes the overall discoverability of a device, allowing it to be placed into a non-discoverable, limited or general discoverable mode. The mode would allow devices to become generally available to other users or it can be restricted to personal use.
Connectability Mode	When determining a baseband connectable state, this mode is used to place a device into a connectable or non-connectable mode.
Pairing	Pairable and non-pairable modes are used to realise the security aspects when operating or intending to use a device. A device may require authentication and, as such, the user would be required to enter a Bluetooth Passkey. The pairing procedure starts the link key generation process, which in turn allows authentication to take place.

period of time or it may require a level of security that differs from one device to another depending upon the services its capable of offering.

In Table 5-3, we consider the specific set of operations that are required for this profile. In the table, features are marked with *M* (Mandatory), *O* (Optional), *X* (Excluded), *C* (Conditional) and *N/A* (Not Applicable); these determine what is expected from the features of the Generic Access Profile. The Intercom Profile requires mandatory support for pairable mode if bonding is supported; bonding is initially offered as optional, see Table 5-5.

Table 5-4 identifies the security requirements for this profile. You may remember from the *Generic Access Profile*, Chapter 2, that Security Mode 1, is a non-secure mode where Bluetooth-enabled devices will never initiate any security procedures; whereas, Security Modes 2 and 3, initiate different levels of security procedures at various stages of connection establishment. In this instance, if authentication is provided, then support should be provided for at least Security Modes 2 or 3.

In our final consideration of the basic rules and procedures that are required from the Generic Access Profile, the idle mode procedures outline behavioural characteristics when DeviceA chooses to initiate them against DeviceB. The procedures that are listed in Table 5-5 provide a clear indication of how a device should operate when performing such an activity.

What we realise here is that there are a specific set of events associated with a procedure and in the *Generic Access Profile*, Chapter 2, we provide an exhaustive presentation and examine how each procedure is conducted.

The mechanism for providing device discoverability is the provision of a well-structured FHS packet, which is shown in Figure 5-6. This packet is used to identify the remote device, where information such as *Bluetooth Device Address* (BD_ADDR) and clock offsets is determined. You may also notice from this packet that the *Class of Device* (CoD)

Table 5-3 The illustration shows specific modes of operation that this profile depends upon to realise its compliant implementation.

MODES	TL
Non-discoverable	M
Limited Discoverable	O
General Discoverable	M
Non-connectable	N/A
Connectable	M
Non-pairable	O
Pairable	C

Table 5-4   The illustration shows specific security procedures that this profile depends upon to realise its compliant implementation.

PROCEDURE	TL
Authentication	C
Security Mode 1	O
Security Mode 2	C
Security Mode 3	C

Table 5-5   The illustration shows specific behavioural procedures that this profile depends upon to realise its compliant implementation.

PROCEDURE	TL
General Inquiry	M
Limited Inquiry	O
Name Discovery	O
Device Discovery	O
Bonding	O

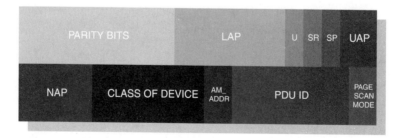

Figure 5-6   The structure of the FHS packet used only for reference to illustrate the position of the Class of Device structure.

field is also provided. This information is relayed to the user interface, which in turn provides common characteristics about discovered devices. The CoD is used during the discovery mechanism to learn more about the type of device and what it may be capable of providing. This structure of information is depicted in Figure 5-7 and is made up of 3-bytes (or 24-bits as shown). The following sections consider the Intercom attributes, which will ultimately make use of the *Service, Major* and *Minor Device Class* fields.

5.5.1.1.1 Service Class.   This high-level form of defining a Bluetooth device identifies where in the Service Class field the Intercom Profile resides; see Table 5-6, which in turn determines the category of service; here, the category of service falls within *Telephony*.

5.5.1.1.2 Major Device Class.   This high-level form of defining a Bluetooth device identifies where in the Major Device Class the Intercom Profile resides; see Table 5-7, which in turn determines the major class grouping. Here, the category falls within phone, since a cordless handset or mobile phone may be used.

5.5.1.1.3 Minor Device Class.   The Minor Device Class in this profile is used to convey further context for the setting within the major class grouping, see Table 5-8. Here the bit may be set appropriately for *Cordless* to denote the type of service available to the user.

5.5.1.2 Service Discovery.   In the *Service Discovery Application Profile*, Chapter 3, we introduced the characteristics of the mechanisms used to retrieve service information from a remote device. Typically, a client will initiate inquiry and discovery procedures, as outlined in our previous section, to learn of the devices in radio range. A client will then make use of an application, which embodies the functionality of the underlying *Service Discovery Protocol* (SDP). The *Service Discovery Application* (`SrvD-scApp`) uses an *SDP Client* to instigate a request to the remote device where the *SDP Server* will respond; as such, both TLs must employ the use of an SDP client and server, as illustrated in Table 5-9.

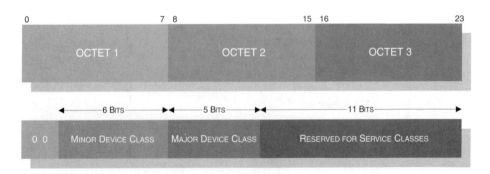

Figure 5-7   The structure of the class of device, illustrating the Minor Device, Major Device and Service Class fields and their respective lengths.

Table 5-6   The Service Class categorisation for the Intercom Profile.

											SERVICE CLASS
23	22	21	20	19	18	17	16	15	14	13	Bit # of CoD
0	1	0	0	0	0	0	0	0	0	0	Telephony

Table 5-7   The Major Device Class for the Intercom Profile.

					MAJOR DEVICE CLASS
12	11	10	9	8	Bit # of CoD
0	0	0	1	0	Phone

Table 5-8   The Minor Device Class for the Intercom Profile.

						MINOR DEVICE CLASS
7	6	5	4	3	2	Bit # of CoD
0	0	0	0	1	0	Cordless

Table 5-9   As a minimum, the local device must support the use of a client application and the remote device must support the use of a server.

FEATURE	TL	TL
SDP Client	M	X
SDP Server	X	M

Table 5-10   The list of PDUs that are required for the operation of the Intercom Profile.

PDU	TL	TL
SDP_ErrorResponse	X	M
SDP_ServiceSearchRequest	M	X
SDP_ServiceSearchResponse	X	M
SDP_ServiceAttributeRequest	M	X
SDP_ServiceAttributeResponse	X	M
SDP_ServiceSearchAttributeRequest	O	X
SDP_ServiceSearchAttributeRequest	X	O

Protocol Data Units (PDUs) are used to instruct the SDP server to undertake browsing procedures and to retrieve service record information about its services; you may recall that these PDUs carry payloads about requests containing AttributeIDs and AttributeValues describing what exactly is being sought. As we previously discussed, the client and server operate a request and response paradigm. SDAP will construct PDUs containing information relating to the AttributeID and Attribute-Values, in turn instructing the server to carry out its operation. The various request and response PDUs that are required are shown Table 5-10.

A service record is maintained for each service a device is capable of supporting and, as such, a *Service Record Handle* is created to uniquely identify this. The Service-RecordHandle is a 32-bit unsigned integer and is stored on the SDP server. The service record shown in Table 5-11 identifies a TL device and provides a list of AttributeIDs, which ultimately would identify the service for the Intercom Profile. A minimum of two AttributeIDs are required to make a service record; these are ServiceRecord-Handle and ServiceClassIDList, where it must contain at least one UUID.

When browsing for services on the remote device, a local device constructs a search pattern using a *Universally Unique Identifier* (UUID). A UUID is a 128-bit value, which has been shortened for use within Bluetooth applications. The shortcut has been provided by first establishing a *Bluetooth Base UUID*, which we discussed in the *Service Discovery Application Profile*, Chapter 3.

The UUIDs that have been presented so far are aliases and take the form of what is referred to as a 16-bit UUID or a 32-bit UUID—but, in turn, they all should refer to the 128-bit notation. These UUIDs have been assigned and can be referenced in the Bluetooth Special Interest Group, Bluetooth Assigned Numbers, v1.1, February 2001. For the search pattern to be successful, they all need to be converted to the 128-bit notation, since they will all be compared at this range. An arithmetic conversion algorithm is used to construct the 128-bit value.

Table 5-11 The list of mandatory and configurable items that make up this profile's service discovery record.

ATTRIBUTE	DESCRIPTION
ServiceRecordHandle	With an `AttributeID` of `0x0000`, this uniquely identifies this service record within the SDP server on the TL device.

ServiceClassIDList
  ServiceClass0
  ServiceClass1
	With an `AttributeID` of `0x0001`, the following `ServiceClass0` would contain the UUID for the *Intercom* and the `ServiceClass1` would identify the *Generic Telephony* service classes. Their respective UUID values are summarised in Table 5-19.

ProtocolDescriptorList
  Protocol0
  Protocol1
	With an `AttributeID` of `0x0004`, the following `Protocol0` would contain a UUID for the protocol *L2CAP*, whereas in `Protocol1` a UUID would contain the protocol identifier for *TCS-AT*. Their respective UUID values are summarised in Table 5-21.

BluetoothProfile-
DescriptorList
  Profile0
    ParameterFor0
	With an `AttributeID` of `0x0009`, the following `Profile0` would identify the UUID for *Intercom* service class, which is summarised in Table 5-19. The `ParameterFor0` accommodates the version number supported by this profile.

ServiceName	With a base `AttributeID` of `0x0006`, this attribute has an offset of `0x0000`. It is a configurable item and has an `AttributeValue` of a `Text` string, where its default setting is *Intercom*.

Table 5-12 summarises the service class UUIDs used to identify the particular profile in use; this also correlates with the identification of the device during a device discovery procedure as previously outlined in Section 5.5.1.1, *Generic Access*.

As part of the service record, the dependent underlying protocols are also identified. The local device retrieves this information, where it can fully understand the exact requirements needed to fulfil the service. The Intercom Profile is dependent on the protocols as shown in Table 5-13, which shows their associated UUID values.

5.5.1.3 TCS in the Intercom Profile. In the *Cordless Telephony Profile,* Chapter 4 we leaned about how signalling messages are created and subsequently constructed to provide us with a telephony service. The extent of the services are governed by the Call

Table 5-12   The list of service classes that match a corresponding profile. This correlates
with our previous Generic Access section.

CLASSES	UUID
Intercom	0x1110
GenericTelephony	0x1204

Control entity and in the following section, we consider its objectives and expectations in
the *profile*.

5.5.1.3.1   Call Control.   The primary responsibility of the CC entity is to coordinate the connection and disconnection of speech and data calls between two participating
TLs. In Table 5-14, we illustrate the set of Call Control procedures that are required to
achieve a compliant Intercom Profile.

5.5.1.4   L2CAP.   The L2CAP layer provides transparency for the upper layers of
the stack from the layers typically found within the host controller. L2CAP payloads are
passed to the *Host Controller Interface*[1] (HCI), which is then subsequently passed onto
the *Link Manager Protocol* (LMP). The range of upper layers, which include RFCOMM,
Service Discovery Protocol (SDP) and TCS all make use of the capabilities offered to us
by L2CAP. Its primary role is to provide *protocol multiplexing*, allowing numerous simultaneous connections to be made, and to also provide the ability for *segmentation* and
reassembly. This refers to the ability to manage large payloads in the application, which
may need to be fragmented into smaller payloads for the lower layers to manage; these are
then transmitted over the air-interface. Finally, the L2CAP layer exchanges *Quality of
Service* (QoS) information, ensuring that sufficient resources are available and that both
Bluetooth devices are attaining the best service.

In Table 5-15, we summarise the broad capabilities that are expected from L2CAP.
In the table, you will notice features are marked appropriately and will determine what is
expected from the L2CAP layer.

Table 5-13   The list of protocols that are used in this profile; their associated UUID values
are also shown.

PROTOCOL	UUID
TCS-AT	0x0006
L2CAP	0x0100

[1]L2CAP payloads are passed directly onto LMP when implemented on a host-less system.

Table 5-14 The illustration shows specific Call Control procedures that this profile depends upon to realise its compliant implementation.

PROCEDURE	TL
Call Request	M
Call Confirmation	M
Call Connection	M
Failure of Call Establishment	M
Call Clearing	M
Call Information	M

5.5.1.4.1 Channel Types. In Table 5-15, we have identified that *Connection-orientated Channels* are mandatory, whereas *Connectionless Channels* are excluded; this type of channel is aimed at broadcasting, where all devices may be targeted. L2CAP uses PDUs to transport connection, signalling and configuration options, which will be discussed below. The higher layers of the Bluetooth protocol stack will instigate a connection with L2CAP using the `L2CA_ConnectReq` request packet, where

Table 5-15 The illustration shows specific procedures that this profile depends upon to realise its compliant implementation.

PROCEDURE	TL
Connection-orientated Channel	M
Connectionless Channel	X
Connection Establishment	M
Configuration	M
Connection Termination	M
Echo	M
Command Rejection	M
Maximum Transmission Unit	M
Flush Timeout	M
Quality of Service	O

Table 5-16   The range of prototypes used to illustrate how L2CAP is architected and how interaction between higher and lower layers is achieved. For this discussion, our concern here is with the higher-layer.

PROTOTYPE	DESCRIPTION
L2CA_	This prefix prototype is used to denote the higher-layer interaction, typically used by RFCOMM, SDP and TCS
L2CAP_	This prefix is used to denote peer-to-peer signalling interaction of L2CAP entities.
LP_	Finally, this prefix denotes lower-layer interaction, where L2CAP interfaces with the LMP layer.

the corresponding result is contained within the L2CA_ConnectRsp response packet.

An L2CA_ConnectRspNeg negative response packet is used to denote a response, where the connection with the remote device was unsuccessful. Since our profile resides above L2CAP and employs its services, we are only concerned with the upper protocol layer of L2CAP. This higher functionality is offered to us through a series of L2CAP events and is denoted through the prefix L2CA_; see Table 5-16.

When creating an L2CAP connection between two devices, a *Protocol/Service Multiplexor* (PSM) value is used to denote the higher-layer protocol that is using the connection; Table 5-17 identifies these values and the corresponding protocols they represent. The value of 0x0005 (TCS-BIN) is used for this profile.

5.5.1.4.2 Signalling.   When establishing communication with a remote device, a *signalling channel* is created and reserved for use during connection, disconnection and configuration of subsequent L2CAP connections. A *channel* is used to describe the communication and data flow that exists between L2CAP entities and Table 5-18 illustrates the range of *Channel Identifies* (CIDs) that are used to identify the channel type. As we

Table 5-17   The PSM values that are used to identify the higher-layer protocol.

PSM	DESCRIPTION
0x0001	SDP
0x0003	RFCOMM
0x0005	TCS-BIN
0x0007	TCS-BIN-CORDLESS

Table 5-18   The CIDs that are used to represent the logical channel.

CID	DESCRIPTION
0x0000	Null
0x0001	Signalling Channel
0x0002	Connectionless Reception Channel
0x0003 to 0x003F	Reserved
0x0040 to 0xFFFF	Dynamically Allocated

can see in Table 5-15, *Connection Establishment* and *Termination* is mandatory in the local device, although the remote device may be capable of initiating and terminating a connection to the local device. The L2CA_DisconnectReq request packet is used to terminate the connection with the remote device and an L2CA_DisconnectRsp response packet is used to ascertain the result of the termination—although all disconnection requests must be completed successfully. The support of *Configuration* is shown as mandatory and we will discuss these specific options in more detail in the following section. Finally, *Echo* and *Command Rejection* are both mandatory for a compliant Intercom Profile.

5.5.1.4.3 Configuration Options.   In establishing a connection with the remote device, the channel is subject to configuration and the higher-layer prototype L2CA_ConfigReq request packet is used to carry configuration requests. Its associated response is contained within the L2CA_ConfigRsp packet; an L2CA_ConfigRspNeg packet is used to denote a negative response during configuration, where for example the suggested *Maximum Transmission Unit* (MTU) is too large. In Table 5-15, we have identified that the MTU and *Flush Timeout* parameters are mandatory, whereas the QoS is optional.

The default MTU setting for the signalling channel is 48 bytes, whereas other channels may be capable of transferring larger payloads; essentially, the MTU determines the size of payloads that are capable of being exchanged between two devices. The Intercom Profile requires that a minimum MTU of 3 bytes should be established to allow support for multiple TLs. During configuration, the local device will inform the remote device that it is potentially capable of accepting larger payloads. If the remote device is unwilling to accept a larger MTU, then the local device is informed with the response contained within the L2CA_ConfigRspNeg packet.

When L2CA_ request and response packets are being exchanged, the Flush Timeout parameter is used to determine how long the local device is prepared to continue to transmit an L2CAP fragment before it gives up; the packet is subsequently flushed (that is, discarded). The suggested Flush Timeout value is sent during the L2CA_ConfigReq request packet. However, if no value is set, then the default value is used. The Intercom Profile uses the default value of 0xFFFF.

As we have already mentioned, the QoS configuration is optional, but if it is used during an `L2CA_ConfigReq` request, then the *best effort* service is established as a default; the available services that are supported by an L2CAP channel are shown in Table 5-19. However, if the QoS service is set at *Guaranteed,* then parameters such *Token Rate, Token Bucket, Peak Bandwidth, Latency* and *Delay Variation,* are used to determine an acceptable guaranteed service, where the `L2CA_ConnectRspNeg` will indicate that these values are unacceptable. These parameters are then subject to further negotiation.

5.5.1.5 Link Manager. The *Link Manager* (LM) layer sits between the HCI and the *Link Controller* (LC), although on a hostless system the LM will have direct interaction with L2CAP. It accepts commands from HCI and translates them into operations for the LC, where *Asynchronous Connectionless* (ACL) and SCO links are created and established. It is during this stage of ACL and SCO establishment that a master-slave switch would be performed as governed by the requirements of this profile. The LM is also responsible for placing the device into a low-power mode, which includes *hold, sniff* and *park.*

In providing *general* error management, devices that operate mandatory procedures during interoperability must either acknowledge their support or provide a reason for procedure failure. The `LMP_Detach` PDU is used to inform the device of the error that occurred; typically, *unsupported LMP feature* (`0x1A`) is reported when an error occurs (see Appendix A).

Next, we take an opportunity to explore the dependencies that make up the Intercom Profile, and we will provide a narrative of the capabilities that are expected at this level. In Table 5-20, we identify the capabilities that are required from this layer and in the following subsections discuss the specific procedures in more detail.

Table 5-19   The range of service definitions that are used during QoS.

SERVICE	DESCRIPTION
No Traffic	This indicates that the channel will not be sending any traffic and, as such, any parameters can be ignored.
Best Effort	This default value attempts to achieve a minimum service with the local remote device, where no guarantees are offered.
Guaranteed	With this service definition, we indicate that we wish to achieve the maximum bandwidth permitted. This is, of course, subject to the nature of a wireless environment.

Table 5-20 The mandatory requirements that are required for a compliant Intercom Profile.

PROCEDURES	SUPPORT
SCO Links	M

5.5.1.5.1 Capabilities. Table 5-20 summarises the broad capabilities that are expected from the LM. These will determine what is expected from the procedures at the LM. Included in the table are a set of deviations that the profile includes, which is above the common set of procedures expected at LM.

5.5.1.5.2 SCO Links. A SCO link is set-up using the `HCI_Add_SCO_Connection` command (see Table 5-21), where a series of `Voice_Setting` parameters are used to denote the type of SCO channel and the audio coding schemes. The `Voice_Setting` parameters are written using the `HCI_Write_Voice_Setting` command and are shown in Table 5-22.

Table 5-21 The command and events that are used in combination to create a SCO connection. The Host Controller first sends the `Command_Status` event, but when the connection has been established the `Connection_Complete` event is generated on both devices.

COMMAND	PARAMETERS
`HCI_Add_SCO_Connection`	`Connection_Handle`
	`Packet_Type`
EVENT	**PARAMETERS**
`Command_Status`	`Status`
	`Num_HCI_Command_Packets`
	`Command_OpCode`
`Connection_Complete`	`Status`
	`Connection_Handle`
	`BD_ADDR`
	`Link_Type`
	`Encryption_Mode`

Table 5-22   The command and events that are used in combination to write the voice setting parameters for a SCO link.

COMMAND	PARAMETERS
HCI_Write_Voice_Setting	Voice_Setting
EVENT	**PARAMETERS**
Command_Complete	Num_HCI_Command_Packets
	Command_OpCode
	Return_Parameters

It assumed that the partying devices have an existing ACL communications link, where pairing, authentication and encryption (if required) have already taken place. The ACL Connection_Handle parameter is used, in part, to then create our SCO connection using the HCI_Add_SCO_Connection command. Although, the host controller generates a Command_Status event, it does not indicate that the SCO connection has been created. The host controller for both devices uses the Connection_Complete event to notify both hosts whether the SCO connection has been successful or not, where the new Connection_Handle and Link_Type identify the new connection. You may also wish to note that the Packet_Type parameter is used to specify the type of high-quality voice transmission, where HV1, HV2 or HV3 can be requested over the SCO link.

The Voice_Setting parameters are shown in more detail in Table 5-23. The parameter makes use of two bytes, but only the first ten bits are useful. The HCI_Write_Voice_Setting command also returns a Status of whether the command succeeded or not. The Voice_Setting parameters define the behaviour of all SCO connections that are active between partying devices.

5.5.1.6 Link Controller.   The LC layer is the lowest layer depicted in the dependencies of this profile and it is responsible for a large number of core capabilities. It manages air-to-interface transactions and determines the fundamental timing of ACL and SCO data packet transmission and reception, as well as coordinating the effort at its upper-edge with the LM. It also encompasses the management of the various packet types and the various inquiry and paging procedures that are available. In turn, the following subsections provide clarity regarding the capabilities that are a requirement at the LC level for the Intercom Profile. In our understanding of the dependencies, we begin by examining in more detail the supported capabilities and a small discussion is offered for each. If you are a developer providing profile-specific applications, then it is unlikely that you will engage in a large part of this component, although in some audio-related applications direct access may be required, where a faster transport mechanism can be supported. Nevertheless, many manufacturers have architected an audio-specific API for intelligible access to this component.

Table 5-23 The `Voice_Setting` parameters that are used to define the behaviour of all active SCO connections.

9	8	7	6	5	4	3	2	1	0	PARAMETERS Bit # of Voice Setting Parameters
0	0	0	0	0	0	0	0	0	0	Linear
0	0	0	0	0	0	0	0	0	1	μ-Law Baseband Coding
0	0	0	0	0	0	0	0	1	0	A-Law Baseband Coding
0	0	0	0	0	0	0	0	0	0	1's Complement
0	0	0	0	0	0	0	1	0	0	2's Complement
0	0	0	0	0	0	1	0	0	0	Sign-magnitude
0	0	0	0	0	0	0	0	0	0	8-bit Input for Linear PCM
0	0	0	0	0	1	0	0	0	0	16-bit Input for Linear PCM
0	0	x	x	x	0	0	0	0	0	Used for denoting the PCM Bit Offset
0	0	0	0	0	0	0	0	0	0	CVSD air-coding format
0	1	0	0	0	0	0	0	0	0	μ-Law air-coding format
1	0	0	0	0	0	0	0	0	0	A-Law air coding format

5.5.1.6.1 Capabilities.   Table 5-24 summarises the broad capabilities that are expected from the LC. In the table, you will notice features are marked appropriately and these will determine what is expected from the LC.

5.5.1.6.1.1 INQUIRY AND INQUIRY SCAN.   An inquiry procedure is used to learn of the other devices in radio range, where the BD_ADDR and clock offsets are obtained; it is DeviceA that will enter an *inquiry substate* to perform this procedure. A device that wishes to be discovered (DeviceB) will enter an *inquiry scan substate*, where the device will respond with an *inquiry response*. In this state, DeviceB is waiting to receive an *Inquiry Access Code* (IAC). From an application perspective, these modes of operation are discussed in more detail in the *Generic Access Profile*, Chapter 2. It is here that specific rules are determined with regard the behaviour of such devices and how long these devices can operate in such modes. When devices have been discovered, this information is passed over to the *Service Discovery Application Profile*, Chapter 3, which manages the specific attributes that make up that device. What is being established here, as a dependency, is that the Bluetooth protocol stack must en-

Table 5-24   The summary of capabilities that are required for the LC to enable a compliant Intercom Profile.

PROCEDURES	DEVICEA	DEVICEB
Inquiry	M	X
Inquiry Scan	X	M
Paging	M	X
Page Scan	X	M
Inter-piconet	O	O
Packet Types	M	M
Voice Codecs	M	M

compass and support such behavioural procedures for this profile to be considered compliant.

5.5.1.6.1.2   PAGING AND PAGING SCAN.   The *inquiry substate* and *inquiry scan substate* procedures are the initial method used to learn of other devices in radio range; to this extent, the device has discovered sufficient information to gain a connection with the remote device. This is achieved when DeviceA has the intent to create a connection with DeviceB; DeviceA is now placed into a *paging substate*, where it will periodically transmit the *Device Access Code* (DAC). The DAC is used to target the device directly and the clock offset is used to gain an idea of the clock cycle of DeviceB. These parameters were originally obtained during our inquiry procedures. If DeviceB wishes to be connected, then it will enter a *page scan substate* and will respond accordingly to DeviceA. An inquiry procedure may be avoided if the BD_ADDR is already known, although a connection may take a little longer as the clock offset is not known.

5.5.1.6.1.3   INTER-PICONET.   Inter-piconet capabilities describe the process that allows the master to manage multiple connections from slave devices. During a connection, other users may temporarily witness degradation in the service that is being provided, but the master must be capable of accepting new participants into the piconet.

5.5.1.6.1.4   PACKET TYPES.   There are numerous packets types available and Table 5-25 identifies those most frequently used for profile support. There are also a number of *common* packet types that are used for general purpose transport; for example, the ID packet is used for inquiry procedures and a POLL packet would be sent by DeviceA to determine if a slave is active on a channel.

The DM1 packet type is used to transmit control data over any connection, but may be used to transport a genuine payload. HV1, HV2 and HV3 are various SCO packet types

Table 5-25   The summary of packet types that are required for the LC to enable a compliant Intercom Profile.

PACKET TYPE	DEVICE A	DEVICE B
DM1	M	M
DH1	M	M
DM3	M	M
DH3	M	M
DM5	M	M
DH5	M	M
HV1	M	M
HV2	M	M
HV3	M	M
DV	X	X

to carry audio-specific data, where a DV packet can combine ACL and SCO specific data; their support in this profile is reflected in Table 5-26. Various ACL packet types are also available. Seven types, including the DM1 type, are attributed to carrying user-specific data.These include DH1, DM3, DH3, DM5, DH5, and AUX1; similarly, Table 5-25 summarises their support in this profile.

5.5.1.6.1.5   VOICE CODECS.   Table 5-26 summarises voice codec support in this profile. Voice coding schemes are used to provide compression and to overcome potential errors in the data transmission.

Continuous Variable Slope Delta (CVSD) provides the second scheme, which is particularly efficient for voice communication; it also tolerates potential errors in the audio data. The *Pulse Code Modulation* (PCM) has two types of logarithmic compression; these

Table 5-26   The summary of voice codec schemes available for voice-related profiles.

VOICE CODEC	DEVICE A	DEVICE B
CVSD	M	M
A-Law	M	M
μ-Law	M	M

are A-law and μ-law, where either compression technique can be applied on the voice channels over the air-interface.

5.6 SUMMARY

- The Intercom Profile falls into the category of the 3-in-1 usage model that is supported by the Cordless Telephony Profile.
- The profile supports terminal-to-terminal direct communication.
- Other usage models may be extended to door intercom and hospital paging schemes.
- The Intercom Profile is built upon the TCS.
- The profile does not mandate a strict master-slave operation and, as such, either terminal may initiate a connection.

6

The Serial Port Profile

6.1 INTRODUCTION

All of the profiles listed in Table 6-1 are based upon the *Serial Port Profile*. Potentially it will impact upon new profile development; in one way or another, you will find yourself returning to it on a regular basis.

With its firm foundation in all the profiles illustrated in Table 6-1, it is clear that a sound knowledge of the Serial Port Profile is one of the key prerequisites of current profile development. Its purpose is to provide a set of protocols and procedures which in turn, allows RFCOMM to provide serial port emulation for Bluetooth-enabled devices. The scenario provided for this profile, as shown in Figure 6-1, illustrates two devices communicating over an emulated serial communications link. The scenario depicted purports legacy application support, providing a transparent wireless transport.

6.2 USAGE MODELS

This section considers existing usage models through scenarios that are typical for the Serial Port Profile. We begin by exploring the existing model where, at face value, the Serial Port Profile provides the ability to impart serial port emulation as part of its application services. Predominately, at the user interface level, the user is notified of an available ser-

Table 6-1   The list of profiles that are built upon the Serial Port Profile.

PROFILE	CHAPTER
Headset	7
Dial-up Networking	8
Fax	9
LAN Access	10
Generic Object Exchange	11
Hands-free	17
Phone Access	17
SIM Access	17

vice which in turn, can be used as a means of data transport. In Figure 6-2, we illustrate the availability of a Bluetooth serial port being made available to the user.

It is important to note that the roles presented by this profile are not restricted to the typical *master-slave* construction, although DeviceA is depicted as the *initiator* and DeviceB as the *acceptor*. Figure 6-3 provides the components that make up the Bluetooth protocol stack and shows where the interface is exposed for *legacy*, *cable replacement* and *intermediate* applications; these are all discussed in more detail later. As a further clarification, Figure 6-3 shows the availability of an interface at the RFCOMM level[1] and illustrates how each type of application would employ its use; developers have a choice as to how they choose to use such an interface and what information to exchange. As such, the RFCOMM protocol itself does not distinguish between types of devices, that is *Type I* and *Type II*.

Figure 6-1   A legacy serial port connection is sustained by two notebooks.

---

[1]The exposure of an interface at this level is not restricted to RFCOMM. A Bluetooth aware helper application may have access to other parts of the Bluetooth protocol stack. For example, to allow registration of new services for the operating system the Bluetooth aware helper application will also have access to an SDP interface.

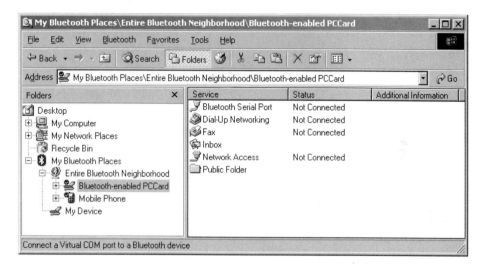

Figure 6-2 The availability of a Bluetooth serial port is made available, where legacy applications can make use of the services it provides. (Courtesy of TDK Systems Europe.)

Before continuing further, it is important from a development point of view to re-acquaint ourselves with both the definition of an *application* and the *types* of devices. The profile offers some explanation of both legacy and Bluetooth aware helper applications, but it is also important when reading this to draw upon our own prior knowledge and experience. This will allow us to fully understand the perspective of the applications from both the developer and the user's point of view.

The following sections have broken the term *application* down into four categories to help us understand the various usage models available and how serial port emulation is provided.

6.2.1   Legacy Applications (Type I)

There are numerous applications[2] readily available that are capable of data transfer through the standard serial communications port. This is primarily achieved by configuring the legacy application to use the serial port reference,[3] which is usually operating system dependent.

From a user's perspective, in the same way as any other profile, the user would perform a device and service discovery to learn of the available Bluetooth-enabled devices in

---

[2]Such applications are typically bundled with various operating systems, such as Microsoft Windows and Linux. These applications can make use of the existing serial communications port and can be configured to transfer data over the serial medium.

[3]In a Microsoft Windows environment, the serial port reference is denoted with the label COMx, where *x* refers to the port number.

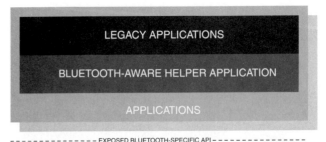

Figure 6-3   From a development perspective, the exposure of the API enables the provision of legacy, cable replacement and intermediate
application support. It also shows where a Bluetooth aware
helper application would reside.

radio range and subsequently any devices would advertise their services. In Figure 6-4,
we illustrate the available services where a Bluetooth serial port can be made available for
use by a legacy application.

In some instances, the user may have to enable this serial port for it to be offered by
the operating system, which then can be subsequently offered to the legacy application. In
Figure 6-4, the user can either double-click[4] the serial port icon or right-click its icon to
begin the process of enabling the device.

In Figure 6-5, we now see the Microsoft Windows Device Manager offers the emulated (or *virtual*[5]) serial ports. Since the virtual ports have been enabled and made available to the operating system, configuration of the port properties can be performed, as
seen in Figure 6-6.

---

[4]The double-click and right-click operations refer to a mouse that is connected to your local device (in this example, a PC or notebook computer running a Microsoft Windows operating system) and where both operations
trigger the two methods of enabling. It is noted that this operation may vary from device to device and, as such,
the number of buttons may vary on a mouse. Indeed, no mouse may be connected. The example just draws your
attention to how it may be possible and acknowledges that implementations may differ.
[5]Virtual and emulated may be used synonymously to describe the software implementation aspect of a physical
serial port.

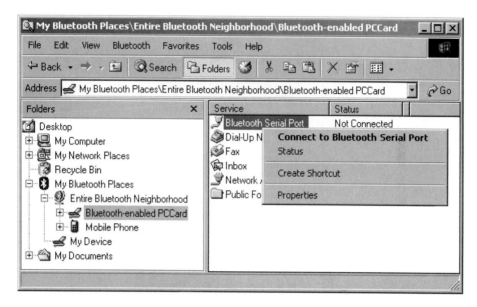

Figure 6-4   Right-clicking the device icon causes a pop-up menu to appear;
the menu offers the ability to enable the serial port emulation.
(Courtesy TDK Systems Europe.)

A legacy application makes use of the emulated serial port model and is therefore classed as a Type I device. The operating system would be offered the virtual serial port through the Bluetooth aware helper application, which we will discuss later in this chapter.

6.2.2   Cable Replacement Applications (Type I)

The purpose of making the distinction between these types of applications is to clarify and understand the composition of RFCOMM. In this particular application context, the creation of an emulated serial port would be transparent to the user. Let us take a look back at Table 6-1; all of these profiles are dependent on the operation of the Serial Port Profile and, as such, each requires the establishment of an emulated serial port as part of their communication link with the remote device.

The phrase "cable replacement application" is not introduced in the profile itself, but is introduced here to attempt to distinguish between the different usages available. It refers to specific Bluetooth applications that create implicit emulated serial ports. These ports remain transparent to the user in order to complete the creation of a communications link; we discuss this in more detail later in this chapter.

The cable replacement application can also be classed as a Type I device. The specific profile would be implemented to use the Bluetooth aware helper application, through an *Application Programming Interface* (API).

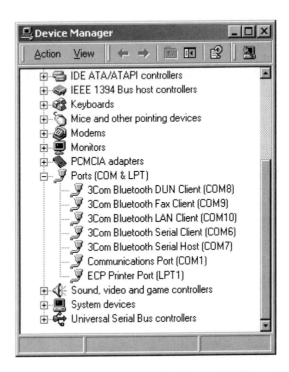

Figure 6-5   In the Microsoft Windows Device Manager, the Bluetooth Virtual Serial Port[6] has been configured ready for use by any legacy application.
(The 3Com Bluetooth Connection Manager has registered with the
operating system a range of virtual serial ports that are ready for use.)

6.2.3   Intermediate Applications (Type II)

This type of application would form part of the communications link, but would still remain transparent to all communicating parties. Figure 6-7 illustrates three devices; DeviceA and DeviceB have Bluetooth capability, whereas DeviceC is a non-Bluetooth
device, such as a wired modem.

DeviceA would communicate with DeviceB through the emulated serial port capability in order to provide DeviceA the service of DeviceC. The provision of services of
the device pair (B and C) would be similar to the usage models provided by the legacy
and cable replacement application.

The intermediate application completes a wired connection (a physical serial port) and
is therefore classed as a Type II device. Some aspects of a Bluetooth aware helper application
may be used to provide the completed and transparent communications link to DeviceC.

---

[6]In the Microsoft Windows environment, a PC or notebook may typically have two physical or standard serial
communication ports available. As such, they are offered to the user as COM1 and COM2. Virtual serial ports offered would then commence from COM3, COM4 and so on, and these are referred to as non-standard ports.

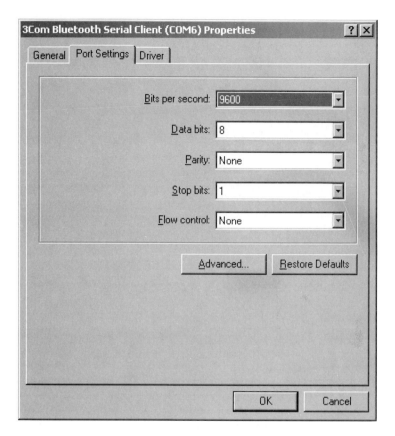

Figure 6-6 When the port is available for application use, its configuration and properties (such as baud rate and data bits) can be managed accordingly. The 3Com Bluetooth Connection Manager has registered with the operating system a range of virtual serial ports, which can now be configured by the user.

Figure 6-7 Three devices form part of this communication link for it to reach the services of the remote party.

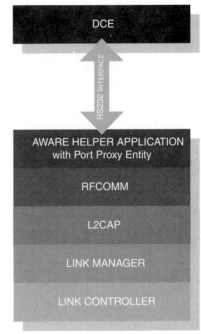

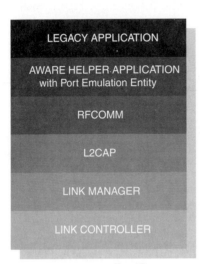

Figure 6-8   The core components of the Bluetooth protocol stack are shown illustrating how the components of Type I and Type II are integrated.

In Figure 6-8, we illustrate the structure of the Bluetooth protocol stack layers with the Type I and Type II applications in mind. In the figure, we can see the two types of applications; of particular interest is the Type II structure, where the Helper-aware application interfaces directly to the physical interface of a *Data Communication Equipment* (DCE) device such as a modem. You will also notice that the Bluetooth helper aware application is accompanied with an additional entity. These entities are used to understand how each type of application interacts with the outside world. The *Port Emulation Entity* is used to describe the API that interfaces to the RFCOMM layer, whereas the *Port Proxy Entity* relays RFCOMM-specific data to the physical serial interface. These are two conceptual structures, which are used to illustrate the two different natures of providing an RFCOMM service.

6.2.4   Bluetooth Aware Helper Applications

Legacy, cable replacement and intermediate applications rely on the use of a *Bluetooth aware helper application*. It achieves this through an API, which is provided to developers when building high-level Bluetooth applications that utilise the emulated serial port function—thus providing an interface to the RFCOMM layer accessing its core functionality.

Table 6-2   Typical APIs that would be used to open and close a communications link as well as transmit and receive data.

API	DESCRIPTION
RFCOMM_OpenConnection	An API function that would be used to open or create a communications link with the peer device.
RFCOMM_CloseConnection	An API function that would be used to close or disconnect a communications link with the peer device.
RFCOMM_TxData	An API function that would be used to transmit data to the peer device.
RFCOMM_RxData	An API function that would be used to receive data from the peer device.

Typically, this is implementation specific and can be managed at various levels on a development platform, such as an embedded or device driver[7] environment. Furthermore, the purpose of this helper aware application is to assist in establishing a legacy and cable replacement application, a virtual serial port presence without disruption to the operating system environment.

Essentially, it succeeds in disguising the underlying wireless transport, which forms most of the Bluetooth protocol stack, and provides a constructive interface to quickly and effectively deploy a communications link.

The two sections that follow provide examples of an implementation on two separate platforms and the role that a helper application would fulfil. In both instances, a common interface can be provided to enable a developer access to the core functionality. In Table 6-2, we identify some common APIs that may be used to routinely exchange data between peer devices and to establish and disconnect the communications link.

6.2.4.1   Applications in the Microsoft Windows Environment.   In the previous examples, we illustrated the presentation of a virtual serial port to the operating system where it could employ the use of that port for legacy type applications. In such implementations, the upper-edge of the helper aware application would expose its interface as a serial port and its lower-edge would present itself to the Bluetooth protocol stack, via an API as we illustrated in Table 6-2. This, in turn, provides a transparent wireless transport for the legacy application and other applications that wish to make use of that service.

Introducing Bluetooth to the Microsoft Windows environment would comprise a *host* and a *host controller*. The host would consist of a Bluetooth library, which contains

---

[7]Device driver refers to the implementation that occurs at an operating system level where the driver itself communicates specifically with an *Hardware Abstraction Layer* (HAL). In this instance, the device driver would act as an intermediate piece of software to interface with the application, independent from the wireless technology.

sufficient software to exist in the new environment and would have sufficient knowledge about the various transport mechanisms, that is, PC Card or USB. In this particular context, the host controller would be enumerated by the Microsoft Windows operating system and, in turn, would acknowledge to the host that it exists. This would be achieved by asking Microsoft Windows to *add new hardware* or through the automated process of introducing the new hardware to the environment, in other words inserting a Bluetooth-enabled PC Card or USB dongle. In most Bluetooth implementations, the host software is active, but no Bluetooth-specific activity is present, since there is no host controller to interact with it. When making available this new device, a number of services will be registered with the operating system. In our earlier illustration, Figure 6-5, the Device Manger recognised the numerous non-standard communications ports.

In Figure 6-9, we illustrate the host and host controller components that are typical of a Bluetooth implementation. Such an environment can be constructed using the Microsoft *Windows Driver Model* (WDM), an architecture, which is inherent in the various development kits currently available.

6.2.4.2 Applications in an Embedded Environment. In this particular instance, an embedded application would provide a minimal set of API function calls in order to quickly facilitate the communications link to the peer device; we illustrated in Table 6-2 some of the possible functions that may be available to a developer.

Embedded applications, such as a *LAN Access Point* (LAP) as presented in the *LAN Access Profile*, Chapter 10, would simply require the communications link to be established transparently. These types of applications would not necessarily advertise a specific serial port service. In the case of the LAP, the LAN Access service would be advertised; this holds well with our explanation of a Cable Replacement Application, as

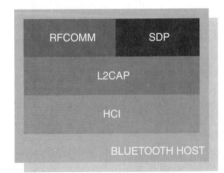
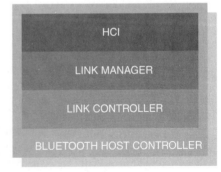

Figure 6-9 An implementation of a host and host controller, where the host resides in the Windows environment awaiting a PC Card or USB dongle to be inserted. When the host software recognises the host controller, Bluetooth specific activity can then take place.

illustrated in our earlier sections. In this context, implementation will vary. With the availability of a Bluetooth protocol stack in one environment, there may be no need to have the host and host controller divide. You may recall that in a Microsoft Windows environment the division of host and host controller was made, as we can see in Figure 6-9.

6.3 PROFILE PRINCIPLES

The profile outlines no specific roles for participating devices, although it does distinguish between the behaviour of *initiator* and *acceptor*.

In Table 6-3, clarification is provided with regard to the roles used within the context of this profile. In general, *DeviceA* represents the initiating party and *DeviceB* represents the accepting party. The terms are often used interchangeably, when describing specific operations in various contexts and are provided here for reference.

There is no distinction made between a master or a slave device in this profile. The relationship exists at the peer-to-peer level. For completeness, the typical scenario created by a *Data Terminal Equipment* (DTE) and a DCE can easily be mapped onto DeviceA and DeviceB, respectively. In Figure 6-10, we can see how the Serial Port components are integrated with the existing Bluetooth protocol stack.

The RFCOMM layer has been architected to provide an independent structure, where concurrent connections can be maintained. In Figure 6-11, we illustrate NotebookB maintaining multiple connections with NotebookA and NotebookC.

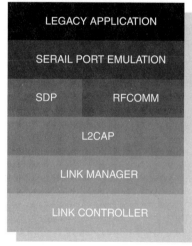
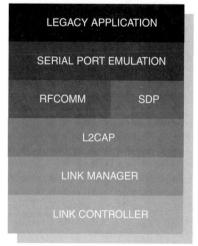

Figure 6-10 The core components of the Bluetooth protocol stack are shown illustrating how the components of the Serial Port Profile are integrated.

Table 6-3   The list of behavioural characteristics that are typical for this profile.

CONFIGURATION	ROLE	DESCRIPTION
DeviceA	Initiator	This configuration describes the device that instigates the original connection or the device that wishes to initiate communication over an existing link.
DeviceB	Acceptor	This configuration describes the process of the device accepting the initiated communication from DeviceA.

The use of authentication and encryption is optional. However, if one device in the relationship requires authentication or encryption, then the participating device should enable the same level of support.

6.4   USER EXPECTATIONS

A large part of the emulated serial communication is typically transparent to the user, alleviating some of the potential complexities involved when configuring legacy serial port-based applications. Here the user is presented with a set of parameters that needs to be determined accurately for the user to create a successful connection with the peer device, although RFCOMM does not strictly impose these restrictions.

Removing this complexity provides a greater sense of 'ease-of-use' for the user, who often does not care about the internal nature of a serial port configuration. With a

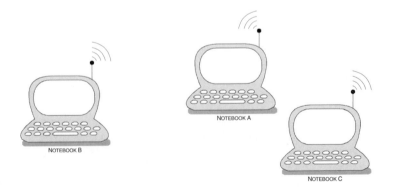

Figure 6-11   This usage model demonstrates the ability to maintain multiple serial connections with many devices. NotebookB maintains a serial connection with NotebookA and NotebookC.

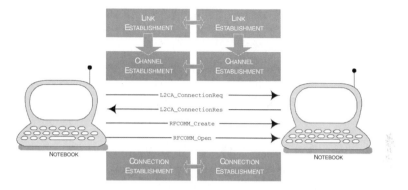

Figure 6-12   The events that take place during the set-up and establishment of a serial communications link.

greater adoption of Bluetooth technology as a means to wireless cable replacement, the typical legacy application would be created in such a manner as to provide transparency, thereby alleviating the user from configuring standard serial port parameters.

In establishing a connection with a peer device to make use of the emulated serial port service, DeviceA initiates the connection by performing inquiry and device discovery procedures. The user may also be given the flexibility to choose specific services available to it through the browsing capabilities. The RFCOMM Server channel number is then made available, which will begin the process of initiating and creating an L2CAP channel for the remote device which in turn, starts a new RFCOMM session using the Server channel number; Figure 6-12 provides an illustration of the events that may occur. We discuss the architecture of the RFCOMM protocol later on in this chapter.

If any existing RFCOMM session is available when a new connection is being established, then the data connection should be created on the existing session; more detail of the procedures for setting up a connection is provided in Section 6.5.1.2, *The RFCOMM Protocol*.

6.5   LIFTING THE LID

6.5.1   Dependencies

Now that we have discussed both existing and future usage models and their respective user expectations, in the following sections, we can an opportunity to explore in greater depth the dependencies that make up this profile. In Figure 6-13, we provide a conceptual illustration representing the dependencies that make up the Serial Port Profile; the areas that are shaded are relevant to this profile. As you can see, the profile depends upon the basic functionality offered to us by the *Generic Access Profile*, Chapter 2 and the *Service Discovery Application Profile*, Chapter 3. We will now discuss, in turn, the basic requirements

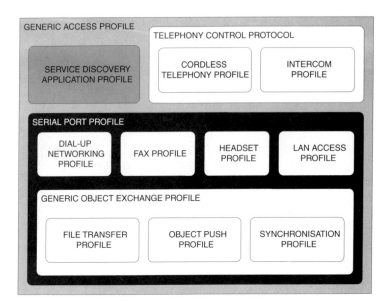

Figure 6-13   The dependent components of the Bluetooth protocol stack that
make up the Serial Port Profile. The areas that are shaded are
relevant to this profile.

of these dependent components and any deviations that may occur from the basic functionality originally offered to us.

6.5.1.1   Service Discovery.   The *Service Discovery Application Profile*, Chapter 3,
introduced the characteristics of the mechanisms used to retrieve service information from
a remote device. Typically, a client will initiate inquiry and discovery procedures as previously outlined, to learn of the devices in radio range. A client can then make use of an
application, carrying the functionality of the underlying *Service Discovery Protocol*
(SDP). The *Service Discovery Application* (SrvDscApp) uses an *SDP Client* to instigate
a request to the remote device where the *SDP Server* will respond; as such, DeviceA and
DeviceB must employ the use of an SDP client and server, as illustrated in Table 6-4.

Protocol Data Units (PDUs) are used to instruct the SDP server to undertake
browsing procedures and to retrieve service record information. You may recall that the
PDUs carry payloads about requests containing AttributeIDs and Attribute-
Values, which describe exactly what is being sought. As we previously discussed, the
client and server operate a request and response paradigm. SDAP will construct PDUs
containing information relating to the AttributeID and AttributeValues, in
turn, instructing the server to carry out its operation. The various request and response
PDUs that are required are shown in Table 6-5, where features indicated are described as
mandatory (M), optional (O) and excluded (X).

Table 6-4   As a minimum, the local device must support the use of a client application and the remote device must support the use of a server.

FEATURE	DEVICEA	DEVICEB
SDP Client	M	X
SDP Server	X	M

A service record is maintained for each service a device is capable of supporting and, as such, a *Service Record Handle* is created to uniquely identify this. The `ServiceRecordHandle` is a 32-bit unsigned integer and is stored on the SDP server. The service record shown in Table 6-6 identifies a device that supports Serial Port emulation and provides a list of `AttributeIDs`, which ultimately would identify the service for the Serial Port Profile. A minimum of two attributes are required to make a service record (`ServiceRecordHandle` and `ServiceClassIDList`), where it must contain at least one `UUID`.

When browsing for services on the remote device, a local device constructs a search pattern using a *Universally Unique Identifier* (UUID). A UUID is a 128-bit value, which has been shortened for use within Bluetooth applications. The shortcut has been provided by first establishing a *Bluetooth Base UUID*, which we discussed in the *Service Discovery Application Profile*, Chapter 3.

The UUIDs that have been presented so far in this chapter are aliases and take the form of what is referred to as a 16-bit UUID or a 32-bit UUID but, in turn, they all should refer to the 128-bit notation. These UUIDs have been assigned and can be referenced in the Bluetooth Special Interest Group, Bluetooth Assigned Numbers, v1.1, February 2001. Since they will all be compared at this range, they all need to be converted to the 128-bit notation. This needs to be done for the search pattern to be successful. An arithmetic conversion algorithm is used to construct the 128-bit value.

Table 6-5   The list of PDUs that are required for the operation of the Serial Port Profile.

PDU	DEVICEA	DEVICEB
SDP_ErrorResponse	X	M
SDP_ServiceSearchRequest	M	X
SDP_ServiceSearchResponse	X	M
SDP_ServiceAttributeRequest	M	X
SDP_ServiceAttributeResponse	X	M
SDP_ServiceSearchAttributeRequest	O	X
SDP_ServiceSearchAttributeRequest	X	O

Table 6-6   The list of mandatory and configurable items that make up this profile's service discovery record.

ATTRIBUTE	DESCRIPTION
`ServiceRecordHandle`	With an `AttributeID` of `0x0000`, this uniquely identifies this service record within the SDP server on the remote device (DeviceB).

`ServiceClassIDList`
 	
   `ServiceClass0`
	With an `AttributeID` of `0x0001`, the following `ServiceClass0` would contain the `UUID` for the *Serial Port*; its respective `UUID` value is summarised in Table 6-7.

`ProtocolDescriptorList`
 	
   `Protocol0`
 	
   `Protocol1`
 	
      `ParameterFor1`
	With an `AttributeID` of `0x0004`, the following `Protocol0` would contain a `UUID` for the protocol *L2CAP*, whereas in `Protocol1` a `UUID` would contain the protocol identifier for *RFCOMM*. Their respective `UUID` values are summarised in Table 6-8. The `ParameterFor1` would contain the relevant server channel number for the RFCOMM transport.

`BluetoothProfile-`
`DescriptorList`
 	
   `Profile0`
 	
   `ParameterFor0`
	With an `AttributeID` of `0x0009`, the following `Profile0` would identify the `UUID` for *Serial Port* service class, which is summarised in Table 6-7. The `ParameterFor0` accommodates the version number supported by this profile.

`ServiceName`	With a base `AttributeID` of `0x0006`, this attribute has an offset of `0x0000`. It is a configurable item and has an `AttributeValue` of a `Text` string, where its default setting is *COMx*, where *x* denotes the internal operating system dependent assigned port number. This typically would be constructed by the Bluetooth aware helper application.

Table 6-7 summarises the service class UUIDs used to identify the particular profile in use; this also correlates with the identification of the device during a device discovery procedure.

As part of the service record, the dependent underlying protocols are also identified. The local device retrieves this information where it can fully understand the exact requirements needed to fulfil the service. The Serial Port Profile is dependent on the protocols as shown in Table 6-8; the table also shows their associated UUID values.

Table 6-7   The service class that matches its corresponding profile. This correlates with our previous Generic Access section.

CLASS	UUID
Serial Port	0x1101

6.5.1.2   The RFCOMM Protocol.   We touched upon the fact that the Serial Port Profile relies upon RFCOMM to provide an emulated serial port presence. Our focus here is to describe the processes used to provide such a service and to establish how the underlying Bluetooth transport is facilitated in achieving this. In doing so, we will develop a fuller understanding of how the various types of applications are supported, that is, Type I and Type II. You may recall from our earlier discussion that Type I devices support an emulated transparent presence, which underlies most of the profiles. Type II devices are intermediary applications, which will ultimately interface with a physical connection.

RFCOMM has been designed to sit above the L2CAP component of the Bluetooth protocol stack, as shown in our earlier illustrations. In our first look at understanding this protocol, we will examine its architecture in more detail and then consider specific aspects of integration over L2CAP. In later sections, we will also discuss how the RFCOMM protocol is used to transport data between peer devices. In our first look at the RFCOMM protocol, we consider how the physical serial port is emulated in software.

6.5.1.2.1   Emulating the Physical Serial Port.   RFCOMM is based upon the *European Telecommunications Standards Institute* (ETSI) digital cellular telecommunications system (Phase 2+); *Terminal Equipment to Mobile Station* (TE-MS) multiplexer protocol (GSM 07.10 Version 6.3.0) specification.[8] The RFCOMM layer emulates RS232 serial ports, where there is also provision for *null modem* capability. In Table 6-9, we identify the typical 9-circuits of an RS232 serial interface.

When two Bluetooth-enabled devices are connected, that, is two *Data Terminal Equipment* (DTE) devices, a null modem connection is created. The translation of these signals is shown in Table 6-10, which shows how the RFCOMM signals are mapped onto

Table 6-8   The list of protocols that are used in this profile; their associated UUID values are also shown.

PROTOCOL	UUID
RFCOMM	0x0003
L2CAP	0x0100

---

[8]©ETSI 1999. Further use, modification, redistribution is strictly prohibited. ETSI standards are available from http://pda.etsi.org/pda/ and http://www.etsi.org/eds/.

Table 6-9   The list of RS232 circuits that are emulated in RFCOMM.

CIRCUIT
Signal Common
Transmit Data (TD)
Received Data (RD)
Request to Send (RTS)
Clear to Send (CTS)
Data Set Ready (DSR)
Data Terminal Ready (DTR)
Data Carrier Detect (DCD)
Ring Indicator (RI)

RS232 control signals. Some devices will be capable of using RS232 control signals, whereas other Bluetooth devices may not. As such, no peer device should be dependent upon receiving this information. To ensure interoperability, the control signals' parameters must be set to default on devices that are using them. These may be defined using the Bluetooth aware helper application, where the parameters are determined through the RFCOMM *Data Link Connection* (DLC) stage; there will be more about this later on. The use of control signals is optional, although flow control, *Ready-to-Receive* (RTR), can be mapped onto *Ready-to-Send* (RTS) and *Clear-to-Send* (CTS), again using the helper application. These mappings are shown in Table 6-10.

The RFCOMM DLC state may dictate that the *Data Set Ready* (DSR), *Data Terminal Ready* (DTR) and *Data Carrier Detect* (DCD) are set to high when creating a new DLC. Doing so indicates that the device is *ready*; conversely, they should be set to low when the connection has terminated.

Table 6-10   In the list of signals, we illustrate how the emulated RFCOMM signals are mapped onto the RS232 signals.

RFCOMM SIGNALS	RS232 SIGNALS
Ready to Communicate (RTC)	DSR, DTR
Ready to Receive (RTR)	RTS, CTS
Incoming Call Indicator (IC)	RI
Data Valid (DV)	DCD

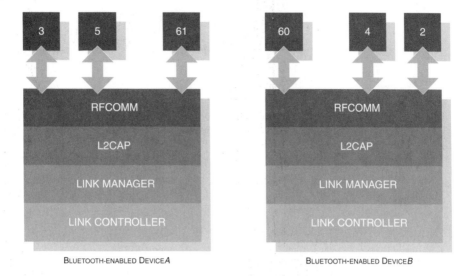

Figure 6-14 A conceptual illustration, providing the notion of multiple emulated serial ports.

In a typical scenario, a notebook or PC would be supplied with one or two RS232 serial port connectors. RFCOMM is capable of supporting up to 60 emulated serial connections, where a unique identifier is assigned for each active connection between two Bluetooth-enabled devices; we will discuss in some more detail the structure of these identifiers later on in this chapter. The provision to support multiple RFCOMM connections is optional and is therefore implementation-specific. In Figure 6-14, we illustrate the conceptual nature of multiple connections with two Bluetooth devices, where each connection maintains its own *Channel Identifier* (CID) with L2CAP.

The Bluetooth aware helper application is exposed to a legacy application and it will encompass the use of a *port emulation entity*. As we touched upon earlier, this provides us with a useful reference model, which the profile refers to as the *service definition model*.

In Figure 6-15 and Table 6-11, we illustrate the structure of these entities and offer an explanation of how each entity interacts with one another. In the previous section, we reinforced the conceptual nature of how each layer interacts and how an emulated serial port service manifests itself to an end-user legacy application. We now turn our attention to the specific structures that make up the transport capability and examine in greater detail RFCOMM *frame types* and *commands*.

6.5.1.2.2 RFCOMM Frames and Commands. In Figure 6-16, we illustrate the RFCOMM frame structure that is used to transport serial data between peer devices. Each device within the communicating party may have a client and server application, concurrently managing multiple sessions in either direction. A DLC is established between two

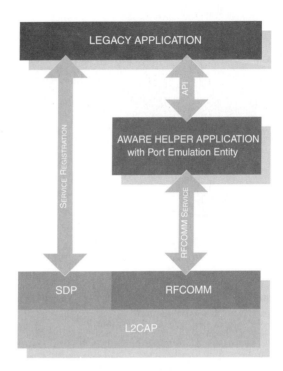

Figure 6-15   The conceptual interaction between components that make up
the emulated serial port service to a legacy application.

Table 6-11   The list of key components that are used to provide an emulated serial port service.

ENTITY	DESCRIPTION
Legacy Application	The end application that will ultimately make use of the serial port services.
Aware Helper Application	This application provides the port emulation entity, which also exposes the API to the legacy application. The port emulation entity will also know how to interact with the RFCOMM layer.
RFCOMM	The entity that provides the serial transport mechanism, which subsequently maintains a CID with the L2CAP layer.
SDP	This layer advertises available RFCOMM services to other interested devices in radio range.
L2CAP	This layer provides segmentation and reassembly (S&R) services, as well as multiplexing capabilities.

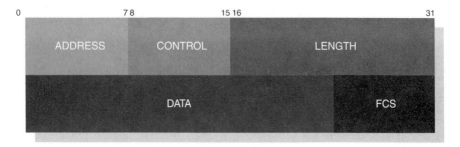

Figure 6-16 The structure of an RFCOMM frame.

devices when there is an active connection. In the ETSI TS 101.369 specification, a *Data Link Connection Identifier* (DLCI) is used to distinguish between connections that have been established; it forms the *Address* field of the frame structure and is illustrated for reference in Figure 6-17. For Bluetooth applications, this structure has been modified to accommodate the concept of an *RFCOMM Server Channel* and a *Direction Bit* (D); we illustrate the format of this adapted structure in Figure 6-18; you have already come across the RFCOMM Server Channel concept in Section 6.5.1.1, *Service Discovery*, where this channel is registered with the service record.

An RFCOMM server application registers the server channel number in the service record, where the channel numbers are in the range of 1 to 30. On closer inspection of Figure 6-18, we can see that the *Server Channel* field is made up of 5-bits, thus providing a potential range of 0 to 31. However, server channel 0 is reserved for transmitting control messages and channel 31 is reserved for backward compatibility with ETSI TS 101.369 specific applications.

The initiating device (DeviceA) is assigned the Direction Bit of 1, whereas the corresponding session at DeviceB is assigned the Direction Bit of 0. We introduced earlier that RFCOMM is capable of managing up to 60 concurrent sessions. This is achieved through the assignment of 30 channels in one direction and 30 channels in the opposing direction. Essentially, the DLCI assignments for DeviceA are available in the range of 3, 5, 7 and so on to 61. DeviceB follows a similar pattern, where the DLCI assignment forms the range of 2, 4, 6 and so on to 60.

In ETSI TS 101.369, the *Extended Address* can be extended over several octets. For the purpose of Bluetooth-enabled applications, the `Extended Address` field is always assigned the value 1. Thus, the address of a session is managed by the DLCI, that is, the

Figure 6-17 The structure of the Address field as described in the ETSI TS 101.369 specification.

0   7

| EXTENDED ADDRESS | COMMAND/ RESPONSE | DIRECTION BIT | SERVER CHANNEL |

Figure 6-18   The structure of the Address field as used in Bluetooth-enabled applications.

combination of D and the ServerChannel. An assignment of 0 would indicate that the address follows over several octets.

Before looking at the *Command/Response* (C/R) field, we need to consider the availability of frame types in RFCOMM; these are presented in Table 6-12. These frames allow RFCOMM to create and control sessions with its peer device. When a command is sent to the peer device, a response will be expected.

In Table 6-13, we illustrate the general notation used to reflect the C/R bit. When the initiator wishes to establish the first connection, the SABM frame is used and carried over DLCI(0); the responder (DeviceB) will reply with the UA frame, which is also on DLCI(0). You may recall from our earlier discussion that DLCI(0) represents our control channel. As such, commands and responses from the initiator will always have the C/R bit set to 1; whereas commands and responses initiated by the responder will always have the C/R bit set to 0. Any data being exchanged between the initiator and responder will carry the C/R bit set to 1 and 0, respectively.

Looking back at our earlier illustration Figure 6-16, the next field forming the RFCOMM frame is the *Control* field. This field is used to identify the type of frame being carried in the payload. The Control field is 8-bits in length and its structure is shown in Table 6-14.

You will notice that bit 4 has been omitted from the table and is referred to as the *Poll/Final* (P/F) bit. The representation of this bit is twofold: in a *command*, the P-bit representation is used, whereas the F-bit representation is used for a *response*. As such, the value of the P/F bit is determined by the command or response payload.

Table 6-12   The available frame types that are supported by RFCOMM.

FRAMES
Set Asynchronous Balanced Mode (SABM)
Unnumbered Acknowledgement (UA)
Disconnected Mode (DM)
Disconnect (DISC)
Unnumbered Information with Header check (UIH)

Table 6-13   The representation of the C/R bit used within the `Address` field.

	DIRECTION	**C/R**
COMMAND	Initiator *to* Responder	1
	Responder *to* Initiator	0
RESPONSE	Initiator *to* Responder	0
	Responder *to* Initiator	1

A payload may need to be carried over several frames; as such, the P bit is set to 1 in a command, where a responder needs to carry its payload over several frames. The responder device provides its frame with the F bit set to 1, acknowledging that more payloads are to follow. Some exceptions of this rule apply to SABM and DISC frames; if the P/F-bit is set to 0, then these frames are discarded. Furthermore, if a spontaneous DM frame is received, then the corresponding device will process the payload regardless of the P/F-bit setting.

In our earlier figure, we showed a *Length* field of two bytes. However, the length of this field may be constructed using one or two bytes, which depends upon the size of the data or payload to be carried. The Length field itself is also constructed using an Extended Address (EA); we illustrate this representation for one and two bytes in Figure 6-19 and Figure 6-20, respectively.

The EA field is used to denote that the Length field has been extended. If EA is set to 0, then the size of the Length field is two bytes and conversely, if the EA-bit is set to 1, then the Length field occupies one byte.

We now turn our attention to the Data field, which is always carried using UIH frames. The default length for an RFCOMM frame is 32-bytes, whereas the maximum payload, as specified by the Length field (over two bytes), is 32,767-bytes. Payload size

Table 6-14   The encoding of the frame type in the `Control` field.

7	6	5	4	3	2	1	0	**FRAME**
								Bit # of Control Field
0	0	1	*x*	1	1	1	1	SABM
0	1	1	*x*	0	0	1	1	UA
0	0	0	*x*	1	1	1	1	DM
0	1	0	*x*	0	0	1	1	DISC
1	1	1	*x*	1	1	1	1	UIH

Figure 6-19   The Length field represented by one byte.

is typically determined by the L2CAP layer's *Maximum Transmission Unit* (MTU). Essentially, the maximum size of a payload in an RFCOMM frame is proportional to the MTU.

The *Frame Check Sequence* (FCS) field is used to verify the payload. In summary, for SABM, DISC, UA and DM frames, the FCS is calculated on the Address, Control and Length fields. For UIH frames, the FCS field is calculated on the Address and Control fields.

6.5.1.2.3   Flow Control.   In a typical physical environment, DTE and DCE devices will use a flow control mechanism to regulate communication between the two devices. A wired environment would have available flow control represented as *Transmission On/Off* (XON/XOFF), RTS/CTS or DTR/DSR. You may recall from our earlier discussion how these signals are mapped in RFCOMM; the use of flow control is optional.

Before continuing our discussion on the use of flow control within RFCOMM, an introduction of the available commands would be useful; these are illustrated in Table 6-15. The FCON/FCOFF and MSC commands are of particular relevance to our flow control discussion; we will discuss the encoding of these commands and other commands in more detail later in this section.

RFCOMM provides two flow control mechanisms. The first affects all RFCOMM frames, that is, the aggregate data flow between two devices. This, in turn, relies upon the FCON/FCOFF command structure. The second affects the individual server channel or DLCI which in turn, is managed through the MSC command. These two mechanisms regulate flow control of UIH frames, which are data payloads being exchanged between peer devices. Flow control has to be negotiated during DLC establishment, since backward compatibility must be retained for earlier versions of Bluetooth-enabled applications.

Figure 6-20   The Length field represented by two bytes.

Table 6-15   The available commands that are supported by RFCOMM.

COMMANDS
Test
Flow Control On (FCON)
Flow Control Off (FCOFF)
Modem Status Command (MSC)
Remote Port Negotiation (RPN)
Remote Line Status (RLS)
DLC Parameter Negotiation (PN)
Non Supported Command (NSC)

You may recall from our earlier discussion that Type I and Type II devices are supported by RFCOMM. Our discussion now turns to support of flow control for these two different types of applications. An application may request flow control support—as such, it must be managed accordingly by RFCOMM. To a greater extent, the RFCOMM protocol can ignore some of the parameters defined by the higher-level legacy application and rely upon its own flow control system. This potentially introduces problems, since RFCOMM and its underlying layers are managing the flow of data between the peer devices. In some circumstances, this may cause confusion for the intended application, since it may be relying on an accurate flow of data. In these instances, the flow control mechanism used by RFCOMM should provide some intelligence to the way it adapts the flow control philosophy. In turn, RFCOMM must do its best to emulate the wired environment, where a combination of flow control mechanisms may also be used; for example, if XON/XOFF support has been selected in the application, then RFCOMM should mirror that same support.

6.5.1.2.4   Credit Based Flow Control.   In the latest Bluetooth specification, credit based flow control has been introduced and has become a mandatory feature. Support is noted within the RFCOMM frame and a frame that supports credit based flow control is illustrated in Figure 6-21. It is a feature that provides flow control on a connection basis.

Both peer devices keep a tally of the number of frames that have been sent to each and, as such, each device knows how many more frames can be sent before their respective buffers fill up. The notion of a credit system is used and while each device has credits, each party can continue sending frames. If a credit reaches zero, then the peer device must pause its transmission until further credits are received.

The amount of credits used for each peer is established during *Parameter Negotiation* (PN), which occurs prior to DLC establishment; we discuss PN in more detail in Section 6.5.1.2.5.6, *Parameter Negotiation (PN)*.

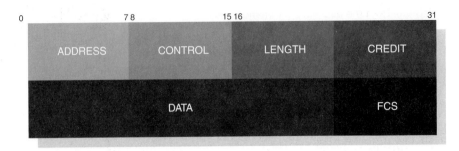

Figure 6-21   The structure of an RFCOMM frame with flow control.

6.5.1.2.5   Encoding Commands and Responses.   In Table 6-15, we introduced the various commands and responses, where FCON/FCOFF and MSC are used to manage and coordinate flow control within the RFCOMM protocol. In this section, we will introduce how these various commands and responses are encoded within the RFCOMM frame. We will also consider the *credit based flow control* mechanism that has been introduced into the latest Bluetooth specification.

In our earlier illustration Figure 6-16, we showed the RFCOMM frame, where the Data field contained information to be transported to its peer. In Figure 6-22, we illustrate the structure used to encode commands and responses.

Commands and responses are all encoded within the UIH frame. The illustration shows us that a *Type*, *Length* and *Value* field make up this new structure. The Type field is further constructed of an Extended Address and a C/R field, which are both similar in nature to our earlier introduction. The EA field is always set to 1, since the Type field always occupies 1-byte and the C/R-bit is used to denote a command or response within the Value field.

The Type field value is assigned, depending upon the command or response being carried out. In Table 6-16, we identify the various values available. Figure 6-23 illustrates the encoded command or response within the RFCOMM frame.

In the following sections, we visit each command and response and examine each structure in detail.

6.5.1.2.5.1   TEST.   This simple command assures the reliability of the communications link between the peer devices. The EA field is set to 1 and the C/R field is set to

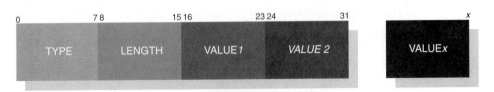

Figure 6-22   The structure of an encoded command or response within the Data field of an RFCOMM frame.

Table 6-16   The encoding of the `Type` field.

7	6	5	4	3	2	TYPE
						Bit # of Type Field
0	0	1	0	0	0	Test
1	0	1	0	0	0	FCON
0	1	1	0	0	0	FCOFF
1	1	1	0	0	0	MSC
1	0	0	1	0	0	RPN
0	1	0	1	0	0	RLS
1	0	0	0	0	0	PN
0	0	0	1	0	0	NSC

reflect a command or response. The `Type` field is assigned the value as shown in Table 6-16 and the `Length` field is assigned the number of bytes contained within the structure. This payload is transmitted to the peer, where it will respond with exactly the same number of bytes as the original payload. This method is used to verify the integrity of the connection.

6.5.1.2.5.2   FLOW CONTROL ON/OFF (FCON/FCOFF).   These commands are used to regulate the aggregate data flow over the RFCOMM connection. The EA field is set to 1 and the C/R field is set to reflect a command or response. The `Type` field is assigned the value as shown in Table 6-16 and the `Length` field is set to zero, since there is no data to carry, other than the acknowledgement of FCON/FCOFF.

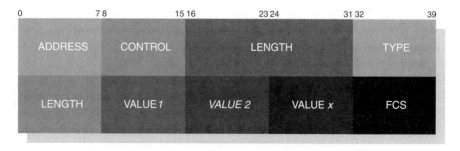

Figure 6-23   An RFCOMM frame illustrating the encoding of a command or response.

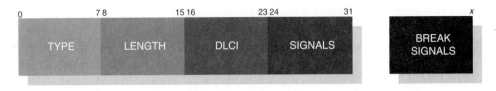

Figure 6-24   The structure of an encoded command or response within the
Data field of an RFCOMM frame showing the inclusion of the
`Break Signals'` field.

During credit based flow control, the FCON/FCOFF control commands should not
be used.

6.5.1.2.5.3   MODEM STATUS COMMAND (MSC).   This command provides the emulated control signals onto the communications link between the peer devices. The `EA`
field is set to 1 and the `C/R` field is set to reflect a command or response. The `Type` field
is assigned the value as shown in Table 6-16 and the `Length` field is assigned the value
two or three. The MSC structure is illustrated in Figure 6-24, where we can see the `Type`,
`Length`, `DLCI`, *Signals* and *Break Signals* fields. The `DLCI` field contains the server
channel or active DLC value for which the MSC is to be applied; this follows the same
structure as illustrated in Figure 6-18.

The new `Signal` field represents the mapped RS232 signals, which were identified in Table 6-10; we illustrate this structure in Figure 6-25. You will also notice in Figure 6-24 the availability of the `Break  Signals` field, which is optional; however, its
structure is shown in Figure 6-26. In Table 6-17 and Table 6-18, we offer an explanation
and usage of the various fields that make up these two new structures.

6.5.1.2.5.4   REMOTE PORT NEGOTIATION (RPN).   This command sets the communication settings, where both devices must ensure that these settings have been defined
prior to sending data. The `EA` field is set to 1 and the `C/R` field is set to reflect a command
or response. The `Type` field is assigned the value as shown in Table 6-16 and the
`Length` field is assigned the value one or eight. In Figure 6-27, we illustrate the parameters that make up the RPN command for an 8-byte length.

The following parameters typically make up the options available at the user-level
application, as we witnessed in Figure 6-6. The `Baud` field represents the baud setting,
where the default value is 9600 baud; the other available settings are shown in Table 6-19

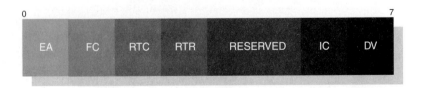

Figure 6-25   The `Signal` field represented by one byte.

Table 6-17   The Signal fields and their usage within MSC.

FIELD	DESCRIPTION
EA	This field is set to 1, since there is only 1-byte of information.
FC	This field is set to 1, when it is not able to accept RFCOMM frames. During credit based flow control, this bit should be set to 0, as it has no meaning for the acceptor device.
RTC	This field is set to 1, when the device is ready to communicate.
RTR	This field is set to 1, when the device is ready to receive data.
IC	This field is set to 1, indicating an incoming call.
DV	This field is set to 1, indicating that data valid has been sent.

Figure 6-26   The Break Signal field represented by one byte.

Table 6-18   The Break Signal fields and their usage within MSC.

FIELD	DESCRIPTION
EA	This field is set to 1, since there is only 1-byte of information.
BREAK	This field is set to 1, indicating that a break signal is encoded.
LENGTH	This field contains the length of the break in units of 200ms.

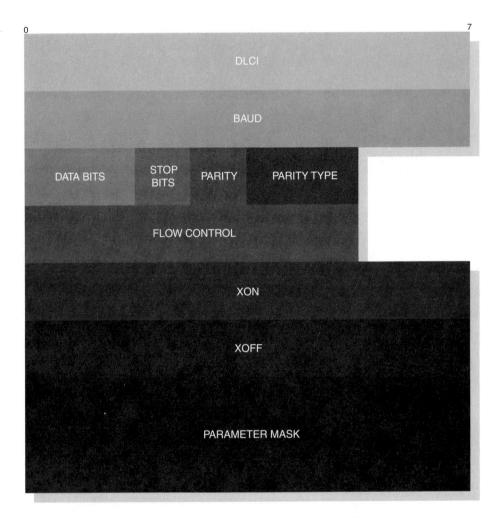

Figure 6-27   The structure of a RPN command, where the blank spaces represent reserved areas.

and are mapped accordingly. The Data Bits field values are illustrated in Table 6-20, where the default setting is 8-bits.

The Stop Bit field has a default value of 0, which represents 1 stop bit; other values include 1, representing 1.5 stop bits. The Parity field has a default value of 0, representing *no parity*, whereas 1 represents *parity*.

In Table 6-21, we illustrate the available values for the Parity Type field and in Table 6-22 we illustrate the available values for the Flow Control field, where the default value is 0, representing *no flow control*. You may recall that these signals are mapped so that RTR is mapped to CTS and RTC is mapped to DTR/DSR. The XON/XOFF field settings are mapped to the default settings of DC1/DC3, respectively.

Table 6-19   Baud settings and their usage within the RPN command.

7	6	5	4	3	2	1	0	BAUD
7	6	5	4	3	2	1	0	Bit # of Baud Field
0	0	0	0	0	0	0	0	2500 bits/s
0	0	0	0	0	0	0	1	4800 bits/s
0	0	0	0	0	0	1	0	7200 bits/s
0	0	0	0	0	0	1	1	9600 bits/s
0	0	0	0	0	1	0	0	19200 bits/s
0	0	0	0	0	1	0	1	38400 bits/s
0	0	0	0	0	1	1	0	57600 bits/s
0	0	0	0	0	1	1	1	115200 bits/s
0	0	0	0	1	0	0	0	230400 bits/s

In our final `Parameter Mask` field, the available values for the first 8-bits are defined in Table 6-23 and the second set are defined in Table 6-24. These values are set according to what will be negotiated as part of the RPN command.

In general, the mask will be interpreted for a command as 1, *change* and 0, *no change*; for a response, the interpretation will be 0, *not accepted* and 1, *accepted*. For reference purposes, the parameter mask is illustrated in Figure 6-28.

6.5.1.2.5.5   REMOTE LINE STATUS (RLS).   This command is optional and is used to indicate the RLS status of the current connection; in a typical scenario, it informs the other end of an error. The `EA` field is set to 1 and the `C/R` field is set to reflect a command or response. The `Type` field is assigned the value as shown in Table 6-16 and the

Table 6-20   Data Bits settings and their usage within the RPN command.

1	0	DATA BITS
1	0	Bit # of Data Bits Field
0	0	5-bits
0	1	6-bits
1	0	7-bits
1	1	8-bits

Table 6-21   Parity Type settings and their usage within the RPN command.

		PARITY TYPE
5	**4**	**Bit # of Parity Type Field**
0	0	Odd Parity
0	1	Even Parity
1	0	Mark Parity
1	1	Space Parity

Length field is assigned the value two. In Figure 6-29, we illustrate the parameters that make up the RLS command.

The DLCI field is constructed in the usual manner as presented in earlier sections and in Table 6-25 we present the available values for the Line Status field, where a default value of 0 indicates *no error* and bit 0, at value 1, will indicate an *error*.

6.5.1.2.5.6   PARAMETER NEGOTIATION (PN).   In our earlier discussion, we introduced the notion that a new DLC is established for every RFCOMM session. As such, a set of parameters are negotiated prior to session establishment. PN is used to define the set of parameters that will be used for a new DLC, see Figure 6-30. The EA field is set to 1 and the C/R field is set to reflect a command or response. The Type field is assigned the value as shown in Table 6-16 and the Length field is assigned the value eight.

The DLCI field is constructed in the usual manner as presented in our earlier sections. The Type field value identifies the type of RFCOMM frame being used and in this

Table 6-22   The Flow Control and their usage within the RPN command.

						FLOW CONTROL
5	**4**	**3**	**2**	**1**	**0**	**Bit # of Flow Control Field**
0	0	0	0	0	0	No Flow Control
0	0	0	0	0	1	XON/XOFF on Input
0	0	0	0	1	0	XON/XOFF on Output
0	0	0	1	0	0	RTR on Input
0	0	1	0	0	0	RTR on Output
0	1	0	0	0	0	RTC on Input
1	0	0	0	0	0	RTC on Output

Table 6-23   The Parameter Mask (1st Byte) and their usage within the RPN command.

								PARAMETER MASK 1st BYTE
7	**6**	**5**	**4**	**3**	**2**	**1**	**0**	**Bit # of Parameter Byte**
0	0	0	0	0	0	0	1	Baud Rate
0	0	0	0	0	0	1	0	Data Bits
0	0	0	0	0	1	0	0	Stop Bits
0	0	0	0	1	0	0	0	Parity
0	0	0	1	0	0	0	0	Parity Type
0	0	1	0	0	0	0	0	XON Character
0	1	0	0	0	0	0	0	XOFF Character

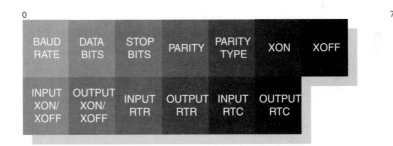

Figure 6-28   The `Parameter Mask` field, which occupies two bytes. The blank spaces represent reserved areas.

Table 6-24   The Parameter Mask (2nd Byte) and their usage within the RPN command.

								PARAMETER MASK 2nd BYTE
7	**6**	**5**	**4**	**3**	**2**	**1**	**0**	**Bit # of Parameter Byte**
0	0	0	0	0	0	0	1	XON/XOFF on Input
0	0	0	0	0	0	1	0	XON/XOFF on Output
0	0	0	0	0	1	0	0	RTR on Input
0	0	0	0	1	0	0	0	RTR on Output
0	0	0	1	0	0	0	0	RTC on Input
0	0	1	0	0	0	0	0	RTC on Output

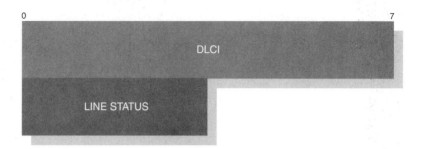

Figure 6-29   The RLS fields represented by two bytes, where the blank
spaces represent reserved areas.

instance it has the value 0, since an `UIH` frame is being used. The `Convergence` field
represents the type of *convergence layer* being used and in all cases the default is Type I
(*unstructured octet streams*). The `Priority` field, as the name suggests, represents the
urgency of the frame, where 0 represents the lowest priority and 63 represents the highest
priority.

In our next field, the `Timer` has a recommended timeout of 20s, which in turn is
applied before a connection is terminated. Different values may be applied depending on
what type of frame is being used. During PN, this timer has a value of 0s, indicating that
this parameter is not negotiable. The `Maximum Frame Size` field has a default value
of 127-bytes, where it has a potential range of up to 32,768-bytes. It defines the `Data` field
range within the RFCOMM frame. The `Maximum Number of Retransmissions`
field has a default value of 0, with a potential range of 255, which implies that there are
no retransmissions for RFCOMM.

Our last field has relevance to the credit based flow control mechanism, which has
been recently introduced into the latest specification and which we also touched upon.
Credit based flow control is enabled as a mandatory feature and the value assigned in the
`Credit` field is used to reflect the initial amount of credit issued to the peer device.

6.5.1.2.5.7   NON-SUPPORTED COMMAND (NSC).   This command is used to indicate
when a command is received but is not recognised. The `EA` field is set to 1 and the `C/R`

Table 6-25   The `Line Status` field and their usage within the RLS command.

				LINE STATUS
3	2	1	0	**Bit # of Line Status Field**
0	0	1	1	Overrun Error
0	1	0	1	Parity Error
1	0	0	1	Framing Error

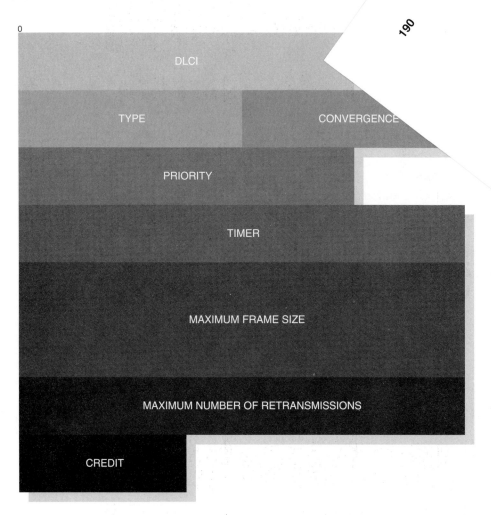

Figure 6-30 The structure of a PN command, where the blank spaces represent padding.

field is set to reflect a response. The `Type` field is assigned the value as shown in Table 6-16 and the `Length` field is assigned the value 1. In Figure 6-31, we illustrate the parameters that make up the NSC command. The `Command Type` field contains the value of the non-supported command and the `C/R`-bit value represents the same value as the non-supported frame.

6.5.1.3 RFCOMM in the Serial Port Profile.

In Section 6.5.1.2, *The RFCOMM Protocol*, we learned about how command and response frames are created to provide us with an emulated serial port presence. We then went on to discuss how we could create an

Figure 6-31 The structure of an NSC command field represented by one byte.

API and expose it to our application so that genuine functionality could be realised in a Bluetooth aware helper application. In this section, we now consider the objectives of RFCOMM in the *profile* and its expectations. In establishing our operations and its primitive functionality, the profile discusses mandatory features that it expects from the protocol and provides guidance with regard to how a Bluetooth aware helper application might achieve these objectives.

Having established the various idiosyncrasies of the RFCOMM protocol, we can see in Table 6-26 and Table 6-27, the features or capabilities that are expected from a compliant Serial Port Profile. In Table 6-26, we illustrate the features of an initiating device, whereas the features expected from a responder device are illustrated in Table 6-27.

The use of the RLS command is encouraged to keep peer devices informed of any state change. In one such instance, an emulated serial port may interface to a Type II ap-

Table 6-26 The illustration shows specific procedures that this profile depends upon to realise its compliant implementation.

PROCEDURE	DEVICEA	DEVICEB
Initialise an RFCOMM Session	M	X
Terminate an RFCOMM Session	M	M
Establish a new DLC Connection	M	X
Disconnect a DLC Connection	M	M
Emulate RS232 Control Signals	C	C
Transfer Data	M	M
Test Command	X	X
Flow Control	C	C
RLS	O	O
PN	O	O
RPN	O	O

Table 6-27   The illustration shows specific procedures that this profile depends upon to realise its compliant implementation.

PROCEDURE	DEVICEA	DEVICEB
Initialise an RFCOMM Session	X	M
Terminate an RFCOMM Session	M	M
Establish a new DLC Connection	X	M
Disconnect a DLC Connection	M	M
Emulate RS232 Control Signals	C	C
Transfer Data	N/A	N/A
Test Command	M	M
Flow Control	M	M
RLS	M	M
PN	M	M
RPN	M	M

plication (physical serial port), where overruns or parity errors may occur. An application that makes use of RS232 port configuration parameters should expose these settings through an appropriate API function; this is of particular relevance when interfacing to Type II applications.

6.5.1.4   L2CAP.   The L2CAP layer provides transparency for the upper layers of the stack from the layers typically found within the host controller. L2CAP payloads are passed to the *Host Controller Interface*[9] (HCI), which is then subsequently passed onto the *Link Manager Protocol* (LMP). The range of upper layers, which include RFCOMM, *Service Discovery Protocol* (SDP) and the *Telephony Control Protocol Specification* (TCS) all make use of the capabilities offered by L2CAP. Its primary role is to provide *protocol multiplexing*, allowing numerous simultaneous connections to be made. It also provides the ability for *segmentation* and *reassembly*; this refers to the ability to manage large payloads in the application, which may need to be fragmented into smaller payloads for the lower-layers to manage; these are then transmitted over the air-interface. Finally, the L2CAP layer exchanges *Quality of Service* (QoS) information, ensuring that sufficient resources are available and that both Bluetooth devices are attaining the best service.

---

[9]L2CAP payloads are passed directly onto LMP when implemented on a hostless system.

Table 6-28   The illustration shows specific procedures that this profile depends upon to realise its compliant implementation.

PROCEDURE	DEVICEA	DEVICEB
Connection-orientated Channel	M	M
Connectionless Channel	X	X
Connection Establishment	M	M
Configuration	M	M
Connection Termination	M	M
Echo	M	M
Command Rejection	M	M
Maximum Transmission Unit	M	M
Flush Timeout	M	M
Quality of Service	O	O

In Table 6-28, we summarise the broad capabilities that are expected from L2CAP. Features are marked with *M* (Mandatory), *O* (Optional), *X* (Excluded), *C* (Conditional) and *N/A*
(Not Applicable); these will determine what is expected from the L2CAP layer.

6.5.1.4.1   Channel Types.   In Table 6-28, we have identified that *Connection-orientated Channels* are mandatory, whereas *Connectionless Channels* are excluded; this
type of channel is aimed at broadcasting, where all devices may be targeted. L2CAP uses
PDUs to transport connection, signalling and configuration options. The higher layers of
the Bluetooth protocol stack will instigate a connection with L2CAP using the `L2CA_
ConnectReq` request packet, where the corresponding result is contained within the
`L2CA_ConnectRsp` response packet. An `L2CA_ConnectRspNeg` negative response
packet is used to denote a response, where the connection with the remote device was unsuccessful. Since our profile resides above L2CAP and employs its services, we are only
concerned with the upper protocol layer of L2CAP. This higher functionality is offered to us
through a series of L2CAP events and is denoted through the prefix `L2CA_`; see Table 6-29.
     When creating an L2CAP connection between two devices, a *Protocol/Service Mul-
tiplexor* (PSM) value is used to denote the higher-layer protocol that is using the connection; Table 6-30 identifies these values and the corresponding protocols they represent.
The value of `0x0003` (RFCOMM) is used for this profile.

6.5.1.4.2   Signalling.   When establishing communication with a remote device, a
signalling channel is created and reserved for use during connection, disconnection and

Table 6-29   The range of prototypes used to illustrate how L2CAP is architected and how interaction between higher- and lower-layers is achieved. For this discussion, our
concern here is with the higher-layer.

PROTOTYPE	DESCRIPTION
L2CA_	This prefix prototype is used to denote the higher-layer interaction, typically used by RFCOMM, SDP, and TCS.
L2CAP_	This prefix is used to denote peer-to-peer signalling interaction of L2CAP entities.
LP_	Finally, this prefix denotes lower-layer interaction, where L2CAP interfaces with the LMP layer.

configuration of subsequent L2CAP connections. A *channel* is used to describe the communication and data flow that exists between L2CAP entities and Table 6-31 illustrates
the range of CID that are used to identify the channel type. As we can see in Table 6-28,
Connection Establishment and *Termination* is mandatory in the local device, although the
remote device may be capable of initiating and terminating a connection to the local device. The L2CA_DisconnectReq request packet is used to terminate the connection
with the remote device. An L2CA_DisconnectRsp response packet is used to ascertain the result of the termination, although all disconnection requests must be completed
successfully. The support of *Configuration* is shown as mandatory and we will discuss
these specific options in more detail in the following section. Finally, *Echo* and *Command
Rejection* are both mandatory for a compliant Serial Port Profile.

6.5.1.4.3   Configuration Options.   In establishing a connection with the remote
device, the channel is subject to configuration and the higher-layer prototype L2CA_
ConfigReq request packet is used to carry configuration requests. Its associated response is contained within the L2CA_ConfigRsp packet; an L2CA_ConfigRspNeg

Table 6-30   The PSM values that are used to identify the higher-layer protocol.

PSM	DESCRIPTION
0x0001	SDP
0x0003	RFCOMM
0x0005	TCS-BIN
0x0007	TCS-BIN-CORDLESS

Table 6-31   The CIDs that are used to represent the logical channel.

CID	DESCRIPTION
0x0000	Null
0x0001	Signalling Channel
0x0002	Connectionless Reception Channel
0x0003 to 0x003F	Reserved
0x0040 to 0xFFFF	Dynamically Allocated

packet is used to denote a negative response during configuration where for example, the suggested MTU is too large. In Table 6-28, we have identified that the MTU and *Flush Timeout* parameters are mandatory, whereas the QoS is optional.

The default MTU setting for the signalling channel is 48-bytes, whereas other channels may be capable of transferring larger payloads; essentially the MTU determines the size of payloads that are capable of being exchanged between two devices. During configuration, the local device will inform the remote device that it is potentially capable of accepting larger payloads. If the remote device is unwilling to accept a larger MTU, then the local device is informed with the response contained within the L2CA_ConfigRspNeg packet.

When L2CA_ request and response packets are being exchanged, the Flush Timeout parameter is used to determine how long the local device is prepared to continue to transmit an L2CAP fragment before it gives up; the packet is subsequently flushed or, in other words, discarded. The suggested Flush Timeout value is sent during the L2CA_ ConfigReq request packet. However, if no value is set, then the default value is used. The Serial Port Profile uses the default value of 0xFFFF.

As we have already mentioned, the QoS configuration is optional, but if it is used during an L2CA_ConfigReq request then the *best effort* service is established as a default; the available services that are supported during an L2CAP channel are shown in Table 6-32. However, if the QoS service is set at *Guaranteed,* then parameters as *Token Rate, Token Bucket, Peak Bandwidth, Latency* and *Delay Variation* are used to determine an acceptable guaranteed service, where the L2CA_ConnectRspNeg will indicate that these values are unacceptable. These parameters are then subject to further negotiation.

6.5.1.5   Link Manager.   The *Link Manager* (LM) layer sits between the HCI and the *Link Controller* (LC), although on a hostless system the LM will have direct interaction with L2CAP. It accepts commands from HCI and translates them into operations for the LC, where *Asynchronous Connectionless* (ACL) and *Synchronous Connection-Orientated* (SCO) links are created and established. It is during this stage of ACL and SCO establishment that a master-slave switch would be performed as governed by the requirements of this profile. The LM is also responsible for placing the device into a low-power mode, which includes *hold, sniff* and *park.*

Table 6-32   The range of service definitions that are used during QoS.

SERVICE	DESCRIPTION
No Traffic	This indicates that the channel will not be sending any traffic and, as such, any parameters can be ignored.
Best Effort	This default value attempts to achieve a minimum service with the local remote device, where no guarantees are offered.
Guaranteed	With this service definition, we indicate that we wish to achieve the maximum bandwidth permitted; this is, of course, subject to the nature of a wireless environment.

In providing *general* error management, devices that operate mandatory procedures during interoperability, must either acknowledge their support or provide the initiator with a reason for failure. The `LMP_Detach` PDU is used to inform the device of the error that occurred; typically, the reason *unsupported LMP feature* (`0x1A`) is reported, see Appendix A.

6.5.1.6   Link Controller.   The LC layer is the lowest layer depicted in the dependencies of this profile and is responsible for a large number of core capabilities. It manages air-interface transactions and determines the fundamental timing of ACL and SCO data packet transmission and reception, as well as coordinating effort at its upper-edge with the LM. It also encompasses the management of the various packet types and the various inquiry and paging procedures that are available. In turn, the following subsections provide clarity with regard to the capabilities that are a requirement at the LC level for the Serial Port Profile. In our understanding of the dependencies, we begin by examining in more detail the supported capabilities and a small discussion is offered for each. If you are a developer providing profile-specific applications, then it is unlikely that you will engage in a large part of this component, although in some audio-related applications direct access may be required, where a faster transport mechanism can be supported. Many manufacturers have architected an audio-specific API for intelligible access to this component.

6.5.1.6.1   Capabilities.   Table 6-33 summarises the broad capabilities that are expected from the LC. In the table, you will notice features are marked appropriately; these will determine what is expected from the features at the LC.

6.5.1.6.1.1   INQUIRY AND INQUIRY SCAN.   An inquiry procedure is used to learn of the other devices in radio range, where the *Bluetooth Device Address* (BD_ADDR)

Table 6-33 The summary of capabilities that are required for the LC to enable a compliant Serial Port Profile.

PROCEDURES	DEVICEA	DEVICEB
Inquiry	M	X
Inquiry Scan	X	M
Paging	M	X
Page Scan	X	M
Inter-piconet	X	X
Packet Types	M	M
Voice Codecs	X	X

and clock offsets are obtained; it is DeviceA that will enter an *inquiry substate* to perform this procedure. A device that wishes to be discovered (DeviceB) will enter an *inquiry scan substate*, where the device will respond with an *inquiry response*. In this state, DeviceB is waiting to receive an *Inquiry Access Code* (IAC). From an application perspective, these modes of operation are discussed in more detail in the *Generic Access Profile*, Chapter 2. It is here that specific rules are determined with regard to the behaviour of such devices and how long these devices can operate in such modes. When devices have been discovered, this information is passed over to the *Service Discovery Application Profile*, Chapter 3, which manages the specific attributes that make up the device. What is being established here, as a dependency, is that the Bluetooth protocol stack must encompass and support such behavioural procedures for this profile to be considered compliant.

6.5.1.6.1.2 PAGING AND PAGING SCAN. The *inquiry substate* and *inquiry scan substate* procedures are the initial method used to learn of other devices in radio range; to this extent, the device has discovered sufficient information to gain a connection with the remote device. This is achieved when DeviceA has the intent to create a connection with DeviceB; DeviceA is now placed into a *paging substate*, where it will periodically transmit the *Device Access Code* (DAC). The DAC is used to target the device directly and the clock offset is used to gain an idea of the clock cycle of DeviceB. These parameters were originally obtained during our inquiry procedures. If DeviceB wishes to be connected, then it will enter a *page scan substate* and will respond accordingly to DeviceA. An inquiry procedure may be avoided if the BD_ADDR is already known, although a connection may take a little longer as the clock offset is not known.

6.5.1.6.1.3 INTER-PICONET. Inter-piconet capabilities describe the process that allows the master to manage multiple connections from slave devices. During a connection,

Table 6-34 The summary of packet types that are required for the LC to enable a compliant Serial Port Profile.

PACKET TYPE	DEVICE A	DEVICE B
DM1	M	M
DH1	M	M
DM3	M	M
DH3	M	M
DM5	M	M
DH5	M	M
HV1	X	X
HV2	X	X
HV3	X	X
DV	X	X

other users may temporarily witness degradation in the service provided; however, the master must be capable of accepting new piconet participants.

6.5.1.6.1.4 PACKET TYPES. There are numerous packet types available and Table 6-34 identifies those most frequently used for profile support. There are also a number of *common* packet types that are used for general purpose transport; for example, the ID packet is used for inquiry procedures and a POLL packet would be sent by DeviceA to determine if a slave is active on a channel.

The DM1 packet type is used to transmit control data over any connection, but may be used to transport a genuine payload. HV1, HV2 and HV3 are various SCO packet types to carry audio-specific data, where a DV packet can combine ACL and SCO specific data; their support in this profile is reflected in Table 6-34. Various ACL packet types are also available—in fact, seven types including the DM1 type are attributed to carrying user-specific data. These include DH1, DM3, DH3, DM5, DH5 and AUX1. Similarly, Table 6-34 summarises their support in this profile.

6.6 SUMMARY

- A large number of other profiles depend on the Serial Port Profile.
- The profile provides a set of protocols and procedures that are incorporated on top of the RFCOMM protocol.

- Two types of devices are supported, which have an implication on the type of application provided.
- Legacy Applications are Type I devices that provide the use of an emulated serial port.
- Cable Replacement Applications are transparent to the user when a serial communications link is created over RFCOMM; these are also classed as Type I devices.
- Intermediate devices are classed as Type II; they usually have a physical port associated with them.
- Bluetooth aware helper applications are used with the two types of devices to provide a suitable API to RFCOMM. These are also used to provide the presence of an emulated serial port to an operating system environment or to provide an illusion to a physical port.
- RS232 Control Signals are not mandatory, but are required when a device requests their use.
- PN is used to establish the DLC prior to creating an RFCOMM session.
- DLCI is used to identify unique RFCOMM concurrent sessions.
- No specific role of master-slave is defined, although DeviceA is the initiator and DeviceB is the acceptor.
- Authentication and encryption is optional, but must be supported if a device requests such functionality.
- Some emulated serial ports may require configuration of the baud, parity bit settings and so on. The Remote Port Negotiation is used to define these parameters.
- Bluetooth devices may concurrently execute multiple sessions.
- The Major Device Class does not specifically class a Serial Port.
- The Remote Line Status command is used to inform the party of any errors or changes.

7

The Headset Profile

7.1 INTRODUCTION

The concept of a *world without wires* maps itself quite well onto the *ultimate headset* as outlined in the *Headset Profile*. A variety of new scenarios are introduced with this profile, some of which are illustrated in Figure 7-1. With an increasing number of ear pieces being introduced by several large well-known companies, coupled with the time[1] needed to bring prices to a more acceptable and affordable level, we will surely see these items as a fashion accessory bundled with your mobile phone handset.

During the course of our discussion, a comparison of this profile is made with other similar telephony profiles, although the usage models do vary. In our first comparison, we examine the overlap between the Headset and the *Car Hands-Free Profile*, Chapter 17, which is introduced later in Part III, *The New Profiles*. We then take our earlier *Cordless Telephony*, Chapter 4, and *Intercom Profiles*, Chapter 5 and examine more closely how these devices may help one another or demonstrate where product overlap may exist.

---

[1]In the early stages of product introduction to the marketplace, it is quite common to see an initial mark-up on the product itself. Indeed, as such products increase in popularity, the price more often is reflected in the numbers sold.

Figure 7-1   The Bluetooth-enabled headset is capable of establishing a connection with a multimedia capable notebook and a mobile phone, both of which act as our audio gateways.

7.1.1   Comparing Headsets with the Hands-Free Profile

In the *Car Profiles*, Chapter 17, we introduce three new profiles that are vehicle orientated. More specifically, we compare the *Hands-Free Profile* with the Headset, as there is some overlap between the usage models for these profiles. Each of these profiles provide audio transfer from one device to another; in the Hands-Free usage model, an in-car hands-free kit is used to provide audio transfer from an *Audio Gateway* (AG) to the *Hands-Free* (HF) unit. The user still has to manipulate the mobile phone handset (AG) to initiate, receive and terminate calls. Furthermore, the protocol structure is also similar in nature, as you can see in Figure 7-2. Both profiles use *AT Command Control* to facilitate control signalling and, as such, both implement a controller component: *headset* and *hands-free*, where these specific components are used to identify the layer that manages the AT command parsing.

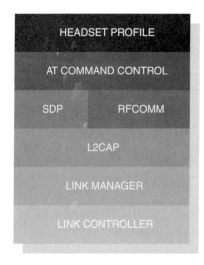
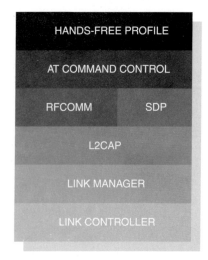

Figure 7-2   In comparing the Headset and Hands-Free Profiles, we can see that both are identical.

The Headset Profile provides functionality through the use of a discreet earpiece, where limited functionality can be provided with on-board button control. In both cases *Voice Recognition* (VR) may also be provided to alleviate the distraction that may be imposed when operating such devices; in particular, it is important that the driver of a moving vehicle keeps his or her eyes focused on the road at all times. In comparison to a Hands-Free kit, a Headset device is overall less intrusive and easier to use (although it is assumed that the user has become familiar with the operation of the Headset product).

7.1.2 Comparing Headsets with the Cordless Telephony Profile

The *Cordless Telephony profile* requires the implementation of the Bluetooth *Telephone Control Protocol Specification* (TCS). In Figure 7-3, we compare the stack components that make up both application types, where the Bluetooth protocol stack architecture can be compared and examined in more detail. As we previously mentioned, the Cordless Telephony Profile is based upon TCS, which resides above L2CAP. As we can see from our illustration, the Headset Profile is dependent upon the implementation provided by RFCOMM. This provides the Headset with the *AT Command Control* and is implemented, as the name suggests, through a series of AT Commands, which enable and control signalling.

In our new usage scenarios, as illustrated in Figure 7-1, the headset makes use of an AG; we will look at this role in more detail later. We can see that a headset device can equally lend itself to the role of a cordless handset, where audio transfer is made between the base station of the cordless gateway and the headset, in the same way it occurs for the cordless handset. However, it would require the headset to be compliant with the Cordless Telephony Profile, that is, have an implementation that encompasses TCS; moreover, a

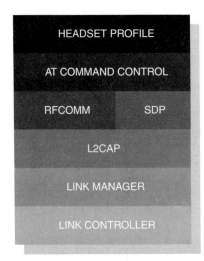
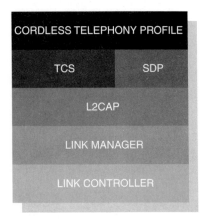

Figure 7-3   The Headset and Cordless Telephony Profiles components are placed side-by-side to illustrate the differences in the stack architecture.

dual implementation of the AT Command Control and the Cordless Telephony may be considered, allowing the user to switch between usage scenarios. The implementation of this switch may be transparent, allowing the user to seamlessly move from one environment to another.

7.1.3 Bluetooth Audio

The Headset Profile mandates the use of the underlying Bluetooth audio capability, where there has to be some degree of certainty that the transport used is able to guarantee the timely delivery of the audio data. A *Synchronous Connection Orientated* (SCO) communications link is used to provide the best quality available through reserving channel bandwidth. Furthermore, audio coding schemes are used to provide compression and to overcome potential errors in the data transmission. The *Pulse Code Modulation* (PCM) has two types of logarithmic compression, these are A-law and μ-law, where either compression technique can be applied on the voice channels over the air-interface; both techniques are detailed in the *International Telecommunications Union* (ITU) Recommendations G.711. *Continuous Variable Slope Delta* (CVSD) provides the second scheme, which is particularly efficient for voice communication; it also tolerates potential errors in the audio data. Audio data can be transferred up to a data rate of 64 Kb/s, which should be sufficient for carrying voice communication. Later on in this chapter we look more specifically at the commands that are used to create an SCO connection and the various optional parameters that define the link.

7.2 USAGE MODELS

This section considers both existing and future usage models through scenarios that may be typical for the Headset Profile. We begin by exploring the existing models, where audio transfer and limited remote control are provided to the headset. In future usage models, we consider other scenarios where the introduction of a headset may provide extended functionality.

7.2.1 Existing Usage Models

At a minimum, the Headset Profile allows a user to wear an earpiece through which audio transfer from a mobile phone is made; it is also capable of providing limited remote control functionality, where it is capable of asserting call connection, termination and rejection. Other remote control capability is extended to volume settings, where the level of the volume can be set in the headset and is subsequently reflected and stored for later retrieval in the AG.

The AG device is used to initially create an Asynchronous Connectionless (ACL) connection between the two devices. The AG discovers the device and then requests whether audio transfer should be made to the HS. Upon confirming that audio transfer should be made, any subsequent incoming or outgoing calls can be heard through the HS.

In Figure 7-4, we show a typical headset product and, by the use of button presses, the user is capable of initiating, terminating and rejecting a. Further functionality is provided

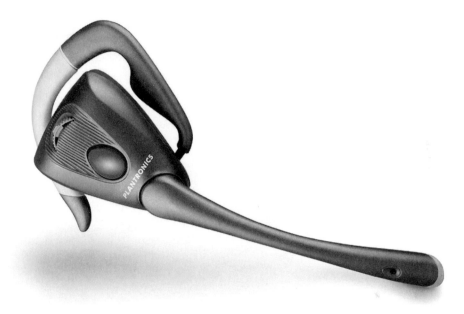

Figure 7-4   A typical headset, which has several button-operated functions. The model shown provides visual confirmation of certain discoverability modes through the use of LEDs. (Courtesy of Plantronics Inc.)

to allow the received volume of the device to be adjusted; the two-position rocking switch can be used to increase or decrease the volume.

7.2.2   Future Usage Models

The headset itself provides limited operation for making outgoing calls; currently, the last number redial is a function offered by many devices. In the *Car Hands-Free Profile*, Chapter 17, the introduction of VR is used to provide greater scope for making outgoing calls. Although not mandated in the profile, the use of VR is a natural step forward for a future usage model.

Furthermore, consideration should also be given to the numerous mobile phones that are currently in circulation, as a large majority of these devices do not support Bluetooth technology. So, do you pass over your existing mobile phone for a new one? Several companies offer the ability to bestow new wireless capabilities upon your non-Bluetooth mobile phone. In Figure 7-5, we illustrate a device that is capable of enabling Bluetooth wireless capability, such as the headset. It is not necessarily restricted to this usage model. Other scenarios, such as dial-up networking, fax and personal area networking can also be supported.

In the *Cordless Telephony Profile*, Chapter 4, we also introduced the headset as a replacement or an addition to the usage model scenarios. In this instance, a headset may be used to allow the user to roam the office quite freely whilst remaining in contact with

Figure 7-5   The device shown is capable of enabling Bluetooth applications
for a mobile phone. (Courtesy of Plantronics Inc.)

the cordless gateway. Similarly, VR may be used to make outgoing calls. This scenario
lends itself well to an office environment with the provision of voice roaming, allowing
the headset to remain connected to the cordless gateway, moving from one cordless gateway station to another. The user is then free to accept and make outgoing calls from any
location within the office.

7.3 PROFILE PRINCIPLES

The Headset Profile provides two new roles: an *AG and a HS*. The HS device can be
placed over the ear, where audio communication and remote control capability has been
transferred to the HS from the AG. The AG and HS support full duplex audio support and
in Figure 7-6 we can see how the Headset components are integrated with the existing
Bluetooth protocol stack.

The profile defines the set of protocols and procedures required to realise its implementation. Support for one SCO audio link is provided and, as such, only the two participating devices can operate at any one time. The profile mandates support for audio
CODECs (see Section 7.1.3, *Bluetooth Audio*), where the resulting audio is monophonic
and has a data rate of 64 Kb/s. The SCO connection is created after the initial ACL connection establishment has taken place.

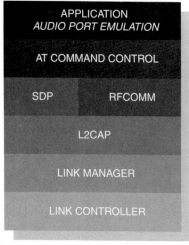
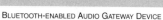
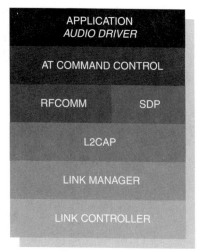

Figure 7-6 The core components of the Bluetooth protocol stack are shown, illustrating how the components of the Headset Profile are integrated.

There are no fixed master-slave roles; this leaves either device free to initiate and terminate a connection, although typically the AG will initiate the primary connection, where inquiry and device discovery procedures are undertaken. The user may determine whether authentication and/or encryption should be used between the two devices; however, if it is used, then the procedures as described for authentication and encryption in the *Generic Access Profile*, Chapter 2, must be adhered to.

In Figure 7-6, we illustrated the components that made up our Headset Profile. The profile is also dependent on the *Serial Port Profile*, Chapter 6, in its implementation. A series of AT commands are also used to enable control signalling, where AT commands are sent to the AG and the HS receives its responses. On closer inspection, you will notice that the AG device provides audio port emulation, whereas the HS provides an audio driver. It is also assumed that some management entity exists, where access to lower components of the stack is provided; in some cases a direct PCM route is used to enable faster audio throughput.

In Table 7-1, clarification is provided with regard to the roles used within the context of this profile. In general, *DeviceA* represents the initiating party and *DeviceB* represents the accepting party. The terms are often used interchangeably, when describing specific operations in various contexts and are provided here for reference.

Since the profile does not prescribe strict master-slave behaviour, either device can be responsible for an initial connection, although it is the AG that initially creates the ACL connection. This general notation is used within the course of this chapter and will always represent participating devices as the *initiator* or *DeviceA* and the *acceptor* or *DeviceB*. In the following section, the *modes of operation* are discussed in more detail.

Table 7-1   The list of behavioural characteristics that are typical for this profile.

CONFIGURATION	ROLE	DESCRIPTION
DeviceA	AG	A device acting as an audio gateway, which may take the form of a mobile phone or hands-free unit. In this particular context, the device is described as initiating the connection with the accepting device.
	Initiator	This configuration describes the device that instigates the original connection or the device that wishes to initiate communication over an existing link.
DeviceB	HS	A device that behaves as a headset, where audio transfer is made between the gateway and headset. It is also the party that accepts incoming connections from the audio gateway. The headset may also instigate a connection with an audio gateway, where the audio gateway will take on the role of acceptor.
	Acceptor	This configuration describes the process of the device accepting the initiated communication from DeviceA.

7.4   USER EXPECTATIONS

7.4.1   Audio Gateway Initiated ACL Connection

The Headset Profile is dependent upon the underlying profiles, where *Connection Establishment* procedures are applicable and are illustrated in the *Generic Access Profile*, Chapter 2. The connection establishment procedures encompass the availability of an initialised RFCOMM session, which includes the capability provided by a virtual serial connection as outlined in the *Serial Port Profile*, Chapter 6. If the device is in Park Mode, then the device is unparked prior to any creation of a SCO connection; if no previous session exists, then one is created and the device may request parked status. It is therefore assumed that the AG and HS devices have previously performed an inquiry, discovery and any authentication and/or encryption.

In this state, the AG device awaits a user action or an internally generated event such as an incoming call. On receiving either notification, the headset is alerted through an unsolicited RING *result code* (see Section 7.5.1.3.1, *AT Command Control*); Figure 7-7 provides further clarification of this sequence of events.

The headset is alerted to the incoming call, which now requires user intervention. At this point, the user may accept or reject the call. On pressing a button on the headset, an alert is sent to the AG device. The HS sends an AT+CKPD command as notification (see Section 7.5.1.3.1, *AT Command Control*). The AG is responsible for creating the SCO connection and can create a SCO connection after connection establishment.

7.4.2 Headset Initiated ACL Connection

The Headset Profile is dependent upon the underlying profiles, where *Connection Establishment* procedures are applicable and are illustrated in the *Generic Access Profile*, Chapter 2. The connection establishment procedures encompass the availability of an initialised RFCOMM session, which includes the capability provided by a virtual serial connection, as outlined in the *Serial Port Profile*, Chapter 6. If the device is in Park Mode, then the device is unparked prior to any creation of a SCO connection; if no previous session exists, then one is created and the device may the request parked status. It is therefore assumed that the AG and HS devices have previously performed an inquiry, discovery and any authentication and/or encryption.

The AG is always responsible for creating the SCO connection and can create a SCO connection after connection establishment. In this state, the AG device awaits a user action initiated from the HS, where the AG is altered through an AT+CKPD command (see Section 7.5.1.3.1, *AT Command Control*); Figure 7-8 provides further clarification of this sequence of events.

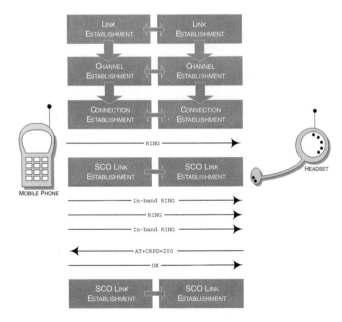

Figure 7-7 The sequence of events that occur during an AG initiated connection.

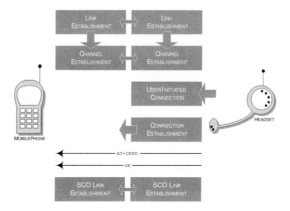

Figure 7-8   The sequence of events that occur during an HS initiated connection.

7.4.3   Transferring an Audio Connection

Either device may transfer an audio connection. In both cases, user intervention is required. On the HS, the user may initiate a transfer from the AG by operating a button, which would then result in a SCO connection being established with the headset. Con-

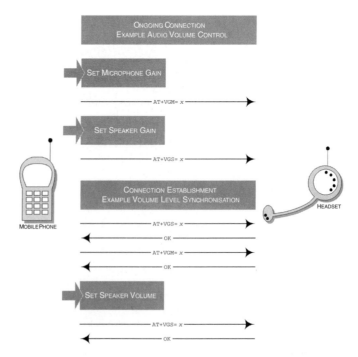

Figure 7-9   The sequence of events that occur during remote volume control operation.

versely, the AG may transfer audio from the HS by operating a function from the AG, which would result in the audio connection being terminated with the HS.

7.4.4 Terminating an Audio Connection

Either device may terminate an audio connection. In both cases, user intervention is required. On the HS, the user may initiate termination by pressing a button, which would result in the SCO and possibly the ACL connection being terminated. Conversely, the AG may terminate the connection with the HS by operating a function available from the AG.

7.4.5 Operating Volume Control

Assuming an ongoing audio connection between the AG and HS, the volume gain of the microphone and speaker of the HS can be controlled using the AT+VGM and AT+VGS, respectively. The specific volume setting is supplied as a parameter to the respective AT command and has the range of 0 to 15; Figure 7-9 provides further clarification of this sequence of events.

The AG and HS may store these settings after connection release for subsequent use during another connection.

Figure 7-10 illustrates a mechanism that is used to increase or decrease volume when operating a dial-type button that is swung in both directions to increase or decrease the volume.

Figure 7-10   A typical headset, which demonstrates the increase and decrease volume operation at the top left of the picture. (Courtesy of Plantronics Inc.)

7.5 LIFTING THE LID

7.5.1 Dependencies

We have already considered both existing and future usage models in relation to user expectations. Now we will take a closer look at the dependencies that make up this particular profile. Figure 7-11, illustrates these conceptually; the shaded areas are those relevant to this profile. As you can see, the Headset Profile is dependent upon the basic functionality offered to us by the *Generic Access Profile*, Chapter 2, the *Service Discovery Application Profile*, Chapter 3 and the *Serial Port Profile*, Chapter 6. Let us now consider, the basic requirements of these dependent components alongside any potential variation from the basic functionality originally offered to us.

7.5.1.1 Generic Access. The Headset Profile is reliant upon the abilities afforded to it by the *Generic Access Profile*, Chapter 2. You may remember from this earlier chapter that a level of basic functionality is attained through the establishment of a set of rules and procedures. Accordingly, the behaviour of such devices is governed by a series of simple rules related to connectivity, discoverability and other common characteristics at the user interface level. These rules help to establish commonality between products, which ultimately results in a predictably beneficial user experience.

This section reflects upon the behavioural aspects of Bluetooth-enabled devices as outlined by the Generic Access Profile, *Chapter 2*. These mandate a number of rules and

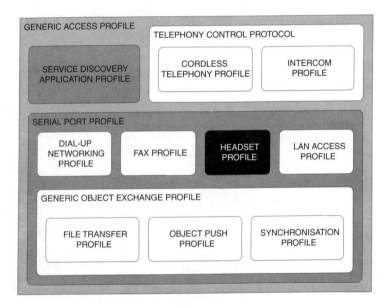

Figure 7-11 The dependent components of the Bluetooth protocol stack that make up the Headset Profile. The areas that are shaded are relevant to this profile.

Table 7-2   The core set of procedures as required by most profiles.

PROCEDURES	DESCRIPTION
Discoverability Mode	This mode prescribes the overall discoverability of a device, allowing it to be placed into a non-discoverable, limited, or general discoverable mode. The mode would allow devices to become generally available to other users or it can be restricted to personal use.
Connectability Mode	When determining a baseband connectable state, this mode is used to place a device into a connectable or non-connectable mode.
Pairing	Pairable and non-pairable modes are used to realise the security aspects when operating or intending to use a device. A device may require authentication and, as such, the user would be required to enter a Bluetooth Passkey. The pairing procedure starts the link key generation process which, in turn, allows authentication to take place.

procedures that ultimately govern the overall connectability, discoverability and security aspects of Bluetooth-enabled devices.

Table 7-2, identifies the basic set of procedures and expectations that determine its operation. These procedures allow us to understand the context in which a device operates; for example, a device may wish to be discoverable for a certain period of time or may require a varying level of security, depending upon the services it is capable of offering.

Table 7-3 identifies the set of operations that are specific to this profile. Features are marked with *M* (Mandatory), *O* (Optional), *X* (Excluded), *C* (Conditional) and *N/A* (Not Applicable) to illustrate the expectations of the Generic Access Profile. The Headset Profile requires mandatory support for pairable modes if bonding is supported; bonding is initially offered as optional (see Table 7-5).

Table 7-4 identifies the security requirements for this profile. You may remember from the *Generic Access Profile*, Chapter 2, that Security Mode 1 is a non-secure mode, where Bluetooth-enabled devices will never initiate any security procedures; whereas, Security Modes 2 and 3 initiate different levels of security procedures at various stages of connection establishment. In this instance, if authentication is provided, then support should be made available for at least Security Modes 2 or 3.

In our final consideration of the basic rules and procedures that are required for the Generic Access Profile, the idle mode procedures outline behavioural characteristics when DeviceA chooses to initiate them against DeviceB. The procedures that are listed in Table 7-5 provide a clear indication of how a device should operate when performing such an activity; let us take our bonding procedure as an example. The term bonding is

Table 7-3 The illustration shows specific modes of operation that this profile depends upon to realise its compliant implementation.

MODES	HS	AG
Non-discoverable	M	N/A
Limited Discoverable	O	N/A
General Discoverable	M	N/A
Non-connectable	N/A	N/A
Connectable	M	M
Non-pairable	O	O
Pairable	O	O

Table 7-4 The illustration shows specific security procedures that this profile depends upon to realise its compliant implementation.

PROCEDURE	HS	AG
Authentication	C	C
Security Mode 1	O	O
Security Mode 2	C	C
Security Mode 3	C	C

Table 7-5 The illustration shows specific behavioural procedures that this profile depends upon to realise its compliant implementation.

PROCEDURE	HS	AG
General Inquiry	N/A	M
Limited Inquiry	N/A	O
Name Discovery	N/A	O
Device Discovery	N/A	O
Bonding	O	O

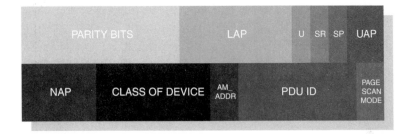

Figure 7-12   The structure of the FHS packet used only for reference to illustrate the position of the CoD structure.

very much associated with the pairing process; however, bonding occurs when the user has the *intent* to initiate a trusted relationship with DeviceB.

With this intent, the user is prompted to enter a Bluetooth Passkey which in turn instigates the pairing process, that is, the generation of the link keys, where subsequent authentication can then occur. In summary, we realise that there is a specific set of events associated with a procedure and in the *Generic Access Profile*, Chapter 2, we provide an exhaustive presentation and examine how each procedure is conducted.

The mechanism for providing device discoverability is the provision of a well-structured FHS packet, which is shown in Figure 7-12. This packet is used to identify the remote device, where information such as *Bluetooth Device Address* (BD_ADDR) and clock offsets is determined. You may also notice from this packet that the *Class of Device* (CoD) field is also provided. This information is relayed to the user interface which, in turn, provides common characteristics about discovered devices. The CoD is used during the discovery mechanism to learn more about the type of device and what it may be capable of providing. The structure of information is depicted in Figure 7-13 and is made up of 3-bytes (or 24-bits as shown). The following sections now consider the Headset attributes, which will ultimately make use of the *Service*, *Major* and *Minor Device Class* fields.

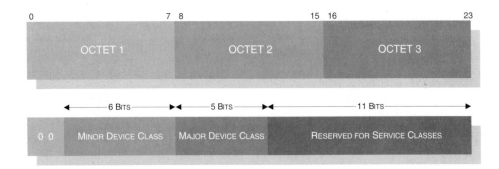

Figure 7-13   The structure of the class of device, illustrating the Minor Device, Major Device and Service Class fields and their respective lengths.

Table 7-6 The Service Class categorisation for the Headset Profile.

											SERVICE CLASS
23	22	21	20	19	18	17	16	15	14	13	Bit # of CoD
0	0	1	0	0	0	0	0	0	0	0	Audio

7.5.1.1.1 Service Class. This high-level form of defining a Bluetooth device identifies where in the Service Class field the Headset Profile resides; see Table 7-6 which, in turn, determines the category of service; here, the category of service falls within *Audio*.

7.5.1.1.2 Major Device Class. This high-level form of defining a Bluetooth device identifies where in the Major Device Class the Headset Profile resides; see Table 7-7 which, in turn, determines the major class grouping. Here, the category falls within *Audio*, since a headset may be used.

7.5.1.1.3 Minor Device Class. The Minor Device Class in this profile is used to provide further context for the setting within the major class grouping, see Table 7-8. Here, the bit may be set appropriately for *Headset* to denote the type of service available to the user.

7.5.1.2 Service Discovery. In the *Service Discovery Application Profile*, Chapter 3, we introduced the characteristics of the mechanisms used to retrieve service information from a remote device. Typically, a client will initiate inquiry and discovery procedures as outlined in our previous section, to learn of the devices in radio range. A client would then make use of an application, which would embody the functionality of the underlying *Service Discovery Protocol* (SDP). The *Service Discovery Application* (SrvDscApp) uses an *SDP Client* to instigate a request to the remote device, where the *SDP Server* will respond; as such, the AG and HS must employ the use of an SDP client and server respectively, as illustrated in Table 7-9.

Protocol Data Units (PDUs) are used to instruct the SDP server to undertake browsing procedures and to retrieve service record information; you may recall that these PDUs carry payloads about requests containing AttributeIDs and Attribute-Values describing what exactly is being sought. As we previously discussed, the client

Table 7-7 The Major Device Class for the Headset Profile.

					MAJOR DEVICE CLASS
12	11	10	9	8	Bit # of CoD
0	0	1	0	0	Audio

Table 7-8   The Minor Device Class for the Headset Profile.

						MINOR DEVICE CLASS
7	6	5	4	3	2	Bit # of CoD
0	0	0	0	0	1	Headset

and server operate a request and response paradigm. SDAP will construct PDUs containing information relating to the `AttributeID` and `AttributeValues`, in turn instructing the server to carry out its operation. The various request and response PDUs that are required are shown in Table 7-10, where features indicated are marked accordingly.

A service record is maintained for each service a device is capable of supporting and, as such, a *Service Record Handle* is created to uniquely identify this. The `Service-RecordHandle` is a 32-bit unsigned integer and is stored on the SDP server. The service record shown in Table 7-11 identifies an HS device and Table 7-12 identifies the AG. Both tables provide a list of `AttributeIDs`, which in combination would identify the services available for the Headset Profile. A minimum of two attributes are required to make a service record; these are `ServiceRecordHandle` and `ServiceClass-IDList`, where it must contain at least one `UUID`.

When browsing for services on the remote device, a local device constructs a search pattern using a *Universally Unique Identifier* (UUID). A UUID is a 128-bit value, which has been shortened for use within Bluetooth applications. The shortcut has been provided by first establishing a *Bluetooth Base UUID*, which we discussed in the *Service Discovery Application Profile*, Chapter 3.

The UUIDs that have been presented so far are aliases and take the form of what is referred to as a 16-bit UUID or a 32-bit UUID but, in turn, they should all refer to the 128-bit notation. These UUIDs have been assigned and can be referenced in the Bluetooth Special Interest Group, Bluetooth Assigned Numbers, v1.1, February 2001. For the search pattern to be successful, they all need to be converted to the 128-bit notation, since they will all be compared at this range. An arithmetic conversion algorithm is used to construct the 128-bit value.

Table 7-13 summarises the service class UUIDs used to identify the particular profile in use; this also correlates with the identification of the device during a device discovery procedure as previously outlined in Section 7.5.1.1, *Generic Access*.

Table 7-9   As a minimum, the local device must support the use of a client application and the remote device must support the use of a server.

FEATURE	AG	HS
SDP Client	M	X
SDP Server	X	M

Table 7-10   The list of PDUs that are required for the operation of the Headset Profile.

PDU	AG	HS
SDP_ErrorResponse	X	M
SDP_ServiceSearchRequest	M	X
SDP_ServiceSearchResponse	X	M
SDP_ServiceAttributeRequest	M	X
SDP_ServiceAttributeResponse	X	M
SDP_ServiceSearchAttributeRequest	O	X
SDP_ServiceSearchAttributeRequest	X	O

As part of the service record, the dependent underlying protocols are also identified. The local device retrieves this information, where it can fully understand the exact requirements needed to fulfil the service. The Headset Profile is dependent on the protocols, as shown in Table 7-14, which also shows their associated UUID values.

7.5.1.3   RFCOMM. In the *Serial Port Profile*, Chapter 6, we introduced the conceptual and functional nature of RFCOMM and how it provides an emulated serial port presence. Several distinctions were made between the various types of applications. The purpose of making these distinctions was to enable clarification and understanding of RFCOMM's composition. In this particular application context, the creation of an emulated serial port would be transparent to the user. The Headset Profile is dependent upon the operation of the Serial Port Profile, and, as such, is required to establish an emulated serial port as part of its communication link with the remote device.

The term cable replacement application was introduced in our earlier chapter and distinguishes between the different scenarios available. It refers to specific Bluetooth applications that create implicit emulated serial ports, which remain transparent to the user to complete the creation of a communications link.

Specific detail has been provided to illustrate how data is communicated over an emulated serial port connection, whereby a *Data Link Connection* (DLC) is established between two peer devices, namely AG and HS. We have also looked at the fields that make up our service record for this profile. The ProtocolDescriptorList field is used to describe the set of protocols that the profile intends to use and, as such, the RFCOMM protocol identifier contains a parameter, which contains the Server Channel number.

The Server Channel is used in combination with a *Data Link Connection Identifier* (DLCI), which is then used to uniquely identify the active DLC. This connection is then mapped onto a connectionless orientated L2CAP *Channel Identifier* (CID).

Table 7-11 The list of mandatory and configurable items that make up the service record for the HS device.

ATTRIBUTE	DESCRIPTION
ServiceRecordHandle	With an `AttributeID` of `0x0000`, this uniquely identifies this service record within the SDP server on the HS device.

ServiceClassIDList
 	
   ServiceClass0
 	
   ServiceClass1
	With an `AttributeID` of `0x0001`, the following `ServiceClass0` would contain the `UUID` for the *Headset* and the `ServiceClass1` would identify the *Generic Audio* service classes. Their respective `UUID` values are summarised in Table 7-13.

ProtocolDescriptorList
 	
   Protocol0
 	
   Protocol1
 	
     ParameterFor1
	With an `AttributeID` of `0x0004`, the following `Protocol0` would contain an `UUID` for the protocol *L2CAP*, whereas in `Protocol1` an `UUID` would contain the protocol identifier for *RFCOMM*. Their respective `UUID` values are summarised in Table 7-14. The `ParameterFor1` would contain the relevant server channel number for the RFCOMM transport.

BluetoothProfile-
DescriptorList
 	
   Profile0
 	
     ParameterFor0
	With an `AttributeID` of `0x0009`, the following `Profile0` would identify the `UUID` for *Headset* service class, which is summarised in Table 7-13. The `ParameterFor0` accommodates the version number supported by this profile.

ServiceName	With a base `AttributeID` of `0x0006`, this attribute has an offset of `0x0000`. It is a configurable item and has an `AttributeValue` of a `Text` string, where its default setting is *Headset*.
RemoteAudio- VolumeControl	With an `AttributeID` of `0x0302`, this attribute identifies whether or not the headset can support volume control. The `AttributeValue` is constructed using a `Boolean`, where the default setting is `FALSE`.

Table 7-12   The list of mandatory and configurable items that make up the service record for the AG device.

ATTRIBUTE	DESCRIPTION
ServiceRecordHandle	With an `AttributeID` of `0x0000`, this uniquely identifies this service record within the SDP server on the AG device.
ServiceClassIDList ServiceClass0 ServiceClass1	With an `AttributeID` of `0x0001`, the following `ServiceClass0` would contain the UUID for the *Headset Audio Gateway* and the `ServiceClass1` would identify the *Generic Audio* service classes. Their respective UUID values are summarised in Table 7-13.
ProtocolDescriptorList Protocol0 Protocol1 ParameterFor1	With an `AttributeID` of `0x0004`, the following `Protocol0` would contain an UUID for the protocol *L2CAP*, whereas in `Protocol1` an UUID would contain the protocol identifier for *RFCOMM*. Their respective UUID values are summarised in Table 7-14. The `ParameterFor1` would contain the relevant server channel number for the RFCOMM transport.
BluetoothProfile- DescriptorList Profile0 ParameterFor0	With an `AttributeID` of `0x0009`, the following `Profile0` would identify the UUID for *Headset* service class, which is summarised in Table 7-13. The `ParameterFor0` accommodates the version number supported by this profile.
ServiceName	With a base `AttributeID` of `0x0006`, this attribute has an offset of `0x0000`. It is a configurable item and has an `AttributeValue` of a `Text` string, where its default setting is *Voice Gateway*.

Table 7-13   The list of service classes that match a corresponding profile. This correlates with our previous Generic Access section.

CLASSES	UUID
Headset	0x1108
HeadsetAudioGateway	0x1112
GenericAudio	0x1203

Table 7-14   The list of protocols that are used in this profile; their associated UUID values are also shown.

PROTOCOL	UUID
RFCOMM	0x0003
L2CAP	0x0100

In this section we highlight the specific features that are required to realise a compliant Headset Profile and illustrate the features or capabilities that are expected from the Serial Port Profile.

The use of the RLS command is encouraged to keep peer devices informed of any state change. In one such instance, an emulated serial port may interface to a Type II application (physical serial port), where overruns or parity errors may occur. An application that makes use of RS232 port configuration parameters should expose these settings through an appropriate Application Programming Interface (API) function; this is of particular relevance when interfacing to Type II applications.

7.5.1.3.1   AT Command Control.   In Section 7.3, *Profile Principles,* we introduced an illustration that identifies the audio port emulation and driver components created with

Table 7-15   The set of capabilities that are required from the initiating party, denoted here by the AG device.

PROCEDURE	AG	HS
Initialise an RFCOMM Session	M	X
Terminate an RFCOMM Session	M	M
Establish a new DLC Connection	M	X
Disconnect a DLC Connection	M	M
Emulate RS232 Control Signals	C	C
Transfer Data	M	M
Test Command	X	X
Flow Control	C	C
RLS	O	O
PN	O	O
RPN	O	O

Table 7-16   The set of capabilities that are required from the responder party, denoted here by the HS device.

PROCEDURE	AG	HS
Initialise an RFCOMM Session	X	M
Terminate an RFCOMM Session	M	M
Establish a new DLC Connection	X	M
Disconnect a DLC Connection	M	M
Emulate RS232 Control Signals	M	M
Transfer Data	N/A	N/A
Test Command	M	M
Flow Control	M	M
RLS	M	M
PN	M	M
RPN	M	M

the help of RFCOMM. It is above this that an audio application would reside, using the serial port emulation provided by RFCOMM. The HS and AG would be capable of supporting the commands and responses as defined in Table 7-18 and Table 7-19, respectively; these are based upon the *International Telecommunications Union* (ITU-T) Telecommunications Sector v.250.[2]

The general format used for the HS to send an AT command to the AG is provided in Table 7-17; the AG, however, will not echo the command and, as such, this is a deviation from the ITU-T Recommendations v.25*ter* specification.

Table 7-17   The default command is used, where no echo from the AG is required. The result code is used to confirm a successful operation, with an OK, where an unsuccessful operation is denoted with an ERROR.

COMMAND	RESULT
AT<CMD>=<VALUE><CR>	<CR><LF>OK<CR><LF> or <CR><LF>ERROR<CR><LF>

---

[2]The new International Telecommunications Union (ITU-T) Telecommunications Recommendation, Series V: Data Communication over the Telephone Network v.25*ter*, supersedes the original v.250 document.

Table 7-18 The `RING` command is used to notify the HS of an incoming call.

COMMAND	DESCRIPTION
RING	This is the incoming call notification to the HS, as indicated in the ITU-T Recommendation.

Table 7-19 provides clarification with regard to the optional AT command capability that may be supported by both the AG and HS. These capabilities extend to the control of the speak and volume gain, which in turn allow the user of the headset to increase or decrease the volume settings of the equipment.

7.5.1.4   L2CAP.   The L2CAP layer provides transparency for the upper layers of the stack from the layers typically found within the host controller. L2CAP payloads are passed to the *Host Controller Interface*[3] (HCI), which is then subsequently passed onto the *Link Manager Protocol* (LMP). The range of upper layers, which include RFCOMM, SDP and the TCS, all make use of the capabilities offered to us by L2CAP. Its primary role is to provide *protocol multiplexing*, allowing numerous simultaneous connections to be made, and it also provides the ability for *segmentation* and *reassembly*. This refers to the ability to manage large payloads in the application, which may need to be fragmented into smaller payloads for the lower-layers to manage; these are then transmitted over the air-interface. Finally, the L2CAP layer exchanges *Quality of Service* (QoS) information, ensuring that sufficient resources are available and that both Bluetooth devices are attaining the best service.

In Table 7-20, we summarise the broad capabilities that are expected from L2CAP. In the table, you will notice features are marked with *M* (Mandatory), *O* (Optional),

Table 7-19 The command set that is optional for the AG and HS to increase and decrease gain levels with the speaker and microphone of the units. A setting of 0 to 15 is used and recommended.

COMMAND	DESCRIPTION
+VGM	The AG issues this command to set the level of gain in the microphone of the HS. The HS reports the level of gain to the AG using the same command structure and setting.
+VGS	The AG issues this command to set the level of gain in the speaker of the HS. The HS reports the level of gain to the AG using the same command structure and setting.

---

[3]L2CAP payloads are passed directly onto LMP when implemented on a hostless system.

Table 7-20 The illustration shows specific procedures that this profile depends upon to re-alise its compliant implementation.

PROCEDURE	AG	HS
Connection-orientated Channel	M	M
Connectionless Channel	X	X
Connection Establishment	M	M
Configuration	M	M
Connection Termination	M	M
Echo	M	M
Command Rejection	M	M
Maximum Transmission Unit	M	M
Flush Timeout	M	M
Quality of Service	O	O

X (Excluded), *C* (Conditional) and *N/A* (Not Applicable); these will determine what is expected from the features at the L2CAP layer.

7.5.1.4.1 Channel Types. In Table 7-20, we have identified that *Connection-orientated Channels* are mandatory, whereas *Connectionless Channels* are excluded; this type of channel is aimed at broadcasting, where all devices may be targeted. L2CAP uses PDUs to transport connection, signalling and configuration options, which will be discussed in a moment. The higher-layers of the Bluetooth protocol stack will instigate a connection with L2CAP using the L2CA_ConnectReq request packet, where the corresponding result is contained within the L2CA_ConnectRsp response packet. An L2CA_ConnectRspNeg negative response packet is used to denote a response, where the connection with the remote device was unsuccessful. Since our profile resides above L2CAP and employs its services, we are only concerned with the upper protocol layer of L2CAP. This higher functionality is offered to us through a series of L2CAP events and is denoted through the prefix L2CA_ (see Table 7-21).

When creating an L2CAP connection between two devices, a *Protocol/Service Multiplexor* (PSM) value is employed to denote the higher-layer protocol that is using the connection; Table 7-22 identifies these values and the corresponding protocols they represent. The value of 0x0003 (RFCOMM) is used for this profile.

7.5.1.4.2 Signalling. When establishing communication with a remote device, a *signalling channel* is created and reserved for use during connection, disconnection and

Table 7-21   The range of prototypes used to illustrate how L2CAP is architected and how interaction between higher- and lower-layers is achieved. For this discussion, our concern here is with the higher-layer.

PROTOTYPE	DESCRIPTION
L2CA_	This prefix prototype is used to denote the higher-layer interaction, typically used by RFCOMM, SDP and TCS.
L2CAP_	This prefix is used to denote peer-to-peer signalling interaction of L2CAP entities.
LP_	Finally, this prefix denotes lower-layer interaction, where L2CAP interfaces with the LMP layer.

configuration of subsequent L2CAP connections. A *channel* is used to describe the communication and data flow that exists between L2CAP entities and Table 7-23 illustrates the range of CID that are used to identify the channel type. As we can see in Table 7-20, *Connection Establishment* and *Termination* is mandatory in the local device, although the remote device may be capable of initiating and terminating a connection to the local device. The L2CA_DisconnectReq request packet is used to terminate the connection with the remote device and an L2CA_DisconnectRsp response packet is used to ascertain the result of the termination; although all disconnection requests must be completed successfully. The support of *Configuration* is shown as mandatory and we will discuss these specific options in more detail in the following section. Finally, *Echo* and *Command Rejection* are both mandatory for a compliant Headset Profile.

7.5.1.4.3   Configuration Options.   In establishing a connection with the remote device, the channel is subject to configuration and the higher-layer prototype L2CA_ConfigReq request packet is used to carry configuration requests. Its associated response is contained within the L2CA_ConfigRsp packet; an L2CA_ConfigRspNeg packet is used to denote a negative response during configuration where, for example, the

Table 7-22   The PSM values that are used to identify the higher-layer protocol.

PSM	DESCRIPTION
0x0001	SDP
0x0003	RFCOMM
0x0005	TCS-BIN
0x0007	TCS-BIN-CORDLESS

Table 7-23 The CIDs that are used to represent the logical channel.

CID	DESCRIPTION
0x0000	Null
0x0001	Signalling Channel
0x0002	Connectionless Reception Channel
0x0003 to 0x003F	Reserved
0x0040 to 0xFFFF	Dynamically Allocated

suggested *Maximum Transmission Unit* (MTU) is too large. In Table 7-20, we have iden-tified that the MTU and *Flush Timeout* parameters are mandatory, whereas the QoS is optional.

The default MTU setting for the signalling channel is 48-bytes, whereas other chan-nels may be capable of transferring larger payloads; essentially, the MTU determines the size of payloads that are capable of being exchanged between two devices. During config-uration, the local device will inform the remote device that it is potentially capable of ac-cepting larger payloads. If the remote device is unwilling to accept a larger MTU, then the local device is informed with the response contained within the L2CA_ConfigRspNeg packet.

When L2CA_ request and response packets are being exchanged, the Flush Time-out parameter is used to determine how long the local device is prepared to continue to transmit an L2CAP fragment before it gives up; the packet is subsequently flushed or, in other words, discarded. The suggested Flush Timeout value is sent during the L2CA_ ConfigReq request packet. However, if no value is set, then the default value is used. The Headset Profile uses the default value of 0xFFFF.

As we have already mentioned, the QoS configuration is optional, but if it is used during an L2CA_ConfigReq request then the *best effort* service is established as a de-fault; the available services that are supported during an L2CAP channel are shown in Table 7-24. However, if the QoS is set at *Guaranteed,* then parameters such *Token Rate*, *Token Bucket*, *Peak Bandwidth*, *Latency* and *Delay Variation*, are used to determine an acceptable guaranteed service, where the L2CA_ConnectRspNeg will indicate that these values are unacceptable. These parameters are then subject to further negotiation.

7.5.1.5 Link Manager. The *Link Manager* (LM) layer sits between the HCI and the LC, although on a host-less system the LM will have direct interaction with L2CAP. It accepts commands from HCI and translates them into operations for the LC, where ACL and SCO links are created and established. It is during this stage of ACL and SCO estab-lishment that a master-slave switch would be performed as governed by the requirements of this profile. The LM is also responsible for placing the device into a low-power mode, which includes *hold*, *sniff* and *park*.

Table 7-24   The range of service definitions that are used during QoS.

SERVICE	DESCRIPTION
No Traffic	This indicates that the channel will not be sending any traffic and, as such, any parameters can be ignored.
Best Effort	This default value attempts to achieve a minimum service with the remote device, where no guarantees are offered.
Guaranteed	With this service definition, we indicate that we wish to achieve the maximum bandwidth permitted. This, of course, is subject to the nature of a wireless environment.

In providing *general* error management, devices that operate mandatory procedures during interoperability must either acknowledge their support or provide a suitable reason for failure. The LMP_Detach PDU is used to inform the device of the error that occurred; typically, the reason *unsupported LMP feature* (0x1A) is reported (see Appendix A).

In our following discussion, we take an opportunity to explore the dependencies that make up the Headset Profile, where we provide a narrative of the capabilities that are expected from this layer. These are identified in Table 7-25; in the following subsections, we discuss the specific procedures in more detail.

7.5.1.5.1   Capabilities.   Table 7-25 summarises the broad capabilities that are expected from the LM and in the table you will notice procedures are marked appropriately; these will determine what is expected from the procedures at the LM. What has been included in the table is a set of profile deviations.

7.5.1.5.2   SCO Links.   A SCO link is set up using the HCI_Add_SCO_Connection command (see Table 7-26), where a series of Voice_Setting parameters are used to denote the type of SCO channel and the audio coding schemes. The Voice_Setting parameters are written using the HCI_Write_Voice_Setting command and are shown in Table 7-27.

It is assumed that the partying devices have an existing ACL communications link, where pairing, authentication and encryption (if required) have already taken place. The ACL Connection_Handle parameter is used, in part, to then create our SCO connection using the HCI_Add_SCO_Connection command.

Although the host controller generates a Command_Status event, it does not indicate that the SCO connection has been created. The host controller for both devices uses the Connection_Complete event to notify both hosts whether the SCO connection

Table 7-25 The mandatory requirements that are required for a compliant Headset Profile.

PROCEDURES	SUPPORT
SCO Links	M

has been successful or not, where the new `Connection_Handle` and `Link_Type` identify the new connection. You may also wish to note that the `Packet_Type` parameter is used to specify the type of high quality voice transmission, where `HV1`, `HV2` or `HV3` can be requested over the SCO link.

The `Voice_Setting` parameters are shown in more detail in Table 7-28; the parameters make use of two bytes, but only the first ten bits are useful. The `HCI_Write_Voice_Setting` command also returns a `Status` of whether the command succeeded or not. The `Voice_Setting` parameters define the behaviour of all SCO connections that are active between partying devices.

7.5.1.6 Link Controller. The LC layer is the lowest-layer depicted in the dependencies of this profile. Furthermore, the LC is responsible for a large number of core capabilities. It manages air-to-interface transactions and determines the fundamental tim-

Table 7-26 The command and event that are used in combination to create a SCO connection. The Host Controller first sends the `Command_Status` event, but when the connection has been established the `Connection_Complete` event is generated on both devices.

COMMAND	PARAMETERS
HCI_Add_SCO_Connection	Connection_Handle
	Packet_Type
EVENT	**PARAMETERS**
Command_Status	Status
	Num_HCI_Command_Packets
	Command_OpCode
Connection_Complete	Status
	Connection_Handle
	BD_ADDR
	Link_Type
	Encryption_Mode

Table 7-27   The commands and events that are used in combination to write the voice setting parameters for a SCO link.

COMMAND	PARAMETERS
HCI_Write_Voice_Setting	Voice_Setting
EVENT	**PARAMETERS**
Command_Complete	Num_HCI_Command_Packets Command_OpCode Return_Parameters

ing of ACL and SCO data packet transmission and reception, as well as coordinating effort at its upper-edge with the LM. It also encompasses the management of the various
packet types and the various inquiry and paging procedures that are available. The following subsections provide clarity with regard to the capabilities that are required at the LM
level for the Headset Profile. In our understanding of the dependencies, we begin by ex-

Table 7-28   The Voice_Setting parameters that are used to define the behaviour of all
active SCO connections.

										PARAMETERS
9	**8**	**7**	**6**	**5**	**4**	**3**	**2**	**1**	**0**	**Bit # of Voice Setting Parameters**
0	0	0	0	0	0	0	0	0	0	Linear
0	0	0	0	0	0	0	0	0	1	μ-Law Baseband Coding
0	0	0	0	0	0	0	0	1	0	A-Law Baseband Coding
0	0	0	0	0	0	0	0	0	0	1's Complement
0	0	0	0	0	0	0	1	0	0	2's Complement
0	0	0	0	0	0	1	0	0	0	Sign-magnitude
0	0	0	0	0	0	0	0	0	0	8-bit Input for Linear PCM
0	0	0	0	0	1	0	0	0	0	16-bit Input for Linear PCM
0	0	x	x	x	0	0	0	0	0	Used for denoting the PCM Bit Offset
0	0	0	0	0	0	0	0	0	0	CVSD air-coding format
0	1	0	0	0	0	0	0	0	0	μ-Law air-coding format
1	0	0	0	0	0	0	0	0	0	A-Law air coding format

amining in more detail the supported capabilities. If you are a developer providing pro-file-specific applications, then it is doubtful that you will engage in much of this compo-nent, although in some audio-related applications direct access may be required, where a faster transport mechanism can be supported. Nevertheless, many manufacturers have ar-chitected an audio-specific API for a intelligible access to this component.

7.5.1.6.1   Capabilities.   Table 7-29 summarises the broad capabilities that are ex-pected from the LC and in the table you will notice features are marked with *M* (Manda-tory), *O* (Optional), *X* (Excluded), *C* (Conditional) and *N/A* (Not Applicable); these dictate the feature expectations at the LC.

7.5.1.6.1.1   INQUIRY AND INQUIRY SCAN.   An inquiry procedure is used to learn of the other devices in radio range, where the BD_ADDR and clock offsets are obtained; it is DeviceA that will enter an *inquiry substate* to perform this procedure. A device that wishes to be discovered (DeviceB) will enter an *inquiry scan substate*, where the device will respond with an *inquiry response*. In this state, DeviceB is waiting to receive an *In-quiry Access Code* (IAC). From an application perspective, these modes of operation are discussed in more detail in the *Generic Access Profile*, Chapter 2. It is here that specific rules are determined with regard to the behaviour of such devices and how long these de-vices can operate in such modes. When devices have been discovered, this information is passed over to the *Service Discovery Application Profile*, Chapter 3, which manages the specific attributes that make up that device. What is being established here, as a depen-dency, is that the Bluetooth protocol stack must encompass and support such behavioural procedures for this profile to be considered compliant.

7.5.1.6.1.2   PAGING AND PAGING SCAN.   The *inquiry substate* and *inquiry scan substate* procedures are the initial methods used to learn of other devices in radio range; to this extent, the device has discovered sufficient information to gain a connection with the

Table 7-29   The summary of capabilities that are required for the LC to enable a compliant Headset Profile.

PROCEDURES	AG	HS
Inquiry	M	X
Inquiry Scan	X	M
Paging	M	X
Page Scan	X	M
Packet Types	M	M
Voice Codecs	M	M

remote device. This is achieved when DeviceA has the intent to create a connection with DeviceB; DeviceA is now placed into a *paging substate*, where it will periodically transmit the *Device Access Code* (DAC). The DAC is used to target the device directly and the clock offset is used to gain an idea of the clock cycle of DeviceB. These parameters were originally obtained during our inquiry procedures. If DeviceB wishes to be connected, then it will enter a *page scan substate* and will respond accordingly to DeviceA. An inquiry procedure may be avoided if the BD_ADDR is already known, although a connection may take a little longer if the clock offset is not known.

     7.5.1.6.1.3 PACKET TYPES. There are numerous packet types available and Table 7-30 identifies those most often used for profile support. There are also a number of *common* packet types that are used for general purpose transport; for example, the ID packet is used for inquiry procedures and a POLL packet would be sent by DeviceA to determine if a slave is active on a channel.

     The DM1 packet type is used to transmit control data over any connection, but it may be used to transport a genuine payload. HV1, HV2, and HV3 are various SCO packet types to carry audio-specific data, where a DV packet can combine ACL and SCO specific data; their support in this profile is reflected in Table 7-30. Various ACL packet types are also available; in fact, seven types including the DM1 type are attributed to carrying user-specific data. These include DH1, DM3, DH3, DM5, DH5, and AUX1; similarly, Table 7-30 summarises their support in this profile.

Table 7-30   The summary of packet types that are required for the LC to enable a compliant Headset Profile.

PACKET TYPE	AG	HS
DM1	M	M
DH1	M	M
DM3	M	M
DH3	M	M
DM5	M	M
DH5	M	M
HV1	M	M
HV2	M	M
HV3	M	M
DV	O	O

Table 7-31   The summary of voice codec schemes available for voice-related profiles.

VOICE CODEC	AG	HS
CVSD	M	M
A-Law	M	M
μ-Law	M	M

7.5.1.6.1.4   VOICE CODECS.   Table 7-31 summarises voice codec support in this profile. Voice coding schemes are used to provide compression and to overcome potential errors in the data transmission. CVSD provides the second scheme, which is particularly efficient for voice communication; it also tolerates potential errors in the audio data. The PCM has two types of logarithmic compression; these are A-law and μ-law, where either compression technique can be applied on the voice channels over the air-interface.

7.6   SUMMARY

- The Headset Profile purports to define the ideal of the *Ultimate Headset*.
- A headset may comprise a small unit with limited functionality allowing the user to establish and accept incoming calls.
- Other headset models may incorporate the Voice Recognition function to enable further outgoing call capabilities.
- There is some overlap of functionality with the Car Hands-Free Profile.
- Some functionality is still provided on the AG.
- The Headset Profile must support SCO links, with the provision of audio CODEC support.
- There are two types of audio CODEC support provided within Bluetooth applications: PCM (A-law and μ-law) and CVSD.
- The AG device discovers the headset and may be prompted to supply a Bluetooth Passkey.
- The Headset Profile is built upon the Generic Access and Serial Port Profiles.
- AT commands are used to provide control.

8

The Dial-up
Networking Profile

8.1 INTRODUCTION

We are becoming more and more mobile in our use of data connectivity and the ability to access information on the move is now as important as being in the office with everything on hand. The Dial-up Networking Profile provides the ability for a user to remotely connect to their data services; for example, to gain access to an *Internet Service Provider* (ISP) or to access the corporate *Local Area Network* (LAN).

It is certainly not a new concept, but the introduction of a *wireless Internet bridge* is used to remove the need to physically connect your mobile phone or modem to a notebook or *Personal Digital Assistant* (PDA). The profile provides the capability of a *data terminal* (DT) device to form a wireless bridge with a *gateway* (GW). Once the connection with the remote service has been established, an Internet bridge is then created. Figure 8-1 and Figure 8-2 show the various scenarios that are supported by this profile.

The profile does not make the range of Internet-related protocols explicit [such as, *Transmission Control Protocol* (TCP), *Internet Protocol* (IP) and *Point-to-Point Protocol* (PPP)] and places no restriction on their use. This is solely due to the fact that the Dial-up Networking Profile outlines the capability to enable the wireless bridge. Indirectly, the Internet-related protocols are supported through various dial-up type applications. There are also numerous similarities to the *LAN Access Profile*; these are explained in the following section.

Figure 8-1   The dial-up networking usage model allows the notebook to behave as our data terminal device; where it can create a wireless
bridge with the mobile phone, which then acts as our gateway.

8.1.1   Comparing Dial-up Networking with the LAN Access Profile

One question often asked is: *what are the differences between the Dial-up Networking
and the LAN Access Profiles,* Chapter 10? In reality, there is little difference between the
two: both profiles depend upon the Serial Port Profile; both enable an IP stack to be supported and both require a PPP implementation. The subtlety in comparison exists primarily in how the Bluetooth link is established; take a look at Figure 8-3. It shows the
components of the *modem driver* and the *modem emulator*, which sit within the data terminal and gateway, respectively. Essentially, the modem component completes a direct
serial cable connection between the DT and GW, forming a wireless bridge. Whereas, the
LAN Access Profile provides the direct services of a LAN through a *LAN Access Point*
(LAP).

The circumstances that determine the different usage can be best illustrated by considering a user sitting in an office where a fixed[1] access point is readily available and

Figure 8-2   In this illustration, the dial-up networking usage model allows
the notebook to behave as our data terminal device; it can create
a wireless bridge with the wireless modem, which then acts as
our gateway.

---

[1]The current v1.1 specification restricts the mobility of a user. In this current state, the user is fixed in one location or in radio range, where the access point resides. However, in the Bluetooth PAN Working Group, a hand-
off technique is currently being architected to allow users to maintain that one, initial connection.

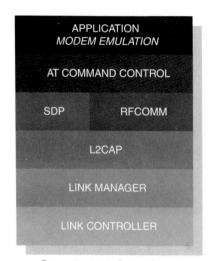

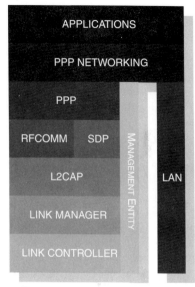

Figure 8-3   The components of the Dial-up Networking and LAN Access
Profiles are shown to illustrate the subtle difference between the
two. The same applications can be used for both profiles.

where the user can make use of the services available via a LAP. However, in the Dial-up
Networking instance, a user may use his or her mobile phone to access those same services across a public telephone network and is not reliant upon a static location. Essentially, the two profiles provide greater flexibility and mobility depending on your current
situation.

The PPP implementation in both profiles is similar and sets out to achieve the same
goals, but the Dial-up Networking Profile requires the use of AT commands to enable
control and dialling. We discuss this aspect of the profile in more detail later on in this
chapter.

8.2   USAGE MODELS

This section now considers our existing usage models through scenarios that may be typical for the Dial-up Networking Profile. We begin by exploring the existing models, where
a notebook or PDA communicates with a mobile phone or wireless modem to obtain a
dial-up service.

The scenarios provided in Figure 8-1 and Figure 8-2 represent our existing usage
models. The role of a notebook or PDA acting as a DT initiates a one-to-one communications link with another Bluetooth-enabled device where it takes on the role of a GW. The

formation of a wireless Internet bridge is created which, in turn, completes the connection. The formation of a wireless bridge between the notebook and PDA (or modem) demonstrates the fundamental Bluetooth philosophy, that is, *removing the need for cables*.[2] A dial-up application on the DT is used to initiate the dial-up connection, with the Bluetooth application serving as the underlying transport. In the following section, we provide clarification on the notion of a wireless Internet bridge and explain how it fits within the Dial-up Networking Profile.

8.2.1 The Wireless Bridge

A wireless bridge is used here to describe the nature of the cableless connection between the DT and GW; this is fundamental to and dominates the profile. Earlier in our introduction, we touched upon the need to connect a cable between a notebook and a mobile phone. This scenario allows the notebook (DT) to perform a dial-up connection through the mobile phone (GW) and then on to a remote service. In this instance, we will access the services provided by an ISP.

To support this profile, a *two-piece* Bluetooth protocol stack is required to complete the wireless bridge. In Figure 8-4, we can see what components of the stack are needed to form the DT and GW wireless relationship. Both the Dial-up Networking and Fax Profiles require the use of the AT Command component, which in turn controls the GW.

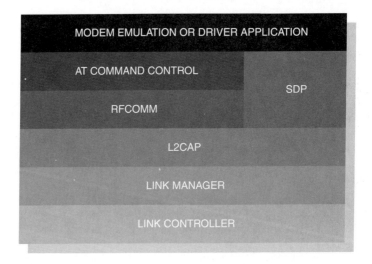

Figure 8-4 This model shows the combination of dial-up networking and facsimile services that are realised in the Bluetooth protocol stack. Essentially, this forms our two-piece stack.

---

[2]The wireless bridge concept is not new. Existing technologies, such as infra-red (IR), provide the ability to communicate with a GW in much the same way as Bluetooth-enabled devices. The advantage of a Bluetooth enabled device is that it does not have to be in line-of-site with the DT; the mobile phone, for example, may be placed in a pocket or kept in a briefcase.

8.2.2   The Internet Bridge

Once our wireless bridge has been successfully established, the dial-up application on the DT would take part in PPP authentication and would subsequently, upon successful negotiation, allow the user to gain access to the services provided. The Internet Bridge is used to describe the complete and successful connection between the DT and the remote services transported via the GW.

8.3   PROFILE PRINCIPLES

The Dial-up Networking Profile provides two new roles: a DT device and a GW device. The GW provides the ability for a DT to connect and to provide remote services; this is achieved by providing modem emulation, where AT commands are used to enable control and dialling. The modem emulation and driver are provided above RFCOMM, where RF-COMM provides serial port capabilities by emulating RS232; see the *Serial Port Profile*, Chapter 6, for more detailed information. The DT incorporates a dial-up networking application, housing the range of networking protocols such as PPP, IP and TCP. Figure 8-5 demonstrates the architecture of the components that would make up the complete dial-up networking model.

In a similar structure to the *LAN Access Profile*, Chapter 10, the DT would incorporate a PPP Client and the remote service would incorporate a PPP Server. This would provide the PPP authentication for accessing the network.

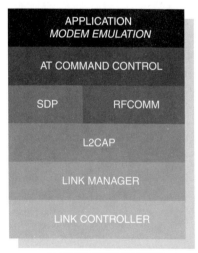
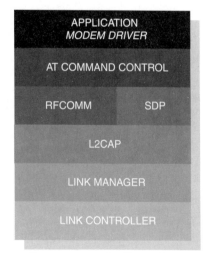

Figure 8-5   The core components of the Bluetooth protocol stack are shown, illustrating how the components of the Dial-up Networking Profile are integrated.

Table 8-1   The list of behavioural characteristics that are typical for this profile.

CONFIGURATION	ROLE	DESCRIPTION
DeviceA	DT	A device acting as a data terminal, which may take the form of a notebook or PDA. In this particular context, the device is described as initiating the connection with the accepting device.
	Initiator	This configuration describes the device that instigates the original connection or the device that wishes to initiate communication over an existing link.
DeviceB	GW	A device that behaves as a gateway, where it manages incoming and outgoing external communication though AT Command control signalling. It is also the party that accepts incoming connections from the data terminal.
	Acceptor	This configuration describes the process of the device accepting the initiated communication from DeviceA.

In Table 8-1, clarification is provided with regard to the roles used within the context of this profile. In general, *DeviceA* represents the initiating party and *DeviceB* represents the accepting party. The terms are often used interchangeably when describing specific operations and are provided here for reference.

In this chapter, the DT is referred to as DeviceA, or the initiator; and the GW is the acceptor and forms DeviceB; DeviceA will remain master, since the GW is permitted to accept only one connection. A GW device is considered to be the *Data Circuit Endpoint* (DCE) and the DT takes the *Data Terminal Equipment* (DTE) role in this conventional mapping.

8.4   USER EXPECTATIONS

8.4.1   Data Terminal

Today, we can openly source products that are capable of supporting the Dial-up Networking Profile; these can be typically found within a PDA, notebook or mobile phone. If you recall from our earlier discussion, the Dial-up Networking Profile is essentially a two-piece solution.

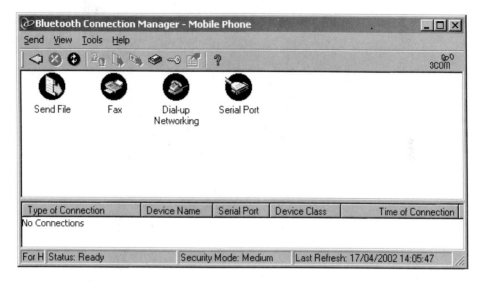

Figure 8-6   The screen shot shows a typical set of attributes that may be seen
when discovering GWs (the 3Com Bluetooth Connection Man-
ager has discovered the services available from a mobile phone).

Bluetooth Profiles supports the general philosophy of a good user experience.
Therefore, it is important to consider how the user would experience the connection and
use of a GW. In later sections, we consider the specific experiences of connecting, terminating and losing connections and how the user may experience such operations.

We will consider the typical attributes that may make up a service discovery of a
GW. The user experience in this particular example is a screen shot from the DT, which
clearly shows that the mobile phone is capable of supporting dial-up networking (see
Figure 8-6).

8.4.1.1   Connecting to a Gateway.   The GW as a mobile phone should be initially enabled, where parameters such as limited discovery and range can be defined; this
would help limit unauthorised access to the GW. As a wireless modem, similar security
features can be employed in addition to the passkey requirement.

In both instances, a passkey would be requested to enable authentication of the DT
and GW. There may be other instances where the passkey may have to be provided, again
possibly due to connection timeouts and/or the mobile phone being re-enabled for dial-up
use. It may be recommended that a timeout occur after a defined period to, again, ensure
and help with unauthorised access. Previously, we touched upon the ability of the GW to
only accept a connection from one DT at any time. This feature restricts use from other
intruders—suffice to say that if it is being used by you, then there is a strong possibility
that it is not being used by anyone else.

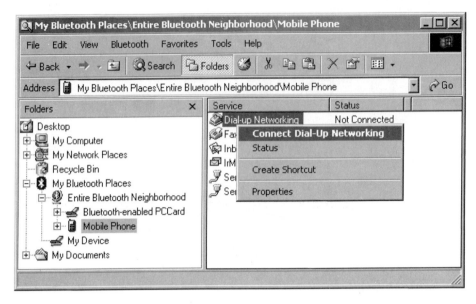

Figure 8-7   Right-clicking the devices icon causes a pop-up menu to appear
                  offering the ability to connect to the device; in this illustration,
                  we can see the user connecting to a service which is offering
                  dial-up networking capabilities. (Courtesy of TDK Systems
                  Europe.)

Once the user has the ability to connect to a device, he or she may continue to make
use of the services it provides. By using a double-click[3] or right-click, the user begins the
process of connecting to the dial-up networking service. This is shown in Figure 8-7.

Prior to using the GW, a user may be required to enter a Bluetooth Passkey. In Figure 8-8, we show the user being prompted with a dialog box requesting the entry of a
passkey.

Underlying all of this high-level user interaction is a sequence of events, which lead
up to the moment of connection. Figure 8-9 illustrates the message sequences that typically occur during a connection set-up. Other implementations may differ slightly, depending upon the user's specific requirements.[4]

During connection establishment, the user may be informed of the dial-up as it progresses. In Figure 8-10, we show the user being informed of the progress of the dial-up

---

[3]The double-click and right-click operations refer to a mouse that is connected to your client device (in this example, a PC or notebook computer running a Microsoft Windows operating system) and where both operations
trigger the same method of access. It is noted that an operation may vary from device to device and, as such, the
number of buttons may vary on a mouse and indeed no mouse may be connected. The example just draws your
attention to how it may be possible and acknowledges that implementations may differ.

[4]The flexibility of the Bluetooth protocol stack, in particular the various HCI and LMP commands available,
allows various methods of creating a successful ACL connection. The text refers to one particular example of a
connection set-up.

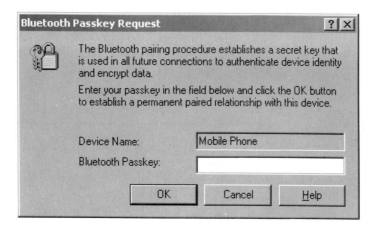

Figure 8-8 The user is requested to enter his or her passkey to authenticate with the GW device.

connection. In Figure 8-11, we now illustrate that the user is being prompted to enter a username and password; this is to comply with PPP authentication.

In Figure 8-12, we now show that PPP authentication is being verified with the remote service; Figure 8-13 shows the registering of the connected computer onto the remote network.

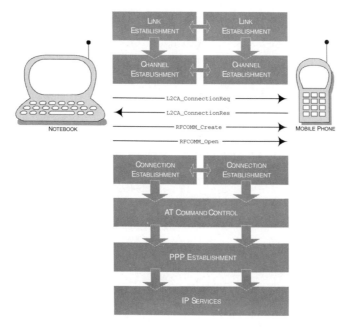

Figure 8-9 The events which takes place during a connection with a DT and a GW.

Figure 8-10 The connection has successfully progressed to the next level;
here, the user is now informed of the GW actually dialling the
service. (Courtesy of TDK Systems Europe.)

8.4.1.2 Ending a Connection with a Gateway. Once a connection is established
with a GW and its services are no longer required, the user may terminate the session. As
shown in Figure 8-14, the user is able to double-click or right-click on the connected device's icon and select disconnect from the pop-up menu to terminate the connection.

Other forms of disconnection may occur if the quality-of-service (QoS) can no
longer be maintained by the remote service; an instance of this specific example may

Figure 8-11 The dial-up connection was successful, and now the user
is prompted to enter their username and password.
(Courtesy of TDK Systems Europe.)

Figure 8-12   The username and password for PPP authentication is being
verified by the remote network. (Courtesy of TDK Systems
Europe.)

Figure 8-13   PPP authentication was successful. The computer can now be
registered with the remote network. (Courtesy of TDK Systems
Europe.)

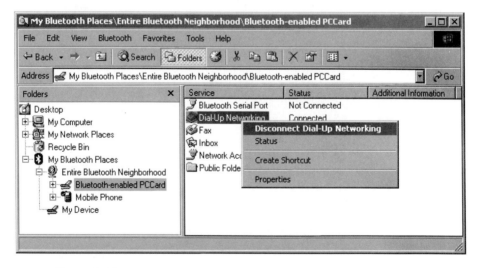

Figure 8-14   Right-clicking the device's icon causes a pop-up menu to appear
offering the ability to disconnect. In this illustration, we can see
the user disconnecting from the dial-up service which, in turn,
will disconnect the GW. (Courtesy of TDK Systems Europe.)

occur when the remote network to which the GW is connected is unexpectedly lost. It is important to remember in such a situation that the appropriate information about the current connection must be conveyed to the user, since the DT may offer a reconnection at a later time.

One other such instance of a terminated connection may occur when a connection is lost due to the DT moving out of range from a GW. Section 8.4.1.3, *Losing a Connection with a GW*, looks at the sequence of events surrounding this possibility and considers how the user should experience this event.

8.4.1.3   Losing a Connection with a Gateway.   It is hard to imagine an instance where a connection would be lost with a GW. However, if the GW is taken out of radio range, or the carrier is unexpectedly lost, then the DT must be able to appropriately manage the user interface aspects and, of course, the application should eventually allow the user to reconnect at a later stage.

In Figure 8-15, the device status is clearly shown when right-clicking the device icon to select its properties. As we saw in an earlier illustration, the device status is also shown alongside the icon (see Figure 8-7). A seamless reconnection can be achieved if both the DT and GW remember their previous respective sessions, where the reconnection time can be dramatically reduced.

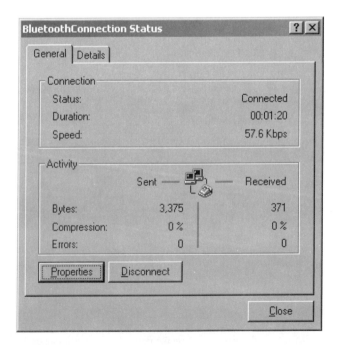

Figure 8-15   The user has chosen to query the device status. (Courtesy of TDK Systems Europe.)

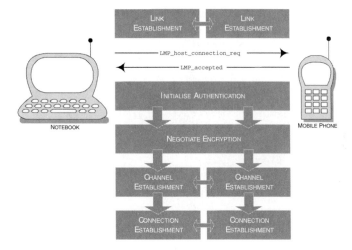

Figure 8-16   The events that place during an incoming connection from a DT.

8.4.2   Gateway

The simplicity of a mobile phone as a GW enables the user to place it in an area where it does not need to be in direct line-of-sight with your PDA or notebook, although it should be within suitable radio range. One classic and most often referred to example is the *brief-case trick*. Here, the user can place the GW into a briefcase or a jacket pocket and make use of the services discreetly. Similarly, wireless modems can be fixed in any location.

   8.4.2.1   Accepting a Connection from a DT.   The GW undertakes a series of events that enable a DT to successfully access its service; Figure 8-16 illustrates these events. When a DT wishes to connect to a GW it initiates bonding, where the GW must accept this request; encryption may also be used on the link.

   8.4.2.2   Refusing a Connection from a DT.   The GW would refuse a connection from a DT in such an instance where the GW refuses to accept bonding, or when an incorrect passkey has been entered. A connection may also be refused if the PPP authentication was unsuccessful.

8.5   LIFTING THE LID

8.5.1   Dependencies

Now that we have covered aspects of existing and future usage models and their respective user expectations, lets take an opportunity to explore in greater depth the dependencies of which this particular profile is comprised. In Figure 8-17 we provide a conceptual

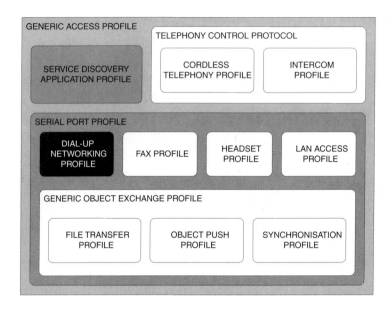

Figure 8-17 The dependent components of the Bluetooth protocol stack that make up the Dial-up Networking Profile. The areas that are shaded are relevant to this profile.

illustration representing the dependencies that make up the Dial-up Networking Profile; the areas that are shaded are relevant to this profile. In this instance, the profile depends upon the basic functionality offered to us by the *Generic Access Profile*, Chapter 2, the *Service Discovery Application Profile*, Chapter 3 and the *Serial Port Profile*, Chapter 6. We now move on to explore the core requirements of these dependent components and reflect upon any variances from their original functionality that may occur.

8.5.1.1 Generic Access. The Dial-up Networking Profile relies upon the capabilities provided by the *Generic Access Profile*, Chapter 2. In our earlier chapter we learned that a level of basic functionality is achieved through establishing a set of rules and procedures. These rules govern the behaviour of such devices and relate to their connectivity, discoverability and common characteristics at the user interface level, with some additional emphasis provided for security. Commonality is established between products through the use of these rules and procedures, resulting in a positive user experience.

Now let's take a look at the behavioural aspects of Bluetooth-enabled devices as outlined by the *Generic Access Profile*, Chapter 2.

In Table 8-2, the basic set of procedures is illustrated identifying functional expectations which, in turn, govern its operation. These procedures help determine the context within which the device would operate.

Table 8-2   The core set of procedures as required by most profiles.

PROCEDURES	DESCRIPTION
Discoverability Mode	This mode prescribes the overall discoverability of a device, allowing it to be placed into a non-discoverable, limited, or general discoverable mode. This mode would allow devices to become generally available to other users or they can be restricted to personal use.
Connectability Mode	When determining a baseband connectable state, this mode is used to place a device into a connectable or non-connectable mode.
Pairing	Pairable and non-pairable modes are used to realise the security aspects when operating or intending to use a device. A device may require authentication and, as such, the user would be required to enter a Bluetooth Passkey. The pairing procedure starts the link key generation process which, in turn, allows authentication to take place.

In Table 8-3, we consider the specific set of operations that are required for this profile. In the table you will notice features are marked with *M* (Mandatory), *O* (Optional), *X* (Excluded), *C* (Conditional) and *N/A* (Not Applicable); these will determine what is expected from the features of the Generic Access Profile.

Security is an important aspect for Bluetooth-enabled devices. Table 8-4 identifies the security requirements for this profile. The *Generic Access Profile*, Chapter 2, taught

Table 8-3   The illustration shows specific modes of operation that this profile depends upon to realise its compliant implementation.

MODES	DT	GW
Non-discoverable	N/A	O
Limited Discoverable	N/A	O
General Discoverable	N/A	O
Non-connectable	N/A	X
Connectable	N/A	M
Non-pairable	M	O
Pairable	O	M

us that Security Mode 1 is a non-secure mode, where Bluetooth-enabled devices will never initiate any security procedures. Security Modes 2 and 3 initiate different levels of security at various stages of connection. In this instance, the profile mandates that support should be provided for at least Security Mode 2 or 3.

Finally, in our consideration of the basic rules and procedures that are required from the Generic Access Profile, we consider the idle mode procedures, which outline behavioural characteristics when DeviceA chooses to initiate them against DeviceB. The procedures that are listed in Table 8-5 provide a clearly indicates how a device should operate when performing such an activity; let us take our bonding procedure as an example. The term bonding is very much associated with the pairing process; however, bonding occurs when the user has the *intent* to initiate a trusted relationship with DeviceB.

With this intent, the user is prompted to enter a Bluetooth Passkey. This, in turn, instigates the pairing process, that is, the generation of the link keys, where subsequent authentication can then occur. In summary, there are a specific set of events associated with a procedure and, in the *Generic Access Profile*, Chapter 2, we further explore how each procedure is conducted.

The provision of a well structured FHS packet is the mechanism for device discoverability and this is shown in Figure 8-18. This packet is used to identify the remote device, where information such as BD_ADDR and clock offsets is determined. You may also notice from this packet that the *Class of Device* (CoD) field is also provided. This information is relayed to the user interface which, in turn, provides common characteristics about discovered devices. During the discovery mechanism the CoD is used to learn more about the type of device and what it may be capable of providing. This structure of information is depicted in Figure 8-19 and is made up of 3 bytes (or 24-bits as shown). The following sections now consider the Dial-up Networking attributes, which will ultimately make use of the *Service, Major* and *Minor Device Classes* fields.

8.5.1.1.1 Service Class. This high-level form of defining a Bluetooth device identifies where in the Service Class field the Dial-up Networking Profile resides; see

Table 8-4 The illustration shows specific security procedures that this profile depends upon to realise its compliant implementation.

PROCEDURE	DT	GW
Authentication	M	M
Security Mode 1	N/A	X
Security Mode 2	C	C
Security Mode 3	C	C

Table 8-5   The illustration shows specific behavioural procedures that this profile depends upon to realise its compliant implementation.

PROCEDURE	DT	GW
General Inquiry	M	N/A
Limited Inquiry	O	N/A
Name Discovery	O	N/A
Device Discovery	O	N/A
Bonding	M	M

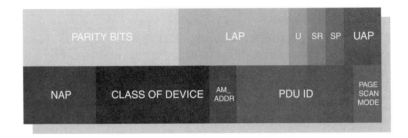

Figure 8-18   The structure of the FHS packet used only for reference to illustrate the position of the Class of Device structure.

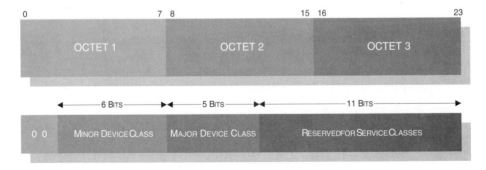

Figure 8-19   The structure of the class of device, illustrating the Minor Device, Major Device and Service Class fields and their respective lengths.

Table 8-6   The Service Class categorisation for the Dial-up Networking Profile.

											SERVICE CLASS
23	22	21	20	19	18	17	16	15	14	13	Bit # of CoD
0	1	0	0	0	0	0	0	0	0	0	Telephony

Table 8-6 which, in turn, determines the category of service; here, the category of service falls within *Telephony*.

    8.5.1.1.2   Major Device Class.   This high-level form of defining a Bluetooth device identifies where in the Major Device Class the Dial-up Networking Profile resides; see Table 8-7 which, in turn, determines the major class grouping. Here, the category falls within phone, since a mobile phone providing modem emulation may be used.

    8.5.1.1.3   Minor Device Class.   The Minor Device Class in this profile is used to convey further contexts for the setting within the major class grouping, see Table 8-8. Here, the bit may be set appropriately for *Mobile Phone* or *Wireless Modem* to denote the type of service available to the user.

    8.5.1.2   Service Discovery.   In the *Service Discovery Application Profile*, Chapter 3, we introduced the characteristics of the mechanisms used to retrieve service information from a remote device. Typically, a client will initiate inquiry and discovery procedures in order to learn of the devices in radio range. A client would then make use of an application, which would embody the functionality of the underlying *Service Discovery Protocol* (SDP). The *Service Discovery Application* (SrvDscApp) uses an *SDP Client* to instigate a request to the remote device, where the *SDP Server* will respond; as such, the DT and GW must employ the use of an SDP client and server, respectively, as illustrated in Table 8-9.

    PDUs are used to instruct the SDP server to undertake browsing procedures and to retrieve service record information; you may recall that these PDUs carry payloads about requests containing `AttributeIDs` and `AttributeValues` describing what exactly is being sought. As we previously discussed, the client and server operate a request

Table 8-7   The Major Device Class for the Dial-up Networking Profile.

					MAJOR DEVICE CLASS
12	11	10	9	8	Bit # of CoD
0	0	0	1	0	Phone

Table 8-8   The Minor Device Class for the Dial-up Networking Profile.

						MINOR DEVICE CLASS
7	6	5	4	3	2	Bit # of CoD
0	0	0	0	0	1	Mobile Phone
0	0	0	1	0	0	Wireless Modem

and response paradigm. SDAP will construct PDUs containing information relating to the `AttributeID` and `AttributeValues`, which, in turn, instruct the server to carry out its operation. The various request and response PDUs required are shown in Table 8-10, where features indicated are described as mandatory (M), optional (O) and excluded (X).

A service record is maintained for each service a device is capable of supporting and, as such, a *Service Record Handle* is created to uniquely identify this. The `Service-RecordHandle` is a 32-bit unsigned integer and is stored on the SDP server. The service record shown in Table 8-11 identifies a GW device and provides a list of `AttributeIDs`, which ultimately identify the service for the Dial-up Networking Profile. A minimum of two attributes are required to make a service record; these are `ServiceRecordHandle`, and a `ServiceClassIDList`, where it must contain at least one `UUID`.

When browsing for services on the remote device, a local device constructs a search pattern using a *Universally Unique Identifier* (UUID). A UUID is a 128-bit value, which has been shortened for use within Bluetooth applications. The shortcut has been provided by first establishing a *Bluetooth Base UUID*, which we discussed in the *Service Discovery Application Profile*, Chapter 3.

The UUIDs that have been presented so far in this chapter are aliases and take the form of what is referred to as a 16-bit UUID or a 32-bit UUID but, in turn, they all should refer to the 128-bit notation. These UUIDs have been assigned and can be referenced in the Bluetooth Special Interest Group, Bluetooth Assigned Numbers, v1.1, February 2001. For the search pattern to be successful, they all need to be converted to the 128-bit notation, since they will all be compared at this range. An arithmetic conversion algorithm is used to construct the 128-bit value.

Table 8-9   As a minimum, the local device must support the use of a client application and the remote device must support the use of a server.

FEATURE	DT	GW
SDP Client	M	X
SDP Server	X	M

The list of PDUs that are required for the operation of the Dial-up Networking Profile.

	DT	GW
~~r_ErrorResponse	X	M
SDP_ServiceSearchRequest	M	X
SDP_ServiceSearchResponse	X	M
SDP_ServiceAttributeRequest	M	X
SDP_ServiceAttributeResponse	X	M
SDP_ServiceSearchAttributeRequest	O	X
SDP_ServiceSearchAttributeRequest	X	O

Table 8-12 summarises the service class UUIDs used to identify the particular profile in use; this also correlates with the identification of the device during a device discovery procedure, as previously outlined in our earlier Section 8.5.1.1, *Generic Access*.

As part of the service record, the dependent underlying protocols are also identified. The local device retrieves this information in order to fully understand the exact requirements needed to fulfil the service. The Dial-up Networking Profile is dependent on the protocols as shown in Table 8-13, which also shows their associated UUID values.

8.5.1.3 RFCOMM. The conceptual and functional nature of RFCOMM was introduced in the *Serial Port Profile,* Chapter 6. In it, we discussed how it provides an emulated serial port presence. Several distinctions were made between the various types of applications. The purpose of making these distinctions was to enable clarification and understanding of RFCOMM's composition. In this particular application context, the creation of an emulated serial port would be transparent to the user. The Dial-up Networking Profile is dependent upon the operation of the Serial Port Profile and as such, is required to establish an emulated serial port as part of its communication link with the remote device.

The term cable replacement application was introduced in our earlier chapter and distinguishes between the different scenarios available. It refers to specific Bluetooth applications that create implicit emulated serial ports, which remain transparent to the user to complete the creation of a communications link.

Specific detail has been provided to illustrate how data is communicated over an emulated serial port connection, whereby a *Data Link Connection* (DLC) is established between two peer devices, namely DT and GW. We have also looked at the fields that make up our service record for this profile. The ProtocolDescriptorList field is used to describe the set of protocols that the profile intends to use and, as such, the RFCOMM protocol identifier contains a parameter, which contains the Server Channel number.

Table 8-11   The list of mandatory and configurable items that make up this profile's service discovery record.

ATTRIBUTE	DESCRIPTION
ServiceRecordHandle	With an `AttributeID` of `0x0000`, this uniquely identifies this service record within the SDP server on the GW device.
ServiceClassIDList ServiceClass0 ServiceClass1	With an `AttributeID` of `0x0001`, the following `ServiceClass0` would contain the `UUID` for the *Dial-up Networking* and the `ServiceClass1` would identify the *Generic Networking* service classes. Their respective `UUID` values are summarised in Table 8-12.
ProtocolDescriptorList Protocol0 Protocol1 ParameterFor1	With an `AttributeID` of `0x0004`, the following `Protocol0` would contain an `UUID` for the protocol *L2CAP*, whereas in `Protocol1` an `UUID` would contain the protocol identifier for *RFCOMM*. Their respective `UUID` values are summarised in Table 8-13. The `ParameterFor1` would contain the relevant server channel number for the RFCOMM transport.
BluetoothProfile- DescriptorList Profile0 ParameterFor0	With an `AttributeID` of `0x0009`, the following `Profile0` would identify the `UUID` for *Dial-up Networking* service class, which is summarised in Table 8-12. The `ParameterFor0` accommodates the version number supported by this profile.
ServiceName	With a base `AttributeID` of `0x0006`, this attribute has an offset of `0x0000`. It is a configurable item and has an `AttributeValue` of a `Text` string, where its default setting is *Dial-up Networking*.
AudioFeedbackSupport	With an `AttributeID` of `0x0305`, this attribute identifies whether or not the GW device is capable of providing audio feedback. The `AttributeValue` is constructed using a `Boolean`, where the default setting is FALSE.

Table 8-12   The list of service classes that match a corresponding profile. This correlates
with our previous Generic Access section.

CLASSES	UUID
Dial-upNetworking	0x1103
GenericNetworking	0x1201

The Server Channel is used in combination with a *Data Link Connection Identifier* (DLCI), which is then used to uniquely identify the active DLC. This connection is then mapped onto a connectionless orientated L2CAP *Channel Identifier* (CID).

In this section we highlight the specific features that are required to realise a compliant Dial-up Networking Profile. Table 8-14 and Table 8-15 illustrate the features or capabilities that are expected from the Serial Port Profile.

The use of the RLS command is encouraged to keep peer devices informed of any state change. In one such instance, an emulated serial port may interface to a Type II application (physical serial port), where overruns or parity errors may occur. An application that makes use of RS232 port configuration parameters should expose these settings through an appropriate API function; this is of particular relevance when interfacing to Type II applications.

8.5.1.3.1   AT Command Control.   In Section 8.3, *Profile Principles,* we introduced an illustration, which identifies the modem emulation and driver components that are created with the help of RFCOMM. It is above this that a dial-up application would reside, using the serial port emulation provided by RFCOMM. The DT and GW would be capable of supporting the commands and responses, as defined in the International Telecommunication Union (ITU-T) Telecommunications Sector v.250.[5] In Table 8-16 and Table 8-17, we identify the supported commands and responses, respectively.

8.5.1.3.2   Call Progress and Audio Feedback.   In our earlier discussion, we introduced the capability of audio feedback, which may be provided during a call progress and is subject to the capability of the GW and DT. If, during a connection establishment, the

Table 8-13   The list of protocols that are used in this profile; their associated UUID values
are also shown.

PROTOCOL	UUID
RFCOMM	0x0003
L2CAP	0x0100

---

[5]The new International Telecommunications Union (ITU-T) Telecommunications Recommendation, Series V: Data Communication over the Telephone Network v.25*ter*, supersedes the original v.250 document.

Table 8-14 The set of capabilities that are required from the initiating party, denoted here by the DT device.

PROCEDURE	DT	GW
Initialise an RFCOMM Session	M	X
Terminate an RFCOMM Session	M	M
Establish a new DLC Connection	M	X
Disconnect a DLC Connection	M	M
Emulate RS232 Control Signals	C	C
Transfer Data	M	M
Test Command	X	X
Flow Control	C	C
RLS	O	O
PN	O	O
RPN	O	O

Table 8-15 The set of capabilities that are required from the responder party, denoted here by the GW device.

PROCEDURE	DT	GW
Initialise an RFCOMM Session	X	M
Terminate an RFCOMM Session	M	M
Establish a new DLC Connection	X	M
Disconnect a DLC Connection	M	M
Emulate RS232 Control Signals	M	M
Transfer Data	N/A	N/A
Test Command	M	M
Flow Control	M	M
RLS	M	M
PN	M	M
RPN	M	M

Table 8-16   The command set that is required and is mandatory for use in the gateway.

COMMAND	DESCRIPTION
&C	Received line signal detector.
&D	Data Terminal Ready
&F	Set to factory defaults
+GCAP	Request complete capabilities list
+GMI	Request manufacturer's identification
+GMM	Request model identification
+GMR	Request revision identification
A	Answer
D	Dial
E	Command Echo
H	Hook control
L	Monitor speaker loudness
M	Monitor speaker mode
O	Return to online data state
P	Select pulse dialling
Q	Result code suppression
S0	Automatic answer
S10	Automatic disconnect delay
S3	Command line termination character
S4	Response formatting character
S5	Command line editing character
S6	Pause before blind dialling
S7	Connection complete timeout
S8	Comma dial modifier time
T	Select tone dialling
V	DCE response format
X	Call progress monitoring control
Z	Reset to default configuration

Table 8-17   The responses that may be produced during any command sequence. These are mandatory implementations for this profile.

RESPONSE	DESCRIPTION
OK	Acknowledges execution of a command as defined in the previous table.
CONNECT	A connection has been established.
RING	The DCE has detected an incoming call signal from the network.
NO CARRIER	The connection has been terminated, or the attempt to establish a connection has failed.
ERROR	An error has occurred during a command operation.
NO DIALTONE	There was no dial tone detected prior to dialling.
BUSY	When a dial attempt was made, the busy signal was detected.

SCO link fails, the call and ACL establishment may still proceed regardless. Furthermore, the GW has the responsibility to manage and establish the SCO connection, see Section 8.5.1.5.2, *SCO Links*.

8.5.1.4   L2CAP.   The L2CAP layer provides transparency for the upper-layers of the stack from the layers typically found within the host controller. L2CAP payloads are passed to the *Host Controller Interface*[6] (HCI), which is then subsequently passed onto the *Link Manager Protocol* (LMP). The range of upper-layers, which include RFCOMM, SDP and the *Telephony Control Protocol Specification* (TCS) all make use of the capabilities offered to us by L2CAP. Its primary role is to provide *protocol multiplexing*, allowing numerous simultaneous connections to be made; it also provides the ability for *segmentation* and *reassembly*. This refers to the ability to manage large payloads in the application, which may need to be fragmented into smaller payloads for the lower-layers to manage; these are then transmitted over the air-interface. Finally, the L2CAP layer exchanges *Quality of Service* (QoS) information, ensuring that sufficient resources are available and that both Bluetooth devices are attaining the best service.

In Table 8-18, we summarise the broad capabilities that are expected from L2CAP. In the table, you will notice features are marked with *M* (Mandatory), *O* (Optional), *X* (Excluded), *C* (Conditional) and *N/A* (Not Applicable); these will determine what is expected from the features at the L2CAP layer.

---

[6]L2CAP payloads are passed directly onto LMP when implemented on a hostless system.

Table 8-18   The illustration shows specific procedures that this profile depends upon to realise its compliant implementation.

PROCEDURE	DT	GW
Connection-orientated Channel	M	M
Connectionless Channel	X	X
Connection Establishment	M	M
Configuration	M	M
Connection Termination	M	M
Echo	M	M
Command Rejection	M	M
Maximum Transmission Unit	M	M
Flush Timeout	M	M
Quality of Service	O	O

8.5.1.4.1   Channel Types.   In Table 8-18, we have identified that *Connection-Orientated Channels* are mandatory, whereas *Connectionless Channels* are excluded; this type of channel is aimed at broadcasting, where all devices may be targeted. L2CAP uses *Protocol Data Units* (PDUs) to transport connection, signalling and configuration options, which will be discussed in a moment. The higher-layers of the Bluetooth protocol stack will instigate a connection with L2CAP using the L2CA_ConnectReq request packet, where the corresponding result is contained within the L2CA_ConnectRsp response packet. An L2CA_ConnectRspNeg negative response packet is used to denote a response, where the connection with the remote device was unsuccessful. Since our profile resides above L2CAP and employs its services, we are only concerned with the upper protocol layer of L2CAP. This higher functionality is offered to us through a series of L2CAP events and is denoted through the prefix L2CA_ (see Table 8-19).

When creating an L2CAP connection between two devices, a *Protocol/Service Multiplexor* (PSM) value is used to denote the higher-layer protocol that is using the connection; Table 8-20 identifies these values and the corresponding protocol they represent. The value of 0x0003 (RFCOMM) is used for this profile.

8.5.1.4.2   Signalling.   When establishing communication with a remote device, a *signalling channel* is created and reserved for use during connection, disconnection and configuration of subsequent L2CAP connections. A *channel* is used to describe the communication and data flow that exists between L2CAP entities and Table 8-21 illustrates the range of CIDs that are used to identify the channel type.

Table 8-19   The range of prototypes used to illustrate how L2CAP is architected and how interaction between higher- and lower-layers is achieved. For this discussion, our concern here is with the higher-layer.

PROTOTYPE	DESCRIPTION
L2CA_	This prefix prototype is used to denote the higher-layer interaction, typically used by RFCOMM, SDP, and TCS
L2CAP_	This prefix is used to denote peer-to-peer signalling interaction of L2CAP entities.
LP_	Finally, this prefix denotes lower-layer interaction, where L2CAP interfaces with the LMP layer.

Table 8-20   The PSM values that are used to identify the higher-layer protocol.

PSM	DESCRIPTION
0x0001	SDP
0x0003	RFCOMM
0x0005	TCS-BIN
0x0007	TCS-BIN-CORDLESS

Table 8-21   The CIDs that are used to represent the logical channel.

CID	DESCRIPTION
0x0000	Null
0x0001	Signalling Channel
0x0002	Connectionless Reception Channel
0x0003 to 0x003F	Reserved
0x0040 to 0xFFFF	Dynamically Allocated

As we can see in Table 8-18, *Connection Establishment* and *Termination* is mandatory in the local device, although the remote device may be capable of initiating and terminating a connection to the local device. The `L2CA_DisconnectReq` request packet is used to terminate the connection with the remote device and an `L2CA_DisconnectRsp` response packet is used to ascertain the result of the termination, although all disconnection requests must be completed successfully. The support of *Configuration* is shown as mandatory and we will discuss these specific options further in the following section. Finally, *Echo* and *Command Rejection* are both mandatory for a compliant Dial-up Networking Profile.

8.5.1.4.3   Configuration Options.   In establishing a connection with the remote device, the channel is subject to configuration and the higher-layer prototype `L2CA_ConfigReq` request packet is used to carry configuration requests. Its associated response is contained within the `L2CA_ConfigRsp` packet; an `L2CA_ConfigRspNeg` packet is used to denote a negative response during configuration where, for example, the suggested *Maximum Transmission Unit* (MTU) is too large. In Table 8-18, we identify that the MTU and *Flush Timeout* parameters are mandatory, whereas the QoS is optional.

The default MTU setting for the signalling channel is 48 bytes, whereas other channels may be capable of transferring larger payloads; essentially, the MTU determines the size of payloads that are capable of being exchanged between two devices. During configuration, the local device will inform the remote device that it is potentially capable of accepting larger payloads. If the remote device is unwilling to accept a larger MTU, then the local device is informed with the response contained within the `L2CA_ConfigRspNeg` packet.

When `L2CA_` request and response packets are being exchanged, the Flush Timeout parameter is used to determine how long the local device is prepared to continue to transmit an L2CAP fragment before it gives up; the packet is subsequently flushed or, in other words, discarded. The suggested Flush Timeout value is sent during the `L2CA_ConfigReq` request packet. However, if no value is set, then the default value is used. The Dial-up Networking Profile uses the default value of `0xFFFF`.

As we have already mentioned, the QoS configuration is optional. If it is used during an `L2CA_ConfigReq` request, then the *best effort* service is established as a default. The available services that support an L2CAP channel are shown in Table 8-22. However, if the QoS service is set at *Guaranteed,* then parameters such *Token Rate, Token Bucket, Peak Bandwidth, Latency* and *Delay Variation* are used to determine an acceptable guaranteed service, where the `L2CA_ConnectRspNeg` will indicate that these values are unacceptable. These parameters are then subject to further negotiation.

8.5.1.5   Link Manager.   The *Link Manager* (LM) layer sits between the HCI and the *Link Controller* (LC), although on a hostless system the LM will have direct interaction with L2CAP. It accepts commands from HCI and translates them into operations for the LC, where *Asynchronous Connectionless* (ACL) and *Synchronous Connection-Orientated* (SCO) links are created and established. It is during this stage of ACL and SCO es-

Table 8-22   The range of service definitions that are used during QoS.

SERVICE	DESCRIPTION
No Traffic	This indicates that the channel will not be sending any traffic and, as such, any parameter can be ignored.
Best Effort	This default value attempts to achieve a minimum service with the local remote device, where no guarantees are offered.
Guaranteed	With this service definition, we indicate that we wish to achieve the maximum bandwidth permitted. This is, of course, subject to the nature of a wireless environment.

tablishment that a master-slave switch would be performed, as governed by the requirements of this profile. The LM is also responsible for placing the device into a low-power mode, which includes *hold*, *sniff* and *park*.

In providing *general* error management, devices that operate mandatory procedures during interoperability must either acknowledge their support or provide the initiator with a reason for procedure failure. The LMP_Detach *Protocol Data Unit* (PDU) is used to inform the device of the error that occurred; typically, the reason *unsupported LMP feature* (0x1A) is reported (see Appendix A).

In the next section, we take an opportunity to explore the dependencies that make up the Dial-up Networking Profile, where we provide a narrative of the capabilities that are expected at this level. In Table 8-23, we identify the capabilities that are required from this layer and, in the following sub-sections, discuss the specific procedures in more detail.

8.5.1.5.1   Capabilities.   Table 8-23 summarises the broad capabilities that are expected from the LM. In the table, you will notice procedures are marked with *M* (Mandatory), *O* (Optional), *X* (Excluded), *C* (Conditional) and *N/A* (Not Applicable); these will determine what is expected from the procedures at the LM. A set of profile deviations are included in the table, which is above the common set of procedures expected at LM.

Table 8-23   The conditional requirements that are required for a compliant Dial-up Networking Profile.

PROCEDURES	DT	GW
SCO Links	C	C

The provision of SCO links, as previously discussed, is based on the capabilities of the DT and GW. If these devices are capable of providing audio feedback, then support for SCO Links should be provided.

8.5.1.5.2 SCO Links. A SCO link is set up using the HCI_Add_SCO_Connection command (see Table 8-24), where a series of Voice_Setting parameters are used to denote the type of SCO channel and the audio coding schemes. The Voice_Setting parameters are written using the HCI_Write_Voice_Setting command and are shown in Table 8-25.

It is assumed that the partying devices have an existing ACL communications link, where pairing, authentication and encryption (if required) have already taken place. The ACL Connection_Handle parameter is used, in part, to then create our SCO connection using the HCI_Add_SCO_Connection command. Although, the host controller generates a Command_Status event, it does not indicate that the SCO connection has been created. The host controller for both devices uses the Connection_Complete event to notify both hosts whether the SCO connection has been successful or not, where the new Connection_Handle and Link_Type identify the new connection. You may also wish to note that the Packet_Type parameter is used to specify the type of high quality voice transmission, where HV1, HV2 or HV3 can be requested over the SCO link.

Table 8-24   The commands and events that are used in combination to create a SCO connection. The Host Controller first sends the Command_Status event. When the connection has been established, the Connection_Complete event is generated on both devices.

COMMAND	PARAMETERS
HCI_Add_SCO_Connection	Connection_Handle
	Packet_Type
EVENT	**PARAMETERS**
Command_Status	Status
	Num_HCI_Command_Packets
	Command_OpCode
Connection_Complete	Status
	Connection_Handle
	BD_ADDR
	Link_Type
	Encryption_Mode

Table 8-25   The commands and events that are used in combination to write the voice setting parameters for a SCO link.

COMMAND	PARAMETERS
HCI_Write_Voice_Setting	Voice_Setting
EVENT	**PARAMETERS**
Command_Complete	Num_HCI_Command_Packets Command_OpCode Return_Parameters

The Voice_Setting parameters are shown in more detail in Table 8-26; the parameter makes use of two bytes, but only the first ten bits are useful. The HCI_Write_ Voice_Setting command also returns a Status of whether the command succeeded or not. The Voice_Setting parameters define the behaviour of all SCO connections that are active between partying devices.

Table 8-26   The Voice_Setting parameters that are used to define the behaviour of all active SCO connections.

										PARAMETERS
9	8	7	6	5	4	3	2	1	0	**Bit # of Voice Setting Parameters**
0	0	0	0	0	0	0	0	0	0	Linear
0	0	0	0	0	0	0	0	0	1	μ-Law Baseband Coding
0	0	0	0	0	0	0	0	1	0	A-Law Baseband Coding
0	0	0	0	0	0	0	0	0	0	1's Complement
0	0	0	0	0	0	0	1	0	0	2's Complement
0	0	0	0	0	0	1	0	0	0	Sign-magnitude
0	0	0	0	0	0	0	0	0	0	8-bit Input for Linear PCM
0	0	0	0	0	1	0	0	0	0	16-bit Input for Linear PCM
0	0	x	x	x	0	0	0	0	0	Used for denoting the PCM Bit Offset
0	0	0	0	0	0	0	0	0	0	CVSD air-coding format
0	1	0	0	0	0	0	0	0	0	μ-Law air-coding format
1	0	0	0	0	0	0	0	0	0	A-Law air coding format

8.5.1.6   Link Controller.   The Link Controller (LC) layer is the lowest layer depicted in the profile dependencies and has responsibilityfor a large number of core capabilities. It manages air-to-interface transactions and determines the fundamental timing of ACL and SCO data packet transmission and reception, as well as coordinating effort at its upper-edge with the LM. It also encompasses the management of the various packet types and the various inquiry and paging procedures that are available. The following subsections provide clarity with regard to the capabilities that are a requirement at the LC level for the Dial-up Networking Profile. In our understanding of the dependencies, we begin by examining the supported capabilities further. If you are a developer providing profile-specific applications, then it is unlikely that you will engage in a large part of this component, although in some audio-related applications, direct access may be required, where a faster transport mechanism can be supported. Nevertheless, many manufacturers have architected an audio-specific API for intelligible access to this component.

8.5.1.6.1   Capabilities.   Table 8-27 summarises the broad capabilities that are expected from the LC. In the table, you will notice features are marked with *M* (Mandatory), *O* (Optional), *X* (Excluded), *C* (Conditional) and *N/A* (Not Applicable); these will determine what is expected from the features at the Link Controller.

8.5.1.6.1.1   INQUIRY AND INQUIRY SCAN.   An inquiry procedure is used to learn of the other devices in radio range, where the BD_ADDR and clock offsets are obtained; it is DeviceA that will enter an *inquiry substate* to perform this procedure. A device that wishes to be discovered (DeviceB) will enter an *inquiry scan substate*, where the device will respond with an *inquiry response*. In this state, DeviceB is waiting to receive an *Inquiry Access Code* (IAC). From an application perspective, these modes of operation are more deeply discussed in the *Generic Access Profile*, Chapter 2. It is here that specific rules are determined with regard to device behaviour and duration of operation.

Table 8-27   The summary of capabilities that are required for the LC to enable a compliant Dial-up Networking Profile.

PROCEDURES	DT	GW
Inquiry	M	X
Inquiry Scan	X	M
Paging	M	X
Page Scan	X	M
Packet Types	M	M
Voice Codecs	O	O

When devices have been discovered, this information is passed over to the *Service Discovery Application Profile*, Chapter 3, which manages the specific attributes that make up that device. Here, we are reinforcing the premise that the Bluetooth protocol stack must encompass and support such behavioural procedures for this profile to be considered compliant.

8.5.1.6.1.2 PAGING AND PAGING SCAN. The *inquiry substate* and *inquiry scan substate* procedures are the initial methods used to learn of other devices in radio range; to this extent, the device has discovered sufficient information to gain a connection with the remote device. This is achieved when DeviceA has the intent to create a connection with DeviceB; DeviceA is now placed into a *paging substate*, where it will periodically transmit the *Device Access Code* (DAC). The DAC is used to target the device directly and the clock offset is used to gain an idea of the clock cycle of DeviceB. These parameters were originally obtained during our inquiry procedures. If DeviceB wishes to be connected, then it will enter a *page scan substate* and will respond accordingly to DeviceA. An inquiry procedure may be avoided if the BD_ADDR is already known, although a connection may take a little longer if the clock offset is not known.

8.5.1.6.1.3 PACKET TYPES. Of the numerous packet types available, Table 8-28 identifies those most often used for profile support. There are also a number of *common* packet types used for general purpose transport; for example, the ID packet is used for in-

Table 8-28   A summary of packet types required for the LC to enable a compliant Dial-up Networking Profile.

PACKET TYPE	DT	GW
DM1	M	M
DH1	M	M
DM3	M	M
DH3	M	M
DM5	M	M
DH5	M	M
HV1	X	X
HV2	X	X
HV3	O	O
DV	X	X

Table 8-29 A summary of voice codec schemes available for voice-related profiles.

VOICE CODEC	DT	GW
CVSD	O	O
A-Law	O	O
μ-Law	O	O

quiry procedures and a POLL packet would be sent by DeviceA to determine if a slave is active on a channel.

The DM1 packet type is used to transmit control data over any connection, but may also be used to transport a genuine payload. HV1, HV2 and HV3 are various SCO packet types to carry audio-specific data, where a DV packet can combine ACL and SCO specific data; their support in this profile is reflected in Table 8-28. Various ACL packet types are also available; in fact, seven types including the DM1 type are attributed to carrying user-specific data. These include DH1, DM3, DH3, DM5, DH5, and AUX1. Similarly, Table 8-28 summarises their support in this profile.

8.5.1.6.1.4 VOICE CODECS. Table 8-29 summarises voice codec support in this profile. Voice coding schemes are used to provide compression and to overcome potential errors in the data transmission. *Continuous Variable Slope Delta* (CVSD) provides the second scheme, which is particularly efficient for voice communication; it also tolerates potential errors in the audio data. The *Pulse Code Modulation* (PCM) has two types of logarithmic compression; these are A-law and μ-law, where either compression technique can be applied on the voice channels over the air-interface.

8.5.1.7 The Point-to-Point Protocol. PPP is typically used for communication between two devices that use a serial interface; it is well described in RFC1661. In the Dial-up Networking context, PPP use is implied with the dial-up networking application. The two applications at either end of the connection will manage the communication and negotiations accordingly.

8.6   SUMMARY

- The Dial-up Networking Profile has many similarities to the LAN Access Profile; both rely on the Generic Access Profile, the Serial Port Profile and have a PPP implementation.
- The Dial-up Networking Profile provides the use of AT commands to enable control and dialling.
- The existing usage models allow a DT to make use of the service provided through a GW; these are the two roles that are defined by this profile.

- The Dial-up Networking Profile provides the ability for a DT and GW to create a wireless bridge, thus creating a two-piece Bluetooth protocol stack.
- An Internet bridge is created when the DT makes use of the remote network services.
- PPP, IP and TCP are supported by the dial-up networking application.
- Bluetooth bonding is mandatory for this profile; failure to provide such support would result in a failed Bluetooth connection.
- The DT is the initiator of the Bluetooth relationship.
- There are no specific master or slave roles, although the DT will be the master as it initiated the connection.
- The DT discovers available GWs in radio range by performing an inquiry.
- A GW may restrict discoverability to further prevent unauthorised access.
- The Bluetooth Passkey is used as part of the authentication and encryption process.
- The service class record must depict the dial-up networking availability in the GW.
- A Service Discovery record is generated, detailing the parameters that apply to a specific service.
- The DT dial-up networking application incorporates a PPP Client and the remote service incorporates a PPP Server, both of which are transparent to the profile and the developer.
- PPP authentication may be required if the remote service requires this, where a username and password must be provided.
- Modem and driver emulation are provided above RFCOMM making use of the serial port emulation model.
- The GW must support the use of dialling and control where AT commands are issued to enable dialling and control.
- An SCO link may be established if it is required and if the GW and DT support this capability.
- A connection would be established regardless of the success of the SCO connection.

9

The Fax Profile

9.1 INTRODUCTION

The *Fax Profile* provides us with the same scenarios as introduced in the previous chapter *Dial-up Networking*, Chapter 8. In Figure 9-1 and Figure 9-2, we show that a fax service can be obtained from a notebook. The notebook behaves as a *gateway* (GW) and connects to a mobile phone or wireless modem, which represents our *data terminal* (DT).

You may recall that the introduction of a dial-up networking service was not a new idea. Nor indeed is the concept of a fax service. What has changed, however, is the introduction of a *wireless bridge,* which is used to remove the need to physically connect your mobile phone or modem to a notebook or *Personal Digital Assistant* (PDA). The Fax Profile provides the capability for a DT device to form a wireless bridge with a GW. Once the connection with the GW has been established, a fax service can then be obtained.

9.2 USAGE MODELS

This section examines our existing usage models through scenarios that may be typical for the Fax Profile. We begin by exploring the existing models, where a notebook or PDA communicates with a mobile phone or wireless modem to obtain a fax service.

Figure 9-1 The fax usage model allows the notebook to behave as our DT device, where it can create a wireless bridge with the mobile phone, which acts as a GW.

The scenarios provided in Figure 9-1 and Figure 9-2 represent our existing usage models. The role of a notebook (or PDA) acting as a DT initiates a one-to-one communications link with another Bluetooth-enabled device. This device, in turn, takes on the role of a GW. A wireless bridge is thereby created, which completes the connection. The formation of a wireless bridge between the notebook and PDA (or modem) demonstrates the fundamental Bluetooth philosophy: *removing the need for cables.*[1] A Fax application on the DT would be used to send a fax, where the Bluetooth device is used as the underlying transport. In the next section, we provide clarification on the notion of a wireless bridge and explain how it fits within the Fax Profile.

9.2.1 The Wireless Bridge

A wireless bridge is used to describe the nature of the cableless connection between the DT and GW; this is fundamental to and dominates the profile. Earlier in our introduction, we touched upon the need to connect a cable between a notebook and a mobile phone.

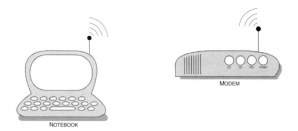

Figure 9-2 In this illustration, the fax usage model allows the notebook to behave as our DT device, where it can create a wireless bridge with the wireless modem, which acts as our GW.

---

[1]The wireless bridge concept is not new, in as much as existing technologies, such as infra-red (IR), provide the ability to communicate with a GW in much the same way as Bluetooth enabled devices. The advantage of a Bluetooth-enabled device is that it does not have to be in line-of-site with the DT. A mobile phone, for example, may be placed in a pocket or kept in a briefcase.

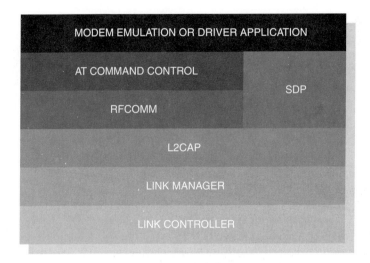

Figure 9-3   This model shows the combination of dial-up networking and facsimile services that are realised in the Bluetooth protocol stack—this essentially forms our two-piece stack.

This scenario allows the notebook (DT) to perform a dial-up connection through the mobile phone (GW) and then on to a remote service.

To support this profile, a *two-piece* Bluetooth protocol stack is required to complete the wireless bridge. In Figure 9-3, we can see what components of the stack are needed to form the DT and GW wireless relationship. Both the Dial-up Networking and Fax Profiles require the use of the AT Command component, which in turn controls the GW.

9.3   PROFILE PRINCIPLES

The Fax Profile provides two new roles: a DT device and a GW device. The GW provides the ability for a DT to connect and to provide the remote services; this is achieved by providing modem emulation, where the operation of AT commands is used to enable control and dialling. The modem emulation and driver are provided above RFCOMM, where RFCOMM provides serial port capabilities by emulating RS232 (see the *Serial Port Profile*, Chapter 6, for more detailed information). Figure 9-4 demonstrates the architecture of the components that make up the complete fax model.

In Table 9-1, clarification is provided with regard to the roles used within the context of this profile. In general, *DeviceA* represents the initiating party and *DeviceB* represents the accepting party. The terms are often used interchangeably when describing specific operations in various contexts and are provided here for reference.

In this chapter, the DT is referred to as DeviceA or the initiator; and the GW is the acceptor and forms DeviceB. DeviceA will remain master, since the GW is permitted to accept only one connection, although there are no strict master-slave roles. A GW device

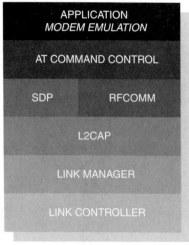

Figure 9-4   The core components of the Bluetooth protocol stack are shown illustrating how the components of the Fax Profile are integrated.

Table 9-1   The list of behavioural characteristics that are typical for this profile.

CONFIGURATION	ROLE	DESCRIPTION
DeviceA	DT	A device acting as a data terminal, which may take the form of a notebook or PDA. In this particular context, the device is described as initiating the connection with the accepting device.
	Initiator	This configuration describes the device that instigates the original connection or the device that wishes to initiate communication over an existing link.
DeviceB	GW	A device that behaves as a gateway, where it manages incoming and outgoing external communication through AT Command control signalling. It is also the party that accepts incoming connections from the data terminal.
	Acceptor	This configuration describes the process of the device accepting the initiated communication from DeviceA.

is considered to be the *Data Circuit Endpoint* (DCE) and the DT takes the *Data Terminal Equipment* (DTE) role in this conventional mapping.

9.4   USER EXPECTATIONS

9.4.1   Data Terminal

Today, we can openly purchase products that are capable of supporting the Fax Profile; these can be typically found within a PDA, notebook or mobile phone. If you recall from our earlier discussion, the Fax Profile is essentially a two-piece solution.

Bluetooth Profiles supports the philosophy of a rewarding user experience. It is therefore important to consider how the user would experience the connection and use of a GW. In later sections, we consider the specific experiences of connecting, terminating and losing connections and how the user may experience such operations.

We will consider the typical attributes that may make up a service discovery of a GW. The user experience in this particular example is a screen shot from the DT, which clearly shows that the mobile phone is capable of supporting the fax profile (see Figure 9-5).

9.4.1.1   Connecting to a Gateway.   The GW as a mobile phone should be initially enabled, where parameters such as limited discovery and range can be defined; this

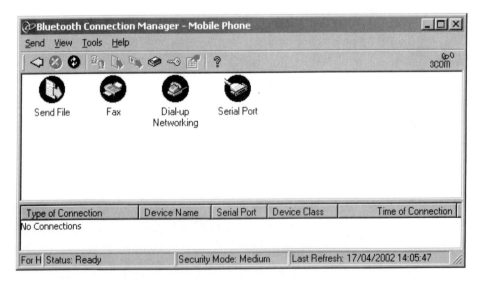

Figure 9-5   The screen shot shows a typical set of attributes that may be seen when discovering GWs (in this instance, the 3Com Bluetooth Connection Manager has discovered the services available from a mobile phone).

helps to limit unauthorised access to the GW. As a wireless modem, similar security features can be employed in addition to the passkey requirement.

In both instances, a passkey would be requested to enable authentication of the DT and GW. There may be other cases where the passkey may have to be provided, again possibly due to connection timeouts and/or the mobile phone being re-enabled for dial-up use. It may be recommended that a timeout occur after a defined period to, again, ensure and help with unauthorised access. In our earlier discussion, we touched upon the ability of the GW to only accept a connection from one DT at any time. This feature restricts use from intruders and, as a result, provides the user with a sense of security.

Once the user has the ability to connect to a device, he or she may now continue to make use of the services it provides. By using a double-click[2] or right-click operation, you can begin the process of connecting to the fax service as shown in Figure 9-6.

Prior to using the GW, a user may be required to enter a Bluetooth Passkey. In Figure 9-7, we show the user being prompted with a dialog box requesting the entry of a passkey.

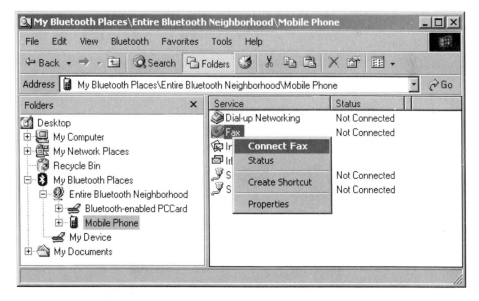

Figure 9-6   Right-clicking the devices icon causes a pop-up menu to appear,
                  offering the ability to connect to the device. In this illustration
                  we can see the user connecting to a service offering fax capabili-
                  ties. (Courtesy of TDK Systems Europe.)

---

[2]The double-click and right-click operations refer to a mouse that is connected to your client device (in this example, a PC or notebook computer running a Microsoft Windows operating system) and where both operations trigger the same method of access. It is noted that an operation may vary from device to device and, as such, the number of buttons may vary. Indeed, no mouse may be connected. The example just draws your attention to how it may be possible and acknowledges that implementations may differ.

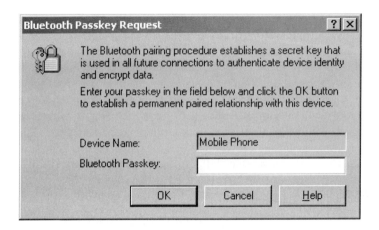

Figure 9-7 The user is requested to enter his or her passkey to authenticate with the GW device.

Underlying this high-level user interaction is a sequence of events that lead up to the moment of connection. Figure 9-8 illustrates the message sequences that typically occur during a connection set-up. Other implementations may differ slightly, depending upon the user's specific requirements.[3]

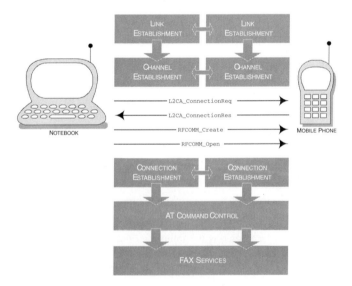

Figure 9-8 The events which takes place during a connection with a DT and a GW.

---

[3]The flexibility of the Bluetooth protocol stack, in particular the various HCI and LMP commands available, allow various methods of creating a successful ACL connection. The text refers to one particular example of a connection set-up.

Figure 9-9   The user has initiated the connection and is now informed of the connection status. (Courtesy of TDK Systems Europe.)

During connection establishment, the user may be informed of the dial-up in progress; in Figure 9-9, we show the user being informed of the progress of the connection. In Figure 9-10, we can see that the connection has made further progress and now the user is informed that the GW has commenced dialling.

9.4.1.2   Ending a Connection with a Gateway.   Once a connection is established with a GW and its services are no longer required, the user may terminate the session. As shown in Figure 9-11, the user is able to right-click on the connected device's icon and select disconnect from the pop-up menu to terminate the connection.

Other forms of disconnection may occur if the quality-of-service can no longer be maintained by the remote service; one example of this would be if the GW connection to the facsimile is unexpectedly lost. It is important to remember that the appropriate information about the current connection must be conveyed to the user, as the DT may offer a reconnection at a later time.

One other such instance of a terminated connection may occur if a connection is lost due to the DT moving out of range from a GW. Section 9.4.1.3, *Losing a connection with a GW*, looks at the sequence of events surrounding this possibility and considers how the user should experience this event.

9.4.1.3   Losing a Connection with a Gateway.   It is hard to imagine an instance where a connection would be lost with a GW. However, if the GW is taken out of radio range or the carrier is unexpectedly lost, then the DT must be able to appropriately

Figure 9-10   The connection has successfully progressed to the next level; the user is now informed of the GW actually dialling the service. (Courtesy of TDK Systems Europe.)

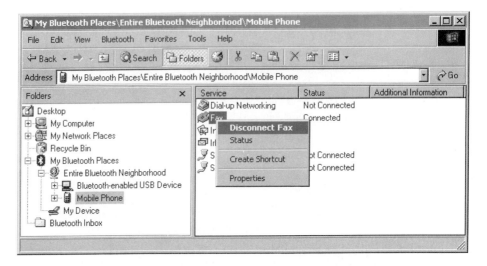

Figure 9-11   The user chooses to right-click the connected device icon and
uses the pop-up menu to terminate the connection with the GW.
(Courtesy of TDK systems Europe.)

manage the user interface aspects and, of course, the application should eventually allow
the user to reconnect at a later stage.

In Figure 9-12, the device status is clearly shown when right-clicking the device
icon to select its properties. As we saw in an earlier illustration, the device status is also
shown alongside the icon (see Figure 9-6). A seamless reconnection can be achieved if
both the DT and GW remember their previous respective sessions, whereby the reconnection time can be dramatically reduced.

9.4.2   Gateway

The simplicity of a mobile phone as a GW enables the user to place it in an area where
it does not need to be in direct line-of-sight with a PDA or notebook, although the GW
should be within suitable radio range. One classic and most often referred to example is
the *briefcase trick*. Here, the user can place the GW into a briefcase or a jacket pocket
and make use of the available services discreetly; similarly, wireless modems can be
fixed in any location.

9.4.2.1   Accepting a Connection from a DT.   The GW undertakes a series of
events that enable a DT to successfully access its service; Figure 9-13 illustrates these
events. When a DT wishes to connect to a GW, it initiates bonding, where the GW must
accept this request; encryption may also be used on the link.

9.4.2.2   Refusing a Connection from a DT.   The GW would refuse a connection
from a DT in such an instance where the GW refuses to accept bonding or when an incorrect

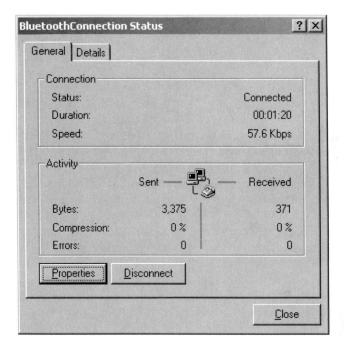

Figure 9-12   The user has chosen to query the device status, where it is
                  shown to be still connected. (Courtesy of TDK Systems
                  Europe.)

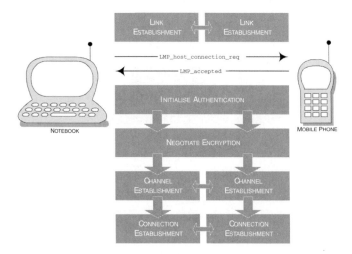

Figure 9-13   The events that take place during an incoming connection from
                  a DT.

passkey has been entered. A connection may also be refused if the fax service is un-available.

9.5 LIFTING THE LID

9.5.1 Dependencies

In our previous discussion, we covered aspects of existing usage models and their respective user expectations. Now we take an opportunity to explore, in greater depth, the dependencies of which this profile comprises.

In Figure 9-14, we illustrate the dependencies that make up the Fax Profile; the areas that are shaded are relevant to this profile. This profile depends upon the basic functionality offered to us by the *Generic Access Profile*, Chapter 2, the *Service Discovery Application Profile*, Chapter 3, and the *Serial Port Profile*, Chapter 6. We will now discuss the basic requirements of these dependent components alongside any deviations that may occur from their basic functionality.

9.5.1.1 Generic Access. The Fax Profile relies upon the capabilities provided by the *Generic Access Profile*, Chapter 2. You may recall that a level of basic functionality is achieved through establishing a set of rules and procedures. It then becomes suffi-

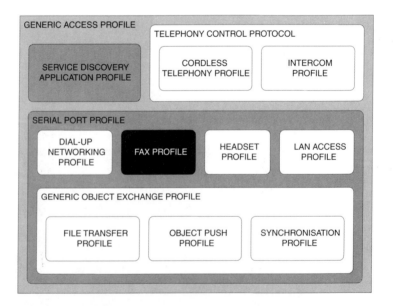

Figure 9-14 The dependent components of the Bluetooth protocol stack that make up the Fax Profile. The areas that are shaded are relevant to this profile.

cient to realise that the behaviour of such devices is governed by simple rules that relate to their connectivity, discoverability and common characteristics at the user interface level, with some additional emphasis provided for security. It is these rules and procedures that are used to establish commonality between products, which will ultimately achieve a cohesive user experience. This section reflects upon the behavioural aspects of Bluetooth-enabled devices as outlined by the Generic Access Profile.

We have dixcussed how the Generic Access Profile mandates certain rules and procedures that help govern the overall connectability, discoverability and security aspects of Bluetooth-enabled devices.

Now, take a look at Table 9-2, the basic set of procedures is illustrated and the functional expectations that govern where operation are also identified. These procedures help to determine the context that the device would operate in; for example, a device may wish to be discoverable for a period of time or it may require a level of security that differs from one device to another depending upon the services it is capable of offering.

In Table 9-3, we consider the specific set of operations that are required for this profile. In the table, you will notice features are marked with *M* (Mandatory), *O* (Optional), *X* (Excluded), *C* (Conditional) and *N/A* (Not Applicable); these will determine what is expected from the features of the Generic Access Profile. Typically, a GW device will operate in a limited discovery mode, where authentication and encryption may be used.

Table 9-4 identifies the security requirements for this profile. Remember that Security Mode 1 is a non-secure mode where Bluetooth-enabled devices will never initiate any security procedures; Security Modes 2 and 3 initiate different levels of security proce-

Table 9-2   The core set of procedures as required by most profiles.

PROCEDURES	DESCRIPTION
Discoverability Mode	This mode prescribes the overall discoverability of a device, allowing it to be placed into a non-discoverable, limited, or general discoverable mode. The mode would allow devices to become generally available to other users or it can be restricted to personal use.
Connectability Mode	When determining a baseband connectable state, this mode is used to place a device into a connectable or non-connectable mode.
Pairing	Pairable and non-pairable modes are used to realise the security aspects when operating or intending to use a device. A device may require authentication and, as such, the user would be required to enter a Bluetooth Passkey. The pairing procedure starts the link key generation process which, in turn, allows authentication to take place.

Table 9-3   The illustration shows specific modes of operation that this profile depends upon
to realise its compliant implementation.

MODES	DT	GW
Non-discoverable	N/A	O
Limited Discoverable	N/A	O
General Discoverable	N/A	O
Non-connectable	N/A	X
Connectable	N/A	M
Non-pairable	M	O
Pairable	O	M

dures at various stages of connection establishment. In this instance, the profile mandates
that support should be provided for at least Security Mode 2 or 3.

In our final consideration of the basic rules and procedures that are required from
the Generic Access Profile, the idle mode procedures outline behavioural characteristics
when DeviceA chooses to initiate them against DeviceB. The procedures that are listed in
Table 9-5 provide a clear indication of how a device should operate when performing
such an activity; let us take our bonding procedure as an example. The term bonding is
very much associated with the pairing process; however, bonding occurs when the user
has the *intent* to initiate a trusted relationship with DeviceB. With this intent, the user is
prompted to enter a Bluetooth Passkey which, in turn, instigates the pairing process that is
the generation of the link keys, where subsequent authentication can then occur. In summary, what we learn here is that there are a specific set of events associated with a procedure. In the *Generic Access Profile*, Chapter 2, we take a closer look at how each
procedure is conducted.

The mechanism for providing device discoverability is the provision of a well structured FHS packet, which is shown in Figure 9-15. This packet is used to identify the re-

Table 9-4   The illustration shows specific security procedures that this profile depends upon
to realise its compliant implementation.

PROCEDURE	DT	GW
Authentication	M	M
Security Mode 1	N/A	X
Security Mode 2	C	C
Security Mode 3	C	C

Table 9-5   The illustration shows specific behavioural procedures that this profile depends
upon to realise its compliant implementation.

PROCEDURE	DT	GW
General Inquiry	M	N/A
Limited Inquiry	O	N/A
Name Discovery	O	N/A
Device Discovery	O	N/A
Bonding	M	M

mote device, where information such as Bluetooth Device Address (BD_ADDR) and clock
offsets is determined. You may also notice from this packet that the *Class of Device*
(CoD) field is also provided. This information is relayed to the user interface which, in
turn, provides common characteristics about discovered devices. The CoD is used during
the discovery mechanism to learn more about the type of device and what it may be capable of providing. This structure of information is depicted in Figure 9-16 and is made up
of 3-bytes (or 24-bits as shown). The following sections now consider the Fax attributes,
which will ultimately make use of the *Service*, *Major* and *Minor Device Class* fields.

9.5.1.1.1   Service Class.   This high-level form of defining a Bluetooth device identifies where in the Service Class field the Fax Profile resides (see Table 9-6) which, in turn,
determines the category of service. Here, the category of service falls within *Telephony*.

9.5.1.1.2   Major Device Class.   This high-level form of defining a Bluetooth device identifies where in the Major Device Class the Fax Profile resides (see Table 9-7)
which, in turn, determines the major class grouping. Here, the category falls within phone,
since a mobile phone providing modem emulation may be used.

9.5.1.1.3   Minor Device Class.   The Minor Device Class in this profile is used to
convey a further context for the setting within the major class grouping (see Table 9-8).

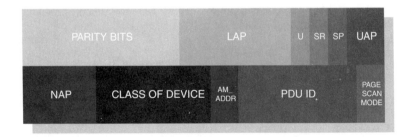

Figure 9-15   The structure of the FHS packet used only for reference to illustrate the position of the Class of Device structure.

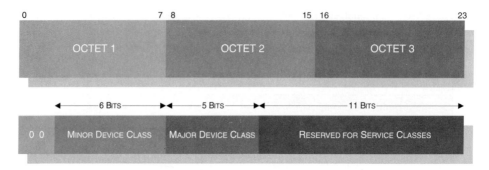

Figure 9-16   The structure of the class of device, illustrating the Minor Device, Major Device and Service Class fields and their respective lengths.

Here, the bit may be set appropriately for *Mobile Phone* or *Wireless Modem* to denote the type of service available to the user.

9.5.1.2   Service Discovery.   In the *Service Discovery Application Profile*, Chapter 3, we introduced the characteristics of the mechanisms used to retrieve service information from a remote device. Typically, a client will initiate an inquiry and discovery procedure as outlined in our previous section, to learn of the devices in radio range. A client can then make use of an application, which embodies the functionality of the underlying *Service Discovery Protocol* (SDP). The *Service Discovery Application* (SrvDscApp) uses an *SDP Client* to instigate a request to the remote device, where the *SDP Server* will respond; as such, the DT and GW must employ the use of an SDP client and server respectively, as illustrated in Table 9-9.

PDUs are used to instruct the SDP server to undertake browsing procedures and to retrieve service record information; you may recall that these PDUs carry payload requests containing `AttributeIDs` and `AttributeValues`, which describe what exactly is being sought. As we previously discussed, the client and server operate a request and response paradigm. SDAP will construct PDUs containing information relating to the `AttributeID` and `AttributeValues`, which in turn instruct the server to carry out its operation. The various request and response PDUs that are required are shown in Table 9-10, where features indicated are described as mandatory (M), optional (O) and excluded (X).

Table 9-6   The Service Class categorisation for the Fax Profile.

											SERVICE CLASS
23	22	21	20	19	18	17	16	15	14	13	Bit # of CoD
0	1	0	0	0	0	0	0	0	0	0	Telephony

Table 9-7   The Major Device Class for the Fax Profile.

					MAJOR DEVICE CLASS
12	11	10	9	8	Bit # of CoD
0	0	0	1	0	Phone

Table 9-8   The Minor Device Class for the Fax Profile.

						MINOR DEVICE CLASS
7	6	5	4	3	2	Bit # of CoD
0	0	0	0	0	1	Mobile Phone
0	0	0	1	0	0	Wireless Modem

Table 9-9   As a minimum, the local device must support the use of a client application and the remote device must support the use of a server.

FEATURE	DT	GW
SDP Client	M	X
SDP Server	X	M

Table 9-10   The list of PDUs that are required for the operation of the Fax Profile.

PDU	DT	GW
SDP_ErrorResponse	X	M
SDP_ServiceSearchRequest	M	X
SDP_ServiceSearchResponse	X	M
SDP_ServiceAttributeRequest	M	X
SDP_ServiceAttributeResponse	X	M
SDP_ServiceSearchAttributeRequest	O	X
SDP_ServiceSearchAttributeRequest	X	O

Table 9-11   The list of mandatory and configurable items that make up this profile's service discovery record.

ATTRIBUTE	DESCRIPTION
`ServiceRecordHandle`	With an `AttributeID` of `0x0000`, this uniquely identifies this service record within the SDP server on the GW device.

`ServiceClassIDList`
 	
`ServiceClass0`
 	
`ServiceClass1`
	With an `AttributeID` of `0x0001`, the following `ServiceClass0` would contain the UUID for the *Fax* and the `ServiceClass1` would identify the *Generic Telephony* service classes. Their respective UUID values are summarised in Table 9-12.

`ProtocolDescriptorList`
 	
`Protocol0`
 	
`Protocol1`
 	
`ParameterFor1`
	With an `AttributeID` of `0x0004`, the following `Protocol0` would contain a UUID for the protocol *L2CAP*, whereas in `Protocol1` a UUID would contain the protocol identifier for *RFCOMM*. Their respective UUID values are summarised in Table 9-13. The `ParameterFor1` would contain the relevant server channel number for the RFCOMM transport.

`BluetoothProfile-DescriptorList`
 	
`Profile0`
 	
`ParameterFor0`
	With an `AttributeID` of `0x0009`, the following `Profile0` would identify the UUID for *Fax* service class, which is summarised in Table 9-12. The `ParameterFor0` accommodates the version number supported by this profile.

`ServiceName`	With a base `AttributeID` of `0x0006`, this attribute has an offset of `0x0000`. It is a configurable item and has an `AttributeValue` of a `Text` string, where its default setting is *Fax*.
`AudioFeedbackSupport`	With an `AttributeID` of `0x0305`, this attribute identifies whether or not the GW device is capable of providing audio feedback. The `AttributeValue` is constructed using a `Boolean`, where the default setting is `FALSE`.

(continued)

Table 9-11   The list of mandatory and configurable items that make up this profile's service discovery record. *Continued.*

ATTRIBUTE	DESCRIPTION
FaxClass1Support	With an `AttributeID` of `0x0302`, this attribute identifies whether or not the GW device is capable of supporting this fax class. The `AttributeValue` is constructed using a `Boolean`, where the default setting is FALSE.
FaxClass2Support	With an `AttributeID` of `0x0304`, this attribute identifies whether or not the GW device is capable of supporting this fax class. The `AttributeValue` is constructed using a `Boolean`, where the default setting is FALSE.
FaxClass2.0Support	With an `AttributeID` of `0x0302`, this attribute identifies whether or not the GW device is capable of supporting this fax class. The `AttributeValue` is constructed using a `Boolean`, where the default setting is FALSE.

A service record is maintained for each service a device is capable of supporting and, as such, a *Service Record Handle* is created to uniquely identify this. The `ServiceRecordHandle` is a 32-bit unsigned integer and is stored on the SDP server. The service record shown in Table 9-11 identifies a GW device and provides a list of `AttributeIDs`, which ultimately would identify the service for the Fax Profile. A minimum of two `AttributeIDs` are required to make a service record; these are `ServiceRecordHandle` and a `ServiceClassIDList`, which must contain at least one `UUID`.

When browsing for services on the remote device, a local device constructs a search pattern using a *Universally Unique Identifier* (UUID). A UUID is a 128-bit value, which has been shortened for use within Bluetooth. The shortcut has been provided by first establishing a *Bluetooth Base UUID*, which we discussed in the *Service Discovery Application Profile*, Chapter 3.

The UUIDs that have been presented so far in this chapter are aliases and take the form of what is referred to as a 16-bit UUID or a 32-bit UUID but, in turn, they should all refer to the 128-bit notation. These UUIDs have been assigned and can be referenced in the Bluetooth Special Interest Group, Bluetooth Assigned Numbers, v1.1, February 2001. For the search pattern to be successful, they all need to be converted to the 128-bit notation, since they will all be compared at this range. An arithmetic conversion algorithm is used to construct the 128-bit value.

Table 9-12 summarises the service class UUIDs used to identify the particular profile in use; this also correlates with the identification of the device during a device discovery procedure, as previously outlined in Section 9.5.1.1, *Generic Access.*

Table 9-12 The list of service classes that match a corresponding profile. This correlates
with our previous Generic Access section.

CLASSES	UUID
Fax	0x1111
GenericTelephony	0x1204

As part of the service record, the dependent underlying protocols are also identified.
The local device retrieves this information, where it can fully understand the exact requirements needed to fulfil the service. The Fax Profile is dependent on the protocols as
shown in Table 9-13, which also shows their associated UUID values.

9.5.1.3 RFCOMM. In the *Serial Port Profile*, Chapter 6, we introduced the
conceptual and functional nature of RFCOMM and discussed how it provides an emulated serial port presence. Several distinctions were made between the various types of applications. The purpose of making these distinctions was to enable clarification and
understanding of RFCOMM's composition. In this particular application context, the creation of an emulated serial port would be transparent to the user. The Fax Profile is dependent upon the operation of the Serial Port Profile and, as such, is required to establish an
emulated serial port as part of its communication link with the remote device.

The term cable replacement application was introduced in our earlier chapter and
distinguishes between the different scenarios available. It refers to specific Bluetooth applications that create implicit emulated serial ports, which remain transparent to the user
to complete the creation of a communications link.

Specific detail has been provided to illustrate how data is communicated over an
emulated serial port connection, whereby a *Data Link Connection* (DLC) is established
between two peer devices, namely DT and GW. We have also looked at the fields that
make up our service record for this profile. The `ProtocolDescriptorList` field
is used to describe the set of protocols that the profile intends to use and, as such, the
RFCOMM protocol identifier contains a parameter, which contains the Server Channel
number.

The Server Channel is used in combination with a *Data Link Connection Identifier*
(DLCI), which is then used to uniquely identify the active DLC. This connection is then
mapped onto a connectionless orientated L2CAP *Channel Identifier* (CID).

Table 9-13 The list of protocols that are used in this profile; their associated UUID values
are also shown.

PROTOCOL	UUID
RFCOMM	0x0003
L2CAP	0x0100

In this section we highlight the specific features that are required to realise a compliant Fax Profile. Table 9-14 and Table 9-15 illustrate the features or capabilities that are expected from the Serial Port Profile.

The use of the RLS command is encouraged to keep peer devices informed of any state change. In one such instance, an emulated serial port may interface to a Type II application (physical serial port), where overruns or parity errors may occur. An application that makes use of RS232 port configuration parameters should expose these settings through an appropriate API function; this is of particular relevance when interfacing to Type II applications.

9.5.1.3.1 AT Command Control. In Section 9.3, *Profile Principles,* we introduced an illustration that identifies the modem emulation and driver components created with the help of RFCOMM. It is above this that a fax application would reside, using the serial port emulation provided by RFCOMM. The DT and GW would be capable of supporting the commands and responses as defined in the *International Telecommunication Union,* Telecommunication Standardisation (ITU Recommendation T.31 and T.32) Sector Asynchronous Facsimile DCE Control, Service Classes 1 and 2. A GW must be capable of supporting at least one fax class, but it may also support all class types. The DT will interrogate the GW to determine the type of fax class support using the AT Command AT+FCLASS.

Table 9-14   The set of capabilities that are required from the initiating party, denoted here by the DT device.

PROCEDURE	DT	GW
Initialise an RFCOMM Session	M	X
Terminate an RFCOMM Session	M	M
Establish a new DLC Connection	M	X
Disconnect a DLC Connection	M	M
Emulate RS232 Control Signals	C	C
Transfer Data	M	M
Test Command	X	X
Flow Control	C	C
RLS	O	O
PN	O	O
RPN	O	O

Table 9-15 The set of capabilities that are required from the responder party, denoted here by the GW device.

PROCEDURE	DT	GW
Initialise an RFCOMM Session	X	M
Terminate an RFCOMM Session	M	M
Establish a new DLC Connection	X	M
Disconnect a DLC Connection	M	M
Emulate RS232 Control Signals	M	M
Transfer Data	N/A	N/A
Test Command	M	M
Flow Control	M	M
RLS	M	M
PN	M	M
RPN	M	M

9.5.1.3.2 Call Progress and Audio Feedback. In our earlier discussion, we introduced the capability of audio feedback, which may be provided during call progress and is subject to the capability of the GW and DT. If, during a connection establishment, the SCO link fails, the call and ACL establishment may still proceed regardless. Furthermore, the GW has the responsibility to manage and establish the SCO connection (see Section 9.5.1.5.2, *SCO Links*).

9.5.1.4 L2CAP. The L2CAP layer provides transparency for the upper-layers of the stack from the layers typically found within the host controller. L2CAP payloads are passed to the *Host Controller Interface*[4] (HCI), which is then subsequently passed onto the *Link Manager Protocol* (LMP). The range of upper layers, which include RFCOMM, SDP and the *Telephony Control Protocol Specification* (TCS) all make use of the capabilities offered to us by L2CAP. Its primary role is to provide *protocol multiplexing*, allowing numerous simultaneous connections to be made and also providing the ability for *segmentation* and *reassembly*. This refers to the ability to manage large payloads in the application, which may need to be fragmented into smaller payloads for the lower-layers to manage; these are then transmitted over the air-interface. Finally, the L2CAP layer exchanges *Quality of Service* (QoS) information, ensuring that sufficient resources are available and that both Bluetooth devices are attaining the best service.

---

[4]L2CAP payloads are passed directly onto LMP when implemented on a hostless system.

Table 9-16   The illustration shows specific procedures that this profile depends upon to realise its compliant implementation.

PROCEDURE	DT	GW
Connection-orientated Channel	M	M
Connectionless Channel	X	X
Connection Establishment	M	M
Configuration	M	M
Connection Termination	M	M
Echo	M	M
Command Rejection	M	M
Maximum Transmission Unit	M	M
Flush Timeout	M	M
Quality of Service	O	O

In Table 9-16, we summarise the broad capabilities that are expected from L2CAP. In the table, you will notice features are marked with *according to*; these will determine what is expected from them at the L2CAP layer.

9.5.1.4.1   Channel Types.   In Table 9-16, we identified that *Connection-Orientated Channels* are mandatory, whereas *Connectionless Channels* are excluded; this type of channel is aimed at broadcasting, where all devices may be targeted. L2CAP uses *Protocol Data Units* (PDUs) to transport connection, signalling and configuration options, which will be discussed in a moment. The higher layers of the Bluetooth protocol stack will instigate a connection with L2CAP using the L2CA_ConnectReq request packet, where the corresponding result is contained within the L2CA_Connect-Rsp response packet. An L2CA_ConnectRspNeg negative response packet is used to denote a response, where the connection with the remote device was unsuccessful. Since our profile resides above L2CAP and employs its services, we are only concerned with the upper protocol layer of L2CAP. This higher functionality is offered to us through a series of L2CAP events and is denoted through the prefix L2CA_ (see Table 9-17).

When creating an L2CAP connection between two devices, a *Protocol/Service Multiplexor* (PSM) value is used to denote the higher-layer protocol that is using the connection; Table 9-18 identifies these values and the corresponding protocols they represent. The value of 0x0003 (RFCOMM) is used for this profile.

Table 9-17   The range of prototypes used to illustrate how L2CAP is architected and how interaction between higher- and lower-layers is achieved. For this discussion, our concern here is with the higher-layer.

PROTOTYPE	DESCRIPTION
L2CA_	This prefix prototype is used to denote the higher-layer interaction, typically used by RFCOMM, SDP and TCS
L2CAP_	This prefix is used to denote peer-to-peer signalling interaction of L2CAP entities.
LP_	Finally, this prefix denotes lower-layer interaction, where L2CAP interfaces with the LMP layer.

9.5.1.4.2   Signalling.   When establishing communication with a remote device, a *signalling channel* is created and reserved for use during connection, disconnection and configuration of subsequent L2CAP connections. A *channel* is used to describe the communication and data flow that exists between L2CAP entities and Table 9-19 illustrates the range of CIDs that are used to identify the channel type. As we can see in Table 9-16, *Connection Establishment* and *Termination* is mandatory in the local device, although the remote device may be capable of initiating and terminating a connection to the local device. The L2CA_DisconnectReq request packet is used to terminate the connection with the remote device and an L2CA_DisconnectRsp response packet is used to ascertain the result of the termination. All disconnection requests must be completed successfully. The support of *Configuration* is shown as mandatory and we will discuss these specific options in more detail in the following section. Finally, *Echo* and *Command Rejection* are both mandatory for a compliant Fax Profile.

9.5.1.4.3   Configuration Options.   In establishing a connection with the remote device, the channel is subject to configuration and the higher-layer prototype L2CA_ConfigReq request packet is used to carry configuration requests. Its associated re-

Table 9-18   The PSM values that are used to identify the higher-layer protocol.

PSM	DESCRIPTION
0x0001	SDP
0x0003	RFCOMM
0x0005	TCS-BIN
0x0007	TCS-BIN-CORDLESS

Table 9-19   The CIDs that are used to represent the logical channel.

CID	DESCRIPTION
0x0000	Null
0x0001	Signalling Channel
0x0002	Connectionless Reception Channel
0x0003 to 0x003F	Reserved
0x0040 to 0xFFFF	Dynamically Allocated

sponse is contained within the L2CA_ConfigRsp packet; an L2CA_ConfigRspNeg packet is used to denote a negative response during configuration where, for example, the suggested *Maximum Transmission Unit* (MTU) is too large. In Table 9-16, we have identified that the MTU and *Flush Timeout* parameters are mandatory, whereas the QoS is optional.

The default MTU setting for the signalling channel is 48-bytes, whereas other channels may be capable of transferring larger payloads; essentially, the MTU determines the size of payloads that are capable of being exchanged between two devices. During configuration, the local device will inform the remote device that it is potentially capable of accepting larger payloads. If the remote device is unwilling to accept a larger MTU, then the local device is informed with the response contained within the L2CA_ConfigRspNeg packet.

When L2CA_ request and response packets are being exchanged, the Flush Timeout parameter is used to determine how long the local device is prepared to continue to transmit an L2CAP fragment before it gives up; the packet is subsequently flushed or, in other words, discarded. The suggested Flush Timeout value is sent during the L2CA_ConfigReq request packet. However, if no value is set then the default value is used. The Fax Profile uses the default value of 0xFFFF.

As we have already mentioned, the QoS configuration is optional. If it is used during an L2CA_ConfigReq request then the *best effort* service is established as a default The available services that are supported for an L2CAP channel are shown in Table 9-20. However, if the QoS service is set at *Guaranteed*, then parameters such *Token Rate*, *Token Bucket*, *Peak Bandwidth*, *Latency* and *Delay Variation*, are used to determine an acceptable guaranteed service, where the L2CA_ConnectRspNeg will indicate that these values are unacceptable. These parameters are then subject to further negotiation.

9.5.1.5   Link Manager.   The *Link Manager* (LM) layer sits between the HCI and the *Link Controller* (LC), although on a hostless system the LM will have direct interaction with L2CAP. It accepts commands from the HCI and translates them into operations for the LC, where *Asynchronous Connectionless* (ACL) and *Synchronous Connection-Orientated* (SCO) links are created and established. It is during this stage of ACL and

Table 9-20   The range of service definitions that are used during QoS.

SERVICE	DESCRIPTION
No Traffic	This indicates that the channel will not be sending any traffic and, as such, any parameters can be ignored.
Best Effort	This default value attempts to achieve a minimum service with the local remote device, where no guarantees are offered.
Guaranteed	With this service definition, we indicate that we wish to achieve the maximum bandwidth permitted. This is, of course, subject to the nature of a wireless environment.

SCO establishment that a master-slave switch would be performed as governed by the requirements of this profile. The LM is also responsible for placing the device into a low-power mode, which includes *hold*, *sniff* and *park*.

In providing *general* error management, devices that operate mandatory procedures during interoperability must either acknowledge their support or provide a suitable reason for failure. The `LMP_Detach` PDU is used to inform the device of the error that occurred; typically, the reason *unsupported LMP feature* (`0x1A`) is reported (see Appendix A).

In the following discussion, we take an opportunity to explore the dependencies that make up the Fax Profile, where we provide a narrative of the capabilities that are expected at this level. In Table 9-21, we identify the capabilities that are required from this layer and in the following subsections we discuss the specific procedures in more detail.

9.5.1.5.1   Capabilities.   Table 9-20 summarises the broad capabilities that are expected from the LM. In the table, you will notice procedures are marked according to what is expected from the procedures at the LM. The table illustrates a set of deviations that the profile includes, which are above the common set of procedures expected at LM.

The provision of SCO links is based on the capabilities of the DT and GW. If these devices are capable of providing audio feedback, then support for SCO Links should also be provided.

Table 9-21   The conditional requirements for a compliant Fax Profile.

PROCEDURES	DT	GW
SCO Links	C	C

9.5.1.5.2 SCO Links. A SCO link is set up using the HCI_Add_SCO_ Connection command (see Table 9-22), where a series of Voice_Setting parameters are used to denote the type of SCO channel and the audio coding schemes. The Voice_Setting parameters are written using the HCI_Write_Voice_Setting command and are shown in Table 9-23.

It assumed that the partying devices have an existing ACL communications link, where pairing, authentication and encryption (if required) have already taken place. The ACL Connection_Handle parameter is used, in part, to then create our SCO connection using the HCI_Add_SCO_Connection command.

Although, the host controller generates a Command_Status event, it does not indicate that the SCO connection has been created. The host controller for both devices uses the Connection_Complete event to notify both hosts whether the SCO connection has been successful or not, where the new Connection_Handle and Link_Type identify the new connection. You may also wish to note that the Packet_Type parameter is used to specify the type of high-quality voice transmission, where HV1, HV2 or HV3 can be requested over the SCO link.

The Voice_Setting parameters are shown in more detail in Table 9-24. The parameters make use of two bytes, but only the first ten bits are useful. The HCI_Write_ Voice_Setting command also returns a Status of whether the command succeeded

Table 9-22   The command and events that are used in combination to create a SCO connection. The Host Controller first sends the Command_Status event. When the connection has been established, the Connection_Complete event is generated on both devices.

COMMAND	PARAMETERS
HCI_Add_SCO_Connection	Connection_Handle
	Packet_Type
EVENT	**PARAMETERS**
Command_Status	Status
	Num_HCI_Command_Packets
	Command_OpCode
Connection_Complete	Status
	Connection_Handle
	BD_ADDR
	Link_Type
	Encryption_Mode

Table 9-23   The command and event that are used in combination to write the voice setting parameters for a SCO link.

COMMAND	PARAMETERS
HCI_Write_Voice_Setting	Voice_Setting
EVENT	**PARAMETERS**
Command_Complete	Num_HCI_Command_Packets Command_OpCode Return_Parameters

Table 9-24   The Voice_Setting parameters that are used to define the behaviour of all active SCO connections.

										PARAMETERS
9	8	7	6	5	4	3	2	1	0	Bit # of Voice Setting Parameters
0	0	0	0	0	0	0	0	0	0	Linear
0	0	0	0	0	0	0	0	0	1	μ-Law Baseband Coding
0	0	0	0	0	0	0	0	1	0	A-Law Baseband Coding
0	0	0	0	0	0	0	0	0	0	1's Complement
0	0	0	0	0	0	0	1	0	0	2's Complement
0	0	0	0	0	0	1	0	0	0	Sign-magnitude
0	0	0	0	0	0	0	0	0	0	8-bit Input for Linear PCM
0	0	0	0	0	1	0	0	0	0	16-bit Input for Linear PCM
0	0	x	x	x	0	0	0	0	0	Used for denoting the PCM Bit Offset
0	0	0	0	0	0	0	0	0	0	CVSD air-coding format
0	1	0	0	0	0	0	0	0	0	μ-Law air-coding format
1	0	0	0	0	0	0	0	0	0	A-Law air coding format

or not. The `Voice_Setting` parameters define the behaviour of all SCO connections that are active between partying devices.

9.5.1.6   Link Controller.   The Link Controller (LC) layer is the lowest layer depicted in the dependencies of this profile. It is responsible for a large number of core capabilities. It manages air-to-interface transactions and determines the fundamental timing of ACL and SCO data packet transmission and reception, as well as coordinating the effort at its upper-edge with the LM. It also encompasses the management of the various packet types and the various inquiry and paging procedures that are available. In turn, the following sub-sections provide clarity with regard to the capabilities that are a requirement at the LC level for the Fax Profile. In our understanding of the dependencies, we begin by examining in more detail the supported capabilities and a small discussion is offered for each. If you are a developer providing profile-specific applications, then the likelihood for you to engage in a large part of this component is unlikely, although in some audio-related applications direct access may be required, where a faster transport mechanism can be supported. Nevertheless, many manufacturers have architected an audio-specific API for an intelligible access to this component.

9.5.1.6.1   Capabilities.   Table 9-25 summarises the broad capabilities that are expected from the LC. In the table, you will notice features are marked according to; these will determine what is expected from the features at the LC.

9.5.1.6.1.1   INQUIRY AND INQUIRY SCAN.   An inquiry procedure is used to learn of the other devices in radio range, where the BD_ADDR and clock offsets are obtained. DeviceA will enter an *inquiry substate* to perform this procedure. A device that wishes to be discovered (DeviceB) will enter an *inquiry scan substate*, where the device will respond

Table 9-25   The summary of capabilities that are required for the LC to enable a compliant Fax Profile.

PROCEDURES	DT	GW
Inquiry	M	X
Inquiry Scan	X	M
Paging	M	X
Page Scan	X	M
Packet Types	M	M
Voice Codecs	O	O

with an *inquiry response*. In this state, DeviceB is waiting to receive an *Inquiry Access Code* (IAC). From an application perspective, these modes of operation are discussed in more detail in the *Generic Access Profile*, Chapter 2. It is here that specific rules are determined with regard to device behaviour and duration of operation. When devices have been discovered, this information is passed over to the *Service Discovery Application Profile*, Chapter 3, which manages its specific attributes. What is being established here, as a dependency, is that the Bluetooth protocol stack must encompass and support such behavioural procedures for this profile to be considered compliant.

9.5.1.6.1.2 PAGING AND PAGING SCAN. The *inquiry substate* and *inquiry scan substate* procedures are the initial method used to learn of other devices in radio range; to this extent, the device has discovered sufficient information to gain a connection with the remote device. This is achieved when DeviceA has the intent to create a connection with DeviceB. DeviceA is now placed into a *paging substate*, where it will periodically transmit the *Device Access Code* (DAC). The DAC is used to target the device directly and the clock offset is used to gain an idea of the clock cycle of DeviceB. These parameters were originally obtained during our inquiry procedures. If DeviceB wishes to be connected, then it will enter a *page scan substate* and will respond accordingly to DeviceA. An inquiry procedure may be avoided if the BD_ADDR is already known, although a connection may take a little longer as the clock offset is not known.

Table 9-26 The summary of packet types that are required for the LC to enable a compliant Fax Profile.

PACKET TYPE	DT	GW
DM1	M	M
DH1	M	M
DM3	M	M
DH3	M	M
DM5	M	M
DH5	M	M
HV1	X	X
HV2	X	X
HV3	O	O
DV	X	X

Table 9-27   The summary of voice codec schemes available for voice-related profiles.

VOICE CODEC	DT	GW
CVSD	O	O
A-Law	O	O
μ-Law	O	O

9.5.1.6.1.3   PACKET TYPES.   There are numerous packet types available. Table 9-26 identifies the most often used packets for profile support. There are also a number of *common* packet types that are used for general-purpose transport; for example, the ID packet is used for inquiry procedures and a POLL packet would be sent by DeviceA to determine if a slave is active on a channel.

The DM1 packet type is used to transmit control data over any connection, but may also be used to transport a genuine payload. HV1, HV2 and HV3 are various SCO packet types to carry audio-specific data, where a DV packet can combine ACL and SCO specific data; their support in this profile is reflected in Table 9-26. Various ACL packet types are also available; in fact, seven types including the DM1 type are attributed to carrying user-specific data. These include DH1, DM3, DH3, DM5, DH5 and AUX1. Similarly, Table 9-26 summarises their support in this profile.

9.5.1.6.1.4   VOICE CODECS.   Table 9-27 summarises voice codec support in this profile. Voice coding schemes are used to provide compression and to overcome potential errors in the data transmission. *Continuous Variable Slope Delta* (CVSD) provides the second scheme, which is particularly efficient for voice communication; it also tolerates potential errors in the audio data. The *Pulse Code Modulation* (PCM) has two types of logarithmic compression; these are A-law and μ-law, where either compression technique can be applied on the voice channels over the air-interface.

9.6   SUMMARY

- The Fax Profile has many similarities to the Dial-up Networking Profile; both rely on the Generic Access Profile, the Serial Port Profile and use AT Commands to enable control and dialling.
- The existing usage models allow a DT to make use of the service provided through a GW; these are the two roles that are defined by this profile.
- The Fax Profile provides the ability for a DT and GW to create a wireless bridge, thus creating a two-piece Bluetooth protocol stack.
- Bluetooth bonding is mandatory for this profile; failure to provide such support would result in a failed Bluetooth connection.
- The DT is the initiator of the Bluetooth relationship.

- There are no specific master or slave roles, although the DT will be the master as it initiated the connection.
- The DT discovers available GWs in radio range by performing an inquiry.
- A GW may restrict discoverability to further prevent unauthorised access.
- The Bluetooth Passkey is used as part of the authentication and encryption process.
- The service class record must depict the fax availability in the GW.
- A service discovery record is generated detailing the parameters, which apply to that specific service.
- Modem and driver emulation are provided above RFCOMM making use of the serial port emulation model.
- The GW must support the use of dialling and control, where AT commands are issued to enable dialling and control.
- A SCO link may be established if it is required and if the GW and DT support this capability.
- A connection would be established regardless of the success of the SCO connection.

The LAN Access Profile

10.1 INTRODUCTION

Take a moment to consider the ease of use that wireless devices provide. The scenario of a wireless notebook or *Personal Digital Assistant* (PDA) user accessing data network services over a fixed network via a *LAN Access Point* (LAP) instantly conjures up images of simplicity and ease-of-use. The *LAN Access Profile* provides the capability of a *data terminal* (DT) device to wirelessly access the services provided by a LAP. Figure 10-1 and Figure 10-2 show the various scenarios that are supported by this profile.

The primary aim of the LAN Access Profile facilitates the support of the networking *Internet Protocol* (IP) over the *Point-to-Point Protocol* (PPP), which is a required component of the profile. This subsequently supports other related networking protocols, such as *Transmission Control Protocol* (TCP) and *Network Basic Input/Output System* (NetBIOS). There are numerous similarities with the *Dial-up Networking* (DUN) Profile, and these are explained in the following section.

10.1.1 Comparing LAN Access with the Dial-up Networking Profile

It is often asked what the differences are between the LAN Access and the Dial-up Networking Profiles. In fact, there is little difference between the two. Both profiles depend upon the Serial Port Profile; both enable an IP stack to be supported and both require a

Figure 10-1   The LAN Access usage model is capable of allowing notebooks
                  or PDAs to behave as DTs, where both devices can access the
                  services provided by the LAN Access Point.

PPP implementation. The subtlety exists in how the Bluetooth link is established. Figure
10-3 shows the components of the *modem driver* and the *modem emulator*, which sit
within the DT and GW, respectively. Essentially, the modem component completes a direct serial cable connection between the DT and GW, forming a wireless bridge. Whereas
the LAN Access Profile provides the direct services of a LAN through a LAP.

The circumstances that arise for the different usages can be best illustrated by considering a user sitting in an office where a fixed[1] access point is readily available and
where the user can make use of the services. However, in the DUN instance, a user may
use his or her mobile phone to access those same services across a public telephone network. Essentially, the two profiles provide greater flexibility and mobility depending on
your situation.

The PPP implementation in both profiles are similar and set out to achieve the same
goals of enabling an IP stack, but the LAN Access Profile omits the use of AT commands
(see the *Dial-up Networking Profile*, Chapter 8).

Figure 10-2   In this illustration, a notebook has been configured to behave as
                  a LAN Access Point, while the other notebook behaves as the
                  DT. The DT is now capable of accessing the services of the
                  LAP.

---

[1]The current v1.1 specification restricts the mobility of a user. The user is fixed in one location and must be
within radio range of where the access point resides. However, in the Bluetooth PAN Working Group, a hand-
off technique is currently being architected to allow the mobility of users so that they can maintain that one initial connection.

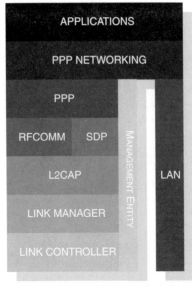
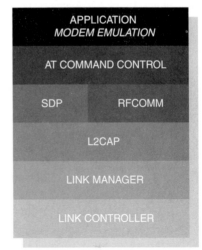

Figure 10-3   The components of the LAN Access and Dial-up Networking Profiles are shown to illustrate the subtle difference. The same applications can be used for both profiles.

10.2   USAGE MODELS

This section considers both existing and future usage models through scenarios that may be typical for the LAN Access Profile. We begin by exploring the existing models where, at face value, the LAN Access Profile provides the wireless ability to make use of a LAN and, in future usage models, we consider alternative means of providing other levels of wireless networking.

10.2.1   Existing Usage Models

Earlier, we touched upon the single, multiple and PC-to-PC scenarios provided in Figure 10-1 and Figure 10-2; these are presently our existing usage models. A single DT is capable of connecting to a LAP and will have its full attention at its disposal. Multiple[2] DTs would inevitably cause the LAP to share its bandwidth resources. Like the single connection, the DT has the ability to utilise the services of the LAP; with multiple DTs, as well as providing the services of the LAP; it would also provide the ability for the DTs to share information with one another.

---

[2]Specifically, the number of active connections permitted would be seven. This is due to the number of concurrent connections that can be maintained by one master device. The AM_ADDR represents the slave member address and is used to identify active participants; this is currently restricted to 3-bits, although slaves that become disconnected or parked give up this address.

The other usage model to discuss here is the PC-to-PC scenario. In this instance, we do not necessarily have a DT or a LAP, but we do have two devices that are capable of supporting LAN Access. The scenario is such that *DeviceA* wishes to connect to *DeviceB* (there are certainly other profiles, which would also accommodate this scenario); DeviceB takes on the role of LAP and DeviceA takes the role of DT. DeviceA is now capable of exploring the services of DeviceB in the usual manner. For a specific PC-to-PC configuration, support is also offered for an independent connection to a PC that is running a PPP Server; for example, a Microsoft Windows 98 installed PC is bundled with a PPP Server. In order for these two devices to create a successful connection, an exchange of text strings must be performed: `CLIENT` and `CLIENTSERVER`.

A LAN Access Point might typically be installed in an area where it is not convenient to either install or continue a cabled network, or it may be installed in an area purely for convenience, such as a conference room. Although, this type of model does provide the image of an embedded device fixed to ceiling or wall, a LAP may take the form of a standalone PC or take a similar form to that of a modem, which may sit alongside or on top of a PC. Here, it has become Bluetooth-enabled and supports the LAN Access Profile. It may then be connected to the LAN or simply offer other resources. The important point here is not to confine our thinking to stereotypical images of what a device should be.

At its core, these models effectively provide the wireless means to connect to a LAN, but there are other numerous applications to be explored.

10.2.2   Future Usage Models

We have talked about the services of a LAP being provided by an existing cabled infrastructure. It would be possible to imagine that an infrastructure could comprise a series of access points that form the basis of a corporate or public network. In the same way that is currently depicted by the LAN Access Profile, users may now freely walk around an office and maintain the connection to the LAN, thereby achieving a seamless connection to the network. Current limitations of the v1.1 specification would dictate that, for each new access point the user is exposed to, a new authentication and encryption procedure would have to be endured. What is achieved from this new usage model is a wireless infrastructure providing ease-of-installation and mobility.

The general availability and low-cost of an access point would provide users with the potential to access data on-the-go, for example, at the train station or in a hotel. Many manufacturers are already considering this potential. It is possible to provide data services such as this in other public spaces, where the user is not confined to a particular area; *Access Point Kiosks* (APK) or similar facilities could be introduced. In the same way that we take public telephones for granted, accessing the services of an APK can be made readily available at a charge to the user (the duration of the connection or a one-off charge can be made). These models are not necessarily restricted to future usage scenarios. Our existing usage model is more than capable of providing these services, but the ability to roam from one device to another further simplifies the user experience.

We have seen these public services already in various guises. For example, we can connect to our corporate network and collect email when we are in a hotel using a standard modem, but how often have we spent time searching through our case looking for the correct connector and cable? With Bluetooth applications, we are building on the fundamental philosophy that sparked its creation: cable replacement technology.

10.3   PROFILE PRINCIPLES

The LAN Access Profile provides two new roles: a DT and a *LAP*. The LAP provides the ability for a DT to connect and to provide its services; this is achieved by running a PPP Server, which transports its packet over RFCOMM. The DT incorporates a PPP Client, again transporting packets over RFCOMM, which in both cases allows it to provide support for an IP stack. Previously, we touched upon the fact that the profile is capable of supporting the range of stereotypical networking protocols; Figure 10-4 demonstrates the architecture of the components that would make up the complete LAN Access model.

During any PPP communication, encryption must be enabled within the *Link Manager* (LM); any attempt to avoid an enforcement of this operation would result in a failure of connection.

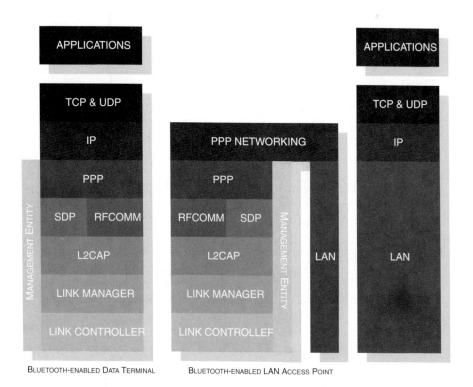

Figure 10-4   The core components of the Bluetooth protocol stack are shown illustrating how the components of the LAN Access Profile are integrated.

Table 10-1 The list of behavioural characteristics that are typical for this profile.

CONFIGURATION	ROLE	DESCRIPTION
DeviceA	DT	A device acting as a DT, which may take the form of a notebook or a PDA. In this particular context, the device is described as initiating the connection with the accepting device.
	Initiator	This configuration describes the device that instigates the original connection or the device that wishes to initiate communication over an existing link.
DeviceB	LAP	A device that behaves as a LAN Access Point, where it manages incoming and outgoing network communication. It is also the party that accepts incoming connections from the DT.
	Acceptor	This configuration describes the process of the device accepting the initiated communication from DeviceA.

In Table 10-1, clarification is provided with regard to the roles used within the context of this profile. In general, *DeviceA* represents the initiating party and *DeviceB* represents the accepting party. The terms are often used interchangeably when describing specific operations in various contexts and are provided here for reference.

10.3.1.1 Additional Parameters. The LAP should support additional parameters to configure the user mode operation. The profile supports various scenarios and, as such, the user mode parameter setting can restrict the number of users accessing remote services.

You may remember that a maximum of seven users can simultaneously access the services of a LAP. In Table 10-2, we illustrate the two user modes available to a LAP administrator.

In Figure 10-5, we can see the LAP administrator setting the number of users capable of accessing this service to one and, as such, places the device into a *Single-User Mode*. Conversely, Figure 10-6 shows the user increasing the number of users capable of accessing the same service, that is, the LAP administrator places the device into *Multi-User Mode*.

In this chapter, the DT is referred to as DeviceA, or the initiator and the LAP is the acceptor and forms DeviceB. Initially, DeviceA takes the role of master of the piconet, but DeviceB will request a master-slave switch, if it is configured for multi-user mode. We will discuss master-slave switching in more detail later in this chapter.

Table 10-2   The LAN Access Point encompasses additional parameters for its operation. Placing the device into a single or multi-user mode can restrict the number of users accessing the remote service.

PARAMETER	DESCRIPTION
Single-User Mode	This places the LAP into single-user mode restricting the number of users to one.
Multi-User Mode	The multi-user mode parameter allows the LAP administrator to set the number of users capable of simultaneously accessing the services of the LAP.

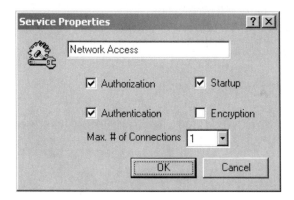

Figure 10-5   The LAP administrator has restricted the number of users to one; the setting has placed the device into a Single-User Mode. (Courtesy of TDK Systems Europe.)

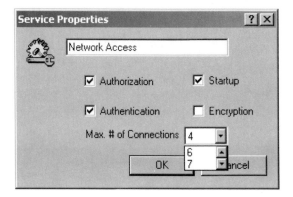

Figure 10-6   The LAP administrator has now increased the number of users capable of accessing the device; this setting has placed the device into Multi-User Mode. (Courtesy of TDK Systems Europe.)

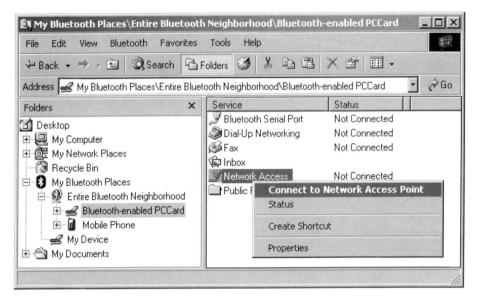

Figure 10-7   Right-clicking the devices icon causes a pop-up menu to appear, offering the ability to connect to the device. In this illustration, we can see the user connecting to a service, which is offering LAN capabilities. (Courtesy of TDK Systems Europe.)

10.4   USER EXPECTATIONS

10.4.1   Data Terminal

10.4.1.1   Connecting to a LAP.   As soon as the user has the ability to connect and has discovered the availability of a LAP, he or she may now continue to make use of the services it provides. The user may now be able to double-click[3] the LAP icon or right-click its icon to begin the process of connecting to the LAP, see Figure 10-7.

In Section 10.3, *Profile Principles*, we touched upon the requirement of authentication and encryption. Before a user can access the full services, he or she is required to enter a *Bluetooth Passkey*. Figure 10-8 shows the user being prompted with a Microsoft Windows dialog box requesting the entry of a passkey. Upon successful entry and authentication, the user may then be required to enter a username or password to fulfill PPP authentication requirements;[4] this would allow further access to the services on the network.

---

[3]The double-click and right-click operations refer to a mouse that is connected to your DT device (in this example, a PC or notebook computer running a Microsoft Windows operating system) and where both operations trigger the same method of access. It is noted that an operation may vary from DT device to DT device; as such, the number of buttons may vary on a mouse and indeed no mouse may be connected. The example just draws your attention to how it may be possible and acknowledges that implementations may differ.

[4]The LAP administrator has an opportunity to enable PPP authentication. If this is disabled, then the user will not be required to enter a username or password.

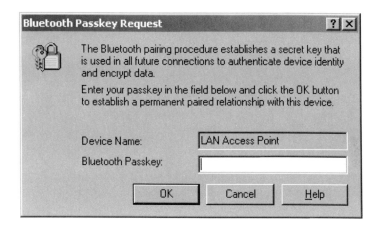

Figure 10-8 The user is requested to enter his or her passkey to authenticate with the LAP device. (Courtesy of TDK Systems Europe.)

It is worth noting that a LAP may offer many services, since its connection to a LAN may be made up of several IP subnets; the subnets, in turn, will offer the user multiple services from that same LAP. The double-clicking or right-clicking operation may expand these services, thus offering the user a greater choice and the initial operation (previously outlined) of connecting would apply to these further expanded services.

10.4.1.2 Ending a connection with a LAP. Once a connection is established with a LAP and its services are no longer required, the user may terminate the session. In Figure 10-7, we illustrated a user right-clicking the device icon to connect to the device. Similarly, the user may choose to perform the same operation to disconnect.

The profile describes this as termination due to *user-intervention*. Other forms of disconnection may occur if the quality of service can no longer be maintained by the LAP; an instance of this specific example may occur when the bandwidth is no longer available or the LAN that the LAP is attached to is unexpectedly lost. It is important to remember that the user must be conveyed the appropriate information about their current situation and to be offered a reconnection at a later time.

One other such instance of a terminated connection may occur when a connection is lost due to the DT moving out of radio range from a LAP; we pick this up in the following section.

10.4.1.3 Losing a connection with a LAP. Current LAP products offer various radio ranges from 10 meters through to 100 meters. With the growing number of Bluetooth-enabled devices in use within an office, there may be some confusion for the user with regard to the radio ranges supported and, as such, if they should walk out of range, the connection is subsequently lost. Advising the user appropriately is paramount and, again, an offer of a reconnection should be made.

The profile covers an instance of this specific operation. It claims to provide the user with the ability to reconnect seamlessly once the DT is within range or other associated disconnection problems are resolved. In addition, it also claims to provide an appropriate warning to the user if their connection is lost. The same method of instigating that initial connection may be used to reconnect to the LAP.

Using the same method of accessing the LAP services, a successful reconnection would occur. This seamless reconnection is achieved due to the fact that both the DT and LAP remember their respective Bluetooth addresses, their passkeys and any previous PPP authentication.

10.4.2   LAN Access Point

Today, LAP devices usually manifest themselves as embedded devices, secured to a ceiling or placed in a similar location. From an administrator's perspective, he or she would typically have an initial contact with the device in order to configure and set-up its internal parameters for connection to a LAN. Other parameters such as the *Dynamic Host Configuration Protocol* (DHCP) configuration, the level of PPP authentication and the number of users can also be defined. The LAP device may also support the use of *Simple Network Management Protocol* (SNMP[5]) to obtain statistical information about its usage and also the configuration of specific SNMP alerts, which may be triggered during a network-related problem.

The administrator may have at his or her disposal an application, which manages these internal parameters and is connected via a dedicated port on the device itself. The administrator may also have a remote management scheme available via a *Hypertext Transfer Protocol* (HTTP) interface (see Figure 10-9).

From a distance, the administrator should be able to determine the successful operation through a series of LEDs that are available on the device itself (see Figure 10-10 and Figure 10-11). Many manufacturers offer a series of LEDs that illuminate, according to the activity and operational status.

In other guises, a LAP may be implemented onto a standalone PC, which itself is connected to a LAN offering users its services. The operational parameters of DHCP configuration and PPP authentication may be managed in a similar manner.

10.4.2.1   Accepting a Connection from a DT.   The LAP undertakes a series of events that enable a DT to successfully access its services. Figure 10-12 illustrates these events. As we have already discussed, encryption is an integral component in a successful Bluetooth connection. The LAP is architected in such a way that it refuses to accept any incoming connections from a DT that does not support encryption.

10.4.2.1.1   Pairing.   During the connection stage, pairing must occur to form part of the authentication process. The passkey is required prior to any successful connection; we discussed the user interface aspect of this in Section 10.4.1.1, *Connecting to a LAP*.

---

[5]SNMP is prescribed in RFC1157.

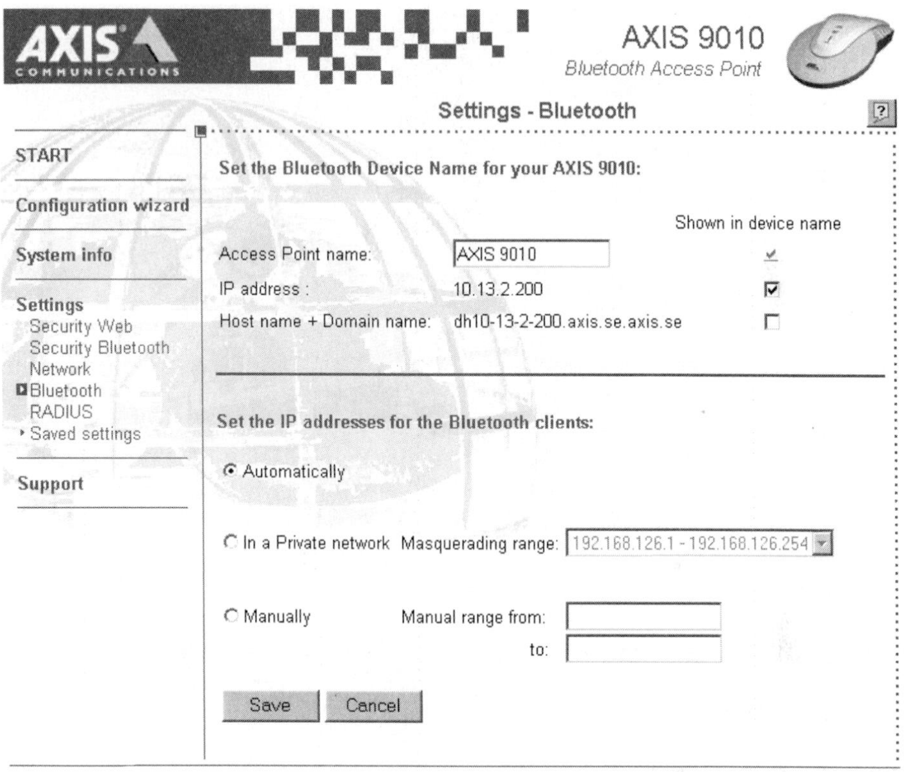

AXIS COMMUNICATIONS   AXIS 9010
                                                                              Bluetooth Access Point

Settings - Bluetooth   [?]

START

Configuration wizard

System info   Shown in device name

Settings   Access Point name: AXIS 9010   ✓
  Security Web   IP address :   10.13.2.200   ☑
  Security Bluetooth   Host name + Domain name: dh10-13-2-200.axis.se.axis.se   ☐
  Network
  ■ Bluetooth
  RADIUS
  ▸ Saved settings   **Set the IP addresses for the Bluetooth clients:**

Support   ⦿ Automatically

                                ○ In a Private network Masquerading range: [192.168.126.1 - 192.168.126.254 ▾]

                                ○ Manually   Manual range from: [   ]
                                                                      to: [   ]

                                [Save] [Cancel]

Set the Bluetooth Device Name for your AXIS 9010:

Figure 10-9   This screen shot shows a number of HTTP interface configuration options. (Courtesy of Axis Communications.)

10.4.2.2   Refusing a Connection from a DT.   There may be several instances when a connection from a DT needs to be refused. The first would be when an incorrect passkey has been entered, where pairing would fail. The second will occur if the PPP authentication fails. The use of the *Challenge Handshake Authentication Protocol* (CHAP[6]) or the *PPP Extensible Authentication Protocol* (EAP[6]) is not mandatory, but nonetheless a connection is refused if this is unsuccessful.

Other such instances may be due to the loss of a LAN connection or if the services the LAP wishes to provide are not available. Lastly, a connection should be refused if the LAP has exhausted most of its bandwidth due to the number of users already connected. The user may be advised to reconnect later or may be offered an alternative LAP.

10.4.2.3   Initialising the LAN Access Service.   As previously indicated, most LAP devices may take the form of an embedded product; as such, this device is switched on once and left to service the DTs. During the power up sequence, most of the initialisa-

---

[6]A discussion on CHAP and EAP are provided in Section 10.5.2.1.3, *Authentication Protocols*.

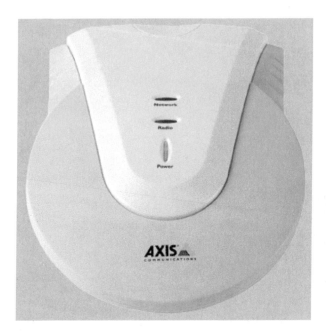

Figure 10-10   One of the many access points widely available today. The
                   Axis' 9010 Bluetooth Access Point clearly shows a series of
                   LEDs that report the operational status of the device. (Cour-
                   tesy of Axis Communications.)

tion parameters can be defined. Table 10-3 outlines some of the initialisation parameters
that are defined in the profile.

In a similar fashion, a PC or notebook that is configured as a LAP may initialise its
power-up parameters when the device is switched on. Alternatively, a PC or notebook
may be configured ad-hoc to behave as a LAP, allowing a DT to connect to it. Table 10-4
provides an example list of implementation-specific parameters.[7]

Figure 10-13 illustrates some of the initialisation-specific parameters that are required to configure the LAP.

The shutdown sequence of the LAP would ultimately terminate the PPP Server and
any active DT connections would be notified of the loss of service.

10.4.2.4   Establishing a LAN Connection.   The DT always initiates a connection with a LAP and it is anticipated that in future profiles a LAP may instigate[8] a connection. There may be several LAPs within radio range offering different levels of

---

[7]The LAN Access Profile outlines the use of IP, DHCP and DNS etc., stating that these components are optional.
[8]In Section 10.2.2, *Future Usage Models*, we stated that a hand-off between a DT and LAP is required for roaming and may require the LAP to initiate a connection with another LAP to pass on information about the *handed-
off* DT.

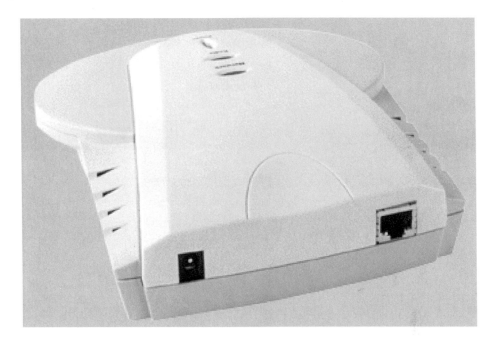

Figure 10-11   In this illustration, the Axis' 9010 Bluetooth Access Point
                   clearly shows the connection ports available for power and
                   LAN. (Courtesy of Axis Communications.)

service. When performing a service discovery, the range of LAPs will be made available to the DT.

Upon creating an RFCOMM connection, the user is required[9] to enter his or her passkey. Subsequently, the PPP application is then started, requiring the user to enter their username and password. This can be optionally postponed to a later stage in the connection process.

10.4.2.5   Losing or Disconnecting a LAN Connection.   The most common or typical form of termination or disconnection from a DT occurs during user-intervention, that is, the user has requested a disconnection. It is also possible that a failure in the LAN may result in the LAP being unable to continue providing its services to the DT. This section considers the probable causes of termination and how a LAP device should manage such scenarios.

The LAP itself may be connected to a LAN, where other administrators may manage this independently, as such its behaviour is always difficult to predict. The LAP itself should be capable of managing instances where the LAN is lost for whatever reason. The LAP may be handling several simultaneous connections, all of which are uploading or downloading data. During this unexpected loss, both the user and LAP administrator

---

[9]If no passkey is required, the default passkey is used, which is a single byte with all its bits set to zero.

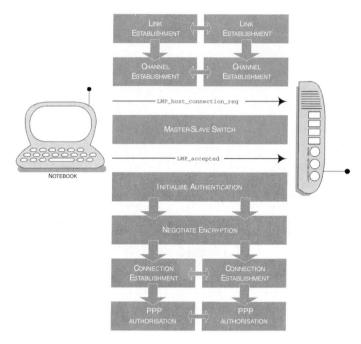

Figure 10-12   The events that take place during an incoming connection from a DT.

Table 10-3   An example of initialisation parameters that may be initialised during the power-up sequence of a LAP.

PARAMETER	DESCRIPTION
PPP Authentication	The LAP administrator determines whether this level of authentication is required and is therefore optional.
PPP Compression	Again, the LAP administrator determines whether compression should be used.
User-mode	The number of users allowed to connect to the LAP at any one time determines this mode. For example, setting the user-mode to allow a single user would place the device in single-*user mode*. Similarly, setting the number of users to two or above would place the LAP configuration into a *multi-user mode*.
Generic Access	This parameter refers to the level of support outlined in Section 10.5.1.1, *Generic Access*. This would determine if specific or all users can make use of its services.

Table 10-4   An example of implementation-specific initialisation parameters that may be initialised during the power-up sequence of a LAP.

PARAMETER	DESCRIPTION
DHCP	This set of parameters will allow connecting DTs to have their unique IP address when connected to the LAN.
DNS	These IP settings allow the correct configuration for routing of data access across the network.
IP	The LAP itself would need a unique IP address.
SNMP	Specific configuration for the request of data usage through the use of an SNMP *Management Information Base* (MIB). The definition of an SNMP alert could be based on statistical information derived from such MIBs.

should be informed (the DT user scenarios are covered in Section 10.4.1.3, *Losing a connection with a LAP*). The administrator would become immediately aware of this, having previously configured his or her installation with an SNMP alert (see Figure 10-14).

The loss of a connection is not restricted to infrastructure related issues. There may be a large demand on the access point, which restricts the *Quality Of Service* (QoS). The bandwidth itself may not be sufficient and one DT may make extraordinary demands, resulting in a poor QoS for other connected DTs. In the same way that an SNMP alert is generated to inform of networking issues, it could be generated to inform the administrator of performance issues.

Once a connection has been established and data has been transferred, there may be an occasion where the DT device has been taken out of range of the LAP. The DT itself has not made a formal request to terminate the session but, as far as the LAP is concerned, it is still connected; this inevitably inhibits other users from making use of the LAP services.

Both the DT and LAP need to be informed if such a connection has been unexpectedly lost. If the DT moves back into range with the LAP, a seamless reconnection[10] can occur, that is, the LAP and DT may "remember" one another. This can be accomplished because they both store the user's passkey, link key, user name and password.

10.5   LIFTING THE LID

10.5.1   Dependencies

In our previous discussion, we covered aspects of existing and future usage models and their respective user expectations. In the following sections, we take an opportunity to explore in greater depth the dependencies that make up this profile. In Figure 10-15, we

---

[10]A reconnection would be subject to the available number of connections and the current QoS available.

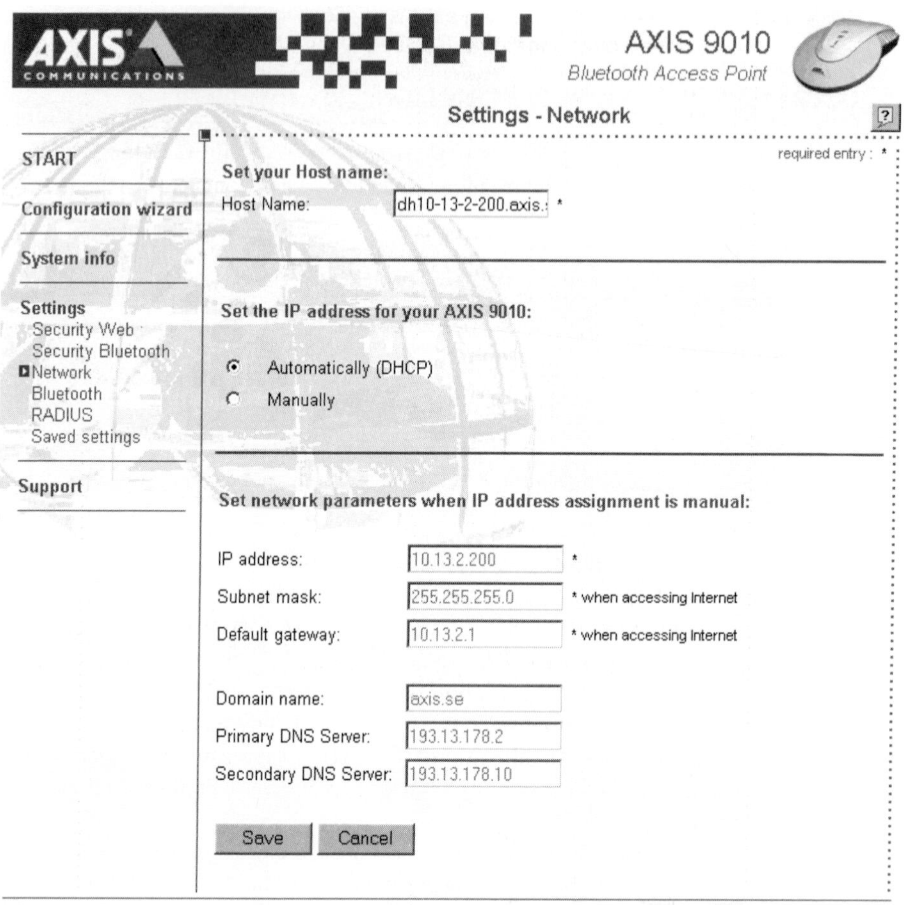

AXIS COMMUNICATIONS

AXIS 9010
Bluetooth Access Point

Settings - Network   [?]

START

Configuration wizard

System info

Settings
 Security Web
 Security Bluetooth
 ▪Network
 Bluetooth
 RADIUS
 Saved settings

Support

required entry : *

Set your Host name:

Host Name: dh10-13-2-200.axis.: *

Set the IP address for your AXIS 9010:

 ⦿   Automatically (DHCP)
 ○   Manually

Set network parameters when IP address assignment is manual:

IP address: 10.13.2.200   *

Subnet mask: 255.255.255.0   * when accessing Internet

Default gateway: 10.13.2.1   * when accessing Internet

Domain name: axis.se

Primary DNS Server: 193.13.178.2

Secondary DNS Server: 193.13.178.10

    Save   Cancel

Figure 10-13 A screen shot showing the number of parameters required in
order to configure the LAP. (Courtesy of Axis Communica-
tions.)

provide a conceptual illustration representing the dependencies that make up the LAN
Access Profile; the areas that are shaded are relevant to this profile. As you can see, the
profile depends upon the basic functionality offered to us by the *Generic Access Profile*,
Chapter 2, the *Service Discovery Application Profile*, Chapter 3 and the *Serial Port Profile*, Chapter 6. We will discuss, in turn, the basic requirements of these dependent components and any deviations that may occur from the basic functionality originally offered
to us.

This section also considers the external components or other dependencies that are
not shown in Figure 10-15, but are required for a product to claim conformity. The LAN
Access Profile is structured in a manner that determines the level of support from the

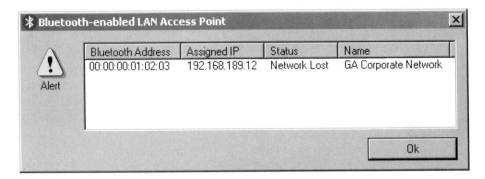

Figure 10-14   An SNMP alert informing the administrator that the LAN
service is lost for the network identified.

Bluetooth core protocol layers; as such, the sections are laid out with the particular layer
reference in mind.

10.5.1.1   Generic Access.   The LAN Access Profile relies upon the capabilities
provided by the *Generic Access Profile*, Chapter 2. You may recall that a level of basic
functionality is achieved through establishing a set of rules and procedures. The behaviour
of such devices is governed by simple rules that relate to their connectivity, discoverability

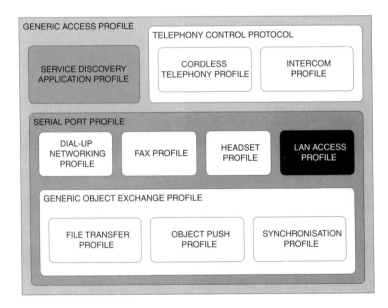

Figure 10-15   The dependent components of the Bluetooth protocol stack
that make up the LAN Access Profile. The areas that are
shaded are relevant to this profile.

Table 10-5   The core set of procedures as required by most profiles.

PROCEDURES	DESCRIPTION
Discoverability Mode	This mode prescribes the overall discoverability of a device, allowing it to be placed into a non-discoverable, limited, or general discoverable mode. The mode would allow devices to become generally available to other users or it can be restricted to personal use.
Connectability Mode	When determining a baseband connectable state, this mode is used to place a device into a connectable or non-connectable mode.
Pairing	Pairable and non-pairable modes are used to realise the security aspects when operating or intending to use a device. A device may require authentication and, as such, the user would be required to enter a Bluetooth Passkey. The pairing procedure starts the link key generation process, which in turn allows authentication to take place.

and common characteristics at the user interface level, with some additional emphasis provided for security. It is these rules and procedures that are used to establish commonality between products, which will ultimately achieve a cohesive user experience. We will now revisit the behavioural aspects of Bluetooth-enabled devices as outlined by the Generic Access Profile.

In Table 10-5, the basic set of procedures is illustrated, identifying functional expectations which, in turn, govern its operation. These procedures help determine the context in which the device would operate. For example, a device may wish to be discoverable for a period of time or it may require a level of security that differs from one device to another depending upon the services it is capable of offering.

In Table 10-6, we consider the specific set of operations that are required for this profile. In the table, you will notice features are marked with *M* (Mandatory), *O* (Optional), *X* (Excluded), *C* (Conditional) and *N/A* (Not Applicable). These will determine what is expected from the features of the Generic Access Profile.

Security is an important aspect for Bluetooth-enabled devices. Table 10-7 identifies the security requirements for this profile. You will also notice that these features are marked in a similar fashion to our previous table. You may remember from the *Generic Access Profile*, Chapter 2, that Security Mode 1 is a non-secure mode where Bluetooth-enabled devices will never initiate any security procedures; whereas Security Modes 2 and 3 initiate different levels of security procedures at various stages of connection establishment. In this instance, the profile mandates that support should be provided for at least Security Mode 2 or 3.

Table 10-6 The illustration shows specific modes of operation that this profile depends upon to realise its compliant implementation.

MODES	DT	LAP
Non-discoverable	X	O
Limited Discoverable	X	X
General Discoverable	X	M
Non-connectable	X	O
Connectable	X	M
Non-pairable	X	O
Pairable	X	M

In our final consideration of the basic rules and procedures that are required from the Generic Access Profile, the idle mode procedures outline behavioural characteristics when DeviceA chooses to initiate them against DeviceB. The procedures that are listed in Table 10-8 provide a clear indication of how a device should operate when performing such an activity. Let us take our bonding procedure as an example. The term bonding is very much associated with the pairing process; however, bonding occurs when the user has the *intent* to initiate a trusted relationship with DeviceB.

With this intent, the user is prompted to enter a Bluetooth Passkey which, in turn, instigates the pairing process, that is, the generation of the link keys, where subsequent authentication can then occur. In summary, we realise that there are a specific set of events associated with a procedure. In the *Generic Access Profile*, Chapter 2, we both presented examine how each procedure is conducted.

The mechanism for providing device discoverability is the provision of a well structured FHS packet, which is shown in Figure 10-16. This packet is used to identify the remote device, where information such as Bluetooth Device Address (BD_ADDR) and clock offsets is determined.

Table 10-7 The illustration shows specific security procedures that this profile depends upon to realise its compliant implementation.

PROCEDURE	DT	LAP
Authentication	M	M
Security Mode 1	M	M
Security Mode 2	C	C
Security Mode 3	C	C

Table 10-8   The illustration shows specific behavioural procedures that this profile depends upon to realise its compliant implementation.

PROCEDURE	DT	LAP
General Inquiry	M	N/A
Limited Inquiry	N/A	N/A
Name Discovery	M	N/A
Device Discovery	M	N/A
Bonding	M	M

You may also notice from this packet that the *Class of Device* (CoD) field is provided. This information is relayed to the user interface which, in turn, provides common characteristics about discovered devices. The CoD is used during the discovery mechanism to learn more about the type of device and what it may be capable of providing. This structure of information is depicted in Figure 10-17 and is made up of 3-bytes (or 24-bits). The following sections now consider the LAN Access attributes, which will ultimately make use of the *Service, Major,* and *Minor Device Class* fields.

10.5.1.1.1   Service Class.   This high-level form of defining a Bluetooth device identifies where in the Service Class field the LAN Access Profile resides (see Table 10-9) which, in turn, determines the category of service. Here, the category of service falls within *Networking.*

10.5.1.1.2   Major Device Class.   This high-level form of defining a Bluetooth device identifies where in the Major Device Class the LAN Access Profile resides (see Table 10-10) which, in turn, determines the major class grouping. Here, the category falls within LAN Access Point.

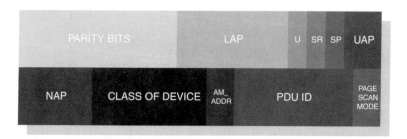

Figure 10-16   The structure of the FHS packet used only for reference to illustrate the position of the CoD structure.

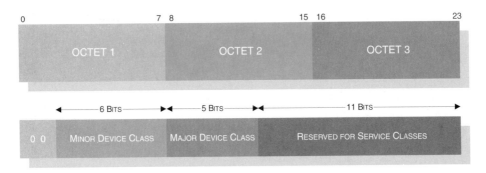

Figure 10-17   The structure of the CoD, illustrating the Minor Device, Major
Device and Service Class fields and their respective lengths.

10.5.1.1.3   Minor Device Class.   The Minor Device Class in this profile is used to
convey further context for the setting within the major class grouping. Here, the bits are
set to reflect the utilisation of the LAN Access Point. Table 10-11 lists the values for the
load ratio, but no standard formula is used to calculate them. Manufacturers are encouraged to adopt a similar mechanism to report this utilisation.

In an area with multiple LAPs, the DT should make use of the service with the lowest utilisation or, in other words, the LAP that is capable of providing the best bandwidth
(assuming that the services available are similar). For completeness, Table 10-12 provides
the remaining lower bits that form the minor device class.

10.5.1.2   Service Discovery.   In the *Service Discovery Application Profile*,
Chapter 3, we introduced the characteristics of the mechanisms used to retrieve service information from a remote device. Typically, a client will initiate inquiry and discovery
procedures as outlined in our previous section, to learn of the devices in radio range. A
client can then make use of an application, which embodies the functionality of the underlying *Service Discovery Protocol* (SDP). The *Service Discovery Application* (SrvD-
scApp) uses an *SDP Client* to instigate a request to the remote device where the *SDP
Server* will respond. As such, the DT and LAP must employ the use of an SDP client and
server respectively, as illustrated in Table 10-13.

Protocol Data Units (PDUs) are used to instruct the SDP server to undertake
browsing procedures and to retrieve service record information about its services. You

Table 10-9   The Service Class categorisation for the LAN Access Profile.

23	22	21	20	19	18	17	16	15	14	13	**SERVICE CLASS**
											Bit # of CoD
0	0	0	0	0	0	1	0	0	0	0	Networking

Table 10-10   The Major Device Class for the LAN Access Profile.

12	11	10	9	8	MAJOR DEVICE CLASS
					Bit # of CoD
0	0	0	1	1	LAN Access Point

may recall that these PDUs carry payloads about requests containing `AttributeIDs` and `AttributeValues` describing what exactly is being sought. As previously discussed, the client and server operate a request and response paradigm. SDAP will construct PDUs containing information relating to the `AttributeID` and `AttributeValues`, which in turn instruct the server to carry out its operation. The various request and response PDUs that are required are shown Table 10-14, where features indicated are described as mandatory (M), optional (O) and excluded (X).

A service record is maintained for each service a device is capable of supporting and, as such, a *Service Record Handle* is created to uniquely identify this. The `ServiceRecordHandle` is a 32-bit unsigned integer and is stored on the SDP server. The service record shown in Table 10-15 identifies a LAP device and provides a list of `AttributeIDs`, which ultimately would identify the service for the LAN Access Profile. A minimum of two attributes are required to make a service record; these are

Table 10-11   The 3-bit upper area of the minor device class that depicts the utilisation of the LAN Access Point.

7	6	5	MINOR DEVICE CLASS
			Bit # of CoD
0	0	0	Fully Available
0	0	1	1 to 17% Utilised
0	1	0	17 to 33% Utilised
0	1	1	33 to 50% Utilised
1	0	0	50 to 67% Utilised
1	0	1	67 to 83% Utilised
1	1	0	83 to 99% Utilised
1	1	1	No Service Available[11]

---

[11]In this instance, the user should either be informed of the unavailability of the service (and be asked to try again later) or offered other similar services from other LAPs within radio range.

Table 10-12   The 3-bit lower area of the minor device class for the LAN Access

			MINOR DEVICE CLASS
4	3	2	Bit # of CoD
0	0	0	Unclassified
0	0	1	Range 0x01 to 0x0F Reserved

`ServiceRecordHandle` and `ServiceClassIDList`, which it must contain at least one `UUID`.

When browsing for services on the remote device, a local device constructs a search pattern using a *Universally Unique Identifier* (UUID). A UUID is a 128-bit value, which has been shortened for use within Bluetooth. The shortcut has been provided by first establishing a *Bluetooth Base UUID*, which we discussed in the *Service Discovery Application Profile*, Chapter 3.

The UUIDs that have been presented are aliases and take the form of what is referred to as a 16-bit UUID or a 32-bit UUID but, in turn, they should all refer to the 128-bit notation. These UUIDs have been assigned and can be referenced in the Bluetooth Special Interest Group, Bluetooth Assigned Numbers, v1.1, February 2001. For the search pattern to be successful, they all need to be converted to the 128-bit notation, since they will all be compared at this range. An arithmetic conversion algorithm is used to construct the 128-bit value.

Table 10-16 summarises the service class UUIDs used to identify the particular profile in use. This also correlates with the identification of the device during a device discovery procedure, as previously outlined in Section 10.5.1.1, *Generic Access*.

As part of the service record, the identification of the dependent underlying protocols are also identified. The local device retrieves this information, where it can fully understand the exact requirements needed to fulfill the service. The LAN Access Profile is dependent on the protocols as shown in Table 10-17, which also shows their associated UUID values.

10.5.1.3   RFCOMM.   In the *Serial Port Profile*, Chapter 6, we introduced the conceptual and functional nature of RFCOMM and how it provides an emulated serial

Table 10-13   As a minimum, the local device must support the use of a client application and the remote device must support the use of a server.

FEATURE	DT	LAP
SDP Client	M	X
SDP Server	X	M

Table 10-14   The list of PDUs that are required for the operation of the LAN Access Profile.

PDU	DT	LAP
SDP_ErrorResponse	X	M
SDP_ServiceSearchRequest	M	X
SDP_ServiceSearchResponse	X	M
SDP_ServiceAttributeRequest	M	X
SDP_ServiceAttributeResponse	X	M
SDP_ServiceSearchAttributeRequest	O	X
SDP_ServiceSearchAttributeRequest	X	O

port presence. Several distinctions were made between the various types of applications. The purpose of making these distinctions was to enable clarification and understanding of RFCOMM's composition. In this particular application context, the creation of an emulated serial port would be transparent to the user. The LAN Access Profile is dependent upon the operation of the Serial Port Profile and, as such, is required to establish an emulated serial port as part of its communication link with the remote device.

The term cable replacement application was introduced in our earlier chapter and distinguishes between the different scenarios available. It refers to specific Bluetooth applications that create implicit emulated serial ports, which remain transparent to the user to complete the creation of a communications link.

Specific detail has been provided to illustrate how data is communicated over an emulated serial port connection, where a *Data Link Connection* (DLC) is established between two peer devices, namely DT and LAP. We have also looked at the fields that make up our service record for this profile. The ProtocolDescriptorList field is used to describe the set of protocols that the profile intends to use and, as such, the RFCOMM protocol identifier contains a parameter, which contains the Server Channel number.

The Server Channel is used in combination with a *Data Link Connection Identifier* (DLCI), which is then used to uniquely identify the active DLC. This connection is then mapped onto a connectionless orientated L2CAP *Channel Identifier* (CID).

In this section we highlight the specific features that are required to realise a compliant LAN Access Profile. Table 10-18 and Table 10-19 illustrate the features or capabilities that are expected from the Serial Port Profile.

The use of the RLS command is encouraged to keep peer devices informed of any state change. In one such instance, an emulated serial port may interface to a Type II application (physical serial port), where overruns or parity errors may occur. An application that makes use of RS232 port configuration parameters should expose these settings through an appropriate Application Programming Interface (API) function; this is of particular relevance when interfacing to Type II applications.

Table 10-15   The list of mandatory and configurable items that make up this profile's service discovery record.

ATTRIBUTE	DESCRIPTION
`ServiceRecordHandle`	With an `AttributeID` of `0x0000`, this uniquely identifies the service record within the SDP server on the LAP device.

`ServiceClassIDList`
 	
`ServiceClass0`
	With an `AttributeID` of `0x0001`, the following `ServiceClass0` would contain the `UUID` for the *LAN Access Using PPP* its respective `UUID` value is summarised in Table 10-16.

`ProtocolDescriptorList`
 	
`Protocol0`
 	
`Protocol1`
 	
`ParameterFor1`
	With an `AttributeID` of `0x0004`, the following `Protocol0` would contain a `UUID` for the protocol *L2CAP*, whereas in `Protocol1` a `UUID` would contain the protocol identifier for *RFCOMM*. Their respective `UUID` values are summarised in Table 10-17. The `ParameterFor1` would contain the relevant server channel number for the RFCOMM transport.

`BluetoothProfile-`
`DescriptorList`
 	
`Profile0`
 	
`ParameterFor0`
	With an `AttributeID` of `0x0009`, the following `Profile0` would identify the `UUID` for the *LAN Access Using PPP* service class, which is summarised in Table 10-16. The `ParameterFor0` accommodates the version number supported by this profile.

`ServiceName`	With a base `AttributeID` of `0x0006`, this attribute has an offset of `0x0000`. It is a configurable item and has an `AttributeValue` of a `Text` string, where its default setting is *LAN Access Using PPP*.
`ServiceDescription`	With a base `AttributeID` of `0x0006`, this attribute has an offset of `0x0001`. It is a configurable item and has an `AttributeValue` of a `Text` string, where its default setting is *LAN Access Using PPP*.

(continued)

Table 10-15 The list of mandatory and configurable items that make up this profile's service discovery record. *Continued.*

ATTRIBUTE	DESCRIPTION
ServiceAvailability	With an `AttributeID` of 0x0008, the following `AttributeValue` would identify the load factor for the LAP. We discussed load factoring in our earlier Section 10.5.1.1.3, *Minor Device Class.* The availability of a useable service is identified in this `AttributeID`.
IPSubnet	With an `AttributeID` of 0x0200, this attribute contains a configurable `Text` string identifying the subnet definition, for example, 192.168.2.23.

Table 10-16 The service class that matches a corresponding profile. This correlates with our previous Generic Access section.

CLASS	UUID
LANAccessUsingPPP	0x1102

Table 10-17 The list of protocols that are used in this profile. Their associated UUID values are also shown.

PROTOCOL	UUID
RFCOMM	0x0003
L2CAP	0x0100

Table 10-18   The set of capabilities that are required from the initiating party, denoted here by the DT device.

PROCEDURE	DT	LAP
Initialise an RFCOMM Session	M	X
Terminate an RFCOMM Session	M	M
Establish a new DLC Connection	M	X
Disconnect a DLC Connection	M	M
Emulate RS232 Control Signals	C	C
Transfer Data	M	M
Test Command	X	X
Flow Control	C	C
RLS	O	O
PN	O	O
RPN	O	O

10.5.1.4   L2CAP.   The L2CAP layer provides transparency for the upper-layers of the stack from the layers typically found within the host controller. L2CAP payloads are passed to the *Host Controller Interface*[12] (HCI), which is then subsequently passed onto the *Link Manager Protocol* (LMP). The range of upper-layers, which include RFCOMM, SDP and the *Telephony Control Protocol Specification* (TCS) all make use of the capabilities offered to us by L2CAP. Its primary role is to provide *protocol multiplexing*, allowing numerous simultaneous connections to be made, and also providing the ability for *segmentation* and *reassembly*. This refers to the ability to manage large payloads in the applications, which may need to be fragmented into smaller payloads for the lower-layers to manage. These are then transmitted over the air-interface. Finally, the L2CAP layer exchanges QoS information, ensuring that sufficient resources are available and that both Bluetooth devices are attaining the best service.

In Table 10-20, we summarise the broad capabilities that are expected from L2CAP. In the table, you will notice features are marked with *M* (Mandatory), *O* (Optional), *X* (Excluded), *C* (Conditional), and *N/A* (Not Applicable); these will determine what is expected from the features at the L2CAP layer.

---

[12]L2CAP payloads are passed directly onto LMP when implemented on a hostless system.

Table 10-19 The set of capabilities that are required from the responder party, denoted here by the LAP device.

PROCEDURE	DT	LAP
Initialise an RFCOMM Session	X	M
Terminate an RFCOMM Session	M	M
Establish a new DLC Connection	X	M
Disconnect a DLC Connection	M	M
Emulate RS232 Control Signals	M	M
Transfer Data	N/A	N/A
Test Command	M	M
Flow Control	M	M
RLS	M	M
PN	M	M
RPN	M	M

Table 10-20 The illustration shows specific procedures that this profile depends upon to realise its compliant implementation.

PROCEDURE	DT	LAP
Connection-orientated Channel	M	M
Connectionless Channel	X	X
Connection Establishment	M	M
Configuration	M	M
Connection Termination	M	M
Echo	M	M
Command Rejection	M	M
Maximum Transmission Unit	M	M
Flush Timeout	M	M
Quality of Service	O	O

10.5.1.4.1 Channel Types. In Table 10-20, we have identified that *Connection-Orientated Channels* are mandatory, whereas *Connectionless Channels* are excluded; this type of channel is aimed at broadcasting, where all devices may be targeted. L2CAP uses PDUs to transport connection, signalling and configuration options, which will be discussed in a moment. The higher layers of the Bluetooth protocol stack will instigate a connection with L2CAP using the L2CA_ConnectReq request packet, where the corresponding result is contained within the L2CA_ConnectRsp response packet. An L2CA_ConnectRspNeg negative response packet is used to denote a response, where the connection with the remote device was unsuccessful. Since our profile resides above L2CAP and employs its services, we are only concerned with the upper protocol layer of L2CAP. This higher functionality is offered to us through a series of L2CAP events and is denoted through the prefix L2CA_ (see Table 10-21).

When creating an L2CAP connection between two devices, a *Protocol/Service Multiplexor* (PSM) value is used to denote the higher-layer protocol that is using the connection. Table 10-22 identifies these values and the corresponding protocols they represent. The value of 0x0003 (RFCOMM) is used for this profile.

10.5.1.4.2 Signalling. When establishing communication with a remote device, a *signalling channel* is created and reserved for use during connection, disconnection and configuration of subsequent L2CAP connections. A *channel* is used to describe the communication and data flow that exists between L2CAP entities. Table 10-23 illustrates the range of CID used to identify the channel type. As we can see in Table 10-20, *Connection Establishment* and *Termination* is mandatory in the local device, although the remote device may be capable of initiating and terminating a connection to the local device. The L2CA_DisconnectReq request packet is used to terminate the connection with the remote device and an L2CA_DisconnectRsp response packet is used to ascertain the result of the termination. All disconnection requests must be completed successfully. The support of *Configuration* is shown as mandatory and we will discuss these specific op-

Table 10-21 The range of prototypes used to illustrate how L2CAP is architected and how interaction between higher- and lower-layers is achieved. For this discussion, our concern here is with the higher-layer.

PROTOTYPE	DESCRIPTION
L2CA_	This prefix prototype is used to denote the higher-layer interaction, typically used by RFCOMM, SDP, and TCS.
L2CAP_	This prefix is used to denote peer-to-peer signalling interaction of L2CAP entities.
LP_	Finally, this prefix denotes lower-layer interaction, where L2CAP interfaces with the LMP layer.

Table 10-22   The PSM values that are used to identify the higher-layer protocol.

PSM	DESCRIPTION
0x0001	SDP
0x0003	RFCOMM
0x0005	TCS-BIN
0x0007	TCS-BIN-CORDLESS

tions in more detail in the following section. Finally, *Echo* and *Command Rejection* are both mandatory for a compliant LAN Access Profile.

10.5.1.4.3   Configuration Options.   In establishing a connection with the remote device, the channel is subject to configuration and the higher-layer prototype L2CA_ ConfigReq request packet is used to carry configuration requests. Its associated response is contained within the L2CA_ConfigRsp packet. An L2CA_ConfigRspNeg packet is used to denote a negative response during configuration where, for example, the suggested *Maximum Transmission Unit* (MTU) is too large. In Table 10-20, we have identified that the MTU and *Flush Timeout* parameters are mandatory, whereas the QoS is optional.

The default MTU setting for the signalling channel is 48 bytes, whereas other channels may be capable of transferring larger payloads. Essentially, the MTU determines the size of payloads that are capable of being exchanged between two devices. During configuration, the local device will inform the remote device that it is potentially capable of accepting larger payloads. If the remote device is unwilling to accept a larger MTU, then the local device is informed with the response contained within the L2CA_ConfigRspNeg packet.

When L2CA_ request and response packets are being exchanged, the Flush Timeout parameter is used to determine how long the local device is prepared to continue to transmit an L2CAP fragment before it gives up; the packet is subsequently flushed or, in

Table 10-23   The CIDs that are used to represent the logical channel.

CID	DESCRIPTION
0x0000	Null
0x0001	Signalling Channel
0x0002	Connectionless Reception Channel
0x0003 to 0x003F	Reserved
0x0040 to 0xFFFF	Dynamically Allocated

other words discarded. The suggested Flush Timeout value is sent during the L2CA_ ConfigReq request packet. However, if no value is set then the default value is used. The LAN Access Profile uses the default value of 0xFFFF.

As we have already mentioned, the QoS configuration is optional. If it is used during an L2CA_ConfigReq request, then the *best effort* service is established as a default. The available services that support an L2CAP channel are shown in Table 10-24. However, if the QoS service is set at *Guaranteed*, then parameters such *Token Rate*, *Token Bucket*, *Peak Bandwidth*, *Latency* and *Delay Variation*, are used to determine an acceptable guaranteed service, where the L2CA_ConnectRspNeg will indicate that these values are unacceptable. These parameters are then subject to further negotiation.

10.5.1.5 Link Manager. The LM layer sits between the HCI and the *Link Controller* (LC), although on a hostless system the LM will have direct interaction with L2CAP. It accepts commands from HCI and translates them into operations for the LC, where *Asynchronous Connectionless* (ACL) and SCO links are created and established. It is during this stage of ACL and SCO establishment that a master-slave switch would be performed as governed by the requirements of this profile. The LM is also responsible for placing the device into a low-power mode, which includes *hold*, *sniff*, and *park*.

In providing *general* error management, devices that operate mandatory procedures during interoperability must either acknowledge support or inform the initiator why the procedure failed. The LMP_Detach PDU is used to inform the device of the error that occurred. Typically, the reason *unsupported LMP feature* (0x1A) is reported (see Appendix A).

The LM may optionally make use of multi-slot packets for both the LAP and DT devices. The behaviour of a LAP configured for single-user and multi-user modes should adhere to the master-slave switch operation, as we will discuss.

Table 10-24   The range of service definitions that are used during QoS.

SERVICE	DESCRIPTION
No Traffic	This indicates that the channel will not be sending any traffic and, as such, any parameters can be ignored.
Best Effort	This default value attempts to achieve a minimum service with the local remote device, where no guarantees are offered.
Guaranteed	With this service definition, we indicate that we wish to achieve the maximum bandwidth permitted. This is, of course, subject to the nature of a wireless environment.

Table 10-25   A feature that is not supported and is part of the requirement for the LAN Access Profile has a specific set of reasons available at the LMP level.

FEATURE	REASON or ERROR
Encryption Disabled	*Host Rejected due to Security Reasons*
LAP Switched to Master when configured for Multi-user Mode	*Unspecified Error*[13]
Number of Users are at its configured[14] maximum	*Other End Terminated Connection: Low Resources*

It is clear during the LM stage that several failures of connection are made evident if the DT fails to endorse the pairing process—specifically, if it is unable to provide encryption on the baseband connection or if there is a clear failure to perform the master-slave switch operation, for eample when it is configured for multi-user mode.

Table 10-25 provides a list of errors that are reported at the LM level, which should, in turn, ultimately inform the user of the reason for the connection failure. This places the user in a position where he or she can rectify the specific problem.

In the next section, we take an opportunity to explore the dependencies that make up the LAN Access Profile. We provide a narrative of the capabilities that are expected at this level. In Table 10-26, we identify the capabilities that are required from this layer and in the following subsections discuss the specific procedures in more detail.

10.5.1.5.1   Capabilities.   Table 10-26 summarises the broad capabilities that are expected from the LM. In the table, you will notice procedures are marked with *M* (Mandatory), *O* (Optional), *X* (Excluded), *C* (Conditional) and *N/A* (Not Applicable); these will

Table 10-26   The change in capabilities for the LAN Access Profile. The table shows that support for pairing, authentication, encryption and master-slave switching are now mandatory.

CAPABILITIES	DT	LAP
Pairing	M	M
Authentication	M	M
Encryption	M	M
Master-Slave Switch	M	M

---

[13]This specific error would not necessarily help the user. The error *Unsupported Feature* may be offered with a possible explanation as to why the connection failed.
[14]The LAP administrator is capable of setting the number of users from one to seven.

determine what is expected from the procedures at the LM. The table includes a set of deviations that the profile includes, which are above the common set of procedures expected at LM.

10.5.1.5.1.1 PAIRING. When the initialisation key is created, the link key can then be generated. The link key is then subsequently used for mutual authentication, thus allowing the devices to communicate. The two devices now share a common link key and are now referred to as *bonded*. Looking at the LMP commands that instigate this process, we note that DeviceA sends the `LMP_in_rand` command (see Table 10-27). DeviceB then responds with the `LMP_accepted` PDU. Both devices then proceed to calculate the initialisation key based upon the parameters provided previously.

A combination key or a unit key is then specifically used to determine the generation of the link key, where a set of rules govern the selection process. Table 10-27 further lists the LMP commands used when pairing occurs between DeviceA and DeviceB. The table shows the `LMP_comp_key` and `LMP_unit_key`, which are used when selecting a combination or unit key method, respectively.

10.5.1.5.1.2 AUTHENTICATION. *Authentication* is used when DeviceA and DeviceB share a common link key or initialisation key, which is typically obtained during the pairing process (see Section 10.5.1.5.1.1, *Pairing*).

The authentication process encompasses LMP Authentication procedures, but all LMP Pairing procedures must have been performed prior to this event. As for the LMP Authentication procedure, this is primarily based on a challenge-response scheme. Here, the verifier or DeviceA sends the `LMP_au_rand` command, containing a random number to the claimant or DeviceB; the random number forms the challenge aspect of this scheme. The response, forming the final part of this scheme, is sent to the verifier using the `LMP_sres` command, which contains the result of the operation. If the operation is what the verifier expected, then it considers the claimant to be authenticated.

The LMP Pairing procedure occurs when there is no link key and, as such, if an `LMP_au_rand` is sent to the claimant it will respond with `LMP_not_accepted`, thus offering the reason as *key missing* (0x06) (see Appendix A). If a key has been previ-

Table 10-27 The range of LMP PDUs available for two units when pairing.

PDU	PARAMETER
`LMP_in_rand`	Random Number
`LMP_au_rand`	Random Number
`LMP_res`	Authentication Response
`LMP_comp_key`	Random Number
`LMP_unit_key`	Key

Table 10-28   The range of LMP PDUs available for authentication.

PDU	PARAMETER
LMP_au_rand	RandomNumber
LMP_sres	AuthenticationResponse
LMP_detach	Reason

ously associated with the claimant, then the claimant proceeds to calculate the response and provides the verifier with a response through LMP_sres. However, if the calculated response is incorrect, the verifier can terminate the connection with the command LMP_detach, offering the reason as *authentication failure* (0x05) (see Appendix A). Table 10-28, summarises the LMP commands used during authentication.

   10.5.1.5.1.3   ENCRYPTION.   The process of encryption commences when at least one device has authenticated[15]. DeviceA (or client) takes the initiative and needs to determine whether to include encryption for point-to-point or broadcast communication. If DeviceB (or server) is agreeable to the parameters offered by the master, the master proceeds to communicate further detailed information about the encryption parameters.
   The actual process is invoked when the two parties agree to use encryption and then L2CAP communication terminates, where the master then sends the LMP_encryption_mode_req command. If this is acceptable to the slave, it too terminates all L2CAP communication and responds with the LMP_accepted command. The next step in this process actually determines the size of the *encryption key* and it is the master that sends the LMP_encryption_key_size_req command, where it offers an initial recommendation of the key size to use. The slave, in turn, then offers its own recommendation, where it informs the master what it thinks it might be capable of. Both master and slave will repeat this process until they reach an agreement; however, if neither party reaches a decision, then the LMP_not_accepted command is sent, offering the reason as *unsupported parameter value* (0x20) (see Appendix A).
   Upon accepting the key size, the LMP_accepted command is issued and the encryption procedure then takes place by issuing the LMP_start_encryption_req command with a random number, which is used to calculate the encryption key. Table 10-29 summarises the available commands for the encryption process.

   10.5.1.5.1.4   MASTER-SLAVE SWITCH.   The master-slave switch operation is required[16] when the LAP is configured for multi-user[17] mode. The failure of a DT to perform this operation prohibits the successful connection to a LAP. Figure 10-18 provides

---

[15]Authentication here refers to the Bluetooth-specific authentication process.
[16]A LAP configured for multi-user mode must remain the master of the piconet.
[17]The DT may refuse the request to become the slave if it needs to remain the master.

Table 10-29   The range of LMP PDUs available for encryption.

PDU	PARAMETER
LMP_encryption_mode_req	Encryption Mode
LMP_encryption_key_size_req	Key Size
LMP_start_encryption_req	Random Number
LMP_stop_encryption_req	*None*

an illustration of the events that occur when the DT fails to comply with the master-slave switch request.[18]

Table 10-30 provides the HCI command and event combination that are used to perform the master-slave switch operation between the DT and LAP. This table represents one such method of performing a switch, where other HCI commands, such as the HCI_Create_Connection command, specify the same request as part of its parameter set up. In this instance, the Allow_Role_Switch parameter is used during the connection establishment to determine if a switch can be performed by the local device, that is, the device initiating the connection (DeviceA). The remote device (DeviceB) is duly notified with its corresponding HCI command, Accept_Connection_Request of whether it can be supported.

Table 10-31 provides the two LMP general response messages, which are mandatory for this profile. During an LMP_accepted operation, the response contains the OpCode of the operation that was successful; whereas the response from the LMP_not_accepted provides the OpCode of the operation that was not successful. Accompanying this OpCode, a *reason* or error code is provided to help to determine why the operation failed; a full list of LMP reasons can be found in Appendix A.

The use of these general response messages is used in combination with the following LMP role-switch specific messages, which are provided in Table 10-32. What follows is a detailed exploration of the behaviour of both these devices when performing the master-slave switch operation. You may remember that the DT is capable of initiating a connection.

When DeviceB (or slave) initiates a master-slave switch, it terminates the final ACL packet and stops any further L2CAP transmissions. It then sends the LMP_slot_offset command, which is immediately followed by the LMP_switch_req command. Similarly, if the master accepts the master-slave switch, it terminates all L2CAP transmissions and then issues a LMP_accepted if the transaction is a success. However, if the operation is rejected, then an LMP_not_accepted is provided as the response, with a specific reason for its failure. Furthermore, when the operation has been completed despite its success or failure, L2CAP communication is resumed.

---

[18]The Bluetooth protocol stack provides the flexibility of issuing a master-slave switch at any time during a Bluetooth connection establishment.

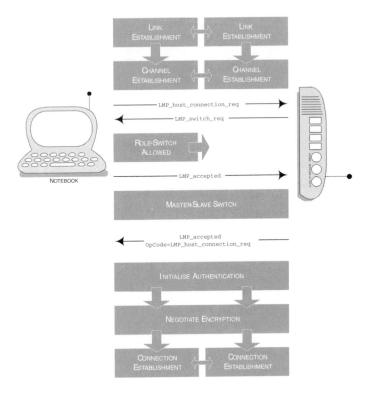

Figure 10-18   The events that take place during a master-slave switch.

Table 10-30   The command and two-stage event notification that are used in combination to perform the master-slave switch.

COMMAND	PARAMETERS
HCI_Switch_Role	BD_ADDR
	Role
EVENT	**PARAMETERS**
Command_Status	Status
	Num_HCI_Command_Packets
	Command_OpCode
Role_Change	Status
	BD_ADDR
	New_Role

Table 10-31   The general response messages used within LMP.

PDU	PARAMETERS
LMP_accepted	OpCode
LMP_not_accepted	OpCode
	Reason

When DeviceA (or master) initiates a master-slave switch, it terminates the final ACL packet and stops any further L2CAP transmissions. It then sends an LMP_switch_ req. Similarly, if the slave accepts the master-slave switch, it terminates all L2CAP transmissions and then issues an LMP_slot_offset command, which is immediately followed by an LMP_accepted command. However, if the operation is rejected, then an LMP_not_accepted is provided as the response, with a specific reason for its failure. Furthermore, when the operation has been completed, despite its success or failure, L2CAP communication is resumed.

10.5.1.6   Link Controller.   The LC layer is the lowest layer depicted in the dependencies of this profile; it is responsible for a large number of core capabilities. It manages air-to-interface transactions and determines the fundamental timing of ACL and SCO data packet transmission and reception, as well as coordinating the effort at its upper-edge with the LM. It also encompasses the management of the various packet types and the various inquiry and paging procedures available. The following subsections provide clarity with regard to the capabilities that are a requirement at the LC level for the LAN Access Profile. To further our understanding of the dependencies, we begin by examining in more detail the supported capabilities. If you are a developer providing profile-specific applications, then you may not wish to engage in a large part of this section, although in some audio-related applications direct access may be required, where a faster transport mechanism can be supported. Many manufacturers have nevertheless architected an audio-specific API for intelligible access to this component.

10.5.1.6.1   Capabilities.   Table 10-33 summarises the broad capabilities that are expected from the LC. In the table, you will notice features are marked with *M* (Mandatory),

Table 10-32   The PDUs available within LMP that are responsible for managing the role-switch behaviour.

PDU	PARAMETERS
LMP_switch_req	Switch instant
LMP_slot_offset	Slot Offset
	BD_ADDR

Table 10-33   The summary of capabilities that are required for the LC to enable a compliant LAN Access Profile.

PROCEDURES	DEVICEA	DEVICEB
Inquiry	M	X
Inquiry Scan	X	M
Paging	M	X
Page Scan	X	M
Inter-piconet	M	M
Packet Types	M	M
Voice Codecs	X	X

O (Optional), *X* (Excluded), *C* (Conditional) and *N/A* (Not Applicable); these determine what is expected from the features at the LC.

10.5.1.6.1.1   INQUIRY AND INQUIRY SCAN.   An inquiry procedure is used to learn of the other devices in radio range, where the BD_ADDR and clock offsets are obtained; it is DeviceA that will enter an *inquiry substate* to perform this procedure. A device that wishes to be discovered (DeviceB) will enter an *inquiry scan substate*, where the device will respond with an *inquiry response*. In this state, DeviceB is waiting to receive an *Inquiry Access Code* (IAC). These modes of operation are discussed from a deeper application perspective in the *Generic Access Profile*, Chapter 2. It is here that specific rules are determined with regard to the behaviour of such devices and how long these devices can operate in such modes. When devices have been discovered, this information is passed over to the *Service Discovery Application Profile*, Chapter 3, which manages the specific attributes that make up that device. What we now understand is that the Bluetooth protocol stack must encompass and support such behavioural procedures for this profile to be considered compliant.

10.5.1.6.1.2   PAGING AND PAGING SCAN.   The *inquiry substate* and *inquiry scan substate* procedures are the initial methods used to learn of other devices in radio range; to this extent, the device has discovered sufficient information to gain a connection with the remote device. This is achieved when DeviceA has the intent to create a connection with DeviceB; DeviceA is placed into a *paging substate*, where it will periodically transmit the *Device Access Code* (DAC). The DAC is used to target the device directly and the clock offset is used to gain an idea of the clock cycle of DeviceB. These parameters were originally obtained during our inquiry procedures. If DeviceB wishes to be connected, then it will enter a *page scan substate* and will respond accordingly to DeviceA.

An inquiry procedure may be avoided if the BD_ADDR is already known, although a connection may take a little longer if the clock offset is not known.

10.5.1.6.1.3 INTER-PICONET. Inter-piconet capabilities describe the process that allows the master to manage multiple connections from slave devices. During a connection other users may temporarily witness degradation in the service that is being provided; however, the master must be capable of accepting new participants into the piconet.

10.5.1.6.1.4 PACKET TYPES. There are numerous packet types available. Table 10-34 identifies those most commonly used for profile support. There are also a number of *common* packet types used for general-purpose transport; for example the ID packet is used for inquiry procedures and a POLL packet would be sent by DeviceA to determine if a slave is active on a channel.

The DM1 packet type is used to transmit control data over any connection, but may be used to transport a genuine payload. HV1, HV2 and HV3 are various SCO packet types to carry audio-specific data, where a DV packet can combine ACL and SCO specific data. Their support in this profile is reflected in Table 10-34. Various ACL packet types are also available; in fact, seven types including the DM1 type are attributed to carrying user-specific data. These include DH1, DM3, DH3, DM5, DH5 and AUX1. Similarly, Table 10-34 summarises their support in this profile.

10.5.1.7 Management Entity. The *Management Entity* (ME) component sits alongside the entire range of layers that make up the Bluetooth protocol stack and the PPP

Table 10-34 The summary of packet types that are required for the LC to enable a compliant LAN Access Profile.

PACKET TYPE	DT	LAP
DM1	M	M
DH1	M	M
DM3	M	M
DH3	M	M
DM5	M	M
DH5	M	M
HV1	X	X
HV2	X	X
HV3	X	X
DV	X	X

layer for this profile (see Figure 10-15). Its role is purely to coordinate the establishment of a connection and to respond and organise appropriate failures for inquiry and paging.

When the DT has a problem in discovering or establishing a connection with a LAP, the link establishment fails and the user may reselect a new LAP in radio range that offers similar services.

The role of the ME extends to the supervision and the behaviour of the master-slave switch when the LAP is configured for the appropriate user-mode. Any reason for the failure of this operation will cause the baseband physical link to fail. Figure 10-19 provides an illustration of the sequence of events that may occur during a master-slave switch operation.

10.5.2   Other Dependencies

Figure 10-15 identifies all the components that make up the LAN Access Profile. This section now considers the components that are provided in the profile, but do not necessarily make up the Bluetooth protocol core.

10.5.2.1   The Point-to-Point Protocol.   The PPP is typically used for communication between two devices that use a serial interface; it is described in RFC1661. In the context of Bluetooth devices, PPP is used to transport packets over RFCOMM, which are subsequently passed over the network, packaged as IP data.

This layer refers to the operational aspects of PPP. It determines the capabilities that are specific to the levels of support and are now described in Sections 10.5.2.1.1, *Initialisation and Shutting Down a PPP Connection* to 10.5.2.1.4, *HDLC Framing*.

10.5.2.1.1   Initialisation and Shutting Down a PPP Connection.   A device that is to behave as a LAP should register its capabilities in the CoD (as previously discussed in Section 10.5.1.1.1, *Service Class*). When the service is no longer required, the registration

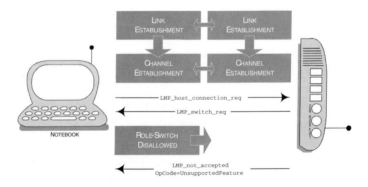

Figure 10-19   The set of events that occur during a failure of the master-slave switch operation.

of its capabilities may be removed or disabled from the database and all active PPP connections terminated.

10.5.2.1.2   Establishing and Disconnecting a PPP Connection.   PPP requires an active RFCOMM session between the LAP and DT; if one does not exist, then the DT can create an RFCOMM session by using the RFCOMM channel as advertised in the LAP service record (see Section 10.5.1.2, *Service Discovery*).

The LAP and DT must then proceed to negotiate a PPP connection though the *Link Control Protocol* (LCP), which is incorporated within PPP. As part of the LCP negotiation process, an MTU will be negotiated as part of the connection; this, in turn, may become implementation-specific, depending on your product.

In Section 10.4.2.5, we discussed the reasons for the termination or disconnection of a service; in the majority of instances, the termination of each protocol layer is managed in an orderly fashion. During instances of a failed radio link, or if the DT device has stayed out of range for an extraordinary length of time, the dismantling of the layers is managed differently.

Each of the layers of the LAN Access Point are shown in Table 10-35, which explains how each should be appropriately managed during disconnection or termination.

10.5.2.1.3   Authentication Protocols.   The use of authentication during a PPP connection is not mandatory. PPP has several methods of authentication available to it and provides the administrator flexibility and additional security measures, along with the existing Bluetooth security, to secure his or her network.

As previously discussed, the user would be required to enter a username and password; failure to enter the correct information would result in a failed PPP connection. A range of authentication models are shown in Table 10-36.

10.5.2.1.4   HDLC Framing.   The *High-level Data Link Control* (HDLC) is a means of organising or encapsulating data into frames over the network. It provides the

Table 10-35   The list of layers, which are made up during a PPP link with a LAP and DT.

LAYER	PROCEDURE
PPP	Received termination notice and begins to inform its sub-layers.
LCP	The procedures for terminating this layer are defined in RFC1661.
IPCP	The producers for terminating this layer are defined in RFC1332, and will cease all IP communication.
RFCOMM	The disconnection of this layer is prescribed in Section 10.5.1.3, *RFCOMM*.
L2CAP	The disconnection of this layer is prescribed in Section 10.5.1.4, L2CAP.

Table 10-36   The various authentication models available to PPP.

AUTHENTICATION	REFERENCE
PPP CHAP	Challenge Handshake Authentication Protocol (CHAP), as prescribed in RFC1994.
MS PPP CHAP Extensions	The Microsoft PPP CHAP Extensions are detailed in RFC2433.
PPP EAP	The PPP Extensible Authentication Protocol (EAP) is defined in RFC2284.

ability to verify that data has been received correctly and is able to control the transmission rate of data. RFCOMM provides a means of HDLC framing and RFC1662 prescribes the HDLC requirements in PPP.

10.5.2.2 Internet Protocol (IP).   An IP interface becomes available when a PPP link has been established; more specifically, this is instantiated when the *Internet Protocol Control Protocol* (IPCP) link has been created and an IP address has been allocated. It is anticipated that a DT would have one active session with a LAP, although multiple sessions can exist when various LAPs provide multiple services. Here, the IP layer would be responsible for correctly routing IP data. It follows that the DT may require the establishment of such parameters as a *default gateway* and a *Domain Name Server* (DNS). These extensions can be found in RFC1877 and describe how the IPCP layer would negotiate DNS and *NetBIOS Name Server* (NBNS) addresses.

During a termination, the PPP link is stopped along with the IPCP layer, which also terminates the IP stack. Prior to termination, the IP stack is responsible for removing the IP address from its routing table.

Table 10-37   The various methods of allocating an IP address.

METHOD	REFERENCE
Fixed IP	A permanent IP address assigned to the DT. Any duplicate IP addresses on the LAN would result in a termination of the duplicated connections.
DHCP	The DHCP provides greater flexibility in the assignment of IP addresses, where administrators can manage a corporation's allocation of addresses. This reduces the risk of duplicate IP addresses being present on the LAN.
Mobile-IP	A specified IP configuration that provides DTs the flexibility to use multiple access points on the same LAN

10.5.2.2.1   IP Address Allocation.   We discussed briefly that the DT would require an authentic IP address to operate correctly on the LAN. PPP dictates three methods on how this can be achieved; these are shown in Table 10-37.

10.6   SUMMARY

- The LAN Access Profile has many similarities to the Dial-up Networking Profile; both rely on the Generic Access Profile, the Serial Port Profile and a PPP implementation.
- The LAN Access Profile omits the use of AT commands.
- The existing usage models allow a DT to make use of the services provided by a LAP; these are the two roles that are defined by this profile.
- A DT may utilize the services of many LAPs within radio range.
- The LAP allows up to seven simultaneous connections from a DT; this provides the scenarios governed by the roles.
- Future usage models will allow a DT to roam around an office whilst maintaining its connection to the LAN.
- Bluetooth authentication and encryption is mandatory for this profile; failure to provide such support would result in a failed Bluetooth connection.
- The DT is the initiator of the Bluetooth relationship.
- The LAP requests to become master if it is configured for multi-user mode; no Bluetooth connection will occur if this switch fails.
- The DT discovers available LAPs in radio range by performing an inquiry.
- A LAP can be configured exclusively for a DT by configuring the LAP into single-user mode.
- A device that wishes to behave as a LAP must register its purpose in the Service Discovery database.
- A Service Discovery record is generated, detailing the parameters that apply to that specific service.
- The DT incorporates a PPP Client and the LAP incorporates a PPP Server, both of which are implemented over RFCOMM.
- PPP is used to enable an IP stack.
- As part of the LCP negotiation, the MTU is also determined.
- IPCP is responsible for allocating an IP address for the DT.
- PPP Authentication is optionally available at this layer, requiring the user to enter a username and password; CHAP or EAP can be used.

11

The Generic Object
Exchange Profile

11.1 INTRODUCTION

The *Generic Object Exchange Profile* (GOEP) establishes a level of basic functionality, abstracted from the *Object Exchange Protocol* (OBEX). In providing this basic set of features and procedures, it then becomes sufficient to realise the object exchange usage models, which is the basis for the *Object Push*, Chapter 12, *File Transfer,* Chapter 13 and *Synchronisation Profiles*, Chapter 14.

In Figure 11-1, we illustrate the components that make up the OBEX functionality. At the upper-edge of the OBEX component, implementers will establish function primitives in the form of an *Application Programming Interface* (API).

In creating such an API, implementers may then realise their object exchange specific applications, where these applications have access to the API. With the various object exchange profiles available, the GOEP simply places a foundation from which these applications can then be developed; remember it is the *governing profile*[1] that will ultimately determine the end function.

---

[1]The reference to *governing profile* is used to distinguish the requirements of the GOEP and that of another object exchange-specific profile. The governing profile will sometimes require other features that may be mandatory, whereas the corresponding feature in the GOEP may be optional.

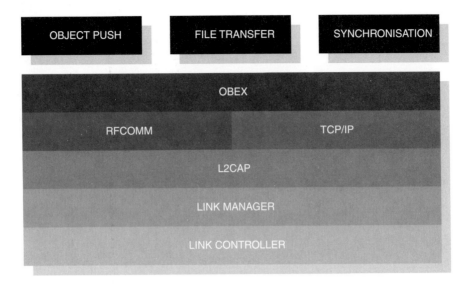

Figure 11-1 The various protocols that form the building blocks of the
Object Exchange specific usage models. It is at the upper-edge
of the OBEX component that function primitives are created
which, in turn, will be used by the higher-applications to realise
usage models.

In this chapter, generic procedures are established for all devices during interoperability. Furthermore, the behaviour of such devices is governed with simple rules that relate to the methods of sending and retrieving data, initialisation and certain characteristics with regard to their discoverability. These features and procedures are used to establish commonality between products, which will ultimately achieve a cohesive user experience.

The lack of a *User Expectation* section in this chapter should demonstrate and remind you that this profile establishes core functionality; it is the governing profile that will ultimately guide the user through specific expectations at the user interface level.

11.2 PROFILE PRINCIPLES

The GOEP provides two new roles: a *Client* and a *Server* device. The client device is capable of pushing and pulling data objects to and from the server, whereas the server provides the facility to allow the client device to push and pull the data objects.

In Figure 11-3, we can see the components that make up the GOEP and it is these building blocks that are required to realise a compliant profile. In our introduction, we touched upon the notion that a set of features and procedures exist to help govern the operation of Bluetooth-enabled devices, which support the GOEP. The profile also provides clarification with regard to the dependencies, as shown in Figure 11-3 and describes how

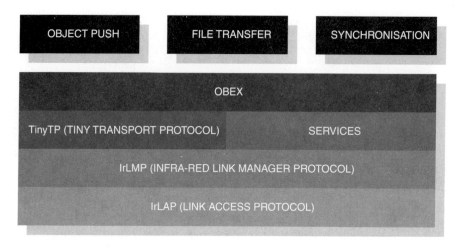

Figure 11-2   The various components that form the building blocks of the
infra-red protocol stack. In similar usage models, the OBEX
function primitives are exposed at the OBEX upper-edge,
where applications have a transparent interface to the underlying mode of transport.

each component realises such functionality. Essentially, what is achieved here is a clear
definition of the core component requirements that make up the Bluetooth protocol stack;
we will discuss this in more detail later on.

Support for IrOBEX[2] in the Bluetooth protocol stack is required, where this component has been adopted by the Bluetooth *Special Interest Group* (SIG). It has been chosen
specifically to allow ad-hoc connections to enable data transfer from one device to another. Tasks such as synchronisation and file transfer can take place between one or more[3]
device, where such objects may include vCalendar, vCard, vMessage and so on. The
OBEX component has been designed with portability in mind and, as such, any existing
infra-red application may reside above OBEX and use Bluetooth as its underlying transport. In Figure 11-2 we provide a comparative illustration, which shows the architecture
of the infra-red protocol stack. Similarly, any Bluetooth OBEX-specific application (that
is, GOEP compliant applications), built upon the OBEX protocol, may use the infra-red
protocol stack as its mode of transport. In Figure 11-1 and Figure 11-2, we illustrated the
common OBEX component where function primitives are exposed and the underlying
transport for the application remains transparent.

There are no fixed master-slave roles; this allows either device free to initiate and
terminate a connection, although typically the client will initiate the primary connection,

---

[2]IrOBEX has been shortened to OBEX and is provided by the non-profit organisation the Infra-red Data Association. The specification itself is the IrDA Object Exchange Protocol (OBEX™), Version 1.2, March 1999.
[3]The GOEP only discusses support for a point-to-point connection; nevertheless, it does not rule out multi-
connection support, where many client devices are capable of pushing and pulling from a server device.

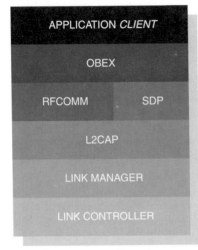

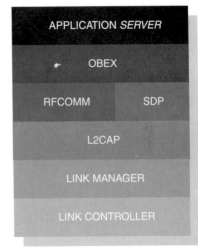

Figure 11-3   The core components of the Bluetooth protocol stack are shown illustrating how the components of the GOEP are integrated.

where inquiry and device discovery procedures are undertaken. Participating devices in this profile are required to perform bonding and pairing, where encryption may be offered as an option. In Figure 11-3, we illustrate the specific Bluetooth protocol stack components that are dependent upon a compliant profile.

In Table 11-1, clarification is provided with regard to the roles used within the context of this profile. In general, *DeviceA* represents the initiating party and *DeviceB* represents the accepting party. The terms are often used interchangeably when describing specific operations in various contexts and are provided here for reference.

This profile does not mandate the operation of a master-slave switch; this is specifically addressed by the needs of the governing profile. It is DeviceB that usually determines whether or not it has a need to become master. In one such example, DeviceB may already be the master of an existing piconet and therefore may insist that it remains master of that relationship. Alternatively, DeviceA may decide that a role-switch is not permitted and choose to remain master. In either case, the device may decide not to continue and fail the link establishment altogether.

It is advisable that the role-switch is performed immediately after the physical-link is established, where the connection request parameters[4] determine whether or not a role-switch can be performed. It is the governing profile that will determine whether or not master-slave switching is mandatory (see *Object Push*, Chapter 12, *File Transfer* Chapter 13 and *Synchronisation Profiles*, Chapter 14, for further examples).

---

[4]The flexibility of the Bluetooth protocol stack, in particular the various HCI and LMP commands available, allow various methods of creating a successful ACL connection. The text refers to one particular example of a connection set-up.

Table 11-1 The list of behavioural characteristics that are typical for this profile.

CONFIGURATION	ROLE	DESCRIPTION
DeviceA	Client	This device is capable of pushing and pulling objects from the server. The client establishes a relationship with the server before data can be exchanged; the client will typically initiate the connection.
	Initiator	This configuration describes the device that instigates the original connection or the device that wishes to initiate communication over an existing link.
DeviceB	Server	A server provides object exchange capability which, in turn, allows client devices to push and pull objects from the server. This type of device would typically accept connections from clients.
	Acceptor	This configuration describes the process of the device accepting the initiated communication from DeviceA.

11.3 LIFTING THE LID

11.3.1 Dependencies

In the following sections, we take an opportunity to explore in greater depth the dependencies that make up this profile. In Figure 11-4, we provide a conceptual illustration, representing the dependencies that make up the GOEP; the areas that are shaded are relevant to this profile. As you can see, the profile depends upon the basic functionality offered to us by the *Generic Access Profile*, Chapter 2, the *Service Discovery Application Profile*, Chapter 3 and the *Serial Port Profile*, Chapter 6. We will now discuss the basic requirements of these dependent components and any deviations that may occur from the basic functionality originally offered to us.

11.3.1.1 Generic Access. The GOEP relies upon the capabilities provided by the *Generic Access Profile*, Chapter 2. You may recall that a level of basic functionality is achieved through establishing a set of rules and procedures. It is these rules and procedures that are used to establish commonality between products, which will ultimately achieve a cohesive user experience. This section discusses the behavioural aspects of Bluetooth-enabled devices as outlined by the Generic Access Profile.

Let us take an opportunity to reflect upon the behavioural aspects of Bluetooth-enabled devices as outlined by the *Generic Access Profile*, Chapter 2. You may remem-

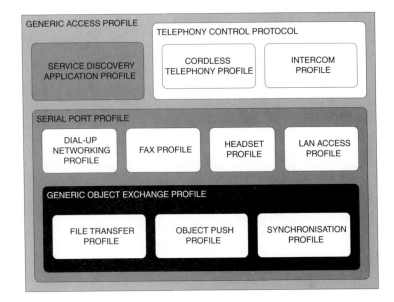

Figure 11-4   The dependent components of the Bluetooth protocol stack that
make up the GOEP. The areas that are shaded are relevant to
this profile.

ber that the Generic Access Profile mandates certain rules and procedures that help govern the overall connectability, discoverability and security aspects of Bluetooth-enabled devices.

In Table 11-2, the basic set of procedures is illustrated, identifying functional expectations, which in turn govern operation. These procedures help us to determine the context in which a device would operate; for example, a device may wish to be discoverable for a period of time or it may require a level of security that differs from one device to another depending upon the services it is capable of offering.

In Table 11-3, we consider the specific set of operations that are required for this profile. In the table, you will notice features are marked with M (Mandatory), O (Optional), X (Excluded), C (Conditional) and N/A (Not Applicable); these determine what is expected from the features of the Generic Access Profile. The GOEP usually operates limited discoverability, but when such devices have no user interface then the general discoverability mode must be used.

Table 11-4 identifies the security requirements for this profile. You will also notice that these features are marked in a similar fashion to our previous table. In the *Generic Access Profile*, Chapter 2, Security Mode 1 is a non-secure mode, where Bluetooth-enabled devices will never initiate any security procedures; whereas Security Modes 2 and 3 initiate different levels of security procedures at various stages of connection establishment. In this instance, the profile mandates that support should be provided for at least Security Mode 2 or 3.

Table 11-2   The core set of procedures as required by most profiles.

PROCEDURES	DESCRIPTION
Discoverability Mode	This mode prescribes the overall discoverability of a device, allowing it to be placed into a non-discoverable, limited or general discoverable mode. The mode would allow devices to become generally available to other users or it can be restricted to personal use.
Connectability Mode	When determining a baseband connectable state, this mode is used to place a device into a connectable or non-connectable mode.
Pairing	Pairable and non-pairable modes are used to realise the security aspects when operating or intending to use a device. A device may require authentication and, as such, the user would be required to enter a Bluetooth Passkey. The pairing procedure starts the link key generation process which, in turn, allows authentication to take place.

In our final consideration of the basic rules and procedures that are required from the Generic Access Profile, the idle mode procedures outline behavioural characteristics when DeviceA chooses to initiate them against DeviceB. The procedures that are listed in Table 11-5 provide a clear indication of how a device should operate when performing such an activity.

Table 11-3   The illustration shows specific modes of operation that this profile depends upon to realise its compliant implementation.

MODES	CLIENT	SERVER
Non-discoverable	N/A	M
Limited Discoverable	N/A	C
General Discoverable	N/A	C
Non-connectable	N/A	O
Connectable	N/A	M
Non-pairable	N/A	M
Pairable	M	M

Table 11-4 The illustration shows specific security procedures that this profile depends upon to realise its compliant implementation.

PROCEDURE	CLIENT	SERVER
Authentication	M	M
Security Mode 1	M	M
Security Mode 2	C	C
Security Mode 3	C	C

The mechanism for providing device discoverability is the provision of a well structured FHS packet, which is shown in Figure 11-5. This packet is used to identify the remote device, where information such as BD_ADDR and clock offsets is determined. You may also notice from this packet that the *Class of Device* (CoD) field is also provided. This information is relayed to the user interface which, in turn, provides common characteristics about discovered devices. The CoD is used during the discovery mechanism to learn more about the type of device and what it may be capable of providing. This structure of information is depicted in Figure 11-6 and is made up of 3-bytes (or 24-bits as shown). The following sections consider the OBEX-based attributes, which will ultimately make use of the *Service*, *Major* and *Minor Device Class* fields.

11.3.1.1.1 Service Class. This high-level form of defining a Bluetooth device identifies where in the Service Class field the OBEX-based Profile resides (see Table 11-6) which, in turn, determines the category of service. Here, the category of service falls within *Object Transfer*.

Table 11-5 The illustration shows specific behavioural procedures that this profile depends upon to realise its compliant implementation.

PROCEDURE	CLIENT	SERVER
General Inquiry	M	N/A
Limited Inquiry	O	N/A
Name Discovery	M	N/A
Device Discovery	M	N/A
Bonding	M	M

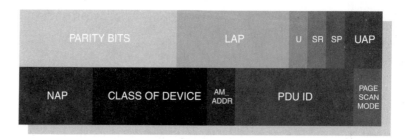

Figure 11-5 The structure of the FHS packet used only for reference to illustrate the position of the CoD structure.

11.3.1.1.2 Major Device Class. This high-level form of defining a Bluetooth device identifies where in the Major Device Class the category of device supporting the OBEX-based Profile resides (see Table 11-7). Here, the various categories of devices that may support the OBEX-based Profile are shown.

11.3.1.1.3 Minor Device Class. The Minor Device Class in this profile is used to convey further context for the setting within the major class grouping (see Table 11-8). Here, the bit may be set appropriately for *Notebook*, *Handheld PDA* or *Palm-sized PDA* to denote the type of device supporting the OBEX-based Profile. Further categorisation can also be provided for a *Phone*.

11.3.1.2 The Object Exchange Protocol. Earlier, we introduced the OBEX concept, whereby it is used as an independent layer and the mode of transport that sits beneath it remains transparent to the application. This provides flexibility in the use of a variety of applications as well as the ability to create ad-hoc connections between devices.

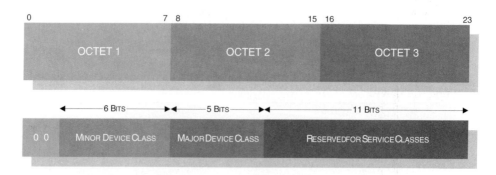

Figure 11-6 The structure of the class of device, illustrating the Minor Device, Major Device and Service Class fields and their respective lengths.

Table 11-6   The Service Class categorisation for OBEX-based Profiles.

											SERVICE CLASS
23	22	21	20	19	18	17	16	15	14	13	Bit # of CoD
0	0	0	1	0	0	0	0	0	0	0	Object Transfer

This section describes the processes used to realise an OBEX-to-OBEX connection and establishes how the underlying Bluetooth transport is facilitated in achieving this.

OBEX has been designed to sit above the RFCOMM component of the Bluetooth protocol stack, as shown in our earlier illustrations. You may remember that the same illustration presented an implementation, where OBEX can be placed above a *Transmission Control Protocol* (TCP), *Internet Protocol* (IP) component, which then resided above L2CAP. In our first look at understanding this protocol, we will look at its architecture in more detail and then consider specific aspects of integration over RFCOMM and TCP/IP. In later sections, we will discuss how OBEX operations such as Put, Get and so on are used to realise function primitives.

11.3.1.2.1   The Object Model and the Session Protocol.   The OBEX specification provides a formal representation to achieve data object exchange between devices, using what is called an *Object Model*. This formal representation includes the provision of a *Session Protocol*, which is used to structure the nature of any communication and is based upon a format that includes a request-response client-server concept. Communication is transported through connection-orientated channels available through RFCOMM and L2CAP; the connectionless-specific transfer would impose interoperability issues between devices.

In our first detailed examination of the OBEX protocol, we look at the structure of the object model, which is used to represent data objects in OBEX. In Figure 11-7, we can see the object encompassing a *Header ID* followed by a number of *Header Values*. The HeaderID is made up of one byte and is further broken down into a two-bit and a six-bit segment. The purpose of such a structure is to provide a descriptive meaning to the objects being transferred and to carry the object itself. The two-bit segment is used to

Table 11-7   The Major Device Class categorisation for a device that supports the OBEX-based Profile.

					MAJOR DEVICE CLASS
12	11	10	9	8	Bit # of CoD
0	0	0	0	1	Computer
0	0	0	1	0	Phone

Table 11-8   The Minor Device Class categorisation for a device that supports the OBEX-based Profile.

7	6	5	4	3	2	MINOR DEVICE CLASS
						Bit # of CoD
0	0	0	0	1	1	Notebook
0	0	0	1	0	0	Handheld PDA
0	0	0	1	0	1	Palm-sized PDA

identify the type of encoding, whereas the six-bit segment is used to identify the header meaning.

In Table 11-9, we show the six-bit segment format that is used in conjunction with Table 11-11; the table describes the header types that are available. The values presented in Table 11-11 provide a known set of header values that can be used for most applications. However, the header value range 0x30 to 0x3F are reserved for user or implementation-specific use. The range should accommodate the upper six bits of the HeaderID value; any user-defined header value must also accommodate the lower two-bit encoding method as shown in Table 11-10.

In establishing the object model, we turn our attention to the session protocol, which forms the request-response nature of exchanging OBEX objects between two devices. In simple terms, the client *requests* and the server *responds*; this essentially forms what is called the *conversational format* between two devices. In Figure 11-8, we can identify an *OpCode*, which is used to denote the type of request being sent to the server; this is followed by the two-byte *Packet Length*. You should further note in Figure 11-8 that the header information may also be included (see Figure 11-7); this, of course, depends upon the type of operation that is being requested.

When managing multi-packets during a request operation, it is the high-order bit in the OpCode that is used to denote the final packet and is referred to as the *final bit*.

One such example is with the PUT operation, where the object may need to be carried over several packets; however, the GET operation is a function that may require multiple responses. Here, the server will indicate to the client that it needs to continue; this is gleaned from the response packet and we will cover this in more detail shortly. In the

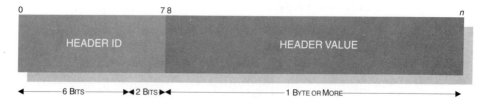

Figure 11-7   The structure of the object model.

Table 11-9 The lower six-bit `HeaderID` segment is used to describe the header type.

						DESCRIPTION
5	**4**	**3**	**2**	**1**	**0**	Bit # of `HeaderID`
x	*x*	*x*	*x*	*x*	*x*	The lower six-bit segment describes the type of header.

meantime, Table 11-12 provides a summary of the operations that are available as function primitives.

We now turn our attention to the format of a response. In Figure 11-9, we can identify a *Response Code*, which is used to denote the type of response being returned to the client, followed by the two-byte *Packet Length*.

When managing multi-packets during a response operation, it is the high-order bit in the `ResponseCode` that is used to denote the final packet and is also referred to as the *final bit*. If you recall from our earlier example, the `GET` operation may require a number of packets to be retrieved from the server to fulfil the original request. The server indicates to the client, by setting the final bit in the `ResponseCode`, that several `GET` operations need to be performed before receiving the final packet. The final bit is also used to inform the client that the server is now ready to receive a new request, but how do we distinguish between more packets and a new operation? It is the `ResponseCode` type that is used to determine what the client should do. In our `GET` operation example, the final bit would be set and the value of the Response Code would be `0x10`, indicating `Continue` (remember the final bit will be set so that the translated value will be `0x90`). A further Response Code of `0x20` (remember that the final bit will be set so our translated value here will be `0xA0`), indicates `Success`. The final bit being set would then appropriately inform the client that it can now continue with a new operation. See IrDA OBEX for a full definition of the response codes.

We have introduced the Object Model and the Session Protocol; in the following sections we consider the implementation of a basic set of APIs that are capable of fulfilling genuine functions for our applications. More specifically, we look at how these opera-

Table 11-10 The higher two-bit segment of the `HeaderID` describes the encoding method for OBEX.

		DESCRIPTION	VALUE
7	**6**	Higher Bit # of `HeaderID`	VALUE
0	0	Two-byte length, null terminated Unicode String.	`0x00`
0	1	Two-byte length, with a byte sequence to follow.	`0x40`
1	0	A single-byte quantity.	`0x80`
1	1	Transmitted with high-byte first; this is a four-byte quantity.	`0xC0`

Table 11-11 The various header identifiers that are encoded in the first six bits of the `HeaderID` byte of the Object Model.

ID	NAME	DESCRIPTION
0xC0	Count	A four-byte unsigned integer, which is used to describe the number of objects joining this transaction.
0x01	Name	An optional description is available to describe the object; an example would be to provide the name of a file during a file transfer operation. This name is constructed using a null terminated `Unicode` string.
0x42	Type	This header is optional and assists in the identification of the type of object being transferred, which may include such objects as *text*, *binary* or *vCard*. If no type is indicated, then the default is assumed to be *binary*.
0xC3	Length	The length of the object is identified with this four-byte unsigned integer and again is optional since the length may be unknown. The *End of Body* may also indicate the end of an object.
0x44 0xC4	Time	This provides the object with a formatted time and date stamp.
0x05	Description	This optional header is used to provide a descriptive meaning to the object being transferred, but can also be used to provide further information in a response code. It is formatted using a null terminated `Unicode` string.
0x46	Target	A number of Bluetooth services exist and this item is used to identify that specific service. In such instances, 128-bit UUIDs[5] can be used to accomplish this identification. This is usually provided in a `CONNECT` or `PUT` operation, where it is directed to a particular service.
0x47	HTTP	An optional header that provides an HTTP 1.x header encompassing many of the features is already present in HTTP.

(continued)

---

[5]A summary of known identifiers can be used where the *Universally Unique Identifiers* (UUIDs) values are used to distinguish the varying services on offer. For example, IrMC-SYNC is used to especially identify IrMC Synchronisation, whereas an identifier value of `F9EC7BC4-953C-11D2-984E-525400DC9E09` is used to identify a folder browsing service.

Table 11-11   The various header identifiers that are encoded in the first six bits of the
`HeaderID` byte of the Object Model. *Continued.*

ID	NAME	DESCRIPTION
0x48	Body	The Body header contains the object being transferred, such as the contents of a file, where several body headers may be used to *chunk* or segment the data. The `End of Body` header is used to
0x49	End of Body	indicate the last chunk or segment and may be used instead of the `Length` header, where the size is unknown.
0x4A	Who	The `Who` header is used to formally identify peer applications and it may be used in a CONNECT response operation. The UUID and target values are matched again using the 128-bit UUIDs encoding.
0xCB	ConnectionID	This optional header value is used to identify the origin of the OBEX connection, especially when multiple connections are being used. This header value is typically the first value to be sent in the request.
0x4C	Application Parameters	The `Application Parameter` header value is used to supply additional information about the application, which resides above the OBEX component.
0x4D	Authentication Challenge	A digest-challenge string is used to initiate the authentication procedures inherent within the remote device.
0x4E	Authentication Response	A digest-response string is used to respond to the authentication challenge originally initiated by the remote device.
0x4F	Object Class	An identification of the class and its associated properties are referenced with the Object Class header.

tions are constructed to enable their intended function. In later sections, we will discuss how OBEX supports the RFCOMM and TCP/IP transport models (see Section 11.3.1.2.8, *OBEX over RFCOMM* and Section 11.3.1.2.9, *OBEX over TCP/IP*).

11.3.1.2.2   Providing Basic Operations.   Having established our functional primitives, we can now turn our attention to the APIs, as shown in Table 11-13. Here, we have a basic set of functions that are capable of being exposed at the upper-edge of our OBEX component; these functions are ready for integration with a chosen OBEX application.

In the following sections, we examine some of the typical functions that we may come across when implementing our OBEX-specific APIs. As such, the OBEX_Connect, OBEX_Disconnect, OBEX_Put, OBEX_Get and OBEX_SetPath will be discussed.

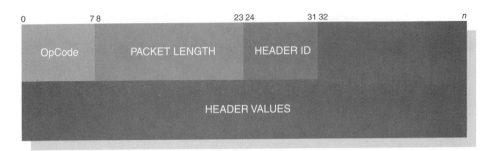

Figure 11-8   The structure of the request packet contains the header parameters of our original object model.

Table 11-12   The range of OBEX-related operations also identifying their specific OpCode values. These can be mapped to specific APIs that can then be exposed to our intended application.

OpCode	DEFINITION	DESCRIPTION
0x80	Connect	Create an OBEX connection.
0x81	Disconnect	Terminate an existing OBEX connection.
0x02	Put	Send a data object.
0x03	Get	Get a data object.
0x85	SetPath	Nominates an area to place the object on the receiving side.
0xFF	Abort	Halt the current operation.

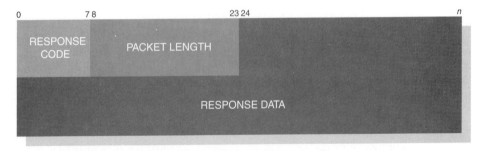

Figure 11-9   The structure of the request packet contains the header parameters of our original object model.

Table 11-13   The range of OBEX-related API functions that can now be exposed to the
OBEX-specific application.

API	OpCode	DEFINITION
OBEX_Connect	0x80	Connect
OBEX_Disconnect	0x81	Disconnect
OBEX_Put	0x02	Put
OBEX_Get	0x03	Get
OBEX_SetPath	0x85	SetPath
OBEX_Abort	0xFF	Abort

11.3.1.2.3   Connecting an OBEX Session.   In our first examination, the OBEX_
Connect function, we look at how the Connect operation is encapsulated within the
request packet (see Figure 11-10).

The Connect request packet is constructed and then used to establish a new
OBEX session. Conversely, its response is shown in Figure 11-11; this will be parsed[6] to
ascertain appropriate instructions by the client device. Let us take a closer look at the parameters that make up these two packets. Our OpCode, shown as 0x80 in Figure 11-10,
always has the final bit set, since it is always communicated in one packet transaction. In
our response, we indicate 0xA0 as our response code, since we are assuming a successful
operation and again the final bit is set, indicating to the client that the server is ready to receive a new request. The PacketLength will accurately reflect the packet size in its
entirety, whereas the OBEXVersion reflects the current IrDA OBEX specification (that
is, Version 1.2). The FLAGS parameter has the default value of zero and is always ignored

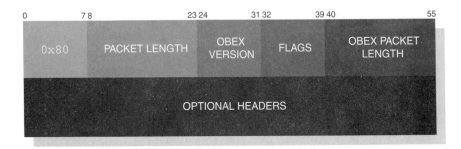

Figure 11-10   The structure of a Connect request packet.

---

[6]When receiving a response from the server, the response packet is parsed or disassembled to learn of the result
(that is, whether it is a success or failure). This information is used to bias what the OBEX component should
do next.

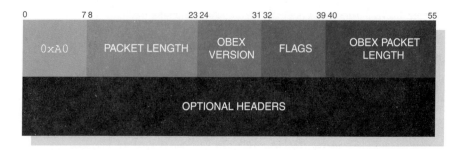

Figure 11-11   The structure of a `Connect` response packet.

by the server. Finally, the `OBEX PacketLength` reflects the maximum packet size capable of being transferred, which is currently 64 KB (less one).

11.3.1.2.4   Disconnecting an OBEX Session.   We have established an OBEX session and naturally we would wish to disconnect it at some point. As such, the `OBEX_Disconnect` function will enable us to disconnect our established session. In Figure 11-12, we provide the structure of a `Disconnect` operation and how it is encapsulated within the request packet.

Conversely, its response is shown in Figure 11-13; this will be parsed to ascertain appropriate instructions by the client device. Let us take a closer look at the parameters that make up these two packets. Our `OpCode`, shown as `0x81` in Figure 11-12, always has the final bit set. It is always communicated in one packet transaction, which informs the server that it is ready to receive its response.

In our response, we indicate `0xA0` as our `ResponseCode`; note that we are assuming a successful operation and that the final bit is set, indicating to the client that the server is ready to receive a new request. The `PacketLength` will accurately reflect the packet size in its entirety.

11.3.1.2.5   Putting Data.   The physical data transfer of objects is achieved through the use of `OBEX_Put` and `OBEX_Get`. In this section, we will consider the

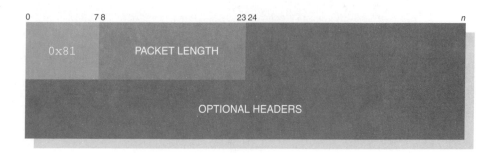

Figure 11-12   The structure of a `Disconnect` request packet.

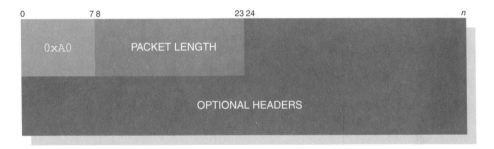

Figure 11-13   The structure of a `Disconnect` response packet.

transfer of data from the client to the server. In Figure 11-14 and Figure 11-15 we provide the structure of a `Put` operation and how it is encapsulated within the request packet.

Conversely, its potential responses are shown in Figure 11-16 and Figure 11-17; subsequently, it will be parsed to ascertain an appropriate action by the client device. Let us take a closer look at the parameters that make up these two packets. Our `OpCode`, shown as `0x02` in Figure 11-14, does not have the final bit set. The client has a large amount of data to transfer and, as such, several packets will be required to transfer its payload. However, in Figure 11-15, the `OpCode` is shown as `0x82`, which indicates to the server that it has now sent the final packet. It sets the final bit of the `OpCode` and is now ready to send a new request.

There are two possible responses during the course of this request. In the first, we may receive a `ResponseCode` of `0x90`, which indicates a *Continue* as a result of the client indicating an `OpCode` of `0x02`. If our `OpCode` does not have the final bit set and we are indicting to the server we have more data to transfer, then its response is *Continue* (see Figure 11-16). In our second indication, see Figure 11-17, we receive `0xA0` in our `ResponseCode`. This informs us that the data transfer was *Successful* on the basis that we sent the last packet and indicated as such with the `OpCode` of `0x82`. Once we have received a successful indication, the client can then begin to send a new request. The `PacketLength` will accurately reflect the packet size in its entirety.

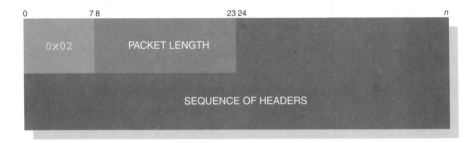

Figure 11-14   The structure of a `Put` request packet indicating that there is more data to be transferred.

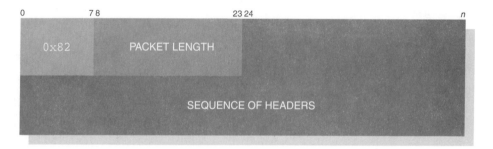

Figure 11-15   The structure of a Put request packet, which indicates that the
final packet has been sent and that the client is now ready to
receive a response.

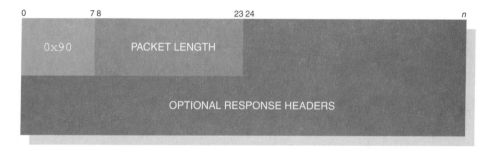

Figure 11-16   The structure of a Put response packet, indicating to the
client that it may continue to transfer the data.

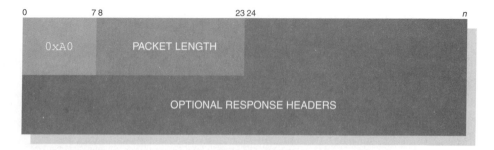

Figure 11-17   The structure of a Put response packet, indicating to the
client that its Put operation has been completed successfully.

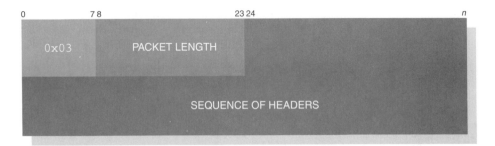

Figure 11-18   The structure of a `Get` request packet, indicating that there is
more data to be retrieved as implied by the `ResponseCode`
`0x90` (*Continue*).

11.3.1.2.6   Getting Data.   We will now consider the transfer of data from the
server to the client. In Figure 11-18 and Figure 11-19, we provide the structure of a `Get`
operation and how it is encapsulated within the request packet.

Conversely, its potential responses are shown in Figure 11-20 and Figure 11-21; it
will be subsequently parsed to ascertain an appropriate action by the client device. Let us
take a closer look at the parameters that make up these two packets. Our `OpCode`, shown
as `0x03` in Figure 11-18, does not have the final bit set. The client has a large amount of
data to collect and, as such, several packets will be retrieved to complete its payload. This
is implied in the `ResponseCode` of `0x90`, which indicates *Continue*. However, in Figure 11-19 the `OpCode` is shown as `0x83`, which now indicates to the server that it has retrieved the final packet and sets the final bit of the `OpCode`; it is now ready to send a new
request. This is implied in the `ResponseCode` of `0xA0`, which indicates that the request has been *Successful*.

We have two possible responses during the course of this request. In the first, we
may receive a `ResponseCode` of `0x90`, which indicates a *Continue* as a result of the
client indicating an `OpCode` of `0x03`. If our `OpCode` does not have the final bit set and

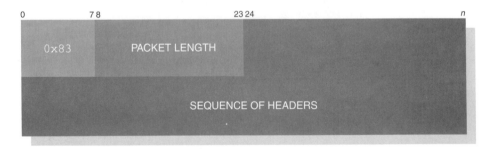

Figure 11-19   The structure of a `Get` request packet, indicating that the final
packet has been collected as implied by the `ResponseCode`
`0xA0` (*Successful*).

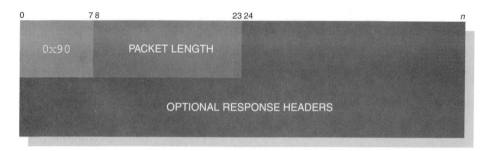

Figure 11-20   The structure of a `Put` response packet, indicating to the
client that it may continue to transfer the data.

we are indicating to the server that we have more data to collect, then its response is *Continue* (see Figure 11-20). In our second indication, see Figure 11-21, we receive 0xA0 in our `ResponseCode`; this informs us that the data transfer was *Successful* on the basis that we sent the last packet and indicated as such with the `OpCode` of 0x83. Once we have received a successful indication, the client can then begin to send a new request. The `PacketLength` will accurately reflect the packet size in its entirety.

   11.3.1.2.7 Setting a Location.   During the transfer of data to and from the client, a specific location may be required to place the data in the directory[7] of the device. The `OBEX_SetPath` function is capable of performing such an operation and we can look specifically at how the `SetPath` operation is encapsulated within the request packet, as shown in Figure 11-20.
   The `SetPath` request packet is constructed and then used to locate an area within the server's file structure. Conversely, its response is shown in Figure 11-23; subse-

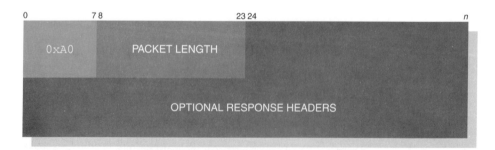

Figure 11-21   The structure of a `Put` response packet, indicating to the
client that its `Put` operation has been completed successfully.

---

[7]A directory structure may be used to store the data objects in a specific location within the system file hierarchy; it should be noted that devices such as notebooks and PDAs utilise such methods of storage. On devices that do not support such a hierarchy, the server may respond with 0xC0, *Bad Request* or 0xC3, *Forbidden*.

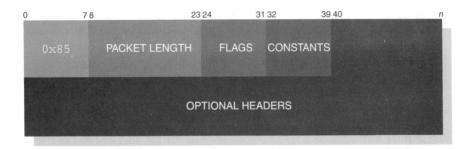

Figure 11-22 The structure of a `SetPath` request packet.

quently, it will be parsed to ascertain an appropriate action by the client device. Let us take a closer look at the parameters that make up these two packets. Our `OpCode`, shown as `0x85` in Figure 11-22, always has the final bit set since it is always communicated in one packet transaction.

In our response, we indicate `0xA0` as our response code, since we are assuming a successful operation and, again, the final bit is set, indicating to the client that the server is ready to receive a new request. The `PacketLength` will accurately reflect the packet size in its entirety, whereas the `FLAGS` parameter always has the default value of zero and is always ignored by the server. The `CONSTANTS` parameter is not used and is reserved for future use.

11.3.1.2.8 OBEX over RFCOMM. RFCOMM has been discussed extensively in the *Serial Port Profile,* Chapter 6. You may remember that RFCOMM provides serial port emulation and is capable of supporting multiple connections. The OBEX protocol has been designed to support RFCOMM, where a server must be capable of supporting several simultaneous connections. These connections must be registered in the *Service Discovery Database*, which we discussed in some detail in the *Service Discovery Application Profile*, Chapter 3. We will learn more of the dependencies of the GOEP as we move forward into the relevant sections later on in this chapter.

There are several assumptions that are made when a client issues a `Connect` request to the server. In the first assumption, we assume that the client is capable of

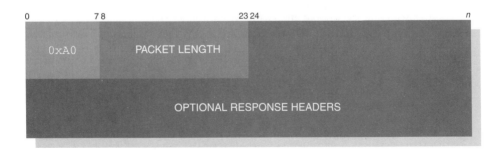

Figure 11-23 The structure of a `SetPath` response packet.

connecting to the server on the basis that it has learned of the RFCOMM channel number from the Service Discovery Database. The second assumption is that the client then initiates the connection to the server, where it is awaiting a connection from the client.

The nature of RFCOMM dictates that it receives data as a byte stream and, as such, the data is collected and sent a byte at a time, using the `Get` and `Put` operations. The OBEX-parsing module of the OBEX component will await and identify an `OpCode` or `ResponseCode`, depending on the type of data it is expecting to receive. How will the parser know the end of the payload? You may remember that request and response packets have a `PacketLength` parameter, which informs us of the size of the payload in its entirety. As such, once the `OpCode` or `ResponseCode` is received, we know that the following two bytes represent the `PacketLength`. To disconnect from the server, the client issues the `Disconnect`-request packet, where the RFCOMM channel is subsequently closed.

11.3.1.2.9 OBEX over TCP/IP. We have come across TCP/IP in earlier chapters, but why does this protocol exist within the OBEX transport mechanism? One fundamental reason for using TCP/IP is the inherent reliability that is achieved by using this protocol; it should not be confused with any networking-related association.

The implementation to use TCP/IP as a mode of transport becomes further complicated. In Table 11-12, we illustrated a series of APIs that can be exposed to our OBEX-specific application. Within our OBEX component, we have to further manage the removal of several layers of encapsulation to retrieve the request or response packet enclosed within the TCP/IP structure (see RFC791 and RFC793). Again, the OBEX protocol has been designed to support TCP/IP, where a server must be capable of supporting several simultaneous connections. These connections must be registered in the *Service Discovery Database*, which we discussed in some detail in the *Service Discovery Application Profile*, Chapter 3.

There are several assumptions that are made when a client issues a `Connect` request to the server. First, we assume that the client is capable of connecting to the server. Since it has learned of the TCP port[8] number, the client subsequently initialises a socket.[9] Secondly, we assume that the client then initiates the connection to the server, where it is awaiting a connection from the client.

Data is sent and retrieved using the `Put` and `Get` request operations. The OBEX-parsing component of your application will await and identify an `OpCode` or `Response-Code`, depending on the type of data it is expecting to receive. To disconnect from the

---

[8]The server registers the appropriate TCP port number in the Service Discovery Database; this is typically port 650. Similarly, a client must assign an internal port number for it to communicate with the server; here a port number above 1023 is recommended, since some operating system deems that port numbers below 1023 are reserved for system use.

[9]The Microsoft Platform Software Development Kit provides a comprehensive set of APIs that allow you to dynamically create sockets (using WinSock) that are associated with specific TCP ports. In some cases, you may find that a minimum amount of parsing may be achieved, where access to the request and response packets can be made directly.

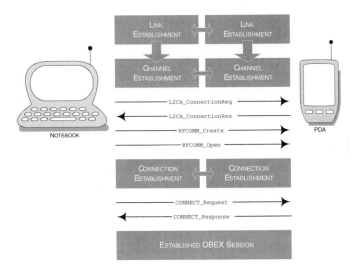

Figure 11-24   The sequence of events that are used to create a successful
connection with the server.

server, the client issues the `Disconnect`-request packet, where the TCP port is subsequently closed.

11.3.1.3   OBEX in the Generic Object Exchange Profile.

In Section 11.3.1.2, *The OBEX Protocol*, we learned how the request and response messages are created to provide us with basic functionality. We then went on to discuss how we could create an API and expose it to our application so that genuine functionality could be realised. We also learned that the OBEX component could parse incoming request and response packets, where an action can be decided based upon the encapsulated data. In this section, we consider the objectives and expectations of OBEX in the *profile*. In establishing our operations and primitive functionality, the profile discusses mandatory features that it expects from the protocol and provides guidance with regard to how a request and response packet should be constructed and subsequently used.

11.3.1.3.1   Initialisation and Establishing an OBEX Session.   Prior to establishing an OBEX session, authentication must occur. An OBEX password may be required and can match the *Bluetooth Passkey*[10] for convenience; this itself reduces user complexity. Further convenience can be provided for the user as both the client and server may store the passkey for future ad-hoc connections.

As a minimum, GOEP must be able to support OBEX without authentication, but if it is requested, then support for the authentication challenge should be provided; we

---

[10]The Bluetooth Passkey is a user-level entered parameter that is required for the pairing procedure and thus enables subsequent authentication.

Table 11-14   The fields and headers that are a mandatory feature of the Connect-request operation.

NAME	TYPE	SUPPORT
OpCode	Field	M
PacketLength	Field	M
OBEXVersion	Field	M
FLAGS	Field	M
OBEXPacketLength	Field	M
Target	Header	C

discuss this in Section 11.3.1.3.2, *OBEX Connection with Authentication*. In Figure 11-24, we provide a series of events that lead up to the establishment of an OBEX session with a server. In Table 11-14, we provide a list of mandatory fields that make up our request packets and provide further information with regard to their usage within the structure.

As you know, the Connect request is used to establish the OBEX session and the Target header is used to identify the targeted service; in some OBEX-specific profiles, this header is mandatory. The Target header is used to identify the intended service; for instance, IrMC-SYNC may be indicated to identify the synchronisation service. The Connect response message is shown in Table 11-15; it is the expected response, where the ResponseCode will indicate 0xA0 if the transfer was successful. The ConnectiontionID and Who headers must be used if the Target header was used in the original Connect request.

Table 11-15   The fields and headers that are a mandatory feature of the Connect-response operation.

NAME	TYPE	SUPPORT
ResponseCode	Field	M
PacketLength	Field	M
OBEXVersion	Field	M
FLAGS	Field	M
OBEXPacketLength	Field	M
ConnectionID	Header	C
Who	Header	C

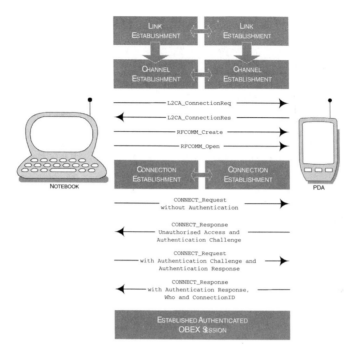

Figure 11-25 The sequence of events that are used to create a successful authenticated connection with the server.

11.3.1.3.2 OBEX Connection with Authentication. In our previous section, we provided the scenario and features that are required to establish an OBEX session without authentication. This section now discusses the features expected from the OBEX protocol when authentication is required. This new authentication procedure is an additional requirement above the Bluetooth specific authentication process, that is, a Bluetooth Passkey is used to instigate the pairing process. The OBEX authentication is used to establish a trusted relationship at the client and server level, where it is the server that will initiate the challenge. The server is unable to commit to an OBEX session, until the authentication features are fully adhered to; in Figure 11-25, we illustrate the sequence of events that are used to establish this relationship. In the first instance of sending a Connect request, the client is unaware that authentication is required and, as such, it sends a request in the usual manner. The fields have been illustrated in Table 11-14.

The client learns of the news when it receives the response from the server. When we look more closely at the fields used in our Connect response (as shown in Table 11-16), we notice that the AuthenticationChallenge header is used. Furthermore, when the client parses the ResponseCode, it will learn of the value 0x41 *Unauthorised*; this notifies the client that it must send a new Connect request with the AuthenticationChallenge and AuthenticationResponse headers (as shown in

Table 11-16 The fields and headers that are a mandatory feature of the first Connect-response for authentication.

NAME	TYPE	SUPPORT
ResponseCode	Field	M
PacketLength	Field	M
OBEXVersion	Field	M
FLAGS	Field	M
OBEXPacketLength	Field	M
AuthenticationChallenge	Header	M

Table 11-17); these headers carry the digest-challenge string and digest-response strings, respectively.

The fields and headers used in the second response are shown in Table 11-18. If the ResponseCode contains the value 0xA0 from the server, then authentication has been successful and the OBEX session can now be established.

11.3.1.3.3 Disconnecting an OBEX Session. At some point, a disconnection of the established OBEX session will be terminated, which may be due to a user request or a loss of connection. The session is terminated using the Disconnect operation, where

Table 11-17 The fields and headers that are a mandatory feature of the second Connect-request for authentication.

NAME	TYPE	SUPPORT
OpCode	Field	M
PacketLength	Field	M
OBEXVersion	Field	M
FLAGS	Field	M
OBEXPacketLength	Field	M
Target	Header	C
AuthenticationChallenge	Header	M
AuthenticationReponse	Header	M

Table 11-18 The fields and headers that are a mandatory feature of the second Connect-response for authentication.

NAME	TYPE	SUPPORT
ResponseCode	Field	M
PacketLength	Field	M
OBEXVersion	Field	M
FLAGS	Field	M
OBEXPacketLength	Field	M
ConnectionID	Header	M
Who	Header	M
AuthenticationReponse	Header	M

the OpCode has the value 0x81. In Table 11-19, we show the remaining fields that are used during this operation.

The Disconnect response message is shown in Table 11-20. The ResponseCode will indicate 0xA0 if the disconnection was successful; this operation is not refused by the server.

11.3.1.3.4 Pushing Data to the Server. Data is transferred to the server using the Put request, where the OpCode may indicate 0x02, for multiple packets and 0x82 to indicate that it has sent the last packet. The features used for this transaction are identified in Table 11-21, where the ConnectionID is mandatory if the Target header was used in the original Connect request.

The Name header is used to identify the object being transferred and the Body/End of Body headers are used to identify the start and end of the object being transferred. In Table 11-22, we identify the features that are required in the Put response, where the ResponseCode may indicate 0x90 for continue in response to the Put OpCode 0x02 or 0xA0 for successful in response to the Put OpCode for successful completion of the transfer.

Table 11-19 The fields and headers that are a mandatory feature of the Disconnect-request operation.

NAME	TYPE	SUPPORT
OpCode	Field	M
PacketLength	Field	M

Table 11-20 The fields and headers that are a mandatory feature of the `Disconnect-` response operation.

NAME	TYPE	SUPPORT
ResponseCode	Field	M
PacketLength	Field	M

11.3.1.3.5 Pulling Data from the Server. Data is transferred from the server using the Get request, where the OpCode may indicate 0x03, for multiple packets and 0x83 to indicate that it has retrieved the last packet. The features used for this transaction are identified in Table 11-21, where the ConnectionID is mandatory if the Target header was used in the original Connect request.

The Name header is used to identify the object being transferred and the Type header is used to identify the type of object being pulled. In Table 11-22, we identify the features that are required in the Get response, where the ResponseCode may indicate 0x90 for *continue* in response to the Get OpCode 0x03 or 0xA0 for *successful* in response to the Get OpCode for successful completion of the transfer. The Name header is used to identify the object being transferred and the Body/End of Body headers are used to identify the start and end of the object being pulled.

11.3.1.3.6 Locating Data Objects. A physical location on the server can be sought using the SetPath request, where the OpCode will indicate 0x85 and the Name header is used to contain the path name. The initial reference used by the server is the root directory. On the basis of this location, the server will reference down into the hierarchy to obtain the new location. For example, if the client requests My Documents in the Name header, it will effectively locate C:\My Documents, on a typical Microsoft Windows based operating system or similar.

The FLAGS parameter is used to denote the type of action to be applied in locating the new directory; for example, where bit 0 is set to indicate that the directory needs to be

Table 11-21 The fields and headers that are a mandatory feature of the `Get`-request operation.

NAME	TYPE	SUPPORT
OpCode	Field	M
PacketLength	Field	M
ConnectionID	Header	C
Name	Header	M
Body/End of Body	Header	M

Table 11-22   The fields and headers that are a mandatory feature of the `Get`-connect operation.

NAME	TYPE	SUPPORT
ResponseCode	Field	M
PacketLength	Field	M
Name	Header	O
Body/End of Body	Header	M

moved up one level before applying the `Name` header. This is equivalent to `..\` on a Microsoft Windows environment or `../` on a Unix environment. Setting bit 1 recommends to the system that it should not create a directory if it already exists; otherwise an error must be reported to the user. The `Constant` parameter is not used and is reserved for future use.

In the request-response packets for the `SetPath` operation, the final bit is always set since this transaction is made in one packet. In Table 11-24, we identify the features that are required in the `SetPath` response, where the `ResponseCode` may indicate `0xA0` for a successful operation. A `ResponseCode` of `0xC4` informs the client that the folder does not exist and a `0xC1` informs the client that folder browsing is not allowed.

11.3.1.4 RFCOMM. In the *Serial Port Profile*, Chapter 6, we introduced the conceptual and functional nature of RFCOMM and how it provides an emulated serial port presence. Several distinctions were made between the various types of applications. The purpose of making these distinctions was to enable clarification and understanding of RFCOMM's composition. In this particular application context, the creation of an emulated serial port would be transparent to the user. The GOEP is dependent upon the operation of the Serial Port Profile and as such, is required to establish an emulated serial port as part of its communication link with the remote device.

The term cable replacement application was introduced in our earlier chapter and distinguishes between the different scenarios available. It refers to specific Bluetooth ap-

Table 11-23   The fields and headers that are a mandatory feature of the `SetPath` request operation for data object location.

NAME	TYPE	SUPPORT
OpCode	Field	M
PacketLength	Field	M
FLAGS	Field	M
Constants	Field	M

Table 11-24 The fields that are a mandatory feature of the `SetPath` response.

NAME	TYPE	SUPPORT
ResponseCode	Field	M
PacketLength	Field	M

plications that create implicit emulated serial ports, which remain transparent to the user to complete the creation of a communications link.

Specific detail has been provided to illustrate how data is communicated over an emulated serial port connection, whereby a *Data Link Connection* (DLC) is established between two peer devices, namely the client and server. We have also looked at the fields that make up our service record for this profile. The `ProtocolDescriptorList` field is used to describe the set of protocols that the profile intends to use and, as such, the RFCOMM protocol identifier contains a parameter, which contains the Server Channel number.

The Server Channel is used in combination with a *Data Link Connection Identifier* (DLCI), which is then used to uniquely identify the active DLC. This connection is then mapped onto a connectionless orientated L2CAP *Channel Identifier* (CID).

In this section we highlight the specific features that are required to realise a compliant GOEP. Table 11-25 and Table 11-26 illustrate the features or capabilities that are expected from the Serial Port Profile.

The use of the RLS command is encouraged to keep peer devices informed of any state change. In one such instance, an emulated serial port may interface to a Type II application (physical serial port), where overruns or parity errors may occur. An application that makes use of RS232 port configuration parameters should expose these settings through an appropriate API function; this is of particular relevance when interfacing to Type II applications.

11.3.1.5 L2CAP. The L2CAP layer provides transparency for the upper-layers of the stack from the layers typically found within the host controller. L2CAP payloads are passed to the *Host Controller Interface*[11] (HCI) and are then subsequently passed onto the *Link Manager Protocol* (LMP). The range of upper layers, which include RFCOMM, *Service Discovery Protocol* (SDP) and the *Telephony Control Protocol Specification* (TCS) all make use of the capabilities offered to us by L2CAP. Its primary role is to provide *protocol multiplexing*, allowing numerous simultaneous connections to be made and it also provides the ability for *segmentation* and *reassembly*. This refers to the ability to manage large payloads in the application, which may need to be fragmented into smaller payloads for the lower-layers to manage; these are then transmitted over the air-interface. Finally, the L2CAP layer exchanges *Quality of Service* (QoS) information, ensuring that

---

[11]L2CAP payloads are passed directly onto LMP when implemented on a hostless system.

Table 11-25   The set of capabilities that are required from the initiating party, denoted here by the client device.

PROCEDURE	CLIENT	SERVER
Initialise an RFCOMM Session	M	X
Terminate an RFCOMM Session	M	M
Establish a new DLC Connection	M	X
Disconnect a DLC Connection	M	M
Emulate RS232 Control Signals	C	C
Transfer Data	M	M
Test Command	X	X
Flow Control	C	C
RLS	O	O
PN	O	O
RPN	O	O

sufficient resources are available and that both Bluetooth devices are attaining the best service.

In Table 11-27, we summarise the broad capabilities that are expected from L2CAP. In the table, you will notice features are marked with *M* (Mandatory), *O* (Optional), *X* (Excluded), *C* (Conditional) and *N/A* (Not Applicable); these will determine what is expected from the L2CAP layer.

11.3.1.5.1   Channel Types.   In Table 11-27, we have identified that *Connection-Orientated Channels* are mandatory, whereas *Connectionless Channels* are excluded; this type of channel is aimed at broadcasting, where all devices may be targeted. L2CAP uses *Protocol Data Units* (PDUs) to transport connection, signalling and configuration options, which will be discussed in a moment. The higher-layers of the Bluetooth protocol stack will instigate a connection with L2CAP using the L2CA_ConnectReq request packet, where the corresponding result is contained within the L2CA_ConnectRsp response packet. An L2CA_ConnectRspNeg negative response packet is used to denote a response, where the connection with the remote device was unsuccessful. Since our profile resides above L2CAP and employs its services, we are only concerned with the upper protocol layer of L2CAP. This higher functionality is offered to us through a series of L2CAP events and is denoted through the prefix L2CA_ (see Table 11-28).

Table 11-26   The set of capabilities that are required from the responder party, denoted here by the server device.

PROCEDURE	CLIENT	SERVER
Initialise an RFCOMM Session	X	M
Terminate an RFCOMM Session	M	M
Establish a new DLC Connection	X	M
Disconnect a DLC Connection	M	M
Emulate RS232 Control Signals	M	M
Transfer Data	N/A	N/A
Test Command	M	M
Flow Control	M	M
RLS	M	M
PN	M	M
RPN	M	M

When creating an L2CAP connection between two devices, a *Protocol/Service Multiplexor* (PSM) value is used to denote the higher-layer protocol that is using the connection. Table 11-29 identifies these values and the corresponding protocol they represent. The value of 0x0003 (RFCOMM) is used for this profile.

11.3.1.5.2   Signalling.   When establishing communication with a remote device, a *signalling channel* is created and reserved for use during connection, disconnection and configuration of subsequent L2CAP connections. A *channel* is used to describe the communication and data flow that exists between L2CAP entities and Table 11-30 illustrates the range of CIDs that are used to identify the channel type. As we can see in Table 11-27, *Connection Establishment* and *Termination* is mandatory in the local device, although the remote device may be capable of initiating and terminating a connection to the local device. The L2CA_DisconnectReq request packet is used to terminate the connection with the remote device and an L2CA_DisconnectRsp response packet is used to ascertain the result of the termination. All disconnection requests must be completed successfully. The support of *Configuration* is shown as mandatory and we will discuss these specific options in more detail in the following section. Finally, *Echo* and *Command Rejection* are both mandatory for a compliant GOEP.

11.3.1.5.3   Configuration Options.   In establishing a connection with the remote device, the channel is subject to configuration and the higher-layer prototype L2CA_

Table 11-27   The illustration shows specific procedures that this profile depends upon to realise its compliant implementation.

PROCEDURE	CLIENT	SERVER
Connection-orientated Channel	M	M
Connectionless Channel	X	X
Connection Establishment	M	M
Configuration	M	M
Connection Termination	M	M
Echo	M	M
Command Rejection	M	M
Maximum Transmission Unit	M	M
Flush Timeout	M	M
Quality of Service	O	O

`ConfigReq` request packet is used to carry configuration requests. Its associated response is contained within the `L2CA_ConfigRsp` packet; an `L2CA_ConfigRspNeg` packet is used to denote a negative response during configuration where, for example, the suggested *Maximum Transmission Unit* (MTU) is too large. In Table 11-27, we show that the MTU and *Flush Timeout* parameters are mandatory, whereas the QoS is optional.

The default MTU setting for the signalling channel is 48-bytes, whereas other channels may be capable of transferring larger payloads; essentially, the MTU determines the

Table 11-28   The range of prototypes used to illustrate how L2CAP is architected and how interaction between higher- and lower-layers is achieved. For this discussion, our concern here is with the higher-layer.

PROTOTYPE	DESCRIPTION
L2CA_	This prefix prototype is used to denote the higher-layer interaction, typically used by RFCOMM, SDP and TCS
L2CAP_	This prefix is used to denote peer-to-peer signalling interaction of L2CAP entities.
LP_	Finally, this prefix denotes lower-layer interaction, where L2CAP interfaces with the LMP layer.

Table 11-29   The PSM values that are used to identify the higher-layer protocol.

PSM	DESCRIPTION
0x0001	SDP
0x0003	RFCOMM
0x0005	TCS-BIN
0x0007	TCS-BIN-CORDLESS

size of payloads that are capable of being exchanged between two devices. During configuration, the local device will inform the remote device that it is potentially capable of accepting larger payloads. If the remote device is unwilling to accept a larger MTU, then the local device is informed with the response contained within the L2CA_ConfigRspNeg packet.

When L2CA_ request and response packets are being exchanged, the Flush Timeout parameter is used to determine how long the local device is prepared to continue to transmit an L2CAP fragment before it gives up; the packet is subsequently flushed or, in other words, discarded. The suggested Flush Timeout value is sent during the L2CA_ConfigReq request packet. However, if no value is set, then the default value is used. The GOEP uses the default value of 0xFFFF.

As we have already mentioned, the QoS configuration is optional. However, if it is used during an L2CA_ConfigReq request, then the *best effort* service is established as a default; the available services that are supported for an L2CAP channel are shown in Table 11-31. However, if the QoS service is set at *Guaranteed*, then parameters such *Token Rate*, *Token Bucket*, *Peak Bandwidth*, *Latency* and *Delay Variation* are used to determine an acceptable guaranteed service, where the L2CA_ConnectRspNeg will indicate that these values are unacceptable. These parameters are then subject to further negotiation.

Table 11-30   The CIDs that are used to represent the logical channel.

CID	DESCRIPTION
0x0000	Null
0x0001	Signalling Channel
0x0002	Connectionless Reception Channel
0x0003 to 0x003F	Reserved
0x0040 to 0xFFFF	Dynamically Allocated

11.3.1.6   Link Manager.   The *Link Manager* (LM) layer sits between the HCI and the *Link Controller* (LC), although on a hostless system the LM will have direct interaction with L2CAP. It accepts commands from HCI and translates them into operations for the LC, where *Asynchronous Connectionless* (ACL) and *Synchronous Connection-Orientated* (SCO) links are created and established. It is during this stage of ACL and SCO establishment that a master-slave switch would be performed as governed by the requirements of this profile. The LM is also responsible for placing the device into a low-power mode, which includes *hold, sniff* and park.

In providing *general* error management, devices that operate mandatory procedures during interoperability must either acknowledge its support or provide a suitable reason informing the initiator why the procedure failed. The LMP_Detach PDU is used to inform the device of the error that occurred; typically, the reason *unsupported LMP feature* (0x1A) is reported (see Appendix A).

11.3.1.7   Link Controller.   The LC layer is the lowest-layer depicted in the dependencies of this profile and is responsible for a large number of core capabilities. It manages air-to-interface transactions and determines the fundamental timing of ACL and SCO data packet transmission and reception, as well as coordinating the effort at its upper-edge with the LM. It also encompasses the management of the various packet types and the various inquiry and paging procedures that are available. In turn, the following subsections provide clarity with regard to the capabilities that are a requirement at the LC level for the GOEP. In our understanding of the dependencies, we begin by examining in more detail the supported capabilities and a small discussion is offered for each. If you are a developer providing profile-specific applications, then the likelihood for you to engage in a large part of this component is improbable, although, in some audio-related applications, direct access may be required, where a faster transport mechanism can be sup-

Table 11-31   The range of service definitions that are used during QoS.

SERVICE	DESCRIPTION
No Traffic	This indicates that the channel will not be sending any traffic and, as such, any parameters can be ignored.
Best Effort	This default value attempts to achieve a minimum service with the local remote device, where no guarantees are offered.
Guaranteed	With this service definition, we indicate that we wish to achieve the maximum bandwidth permitted. This is, of course, subject to the nature of a wireless environment.

ported. Nevertheless, many manufacturers have architected an audio-specific API for intelligible access to this component.

11.3.1.7.1 Capabilities. Table 11-32 summarises the broad capabilities that are expected from the LC. In the table, you will notice features are marked with *M* (Mandatory), *O* (Optional), *X* (Excluded), *C* (Conditional) and *N/A* (Not Applicable); these will determine what is expected from the features at the LC.

11.3.1.7.1.1 INQUIRY AND INQUIRY SCAN. An inquiry procedure is used to learn of the other devices in radio range, where the BD_ADDR and clock offsets are obtained; it is DeviceA that will enter an *inquiry substate* to perform this procedure. A device that wishes to be discovered (DeviceB) will enter an *inquiry scan substate*, where the device will respond with an *inquiry response*. In this state, DeviceB is waiting to receive an *Inquiry Access Code* (IAC). From an application perspective, these modes of operation are discussed in more detail in the *Generic Access Profile*, Chapter 2. It is here that specific rules are determined with regard to the behaviour of such devices and how long these devices can operate in such modes. When devices have been discovered, the information is passed over to the *Service Discovery Application Profile*, Chapter 3, which manages the specific attributes that make up that device. What is being established here, as a dependency, is that the Bluetooth protocol stack must encompass and support such behavioural procedures for this profile to be considered compliant.

11.3.1.7.1.2 PAGING AND PAGING SCAN. The *inquiry substate* and *inquiry scan substate* procedures are the initial methods used to learn of other devices in radio range; to this extent, the device has discovered sufficient information to gain a connection with the remote device. This is achieved when DeviceA has the intent to create a connection with

Table 11-32   The summary of capabilities that are required for the LC to enable a compliant GOEP.

PROCEDURES	CLIENT	SERVER
Inquiry	M	X
Inquiry Scan	X	M
Paging	M	X
Page Scan	X	M
Inter-piconet	O	O
Packet Types	M	M
Voice Codecs	X	X

DeviceB; DeviceA is now placed into a *paging substate*, where it will periodically transmit the *Device Access Code* (DAC). The DAC is used to target the device directly and the clock offset is used to gain an idea of the clock cycle of DeviceB. These parameters were originally obtained during our inquiry procedures. If DeviceB wishes to be connected, then it will enter a *page scan substate* and will respond accordingly to DeviceA. An inquiry procedure may be avoided if the BD_ADDR is already known, although a connection may take a little longer if the clock offset is not known.

11.3.1.7.1.3 INTER-PICONET. Inter-piconet capabilities describe the process that allows the master to manage multiple connections from slave devices. During a connection, other users may temporarily witness degradation in the service that is being provided; however, the master must be capable of accepting new participants in the piconet.

11.3.1.7.1.4 PACKET TYPES. There are numerous packet types available and Table 11-33 identifies the most often used packets for profile support. There are also a number of *common* packet types used for general-purpose transport; for example, the ID packet is used for inquiry procedures and a POLL packet would be sent by DeviceA to determine if a slave is active on a channel.

The DM1 packet type is used to transmit control data over any connection, but may also be used to transport a genuine payload. HV1, HV2 and HV3 are various SCO packet types to carry audio-specific data, where a DV packet can combine ACL and SCO specific data; their support in this profile is reflected in Table 11-33. Various ACL packet types

Table 11-33   The summary of packet types that are required for the LC to enable a compliant GOEP.

PACKET TYPE	CLIENT	SERVER
DM1	M	M
DH1	M	M
DM3	M	M
DH3	M	M
DM5	M	M
DH5	M	M
HV1	X	X
HV2	X	X
HV3	X	X
DV	X	X

are also available. In fact, seven types including the DM1 type are attributed to carrying user-specific data. These include DH1, DM3, DH3, DM5, DH5 and AUX1; similarly, Table 11-33 summarises their support in this profile.

11.4 SUMMARY

- All OBEX-specific profiles, such as the Object Push, File Transfer and Synchronisation are dependent upon the GOEP.
- A governing profile may change the basic requirements of the GOEP to accommodate its own needs.
- Features are defined to determine the behaviour of certain operations that govern connection, disconnection and push and pull behaviour.
- The GOEP is based upon the OBEX protocol within the Bluetooth protocol stack.
- An OBEX component would be responsible for exposing an API to the OBEX-specific profiles.
- The OBEX protocol can be implemented upon RFCOMM and TCP/IP.
- Certain characteristics define the OBEX features expected from the profile.
- There are two levels of authentication for the client and server at the application level (Bluetooth and OBEX) although this is not mandatory.
- No user expectations are described in the profile, as the governing profile determines the user characteristics.

12

The Object Push Profile

12.1 INTRODUCTION

In our everyday lives, we constantly exchange business or personal information. In a business context, we often exchange business cards, which contain information relating to our business address, a range of contact telephone numbers and more often than not an email address. This practice is commonly referred to as *Personal Data Interchange* (PDI). It simply refers to the exchange of personal data in the various contexts in which we find ourselves, whether in a business meeting or at a trade exhibition. The nature of the information we exchange is often varied; when passing time and dates for an appointment or an agenda at a conference, there has to be a more convenient way to accurately exchange such information.

The natural transition of PDI is to provide an electronic method where we can conveniently exchange personal details. What the object exchange usage models provide is a foundation for creating ad-hoc connections between Bluetooth-enabled devices. In particular, the *Object Push Profile* achieves a more formal and convenient method for exchanging this data accurately and electronically.

It is primarily focused at the exchange of electronic data that takes the format of *vCard* and *vCalendar* objects; moreover, the Object Push Profile mandates how the vCard and vCalendar objects are exchanged between two Bluetooth-enabled devices. In Figure 12-1 and Figure 12-2, we illustrate the typical usage models that are provided by this pro-

Figure 12-1   The Object Push usage model shown in this illustration allows
                  the user to exchange business cards with a PDA and mobile
                  phone.

file. vCard[1] and vCalendar[2] are specifications that identify an object's structure and content. In this chapter, we discuss the requirements of the profile itself and the expectations
of the underlying dependency, the *Generic Object Exchange Profile* (GOEP), Chapter 11.
It is important to remember that there are numerous applications that already support
vCard and vCalendar data object exchange and we are simply adding another transport
mechanism for these existing applications. You may remember from our discussion of
GOEP that transparency is provided for applications that reside above the Object Exchange (OBEX) Protocol.

   The Object Push Profile is dependent upon the features and procedures that are described in the GOEP. These features are, in turn, dependent upon the *Generic Access*,
Chapter 2, the *Service Discovery Application*, Chapter 3 and the *Serial Port Profiles*,
Chapter 6. The core dependency illustrated in this chapter relates to the capabilities as described in the GOEP.

Figure 12-2   The Object Push usage model shown in this illustration allows
                  the user to exchange business cards and appointment informa-
                  tion between a mobile phone and a notebook.

---

[1]The vCard specification is discussed in detail in The Internet Mail Consortium, "vCard: The Electronic Business Card," Version 2.1, September 1996.
[2]The vCalendar specification is discussed in detail in The Internet Mail Consortium, "vCalendar: The Electronic
Calendaring and Scheduling Exchange Format," Version 1.0, September 1996.

12.2 USAGE MODELS

This section considers our existing usage model through scenarios that may be typical for the Object Push Profile. We begin by exploring the existing model, where a *mobile phone*, *PDA* or *notebook* communicates with a similar device to exchange vCard and vCalendar objects.

Figure 12-1 and Figure 12-2 illustrate our existing usage models. The role of the mobile phone acting as a client initiates a one-to-one communications link with another Bluetooth-enabled device, where it takes on the role of a server. The Object Push Profile usage model prescribes short-range communication typically found in an environment where individuals wish to exchange personal information. The Object Push Profile is one of the simplest usage models within the Bluetooth technology.

12.3 PROFILE PRINCIPLES

The Object Push Profile provides two new roles: a *Push Client* and a *Push Server*. The Push Client device is capable of pushing and pulling data objects to and from the Push Server, whereas the server provides the facility to allow the client device to push and pull the data objects.

In our introduction, we touched upon the notion that a set of features and procedures exist to help govern the operation of Bluetooth-enabled devices, which support the Object Push Profile. At the heart of this profile, the GOEP establishes core capabilities that are realised in the Object Push Profile. Tasks such as object push and synchronisation can take place between devices, where such objects may include vCalendar and vCard, as previously outlined. The GOEP and its underlying capabilities have been designed with portability in mind and, as such, any existing application may make use of the GOEP.

There are no fixed master-slave roles; this allows either device free to initiate and terminate a connection, although typically the client will initiate the primary connection, where inquiry and device discovery procedures are undertaken. Participating devices in this profile must be required to perform bonding, pairing, authentication and encryption when requested to do so. Their use within this profile is optional. The OBEX authentication procedures are not required for this profile. In Figure 12-3, we illustrate the specific Bluetooth protocol stack components that are dependent upon a compliant profile.

In Table 12-1, clarification is provided with regard to the roles used within the context of this profile. In general, *DeviceA* represents the initiating party and *DeviceB* represents the accepting party. The terms are often used interchangeably when describing specific operations and are provided here for reference.

12.4 USER EXPECTATIONS

The Object Push Profile should enable three core features, which include the ability to *Object Push*, *Business Card Pull* and *Business Card Exchange* as shown in Table 12-2. As a minimum, support for vCard is mandatory, where other objects such as vCalendar,

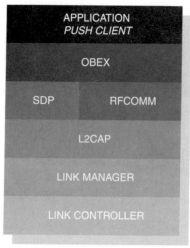 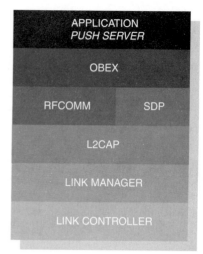

BLUETOOTH-ENABLED PUSH CLIENT   BLUETOOTH-ENABLED PUSH SERVER SERVER

Figure 12-3 The core components of the Bluetooth protocol stack are shown illustrating how the components of the Object Push Profile are integrated.

Table 12-1 The list of behavioural characteristics that are typical for this profile.

CONFIGURATION	ROLE	DESCRIPTION
DeviceA	Client	This device is capable of pushing and pulling objects from the server. The client establishes a relationship with the server before data can be exchanged; the client will typically initiate the connection.
	Initiator	This configuration describes the device that instigates the original connection or the device that wishes to initiate communication over an existing link.
DeviceB	Server	A server provides object exchange capability which, in turn, allows client devices to push and pull objects from the server. This type of device would typically accept connections from clients.
	Acceptor	This configuration describes the process of the device accepting the initiated communication from DeviceA.

Table 12-2   The illustration shows specific behavioural procedures that this profile depends
upon to realise its compliant implementation.

FEATURE	CLIENT	SERVER
Object Push	M	M
Business Card Pull	O	O
Business Card Exchange	O	O

vMessage and vNotes are optional; however, if an object is used and is not supported by the server, an appropriate error message should be conveyed to the user. These particular features and their associated functionality are now described in more detail, with an emphasis provided for user expectation. Devices whose behaviour mimic that of a server should be configured as such, where Figure 12-4 illustrates the configuration options available to some Bluetooth-enabled devices. In this particular mode of operation, server devices should be configured for *limited* discovery or where the device is public should be configured for *general* discovery; see *Generic Access Profile*, Chapter 2 for more information.

12.4.1.1   The Object Push Feature.   This function permits the pushing of data objects to a server, where the user may be prompted to enter a Bluetooth Passkey if authentication is required, although no OBEX authentication is used during this process.

Interoperability at the application level is achieved through the support of the various object data types that are available. In Table 12-3, we identify the various data object formats and their associated specification. It is the application that is responsible for providing the relevant data object support; Bluetooth wireless technology is used as the transport medium.

The user should perform inquiry and discovery procedures to ascertain the capabilities of the server device. Once he or she has identified the appropriate server, the user can select and make use of the facilities it has available. Users should not use the services of a server that does not support a data object type; however, if a data object is used inadvertently, then the server should report an appropriate error message indicating that the object is not supported. As illustrated in Figure 12-4, the user must configure the server into the *Object Exchange* mode, although this would remain transparent.[3] The server is now capable of supporting the various object types; in this particular example, these objects relate to the checked items as shown in the illustration (that is, *Business Cards*, *Calendar Items*, *E-Mail Messages* and *Notes*).

Push Servers must be capable of managing multiple objects during an OBEX connection, although it is not mandatory for Push Clients to support multiple object transfer. You may recall from the *Generic Object Exchange Profile*, Chapter 11, that a push

---

[3]No explicit reference is made to this particular mode of operation at the user-interface level; however, activating this capability intrinsically enables this operation.

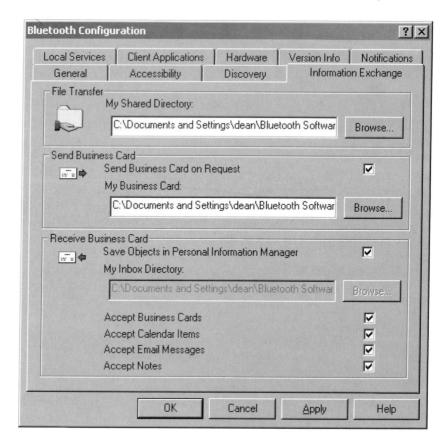

Figure 12-4   The generic options available to the user. The user can configure their set-up and regulate how information is exchanged
between two devices. (Courtesy of TDK Systems Europe.)

function is managed through a `Put` operation, where an OBEX session has been established beforehand with a `Connect` operation. The disconnection of an OBEX session is
managed with the `Disconnect` operation and so on; this is discussed in more detail in
Section 12.5.1.2, *OBEX in the Object Push Profile*.

12.4.1.2   Business Card Pull.   This feature allows the pulling of a business card
from a server, where this support is offered as optional; however, a suitable error message
must be used to inform the user where no such support exists.

During this operation, the Push Client wishes to retrieve the business card from the
Push Server. If authentication is required, the user may be prompted to enter a Bluetooth
Passkey, although no OBEX authentication is used during this process. In this example,
Figure 12-5 shows the user being prompted with a Microsoft Windows dialog box re-
questing the entry of a passkey to authenticate with the server (Mobile Phone).

Table 12-3 The table identifies the object types and formats available that must be supported by any application using the Object Push Profile.

FORMAT	DESCRIPTION
vCard	Object Push applications must support the capabilities and format provided within the Internet Mail Consortium, "vCard: The Electronic Business Card," Version 2.1, September 1996.
vCalendar	Object Push applications must support the capabilities and format provided within the vCalendar specification as discussed in further detail in The Internet Mail Consortium, "vCalendar: The Electronic Calendaring and Scheduling Exchange Format," Version 1.0, September 1996.
vMessaging	Object Push applications must support the capabilities and format provided within the Infra-red Data Association, "Specification for Ir Mobile Communications (IrMC)," Version 1.1, March 1999.
vNotes	Object Push applications must support the capabilities and format provided within the Infra-red Data Association, "Specification for Ir Mobile Communications (IrMC)," Version 1.1, March 1999.

It is assumed that the server device the object is being pulled from has been configured and that the inquiry and discoverability procedures have already been performed. It is also assumed that the server device the object is being pulled from is capable of supporting this profile. Once the user has the ability to connect to a device, he or she may now continue to make use of the services it provides; the user does so by using a

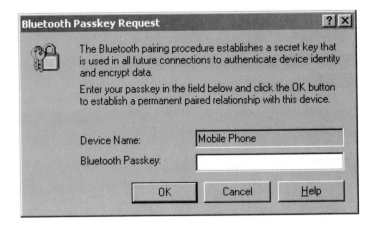

Figure 12-5 The provision of pairing and authentication is optional, but in this instance the user is prompted to enter a Bluetooth Passkey. (Courtesy of TDK Systems Europe.)

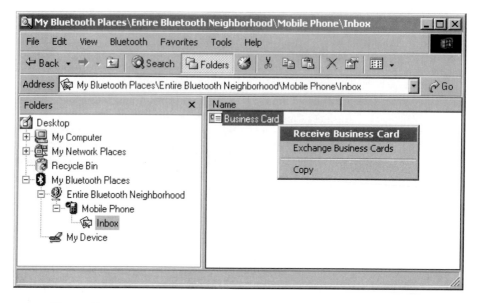

Figure 12-6   Right-clicking the icon causes a pop-up menu to appear which
                  offers the ability to receive the business card. (Courtesy of
                  TDK Systems Europe.)

double-click[4] or right-click operation to begin the process of receiving the business card
as we can see in Figure 12-6.

When the user has selected the *Receive Business Card* option from the menu, he or
she is prompted with a dialog box, informing them of the progress of their request; Figure
12-7 provides such an illustration.

Push Servers must be capable of managing multiple objects during an OBEX connection, although it is not mandatory for Push Clients to support multiple object transfer.
A pull function is managed through a Get operation, where an OBEX session has been
established beforehand with a Connect operation. Devices that support the Business
Card Pull feature must use the default location for storing the Business Card. In our earlier illustration, Figure 12-6, we can see in the Mobile Phone device that the Business
Card is stored in the *Inbox* area; this is the default location. The default function of the
Get operation is used to retrieve data from that location; to achieve successful interoperability, both the Push Client and Server must support the vCard format specification (as
we illustrated in Table 12-3).

---

[4]The double-click and right-click operations refer to a mouse that is connected to your client device (in this example, a PC or notebook computer running a Microsoft Windows operating system) and where both operations
trigger the same method of access. It is noted that an operation may vary from device to device and, as such, the
number of buttons may vary on a mouse. Indeed, no mouse may be connected. The example draws your attention to how it may be possible and acknowledges that implementations may differ.

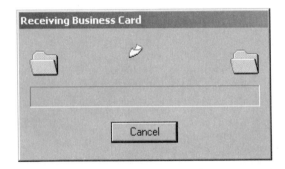

Figure 12-7   The user is informed that the business card is being received.
(Courtesy of TDK Systems Europe.)

12.4.1.3   Business Card Exchange.   During this operation, both devices wish to exchange business cards, where support may be offered as optional; however, a suitable error message must be used to inform the user where no such support exists. If authentication is required, each user may be required to enter a Bluetooth Passkey, although no OBEX authentication is used during this process.

It is assumed that both devices have been configured to allow the exchange of objects and that the inquiry and discoverability procedures have already been performed. It is also assumed that both devices are capable of supporting this profile. Once the user has the ability to connect to a device, he or she may now continue to make use of the services it provides. They do so by using a double-click or right-click operation to begin the process of exchanging the business cards (as we can see in Figure 12-8).

When the user has selected the *Exchange Business Card* option from the menu, he or she is prompted with a dialog box, informing them of the progress of their request; Figure 12-9 provides such an illustration.

Push Servers must be capable of managing multiple objects during an OBEX connection, although it is not mandatory for Push Clients to support multiple object transfer. A pull function is managed through a `Get` operation and a push function is managed through a `Put` operation, where an OBEX session has been established beforehand with a `Connect` operation. Devices that support the Business Card Exchange feature must use the default location for storing the Business Card. In our earlier illustration, Figure 12-8, we can see that the Business Card is stored in the *Inbox* area; this is the default location. The default function of the `Get` operation is used to retrieve data from that location. In order to achieve successful interoperability, both the Push Client and Server must support the vCard format specification (as we illustrated in Table 12-3). The disconnection of an OBEX session is managed with the `Disconnect` operation and so on; this is discussed in more detail in Section 12.5.1.2, *OBEX in the Object Push Profile*.

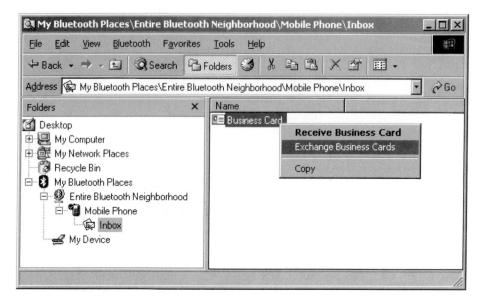

Figure 12-8   Right-clicking the icon causes a pop-up menu to appear offering
the ability to exchange business cards. (Courtesy of TDK Systems Europe.)

12.5   LIFTING THE LID

12.5.1   Dependencies

In our previous discussion, we covered aspects of existing usage models and their respective user expectations. In the following sections, we take an opportunity to explore in greater depth the dependencies that make up this profile. In Figure 12-10, we provide a

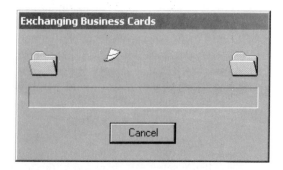

Figure 12-9   The user is informed that the exchange of business cards is in
progress. (Courtesy of TDK Systems Europe.)

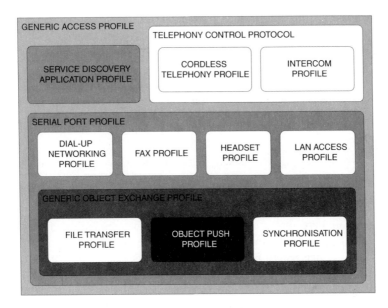

Figure 12-10   The dependent components of the Bluetooth protocol stack
that make up the Object Push Profile. The areas that are
shaded are relevant to this profile.

conceptual illustration representing the dependencies that make up the Object Push Profile; the areas that are shaded are relevant to this profile. As you can see, the profile depends upon the basic functionality offered to us by the *Generic Access Profile*, Chapter 2,
the *Service Discovery Application Profile*, Chapter 3, the *Serial Port Profile*, Chapter 6
and the *Generic Object Exchange Profile*, Chapter 11. We will now discuss the basic requirements of these dependent components and any deviations that may occur from the
basic functionality originally offered to us.

12.5.1.1 Service Discovery. In the *Service Discovery Application Profile*,
Chapter 3, we introduced the characteristics of the mechanisms used to retrieve service information from a remote device. Typically, a client will initiate inquiry and discovery
procedures as outlined in our previous section, to learn of the devices in radio range. A
client can then make use of an application, embodying the functionality of the underlying
Service Discovery Protocol (SDP). The *Service Discovery Application* (SrvDscApp)
uses an *SDP Client* to instigate a request to the remote device where the *SDP Server* will
respond; as such, the client and server must employ the use of an SDP client and server,
respectively, as illustrated in Table 12-4.

   Protocol Data Units (PDUs) are used to instruct the SDP server to undertake
browsing procedures and to retrieve service record information; you may recall that these
PDUs carry payloads about requests containing AttributeIDs and Attribute-

Table 12-4   As a minimum, the local device must support the use of a client application and the remote device must support the use of a server.

FEATURE	CLIENT	SERVER
SDP Client	M	X
SDP Server	X	M

Values describing what exactly is being sought. As we previously discussed, the client and server operate a request and response paradigm. SDAP will construct PDUs containing information relating to the AttributeID and AttributeValues, which in turn instruct the server to carry out its operation. The various request and response PDUs that are required are shown in Table 12-5, where features indicated are described as mandatory (M), optional (O) and excluded (X).

A service record is maintained for each service a device is capable of supporting and, as such, a *Service Record Handle* is created to uniquely identify this. The Service-RecordHandle is a 32-bit unsigned integer and is stored on the SDP server. The service record shown in Table 12-6 identifies an Object Push server device and provides a list of AttributeIDs, which ultimately identify the service for the Object Push Profile. A minimum of two attributes are required to make a service record; these are Ser-viceRecordHandle, and a ServiceClassIDList, where it must contain at least one UUID.

When browsing for services on the remote device, a local device constructs a search pattern using a *Universally Unique Identifier* (UUID). A UUID is a 128-bit value, which has been shortened for use within Bluetooth applications. The shortcut has been provided by first establishing a *Bluetooth Base UUID*, which we discussed in the *Service Discovery Application Profile*, Chapter 3.

Table 12-5   The list of PDUs that are required for the operation of the Object Push Profile.

PDU	CLIENT	SERVER
SDP_ErrorResponse	X	M
SDP_ServiceSearchRequest	O	X
SDP_ServiceSearchResponse	X	O
SDP_ServiceAttributeRequest	O	X
SDP_ServiceAttributeResponse	X	O
SDP_ServiceSearchAttributeRequest	M	X
SDP_ServiceSearchAttributeRequest	X	M

Table 12-6   The list of mandatory and configurable items that make up this profile's service discovery record.

ATTRIBUTE	DESCRIPTION
`ServiceRecordHandle`	With an `AttributeID` of `0x0000`, this uniquely identifies this service record within the SDP server for the Object Push server device.

`ServiceClassIDList`
 	
`ServiceClass0`
	With an `AttributeID` of `0x0001`, the following `ServiceClass0` would contain the `UUID` for the *OBEX Object Push*; its respective `UUID` value is summarised in Table 12-7.

`ProtocolDescriptorList`
 	
`Protocol0`
 	
`Protocol1`
 	
`ParameterFor1`
 	
`Protocol2`
	With an `AttributeID` of `0x0004`, the following `Protocol0` would contain a `UUID` for the protocol *L2CAP*, whereas in `Protocol1` a `UUID` would contain the protocol identifier for *RFCOMM*. The `ParameterFor1` would contain the relevant server channel number for the RFCOMM transport. Finally, `Protocol2` would contain the `UUID` for *OBEX*. Their respective `UUID` values are summarised in Table 12-8.

`BluetoothProfile-`
`DescriptorList`
 	
`Profile0`
 	
`ParameterFor0`
	With an `AttributeID` of `0x0009`, the following `Profile0` would identify the `UUID` for *OBEX Object Push* service class, which is summarised in Table 12-7. The `ParameterFor0` accommodates the version number supported by this profile.

`ServiceName`	With a base `AttributeID` of `0x0006`, this attribute has an offset of `0x0000`. It is a configurable item and has an `AttributeValue` of a `Text` string, where its default setting is *OBEX Object Push*.
`SupportedFormats`	With an `AttributeID` of `0x0303`, this attribute identifies what object formats the Object Push server device currently supports. Table 12-9 summarises the types available.

Table 12-7   The service class that matches its corresponding profile.

CLASSES	UUID
OBEXObjectPush	0x1105

The UUIDs that have been presented so far in this chapter are aliases and take the form of what is referred to as a 16-bit UUID or a 32-bit UUID but, in turn, they all should refer to the 128-bit notation. For the search pattern to be successful, they all need to be converted to the 128-bit notation, since they will all be compared at this range. An arithmetic conversion algorithm is used to construct the 128-bit value.

Table 12-7 summarises the service class UUIDs used to identify the particular profile in use; this also correlates with the identification of the device during a device discovery procedure as previously discussed in the *Generic Object Exchange Profile*, Chapter 11.

As part of the service record, the identification of the dependent underlying protocols is also made. The local device retrieves this information, where it can fully understand the exact requirements needed to fulfil the service. The Object Push Profile is dependent on the protocols as shown in Table 12-8; the table also shows their associated UUID values.

The Object Push sever device is capable of supporting several object formats, which are summarised in Table 12-9. The `AttributeValue` that would follow is an 8-bit unsigned integer used to uniquely identify the particular format; these values are also shown.

12.5.1.2   OBEX in the Object Push Profile.   In this section, we consider the objectives of OBEX in the *profile* and its expectations. In establishing our operations and its primitive functionality, the profile discusses mandatory features that it expects from the protocol and provides guidance with regard to how a request and response packet should be constructed and subsequently used. In Table 12-10, we identify the operations that must be supported by the Push Client and Server devices to enable a compliant Object Push Profile.

Table 12-8   The list of protocols that are used in this profile; their associated UUID values are also shown.

PROTOCOL	UUID
OBEX	0x0008
RFCOMM	0x0003
L2CAP	0x0100

Table 12-9 The list of supported formats that a server device is capable of supporting.

FORMATS	VALUE
vCard 2.1	0x01
vCard 3.0	0x02
vCal 1.0	0x03
iCal 2.0	0x04
VNote	0x05
VMessage	0x06
Other	0xFF

In Table 12-11, we identify the optional and mandatory OBEX headers that are used during the *Object Push* feature, where no OBEX authentication is required. The OBEX headers that are not shown are excluded from the operation of this feature.

In Table 12-12, we identify the optional and mandatory OBEX headers that are used during the *Business Card Pull* and *Exchange* features, where no OBEX authentication is required. The OBEX headers that are not shown are excluded from the operation of this feature.

In the following sections, we discuss the specific operations as outlined in Table 12-10 in more detail and consider their support in this profile.

12.5.1.2.1   Initialisation and Establishing an OBEX Session.   As you may recall, the Connect request is used to establish the OBEX session. In Table 12-13, we provide

Table 12-10 The required OBEX operations that should be supported in the Push Client and Server devices.

OPERATION	CLIENT	SERVER
Connect	M	M
Disconnect	M	M
Put	M	M
Get	O	M
Abort	M	M

Table 12-11   The required OBEX headers that should be supported by the Object Push feature.

HEADER	CLIENT	SERVER
Name	M	M
Type	O	O
Length	M	M
Time	O	O
Description	O	O
HTTP	O	O
Body	M	M
End of Body	M	M

a list of mandatory and conditional fields that make up our *request* packets and provide further information with regard to their usage within the structure.

The Connect response message as shown in Table 12-14 is the expected response, where the ResponseCode will indicate 0xA0 if the transfer was successful.

12.5.1.2.2 Disconnecting an OBEX Session.   At some point, an established OBEX session will be terminated, which may be due to a user request or a loss of connec-

Table 12-12   The required OBEX headers that should be supported by the Business Card Pull and Exchange features.

HEADER	CLIENT	SERVER
Name	M	M
Type	M	M
Length	M	M
Time	O	O
Description	O	O
HTTP	O	O
Body	M	M
End of Body	M	M

Table 12-13   The fields that are a mandatory feature of the `Connect-Request` operation.

NAME	TYPE	SUPPORT
OpCode	Field	M
PacketLength	Field	M
OBEXVersion	Field	M
FLAGS	Field	M
OBEXPacketLength	Field	M

Table 12-14   The fields that are a mandatory feature of the `Connect-Response` operation.

NAME	TYPE	SUPPORT
ResponseCode	Field	M
PacketLength	Field	M
OBEXVersion	Field	M
FLAGS	Field	M
OBEXPacketLength	Field	M

Table 12-15   The fields and headers that are a mandatory feature of the `Disconnect-request` operation.

NAME	TYPE	SUPPORT
OpCode	Field	M
PacketLength	Field	M

Table 12-16   The fields and headers that are a mandatory feature of the `Disconnect-response` operation.

NAME	TYPE	SUPPORT
ResponseCode	Field	M
PacketLength	Field	M

Table 12-17 The fields and headers that are a mandatory feature of the Put-request operation.

NAME	TYPE	SUPPORT
OpCode	Field	M
PacketLength	Field	M
Name	Header	M
Body/End of Body	Header	M

tion. The session is terminated using the Disconnect operation, where the OpCode has the value 0x81. In Table 12-15, we show the rest of the fields that are used during this operation.

The Disconnect response message is shown in Table 12-16. The Response-Code will indicate 0xA0 if the disconnection was successful. This operation is not refused by the server.

12.5.1.2.3 Pushing Data to the Server.

Data is transferred to the server using the Put request, where the OpCode may indicate 0x02 for multiple packets and 0x82 to indicate that it has sent the last packet. The features used for this transaction are identified in Table 12-17.

The Name header is used to identify the object being transferred and the Body/End of Body headers are used to identify the start and end of the object being transferred. In Table 12-18, we identify the features that are required in the Put response. In the table, the ResponseCode may indicate 0x90 for *continue* in response to the Put OpCode 0x02 or 0xA0 for *successful* in response to the Put OpCode for successful completion of the transfer.

12.5.1.2.4 Pulling Data from the Server.

Data is transferred from the server using the Get request, where the OpCode may indicate 0x03 for multiple packets and 0x83 to indicate that it has retrieved the last packet. The features used for this transaction are identified in Table 12-19.

The Name header is used to identify the object being transferred; the Type header is used to identify the type of object being pulled. For example, the Type header may contain text/x-vcard as its default object. In Table 12-20, we identify the features

Table 12-18 The fields and headers that are a mandatory feature of the Put-response operation.

NAME	TYPE	SUPPORT
ResponseCode	Field	M
PacketLength	Field	M

Table 12-19   The fields and headers that are a mandatory feature of the Get-request operation.

NAME	TYPE	SUPPORT
OpCode	Field	M
PacketLength	Field	M
Type	Header	M
Name	Header	M

that are required in the Get response, where the ResponseCode may indicate 0x90 for *continue* in response to the Get OpCode 0x03 or 0xA0 for *successful* in response to the Get OpCode for successful completion of the transfer.

The Name header is used to identify the object being transferred and the Body/End of Body headers are used to identify the start and end of the object being pulled.

12.5.1.2.5   The Default Get Object.   In our earlier discussion, we touched upon the ability to retrieve a business card from a default location, which we identified as the *Inbox*. The purpose of using a default method is to retrieve basic information from the server rather than having both devices perform the exchange. In the request packet of the Get operation, the type of object to be retrieved is identified as text/x-vCard; in the response packet, the Body/End of Body headers are used to denote the start and end of the object data as the size will be unknown.

12.6   SUMMARY

- The Object Push profile is based upon the GOEP.
- We exchange information with each other all the time and this profile allows us to do this electronically.

Table 12-20   The fields and headers that are a mandatory feature of the Request-connect operation.

NAME	TYPE	SUPPORT
ResponseCode	Field	M
PacketLength	Field	M
Name	Header	M
Body/End of Body	Header	M

- Our current usage models allow us to exchange vCard, vCalendar, vMessage and vNotes.
- These objects can be pushed and pulled and, as such, the profile defines two roles: Push Client and a Push Server.
- Many devices are capable of supporting the Object Push Profile, such as mobile phones, notebooks and PDAs.
- The Object Push Profile enables three core features: Object Push, Business Card Pull and Exchange.
- The inherent capabilities within the GOEP provide the profile with its generic operations.
- The default operation retrieves a business card from a default location.

The File Transfer Profile

13.1 INTRODUCTION

In this, the second of our *Object Exchange* (OBEX) profiles, we consider the features and procedures that are required to realise a compliant *File Transfer Profile*. This profile allows users to create ad-hoc connections between Bluetooth-enabled devices that support the File Transfer Profile; what is achieved here with this profile is *simplicity*. With supported devices, users can exchange data files and manipulate their directory structure. In Figure 13-1 and Figure 13-2, we illustrate the type of devices that may support the File Transfer Profile. In Figure 13-2, we can see a Bluetooth-enabled digital camera supporting file transfer to a notebook, where still or moving images may be transferred.

In this chapter, we discuss the requirements of the profile itself and the expectations of the underlying dependency, the *Generic Object Exchange Profile* (GOEP), Chapter 11. It is important to remember that there are numerous applications that already support file transfer, where the underlying transport may vary. In most Bluetooth-enabled devices, the ability to transfer files from one device to another has been integrated seamlessly, as we will demonstrate later on in this chapter. You may remember from our discussion of the GOEP that transparency is provided for applications that reside above the Object Exchange OBEX.

The File Transfer Profile is dependent upon the features and procedures that are described in the GOEP. The GOEP is, in turn, dependent upon the *Generic Access*, Chapter 2,

Figure 13-1   The File Transfer usage model allows the user to exchange files
between two notebooks.

the *Service Discovery Application*, Chapter 3 and the *Serial Port Profiles*, Chapter 6. The
core dependency illustrated in this chapter relates to the capabilities as described in the
GOEP.

13.2 USAGE MODELS

This section considers our existing usage model through scenarios that may be typical for
the File Transfer Profile. We begin by exploring the existing model, where a Bluetooth-
enabled *still* or *moving camera* and a *notebook* communicates with a similar device to exchange and manipulate data objects.

Figure 13-1 and Figure 13-2, illustrate our existing usage models. The role of the notebook acting as a client initiates a one-to-one communications link with another Bluetooth-
enabled device, where it takes on the role of a server. The File Transfer Profile usage
model prescribes short-range and ad-hoc communication typically found in an environment where individuals wish to exchange information.

Figure 13-2   The File Transfer usage model allows the user to exchange files
between a digital camera and a notebook.

13.3   PROFILE PRINCIPLES

The File Transfer Profile provides two new roles: a *Client* and a *Server*. The Client device is capable of pushing and pulling data objects to and from the Server, whereas the server provides the facility to allow the client device to push and pull the data objects. In this context, a data object refers to the files and folders that can be created or manipulated within a traditional directory hierarchy.

In our introduction, we touched upon the notion that a set of features and procedures exist to help govern the operation of Bluetooth-enabled devices, which support the File Transfer Profile. At the heart of this profile, the GOEP establishes core capabilities that are realised in the File Transfer Profile. Tasks such as object push and manipulation can take place between devices, where such objects may include large files or complete directory structures, as previous outlined. The GOEP and its underlying capabilities have been designed with portability in mind and, as such, any existing application may make use of the GOEP.

There are no fixed master-slave roles; this allows either device to initiate and terminate a connection, although typically the client will initiate the primary connection, where inquiry and device discovery procedures are undertaken. Participating devices in this profile must be required to perform bonding, pairing, authentication and encryption when requested to do so, but its use within this profile is optional. The use of OBEX authentication is supported, but its use is also optional. In Figure 13-3, we illustrate the specific Bluetooth protocol stack components that are dependent upon a compliant profile.

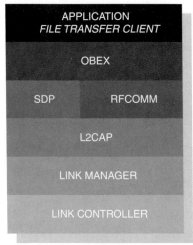
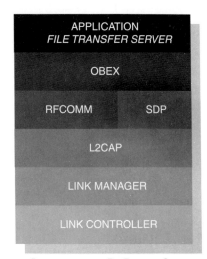

BLUETOOTH-ENABLED FILE TRANSFER CLIENT   BLUETOOTH-ENABLED FILE TRANSFER SERVER

Figure 13-3   The core components of the Bluetooth protocol stack are shown, illustrating how the components of the File Transfer Profile are integrated.

Table 13-1   The list of behavioural characteristics that are typical for this profile.

CONFIGURATION	ROLE	DESCRIPTION
DeviceA	Client	This device is capable of pushing and pulling objects from the server. The client establishes a relationship with the server before data objects can be exchanged and manipulated; the client will typically initiate the connection.
	Initiator	This configuration describes the device that instigates the original connection or the device that wishes to initiate communication over an existing link.
DeviceB	Server	A server provides object exchange capability which, in turn, allows client devices to push and pull objects from the server. This type of device would typically accept connections from clients and allow the client to create or manipulate data objects.
	Acceptor	This configuration describes the process of the device accepting the initiated communication from DeviceA.

In Table 13-1, clarification is provided with regard to the roles used within the context of this profile. In general, *DeviceA* represents the initiating party and *DeviceB* represents the accepting party. The terms are often used interchangeably when describing specific operations in various contexts and are provided here for reference.

13.4 USER EXPECTATIONS

The File Transfer Profile should enable three core features, which include the ability to *Folder Browse*, *Object Transfer*; this is further divided into two types (*File Transfer* and *Folder Transfer*) and *Object Manipulation,* as shown in Table 13-2. A server may provide functions to aid in the manipulation of a data object. Such capabilities include *navigation* through folders, as well as the ability to *copy a file or folder* to and from the server, *delete a file or folder* and to *create a file or folder*. These particular features and their associated functionality are described in more detail with an emphasis provided for user expectation. Devices whose behaviours mimic a server should be configured as such, where Figure 13-4 illustrates the available configuration options available to some Bluetooth-enabled devices. In this particular mode of operation, server devices should be configured for *lim-*

Table 13-2 The illustration shows specific behavioural procedures that this profile depends upon to realise its compliant implementation.

FEATURE	CLIENT	SERVER
Folder Browse	M	M
Object Transfer: File Transfer	M	M
Object Transfer: Folder Transfer	O	O
Object Manipulation	O	O

ited discovery or, where the device is public, should be configured for *general* discovery; see *Generic Access Profile*, Chapter 2, for more information.

13.4.1.1 The Folder Browsing Feature. This function allows the user to navigate through the files and folders of the remote device or server. If authentication is required, the user may be prompted to enter a Bluetooth Passkey. OBEX authentication may be used during this process.

The user should perform inquiry and discovery procedures to ascertain the capabilities of the server device. Once he or she has identified the appropriate server to use, the user can then select and make use of the facilities it has available.

On initial connection, the server will establish the `root` directory as a starting reference. The server may decide to reveal its sub-directories, where the `Get` request operation may return an *Unauthorised* or *Forbidden* response when access is not allowed. When the server shows its `root` contents, it uses the capabilities provided by the *Format Listing* functions. We will discuss this later on in Section 13.5.1.2.7, *Providing Folder Services*. As illustrated in Figure 13-4, the user must configure the server into the *File Transfer* mode, although this would remain transparent[1] to the user.

A server must be capable of supporting the `SetPath` operation, where the default directory is set at the `root`. In Figure 13-4, we saw a default location being created on an area of the local drive[2] in the *File Transfer* group. The Bluetooth connection will establish this default location and use it as the `root` directory, where in Figure 13-5 we see it displayed as `Public Folder`. The server device reveals the folder information using the `Get` operation, where the initial `root` is retrieved along with its subdirectories. The current directory will be set using the `SetPath` operation, where subsequent retrieval of subdirectory information is obtained using the `Get` operation. You may recall from the

---

[1]No explicit reference is made to this particular mode of operation at the user-interface level; however, activating this capability intrinsically enables this operation.

[2]During the Bluetooth product installation process, an area of the personal `My Documents` directory was used as a reference point for all file transfers, where Figure 13-4 depicted the default location. The local drive reference refers to the hard drive of your notebook or PC system, which houses the operating system as well as associated program files.

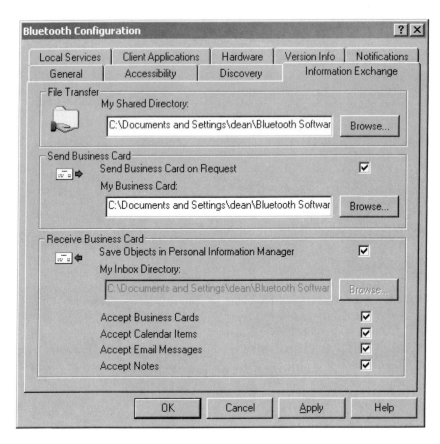

Figure 13-4 The generic options available to the user. The user can configure their set-up relating to where the default shared directory is
created for the *Public Folder* view. (Courtesy of TDK Systems
Europe.)

Generic Object Exchange Profile, Chapter 11, that a pull function is managed through a
`Get` operation, where an OBEX session has been established beforehand with a `Connect`
operation. The disconnection of an OBEX session is managed with the `Disconnect` operation and so on; this is discussed in more detail in Section 13.5.1.2, *OBEX in the File
Transfer Profile.*

13.4.1.2 Object Transfer. This feature allows the pushing and pulling of data
objects to and from the server, where supported data objects may include files or folders.
Folder support is offered as optional; however, a suitable error message must be used to
inform the user where no such support exists.

During this operation, the client wishes to retrieve files or folders from the server. If
authentication is required, the user may be required to enter a Bluetooth Passkey; OBEX

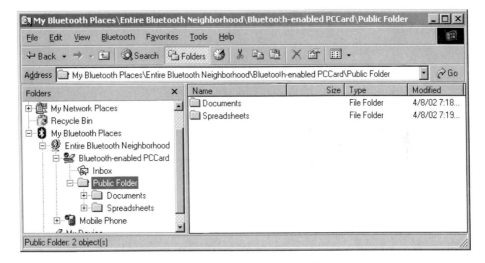

Figure 13-5   The server uses the `Public Folder` as the `root` directory, where its sub-directories may be shown. (Courtesy of TDK Systems Europe.)

authentication may be used during this process. In this example, Figure 13-6 shows the user being prompted with a Microsoft Windows dialog box requesting the entry of a passkey to authenticate with the server (Bluetooth-enabled PCCard).

It is assumed the server device the object is being pulled from has been configured and that the inquiry and discoverability procedures have already been performed. It is also

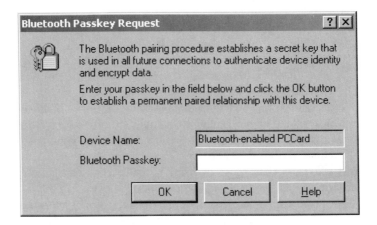

Figure 13-6   The provision of pairing and authentication is optional, but in this instance the user is prompted to enter a Bluetooth Passkey. (Courtesy of TDK Systems Europe.)

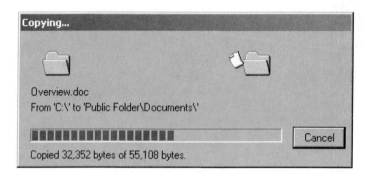

Figure 13-7   With a copy and paste operation, the `Overview.doc` file is
transferred and the user is informed of its progress. (Courtesy
of TDK Systems Europe.)

assumed that the server device the object is being pulled from is capable of supporting
this profile. Once the user has the ability to connect to a device, he or she may now continue to make use of the services it provides. Using a *drag and drop* or *copy and paste* operation, the devices can then begin to transfer the data. In Figure 13-7, the user is notified
with a Microsoft Windows dialog as to the copy in progress.

Servers must be capable of managing multiple objects during an OBEX connection,
although it is not mandatory for clients to support multiple object transfer. A pull function
is managed through a `Get` operation, where an OBEX session has been established beforehand with a `Connect` operation. The disconnection of an OBEX session is managed
with the `Disconnect` operation and so on.

13.4.1.3   Object Manipulation.   This feature enables the capability for the user
to create, delete and rename data objects. The server may have not enabled such privileges and should inform the user with an appropriate error message. If authentication is
required, the user may be promted to enter a Bluetooth Passkey; OBEX authentication
may be used during this process.

It is assumed that both devices have been configured to allow the exchange of data
objects and that the inquiry and discoverability procedures have already been performed.
It is also assumed that both devices are capable of supporting this profile. Once the user
has the ability to connect to a device, he or she may now continue to make use of the services it provides. They do so by using a double-click or right-click operation to begin
the process of creating or renaming data objects, as we can see in Figure 13-8 and Figure 13-9, respectively. New folders are created in the current folder on the server device
using the `SetPath` operation, where the `Name` header contains the name of the folder
to be created.

Furthermore, with privileges permitting, the user may continue to delete files and
folders using the `Put` operation, where the `Name` header contains the file or folder to be
deleted. An OBEX session is established using the `Connect` operation and the discon-

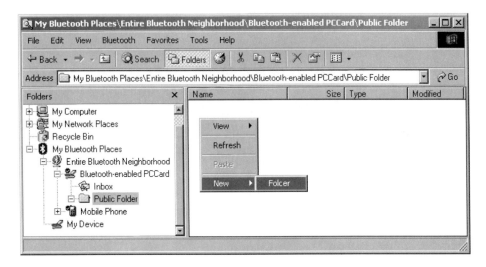

Figure 13-8   Right-clicking the icon causes a pop-up menu to appear offering the ability to create a new folder. (Courtesy of TDK Systems Europe.)

nection of an OBEX session is managed with the `Disconnect` operation; this is discussed in more detail in Section 13.5.1.2, *OBEX in the File Transfer Profile*.

When the user wishes to delete files or folders, they are prompted as to their progress with a dialog box. In Figure 13-10, we can see that the user has deleted a folder which is in the process of being deleted from the server; whereas in Figure 13-11, we can see that the user has deleted a file.

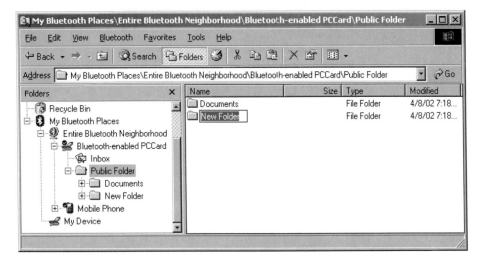

Figure 13-9   The user has selected to rename the new folder that was created in a previous operation. (Courtesy of TDK Systems Europe.)

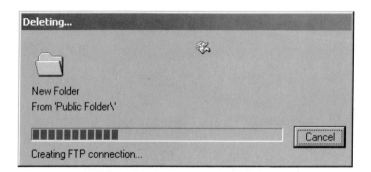

Figure 13-10   In this instance, the user has chosen to delete the new folder and is promoted as to its progress. (Courtesy of TDK Systems Europe.)

13.5   LIFTING THE LID

13.5.1   Dependencies

We have previously considered the aspects of existing usage models and their respective user expectations. Here, we take an opportunity to further examine the dependencies that make up this profile. In Figure 13-12, we provide a conceptual illustration representing the dependencies that make up the File Transfer Profile; the areas that are shaded are relevant to this profile. As you can see, the profile depends upon the basic functionality offered to us by the *Generic Access Profile*, Chapter 2, the *Service Discovery Application Profile*, Chapter 3, the *Serial Port Profile*, Chapter 6 and the *Generic Object Exchange Profile*, Chapter 11. We will now discuss the basic requirements of these dependent components and consider any deviations that may occur from their original basic functionality.

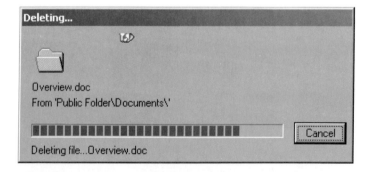

Figure 13-11   Here, we see the user choosing to delete a file. The user is informed as to its progress. (Courtesy of TDK Systems Europe.)

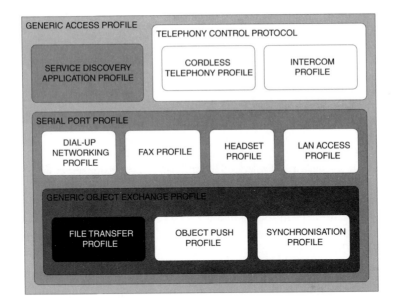

Figure 13-12   The dependent components of the Bluetooth protocol stack
that make up the File Transfer Profile. The areas that are
shaded are relevant to this profile.

13.5.1.1   Service Discovery.   In the *Service Discovery Application Profile*,
Chapter 3, we introduced the characteristics of the mechanisms used to retrieve service information from a remote device. Typically, a client will initiate an inquiry and discovery
procedure to learn of the devices in radio range. A client would then make use of an application, which would embody the functionality of the underlying *Service Discovery Protocol* (SDP). The *Service Discovery Application* (SrvDscApp) uses an *SDP Client* to
instigate a request to the remote device, where the *SDP Server* will respond; as such, the
client and server must employ the use of an SDP client and server respectively, as illustrated in Table 13-3.

Protocol Data Units (PDUs) are used to instruct the SDP server to undertake
browsing procedures and to retrieve service record information. PDUs carry payloads
about requests containing AttributeIDs and AttributeValues, which describe
what exactly is being sought. As we previously discussed, the client and server operate a
request and response paradigm. SDAP will construct PDUs containing information relating to the AttributeID and AttributeValues which, in turn, instruct the server to
carry out its operation. The various request and response PDUs that are required are
shown Table 13-4, where features indicated are described as mandatory (M), optional (O)
and excluded (X).

A service record is maintained for each service a device is capable of supporting
and, as such, a *Service Record Handle* is created to uniquely identify this. The Service-
RecordHandle is a 32-bit unsigned integer and is stored on the SDP server. The ser-

Table 13-3 As a minimum, the local device must support the use of a client application and the remote device must support the use of a server.

FEATURE	CLIENT	SERVER
SDP Client	M	X
SDP Server	X	M

vice record shown in Table 13-5 identifies a File Transfer server device and provides a list of `AttributeIDs`, which ultimately would identify the service for the File Transfer Profile. A minimum of two attributes are required to make a service record. These are `ServiceRecordHandle` and a `ServiceClassIDList`, where it must contain at least one `UUID`.

When browsing for services on the remote device, a local device constructs a search pattern using a *Universally Unique Identifier* (UUID). A UUID is a 128-bit value, which has been shortened for use within Bluetooth-enabled devices. The shortcut has been provided by first establishing a *Bluetooth Base UUID*, which we discussed in the *Service Discovery Application Profile*, Chapter 3.

The UUIDs that have been presented so far in this chapter are aliases and take the form of what is referred to as a 16-bit UUID or a 32-bit UUID, but in turn they all should refer to the 128-bit notation. For the search pattern to be successful, they all need to be converted to the 128-bit notation, since they will all be compared at this range. An arithmetic conversion algorithm is used to construct the 128-bit value.

Table 13-6 summarises the service class UUIDs used to identify the particular profile in use; this also correlates with the identification of the device during a device dis-

Table 13-4 The list of PDUs that are required for the operation of the File Transfer Profile.

PDU	CLIENT	SERVER
SDP_ErrorResponse	X	M
SDP_ServiceSearchRequest	O	X
SDP_ServiceSearchResponse	X	O
SDP_ServiceAttributeRequest	O	X
SDP_ServiceAttributeResponse	X	O
SDP_ServiceSearchAttributeRequest	M	X
SDP_ServiceSearchAttributeRequest	X	M

Table 13-5 The list of mandatory and configurable items that make up this profile's service discovery record.

ATTRIBUTE	DESCRIPTION
`ServiceRecordHandle`	With an `AttributeID` of `0x0000`, this uniquely identifies this service record within the SDP server for the File Transfer server device.

`ServiceClassIDList`
 	
   `ServiceClass0`
	With an `AttributeID` of `0x0001`, the following `ServiceClass0` would contain the UUID for the *OBEX File Transfer*. Its respective UUID value is summarised in Table 13-6.

`ProtocolDescriptorList`
 	
   `Protocol0`
 	
   `Protocol1`
 	
      `ParameterFor1`
 	
   `Protocol2`
	With an `AttributeID` of `0x0004`, the following `Protocol0` would contain a UUID for the protocol *L2CAP*, whereas in `Protocol1` a UUID would contain the protocol identifier for *RFCOMM*. The `ParameterFor1` would contain the relevant server channel number for the RFCOMM transport. Finally, `Protocol2` would contain the UUID for *OBEX*. Their respective UUID values are summarised in Table 13-7.

`BluetoothProfile-`
`DescriptorList`
 	
   `Profile0`
 	
      `ParameterFor0`
	With an `AttributeID` of `0x0009`, the following `Profile0` would identify the UUID for *OBEX File Transfer* service class, which is summarised in Table 13-6. The `ParameterFor0` accommodates the version number supported by this profile.

`ServiceName`	With a base `AttributeID` of `0x0006`, this attribute has an offset of `0x0000`. It is a configurable item and has an `AttributeValue` of a `Text` string, where its default setting is *OBEX File Transfer*.

covery procedure as previously discussed in the *Generic Object Exchange Profile*, Chapter 11.

As part of the service record, the dependent underlying protocols are also identified. The local device retrieves this information, where it can fully understand the exact requirements needed to fulfil the service. The File Transfer Profile is dependent on the protocols, as shown in Table 13-7, which also show their associated UUID values.

Table 13-6   The service class that matches its corresponding profile.

CLASS	UUID
OBEXFileTransfer	0x1106

13.5.1.2   OBEX in the File Transfer Profile.   In this section, we now consider the objectives of OBEX in the *profile* and its expectations. In establishing our operations and its primitive functionality, the profiles discuss mandatory features that it expects from the protocol and provides guidance with regard to how a request and response packet should be constructed and subsequently used. In Table 13-8, we identify the operations that must be supported by the client and server devices to enable a compliant File Transfer Profile.

In Table 13-9, we identify the optional and mandatory OBEX headers that are used during the generic operation of all file transfer features, where OBEX authentication is supported. The OBEX headers that are not shown are excluded from the operation of this profile. In the following sections, we discuss the specific operations as outlined in Table 13-9 in more detail and consider their support in this profile.

13.5.1.2.1   Initialisation and Establishing an OBEX Session.   Prior to establishing an OBEX session, authentication may occur. An OBEX password may be required and can match the Bluetooth Passkey for convenience; this itself reduces the user complexity. Further convenience can be provided for the user, as both the client and server may store the passkey for future ad-hoc connections.

As a minimum, GOEP must be able to support OBEX without authentication; however, if it is requested, then support for the authentication challenge should be provided. We discuss this later in Section 13.5.1.2.2, *OBEX Connection with Authentication*. In Table 13-10, we provide a list of mandatory fields that make up the request packet and provide further information with regard to its usage within the structure.

As you know, the Connect request is used to establish the OBEX session and the Target header is used to identify the targeted service. In this instance, the Target header is used to denote the *File Browsing* UUID F9EC7BC4-953C-11D2-984E-525400DC9E09, where its transmission order is from left to right. The Connect response message is shown in Table 13-11, where the ResponseCode will indicate 0xA0

Table 13-7   The list of protocols that are used in this profile; their associated UUID values are also shown.

PROTOCOL	UUID
OBEX	0x0008
RFCOMM	0x0003
L2CAP	0x0100

Table 13-8   The required OBEX operations that should be supported in the Push Client and Server devices.

OPERATION	CLIENT	SERVER
Connect	M	M
Disconnect	M	M
Put	M	M
Get	M	M
Abort	M	M
SetPath	M	M

Table 13-9   The required OBEX headers that should be supported by the File Transfer feature.

HEADER	CLIENT	SERVER
Count	O	O
Name	M	M
Type	M	M
Length	M	M
Time	O	O
Description	O	O
Target	M	M
HTTP	O	O
Body	M	M
End of Body	M	M
Who	M	M
ConnectionID	M	M
Authentication Challenge	M	M
Authentication Response	M	M

Table 13-10   The fields and headers that are a mandatory feature of the `Connect-Request`
operation.

NAME	TYPE	SUPPORT
OpCode	Field	M
PacketLength	Field	M
OBEXVersion	Field	M
FLAGS	Field	M
OBEXPacketLength	Field	M
Target	Header	C

if the connection was successful. The `ConnectionID` and `Who` headers must be used if
the `Target` header was used in the original `Connect` request.

13.5.1.2.2   OBEX Connection with Authentication.   In our previous section, we
provided the scenario and features that are required to establish an OBEX session without
authentication. This section now discusses the features expected from the OBEX protocol
when authentication is required. This new authentication procedure is an additional requirement above the Bluetooth-specific authentication process, that is, a Bluetooth
Passkey is used to instigate the pairing process, where Bluetooth authentication can then
occur. The OBEX authentication is used to establish a trusted relationship at the client
and server level, where it is the server that will initiate the challenge. The server is unable
to commit to an OBEX session until the authentication features are fully adhered to. In the

Table 13-11   The fields and headers that are a mandatory feature of the `Connect-Response`
operation.

NAME	TYPE	SUPPORT
ResponseCode	Field	M
PacketLength	Field	M
OBEXVersion	Field	M
FLAGS	Field	M
OBEXPacketLength	Field	M
ConnectionID	Header	M
Who	Header	M

Table 13-12   The fields and headers that are a mandatory feature of the first `Connect`-response for authentication.

NAME	TYPE	SUPPORT
ResponseCode	Field	M
PacketLength	Field	M
OBEXVersion	Field	M
FLAGS	Field	M
OBEXPacketLength	Field	M
AuthenticationChallenge	Header	M

first instance of sending a `Connect` request, the client is unaware that authentication is required; as such, it sends a request in the usual manner, the fields of which have been previously illustrated in Table 13-10.

The client learns of the news when it receives the response from the server. When we look more closely at the fields used in our `Connect` response as shown in Table 13-12, we notice that the `AuthenticationChallenge` header is used. Furthermore, when the client parses the `ResponseCode` it will learn of the value $0x41$ *Unauthorised*; this notifies the client that it must send a new `Connect` request with the `Authentication-Challenge` and `AuthenticationResponse` headers, as shown in Table 13-13; these headers carry the digest-challenge string and digest-response strings, respectively.

Table 13-13   The fields and headers that are a mandatory feature of the second `Connect`-request for authentication.

NAME	TYPE	SUPPORT
OpCode	Field	M
PacketLength	Field	M
OBEXVersion	Field	M
FLAGS	Field	M
OBEXPacketLength	Field	M
Target	Header	C
AuthenticationChallenge	Header	M
AuthenticationReponse	Header	M

Table 13-14   The fields and headers that are a mandatory feature of the second `Connect`-response for authentication.

NAME	TYPE	SUPPORT
ResponseCode	Field	M
PacketLength	Field	M
OBEXVersion	Field	M
FLAGS	Field	M
OBEXPacketLength	Field	M
ConnectionID	Header	M
Who	Header	M
AuthenticationReponse	Header	M

The fields and headers used in the second response are shown in Table 13-14. If the `ResponseCode` contains the value `0xA0` from the server, then authentication has been successful. The OBEX session can now be established.

13.5.1.2.3 Disconnecting an OBEX Session.   At some point, an established OBEX session will be terminated. This may be due to a user request or a loss of connection. The session is terminated using the `Disconnect` operation where the `OpCode` has the value `0x81` and in Table 13-15 we show the rest of the fields that are used during this operation.

The `Disconnect` response message is shown in Table 13-16, where the `ResponseCode` will indicate `0xA0` if the disconnection was successful. This operation is not refused by the server.

13.5.1.2.4 Pushing Files to the Server.   Data is transferred to the server using the `Put` request, where the `OpCode` may indicate `0x02` for multiple packets and `0x82` to indicate that it has sent the last packet. The features used for this transaction are identified in Table 13-17, where the `ConnectionID` is mandatory if the `Target` header was

Table 13-15   The fields and headers that are a mandatory feature of the `Disconnect`-request operation.

NAME	TYPE	SUPPORT
OpCode	Field	M
PacketLength	Field	M

Table 13-16   The fields and headers that are a mandatory feature of the `Disconnect-`
response operation.

NAME	TYPE	SUPPORT
ResponseCode	Field	M
PacketLength	Field	M

used in the original `Connect` request. You may recall that the OBEX connection establishment used the `Target` header.

The `Name` header is used to identify the object being transferred and the `Body/`
`End of Body` headers are used to identify the start and end of the object being transferred. In Table 13-18, we identify the features that are required in the `Put` response,
where the `ResponseCode` may indicate `0x90` for *continue* in response to the `Put`
`OpCode 0x02` or `0xA0` for *successful* in response to the `Put` `OpCode` for successful
completion of the transfer.

13.5.1.2.5   Pulling Files from the Server.   Data is transferred from the server
using the `Get` request, where the `OpCode` may indicate `0x03` for multiple packets and
`0x83` to indicate that it has retrieved the last packet. The features used for this transaction
are identified in Table 13-19, where the `ConnectionID` is mandatory if the `Target`
header was used in the original `Connect` request.

The `Name` header is used to identify the object being transferred and the `Type`
header is used to identify the type of object being pulled. In Table 13-20, we identify the
features that are required in the `Get` response, where the `ResponseCode` may indicate
`0x90` for *continue* in response to the `Get` `OpCode 0x03` or `0xA0` for successful in response to the `Get` `OpCode` for successful completion of the transfer. The Name header is
used to identify the object being transferred and the `Body/End of Body` headers are
used to identify the start and end of the object being pulled.

Table 13-17   The fields and headers that are a mandatory feature of the `Put`-request
operation.

NAME	TYPE	SUPPORT
OpCode	Field	M
PacketLength	Field	M
ConnectionID	Header	M
Name	Header	M
Body/End of Body	Header	M

Table 13-18 The fields and headers that are a mandatory feature of the `Put`-response operation.

NAME	TYPE	SUPPORT
ResponseCode	Field	M
PacketLength	Field	M

13.5.1.2.6 Locating Data Objects. A physical location on the server can be sought using the `SetPath` request, where the `OpCode` will indicate `0x85` and the `Name` header is used to contain the path name. The initial reference used by the server is the `root` directory. On the basis of this location, the server will reference down into the hierarchy to obtain the new location. For example, if the client requests `My Documents` in the `Name` header, it will effectively locate `C:\My Documents` on a typical Microsoft Windows based operating system.

The `FLAGS` parameter is used to denote the type of action to be applied in locating the new directory; for example, where bit 0 is set to indicate that the directory needs to be moved up one level before applying the `Name` header; this is equivalent to `..\` on a Microsoft Windows environment or `../` on an Unix environment. Setting bit 1 recommends to the system that it should not create a directory if it already exists, otherwise an error must be reported to the user. The `Constant` parameter is not used and is reserved for future use.

In the request-response packets for the `SetPath` operation, the final bit is always set since this transaction is made in one packet. In Table 13-22, we identify the features that are required in the `SetPath` response, where the `ResponseCode` may indicate `0xA0` for a successful operation. A `ResponseCode` of `0xC4` informs the client that the folder does not exist and a `0xC1` informs the client that folder browsing is not allowed.

13.5.1.2.7 Providing Folder Services. This profile mandates the use of navigational features of a directory hierarchy and possible manipulation of the hierarchy itself as

Table 13-19 The fields and headers that are a mandatory feature of the `Get`-request operation.

NAME	TYPE	SUPPORT
OpCode	Field	M
PacketLength	Field	M
ConnectionID	Header	M
Type	Header	C
Name	Header	C

Table 13-20   The fields and headers that are a mandatory feature of the `Get`-response
operation.

NAME	TYPE	SUPPORT
ResponseCode	Field	M
PacketLength	Field	M
Name	Header	O
Body/End of Body	Header	M

well as its contents. The OBEX protocol is used to facilitate these fundamental features.
In previous sections, we concentrated on the moving of files between the client and
server; in the sections that follow, we discuss the characteristics that are expected from
the OBEX protocol.

13.5.1.2.7.1   PULLING AND PUSHING A FOLDER.   Pulling folders from the server
encompasses the same procedures as outlined in our earlier section, discussing the `Get`
operation for retrieving files. The `Name` header is used to identify the name of the folder
to be retrieved, whereas using the `Get` operation without a `Name` header illustrates the retrieval of the entire folder contents. It also mandates the use of the `ConnectionID` and
`Type` headers, where the `Type` header is set to `x-obex/folder-listing`.

In Section 13.5.1.2.6, *Locating Data Objects*, we discussed the use of using the
`SetPath` operation to set a *working*[3] directory, this is the fundamental operation used to

Table 13-21   The fields and headers that are a mandatory feature of the `SetPath` request
operation for data object location.

NAME	TYPE	SUPPORT
ResponseCode	Field	M
PacketLength	Field	M
FLAGS	Field	M
Constants	Field	M
Name	Header	M
ConnectionID	Header	M

---

[3]The working directory reference relates to the area in which files and folders will be placed, that is, a known
location.

Table 13-22   The fields that are a mandatory feature of the `SetPath` response.

NAME	TYPE	SUPPORT
ResponseCode	Field	M
PacketLength	Field	M

create a new folder. In the section that follows, we learn of the procedures involved to allow users to navigate and manipulate a directory hierarchy.

13.5.1.2.7.2   MANIPULATING FILES AND FOLDERS.   The manipulation of files and folders extends to the deletion of such entities. In Section 13.5.1.2.4, *Pushing Files to the Server*, the *Put* operation is used to delete a file from the server; this includes the `ConnectionID` and `Name` headers, but excludes the `Body/End of Body` headers. A similar operation is used to delete a folder, but a `ResponseCode` of `0xCC` would indicate that the folder is not empty and the operation is therefore not allowed.

13.6   SUMMARY

- The File Transfer profile is based upon the GOEP.
- We exchange information with each other all the time and this profile allows us to do this on an ad-hoc basis.
- Our current usage models allow us to exchange files.
- These objects can be pushed and pulled and, as such, the profile defines two roles: client and server.
- Many devices are capable of supporting the File Transfer Profile, such as mobile phones, notebooks and Bluetooth-enabled video cameras.
- The File Transfer Profile enables three core features: Folder Browsing, Object Transfer and Object Manipulation.
- The inherent capabilities within the GOEP provide the profile with its generic operations.

14

The Synchronisation
Profile

14.1 INTRODUCTION

In our discussion of the final *Object Exchange* (OBEX) foundation profile, we consider the features and procedures that are required to realise a compliant *Synchronisation Profile*. In our earlier discussion ˙of the *Object Push Profile*, Chapter 12, we discussed our everyday ability to exchange a varied amount of data in various contexts. For example, at conferences or exhibitions we may collect business cards, which contain information relating to a business address, a range of contact telephone numbers and an email address. This type of exchange is referred to as *Personal Data Interchange* (PDI), where this data may be transferred to several electronic devices, such as a mobile phone, *Personal Digital Assistant* (PDA) or a notebook. With the amount of data held on these various devices, synchronisation is used to ensure its accuracy and that the data is consistent for all devices. This profile defines a set of features and procedures which, in turn, allow users to synchronise the information contained on these separate devices.

In Figure 14-1 and Figure 14-2, we demonstrate the types of devices that are capable of synchronisation. In this chapter, we discuss the requirements of the profile itself and the expectations of the underlying dependency, the *Generic Object Exchange Profile* (GOEP), Chapter 11. It is important to remember that there are numerous applications that already support synchronisation, where the underlying transport may vary. You may

Figure 14-1   The Synchronisation usage model shown allows the user to exchange Object Stores between a mobile phone and a notebook.

remember from our discussion of the GOEP that transparency is provided for applications
that reside above the OBEX Protocol.

The Synchronisation Profile is dependent upon the features and procedures that are
described in the GOEP. The GOEP is, in turn, dependent upon the *Generic Access*, Chapter 2, the *Service Discovery Application*, Chapter 3 and the *Serial Port Profiles*, Chapter
6; the core dependency illustrated in this chapter relates to the capabilities as described in
the GOEP.

14.2   USAGE MODELS

This section considers our existing usage model through scenarios that may be typical for
the Synchronisation Profile. We begin by exploring the existing model where a Bluetooth-
enabled *notebook*, *PDA* and *mobile phone* are capable of synchronising *Object Stores*.
There will be more about this later in the chapter.

Figure 14-1 and Figure 14-2 show the current usage models in this scenario. The
role of the notebook acting as a client initiates a one-to-one communications link with
another Bluetooth-enabled device, where it takes on the role of a server. The Synchronisation Profile usage model prescribes the ability to synchronise data between Bluetooth-
enabled devices.

Figure 14-2   The Synchronisation usage model shown allows the user to
exchange Object Stores between a notebook and a PDA.

14.3 PROFILE PRINCIPLES

The Synchronization Profile provides two new roles: a *Client* and a *Server*. The client device is capable of pushing and pulling objects to and from the server, whereas the server provides the facility to allow the client device to push and pull the objects. In this context, an object refers to an Object Store, which is a database containing many *IrMC*[1] *Objects*.

In our introduction, we touched upon the notion that a set of features and procedures exist to help govern the operation of Bluetooth-enabled devices, which support the Synchronisation Profile. At the heart of this profile, the GOEP establishes core capabilities that are realised in the Synchronisation Profile. Tasks such as object push and manipulation can take place between devices, where such objects may include large files or complete directory structures, as previous outlined. The GOEP and its underlying capabilities have been designed with portability in mind and, as such, any existing application may make use of the GOEP.

There are no fixed master-slave roles. This leaves either device free to initiate and terminate a connection, although typically the client will initiate the primary connection, where inquiry and device discovery procedures are undertaken. Participating devices in this profile must be required to perform bonding, pairing, authentication and encryption when requested to do so, but their use within this profile is optional. The use of OBEX authentication is supported, but its use is also optional. In Figure 14-3, we illustrate the specific Bluetooth protocol stack components that are dependent upon a compliant profile.

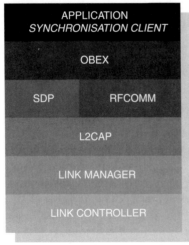

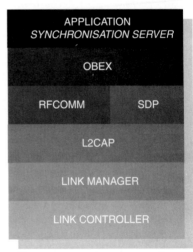

BLUETOOTH-ENABLED SYNCHRONISATION CLIENT   BLUETOOTH-ENABLED SYNCHRONISATION SERVER

Figure 14-3   The core components of the Bluetooth protocol stack are shown, illustrating how the components of the Synchronisation Profile are integrated.

---

[1]The *Infra-red Mobile Communications* (IrMC) Object refers to the inclusion of vCard, vCalendar and vNotes.

Table 14-1   The list of behavioural characteristics that are typical for this profile.

CONFIGURATION	ROLE	DESCRIPTION
DeviceA	Client	This device is capable of pushing and pulling objects from the server. The client establishes a relationship with the server before data objects can be exchanged and manipulated; the client will typically initiate the connection.
	Initiator	This configuration describes the device that instigates the original connection or the device that wishes to initiate communication over an existing link.
DeviceB	Server	A server provides object exchange capability which, in turn, allows client devices to push and pull objects from the server. This type of device would typically accept connections from clients and allow the client to create or manipulate data objects.
	Acceptor	This configuration describes the process of the device accepting the initiated communication from DeviceA.

In Table 14-1, clarification is provided with regard to the roles used within the context of this profile. In general, *DeviceA* represents the initiating party and *DeviceB* represents the accepting party. The terms are often used interchangeably when describing specific operations in various contexts and are provided here for reference.

14.4   USER EXPECTATIONS

The Synchronisation Profile should enable three core features, which include the ability to *Synchronise*; this is further divided into four types (*Phonebooks, Calendars, Emails* and *Notes*), *Sync Command* and *Automatic Synchronisation* as shown in Table 14-2. During the *Initialisation Sync Mode*, the server is placed into *limited* or *general* discovery and permits the connection and pairing of client devices. During *General Sync Mode*, both the server and client may enter this mode allowing devices to connect. When a client initiates a connection with a server and the intent is to synchronise, the server will then enter this mode. Similarly, when a *server* initiates a connection with the client, the client will also enter the General Sync Mode. User intervention is required to enable these two modes of operation. These particular features and their associated functionality are now described in more detail with an emphasis provided for user expectation. Devices whose behaviour

Table 14-2   The illustration shows specific behavioural procedures that this profile depends upon to realise its compliant implementation.

FEATURE	CLIENT	SERVER
Synchronisation	M	M
Sync Command	M	O
Automatic Synchronisation	O	M

mimic a server should be configured as such, where Figure 14-4 illustrates the configuration options available to some Bluetooth-enabled devices.

14.4.1.1   The Synchronisation Feature.   This feature provides synchronisation capabilities on both the client and server; as such, its support is considered mandatory. If authentication is required, the user may be prompted to enter a Bluetooth Passkey; OBEX authentication may be used during this process.

Interoperability at the application level is achieved through the support of the various object data types that are available. In Table 14-3, we identify the various data object formats and their associated specifications. It is the application that is responsible for providing the relevant data object support; Bluetooth wireless technology is used as the transport medium.

Table 14-3   The table identifies the object types and formats available that must be supported by any application using the Synchronisation Profile.

FORMAT	DESCRIPTION
vCard	Synchronisation applications must support the capabilities and format provided within the Internet Mail Consortium, "vCard: The Electronic Business Card," Version 2.1, September 1996.
vCalendar	Synchronisation applications must support the capabilities and format provided within the vCalendar specification. This is discussed in further detail in The Internet Mail Consortium, "vCalendar: The Electronic Calendaring and Scheduling Exchange Format," Version 1.0, September 1996.
vMessaging	Synchronisation applications must support the capabilities and format provided within the Infrared Data Association, "Specification for Ir Mobile Communications (IrMC)," Version 1.1, March 1999.
vNotes	Synchronisation applications must support the capabilities and format provided within the Infrared Data Association, "Specification for Ir Mobile Communications (IrMC)," Version 1.1, March 1999.

   The user should perform an inquiry and discovery procedure to ascertain the capabilities of the server device. Once he or she has identified the appropriate server, the user
can select and make use of the facilities it has available. Users should not use the services
of a server that does not support a data object type; however, if a data object is used inadvertently, then the server should report an appropriate error message indicating that the
object is not supported. As illustrated in Figure 14-4, the user can configure the server to
support the various object types; as such, it is capable of supporting these objects when
requested by the client to do so. Here, the mode of operation is supported by the General
Sync Mode. In this particular example, these objects relate to the checked items as shown
on the illustration (that is, *Business Cards, Calendar Items, E-Mail Messages* and *Notes*).
   The client device typically initiates the synchronisation sequence, where the user
may now continue to make use of the services it provides. The user can use a double-
click[2] or right-click operation to begin the process of synchronisation. In Figure 14-5 and

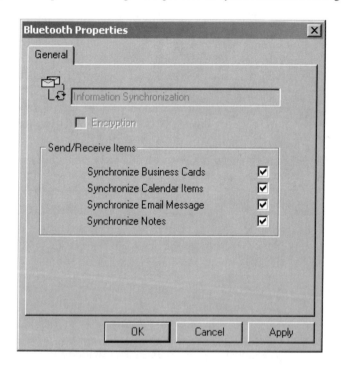

Figure 14-4   The generic options available to the user. The user can config-
                ure their set-up relating to how information is exchanged be-
                tween two devices. (Courtesy of TDK Systems Europe.)

---

[2]The double-click and right-click operations refer to a mouse that is connected to your client device (in this example, a PC or notebook computer running a Microsoft Windows operating system) and where both operations
trigger the same method of access. It is noted that an operation may vary from device to device and, as such, the
number of buttons may vary on a mouse. Indeed, no mouse may be connected. The example just draws your attention to how it may be possible and acknowledges that implementations may differ.

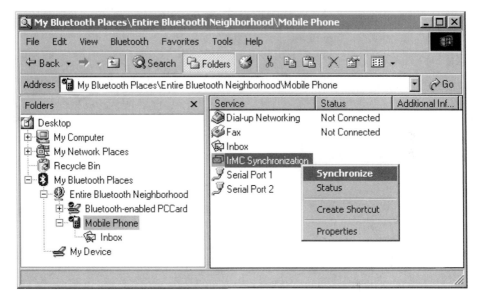

Figure 14-5   Right-clicking the icon causes a pop-up menu to appear offering
the ability to synchronise. (Courtesy of TDK Systems Europe.)

in Figure 14-6, we illustrate the effect of a successful synchronisation where all the object stores are the same on both devices.

Servers must be capable of managing multiple objects during an OBEX connection, although it is not mandatory for clients to support multiple object transfer. You may recall from the *Generic Object Exchange Profile*, Chapter 11, that a push function is managed through a `Put` operation, a pull function is managed through a `Get` operation, where an OBEX session has been established beforehand with a `Connect` operation. The disconnection of an OBEX session is managed with the `Disconnect` operation and so on; this is discussed in more detail in Section 14.5.1.2, *OBEX in the Synchronisation Profile*.

14.4.1.2   The Sync Command Feature.   This feature is used during the condition where the server wishes to initiate synchronisation. With this feature, the client is placed into General Sync Mode. This is done without the need for user intervention. Again, the user will select the ability to synchronise in very much the same way as previously illustrated in Figure 14-5. The user may be prompted to authenticate with the device, where he or she may be required to enter a Bluetooth Passkey as shown in Figure 14-7; furthermore, the user may also be requested to use OBEX authentication, which is discussed in more detail later in this chapter.

14.4.1.3   The Automatic Synchronisation Feature.   During this operation, both devices will automatically synchronise their object stores. The client will initiate this automation, as the server moves closer into radio range and the server will remain in General

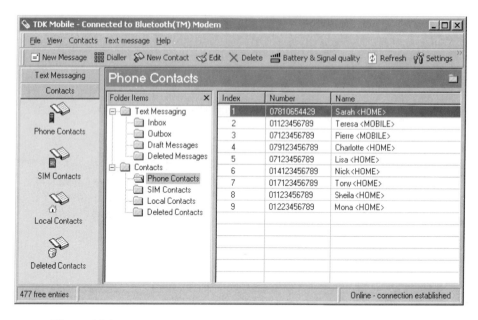

Figure 14-6   As a result of a successful synchronisation, the application is updated to reflect the phone contacts as stored on the mobile phone handset. (Courtesy of TDK Systems Europe.)

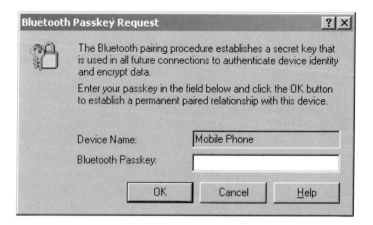

Figure 14-7   The provision of pairing and authentication is optional, but in this instance the user is prompted to enter a Bluetooth Passkey. (Courtesy of TDK Systems Europe.)

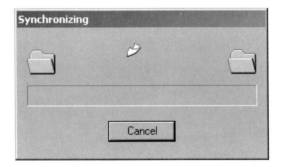

Figure 14-8   The user is prompted indicating synchronisation is in progress.
(Courtesy of TDK Systems Europe.)

Sync Mode. During this operation, the user may be prompted as to the progress of the automatic synchronisation as we have illustrated in Figure 14-8.

14.5   LIFTING THE LID

14.5.1   Dependencies

In the following sections, we take an opportunity to explore in greater depth the dependencies that make up this profile.

In Figure 14-9, we provide a conceptual illustration representing the dependencies that make up the Synchronisation Profile; the areas that are shaded are relevant to this profile. As you can see, the profile depends upon the basic functionality offered to us by the *Generic Access Profile*, Chapter 2, the *Service Discovery Application Profile*, Chapter 3, the *Serial Port Profile*, Chapter 6 and the *Generic Object Exchange Profile*, Chapter 11. We will now discuss the basic requirements of these dependent components and any deviations that may occur from the basic functionality originally offered to us.

14.5.1.1   Service Discovery. In the *Service Discovery Application Profile*, Chapter 3, we introduced the characteristics of the mechanisms used to retrieve service information from a remote device. Typically, a client will initiate an inquiry and discovery procedure as outlined in our previous section, to learn of the devices in radio range. A client would then make use of an application, which would embody the functionality of the underlying *Service Discovery Protocol* (SDP). The *Service Discovery Application* (SrvDscApp) uses an *SDP Client* to instigate a request to the remote device where the *SDP Server* will respond; as such, the client and server must employ the use of an SDP client and server respectively, as illustrated in Table 14-4.

Protocol Data Units (PDUs) are used to instruct the SDP server to undertake browsing procedures and to retrieve service record information; you may recall that these PDUs carry payloads about requests containing `AttributeIDs` and `Attribute-`

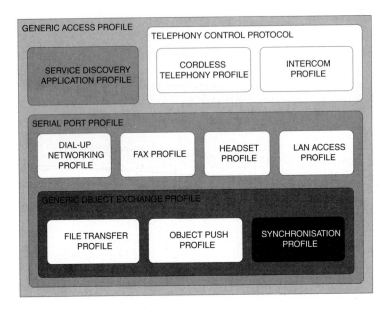

Figure 14-9 The dependent components of the Bluetooth protocol stack that make up the Synchronisation Profile. The areas that are shaded are relevant to this profile.

Values describing exactly what is being sought. As we previously discussed, the client and server operate a request and response paradigm. SDAP will construct PDUs containing information relating to the `AttributeID` and `AttributeValues` which, in turn, instruct the server to carry out its operation. The various request and response PDUs that are required are shown Table 14-5, where features indicated are described as mandatory (M), optional (O) and excluded (X).

A service record is maintained for each service a device is capable of supporting and, as such, a *Service Record Handle* is created to uniquely identify this. The `ServiceRecordHandle` is a 32-bit unsigned integer and is stored on the SDP server. The service record shown in Table 14-6 identifies a synchronisation server (IrMC Server) and Table 14-7 identifies the sync command server (IrMC Client). Both tables provide a list

Table 14-4 As a minimum, the local device must support the use of a client application and the remote device must support the use of a server.

FEATURE	CLIENT	SERVER
SDP Client	M	X
SDP Server	X	M

Table 14-5 The list of PDUs that are required for the operation of the Syncronisation Profile.

PDU	CLIENT	SERVER
SDP_ErrorResponse	X	M
SDP_ServiceSearchRequest	O	X
SDP_ServiceSearchResponse	X	O
SDP_ServiceAttributeRequest	O	X
SDP_ServiceAttributeResponse	X	O
SDP_ServiceSearchAttributeRequest	M	X
SDP_ServiceSearchAttributeRequest	X	M

of AttributeIDs, which ultimately identify the services that make up the Synchronisation Profile. A minimum of two attributes are required to make a service record; these are ServiceRecordHandle and ServiceClassIDList, where it must contain at least one UUID.

When browsing for services on the remote device, a local device constructs a search pattern using a *Universally Unique Identifier* (UUID). A UUID is a 128-bit value, which has been shortened for use within Bluetooth. The shortcut has been provided by first establishing a *Bluetooth Base UUID*, which we discussed in the *Service Discovery Application Profile*, Chapter 3.

The UUIDs that have been presented in this chapter are aliases and take the form of what is referred to as a 16-bit UUID or a 32-bit UUID but, in turn, they all should refer to the 128-bit notation. These UUIDs have been assigned and can be referenced in the Bluetooth Special Interest Group, Bluetooth Assigned Numbers, v1.1, February 2001. For the search pattern to be successful, they all need to be converted to the 128-bit notation, since they will all be compared at this range. An arithmetic conversion algorithm is used to construct the 128-bit value.

Table 14-8 summarises the service class UUIDs used to identify the particular profile in use; this also correlates with the identification of the device during a device discovery procedure, as previously discussed in the *Generic Object Exchange Profile*, Chapter 11.

As part of the service record, the identification of the dependent underlying protocols are also identified. The local device retrieves this information, where it can fully understand the exact requirements needed to fulfil the service. The Synchronisation Profile is dependent on the protocols as shown in Table 14-9 also showing their associated UUID values.

The IrMC server device is capable of supporting several data objects, which are summarised in Table 14-10. The AttributeValue that would follow is an 8-bit unsigned integer used to uniquely identify the particular object; these values are also shown.

Table 14-6   The list of mandatory and configurable items that make up IrMC Server service discovery record.

ATTRIBUTE	DESCRIPTION
ServiceRecordHandle	With an `AttributeID` of `0x0000`, this uniquely identifies this service record within the SDP server for the IrMC server device.
ServiceClassIDList ServiceClass0	With an `AttributeID` of `0x0001`, the following `ServiceClass0` would contain the `UUID` for the *IrMC Sync*. Its respective `UUID` value is summarised in Table 14-8.
ProtocolDescriptorList Protocol0 Protocol1 ParameterFor1 Protocol2	With an `AttributeID` of `0x0004`, the following `Protocol0` would contain a `UUID` for the protocol *L2CAP*, whereas in `Protocol1` a `UUID` would contain the protocol identifier for *RFCOMM*. The `ParameterFor1` would contain the relevant server channel number for the RFCOMM transport. Finally, `Protocol2` would contain the `UUID` for *OBEX*. Their respective `UUID` values are summarised in Table 14-9.
BluetoothProfile- DescriptorList Profile0 ParameterFor0	With an `AttributeID` of `0x0009`, the following `Profile0` would identify the `UUID` for *IrMC Sync* service class, which is summarised in Table 14-8. The `ParameterFor0` accommodates the version number supported by this profile.
ServiceName	With a base `AttributeID` of `0x0006`, this attribute has an offset of `0x0000`. It is a configurable item and has an `AttributeValue` of a `Text` string, where its default setting is *IrMC Synchronisation*.
SupportedDataStores	With an `AttributeID` of `0x0301`, this attribute identifies what data object the IrMC server device currently supports. Table 14-10 summarises the types available.

Table 14-7   The list of mandatory and configurable items that make up IrMC Client service discovery record.

ATTRIBUTE	DESCRIPTION
ServiceRecordHandle	With an `AttributeID` of `0x0000`, this uniquely identifies this service record within the SDP server for the IrMC client device.
ServiceClassIDList ServiceClass0	With an `AttributeID` of `0x0001`, the following `ServiceClass0` would contain the `UUID` for the *IrMC Sync Command*. Its respective `UUID` value is summarised in Table 14-8.
ProtocolDescriptorList Protocol0 Protocol1 ParameterFor1 Protocol2	With an `AttributeID` of `0x0004`, the following `Protocol0` would contain a `UUID` for the protocol *L2CAP*, whereas in `Protocol1` a `UUID` would contain the protocol identifier for *RFCOMM*. The `ParameterFor1` would contain the relevant server channel number for the RFCOMM transport. Finally, `Protocol2` would contain the `UUID` for *OBEX*. Their respective `UUID` values are summarised in Table 14-9.
BluetoothProfile-DescriptorList Profile0 ParameterFor0	With an `AttributeID` of `0x0009`, the following `Profile0` would identify the `UUID` for *IrMC Sync* service class, which is summarised in Table 14-8. The `ParameterFor0` accommodates the version number supported by this profile.
ServiceName	With a base `AttributeID` of `0x0006`, this attribute has an offset of `0x0000`. It is a configurable item and has an `AttributeValue` of a `Text` string, where its default setting is *Sync Command Service*.

14.5.1.2   OBEX in the Synchronisation Profile.   In this section, we consider the objectives of OBEX in the *profile* and its expectations. In establishing our operations and its primitive functionality, the profile discusses mandatory features that it expects from the protocol and provides guidance with regard to how a request and response packet should be constructed and subsequently used. In Table 14-11, we identify the operations that must be supported by the client and server devices to enable a compliant Synchronisation Profile.

Table 14-8   The list of service classes that match a corresponding profile.

CLASSES	UUID
IrMCSync	0x1104
IrMCSyncCommand	0x1107

Table 14-9   The list of protocols that are used in this profile; their associated UUID values are also shown.

PROTOCOL	UUID
OBEX	0x0008
RFCOMM	0x0003
L2CAP	0x0100

Table 14-10   The list of supported objects that a client device is capable of supporting.

OBJECTS	VALUE
Phonebook	0x01
Calendar	0x03
Notes	0x05
Messages	0x06

Table 14-11   The required OBEX operations that should be supported in the client and server devices.

OPERATION	CLIENT	SERVER
Connect	M	M
Disconnect	M	M
Put	M	M
Get	M	M
Abort	M	M

In Table 14-12, we identify the optional and mandatory OBEX headers that are used during the generic operation of all synchronisation features, where OBEX authentication is supported. The OBEX headers that are not shown are excluded from the operation of this profile. In the following sections, we discuss the specific operations as outlined in Table 14-12 and consider their support in this profile.

14.5.1.2.1   Initialisation and Establishing an OBEX Session.   Prior to establishing an OBEX session, authentication may occur prior to an OBEX session establishment. An OBEX password may be required and can match the Bluetooth Passkey for convenience; this itself reduces the user complexity. Further convenience can be provided for the user as both the client and server may store the passkey for future ad-hoc connections.

As a minimum, GOEP must be able to support OBEX without authentication. If it is requested, then support for the authentication challenge should be provided; we discuss this in Section 14.5.1.2.2, *OBEX Connection with Authentication*. In Table 14-13, we provide a list of mandatory fields that make up or request packets and provide further information with regard to its usage within the structure.

Table 14-12   The required OBEX headers that should be supported by the general features that are available during synchronisation.

HEADER	CLIENT	SERVER
Name	M	M
Length	M	M
Time	O	O
Description	O	O
Target	M	M
HTTP	O	O
Body	M	M
End of Body	M	M
Who	M	M
ConnectionID	M	M
Authentication Challenge	M	M
Authentication Response	M	M
Application Parameters	M	M

Table 14-13 The fields and headers that are a mandatory feature of the `Connect`-request operation.

NAME	TYPE	SUPPORT
OpCode	Field	M
PacketLength	Field	M
OBEXVersion	Field	M
FLAGS	Field	M
OBEXPacketLength	Field	M
Target	Header	C

As you know, the `Connect` request is used to establish the OBEX session and the `Target` header is used to identify the targeted service. In this instance, the `Target` header is used to denote *IrMC Sync*. The `Connect` response message is shown in Table 14-14, where the `ResponseCode` will indicate 0xA0 if the connection was successful. The `ConnectionID` and `Who` headers must be used if the `Target` header was used in the original `Connect` request.

14.5.1.2.2 OBEX Connection with Authentication. In our previous section, we provided the scenario and features that are required to establish an OBEX session without authentication. This section now discusses in more detail the features expected from the OBEX protocol when authentication is required. This new authentication procedure is an additional requirement above the Bluetooth specific authentication process, that is, a

Table 14-14 The fields and headers that are a mandatory feature of the `Connect`-response operation.

NAME	TYPE	SUPPORT
ResponseCode	Field	M
PacketLength	Field	M
OBEXVersion	Field	M
FLAGS	Field	M
OBEXPacketLength	Field	M
ConnectionID	Header	M
Who	Header	M

Bluetooth Passkey is used to instigate the pairing process, where Bluetooth authentication can then occur. The OBEX authentication is used to establish a trusted relationship at the client and server level, where it is the server that will initiate the challenge. The server is unable to commit to an OBEX session, until the authentication features are fully adhered to. In the first instance of sending a `Connect` request, the client is unaware that authentication is required and, as such, it sends a request in the usual manner, the fields of which have been previously illustrated in Table 14-13.

The client learns of the news when it receives the response from the server. When we look more closely at the fields used in our `Connect` response as shown in Table 14-15, we notice that the `AuthenticationChallenge` header is used. Furthermore, when the client parses the `ResponseCode` it will learn of the value `0x41` *Unauthorised*; this notifies the client that it must send a new `Connect` request with the `Authentication-Challenge` and `AuthenticationResponse` headers as shown in Table 14-16. These headers carry the digest-challenge string and digest-response strings, respectively.

The fields and headers used in the second response are shown in Table 14-17. If the `ResponseCode`, contains the value `0xA0` from the server, then authentication has been successful. The OBEX session can now be established.

14.5.1.2.3 Disconnecting an OBEX Session. At some point an established OBEX session will be terminated, which may be due to a user request or a loss of connection. The session is terminated using the `Disconnect` operation, where the `OpCode` has the value `0x81`. In Table 14-18, we show the rest of the fields that are used during this operation.

The `Disconnect` response message is shown in Table 14-19, where the `ResponseCode` will indicate `0xA0` if the disconnection was successful; this operation is not refused by the server.

14.5.1.2.4 Pushing Files to the Server. Data is transferred to the server using the `Put` request, where the `OpCode` may indicate `0x02` for multiple packets and `0x82` to

Table 14-15 The fields and headers that are a mandatory feature of the first `Connect`-response for authentication.

NAME	TYPE	SUPPORT
ResponseCode	Field	M
PacketLength	Field	M
OBEXVersion	Field	M
FLAGS	Field	M
OBEXPacketLength	Field	M
AuthenticationChallenge	Header	M

Table 14-16   The fields and headers that are a mandatory feature of the second `Connect`-request for authentication.

NAME	TYPE	SUPPORT
OpCode	Field	M
PacketLength	Field	M
OBEXVersion	Field	M
FLAGS	Field	M
OBEXPacketLength	Field	M
Target	Header	C
AuthenticationChallenge	Header	M
AuthenticationReponse	Header	M

indicate that it has sent the last packet. The features used for this transaction are identified in Table 14-20, where the `ConnectionID` is mandatory if the `Target` header was used in the original `Connect` request. You may recall that the OBEX connection establishment used the `Target` header.

The `Name` header is used to identify the object being transferred and the `Body/End of Body` headers are used to identify the start and end of the object being transferred. In Table 14-21, we identify the features that are required in the `Put` response,

Table 14-17   The fields and headers that are a mandatory feature of the second `Connect`-response for authentication.

NAME	TYPE	SUPPORT
ResponseCode	Field	M
PacketLength	Field	M
OBEXVersion	Field	M
FLAGS	Field	M
OBEXPacketLength	Field	M
ConnectionID	Header	M
Who	Header	M
AuthenticationReponse	Header	M

Table 14-18   The fields and headers that are a mandatory feature of the `Disconnect`-request operation.

NAME	TYPE	SUPPORT
OpCode	Field	M
PacketLength	Field	M

Table 14-19   The fields and headers that are a mandatory feature of the `Disconnect`-response operation.

NAME	TYPE	SUPPORT
ResponseCode	Field	M
PacketLength	Field	M

Table 14-20   The fields and headers that are a mandatory feature of the `Put`-request operation.

NAME	TYPE	SUPPORT
OpCode	Field	M
PacketLength	Field	M
ConnectionID	Header	M
Name	Header	M
Body/End of Body	Header	M

Table 14-21   The fields and headers that are a mandatory feature of the `Put`-response operation.

NAME	TYPE	SUPPORT
ResponseCode	Field	M
PacketLength	Field	M

Table 14-22   The fields and headers that are a mandatory feature of the `Get`-request
operation.

NAME	TYPE	SUPPORT
OpCode	Field	M
PacketLength	Field	M
ConnectionID	Header	M
Type	Header	C
Name	Header	C

where the `ResponseCode` may indicate `0x90` for *continue* in response to the `Put`
`OpCode 0x02` or `0xA0` for *successful* in response to the `Put OpCode` for successful
completion of the transfer.

14.5.1.2.5   Pulling Files from the Server.   Data is transferred from the server
using the `Get` request, where the `OpCode` may indicate `0x03` for multiple packets and
`0x83` to indicate that it has retrieved the last packet. The features used for this transaction
are identified in Table 14-22, where the `ConnectionID` is mandatory if the `Target`
header was used in the original `Connect` request.

The `Name` header is used to identify the object being transferred and the `Type`
header is used to identify the type of object being pulled. In Table 14-23, we identify the
features that are required in the `Get` response, where the `ResponseCode` may indicate
`0x90` for *continue* in response to the `Get OpCode 0x03` or `0xA0` for *successful* in response to the `Get OpCode` for successful completion of the transfer. The `Name` header is
used to identify the object being transferred and the `Body/End of Body` headers are
used to identify the start and end of the object being pulled.

Table 14-23   The fields and headers that are a mandatory feature of the `Get`-response
operation.

NAME	TYPE	SUPPORT
ResponseCode	Field	M
PacketLength	Field	M
Name	Header	O
Body/End of Body	Header	M

14.6 SUMMARY

- The Synchronisation Profile is based upon the GOEP.
- We exchange information with each other all the time and this profile allows us to keep this information consistent between our personal devices.
- Our current usage models allow us to synchronise vCard, vCalendar, vMessage and vNotes.
- These objects can be pushed and pulled and, as such, the profile defines two roles: a client and a server.
- Many devices are capable of supporting the Synchronisation Profile, such as mobile phones, notebooks and PDAs.
- The Synchronisation Profile enables three core features: Synchronisation, Sync Command and Automatic Synchronisation.
- The inherent capabilities within the GOEP provide the profile with its generic operations.

Part 3

THE NEW PROFILES

BACKGROUND

This section begins with an overview of the currently architected profiles in various stages of release and goes on to discuss the newer profiles by exploring the more popular choices. This exploration is limited to an overview of the profiles rather than an in-depth review of their dependencies; it is intended to provide the reader with "food for thought" on how future profiles might be extended or moulded.

15

Defining New Profiles

15.1 INTRODUCTION

In *My Bluetooth Application*, Chapter 1, we introduced the conceptual nature of a Bluetooth Profile and how it relates to the Bluetooth protocol stack. This described how each profile facilitated the underlying protocol to ultimately achieve an end-user experience. It also introduced the importance of establishing a common set of parameters and user interface characteristics to ensure interoperability with all manufacturers' devices.

The Bluetooth *Special Interest Group* (SIG) openly welcomes all member[1] companies to contribute to the growth of new profiles, adopting new usage models and increasing the Bluetooth application potential. Typical facets to creating a new profile must combine interoperability features, where integration of a common set of parameters and a clear definition of structured procedures provide a holistic user experience.

It is envisaged that the next release from the Bluetooth SIG shall combine new profiles that are being currently architected. In Section 15.3, *Profiles and Protocols Under Development*, we provide a list of profiles that are in the process of reaching *maturity* in development, where they are expected to be in the next release.

15.2 IDENTIFYING NEW PROFILES

Any member company can contribute to the new definition of a profile, which must adhere to the interoperability requirements defined by the Bluetooth SIG. A more formal process will be made available on their web site,[2] where member companies can choose to submit profile suggestions and documentation online. During profile development, revisions of related documentation are incremented to reflect the significant changes in devel-

---

[1]Member companies refer to companies that have signed and agreed to the terms and conditions as prescribed by the Bluetooth SIG. As such, each member company is free to develop Bluetooth specific technologies. The type of membership, whether adopter or associate, entitles you to various evolutionary phases of the documentation being drafted.

[2]The Bluetooth member company web site access is obtained through http://www.bluetooth.org.

opment and the approval from the *Bluetooth Architecture Review Board* (BARB). As such, Table 15-1 clarifies the time at which membership companies can become privy to the evolution of such documentation.

In the following section, we clarify the formal processes involved in establishing a working group where new specifications and subsequently new profiles can be architected.

15.2.1   Market Requirements and Usage Models

Any member (adopter, associates or promoter) of the SIG can submit to the BARB that they wish to create a new working group to undertake the creation of a new profile. Clear objectives and usage models must be identified accompanied with any overlaps of other profiles. It is suggested that the submission should also be supported by a number of companies wishing to adopt the same profile.

The BARB will make a decision based upon the information submitted and, upon successful acceptance, will initially create a study group. It is here that the members involved elect a chair and sufficient interest must be sustained within the group or the BARB will suspend its activities. Within the study group the members must then set out their charter or objectives.

The study group will also undertake an analysis of the market acceptance and the range of usage models that can be expected from it. A *profile plan*[3] is established outlin-

Table 15-1   The evolution of a protocol and profile are mapped directly on phases of release, where working groups are privy to early revisions. Higher revisions of the documents are made available to the member company audience.

VERSION	DESCRIPTION
V0.5	A number of internal working group changes are made from its initial draft of v0.1 to the final adopted release of v0.5. Prior to its submission to the adopter and associates, it is passed onto the BARB for approval. All early revisions are released internally within the working group for review.
V0.5 and above	The new profile or protocol undergoes the natural evolution process and is generally released when there are significant changes made; adopters and associates will have access to these further revisions.
V1.0	Further revisions and additions are made to the existing architecture before again meeting with BARB for its approval and subsequent release for incorporation into the Bluetooth Specification.

---

[3]A profile plan is typically a Bluetooth *Marketing Requirement Document* (MRD).

ing the evolution and market analysis. With identifiable project deliverables and project planning a working group can then be formally created with the approval of the BARB to undertake the effort required.

15.3 PROFILES AND NEW PROTOCOLS UNDER DEVELOPMENT

This section describes in full all of the profiles and protocols that are still under development; some of which have already been adopted by the SIG. It is expected, as they reach maturity,[4] that they will be incorporated into the Specification of the Bluetooth System.

15.3.1 Audio and Video

Table 15-2   The introduction of these new profiles is expected in the new release of the Specification of the Bluetooth System.

PROFILE	DESCRIPTION
Advanced Audio Distribution Profile (A2DP)	This new addition to the profile suite prescribes how Bluetooth-enabled devices support distribution of high quality audio. It outlines a set of new protocols and procedures that enable advanced audio capabilities for a range of Bluetooth-enabled products.
Audio/Video Remote Control Profile (AVRCP)	This profile defines a new set of protocols and user features for the adoption of remote control functionality within Bluetooth-enabled devices. It also outlines, as with any other profile, how such devices should interoperate.
Generic Audio/Video Distribution Profile (GAVDP)	The GAVDP forms a small part of the comprehensive introduction of the range of audio/video-related services. This profile specifically addresses the necessary requirements to achieve streaming channels for audio and video distribution.
Video Conferencing Profile (VCP)	In this last set of audio/video-related profiles, the video conferencing profiles provides a set of protocols and procedures that are required to enable the support of this feature.

---

[4]A profile is ready for incorporation as part of the specification when it has reached v1.0. Thus, it has been reviewed by member companies and they have agreed to adopt it.

Table 15-3   The set of new Audio/Video-related protocols.

PROTOCOL	DESCRIPTION
Audio/Video Control Transport Protocol (or AVCTP)	To achieve the functionally prescribed in the audio/video-related profiles, this protocol is specifically used to address the transportation of command and response messages in compliant Bluetooth-enabled devices.
Audio/Video Distribution Transport Protocol (or AVDTP)	This protocol further defines procedures for the establishment, initial negotiation and transmission methods for audio/video-enabled devices.

15.3.2   Printing and Imaging

Table 15-4   The Basic Printing, Imaging and Hardcopy Cable Replacement Profiles.

PROFILE	DESCRIPTION
Basic Printing Profile (BPP)	This profile establishes the fundamental requirements to enable basic printing, outlining a common set of protocols and procedures. It is primarily aimed, although not limited, to mobile devices, such as mobile phones and PDAs, where more larger and static devices may use the Hardcopy Cable Replacement Profile. We discuss this profile in *The Basic Printing and Basic Imaging Profiles: An Overview*, Chapter 19.
Basic Imaging Profile (BIP)	This profile outlines the requirements necessary to enable the imaging usage model. It manages a series of procedures which, in turn, negotiate the size and encoding of the image-related data to be exchanged. We discuss this profile in *The Basic Printing and Basic Imaging Profiles: An Overview*, Chapter 19.
Hardcopy Cable Replacement Profile (HCRP)	This profile prescribes the capabilities of Bluetooth-enabled devices that support the HCRP. Specific usage models can be extended to printing and scanning of documents. The printing of images would be managed by the capabilities offered to us by the Basic Imaging Profile.

15.3.3   Car

Table 15-5   The set of car profiles.

PROFILE	DESCRIPTION
Car Hands-Free Profile (HFP)	A set of protocols and procedures outline the capabilities that are offered to us though the HFP. It outlines the ability to operate a hands-free phone device within a vehicle environment that has a hands-free unit, where connection establishment is achieved through Bluetooth wireless means. We discuss this profile in *The Car Profiles: An Overview*, Chapter 17.
Car Phone Access Profile (PAP)	In this suite of car-specific capability, the PAP provides a set of protocols and procedures that allow the remote operation of a phone using an in-car device, which may include a cordless handset, hands-free units and car-embedded mobile phones. We discuss this profile in *The Car Profiles: An Overview*, Chapter 17.
Car SIM Access Profile (SAP)	This final suite of profiles provides the diversity required to enable users to make use of SIM-specific information which, in turn, allows the user to make use of the in-car embedded phone. We discuss this profile in *The Car Profiles: An Overview*, Chapter 17.

15.3.4 Extended Services Discovery

Table 15-6   The set of Extended Service Discovery Profiles.

PROFILE	DESCRIPTION
Extended Service Discovery Profiles for Universal Plug and Play (ESDP for UPnP)	This profile is considered to be an enhancement to the existing Service Discovery Protocol. It describes how support should be provided in Bluetooth-enabled devices that use UPnP. This support manifests itself through the SDP and embodies other protocols such as L2CAP and IP. We discuss this profile in *ESDP: An Overview*, Chapter 18.
Extended Service Discovery Profiles Device Identification (ESDP DI)	This profile is also an enhancement to the existing SDP. It describes how device identification is provided in the service record, where characteristics such as manufacture and model description are further used to ensure that a user is making use of the best available service. This document describes how this is achieved.

15.3.5 Personal Area Networking

Table 15-7   The Personal Area Networking Profile.

PROFILE	DESCRIPTION
Personal Area Networking Profile (PAN)	This new profile is considered to be an extension of the existing functionality already offered to us by the foundation profiles. It defines three new scenarios to encompass Group Ad-hoc Networking and Network Access Point. A PAN User is described as a device that accesses these services. In general, it offers a more comprehensive IP solution and is introduced in *The PAN Profile: An Overview*, Chapter 16.

Table 15-8   The Bluetooth Network Encapsulation Protocol.

PROTOCOL	DESCRIPTION
Bluetooth Network Encapsulation Protocol (BNEP)	The PAN Profile requires the implementation of the BNEP to facilitate the use of unmodified Ethernet payloads transported over the L2CAP. This feature enables the incorporation of a large number of networking-related technologies.

15.3.6   Radio

Table 15-9   The Radio working groups undertaking improvements and increased bandwidth capability.

PROFILE	DESCRIPTION
Radio 1.x	This working group is undertaking *enhancements* to the existing functionality already offered to us in the Bluetooth Specification v1.1. The improvements that are addressed in the short term are radio and baseband-specific as well as increased bandwidth (2 Mb/s) in combination with errata raised against v1.1. It is, of course, expected that any future functionality would be backward compatible.
Radio 2	The Radio 2 working group is concentrating efforts to allow Bluetooth wireless communications to provide greater bandwidth capability (11 Mb/s), whilst ensuring backward capability of v1.1 compliant devices. Increased adoption and the embodiment of other wireless and static technologies are enabled. It is also suggested that the release of this specification and subsequent adoption by the BARB will form the much speculated and hyped Bluetooth v2.0.

15.3.7   Others

Table 15-10   The services offered by the HID, ISDN Access and Local Positioning Profiles.

PROFILE	DESCRIPTION
Human Interface Device Profile (HID)	The HID Profile describes how Bluetooth-enabled devices can make use of HID capabilities and then communicate and support them. Such examples of Bluetooth HID devices include keyboards, mice and gaming devices.
Common ISDN Access Profile	This profile describes how ISDN can be used over Bluetooth-enabled devices. More specifically, it outlines how existing ISDN applications can make use of the Bluetooth transport.
Local Positioning Profile (LP)	In the last collection of profiles that have been introduced in this chapter, the LP Profile defines a set of protocols and procedures that allow position-related information to be communicated over Bluetooth-enabled devices. Support is provided for position determination, location awareness and time transfer.
Co-existence Profile	With the increase of wireless communications operating within the 2.4 GHz band, it is becoming increasingly important to help identify how these wireless products can co-exist. This profile outlines a set of procedures and protocols to overcome and help such devices cooperate in all environments.
Unrestricted Digital Information (UDI)	With the global vision of Bluetooth communication, the adoption of this technology in various countries has an effect on bandwidth requirements. One such country is Japan, where the use of mobile phones differs from those of their American and European counterparts. This profile outlines how Bluetooth-enabled devices can be used with 3rd *Generation* (3G) mobile handsets, where the initial application being considered is the use of video.

16

The PAN Profile: An Overview

16.1 INTRODUCTION

Having considered the simplicity and ease-of-use offered to us by the LAN Access Profile and the diversity and flexibility of the Dial-up Networking Profile, we can further reflect on the number of potential scenarios that are introduced when we consider the implementation of the *Personal Area Networking Profile* (PAN).

The introduction of the *Group Ad-hoc Networking* (GN) and *Network Access Point* (NAP) scenarios, as shown in Figure 16-1 and Figure 16-2, provide a *Personal Area Networking User* (PAN User) with an opportunity to access either service. The NAP is well suited to our earlier introduction of the *Access Point Kiosk* (APK), where a range of public services can be made available. The GN provides greater flexibility in the creation of an ad-hoc network amongst its peers, providing simpler data transfer and exchange between *familiar* users; whereas a NAP may potentially embody the comprehensive range of networking technologies offered to us as a viable range of services.

At this stage of development, the PAN Profile is considered to be the first phase, where subsequent phases[1] will confront the technical challenges imposed by architecting solutions to resolve *Inter-piconet Scheduling* (IPS) and *Access Point Roaming* (APR).

---

[1] The IPS and APR are two working groups created from the PAN working group. They have been specifically constructed to overcome the technical issues raised by providing access point roaming, thus allowing users the flexibility to move from one area to another. The IPS working group is studying a means of allowing a user to move between inter-piconets or scatternets with the same ease as outlined in APR. Companies who have specialised in providing Bluetooth networking products have been eager to promote their roaming solutions as a de facto standard; this, in turn, may lead to a great deal of confusion for the end-user.

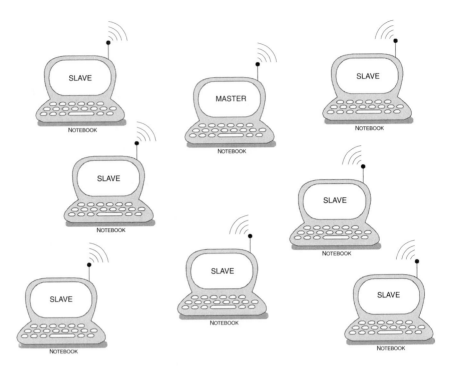

Figure 16-1   The new Group Ad-hoc Networking scenario provided by the
PAN Profile, where the relationship is still coordinated by a
master if it is configured for multi-user mode.

As with any introduction of a new technological solution, there is an immediate fa-
naticism to be the first to produce a product that embodies the PAN functionality. This
eruption of emotion can be likened to the first manufacturer to produce the first Bluetooth-
enabled product.

With this high-emotion and excitement, we cannot help, but wonder what will become of our *foundation profiles*? Can these profiles coexist within the new model? Does
the PAN Profile ultimately replace these? In the following sections, we compare the ar-
chitectures of the PAN, the LAN Access and Dial-up Networking Profiles, where considerable differences and, of course, usage scenarios have been introduced.

16.1.1   Comparing Personal Area Networking with the LAN Access and Dial-up Networking Profiles

In the *LAN Access Profile*, Chapter 10, we introduced the simplicity provided by this profile and the range of scenarios that are available to the user. Similarly, in the *Dial-up Networking Profile*, Chapter 8, we also introduced the mobility and flexibility usage
scenarios that enable a user to be in any location to access their services. The introduction
of the PAN Profile further provides a range of network-related scenarios to essentially en-

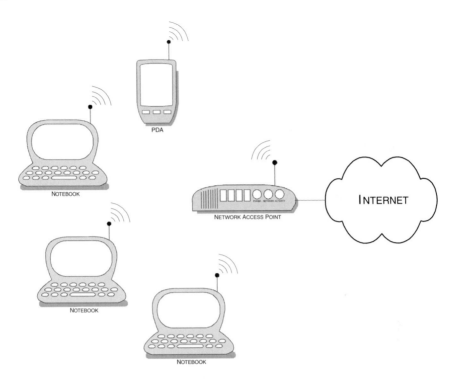

Figure 16-2   The new Network Access Point scenario provided by the PAN
Profile, where the relationship is still coordinated by a master if it
is configured for multi-user mode. As you can see, the potential
for the range of networking technologies are quite tremendous.

hance the user's experience of Bluetooth technology as a real networking solution. The
very nature of the availability and adoption of Bluetooth-enabled devices provides us with
the opportunity to create dynamic and ad-hoc connections to neighbouring Bluetooth devices. The emphasis here is the dynamic nature in which we are able to exchange data; we
will look more closely at the new usage models in detail in Section 16.2, *Usage Models*.

One noticeable and significant difference between the LAN Access, Dial-up Networking and PAN Profiles is the introduction of the *Bluetooth Networking Encapsulation
Protocol* (BNEP) and the subsequent omission of the *Point-to-Point Protocol* (PPP) component. The LAN Access, and similarly the Dial-up Networking Profile, both depend on
the implementation or the existence of a PPP[2] server and client, where the support of networking-related protocols are then instantiated above it; PPP also provides authentication

---

[2]In our earlier discussion of the LAN Access Profile, PPP support is required within the profile itself, which
then implicitly enables the creation of a TCP/UDP/IP stack. Support of a PPP Client/Server implementation is
not made explicit in the Dial-up Networking Profile, but is a requirement of the dial-up networking legacy
application.

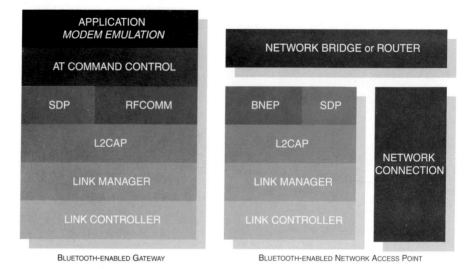

BLUETOOTH-ENABLED GATEWAY   BLUETOOTH-ENABLED NETWORK ACCESS POINT

Figure 16-3   The components of the Dial-up Networking Profile as compared with the PAN Profile.

and, in some instances, compression. In Figure 16-3, we compare the implementation of the Dial-up Networking components to the PAN Profile. In contrast, Figure 16-4 shows the LAN Access components as compared with the PAN Profile. In Figure 16-5 we illustrate the components of the data terminals from both foundation profiles and compare this with the components of the PAN User.

BNEP itself facilitates in a greater adoption of the network-related protocols that can be made available. Such protocols include IPv4,[3] IPv6[4] and IPX.[5] The BNEP transports packets over the L2CAP protocol, encapsulating the various upper-networking payloads. The introduction of this new protocol provides forwarding of complete Ethernet payloads, which may remain unmodified during data exchange.

As part of this exploration, we need to look at the usage models that all these profiles offer and determine if there is any redundancy and/or overlap. In our introduction, we touched upon the new scenarios that the PAN Profile introduced. The GN and NAP each offer different usage models, depending upon the requirements of how the data needs to be accessed or exchanged. The GN offers the ability to dynamically create a network shared between familiar users, whereas the LAN Access Profile can provide this ability through a *LAN Access Point* (LAP). Using a LAP, each *Data Terminal* (DT) would, subject to Bluetooth authentication and authorisation, have access to the shared re-

---

[3]Internet Protocol version 4 is the current and widely available version of the Internet protocol. It is the standard communications protocol used for the Internet.

[4]Internet Protocol version 6 is the next version after IPv4 and is sometimes referred to as IP Next Generation (IPng). Essentially, it will provide the Internet with new functionality, that is, it will offer longer addresses. It will thus be capable of supporting more Internet users.

[5]The Internetwork Packet Exchange (IPX) is a networking protocol from Novell.

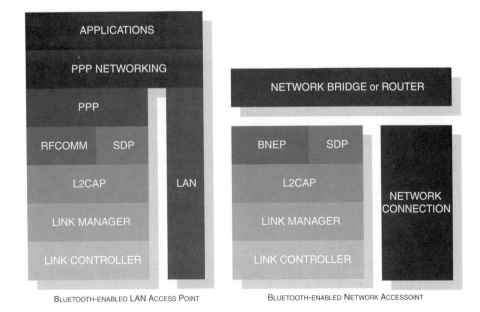

Figure 16-4   The components of the LAN Access Profile as compared with the PAN Profile.

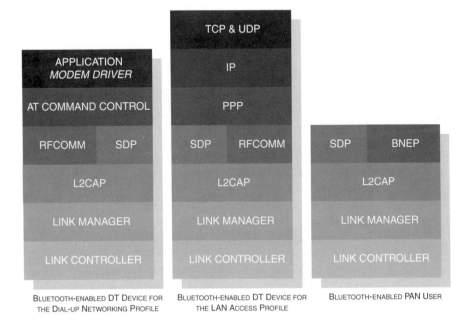

Figure 16-5   The components of the Dial-up Networking and LAN Access Data Terminal devices, as compared with the PAN User.

sources of its peer. The Dial-up Networking Profile offers the ability to create a wireless bridge, which in turn allows the user to connect to an *Internet Service Provider* (ISP) or a corporate network. Having access to a corporate network would also allow the user to access shared resources. The LAN Access and Dial-up Networking Profiles effectively provide an access point, where other remote services can be accessed. This is the provision of the latter scenario introduced by the PAN Profile. The NAP allows a user to access a larger or broader resource base; this is similar in nature to what has already been introduced by our foundation profiles.

It is here that we need to broach the question that has undoubtedly been raised as a result of this new profile. We have witnessed manufacturers investing development time and money in producing products that conform to the LAN Access and Dial-up Networking Profiles. What then is the expected longevity of these core profiles? Can all these profiles each provide a user a benefit or will it ultimately confuse the user population? In the following section, we consider their future and propose whether they can coexist?

16.1.2   What is the Future of the LAN Access and Dial-up Networking Profiles?

Redundancy is not an immediate thought: the expected arrival of such products supporting the PAN Profile is already emerging onto the market; as such, users are still familiarising themselves with their existing Bluetooth-enabled LAN Access and Dial-up Networking products. Furthermore, should the introduction of a PAN Profile product exclude the ability to cooperate in an inter-piconet and roaming environment? If manufacturers were eager to be the first to produce a PAN compliant product, then the omission of IPS and APR would, again, constrain its capability. Timing seems to be a critical consideration in the provision of new products to the wider user population.

The introduction of PAN products in the short-term should provide legacy support. This legacy support would alleviate the existing user population abandoning their initial investment, although an equal awkwardness for manufacturers is to encourage the user population to adopt and to benefit from the new features. Consideration should also be given to provide a happy medium, where upgrade options can be supplied. Over time, as wider adoption of the PAN Profile is undertaken, legacy support can then be subsequently removed.

We can easily identify some redundancy and overlap of the foundation profiles with the PAN Profile. The mobile phone as a Network Access Point replaces the need for a modem emulator because it is already connected to a *General Packet Radio Service* (GPRS) network or a *Universal Mobile Telecommunications Service* (UMTS) network, where Internet access is permanently available (see Section 16.2.2, *Future Usage Models*). Putting aside the architectural differences of the PAN Profile, the LAN Access Profile provides the same capabilities as the NAP, albeit the NAP provides a much broader base of networking technologies. We should take into account the current costs of using a GPRS network. Typically, network operators charge for the amount of data that is exchanged; however, using the existing dial-up method would at least alleviate some of the cost burden, until GPRS connectivity is as second nature as a permanent Internet connection in the home or office.

The PAN Profile provides several new usage models. Such models enhance the user's experience of creating ad-hoc networks and forming relationships with Network Access Points; overall, the simplicity and ease-of-use of accessing and exchanging data is greatly improved.

16.2 USAGE MODELS

This section considers both existing and future usage models through scenarios that may be typical for the Personal Area Networking Profile. We begin by exploring the existing models. At face value, the PAN Profile provides group ad-hoc networking and network access points. In future usage models, we consider alternative means of providing other levels of simple wireless networking.

16.2.1 Existing Usage Models

In our introduction, we touched upon the Network Access Point and Group Ad-hoc Networking scenarios. These represent our new usage models for this profile, where a PAN User is capable of selecting either advertised service. The Group Ad-hoc Networking scenario represents a dynamically created network, which is administered by a master; the maximum number of users that can take part in this relationship is eight (one master and seven slaves[6]).

Once the GN is created, each PAN User member will have access to the shared resources. This is subject to each user defining an area that can be shared safely. Using a suitable application, the user can configure an area and place documents and other items that he or she wishes to share with other PAN Users. Typically, a PAN User would initiate a connection to a GN, which is advertising the available service, although a GN can engage in an initiation to a PAN User device. Again, the PAN User device must be advertising the appropriate service. This scenario also lends itself well to networking type games, where the master would host the game and others would choose to join in. This could be further extended in the *Service Discovery Protocol,* where the game type itself is advertised.

The Network Access Point is very similar in nature to the LAN Access Point. When a PAN User is connected to it, a whole range of services and shared resources become available. The current restriction imposed by a LAN Access Point is the maximum number of users, which we have previously covered in some detail. The NAP overcomes this restriction by employing multiple radio units and, for each radio unit, seven users would be able to access a service through that *radio port.*[7] The greater the number of radio units, then the greater the number of users that can access the NAP.

---

[6]This restriction is due to the number of concurrent connections that can be maintained by one master device. The AM_ADDR represents the slave member address and is used to identify active participants; this is currently restricted to 3 bits, although slaves that become disconnected or parked give up this address. The Network Access Point must be configured for multi-user mode for it to accept more than one connection.

[7]The radio port reference is used in this context to describe the nature of a NAP, where multiple radios are available to the user. The *Service Discovery Application Protocol,* Chapter 3, will manage the presentation of this service appropriately, allowing the user to access the best available port.

The NAP itself behaves as a transparent medium, where the core services are those offered by the networking technologies attached to it. In a similar manner to the LAN Access Profile, the NAP may be installed in an area that is inconvenient to either install or continue a cabled network.

16.2.2   Future Usage Models

The development of the Personal Area Networking Profile is predicted to be coordinated in phases and, as such, the current[8] specification has been deemed the first phase. To increase the popularity of Bluetooth technology as a networking solution, inter-piconet scheduling has to be drafted and subsequently implemented. Such a Bluetooth device would be capable of participating in multiple piconets and would also be capable of handing off between access points. Both Radio Working Groups are also looking at increasing the availability of bandwidth, which would need to be on par with the throughput currently available with WiFi[9] and other similar wireless networking technologies.

We introduced the APK in the *Dial-up Networking Profile*, Chapter 8 and the *LAN Access Profile*, Chapter 10, where it was described as a means for which public access services could be provided at a charge to the user. The nature of the PAN Profile potentially provides a greater range of public services that can be made available. It is expected that technologies such as ISDN, home PNA, cable modems and mobile phones would be available in the future and incorporated into the backbone of the PAN infrastructure.

In Section 16.1.2, *What is the Future of the LAN Access and Dial-up Networking Profiles?*, we also introduced the concept of a mobile phone behaving as a NAP. Such behaviour would remove the need for it to provide modem emulation, although legacy support may be provided for reasons previously discussed. As an access point, emerging and available technologies, such as GPRS or UMTS, would provide a permanent connection to the Internet. This *always on* feature would allow your mobile phone or a PDA to be permanently active to receive emails, faxes and other Internet-related alerts such as the latest headline news.

The incredible growth of digital TV could see the introduction of Bluetooth-enabled digital transceivers. Users would employ their Bluetooth-enabled notebook or home PC to connect to the Internet and receive email and other standard Internet features through this new wireless service. Consideration may also be offered to provide other services from your PC, where specific applications are available to allow the consumer access to the daily TV listings, record programs and playback TV through their PC.

The introduction of a wireless infrastructure, as introduced in the *LAN Access Profile*, Chapter 10, becomes more of a genuine reality when considering the use of NAPs. As it stands, NAPs and indeed the LAN Access Point, will provide you with a functional, albeit limited, infrastructure. Limited is used here in this context to emphasise the term *mobility*; the PAN User, at present, is not able to roam between access points or piconets.

---

[8]Bluetooth Special Interest Group, "Personal Area Networking (PAN) Profile," Version 0.95a, June 2001.
[9]*Wireless Fidelity* (WiFi) is the standard for *Wireless Local Area Networking* (WLAN) (IEEE 802.11b), supporting a bandwidth of up to 11 Mb/s.

The viability of furnishing new office suites as a wireless-based solution will become the ultimate *wireless showcase* for the office of the future.

16.3   PROFILE PRINCIPLES

The profile defines three new configurations: a PAN User, a GN and a NAP. These new scenarios were defined in Figure 16-1 and Figure 16-2. Both the GN and NAP provide the ability for a PAN User to connect and to offer the services available, either via shared resources or access to the Internet.

The new architecture removes the need for a PPP component and the introduction of BNEP, implemented directly over L2CAP as the transport mechanism, is used to transport unmodified Ethernet payloads. In turn, a range of various networking protocols can then be instantiated above BNEP. Figure 16-6 and Figure 16-7 illustrate the components that constitute the Group Ad-hoc Network and the Network Access Point, respectively. A *Management Entity* (ME) is recommended and typically will coexist alongside the entire range of layers. Its primary objective is to coordinate the establishment of a connection and to respond and organise appropriate failures for inquiry and paging, which is very much similar to the LAN Access Profile.

In Table 16-1, clarification is provided with regard to the roles used within the context of this profile. In general, *DeviceA* represents the initiating party and *DeviceB* represents the accepting party. The terms are often used interchangeably when describing specific operations in various contexts and are provided here for reference.

In Figure 16-8, we provide a conceptual illustration, representing the dependencies that make up the PAN Profile; the areas that are shaded are relevant to this profile. As you can see, the profile depends upon the basic functionality offered to us by the *Generic Access Profile*, Chapter 2 and the *Service Discovery Application Profile*, Chapter 3.

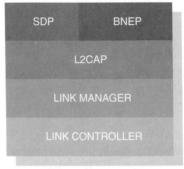

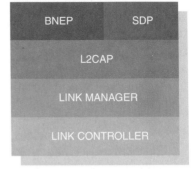

Figure 16-6   The range of components from the Bluetooth protocol stack and the Group Ad-hoc Network. The illustration shows the placement of the BNEP above L2CAP.

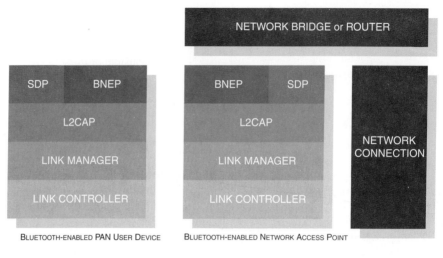

Figure 16-7   The range of components from the Bluetooth protocol stack and
the Network Access Point. The illustration shows the placement
of the BNEP above L2CAP.

We now take an opportunity to reflect upon the behavioural aspects of Bluetooth-
enabled devices as outlined by the *Generic Access Profile*, Chapter 2. You may remember
that the Generic Access Profile mandates certain rules and procedures that help govern
the overall connectability, discoverability and security aspects of Bluetooth-enabled
devices.

In Table 16-2, the basic set of procedures is illustrated, identifying functional expectations, which in turn govern its operation. These procedures help determine the context that the device would operate; for example, a device may wish to be discoverable for
a period of time or it may require a level of security that differs from one device to another depending upon the services it is capable of offering.

In Table 16-3, we consider the specific set of operations that are required for this
profile. In the table, you will notice features are marked with *M* (Mandatory), *O* (Optional), *X* (Excluded), *C* (Conditional) and *N/A* (Not Applicable); these will determine
what is expected from the features of the Generic Access Profile. The administrator has
the option to use pairing and, as such, has the option to increase the level of security for
all users. If pairing is supported, then bonding becomes mandatory as it is defined as optional at this stage, see Table 16-5.

Security is an important aspect for Bluetooth-enabled devices and Table 16-4 identifies the security requirements for this profile. You will also notice that these features are
marked in a similar fashion to our previous table. You may remember from the *Generic
Access Profile*, Chapter 2, that Security Mode 1 is a non-secure mode, where Bluetooth-
enabled devices will never initiate any security procedures; whereas Security Modes 2
and 3 initiate different levels of security procedures at various stages of connection estab-

Table 16-1 The list of behavioural characteristics that are typical for this profile.

CONFIGURATION	ROLE	DESCRIPTION
DeviceA	PANU	A PAN User is capable of initiating a connection to a GN or a NAP.
	GN or NAP	A GN and NAP are also capable of initiating a connection with a PAN User and, as such, they are considered to undertake the role of DeviceA.
	Initiator	This configuration describes the device that instigates the original connection or the device that wishes to initiate communication over an existing link.
	Client	This is the device that supports the client relationship.
DeviceB	GN or NAP	The GN and NAP accept incoming connections from a PAN User and, as such, the role depicted here is of DeviceB.
	PANU	A PAN User is also capable of accepting a connection from a GN or NAP and as such the role undertaken here is of DeviceB.
	Acceptor	This configuration describes the process of the device accepting the initiated communication from DeviceA.
	Server	The GN and NAP provide the server relationship of two participating devices.

lishment. In addition to the Generic Access Profile security procedures, additional security mechanisms are also provided for the PAN Profile. NAP, GN and PANU devices each have varying authorisation methods built upon the Generic Access Profile; these are discussed in more detail in Section 16.4.4, *Security Levels Available to the PAN Profile*.

In our final consideration of the basic rules and procedures that are required from the Generic Access Profile, the idle mode procedures outline behavioural characteristics when DeviceA chooses to initiate them against DeviceB. The procedures that are listed in Table 16-5 provide a clear indication of how a device should operate when performing such an activity; let us take our bonding procedure as an example. The term bonding is very much associated with the pairing process; however, bonding occurs when the user

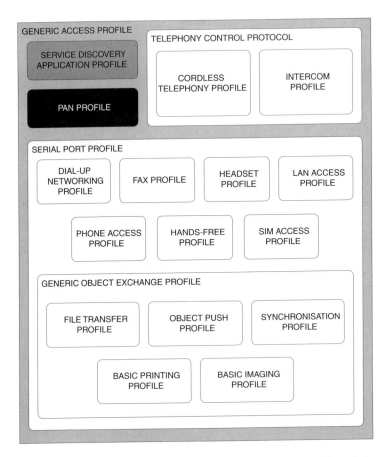

Figure 16-8   The dependent components of the Bluetooth protocol stack that make up the PAN Profile. The areas that are shaded are relevant to this profile.

has the *intent* to initiate a trusted relationship with DeviceB. With this intent, the user is prompted to enter a Bluetooth Passkey which, in turn, instigates the pairing process that is the generation of the link keys, where subsequent authentication can then occur. In summary, we realise that there are a specific set of events associated with a procedure and in the *Generic Access Profile*, Chapter 2, we provide an exhaustive presentation and examine how each procedure is conducted.

In this chapter, the PAN User is referred to as DeviceA, or the initiator; and the GN and NAP are the acceptors and form DeviceB, although the GN and NAP may initiate a connection. Initially, DeviceA takes the role of the master of the piconet, but DeviceB will request a master-slave switch if it is configured for multi-user mode. During the instance where a GN or NAP initiates a connection, no master-slave switch will be required.

Table 16-2   The core set of procedures as required by most profiles.

PROCEDURES	DESCRIPTION
Discoverability Mode	This mode prescribes the overall discoverability of a device, allowing it to be placed into a non-discoverable, limited or general discoverable mode. The mode would allow devices to become generally available to other users or it can be restricted to personal use.
Connectability Mode	When determining a baseband connectable state, this mode is used to place a device into a connectable or non-connectable mode.
Pairing	Pairable and non-pairable modes are used to realise the security aspects when operating or intending to use a device. A device may require authentication and, as such, the user would be required to enter a Bluetooth Passkey. The pairing procedure starts the link key generation process, which in turn allows authentication to take place.

16.4   USER EXPECTATIONS

16.4.1   Personal Area Networking (PAN) User

There are a large number of emerging products that support the LAN Access Profile and the behaviour of a PAN User can be likened to the DT. In much the same way, a PAN User would instigate the connection to a GN or a NAP.

Table 16-3   The illustration shows specific modes of operation that this profile depends upon to realise its compliant implementation.

MODES	NAP	GN	PANU
Non-discoverable	O	O	O
Limited Discoverable	O	O	O
General Discoverable	M	M	O
Non-connectable	O	O	O
Connectable	M	M	O
Non-pairable	O	O	O
Pairable	C	C	C

Table 16-4 The illustration shows specific security procedures that this profile depends upon to realise its compliant implementation.

PROCEDURE	NAP	GN	PANU
Authentication	O	O	O
Security Mode 1	M	M	M
Security Mode 2	C	C	C
Security Mode 3	C	C	C

Bluetooth Profiles supports the general philosophy of a good user experience. It is therefore important to consider how the user would experience accessing and using the services of a GN or NAP. In later sections, we consider the specific experience of connecting, terminating and refusing connections and how the user may experience such operations.

16.4.1.1 Connecting to a GN or NAP. As soon as the user has the ability to connect and has discovered the availability of a GN or NAP, he or she may now continue to make use of the services it provides. Before a user can access the full services, he or she is required to enter a *Bluetooth Passkey*. This is similar to the LAN Access Profile previously illustrated. Upon successful entry and authentication, the user may then be required to enter a username or password to fulfil network authorisation; this would allow further access to the services on the network.

The availability of numerous backbone networking technologies can be provided through a NAP; as such, they offer a wider variety of services than those initially conceived with the LAN Access Point. Further expansion of these services, may offer the user a greater choice.

16.4.1.2 Ending a Connection with a GN or NAP. Once a connection is established with a GN or NAP and its services are no longer required, the user may terminate

Table 16-5 The illustration shows specific behavioural procedures that this profile depends upon to realise its compliant implementation.

PROCEDURE	NAP	GN	PANU
General Inquiry	N/A	N/A	M
Limited Inquiry	N/A	N/A	O
Name Discovery	N/A	N/A	M
Device Discovery	N/A	N/A	M
Bonding	O	O	O

the session. In a similar operation as provided by the LAN Access Profile, the user may select an option from the pull-down menu after highlighting the connected device. Disconnect is then chosen to terminate the connection.

This termination process is due to *user-intervention*; other forms of disconnection may occur if the *Quality of Service* (QoS) can no longer be maintained by the GN or NAP. An instance of this specific example may occur when the number of available radio ports have been exhausted or the backbone, which the NAP is connected to, is unexpectedly lost. It is important to remember that, in such a situation, the user must be conveyed the appropriate information about their current situation and may be offered a reconnection at a later time.

16.4.2 Group Ad-hoc Networking

The GN provides the flexibility to create dynamic networks that are provided to familiar or known users. The GN master, or the individual who wishes to host the session, may choose to limit the number of users participating or restrict specific users from entering the ad-hoc network. The GN master can be considered as an administrator, that is, someone who is responsible for the configuration and management of the ad-hoc network session.

16.4.2.1 Refusing a Connection from a PAN User. There may be several instances when a connection from a PAN User needs to be refused. The first would be when an incorrect passkey has been entered, where authentication would fail. The second will occur if the PAN User has been excluded to participate in the ad-hoc network; and a third consideration should also be given to the maximum number of users having been reached, where an opportunity to reconnect at a later stage may be offered.

16.4.2.2 A GN Initiating a Connection with a PAN User. The PAN User Bluetooth-enabled device has to advertise the capability of being addressed in this manner. Once the inquiring GN device has established, then the establishment of this connection may begin. The GN is also subject to authentication and authorisation. No master-slave switch operation needs to be performed.

16.4.3 Network Access Points

In a similar manner to the LAN Access Point, the new Network Access Point may be primarily an embedded device placed in a location for convenience, such as a ceiling or a wall. From an administrator's perspective, he or she would typically have an initial contact with the device in order to configure and set-up its internal parameters for connection to the backbone networking technologies. Other parameters such as the *Dynamic Host Configuration Protocol* (DHCP) configuration and support for the use of *Simple Network Management Protocol* (SNMP[10]) to obtain statistical information about its usage and also the configuration of specific SNMP alerts, which may be triggered during a networking-related

---

[10]SNMP is prescribed in RFC1157.

problem. Other configuration schemes may be available for the administrator to view or change these parameters.

16.4.3.1   Refusing a Connection from a PAN User.   There may be several instances when a connection from a PAN User needs to be refused. The first would be when an incorrect passkey has been entered, where authentication would fail. The second consideration should be given when the maximum number of users has been reached, where an opportunity to reconnect at a later stage may be offered. The third possibility may be due to the backbone networking infrastructure having been lost and no services can be made available to the PAN User. Suitable notification should be provided and an offer to reconnect at a later stage should be made.

16.4.3.2   A NAP Initiating a Connection with a PAN User.   The PAN User Bluetooth-enabled device has to advertise the capability of being addressed in this manner. Once the inquiring NAP device has established this, then connection establishment may begin. The NAP is also subject to authentication and authorisation. No master-slave switch operation needs to be performed.

16.4.4   Security Levels Available to the PAN Profile

The PAN User, GN and NAP are all based upon the baseband link manager and link controller protocols. As such, the requirement for authentication and encryption has been well prescribed in our earlier chapters. Other BNEP and higher-level authorisation mechanisms are optional. When a PAN User member has obtained trusted access to the GN or NAP shared resource environment, other measures of security should also be enforced. Some examples would be to restrict users to defined areas and to limit their permission level within that area.

The PAN Profile is dependent on the *Generic Access Profile*, Chapter 2, like all other profiles. As such, the three standard levels of security also apply here; that is, *non-secure, service-level enforced security* and *link-level enforced security*.

16.4.4.1   Modes of Security.   The availability of PAN-specific security operations is also provided, where access to a GN or NAP is further defined by operational parameters defined within the SDP service record.

A PAN can be deemed as *open* and, as such, no authorisation and authentication is required. Authentication (Bluetooth-specific) and/or authorisation may be required to gain access to the range of services available. In all cases, if authentication and/or authorisation fails the PAN User is refused connection to the GN or NAP.

A further definition is used to prescribe other security levels, where the data communicated within the PAN is protected. *PAN Secrecy Modes* are used to denote this level of confidentiality. During a *clear mode* operation, no encryption is used and the *encryption mode* operation enforces all data transmitted within the PAN group to be encrypted. These modes of operation may change when the group is constructed and any device failing to acknowledge the shift in operation will be excluded from the PAN group. Any failure to comply with these modes of operation will also result in the connection being refused.

Similarly, the above applies to a GN or NAP wishing to instigate the connection to a PAN User. The PAN User would also refuse a connection if authentication and/or authorisation failed.

16.5 SUMMARY

- The PAN Profile defines three further configurations: PAN User, Group Ad-hoc Networking and Network Access Points.
- These new configurations offer further usage scenarios allowing the PAN User to either create a dynamic network (GN) or to access the services of a Network Access Point where, a greater variety of backbone networking technologies may be available.
- The current specification is considered to be the first phase of development for the PAN Profile.
- Further phases will tackle such issues as IPS and APR to enable access point roaming and inter-piconet roaming.
- Within the typical roles, a PAN User can initiate a connection; the PAN Profile also allows the GN and NAP to initiate connections.
- The GN is restricted to a maximum of eight users: one master and up to seven slaves.
- The NAP may offer several radio units where, it can increase the number of users, which is determined by the number of radio units multiplied by the maximum number of users.
- Bluetooth authentication may optionally be required for a PAN User to gain access to the PAN group.
- Higher-level authorisation may be required, which is prescribed by the backbone networking technology.

17

The Car Profiles:
An Overview

17.1 INTRODUCTION

The variety and diversity in the range of vehicles on the marketplace today is incredible; manufacturers constantly tempt us with cost-effective finance schemes, along with handsome options for additional features. Automotive industries continually strive to incorporate better and more luxurious features into their range of models, increasing the *gadget-factor* and, as such, tempting potential new owners into purchasing their vehicles. The high-end, more luxurious vehicles continually struggle to compete with lower-end vehicle packages, as these nowadays find themselves technically on par with the higher-end range. With the introduction of Bluetooth-enabled applications and its low-cost attraction, it would seem that both-end vehicle market ranges would also benefit from another gadget: wireless technology. Indeed, some major manufacturers have already announced their intention to incorporate Bluetooth technology. It is open and widely available and, in turn, three new car-specific profiles have been introduced.

The number of car profiles currently under development comprises the *Hands-Free*, *Phone Access* and *SIM Access Profiles*. Each profile addresses specific functionality enabled within the vehicle environment; we discuss this in more detail in the following section.

17.2   USAGE MODELS

This section now considers both existing and future usage models through scenarios that may be typical for the Car Profiles, as illustrated in our introduction. We begin by exploring the existing models, where at face value the Car Profiles provide us with the ability to combine our Bluetooth-enabled mobile phone with hands-free or in-car embedded Bluetooth units. In future usage models, we consider other usage scenarios that lend themselves quite well to the diversity of these new profiles.

In exploring our existing usage models, we compare each profile; as such, we clearly demonstrate their differences and specific usage cases. However, before moving on to discuss the range of possibilities, we need to consider some safety aspects of using these features in a moving vehicle. The immediate two sections that follow help us understand what considerations should be made and when exactly the user should be allowed to operate such devices.

17.2.1   In-Car Safety

The exploration of the usage models takes into consideration the safety requirements and common sense that drivers should apply in their vehicles. It is assumed that appropriate safety measures have been integrated within the car environment to ensure driver and passenger safety which, in turn, will have a positive effect upon fellow road users and pedestrians. Current research in the United Kingdom places the same emphasis on using a mobile or hands-free device as driving when over the legal alcohol limit. However, attempts at enforcing a ban on using a hands-free device, for example, have recently been thwarted. Officers are unsure if a driver is using a hands-free device or just singing along to music. Nonetheless, if legislation is drafted enforcing new laws that make it illegal for any type of device to be operated in a vehicle, vehicle manufactures will be forced to consider alternative methods of in-car communication.

Safety is paramount in a moving vehicle and the temptation to peruse your calendar or other mobile-menu specific items on your in-car display unit is clearly a serious distraction and potentially dangerous. The increase in voice-activated functionality would help alleviate the distraction from the road to your in-car display unit, as would an incorporated microphone and speaker system, which are indeed becoming more common. Voice announcements would equally lend themselves well to incoming call notification.[1] If a caller's name is in the phonebook of the mobile phone unit, then an audible announcement of the caller can be made. Otherwise, a ring tone accompanied by an announcement of caller unknown or number withheld would also help keep the driver's eyes firmly focused on the road. Similarly, using voice activated dialling would also help alleviate the fingering required to navigate through your list of names and numbers. In reducing the

---

[1]The temptation here is to look down at your in-car display to identify the caller, in much the same way we look at our mobile phone. With an announcement, the caller can be audibly identified. This removes the need to seek further information from the in-car display unit.

amount of time needed to bring the eyes down to focus on your in-car display unit, the more confident manufacturers can concern themselves with driver and passenger safety when they operate such devices.

17.2.2 When to Enable Functionality

Most mobile phone manufacturers provide the ability to configure a mobile phone for a particular operating environment. In this context, it refers to a specific configuration that meets with environmental needs. Such examples may include *Silent*, for discreet operation in a restaurant or *Outdoors*, where the ring volume needs to be a little louder, since the surrounding noise is a distraction. In-car configurations may be supported to allow the exporting of mobile phone or PDA-specific data for perusal within the in-car display unit and control by a button-operated steering wheel. Furthermore, the configuration would also identify what specific functionality can be operated by the in-car system, and therefore restrict the perusal of certain data. Using the Phone Access or SIM Access Profiles, a user would be able to select what specific data to export and perhaps limit the temptation to scan the names and addresses. Any calendar or reminder function can also be exported, but again using voice audible announcements rather than beeps, or the like. Such audible triggers can be used to uniquely identify the alert, which again would allow the driver to keep his or her eyes on the road.

One luxury automotive manufacturer inhibits the use of the vehicle's extended menu functionality while the vehicle is in motion. That is, the menu can only be accessed when the vehicle has become stationary, such as at a set of traffic lights or during the more commonplace traffic delays. This restriction removes the temptation to play with your device while it is moving. Nevertheless, even while your vehicle is stationery, scanning the names and numbers still poses a distraction. This is because your eyes are not focused on the traffic ahead or indeed on the colour of the traffic lights. You may experience other drivers' frustration as the driver behind beeps his or her horn to alert you that you need to move forward.

There has to be a satisfactory consensus on how we choose to develop and subsequently integrate this technology into our vehicles. Above all removing temptation, adding safety features and providing a satisfactory user experience are three key immediate considerations.

17.2.3 Existing Usage Models

We see more and more in-car display units being integrated, providing on-board statistics such as average speed and average fuel consumption. The availability of this display unit lends itself quite well to the profiles illustrated in this chapter. Each will require the use of some output display, informing the user what activity or function they wish to enable or select. Furthermore, button-operated steering wheels are also commonly available. Extending the functionality to the steering wheel removes the need to reach for the centre console and change environment settings. Drivers already have the ability to change the volume level or select a track or disc on their integrated multi-CD player.

Figure 17-1 The new Car Hands-Free Profile enables mobile phone users
to interoperate their devices with existing car hand-free kits,
where the audio functionality has been integrated within the
vehicle's speaker and microphone system.

The Car Hands-Free Profile provides the ability for a user to enable their mobile handset
to function with a hands-free kit within the vehicle. The hands-free unit may already be integrated into the in-car speaker and microphone system, thus allowing the user to accept incoming and make outgoing calls from the mobile phone handset. Figure 17-1 provides an
illustration representing the scenario created by this profile. A hands-free unit may also interoperate with a Headset compliant product when no such hands-free kit is present. We talked in
some detail about the headset usage models in our earlier chapter (see the *Headset Profile*,
Chapter 7). The provision here is that the user has the ability to select either environment to
make use of the mobile phone. You may remember that the user already has the ability to move
audio functions from the mobile phone to the headset and vice versa; similarly, audio functions
and control can be exported between the mobile phone and the hands-free car kit.

As we mentioned, the introduction of button-operated steering wheels and in-car
display units is feasible as a means to control the function provided within your mobile
phone, PDA or notebook. The Phone Access Profile allows you to export the functionality
inherent within your mobile devices to your in-car system and Figure 17-2 provides an illustration, representing the scenario created by this profile.

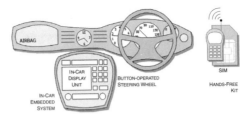

Figure 17-2 The new Car Phone Access Profile follows from the Car
Hands-Free Profile, where remote control capability, phonebook and possibly calendar access are exported to the in-car
embedded system. These are provided by the button-operated
steering wheel and in-car display unit.

Figure 17-3   The new Car SIM Access Profile enables a user to communicate with the in-car embedded phone unit. Data such as the
phonebook, as well as calendar information, can be exported.
Other data, such as seat and mirror positions may also be saved
within a mobile phone for later use in a company car.

In the final car profile, the SIM Access allows the downloading of SIM-specific
data from your mobile phone or PDA to an in-car embedded unit and, as such, the vehicle
would have its own integrated Bluetooth device. The advantage of this profile allows the
user to occupy a company car and to be able to personalise it with their own configuration
previously saved on their mobile phone. Similarly, any changes made within the vehicle
can also be saved back into the mobile phone for later retrieval. Using your mobile phone
as a keyless system would enable the driver to enter the vehicle. During his or her ap-
proach to the car, the vehicle would automatically detect their mobile device and begin
downloading their *in-car personality*. It is also important to note that relevant billing information is addressed to the driver accordingly. Finally, Figure 17-3 provides the illustration representing the scenario created by this profile.

17.2.4   Future Usage Models

The potential number of usage models is numerous, but at the same time we must consider all safety aspects imposed by the nature of a moving vehicle. Some functionality can
be made available under certain conditions, as previously outlined. Functionality can be
offered when stationary, although passengers may access some functionality when the car
is in motion.

The use of a mobile phone as a keyless entry system to your vehicle is quite attrac-
tive; we introduced this concept in Section 17.2.3, *Existing Usage Models*. This is not just
limited to a car, but the mobile phone can act as a keyless entry system to a variety of environments, such as the office or accessing a computer, although we are moving out of
scope with these ideas for this profile.

In the *PAN Profile: An Overview*, Chapter 16, we introduced the concept of a mobile
phone acting as a *Network Access Point* (NAP) and, as such, the ability for passengers to access the Internet or the corporate office is a seamless and natural extension to our in-car personality. As we previously described, such technologies as *General Packet Radio Service*

(GPRS) network or a *Universal Mobile Telecommunications Service* (UMTS) network may exist to provide a permanent connection, although a charge is imposed according to the amount of data transferred. The *Dial-up Networking Profile*, Chapter 8, may also be part of the profile already supported by the mobile phone and, as such, this may be an alternative and cheaper solution. Providing such networking capability within the car must be used safely; clearly, the driver would not be able to use such functionality. However, passengers with appropriately enabled Bluetooth devices can use such facilities.

A more adventurous usage model for Bluetooth devices within the vehicle environment is to provide the ability to configure certain personality characteristics. *Bluetooth Driver Personalities* (BDP) would allow you to provide other interested drivers, within suitable radio range, with your individual information, physical characteristics and other interests.

A more pragmatic use, aimed at the more safety conscious audience Bluetooth-enabled in-car units would provide the ability for police traffic enforcement units to interrogate the vehicle, where your current speed may be requested and whether the vehicle is insured and serviced. The provision here is that the driver has enabled such a feature and has openly allowed the car to be interrogated in this manner. People who demonstrate repeated traffic offences may find themselves having such a unit enforced upon them.

Taking this one step further, in areas where your speed is an important observation, such as in close proximity to a school, *Bluetooth speed* units may be installed and your car, and subsequently the driver, informed of the speed in the area. Furthermore, the driver has configured his car to operate at the speed governed within the area and, as such, the car accommodates the new speed limit whilst the vehicle remains under the driver's control.

A more obvious usage model is the ability to interrogate a car when it is brought into a dealership for a regular service or when the car has a problem. Diagnostic and service-related data is passed onto the technician who can quickly identify any problems. This can also be extended to racing car technicians who need to diagnose quickly the problems that the car may have.

A convenient use of in-car wireless systems is to provide automatic access to home garages, allocated parking spaces or entry systems and public use parking areas, where a subscription has been previously paid. Similarly, toll bridges may also benefit from automatic wireless entry systems with the provision of a valid *Bluetooth ticket*.

This chapter addresses three new car profiles. We introduce a breakdown of the three profiles into their respective sections and cover the typical components, such as Profile Principles and User Expectations, which we have already become familiar with in previous chapters.

17.3 THE HANDS-FREE PROFILE BASICS

17.3.1 Profile Principles

The Hands-Free Profile provides two new roles: an *Audio Gateway* (AG) and a *Hands-Free* unit (HF). The HF device may already be installed as part of the in-car hands-free kit, where it is configured to use in-car audio functionality that extends to the speaker and

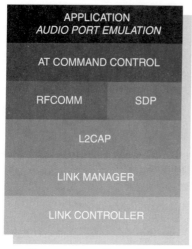
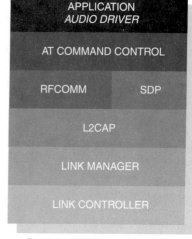

BLUETOOTH-ENABLED GATEWAY DEVICE   BLUETOOTH-ENABLED HANDS-FREE DEVICE

Figure 17-4   The components of the Bluetooth protocol stack are shown,
illustrating the newer components of the Hands-Free Profile.

microphone system. The AG provides full duplex audio support, where such devices include a mobile phone. In Figure 17-4, we can see how the new Hands-Free components
are integrated with the existing Bluetooth protocol stack.

The profile defines a set of protocols and procedures, which are required to realise
the profile implementation. Support for one *Synchronous Connection Oriented* (SCO)
audio link is provided and, as such, only the two participating devices can operate at any
one time. The profile mandates support for audio CODECs,[2] where the resulting audio is
monophonic and has a data rate of 64 Kb/s, although no obvious degradation should be
observed.

In Figure 17-5, we provide a conceptual illustration representing the dependencies
that make up the Hands-Free Profile; the areas that are shaded are relevant to this profile.
As you can see, the profile depends upon the basic functionality offered to us by the
Generic Access Profile, Chapter 2, the *Service Discovery Application Profile*, Chapter 3
and the *Serial Port Profile*, Chapter 6.

The Hands-Free Profile does not operate strict master-slave roles and either the AG
or HF may initiate the connection. As such, the initiating party is referred to as DeviceA,
or the initiator; and DeviceB is the acceptor. Any initiating device is the master of the relationship, but no master-slave role switch is required from the accepting device.

---

[2]Bluetooth technology has provision for two types of audio-encoding schemes. The *Pulse Code Modulation*
(PCM) has two types of logarithmic compression, these are A-law and μ-law; *Continuous Variable Slope Delta*
(CVSD) provides the second scheme, which is particularly efficient for voice communication. Further information about Bluetooth Audio can be found in the *Cordless Telephony*, Chapter 4, *Intercom*, Chapter 5 and *Headset Profiles*, Chapter 7.

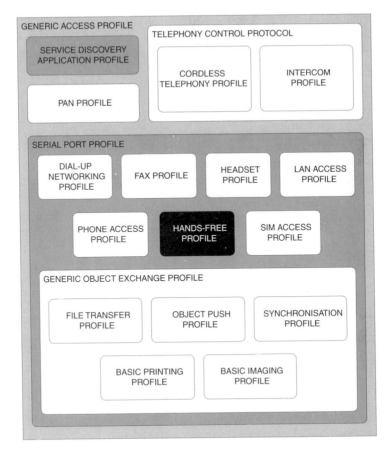

Figure 17-5   The dependent components of the Bluetooth protocol stack that make up the Hands-Free Profile. The areas that are shaded are relevant to this profile.

Figure 17-4 illustrated the components that made up our Hands-Free Profile. The profile is also dependent on the *Serial Port Profile*, Chapter 6, in its implementation. Like the *Headset Profile*, Chapter 7, a series of AT commands are also used to enable control signalling. On closer inspection, you will also notice that the AG device provides audio port emulation, whereas the HF provides an audio driver. It is also assumed that some management entity exists, where access to lower components of the stack is provided; in some cases, a direct *Pulse Code Modulation* (PCM) route is used to enable faster audio throughput.

17.3.2   User Expectations

17.3.2.1   Audio Gateway and the Hands-Free Unit.   In this example, we will use our mobile phone and our in-car hands-free kit as our usage models to explain the interaction and sequence of events between these two devices. There is some degree of overlap with the Headset Profile, since this itself achieves exactly the same functionality as the Hands-Free Profile. Nevertheless, as it is, more and more products on the market now offer support for dual capability encompassing both the Headset and Hands-Free Profiles; refer back to our previous chapter the *Headset Profile*, Chapter 7, for more information.

As you know and have become more familiar with, *Bluetooth Profiles* supports the general philosophy of a good user experience. It is therefore important to consider how the user would experience the access and usability of the services provided by an HF. In the following sections, we consider the specific actions of creating a connection, terminating and losing the connection between the AG and HF and how the user may experience such operations. With a small display, the mobile phone may only provide a user-friendly description of the discovered HF device, although an extended menu may exist to specifically interrogate the device further; whereas a PDA however, may typically have a larger display offering further details about the discovered device. Nonetheless, each device may have an option to allow you to customise the HF device.

17.3.2.1.1 Service Level and Audio Connection Set-Up. A user or an internal event would realise the creation of an audio connection, where a SCO link is established between the AG and HF, although it is implied that a *Service Level Connection* already exists, see Figure 17-6. This pre-condition to setting up the SCO connection essentially mandates that these two devices already have a prior relationship, where an inquiry, discovery and optional authentication has already taken place, although if no prior relationship exists between both parties then one is created. Formal procedures also exist to accommodate parking,[3] unparking, connection termination and release.

17.3.2.1.2 Creating a Call. It is assumed that both the AG and HF already have an existing SCO connection ready for use, as outlined in our previous section. The AG may initiate a call by using the function already inherent in the mobile phone device, using the buttons provided by the handset. This does require the driver or user to reach down or across to operate the device. Figure 17-7 shows the specific set of events that are used to enable a call and how the AG and HF coordinate the audio effort.

17.3.2.1.3 Accepting a Call. A call can be accepted by the function already provided by the mobile phone using the buttons provided on the handset. The in-car system has alerted the driver to an incoming call through the use of an in-band ringing tone or through a voice announcement, as we previously described. Figure 17-8 shows the specific set of events that are used to accept a call and how the AG and HF coordinate the audio effort.

17.3.2.1.4 Rejecting and Terminating a Call. A call can be rejected by the function already provided by the mobile phone handset. The in-car system has alerted the dri-

---

[3]The parking and unparking operations refer to the baseband connection state, where devices may be placed into park mode and subsequently unparked. This state is a lower power usage model where partying devices conserve their battery life.

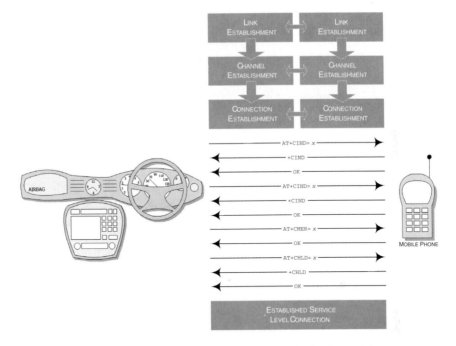

Figure 17-6   The events that take place during a service level connection set-up.

ver to an incoming call through the use of an in-band ringing tone or through a voice an-nouncement. The driver would depress the associated button provided by the mobile handset to reject the call and have it diverted to voice mail. Similarly, a call can be termi-nated using the same function. In both instances, an audible confirmation may be used to alert the driver that the call has been rejected or terminated.

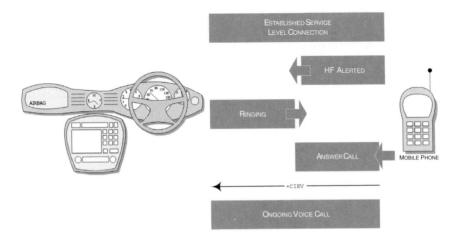

Figure 17-7   The events that take place during the creation of a call.

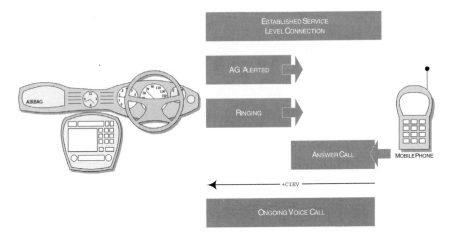

Figure 17-8   The events that take place when the driver accepts a call.

17.3.2.1.5   Voice Recognition.   It is assumed that the HF unit is capable of supporting this function through the AG and, as such, has the ability to retrieve numbers using voice activation from the AG and to subsequently dial them. Voice activation is enabled through the use of the mobile phone handset, which places the AG unit into a *momentary-on* state, where it waits for the driver's announcement. This function, if not used, may timeout or be deactivated using the same or similar function from the mobile phone handset. Figure 17-9 shows the activation events that occur during the use of the voice function; it also demonstrates the coordinated audio effort between the AG and HF.

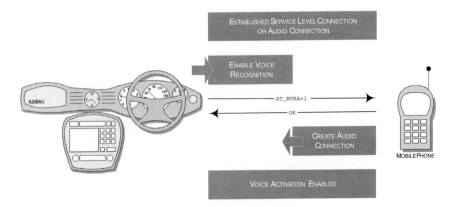

Figure 17-9   The events that take place during activation of the voice control capability for the Hands-Free Profile.

17.4   THE PHONE ACCESS PROFILE BASICS

17.4.1   Profile Principles

The Phone Access Profile provides two new roles: a *Mobile Equipment* (ME) and a *Terminal Equipment* unit (TE). In a similar manner to the AG, the ME provides full duplex audio support and such devices include a mobile phone. The TE is the device that provides remote control functionality and such devices would include an in-car kit or in-car embedded unit. In Figure 17-10, we can see the new Phone Access components integrated with the existing Bluetooth protocol stack.

   The functionality of the ME is exported to the TE for control and operation and only one TE can control an ME. As such, only one audio connection exists between the two devices. Like the Hands-Free Profile, the profile mandates support for audio CODECs where the resulting audio is monophonic and has a data rate of 64 Kb/s.

   In Figure 17-11, we provide a conceptual illustration representing the dependencies that make up the Phone Access Profile; the areas that are shaded are relevant to this profile. As you can see, the profile depends upon the basic functionality offered to us by the *Generic Access Profile*, Chapter 2, the *Service Discovery Application Profile*, Chapter 3 and the *Serial Port Profile*, Chapter 6.

   In Figure 17-10, we illustrated the components that made up our Phone Access Profile. The profile is also dependent on the *Serial Port Profile*, Chapter 6, in its implementation. Like the *Hands-Free Profile*, we introduced earlier, a series of AT commands are also used to enable control signalling. On closer inspection, you will notice that the ME device provides audio-port emulation, whereas the TE provides an audio driver. It is

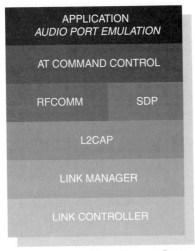

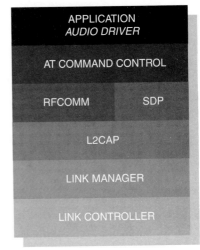

Figure 17-10   The components of the Bluetooth protocol stack are shown, illustrating the newer components of the Phone Access Profile.

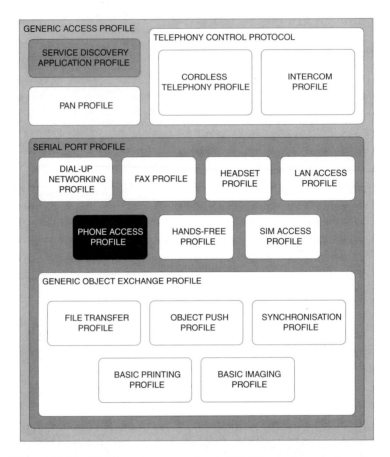

Figure 17-11   The dependent components of the Bluetooth protocol stack
that make up the Phone Access Profile. The areas that are
shaded are relevant to this profile.

also assumed that some management entity exists, where access to lower components of
the stack is provided; in some cases, a direct PCM route is used to enable faster audio
throughput.

Like the Hands-Free Profile, the Phone Access Profile does not operate strict master-
slave roles and either the ME or TE may initiate the connection.

17.4.2   User Expectations

17.4.2.1   The Mobile and Terminal Equipment Units.   There is some degree
of overlap with the Phone Access and Hands-Free Profiles; the extent of the overlap
goes as far as the audio transfer between the two devices. In addition to the audio transfer, this profile provides remote control support to allow the user to control the ME
using the TE. In this example, we use a mobile phone and our in-car embedded device

to best illustrate our usage model in explaining the interaction and sequence of events between these two devices.

The profile mandates a minimum set of key features that is required for any device to be considered compliant with the Phone Access Profile. These are shown in Table 17-1.

17.4.2.1.1 Service Level and Audio Connection Set-up. A user or an internal event would realise the creation of an audio connection, where a SCO link is established between the TE and ME, although it is implied that a *Service Level Connection* already exists. This pre-condition to setting up the SCO connection essentially mandates that these two devices already have a prior relationship. That is an inquiry, discovery and optional authentication has already taken place. If no prior relationship exists between both

Table 17-1   The minimum set of key features that are required for this profile.

	FEATURE	DESCRIPTION
1	Call control support	This feature provides core functionality to include accepting, terminating and making calls.
2	Phonebook support	This support provides the user with the ability to sort, scroll and select entries from their phonebook.
3	Phone status information	This feature provides general information about the status of the phone to include support for signal strength, call status and operator name.
4	SIM PIN status information	Here the user may request the status indication of the PIN code and entry status.
5	Supplementary services	The features supported can normally be found with any mobile phone; they provide the user with a common set of features, to include three-way calling, call forwarding, and barring.
6	Short Message Service (SMS)	This provides extended functionality to the user, that is, all the SMS capabilities of a mobile phone.
7	Miscellaneous	This feature allows the user to query and configure capabilities within the device to provide such information as voice recognition activation, volume control and data call indication.

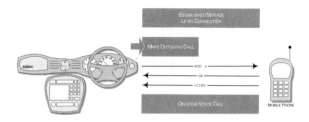

Figure 17-12   The events that take place during the creation of a call.

parties, then one is created. Formal procedures also exist to accommodate parking and un-parking, connection, termination and release.

   17.4.2.1.2   Creating a Call.   It is assumed that both the TE and ME already have an existing SCO connection ready for use. The TE may initiate a call by using the function available though the in-car embedded unit. A button-operated steering wheel and in-car display unit, inherent in the vehicle, would be used to provide navigation for the phonebook in order to select the name of the person to call. Figure 17-12 shows the specific set of events that are used to enable a call and illustrates how the TE and ME coordinate the audio and remote control effort.

   17.4.2.1.3   Accepting a Call.   A call can be accepted by the function already provided by the mobile phone. The exported functionality to a vehicle environment allows the user to accept a call from the button-operated steering wheel. The in-car system has alerted the driver to an incoming call through the use of an in-band ringing tone or through a voice announcement. Figure 17-13 shows the specific set of events that are used to accept a call and how the TE and ME coordinate the audio and remote control effort.

   17.4.2.1.4   Rejecting and Terminating a Call.   A call can be rejected by the function already provided by the mobile phone. The in-car system has alerted the driver to an incoming call through the use of an in-band ringing tone or through a voice announcement. The exported functionality to a vehicle environment would allow the user to reject

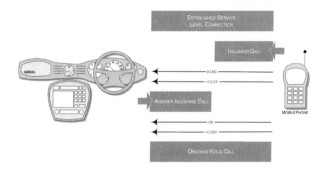

Figure 17-13   The events that take place when the driver accepts a call.

the call from the button-operated steering wheel. The remote control handling of this sequence would allow the caller to be transferred to voice mail. Similarly, the call can be terminated using the same function. In both instances, an audible confirmation can be used notifying the user that the call as been rejected or terminated.

17.4.2.1.5   Voice Recognition.   It is assumed that the ME unit is capable of supporting this function through the TE and, as such, has the ability to retrieve numbers using voice activation from the ME and to subsequently dial them. Voice activation can be entered using the button-operated steering wheel, as well as the feature already provided by the mobile phone handset, which places the ME unit into a *momentary-on* state, where it waits for the driver's announcement. This function, if not used, may timeout or be deactivated using the same or similar functions from the steering wheel and mobile phone handset. Figure 17-9 showed the activation events that occur during the use of the voice function. It demonstrates the coordinated audio and remote control efforts between the TE and ME.

17.4.2.1.6   Other Functionality.   As illustrated in Table 17-1, the range of functionality that is exported by the ME allows the TE to effectively take control of the unit, where the driver can safely operate the device without too much distraction.

17.4.2.2   Security.   The application determines if authentication and encryption is enforced and if the procedures as prescribed in the *Generic Access Profile*, Chapter 2, are applied. However, the Phone Access Profile does mandate several security features.

During pairing *Link Level Enforced Security* and *Service Level Enforced Security* (see the *Generic Access Profile*, Chapter 2, for more information) are recommended with the addition of authentication and encryption. User intervention is required during this process when first establishing a connection.

17.5   THE SIM ACCESS PROFILE BASICS

17.5.1   Profile Principles

The *Subscriber Identity Module* (SIM) *Access Profile* provides two new roles: a *SIM Client* and a *SIM Server*. This profile mandates the exchange of SIM-specific data between a SIM client and SIM server. As such, it is not limited to the car profiles and may be used for other application usage models. The SIM client unit forms part of an in-car embedded environment, where its backbone supports the audio and remote control nature of the usage scenarios, as previously outlined in our earlier sections. No audio and remote control hand-off is required, since the in-car SIM client Bluetooth-enabled device is an integral component to the operation of the in-car embedded phone unit. Furthermore, since the embedded device is a GSM capable unit, calls can be connected, terminated and rejected in the usual manner. In Figure 17-14, we can see the new SIM Access components integrated with the existing Bluetooth protocol stack.

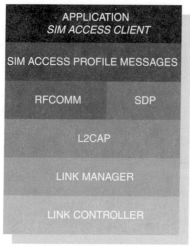

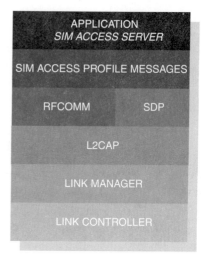

Figure 17-14   The components of the Bluetooth protocol stack are shown, illustrating the newer components of the SIM Access Profile.

The profile defines a set of protocols and procedures, which are required to realise the profile implementation. The functionality of the SIM server exports its SIM-specific data to the SIM client to allow it to make use of phonebook, calendar and other mobile phone or PDA related data.

In Figure 17-15, we provide a conceptual illustration representing the dependencies that make up the SIM Access Profile; the areas that are shaded are relevant to this profile. As you can see, the profile depends upon the basic functionality offered to us by the *Generic Access Profile*, Chapter 2, the *Service Discovery Application Profile*, Chapter 3 and the *Serial Port Profile*, Chapter 6.

The SIM Access Profile does not operate strict master-slave roles and either the SIM Client or the SIM Server may initiate the connection.

17.5.2   User Expectations

17.5.2.1   The SIM Client and Server.   The user expectations are almost transparent to the usage model prescribed by this profile. With the inquiry and discovery procedures that are typical for a Bluetooth connection, no other visual process occurs. The profile mandates the transfer of SIM subscription and other related data to the SIM client, where it can then register the client on a GSM network. Furthermore, existing procedures are available within the in-car embedded unit to conduct the operation of making and receiving GSM network calls as you would expect from your mobile phone handset. As a result of data sharing with the SIM client, the in-car embedded unit has access to the phonebook and, in some cases, calendar specific information. As a minimum, the SIM Access Profile provides the ability to exchange data from one SIM to another.

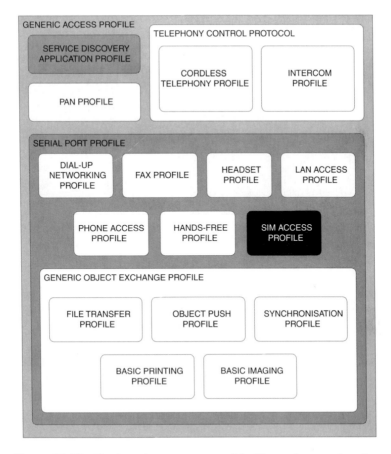

Figure 17-15 The dependent components of the Bluetooth protocol stack
that make up the SIM Access Profile. The areas that are
shaded are relevant to this profile.

In part, the profile has been based upon the GSM 11.11 Specification of the *Subscriber Identity Module – Mobile Equipment* (SIM-ME) Interface. It is also based on the GSM 11.14 Specification of the SIM Application Toolkit for the Subscriber Identity Module – Mobile Equipment (SIM-ME) Interface, see Figure 17-14, which provides an illustration outlining how these components are integrated within the Bluetooth protocol stack.

The profile mandates a minimum set of key application features that is required for any device to be considered compliant with the SIM Access Profile. These are shown in Table 17-2.

17.5.2.2 Security. Stronger Bluetooth security methods are encouraged for this profile, inasmuch as particularly sensitive and confidential data are being exchanged be-

Table 17-2 The minimum set of key features that are required for this profile.

	FEATURE	DESCRIPTION
1	Connection Management	This feature provides core functionality to allow the connection, disconnection and status procedures for both parties.
2	Transfer Application Protocol Data Units (APDUs)	This feature provides the ability to communicate over the connection using APDUs. It is the client that initiates the APDU, where the payload data relates to the transfer of client-server specific parameters.
3	Transfer Answer to Reset (ATR)	This denotes the ability of the server to send the ATR in response to a reset. The process may be initiated by the client requesting the server to send it from the SIM.
4	Power SIM On/Off	The client may request that the server switch off the SIM, where all GSM connections have ended. Similarly, it may also request that it be switched on if it has been previously switched off.
5	Reset SIM	The client may request the server to reset the SIM if all GSM connections have been terminated.
6	Report Status	This feature is used to identify any changes within the client-server relationship (connection status) and during the connection set-up procedure.
7	Transfer Card Read Status	The client may request Card Reader Status which, in turn, provides the client operation status of the SIM. In turn, details regarding the SIM size and so on are reported.
8	Error Handling	Generic handling procedures are an inherent process for the features presented in this table.

tween the two parties. Any eavesdropping could result in unwanted identification of personal data. Support should be provided for at least *Link Level Enforced Security* and *Service Level Enforced Security* (see the *Generic Access Profile*, Chapter 2, for more information) and pairing is mandatory for both devices.

Furthermore, the use of encryption is strongly recommended, along with use of longer Bluetooth Passkeys,[4] where the navigation of user interaction is encouraged during all exchanges between SIM devices.

17.6 SUMMARY

- The Car Profiles have three new profiles: Hands-Free, Phone Access and SIM Access.
- The Hands-Free Profile provides audio hand-off to an in-car hands-free kit, but its operation is still coordinated through the mobile phone handset interface.
- There is an overlap of the Hands-Free Profile with the Headset Profile since both provide audio hand-off.
- The Phone Access Profile also provides audio hand-off, but extends this to remote control of the ME, where navigation of a phonebook can be managed through the button-operated steering wheel and visual output is provided by the in-car display unit.
- The SIM Access Profile provides the exchange of SIM-specific data between two devices, primarily a mobile phone handset and an in-car embedded handset, where the in-car unit can take control.
- When SIM-specific data has been exchanged with the in-car embedded handset, the user can make and disconnect calls using the button-operated steering wheel and the in-car display unit.

---

[4]The Bluetooth Passkey is a user-level entered parameter that is required for the pairing procedure and thus enables subsequent authentication.

18

The ESDP: An Overview

18.1 INTRODUCTION

In our introduction of the *Service Discovery Application Profile* (SDAP) and the *Service Discovery Protocol* (SDP), Chapter 3, we discussed in some detail that in combination these two components provided us with a foundation on which we can establish user-level clarity with the discovered services of Bluetooth enabled devices that are in radio range. The SDAP establishes a level of basic functionality, abstracted from SDP. SDAP collects and organises service information from the remote device, allowing the user to make an informed decision about the services on offer.

The *Extended Service Discovery Profile* (ESDP) is an extension of the SDP, where its primary aim is to help extend the availability of services from devices that may be in radio range or from devices that offer services beyond the capabilities of a Bluetooth enabled device. A Bluetooth enabled device that is part of a piconet, for example, may be part of a larger community of devices possibly connected through an IP-based network. Utilising *Universal Plug and Play* (UPnP) device architecture, it becomes possible for many devices to communicate with each other, without the restriction of formality. The UPnP open architecture is an industry initiative, where committees create various standards for a range of services. Essentially, what we create is a dynamic solution for ad-hoc communication; furthermore, what we achieve is a global community of devices that are capable of sharing resources and services with each other. In providing extended services,

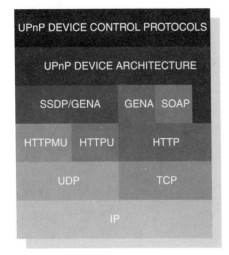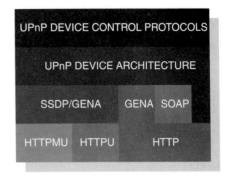

Figure 18-1   In our illustration, we can see two new stacks that make up the UPnP Device Architecture. The stack shown on the left forms part of an IP-based solution, whereas the stack shown on the right forms part of an L2CAP-based solution.

it is also possible to allow control of these devices in the larger community. It should be noted that these devices may not necessarily be Bluetooth-enabled. SDAP will still assume the responsibility for organising and providing user-level clarity with the availability of services.

To enable Bluetooth-enabled devices to become part of this wider community, ESDP is supported and, as such, Figure 18-1 illustrates the components that make up the UPnP device architecture for an IP-based and L2CAP-based solution. In the following sections, we discuss the architecture and features in more detail.

18.2   PROFILE PRINCIPLES

The UPnP ESDP provides two new roles: a *local* device and a *remote* device. The local device typically initiates the service discovery procedure, whereas the remote device responds to the inquiries made by the local device. You may recall from our discussion in the *Service Discovery Application Profile*, Chapter 3, that a local device would make use of an application (SrvDscApp) and an SDP client; similarly, the remote device would utilise an SDP server and database. These mechanisms and processes are inherent within ESDP and provide the same capabilities as previously discussed.

We now turn our attention to the components that make up the new UPnP device architecture and, more specifically, how each component operates with the components of the Bluetooth protocol stack. Put simply, devices that embody this architecture facilitate services through control protocols, which form the highest layer in the UPnP device architecture—see Figure 18-1 as our first example. Devices that are making use of the services of another device are referred to as *control points*; these are also referred to as our local and remote devices. The control protocol interfaces to higher-layers, such as a user interface, which provides information about the device. This information is then encoded in a variety of formats by the device architecture layer using the *Simple Service Discovery Protocol* (SSDP), *General Event Notification Architecture* (GENA) and the *Simple Object Access Protocol* (SOAP). This is then delivered to the *Hypertext Transfer Protocol* (HTTP) layer through a variety of mechanisms, such as standard HTTP, *Multicast* HTTP (HTTPMU) or *Unicast* HTTP (HTTPU).

Earlier, we touched upon the two possible implementations available for a UPnP device architecture: L2CAP-based or IP-based. In Figure 18-2, we illustrate the components that make up our L2CAP-based solution. UPnP uses the connection-orientated transport mechanism inherent within L2CAP, where an Asynchronous Connectionless (ACL) peer-to-peer connection is used to transport data over the air-interface. When you compare the L2CAP-based and IP-based implementations, you will notice the difference in protocol usage (compare Figure 18-2, Figure 18-3 and Figure 18-4).

The IP-based solution is twofold: either through the *LAN Access Profile*, Chapter 10 or the *PAN Profile*, Chapter 16. Both solutions utilise the *User Datagram Protocol* (UDP) and the *Transmission Control Protocol* (TCP) over an IP stack. In the scenario offered to

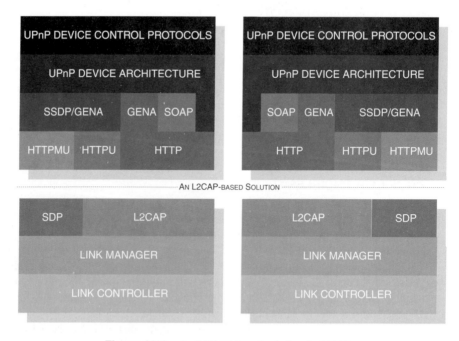

Figure 18-2   An L2CAP-based solution for ESDP.

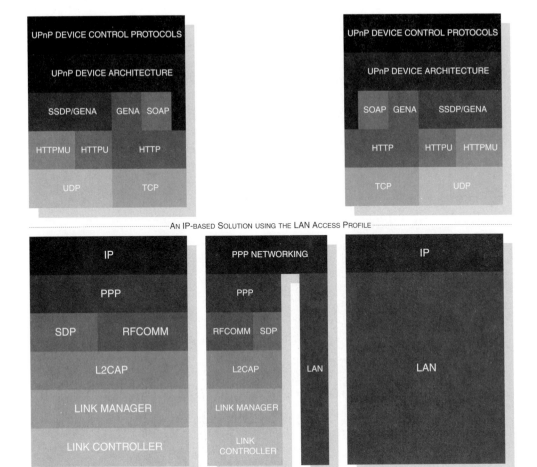

Figure 18-3   An IP-based Solution using the LAN Access Profile, for ESDP.

us by the LAN Access Profile, a *data terminal* (DT) device will typically request the services of a *LAN Access Point* (LAP). If the DT device supports ESDP, then UPnP can discover other UPnP services using the SSDP and GENA mechanisms. The LAP does not necessarily have to understand UPnP. We illustrate the architecture for the IP-based solution using the LAN Access Profile in Figure 18-3.

Similarly, the PAN Profile allows a *PAN User* (PANU) to seek *Network Access Points* (NAPs) or *Group Ad-hoc Networks* (GNs) and will then subsequently utilise the UPnP device architecture though SSDP and GENA to discover other UPnP-enabled services. The NAP and GN do not necessarily have to understand UPnP. In both cases, fur-

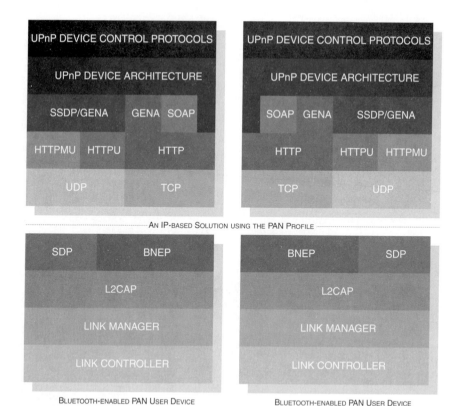

Figure 18-4   An IP-based Solution using the PAN Profile, for ESDP.

ther information pertaining to services, control and presentation can then be offered. We illustrate the architecture for the IP-based solution using the PAN Profile in Figure 18-4.

In Figure 18-5, we provide a conceptual illustration representing the dependencies that make up the IP-based solution using the PAN Profile for ESDP; the areas that are shaded are relevant to this profile. As you can see, the profile depends upon the basic functionality offered to us by the *Generic Access Profile*, Chapter 2 and the *Service Discovery Application Profile*, Chapter 3.

In Figure 18-6, we provide a conceptual illustration representing the dependencies that make up the IP-based solution using the LAN Access Profile for ESDP; the areas that are shaded are relevant to this profile. As you can see, the profile depends upon the basic functionality offered to us by the *Generic Access Profile*, Chapter 2, the *Service Discovery Application Profile*, Chapter 3 and the *Serial Port Profile*, Chapter 6.

In Table 18-1, clarification is provided with regard to the roles used within the context of this profile. In general, *DeviceA* represents the initiating party and *DeviceB* represents the accepting party. The terms are often used interchangeably when describing specific operations in various contexts and are provided here for reference.

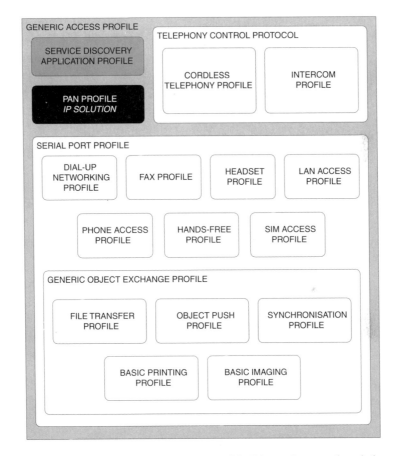

Figure 18-5   The dependent components of the Bluetooth protocol stack that make up the IP solution for the PAN Profile. The areas that are shaded are relevant to this profile.

18.3   USER EXPECTATIONS

In this section, we turn our attention to the features for devices that use ESDP for UPnP. In the first instance, SDP shall learn of the services that are available; in the second instance, a discovery of UPnP services shall be made. The various features that form the two solutions within ESDP create the scenarios available to a user.

18.3.1   L2CAP-based Solution

Devices utilising an L2CAP-based solution would create a peer-to-peer connection, where the initiating device will learn of the services the remote device has available. In Table 18-2, we identify the list of features that are supported during the operation of an L2CAP-based solution; features are marked with *Mandatory* (M) or *Optional* (O).

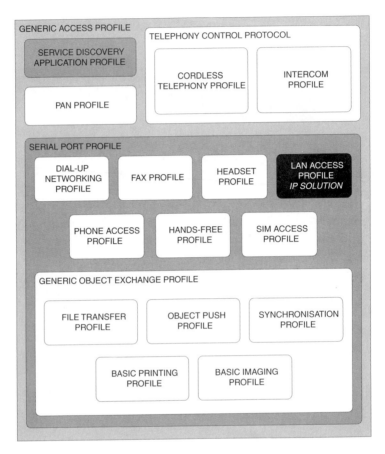

Figure 18-6   The dependent components of the Bluetooth protocol stack that
make up the IP solution for the LAN Access Profile. The areas
that are shaded are relevant to this profile.

18.3.1.1   Discover and Advertise UPnP Services.   The local and remote devices
are in a state where services can be discovered. In a discovery operation, the local device
initiates the discovery of UPnP services that are in radio range. Conversely, the remote
device will advertise any UPnP services. These services are created using the SDP service
records, where information relating to the specific nature of the service on offer can be
advertised. In both instances, the existing SDAP mechanisms will be used to facilitate the
exchange of information.

18.3.1.2   Operating UPnP Services.   When UPnP services have been discovered, a user may now choose to make use of the advertised services. A peer-to-peer connection is established when the user wishes to make use of an advertised service. The
UPnP device architecture components that make up an L2CAP-based solution shall be

Table 18-1   The list of behavioural characteristics that are typical for this profile.

CONFIGURATION	ROLE	DESCRIPTION
DeviceA	Local	This device is capable of initiating a service discovery making use of an application and a SDP client.
	Initiator	This configuration describes the device that instigates the original connection or the device that wishes to initiate communication over an existing link.
DeviceB	Remote	A remote device is capable of accepting connections from a local device and responding to the inquiries made. The remote device relies upon a SDP server and database.
	Acceptor	This configuration describes the process of the device accepting the initiated communication from DeviceA.

used to transport information between devices. The *Bluetooth Device Address* (BD_ADDR) will be used to uniquely identify the participating devices, whereas an IP address would be used in an IP-based solution.

18.3.2   IP-based Solutions

Devices utilising an IP-based solution, using the PAN or LAN Access Profiles would create a peer-to-peer connection, where the initiating device will learn of the services the remote device has available. In Table 18-3, we identify the list of features that are supported during the operation of the PAN and LAN Access Profiles; features are marked with *Mandatory* (M) or *Optional* (O).

The discovery, advertising and operational features of the L2CAP-based solution are similar to the features available to the IP-based solution. Both solutions require

Table 18-2   The list of features that are available for an L2CAP-based solution.

FEATURE	LOCAL	REMOTE
Discover UPnP Services	M	O
Advertise UPnP Services	O	M
Operation of UPnP Services	M	M

Table 18-3   The list of features that are available for an IP-based solution to include the PAN and LAN Access Profiles.

FEATURE	LOCAL	REMOTE
Discover IP Support	M	M
Discover UPnP Services	O	O
Advertise UPnP Services	O	O
Operation of UPnP Services	M	O

discovery and creation of service records to appropriately advertise the services. The exception here is that the IP-based solution would inform the local device that IP-support can be obtained. The local device shall initiate a service discovery of the remote devices that are within radio range, although in this instance the local device will also learn of devices that support IP. Devices that support IP are shown using the capabilities provided by SDAP. If multiple devices are shown to have IP support, then the local device may choose to use just the one service.

18.4   SUMMARY

- ESDP extends the SDP.
- ESDP utilises the UPnP device architecture, which is used to allow devices that do not have to be Bluetooth-enabled to talk to each other.
- The UPnP architecture is made up of several new layers, which can be built upon L2CAP or an IP-based solution.
- An L2CAP-based solution takes communication directly from the HTTP layer.
- An IP-based solution makes use of an IP-stack and further uses UDP and TCP; HTTP then sits above UDP and TCP.
- From a user's perspective, several features are available: discovery of IP-support and UPnP services, advertising of relevant UPnP services and the control and operation of such devices.

19

The Basic Printing and Basic Imaging Profiles: An Overview

19.1 INTRODUCTION

Both the *Basic Printing* and *Imaging Profiles* depend upon the functionality offered to us by the underlying *Generic Object Exchange Profile* (GOEP). You may recall that the GOEP establishes a level of basic functionality, abstracted from the *Object Exchange Protocol* (OBEX). These basic set of features and procedures establish the functionality already offered to us in the *Object Push*, Chapter 12, *File Transfer,* Chapter 13 and *Synchronisation Profiles*, Chapter 14.

The Basic Printing and Imaging Profiles use the inherent push and pull capabilities that are provided in the GOEP. Using the basics of this functionality, we can then realise simple, but effective usage models, which we will discuss later in this chapter.

In Figure 19-1, we illustrate the components that make up the OBEX functionality. At the upper-edge of the OBEX component, implementers will establish function primitives in the form of an *Application Programming Interface* (API); you may recall from the *Generic Object Exchange Profile*, Chapter 11, we had a very similar discussion. In the same way, other OBEX-related usage models would utilise an API, so too will the Basic Printing and Imaging Profiles.

You will find that generic procedures are established for all devices during interoperability. Furthermore, the behaviour of such devices is governed with simple rules that relate to the methods of sending and retrieving data, initialisation and certain characteristics with

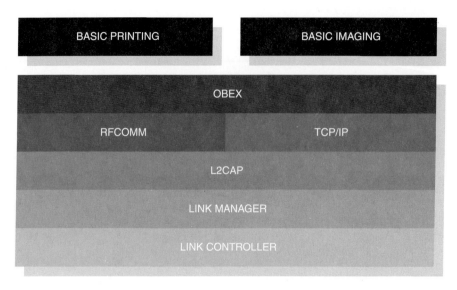

Figure 19-1   The various protocols that form the building blocks of the Object Exchange specific usage models. It is at the upper-edge of the OBEX component that function primitives are created which, in turn, will be used by the higher-applications to realise the usage models.

regard to their discoverability. It is these features and procedures that are used to establish commonality between products, which will ultimately achieve a cohesive user experience.

19.2   THE BASIC PRINTING PROFILE

Bluetooth enables the ad-hoc nature of connecting to devices with ease and transparency. The Basic Printing Profile adds yet another usage model to its already incredible portfolio. This profile allows a user to create an ad-hoc connection to a Bluetooth-enabled printer which, in turn, enables all types of devices, such as *notebooks, Personal Digital Assistants* (PDAs) and *mobile phones* to send a variety of documents to a printer.

In Figure 19-2 and Figure 19-3, we illustrate the scenarios that are available to the Basic Printing models. In the illustrations, we demonstrate that a notebook, PDA and mobile phone are all capable of communicating to a Bluetooth-enabled printer. In Figure 19-4, we show a printer server product, which in turn connects the printer to a network.

19.2.1   Usage Models

This section considers our existing usage model through scenarios that may be typical for the Basic Printing Profile. We begin by exploring the existing model where a notebook, mobile phone, PDA or similar device communicates and establishes a connection with a Bluetooth-enabled printer.

Figure 19-2 The new Basic Printing Profile enables notebook users to interoperate their devices with a Bluetooth-enabled printer.

Figure 19-2 and Figure 19-3 illustrate our existing usage models. The role of the notebook acting as a sender initiates a one-to-one communications link with the Bluetooth enabled printer device. The Basic Printing Profile usage model prescribes short-range and ad-hoc communication typically found in an environment where individuals wish to quickly and transparently print documentation.

The printer may be capable of supporting a variety of formats, which include emails, plain or formatted text, structured information, such as vCard and vCalendar, and a variety of downloadable information from an intranet or from the Internet.

19.2.2 Profile Principles

The Basic Printing Profile provides two new roles: a *Sender* and a *Printer*. The Sender device is capable of pushing data objects to the Printer, whereas the Printer provides the facility to allow the Sender device to push the data objects. In this context, a data object refers to a document type, which we will discuss in more detail later.

In our introduction, we touched upon the notion that a set of features and procedures exist to help govern the operation of Bluetooth-enabled printer devices. At the heart of this profile, the GOEP establishes core capabilities that are realised in the Basic Printing Profile. A task such as object push takes place between the sender and the printer, where documents can then be printed.

Figure 19-3 The new Basic Printing Profile also enables mobile phone and
PDA users to interoperate their devices with a Bluetooth-
enabled Printer.

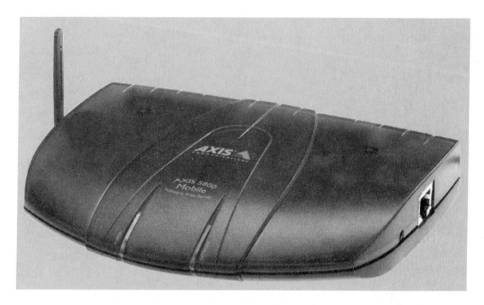

Figure 19-4   A Bluetooth-enabled Printer Server. (Courtesy of Axis
                   Communications.)

There are no fixed master-slave roles. This allows either device the freedom to initiate
and terminate a connection, although typically the sender will initiate the primary connection, where inquiry and device discovery procedures are undertaken. Participating devices
in this profile must be required to perform bonding, pairing authentication and encryption
when requested to do so. Their use within this profile is optional. Printers should not engage OBEX authentication if the sender device does not have a user interface. In general,
OBEX authentication should not be supported. In Figure 19-5, we illustrate the specific
Bluetooth protocol stack components that are dependent upon a compliant profile.

In Table 19-1, clarification is provided with regard to the roles used within the context of this profile. In general, *DeviceA* represents the initiating party and *DeviceB* represents the accepting party. The terms are often used interchangeably when describing
specific operations in various contexts and are provided here for reference.

In Figure 19-6, we provide a conceptual illustration representing the dependencies
that make up the Basic Printing Profile; the areas that are shaded are relevant to this profile. As you can see the profile depends upon the basic functionality offered to us by the
Generic Access Profile, Chapter 2, the *Service Discovery Application Profile*, Chapter 3
and the *Serial Port Profile*, Chapter 6.

19.2.3   User Expectations

19.2.3.1   Printer Modes and Services.   A printer device is capable of supporting
four modes of operation, which are illustrated in Table 19-2. You will also notice that
these modes are depicted as *Optional* (O) or *Mandatory* (M). An administrator who

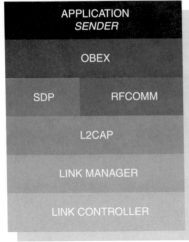
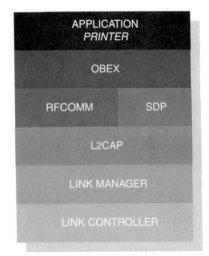

Figure 19-5 The components of the Bluetooth protocol stack are shown illustrating the newer components of the Basic Printing Profile.

Table 19-1 The list of behavioural characteristics that are typical for this profile.

CONFIGURATION	ROLE	DESCRIPTION
DeviceA	Sender	This device is capable of pushing data objects to the Printer. The sender establishes a relationship with the server before data objects can be sent; the sender will typically initiate the connection.
	Initiator	This configuration describes the device that instigates the original connection or the device that wishes to initiate communication over an existing link.
DeviceB	Printer	A printer provides object exchange capability, which in turn allows sender devices to push data objects to the printer. This type of device would typically accept connections from the sender.
	Acceptor	This configuration describes the process of the device accepting the initiated communication from DeviceA.

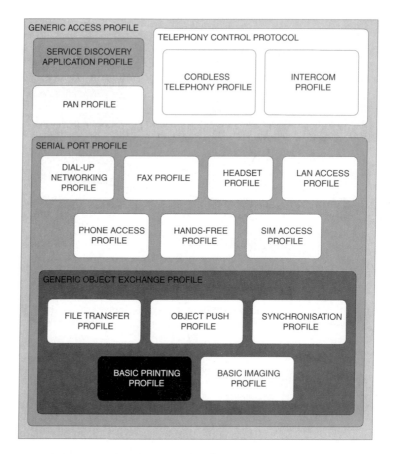

Figure 19-6   The dependent components of the Bluetooth protocol stack that
make up the Basic Printing Profile. The areas that are shaded
are relevant to this profile.

wishes to restrict or provide open access to the printer services may configure these
modes of operation. In Table 19-3, we illustrate the types of printing services that are
available.

   19.2.3.2   Configuration.   The Basic Printing Profile provides an optional configuration capability to allow users to control and select printing features. Using a *Reflected
User Interface* (RUI) for Bluetooth-enabled printers, documents and other objects can be
controlled or their current printing status can be tracked. This method applies to both direct and reference printing services.
   Similarly, administrators may use the RUI to place the printer into one of the modes
as illustrated in Table 19-2. In Figure 19-7, we illustrate a sample interface, where in this
instance a user has control over the object he or she is about to print.

Table 19-2   The list of modes that a printer device is capable of supporting.

MODE	SUPPORT	DESCRIPTION
Offline	O	This mode may describe the printer as non-discoverable or in a state where it cannot be accessed.
Private Online	O	A printer device operating in this mode would restrict general users from making use of the services. For a user to be able to connect to the device, he or she must know the Bluetooth Device Address.
Public Online	M	This mode allows all users to discover and connect to the device using a general or limited inquiry.
Bonding	M	This mode denotes that the printer is ready to pair with the sender.

19.2.3.3   Printing a Single Object.   A user wishing to make use of a printer will undertake inquiry and device discovery procedures to learn of the devices that are in radio range. The service discovery procedure will allow the user to determine if the printer is capable of supporting a *Simple Push Transfer*. When a user wishes to print a document, he or she will use existing procedures inherent within any word-processing application. The sender device will create a connection with the printer, where pairing and authentication may be required.

Objects are pushed to the printer using the *Simple Push Transfer Model*. This particular model provides the basic printing capability that any Bluetooth-enabled printer should support, although a printer may also support more complex print operations, as we will learn in the following section.

You may recall from the *Generic Object Exchange Profile*, Chapter 11, that an OBEX `Put` operation is used to instigate a push procedure from one device to another. When the sender device wishes to print an object, it will use the `Put` operation to send the object to the printer. In Figure 19-8, we illustrate the sequence of events that occur for a direct service; in this instance, the sender pushes the entire object to the printer. In a

Table 19-3   The list of modes that a printer device is capable of supporting.

SERVICE	DESCRIPTION
Direct	The object to be printed is located on the sender device.
Reference	In this service, the object to be printed is located in another area, such as a network, but the sender device is capable of providing a reference to it.

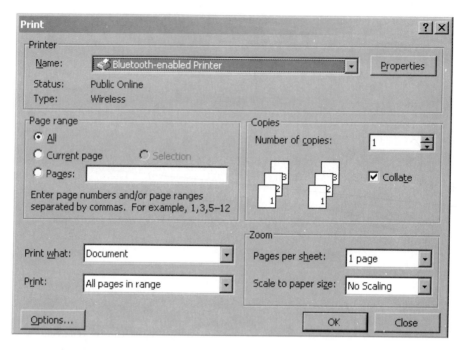

Figure 19-7   The screen shot shows the typical options that are available to a
user when he or she wishes to print a document.

reference service, the sender will indicate to the printer where it can find it. The printer
will then locate the object and then print it.

19.2.3.4 Printing Multiple Objects.   A user wishing to make use of a printer
will undertake inquiry and device discovery procedures to learn of the devices that are in
radio range. The service discovery procedure will allow the user to determine if the
printer is capable of supporting a *Job-Based Transfer*. When a user wishes to print a doc-

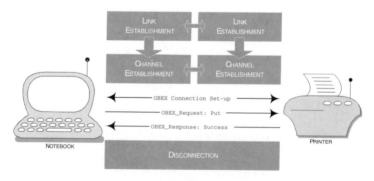

Figure 19-8   The sequence of events that occur when the sender wishes to
use the direct service which, in turn, prints a single object.

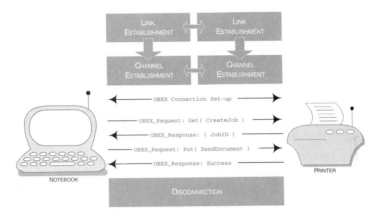

Figure 19-9   The sequence of events that occur when the sender wishes to
perform more complex print operations.

ument, he or she will use existing procedures inherent within any word-processing application. The sender device will create a connection with the printer, where pairing and authentication may be required.

The nature of a Job-Based Transfer is to enable more complex print operations. The
sender and printer exchange instructions using the *Simple Object Access Protocol*
(SOAP), which is encoded within an OBEX operation. The mechanisms underlying a
Job-Based Transfer Model differ from the Simple Push Transfer Model. The Job-Based
Transfer Model is capable of supporting direct and reference printing, but manages more
complex object types, as well as providing the sender with control and status capabilities.
The activities that ensure a print activity also differ from the Simple Push Transfer Model.
Our simple transfer involved an OBEX Put operation, where either the document was
handed-over or a reference to the document location was passed onto the printer device.
In our Job-Based transfer, a *session* is first created with the printer device. Once establishing a session with the printer, the sender device can then perform a series of activities
using commands which, in turn, instruct the printer.

A session with the printer has to be first established with an encoded SOAP operation within the OBEX Get request. The CreateJob command is used to establish a session with the printer, where the encoded OBEX Get response contains a JobID. In
establishing this session, a document can then be sent for printing. This is done using the
OBEX Put operation with an encoded SendDocument command. In Figure 19-9, we
illustrate the sequence of events that occur for this particular service.

19.3   THE BASIC IMAGING PROFILE

The diversity of Bluetooth-enabled devices that are continually becoming available is ac-
celerating at an amazing rate. With the introduction of many Bluetooth-enabled Printer
kits already appearing on the market, we will surely see the emergence of imaging-related

Figure 19-10   The new Basic Imaging Profile enables notebook users to interoperate their devices with a Bluetooth-enabled imaging device.

products. One such manufacturer has released Bluetooth-enabled digital still and moving cameras. The Basic Imaging Profile also adds another usage model to an incredible portfolio. This profile allows a user to create an ad-hoc connection to a Bluetooth-enabled imaging device which, in turn, enables all types of devices, such as notebooks, PDAs and mobile phones to send and retrieve a variety of image formats.

In Figure 19-10 and Figure 19-11, we illustrate the scenarios that are available to the Basic Imaging models. In the illustrations, we demonstrate that a notebook, PDA and mobile phone are all capable of communicating to a Bluetooth-enabled imaging device.

19.3.1   Usage Models

This section considers our existing usage model through scenarios that may be typical for the Basic Imaging Profile. We begin by exploring the existing model where a notebook, mobile phone, PDA or similar device communicates and establishes a connection with a Bluetooth-enabled imaging device.

Figure 19-10 and Figure 19-11 represent our existing usage models. The notebook acting as an imaging initiator, initiates a one-to-one communications link with the Bluetooth-enabled imaging device. The Basic Imaging Profile usage model prescribes short-range

Figure 19-11   The new Basic Imaging Profile also enables mobile phone and PDA users to interoperate their devices with a Bluetooth-enabled imaging device.

and ad-hoc communication typically found in an environment where individuals wish to quickly and transparently exchange images between Bluetooth-enabled devices.

The usage models extend beyond those illustrated in our earlier figures. A mobile phone is capable of retrieving images from an imaging device, where the image can then be used as a background image or forwarded onto a colleague or friend. In similar scenarios, a notebook device is capable of sensing a digital camera in radio range and automatically retrieves the images that it has stored. Furthermore, a notebook at a conference can be used to pass images to a Bluetooth-enabled projector.

19.3.2   Profile Principles

The Basic Imaging Profile provides two new roles: an *Imaging Initiator* and an *Imaging Responder*. The Initiator device is capable of initiating an image feature, whereas the Responder provides the capability to respond and support such imaging features.

In our introduction, we touched upon the notion that a set of features and procedures exist to help govern the operation of Bluetooth-enabled imaging devices, which support the Basic Imaging Profile. At the heart of this profile, the GOEP establishes core capabilities that are realised in the Basic Imaging Profile. A task such as object pull and push takes place between the initiator and the responder, where various types of images can be exchanged.

There are no fixed master-slave roles. This allows either device free to initiate and terminate a connection, although typically the initiator device will initiate the primary connection, where inquiry and device discovery procedures are undertaken. Participating devices in this profile must be required to perform bonding, pairing authentication and encryption when requested to do so, but their use within this profile is optional. Imaging devices should not engage OBEX authentication if the initiator device does not have a user interface. In general, OBEX authentication should not be supported. In Figure 19-12, we illustrate the specific Bluetooth protocol stack components that are dependent upon a compliant profile.

In Table 19-4, clarification is provided with regard to the roles used within the context of this profile. In general, *DeviceA* represents the initiating party and *DeviceB* represents the accepting party. The terms are often used interchangeably when describing specific operations in various contexts and are provided here for reference.

In Figure 19-13, we provide a conceptual illustration representing the dependencies that make up the Basic Printing Profile; the areas that are shaded are relevant to this profile. As you can see, the profile depends upon the basic functionality offered to us by the *Generic Access Profile*, Chapter 2, the *Service Discovery Application Profile*, Chapter 3 and the *Serial Port Profile*, Chapter 6.

19.3.3   User Expectations

19.3.3.1   Imaging Modes and Features.   An imaging responder device is capable of supporting several modes of operation, which include the ability to be non-discoverable, limited discoverable or general discoverable; each mode is user configured. Furthermore, an imaging device may also be configured to operate with a certain capability; these are

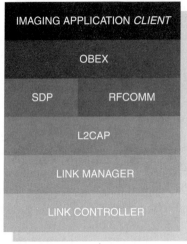
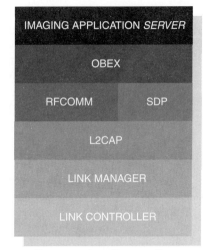

Figure 19-12   The components of the Bluetooth protocol stack are shown illustrating the newer components of the Basic Imaging Profile.

Table 19-4   The list of behavioural characteristics that are typical for this profile.

CONFIGURATION	ROLE	DESCRIPTION
DeviceA	Imaging Initiator	This device is capable of pulling and pushing image objects to the imaging device. The initiator establishes a relationship with the responder before image objects can be sent; the initiator will typically initiate the connection.
	Initiator	This configuration describes the device that instigates the original connection or the device that wishes to initiate communication over an existing link.
DeviceB	Imaging Responder	A responder provides image object exchange capability which, in turn, allows an initiator device to push image objects to the responder. This type of device would typically accept connections from the initiator.
	Acceptor	This configuration describes the process of the device accepting the initiated communication from DeviceA.

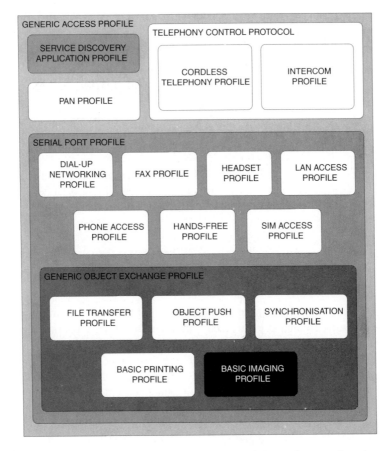

Figure 19-13 The dependent components of the Bluetooth protocol stack that make up the Basic Printing Profile. The areas that are shaded are relevant to this profile.

shown in Table 19-5. You will also notice that these capabilities are depicted as *Optional* (O) or *Mandatory* (M).

The Basic Imaging Profiles supports several imaging features. As indicated in Table 19-5, the generic imaging capability should be supported as a minimum, where the support of other capabilities is considered optional. These features are now discussed in the following sections.

19.3.3.2 Image Push and Pull. An imaging initiator device is capable of pushing an image object to an imaging responder using four commands. These commands form part of the OBEX push procedure using the `Put` operation. Conversely, an OBEX pull procedure is accomplished through the use of a `Get` operation.

Table 19-5   The list of modes that a imaging device is capable of supporting.

CAPABILITY	SUPPORT	DESCRIPTION
Imaging	M	As a minimum, a device should support generic imaging capabilities, where an image can be pushed or pulled.
Capturing	O	The ability to capture an image through a Bluetooth wireless optical interface.
Printing	O	A device that is capable of printing images through a Bluetooth wireless interface.
Display	O	Using a Bluetooth-enabled projector device as an example, we can create the ability to transfer image objects to this device, where they are subsequently displayed.

The image push feature places an image onto the image responder, where a `PutImage` command is encoded within an OBEX `Put` operation. In this instance, the only possible outcome is for the responder to print the image. However, the imaging initiator should determine if these capabilities are supported using a `GetCapabilities` command encoded within the OBEX `Get` operation; this is illustrated in Figure 19-14.

In a typical scenario, an imaging responder will be a Bluetooth-enabled digital still or moving camera, where the imaging initiator has already determined its capabilities using the `GetCapabilities` command. With a series of images available on the responder, a `GetImage` command is used to retrieve the image from the responder and is shown in Figure 19-15. When an image is no longer required, the image initiator device may choose to delete an image using the `DeleteImage` command encoded within an OBEX operation.

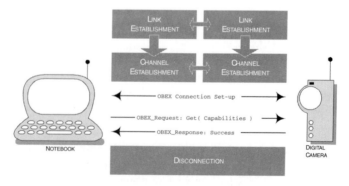

Figure 19-14   The sequence of events that occur when the initiator wishes to determine the capabilities of the responder.

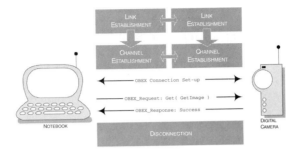

Figure 19-15   The sequence of events that occur when the sender wishes to retrieve an image from a responder device.

19.3.3.3   Advanced Imaging Printing.   The *Advanced Imaging* features prescribe specifically how an image should be printed. Parameters during a typical push operation, such as the number of copies or how an image should be laid out on a page, are not provided. In the first instance, an imaging initiator would determine if the responder is capable of these advanced features using the `GetCapabilities` command. To commence the printing process, the OBEX `Put` operation is encoded with the `StartPrint` command.

An additional function is also provided to allow the printing of images where in some cases the image may be too large and the buffering capabilities of the responder device may not be sufficient to accommodate it in its entirety. As such, the `GetPartial-Image` command, which is encoded in an OBEX operation, is used to retrieve the image in sections. In Figure 19-16, we illustrate the sequence of events that occur during the operation of sending a large image to an imaging responder device.

19.3.3.4   Archiving Images.   We have discussed many features of the Basic Imaging Profile; to complement this, an *Automatic Archiving* process is used by the imaging responder to automatically retrieve images. In a typical scenario, a digital camera would instigate a connection, where all the images that it has stored can be downloaded onto a notebook.

As usual, the `GetCapabilities` command is used to determine if the device supports the feature, where further commands, such as `GetImageList`, `GetImage`, `DeleteImage` and `StartArchive` are also used. In Figure 19-17, we demonstrate the events that occur during this process.

19.3.3.5   Remote Camera.   With the ability to already connect and determine the capabilities of an imaging responder, the initiator may undertake control of the responder device. The *Remote Camera* feature allows the initiator to control the monitoring of an image and then to subsequently control the triggering of the shutter.

The feature provides further commands to enable the remote control capability. Through the use of `GetMonitoringImage`, `GetImageProperties` and `GetImage`, images can be previewed before they are actually captured and transferred. In Figure 19-18, we demonstrate the events that occur during this process.

19.3.3.6   Remote Display.   In our final examination of the features available within the Basic Imaging Profile, we look at the capabilities provided to us through the *Remote Display*.

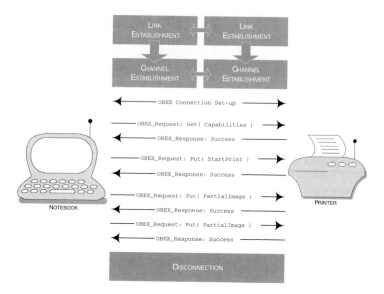

Figure 19-16   The sequence of events that occur when the initiator wishes to use the responder device to print a large image. In this illustration, the notebook assumes the role of imaging initiator and the printer takes on the role of the image responder.

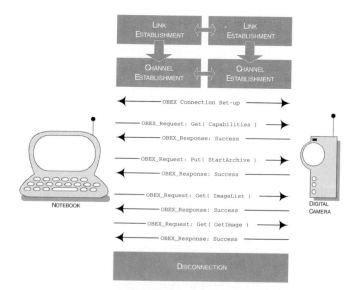

Figure 19-17   The sequence of events that occur when the initiator wishes to use the responder device to retrieve a set of images. In this illustration, the camera assumes the role of imaging initiator and the notebook takes on the role of the image responder.

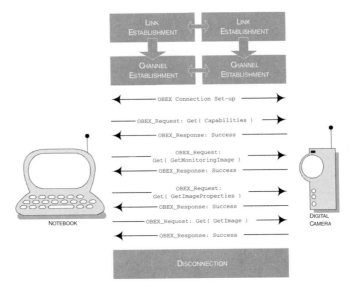

Figure 19-18 The sequence of events that occur when the initiator wishes to take control of the remote camera device

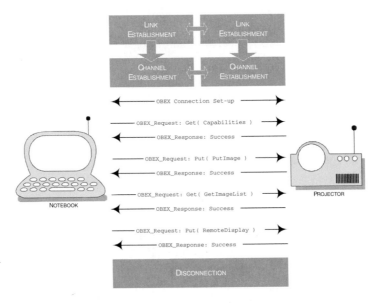

Figure 19-19 The sequence of events that occur during the operation of using the imaging responder to display images.

An imaging initiator has the inherent core functionality to push images to an imaging responder which, in turn, the imaging responder has the capability to display the images that it receives.

The sequence, as illustrated in Figure 19-19, shows that an image is transferred to the responder using the `PutImage` command, encoded within an OBEX `Put` operation. In the sequence, the `GetCapabilities` is used to determine if the responder supports the display feature and then issues the `PutImage` command. In the next event, the `Remote-Display` command is then issued to actually instruct the responder to display the image.

19.4   SUMMARY

- The Basic Printing and Imaging Profiles provide seamless and transparent connections to Bluetooth-enabled printers and imaging responders, respectively.
- Both profiles are dependent upon the capabilities provided in the GOEP.
- Both profiles form part of the new set of profiles that are currently being drafted for adoption into the specification.
- Authentication and encryption is optional for both the printing and imaging.
- There are no strict master-slave roles operated by these profiles.
- When operating the printing profile, a number of Bluetooth-enabled devices can connect and make use of the services provided, where two new roles are created: sender and printer.
- Similarly, a range of Bluetooth-enabled devices can connect to and make use of the imaging responder features. Two new roles are also created: an imaging initiator and an imaging responder.
- The printing profile operates four modes of operation: offline, private online, public online and bonding.
- A Bluetooth-enabled printer may operate direct or reference printing.
- During the operation of the direct printing feature, the sender device pushes the object directly to the printer.
- The reference printing feature offers the printer a reference for it to locate the intended object for printing.
- A Bluetooth-enabled printer is capable of managing single and multiple object types and can be configured for more complex operations.
- The imaging profile provides four core capabilities: imaging, capturing, printing and display.
- The imaging feature is the basic functionality offered to us as a minimum by any device supporting the Basic Imaging Profile.
- Capturing allows an imaging initiator to retrieve images dynamically.
- Using the printer capability allows the initiator to send images directly to a printer, where segmentation is offered if the image is too large.
- Using the display feature allows an initiator to send images to a responder that has display capabilities.

Appendix A

Link Manager Protocol Reasons

Table A-1 The list of LMP error reasons.

	REASON	DESCRIPTION
1	0x05	Authentication Failure
2	0x06	Key Missing
3	0x0A	Max Number Of SCO Connections To A Device (The maximum number of SCO connections to a particle device has been reached. All allowed SCO connection handles to that device are used.)
4	0x0D	Host Rejected due to limited resources (The host at the remote side has rejected the connection because the remote host did not have enough additional resources to accept the connection.)
5	0x0E	Host Rejected due to security reasons (The host at the remote side has rejected the connection because the remote host determined that the local host did not meet its security criteria.)
6	0x0F	Host Rejected due to remote device is only a personal device (The host at the remote side has rejected the connection because the remote host is a personal device and will only accept the connection from one particle remote host.)
7	0x10	Host Timeout (Used at connection accept timeout, the host did not respond to an incoming connection attempt before the connection accept timer expired.)
8	0x13	Other End Terminated Connection: User Ended Connection
9	0x14	Other End Terminated Connection: Low Resources
10	0x15	Other End Terminated Connection: About to Power Off

(continued)

Table A-1   The list of LMP error reasons. *Continued.*

	REASON	DESCRIPTION
11	0x16	Connection Terminated by Local Host
12	0x17	Repeated Attempts (An authentication or pairing attempt is made too soon after a previously failed authentication or pairing attempt.)
13	0x18	Pairing Not Allowed
14	0x19	Unknown LMP PDU
15	0x1A	Unsupported LMP Feature
16	0x1B	SCO Offset Rejected
17	0x1C	SCO Interval Rejected
18	0x1D	SCO Air Mode Rejected
19	0x1E	Invalid LMP Parameters
20	0x1F	Unspecified Error
21	0x20	Unsupported parameter value
22	0x21	Switch not allowed
23	0x23	LMP Error Transaction Collision
24	0x24	PDU not allowed
25	0x25	Encryption mode not acceptable
26	0x26	Unit key used
27	0x27	QoS not supported
28	0x28	Instant passed
29	0x29	Pairing with unit key not supported

Appendix B

Host Controller Interface Reasons

Table B-1 The list of HCI error reasons.

	REASON	DESCRIPTION
1	0x01	Unknown HCI Command
2	0x02	No Connection
3	0x03	Hardware Failure
4	0x04	Page Timeout
5	0x05	Authentication Failure
6	0x06	Key Missing
7	0x07	Memory Full
8	0x08	Connection Timeout
9	0x09	Max Number Of Connections
10	0x0A	Max Number Of SCO Connections To A Device
11	0x0B	ACL connection already exists
12	0x0C	Command Disallowed
13	0x0D	Host Rejected due to limited resources
14	0x0E	Host Rejected due to security reasons
15	0x0F	Host Rejected due to remote device being only a personal device
16	0x10	Host Timeout

(continued)

Table B-1 The list of HCI error reasons. *Continued.*

	REASON	DESCRIPTION
17	0x11	Unsupported Feature or Parameter Value
18	0x12	Invalid HCI Command Parameters
19	0x13	Other End Terminated Connection: User Ended Connection
20	0x14	Other End Terminated Connection: Low Resources
21	0x15	Other End Terminated Connection: About to Power Off
22	0x16	Connection Terminated by Local Host
23	0x17	Repeated Attempts
24	0x18	Pairing Not Allowed
25	0x19	Unknown LMP PDU
26	0x1A	Unsupported Remote Feature
27	0x1B	SCO Offset Rejected
28	0x1C	SCO Interval Rejected
29	0x1D	SCO Air Mode Rejected
30	0x1E	Invalid LMP Parameters
31	0x1F	Unspecified Error
32	0x20	Unsupported LMP Parameter Value
33	0x21	Role Change Not Allowed
34	0x22	LMP Response Timeout
35	0x23	LMP Error Transaction Collision
36	0x24	LMP PDU Not Allowed
37	0x25	Encryption Mode Not Acceptable
38	0x26	Unit Key Used
39	0x27	QoS is Not Supported
40	0x28	Instant Passed
41	0x29	Pairing with Unit Key Not Supported
42	0x2A–0xFF	Reserved for Future Use

Glossary & Definitions

3G

Third generation. A term used to describe the next generation of wireless communication; see *UMTS*.

3-in-1 Phone

A usage scenario, which describes the additional capability provided for mobile phones. Typical scenarios can be found in the *Cordless Telephony* and *Intercom Profiles*.

802.11b

This standard is part of a family of other specifications, which offer varying solutions of wireless connectivity to a fixed LAN. Like the Bluetooth specification, 802.11b operates at the 2.4GHz range and is often referred to as Wi-Fi. It has been developed by a working group of the IEEE.

Acceptor

A device that accepts a connection from an initiating device. In a typical scenario, a master will *initiate* a connection and the slave will *accept*; see *Initiator*.

Access Point

A Bluetooth enabled device that allows multiple users to make use of the remote service. In one example, a LAN Access Point allows multiple users to access the services of a connected LAN.

Access Point Kiosk	This refers to the provision of data services through a *public access point* in the same way that a telephone service is presently provided.
ACL	Asynchronous Connectionless; see *ACL Link*.
ACL Link	A packet-switched connection between two devices that is used to carry generic data. ACL data is transmitted over the air-interface in unreserved bandwidth. ACL data is retransmitted to ensure data integrity; see *SCO* and *SCO Link*.
Active Mode	see *Mode (Active)*.
AM_ADDR	Active Member Address. When a slave is active, it is assigned a 3-bit address to uniquely distinguish it from other slaves; see *Mode (Active)*, *Mode (Park)*, *AR_ADDR* and *PM_ADDR*.
AG	Audio Gateway; see *Audio Gateway*.
AP	Access Point; see *Access Point*.
APDU	Application Protocol Data Unit.
API	Application Programming Interface. An API would be used to allow developers to interface to an underlying piece of software. For example, a Bluetooth protocol stack would provide an API. In turn, the API would allow developers to create end-user functionality with ease and transparency.
APK	Access Point Kiosk; see *Access Point Kiosk*.
APR	Access Point Roaming.
AR_ADDR	Access Request Address. An address used by the slave during a slave-initiated unpark procedure; see *Mode (Active)*, *Mode (Park)*, *AM_ADDR* and *PM_ADDR*.
ASCII	American Standard Code for Information Interchange. A format used to exchange text files between computers.
ATR	Answer to Reset.
AT	Attention.
AT Command	AT Commands are used as part of the emulation and driver components of the protocol stack. They enable control and signalling of a connected device. For example, an external call can be created and terminated in the dial-up networking model.

Authenticated (Device)	An authenticated device indicates that two devices have undertaken the process of authentication; see *Authentication*.
Authentication	Authentication is performed to allow verification of "who" is at the other end. This encompasses using a stored link key or the use of a Bluetooth Passkey.
Authorisation	A process that grants access to a user of a Bluetooth device.
Audio Driver	A component of the Bluetooth protocol stack that provides AT Command management for signalling and control. An audio driver may be used on a headset device to allow it to control the gateway; see *Audio Emulation*.
Audio Emulation	A component of the Bluetooth protocol stack that provides AT Command management for signalling and control. An audio emulator may be used on a mobile phone to allow it to be controlled by the headset device; see *Audio Driver*.
Audio Gateway	A Bluetooth-enabled device that provides duplex audio support for connected headset devices.
Baseband	see *LC*.
BB	Baseband; see *LC*.
BD_ADDR	Bluetooth Address. A unique Bluetooth address based upon the same philosophy as the MAC address. The BD_ADDR is made up of a 48-bit address, which is further broken down into three parts: a 24-bit LAP field, a 16-bit NAP field and an 8-bit UAP field; see *MAC*.
BIP	Basic Imaging Profile.
BNEP	Bluetooth Network Encapsulation Protocol. A protocol created to be used with the PAN specific profiles. It facilitates transportation of networking protocols over Bluetooth enabled devices.
Bond	see *Bondable* and *Bonding*.
Bondable	A term used to describe the state of a device, which has learned of other devices in radio range. With an intent to connect to a remote device, the user may choose to pair with it in order to make use of its services; see *Pairing* and *Bonding*.
Bonding	A term used to describe the intention of another user to connect to a Bluetooth device. A user who has performed device and service discovery procedures, places those discovered devices into a bondable state,

where pairing is performed to authenticate the user to access its services; see *Pairing* and *Bondable*.

BPP   Basic Printing Profile.

BQA   Bluetooth Qualification Administrator.

BQB   Bluetooth Qualification Body.

BQP   Bluetooth Qualification Programme.

BQRB   Bluetooth Qualification Review Board.

BQTF   Bluetooth Qualification Test Facility.

BTAB   Bluetooth Technical Advisory Board.

CAC   Channel Access Code; see *Channel Access Code*.

Call Control   An entity of the TCS protocol, which manages and co-ordinates the connection and termination of speech and data calls between two devices; see *Connectionless TCS*, *Group Management* and *Supplementary Services*.

CC   Call Control; see *Call Control*.

CHAP   Challenge-Handshake Authentication Protocol. A secure procedure that allows a user to make use of a remote service. In a typical relationship a server issues a challenge, where the client device responds with a calculated value. The server verifies this value before access is granted. CHAP is considered to be more secure than PAP.

Channel Access Code   This access code is used to identify a piconet and is included in all packets for that piconet; see *Device Access Code* and *Inquiry Access Code*.

Channel (Logical)   Bluetooth defines five logical channel types: an LC channel, LM channel, a UA channel, a UI channel and a US channel. The LC and LM are two control channels, whereas UA, UI and US transport asynchronous, isosynchronous and synchronous data, respectively.

Channel (Physical)   This channel represents the physical over the air-interface connection that exists between Bluetooth devices.

Channel (Secure)   A physical channel becomes secure when encryption is used over the air-interface. Other users are not able to eavesdrop on the ensuing conversation.

CHV

Card Holder Verification. This refers to a PIN that is used to access a SIM; see *PIN* and *SIM*.

CLI

Command Line Interface.

CL^1

Connectionless; see *Connectionless*.

CL^2

Connectionless TCS; see *Connectionless TCS*.

Client

In a client-server relationship, a client requests information from a server; see *Server*.

CO

Connection-orientated; see *Connection-orientated*.

CoD

Class of Device. A series of attributes that form part of an FHS packet which, in turn, is used to characterise a type of device. For example, such devices may include mobile phones, notebooks and so on.

CODEC

COder DECoder. A process that combines analogue to digital conversion and digital to analogue conversion in a single-chip.

Common Link Key

A term used to describe a key that is shared between two Bluetooth devices, prior to authentication taking place. A link key may have been derived from the Bluetooth Passkey; see *Link Key*.

COM Port

see *RS232* and *Serial Port*.

Connection (Bluetooth)

The term connection is used to describe the state of two Bluetooth devices and to indicate an active conversation; see *ACL Link* and *SCO Link*.

Connectionless

A term used to describe a connection that is not associated with any particular device. For example, a broadcast is described as connectionless; see *Connection-orientated*.

Connection-orientated

A connection state that is used to describe the specific direction of data to a Bluetooth device. For example, L2CAP may use a connection-orientated channel to direct data to a specific protocol that may reside above it; see *Connectionless*.

Connectionless TCS

A characteristic of the TCS protocol, which allows control data to be communicated to other devices without the need to establish a TCS connection; see *Call Control*, *Group Management* and *Supplementary Services*.

Connection (Secure)

This reference is used to describe the nature of a secure Bluetooth connection between two devices. These devices are capable of supporting *encryption* and, as such, no third-party is able to eavesdrop on the ensuing conversation; see *Encryption*.

Control Point   A term used within ESDP that is used to describe a device that is making use of the services provided by another.

CTP   Cordless Telephony Profile.

CTS   Clear To Send.

Current Link Key   This refers to the link key that is currently in use by two Bluetooth devices. A link key may have been derived from the Bluetooth Passkey; see *Link Key*.

CVSD   Continuous Variable Slope Delta. A process that is used to help reduce the probability of errors when transmitting audio-specific communication.

D   Direction Bit; see *Direction Bit*.

DAC   Device Access Code; see *Device Access Code*.

Data Terminal   A device that is capable of initiating a connection with a gateway in order to make use of the remote services. For example, a data terminal may access the services of a LAP, where the LAP adopts the characteristics of a gateway device; see *Gateway*.

DCD   Data Carrier Detect.

DCE   Data Communications Equipment.

DeviceA   DeviceA, represents a device that intends to initiate a connection with DeviceB; see *Initiator*, *Acceptor* and *DeviceB*.

Device Access Code   This access code is used during procedures that manage paging and responses to paging; see *Channel Access Code* and *Inquiry Access Code*.

DeviceB   DeviceB, represents the accepting party that accepts a connection from DeviceA; see *Acceptor*, *Initiator* and *DeviceA*.

Device (Connectable)   A device that has been placed into this mode is capable of allowing connections from other devices.

Device Description   A device description is used to provide meaningful information about a discovered device.

Device Discovery   see *Discovery (Device)*.

Device (Local)   see *DeviceA* and *Initiator*.

Device Name   see *Discovery (Name)*.

Device (Remote)	see *DeviceB* and *Acceptor*.
DH	Data High. An ACL packet type used for achieving high data rates.
DHCP	Dynamic Host Configuration Protocol. A networking protocol that coordinates the automatic assignment of IP addresses for use on a network.
DIAC	Dedicated Inquiry Access Code. This type of access code is used to discover Bluetooth devices with particular characteristics that are in radio range; see *Inquiry Access Code* and *GIAC*.
Direction Bit	A bit used to denote the direction of data flow between two RFCOMM peer entities. It is used in combination with the RFCOMM Server Channel to create a DLCI; see *RFCOMM Server Channel* and *DLCI*.
DISC	Disconnect.
Discoverable (General)	A Bluetooth device can be placed into a general discoverable mode, where it will respond to all inquiries without any time restriction; see *Discoverable (Limited)* and *Discoverable (Non)*.
Discoverable (Limited)	A Bluetooth device can be placed into a discoverable mode for a limited time period. When this time period expires the device is no longer available to respond to an inquiry; see *Discoverable (General)* and *Discoverable (Non)*.
Discoverable (Non)	A Bluetooth device can be placed into non-discoverable mode to restrict it being discovered from inquiring devices; see *Discoverable (General)* and *Discoverable (Limited)*.
Discovery (Device)	A procedure, which describes the mechanism used to determine the availability of other Bluetooth devices that are in radio range.
Discovery (Name)	A procedure, which describes the mechanism used to determine the names of the Bluetooth devices that are in radio range.
Discovery (Service)	A procedure, which describes the mechanism used to determine the availability of services of other Bluetooth enabled devices.
DLC	Data Link Connection. An RFCOMM active connection; see *DLCI*.
DLCI	Data Link Connection Identifier. An RFCOMM server channel number used in combination with a direction bit, which uniquely identifies the RFCOMM channel; see *RFCOMM Server Channel, Direction Bit* and *DLC*.
DM[1]	Data Medium. A packet type used to carry data only.

DM²	Disconnect Mode.
DNS	Domain Name Server. A DNS is used to enable the translation of domain names to Internet addresses.
DSR	Data Set Ready.
DT	Data Terminal; see *Data Terminal*.
DTE	Data Terminal Equipment.
DTR	Data Terminal Ready.
DUN	Dial-up Networking.
DUNP	Dial-up Networking Profile.
DV¹	Data Valid.
DV²	Data Voice. A packet capable of combining data and voice information.
EA	Extended Address.
EAP	Extensible Authentication Protocol.
Encryption	A process that is used to secure a Bluetooth connection between two devices and, as such, no third-party is able to eavesdrop on the ensuing conversation.
Encryption Key	An encryption key is generated, in part, using the *current link key* which, in turn, is used to secure the conversation between two devices; see *Current Link Key* and *Encryption*.
ESDP	Extended Service Discovery Profile.
Establishment (Channel)	This term is used to describe the establishment of a logical channel between two devices; see *Channel (Physical)* and *Establishment (Link)*.
Establishment (Connection)	This term is used to describe the establishment of a connection between two applications each residing on a Bluetooth device.
Establishment (Link)	This term is used to describe the establishment of a physical channel between two devices; see *Channel (Physical)* and *Establishment (Channel)*.
Ethernet	The most common networking protocol used on a fixed or wireless network; it is a standard governed by the IEEE.
ETSI	European Telecommunications Standards Institute.

FCOFF	Flow Control Off.
FCON	Flow Control On.
FCS	Frame Check Sequence.
FHS	Frequency Hopping Synchronisation. The BD_ADDR, clock offset and CoD are encapsulated in this data packet.
FTP	File Transfer Profile.
GAP	Generic Access Profile.
Gateway	A gateway device will typically have a remote service, which is accessed through the use of a data terminal. For example, a mobile phone, acting as a gateway will allow a data terminal device, such as a notebook to make a dial-up connection to an ISP; see *Data Terminal*.
GENA	General Event Notification Architecture.
General Discovery	see *Mode (General Discoverable)*.
General Sync	see *Mode (General Sync)*.
GIAC	General Inquiry Access Code. This type of access code is used to discover all Bluetooth devices of any type that are in radio range; see *Inquiry Access Code* and *DIAC*.
GM	Group Management; see *Group Management*.
GN	Group Network; see *Group Network*.
GOEP	Generic Object Exchange Protocol.
GPRS	General Packet Radio Services. A packet-switched wireless communications protocol that provides increased data rates for mobile phones. It also promotes a permanent connection to the Internet; see *UMTS*.
Group Management	An entity of the TCS protocol, which manages and co-ordinates the activities of a group of devices; see *Connectionless TCS*, *Call Control* and *Supplementary Services*.
Group Network	A usage model described by the PAN Profile that illustrates the ability of a PANU to create ad-hoc connections.
GSM	Global System for Mobile communications. A digital wireless communication system commonly used within mobile phones. Other wireless technologies, such as HSCSD, GPRS and UMTS are used in combination to provide faster data rates and better applications; see *HSCSD*, *GPRS* and *UMTS*.

GW   Gateway; see *Gateway*.

Hand-off   A procedure that transfers control from one device to another. For ex-
                                          ample, an office may be fitted with a series of APs. When a user roams
                                          the office, a hand-off occurs between APs: a user moves out of radio
                                          range of one AP and into radio range of another; see *Roaming*.

HAL   Hardware Abstraction Layer.

HCI   Host Controller Interface.

HDLC   High-level Data Link Control. A networking protocol that describes the
                                          end-point encapsulation of data; see *PPP*.

HF   Hands-Free.

HFP   Hands-free Profile.

Hold Mode   see *Mode (Hold)*.

Host   A device, which typically houses the higher layers of the Bluetooth
                                          protocol stack: HCI, L2CAP, RFCOMM and SDP. In one particular ex-
                                          ample a Microsoft Windows operating system may have integrated host
                                          software which, in turn, will control a host controller through a defined
                                          transport layer; see *Host Controller* and *Transport Layer*.

Host Controller   A device, which typically houses the lower layers of the Bluetooth pro-
                                          tocol stack: LC and LM. In one particular example, a PCCard and USB
                                          dongle device will contain the lower layers and the radio. When placed
                                          into a host, the host can then control the host controller enabling Blue-
                                          tooth-specific activity; see *Host*.

HS   Headset.

HSCSD   High-speed Circuit Switched Data. A wireless communication protocol
                                          that offers a higher data rate for mobile phones. HSCSD is capable of
                                          offering data rates four times faster than GSM.

HSP   Headset Profile.

HTTP   Hypertext Transfer Protocol. HTTP defines a set of rules that allow
                                          users to exchange files across the WWW.

HTTPMU   HTTP Multicast.

HTTPU   HTTP Unicast.

HV   High quality Voice. A data packet that is used to carry SCO data.

IAC	Inquiry Access Code; see *Inquiry Access Code*.
IC	Incoming Call Indicator.
ICS	Implementation Conformance Statement.
Idle Mode	see *Mode (Idle)*.
IETF	Internet Engineering Task Force.
Imaging Initiator	A device in the Basic Imaging Profile, which initiates a connection with an *Imaging Responder*. This, in turn, allows it to access the imaging capabilities of the responder device; see *Imaging Responder*.
Imaging Responder	A device in the Basic Imaging Profile, which accepts a connection from an Imaging Initiator. In turn, the responder is capable of providing imaging features to the initiating device; see *Imaging Initiator*.
Initiator	A device that initiates a connection to another device, where the remote device accepts the connection. In a typical scenario, a master will *initiate* a connection and the slave will *accept*; see *Acceptor*.
Inquiry	A procedure that is used to discover the availability of devices in radio range; see *Discovery (Device)* and *Discovery (Service)*.
Inquiry Access Code	The IAC encompasses two variations: a GIAC and a DIAC; see *GIAC, DIAC, Channel Access Code* and *Device Access Code*.
Inquiry (scan substate)	A device is said to be in a discoverable mode when it wishes to be discovered by other devices. For it to be able to respond to inquiring devices it has to be placed into an Inquiry Scan Substate; see *Mode (Discoverable)*.
Inquiry (substate)	A device is said to be discovering when it wishes to learn of the devices that are in radio range. For a device to discover other devices it has to be placed into an Inquiry Substate.
Initialisation Key	An initialisation key is generated based upon the BD_ADDR, passkey (or PIN) and the length of the PIN. This key is then used to generate the link key; see *BD_ADDR* and *PIN*.
Initialisation Sync	see *Mode (Initialisation Sync)*.
Internet Bridge	With the use of a data terminal and a gateway a wireless bridge is created. The purpose of instantiating this connection is to access the remote services of an ISP through dial-up networking. Once a connection has been authorised to the remote service, an Internet bridge is created; see *Wireless Bridge*.

IP[1]

Internet Protocol. A networking protocol that is used to transmit data over the Internet or a network; see *IPv4, IPv6, UDP* and *TCP*.

IP[2]

Intercom Profile.

IP-based Solution

A term used in the ESDP, which describes the placement of UPnP over an IP stack which, in turn, is provided by the PAN Profile or the LAN Access Profile; see *L2CAP-based Solution, ESDP* and *UPnP*.

IPCP

Internet Protocol Control Protocol.

IPS

Inter-piconet Scheduling.

IP Subnet

Internet Protocol Subnetwork. A subnet may be used to uniquely identify a particular set of computers that are connected to a network. For example, a set of IP addresses can be allocated to engineering on a particular subnet, whereas the administration department may use another subnet.

IPv4

Internet Protocol version 4. This is the most common version of IP being used today.

IPv6

Internet Protocol version 6. A new version of IP, which extends the number of available IP addresses.

IR

Infrared. A wireless technology that requires devices to be in line-of-sight.

IrDA

Infrared Data Association. An organisation that is responsible for maintaining and defining the infrared-related protocols.

IrLAP

Infrared Link Access Protocol.

IrLMP

Infrared Link Management Protocol.

IrMC

Infrared Mobile Communications.

IrMC Client

An IrMC Client initiates a connection with an IrMC Server, where IrMC Objects can be exchanged between the two devices; see *IrMC Server* and *IrMC Objects*.

IrMC Device

A typical IrMC Device may be a notebook or PC and will contain an IrMC client of Server; see *IrMC Server* and *IrMC Client*.

IrMC Object

An IrMC Client and Server device will exchange IrMC Objects. These objects typically are vNotes, vCalendar, vCard and vMessage objects; see *IrMC Server, IrMC Client, vNotes, vCalendar, vMessage* and *vCard*.

IrMC Server	An IrMC Server listens for and accepts connections from an IrMC Client. An IrMC Client will request an IrMC Object from the IrMC Server; see *IrMC Client* and *IrMC Object*.
IrOBEX	Infrared Object Exchange. This defines the protocol that allows IrMC Client and Server devices to exchange IrMC Objects. The protocol is portable enough to be used within Bluetooth applications.
ISDN	Integrated Services Digital Network. A standard for digital communication over traditional copper wire. This type of network provides an increase in the delivery of web page orientated content offering speeds of up to 128Kb/s.
ISM	Industrial Scientific Medicine. A radio frequency band that operates at 2400 to 2483.5 MHz and is the adopted frequency for Bluetooth-enabled devices.
ISP	Internet Service Provider. A company that specialises in providing businesses and home users with dial-up connections to gain access to the Internet.
IT	Information Technology.
ITU	International Telecommunications Union.
ITU-T	The Telecommunications standardisation division of the ITU.
IXIT	Implementation Extra Information for Testing.
Known (Device)	A term used to describe that current state of a device. A device is known when it has responded to an inquiry.
L2CAP	Logical Link Control and Adaptation Protocol. A protocol that supports multiplexing, packet segmentation and reassembly.
L2CAP-based Solution	A term used in the ESDP, which describes the placement of UPnP over the L2CAP layer within the Bluetooth protocol stack; see *IP-based Solution*, *L2CAP*, *ESDP* and *UPnP*.
LAN	Local Area Network. A LAN is a localised collection of computers that are connected together. Data is transported over the network using protocols such as Ethernet, TCP and IP; see *Ethernet*, *TCP* and *IP*.
LAN Access Point	A Bluetooth device that provides networking services to connected data terminal devices.
LAP[1]	Lower Address Part. A 24-bit portion of the BD_ADDR; see *BD_ADDR*, *NAP* and *UAP*.

LAP²   LAN Access Point; see *LAN Access Point.*

LAP³   LAN Access Profile.

Laptop (Computer)   see *Notebook.*

LC   Link Controller; see *Link Controller.*

LCP   Link Control Protocol.

LED   Light Emitting Diode. An electrical component that emits light and may be used as an indication for power being on.

Limited Discovery   see *Mode (Limited Discoverable).*

Link   see *SCO Link* and *ACL Link.*

Link Controller   The LC is the lowest layer in the protocol stack and forms the final end-point for the creation of connections to other Bluetooth devices. The LC is often used interchangeably with the *BB.*

Link Key   A link key is used during the authentication process and can be common or current; see *Common Link Key* and *Current Link Key.*

Link Level Enforced Security   A security mode within the Generic Access Profile, which is also referred to as Security Mode 3. During this security mode, procedures are initiated prior to link establishment; see *Establishment (Link), Non-Secure* and *Service Level Enforced Security.*

Link Manager   The link manager resides above LC and is responsible for link set-up, authentication and security.

LM   Link Manager; see *Link Manager.*

LMP   Link Manager Protocol; see *Link Manager.*

LMP Authentication   Link Manager Protocol Authentication. The LM is responsible for the management and co-ordination of the authentication process. This definition refers to the encapsulated processes that are undertaken at this level; see *Link Manager* and *Authentication.*

LMP Pairing   Link Manager Protocol Pairing. The LM is responsible for the management and coordination of the pairing process. This definition refers to the encapsulated processes that are undertaken at this level; see *Link Manager* and *Pairing.*

Local Device   see *DeviceA* and *Initiator.*

Logical Channel   see *Channel (Logical).*

LSB	Least Significant Byte or Bit.
Management Entity	A common component that sits alongside the protocol stack and co-ordinates the effort required between protocol layers; see *Protocol Stack (Bluetooth)*.
Master	A master is a device that may have initially created a Bluetooth connection, but is primarily responsible for coordinating air-interface traffic for devices in a piconet; see *Piconet* and *Slave*.
Master-Slave Switch	A procedure that occurs when a device wishes to become master of a piconet. For example, a LAP configured for multi-user mode will request a role switch. The device then assumes responsibility for co-ordinating air-interface traffic; see *Master* and *Slave*.
Maximum Frame Size	A negotiated value used to determine the maximum allowable frame to be used for a DLC; see *DLC*.
Maximum Transmission Unit	A negotiated value used to determine the maximum allowable packet size that can be transmitted.
ME[1]	Management Entity; see *Management Entity*.
ME[2]	Mobile Equipment; see *Mobile Equipment*.
MAC	Media Access Control. A MAC address is used to uniquely identify a computer that is connected to a network. The BD_ADDR in Bluetooth is based upon the MAC address; see *BD_ADDR*.
MIB	Management Information Base. A format that describes how a series of network objects can be managed by SNMP; see *SNMP*.
Mobile Equipment	A device that has similar capabilities to a gateway. To provide further context, this role is used in the PAP; see *Gateway*.
Mode (Active)	This mode relates to active devices, where a master will schedule transmissions to a slave and similarly, a slave will listen for the master. Essentially, this describes Bluetooth units that are active on a channel.
Mode (Connectable)	A device is described to be in a connectable mode if other devices can connect to it.
Mode (Discoverable)	A device is described to be in a discoverable mode if other devices can discover it.
Mode (General Discoverable)	A device may enter General Discoverable Mode if it wishes to be discovered by other devices; see *Mode (Limited Discoverable)*.
Mode (General Sync)	A term used within the Synchronisation Profile, which is used to describe an IrMC Client and Server device in a connectable mode. The

behaviour of the two devices are different: for a client device, it is used to describe an initiated connection from the server, whereas a server device accepts the connection from a client who then starts synchronisation and pairing; see *Mode (Initialisation Sync)*.

Mode (Hold)

During the operation of this mode an ACL link may temporarily be suspended to allow the device to perform other activities. It is also possible for the device to enter a low-power state, where the slave still retains its AM_ADDR; see *ACL Link, AM_ADDR, Mode (Active), Mode (Hold)* and *Mode (Sniff)*.

Mode (Idle)

A Bluetooth enabled device may undertake several activities during this mode. General and limited inquiry procedures may be performed in addition to device and name discovery.

Mode (Initialisation Sync)

A term used within the Synchronisation Profile, which is used to describe an IrMC Server device in a limited or general discoverable mode; see *Mode (Initialisation Sync)*.

Mode (Limited Discoverable)

A device may enter Limited Discoverable Mode if it wishes to be discovered by other devices for a limited period of time; see *Mode (General Discoverable)*.

Mode (Non-Connectable)

A device is described to be in a non-connectable mode if no other device can connect to it.

Mode (Non-Discoverable)

A device is described to be in a non-discoverable mode if no other device can discover it.

Mode (Non-Pairable)

A device is described to be in a non-pairable mode if no other device can pair with it.

Mode (Pairable)

A device is described to be in a pairable mode if other devices can pair with it.

Mode (Park)

A device may not want to participate on an active piconet channel, but still wishes to remain synchronised to it. In this mode, the slave releases its AM_ADDR and is assigned two new addresses: PM_ADDR and AR_ADDR. In this mode, a slave can enter a low-power state, where there is very little activity; see *Mode (Active), Mode (Hold), Mode (Sniff), AM_ADDR, PM_ADDR* and *AR_ADDR*.

Mode (Security)

A term used within the Generic Access Profile, which is used to describe a device in a particular security state. The profile defines three modes: non-secure, service level enforced security and link level enforced security.

Mode (Sniff)

In this mode, the ACL activity for a device is reduced, which also acts as a low-power mode; see *Mode (Hold)* and *Mode (Park)*.

Modem	A device, which allows you to make outgoing calls to an ISP. It takes digital signals from a notebook or PC and converts them to analogue signals in order to send them over copper cable.
Modem Driver	A component of the Bluetooth protocol stack that provides AT Command management for signalling and control. A modem driver may be used on a data terminal device to allow it to control the gateway; see *Modem Emulation*.
Modem Emulation	A component of the Bluetooth protocol stack that provides AT Command management for signalling and control. A modem emulator may be used on a mobile phone to allow it to be controlled by the data terminal device; see *Modem Driver*.
Modem (Null)	A device that allows a notebook or PC to connect to another notebook or PC. A null modem allows two DTE devices to communicate with each other.
MRD	Marketing Requirement Document.
MSB	Most Significant Byte or Bit.
MSC	Modem Status Command.
MS Switch	Master-Slave Switch; see *Master-Slave Switch*.
MTU	Maximum Transmission Unit; see *Maximum Transmission Unit*.
Multiple-point	A configuration within the TCS protocol that allows one Bluetooth-enabled device to communicate with multiple devices that are in radio range over an L2CAP connectionless channel. The TCS protocol also supports a single-point configuration; see *Single-point*.
NAP[1]	Network Access Point; see *Network Access Point*.
NAP[2]	Non-significant Address Part. A 16-bit portion of the BD_ADDR; see *BD_ADDR*, *LAP* and *UAP*.
NetBIOS	Network Basic Input/Output System. A piece of software that allows various computers connected to a LAN to create a peer network which, in turn, allows each computer connected to communicate with one another.
Network Access Point	A usage model described by the PAN Profile that illustrates the ability of a PANU to access the services available through a NAP.
Non-secure	A security mode within the Generic Access Profile, which is also referred to as Security Mode 1. During this security mode, no security

procedures are initiated; see *Service Level Enforced Security* and *Link Level Enforced Security*.

Notebook (Conputer)   A portable and battery operated PC; also called a *laptop*.

NSC   Non-supported Command.

OBEX   Object Exchange. A protocol that is based upon IrOBEX and facilitates the exchange of data objects between a client and server device.

Object Store   A secure container used to store objects when they are transferred during an OBEX operation; see *OBEX*.

OpCode   Operation Code.

Open Source   A term that refers to the open availability of source code; as such other developers can improve and modify it to meet with their own development expectations.

OPP   Object Push Profile.

OS   Operating System. A piece of software loaded onto a PC or an embedded device; as such, the OS interacts with applications and hardware.

Packet   A term often used interchangeably throughout the Bluetooth specification to describe the nature of a data structure. Such data structures include an RFCOMM frame, a signalling message from the TCS protocol, an SDP PDU or an OBEX operation.

Page (Scan)   A device in this state will periodically transmit the DAC in order to attract the attention of the remote device. If the remote device wishes to be connected, then it will enter a page scan substate and will respond accordingly.

Page (Scan substate)   During a Page Scan state, a DAC is transmitted to attract the attention of the remote device. The remote device will enter a Page Scan Substate if it wishes to be connected to and will respond accordingly; see *Page (Scan)*.

Paired (Device)   A device that has exchanged link keys and is now ready to begin the process of authentication; see *Link Key* and *Authentication*.

Pairing   A device is pairing when it is exchanging and creating link keys with another device it intends to connect to; see *Link Key*.

PAN[1]   Personal Area Network.

PAN[2]   Personal Area Networking. This reference is usually made to describe the personal collection of devices that may typically surround an office environment. A user may have a notebook, LAN Access Point and a Bluetooth-enabled printer. This collection of devices for a user would form their PAN.

PAN Profile	Personal Area Network Profile.
PANU	Personal Area Network User.
PAP	Phone Access Profile.
Park Mode	see *Mode (Park)*.
Passkey (Bluetooth)	see *PIN*.
Payload	A term often used to describe a data structure containing instructions for a peer device.
PC	Personal Computer.
PCCard	Personal Computer Card; see *PCMCIA*.
PCM	Pulse Code Modulation. A digital method for transmitting voice data.
PCMCIA	Personal Computer Memory Card International Association. An organisation that promotes the standard for credit card-sized devices that typically fit into a notebook.
PD	Programme Directive.
PDA	Personal Digital Assistant. A personal organiser that provides calendar, phonebook and other information storage and retrieval for personal or business use.
Physical Channel	see *Channel (Physical)*.
Piconet	An ad-hoc collection of Bluetooth devices, where one device behaves as a master and the other connected devices are slaves; see *Slave*, *Master* and *Scatternet*.
PIM	Personal Information Management.
PIN	Personal Identification Number. A secret number, used to authenticate with other Bluetooth devices. At the user interface level, the user will be prompted to enter a *Passkey*; see PIN_{UI} and PIN_{BB}.
PIN_{BB}	A PIN value that is represented at the baseband level; see *PIN* and PIN_{UI}.
PIN_{UI}	A PIN value that is represented at the user-interface level; see *PIN* and PIN_{BB}.

PM_ADDR

Parked Member Address. A unique address that is assigned to a slave that is parked. This address is used in the master-initiated unpark procedure; see *Mode (Active)*, *Mode (Park)*, *AM_ADDR* and *AR_ADDR*.

PN

Parameter Negotiation.

PPP

Point-to-Point Protocol. A serial communications protocol that supports full duplex communication between two devices. HDLC may be used to encapsulate the endpoint; see *HDLC*.

PPP Client

A device that encompasses the ability to make requests from a *PPP Server*; see *PPP* and *PPP Server*.

PPP Server

A device that encompasses the ability to respond to a *PPP Client*; see *PPP* and *PPP Client*.

Pre-paired (Device)

This term describes a state of a device that has a previous history with another Bluetooth-enabled device. It describes the device as previously paired or known; see *Pairing*.

Printer

A device in the Basic Printing Profile that is capable of accepting connections from a sender device in order for it to print a document; see *Sender*.

Profile (Bluetooth)

A Bluetooth Profile utilises the capabilities provided within a Bluetooth protocol stack, which in turn provides end-user functionality and ensures interoperability and a cohesive user experience; see *Bluetooth protocol Stack*.

Protocol Stack (Bluetooth)

A Bluetooth protocol stack is a series of layers that form the end function from host controller to the host. Each component within the stack has a unique responsibility, where end-user functionality is realised with a Bluetooth Profile; see *LC*, *LM*, *HCI*, *L2CAP*, *RFCOMM SDP* and *Profile (Bluetooth)*.

PSTN

Public Switched Telephone Network. The most common collection of interconnected public telephone networks, which is capable of carrying voice and data communication.

QoS

Quality of Service.

Radio (Bluetooth)

A physical component within the Bluetooth hardware infrastructure and operated through the LC layer; it provides the capability of a device to essentially communicate with other Bluetooth enabled devices. A Bluetooth transceiver operates in the 2.4 GHz ISM band, where different countries have their individual requirements and restrictions; see *Radio (Range)*.

Radio (Range)

A Bluetooth radio is capable of transmitting and receiving data from other devices within a defined range or distance. Some devices support

	ranges of 10m and others offer ranges of up to 100m; see *Radio (Bluetooth)*.
Remote Device	see *DeviceB* and *Acceptor*.
RD	Received Data.
RFC	Request For Comments.
RFCOMM	A protocol based upon a subset of the ETSI TS 101.369 standard for Serial Port Emulation, which has been adapted for the Bluetooth specification.
RFCOMM Server Channel	A unique number, which is registered in the Service Record. It is used in combination with a Direction Bit, to identify the flow of data for that channel; see *Service Record* and *Direction Bit*.
RI	Ring Indicator.
Roaming	A device that is capable of moving between APs, where transfer of control is passed from one AP to another; see *Hand-off*.
Role	An adopted set of characteristics and capabilities that are inherent within a Bluetooth enabled device.
Role-Switch	see *Master-Slave Switch*.
RLS	Remote Line Status.
RPN	Remote Port Negotiation.
RS232	A protocol that describes how a serial interface should be addressed and how data should be transmitted and received by the connected devices; see *Serial Port* and *UART*.
RTC	Ready To Communicate.
RTR	Ready To Receive.
RTS	Ready To Send.
RUI	Reflected User Interface.
Rx	Receive.
SABM	Set Asynchronous Balanced Mode.
SAP	SIM Access Profile.
Scatternet	A collection of piconets form a scatternet; see *Piconet*.

SCO	Synchronous Connection Orientated; see *SCO Link*.
SCO Link	A symmetric connection between two devices that is used to carry audio data. Bandwidth is reserved over the air-interface to achieve greater throughput. SCO data is not retransmitted which, in, turn, ensures time integrity; see *ACL* and *ACL Link*.
SDAP	Service Discovery Application Profile.
SDDB	Service Discovery Database.
SDK	Software Development Kit. Many vendors of Bluetooth protocol stacks provide ease-of-use and transparency alleviating the complexity of a stack through the use of an API; see *Protocol Stack (Bluetooth)* and *API*.
SDP	Service Discovery Protocol.
Secure Channel	see *Channel (Secure)*.
Security Mode 1	see *Non-Secure*.
Security Mode 2	see *Service Level Enforced Security*.
Security Mode 3	see *Link Level Enforced Security*.
Sender	A role in the Basic Printing Profile that is capable of pushing objects to a Bluetooth enabled printer; see *Printer*.
Serial Port	An RS232 communications port that is part of your PC or notebook, where such devices as modems are connected.
Server	In a client-server relationship, a server responds to a client who initially requested information; see *Client*.
Service Class	A categorisation that is used to group a type of device. Such categorisations include *Networking* and *Telephony*. The CoD contains information relevant to a device and a device discovery will be used to learn of the available devices; see *Discovery (Device)*.
Service Discovery	see *Discovery (Service)*.
Service Level Enforced Security	A security mode within the Generic Access Profile, which is also referred to as Security Mode 2. During this security mode, procedures are initiated prior to channel establishment; see *Establishment (Channel)*, *Non-Secure* and *Link Level Enforced Security*.

Service Record   A collection of fields, which are used to uniquely identify a service that a Bluetooth device is capable of supporting. A service discovery procedure is used to discover the available services; see *Discovery (Service)*.

Session   In the context of a Job-Based Transfer within the Basic Printing Profile, a session is first created with a printer device before printing commences. Once a successful session has been created the sender device can print, query and request status information from the printer; see *Sender* and *Printer*.

SIG   Special Interest Group (Bluetooth).

Silent (Device)   A device may be configured for general or limited discoverability, but is unable to respond to an inquiry due to activities at the LC. When a device fails to respond because of this reason, it is said to be silent; see *Discovery (General)* and *Discovery (Limited)*.

SIM   Subscriber Identity Module. A SIM is a processor or memory chip of a specified size that is typically used within a mobile phone. Its primary role is to store addresses and phonebook information, but it also contains information relating to the user's telecom provider.

SIM Client   Subscriber Identity Module Client. A SIM Client will request from a SIM Server to use the services and files of a SIM; see *SIM* and *SIM Server*.

SIM Server   Subscriber Identity Module Server. A SIM Server provides access for a SIM Client to the services and files of a SIM; see *SIM* and *SIM Client*.

Single-point   A configuration within the TCS protocol that allows one Bluetooth enabled device to communicate with another device over an L2CAP connection-orientated channel. The TCS protocol also supports a multiple-point configuration; see *Multiple-point*.

Slave   A slave is a device that accepts an incoming connection from a master and will take instructions as to how it should co-ordinate air-interface traffic; see *Piconet* and *Master*.

SMS   Short Message Service. A text messaging service typically found with mobile phones that have GSM capability.

Sniff Mode   see *Mode (Sniff)*.

SNMP   Simple Network Management Protocol. This network protocol is used to specifically monitor and manage network objects and their related processes; see *MIB*.

SOAP[1]   Simple Object Access Protocol. A protocol that is encoded within an OBEX operation which, in turn, provides greater flexibility and complexity for printer operations; see *Sender* and *Printer*.

SOAP²	Simple Object Access Protocol. A protocol that is used in the UPnP Device Architecture for ESDP which, in turn, transports packets directly to HTTP, through multicast or unicast operations.
SP	Synchronisation Profile.
SPP	Serial Port Profile.
SS	Supplementary Services; see *Supplementary Services*.
SSDP	Simple Service Discovery Protocol.
Subnet (IP)	see *IP Subnet*.
Supplementary Services	A term used in the TCS protocol, which describes additional telephony related features that may be available to a device; see *Call Control*, *Connectionless TCS* and *Group Management*.
Sync Command	This service allows the IrMC Server to initiate synchronisation; see *IrMC Client* and *Server*.
TCS	Telephony Control Protocol Specification.
TCS-BIN	Telephony Control Protocol Specification Binary.
TCP	Transmission Control Protocol. A networking protocol that is often used in combination with an IP stack to transport data over a network. TCP may be used as an alternative to UDP. TCP offers correct sequencing of data packets and a guaranteed service; see *IP* and *UDP*.
TD	Transmit Data.
Terminal Equipment	A device that has similar capabilities to a data terminal. To provide further context, this role is used in the PAP; see *Data Terminal*.
TE	Terminal Equipment; see *Terminal Equipment*.
Transport Layer	An intermediary layer that enables a host and host controller to communicate. A developer will have access to a number of layers to include: USB, RS232, UART and PCCard; see *Host* and *Host Controller*.
Trusted (Device)	A device that has undertaken pairing and authentication is considered to be a trusted device.
Tx	Transmit.
UA¹	Unnumbered Acknowledgement.

UA²   User Asynchronous data; see *Channel (Logical)*.

UAP   Upper Address Part. An 8-bit portion of the BD_ADDR; see *BD_ADDR*, *LAP* and *NAP*.

UART   Universal Asynchronous Receiver/Transmitter. A microchip that controls the serial interface, providing the RS232 DTE interface to allow the exchange of data between devices; see *Serial Port*, *RS232* and *DTE*.

UDP   User Datagram Protocol. A networking protocol that is often used in combination with an IP stack to transport data over a network. UDP may be used as an alternative to TCP, but UDP does not offer correct sequencing of data packets nor a guaranteed service; see *IP* and *TCP*.

UI¹   User Interface.

UI²   User Isynchronous data; see *Channel (Logical)*.

UIH   Unnumbered Information with Header check.

UMTS   Universal Mobile Telecommunications Service. A 3G wireless communication packet-based protocol that aims to increase data rates in mobile phones. It is based upon GSM; because of the higher data rates possible, it will provide the potential for applications such as streaming video and digitised voice.

Unicode   A relatively new format used to allow the exchange and process of information between computers; it is also used to encode data within a software application. Unicode is a fixed-width standard for which 8-bit or 16-bit encoding can be used; see *UTF-8* and *ASCII*.

Unknown (Device)   A device that has not been discovered by another device is said to be unknown.

Un-paired (Device)   A device that has not undertaken pairing and authentication is said to be an un-paired device.

UPnP   Universal Plug and Play.

US   User Synchronous; see *Channel (Logical)*.

USB   Universal Serial Bus. A common serial interface available on most PCs, notebooks and peripheral devices, such as mice and keyboards.

User-Friendly Name   see *Discovery (Name)*.

UTF-8   A particular Unicode scheme used to encode data within a software application. The UTF-8 format is used to encode English characters that occupy one byte, whereas Asian or Arabic characters occupy two bytes; see *Unicode*.

UUID   Universally Unique Identifier.

vCard   A format and specification used to allow devices that support it to exchange business cards electronically.

vCalendar   A format and specification used to allow devices that support it to exchange calendar and appointment data electronically.

vMessage   A format and specification used to allow devices that support it to exchange email data electronically.

vNotes   A format and specification used to allow devices that support it to exchange text data electronically.

Voice Recognition   The ability of a Bluetooth device to execute instructions with a verbal command. For example, in the HSP outgoing calls can be made by verbally announcing the caller.

VR   Voice Recognition; see *Voice Recognition*.

WDM   Windows Driver Model.

Wi-Fi   Wireless Fidelity; see *802.11*.

Wireless Bridge   An instance where a wireless connection is made between two devices. A data terminal and gateway device is capable of supporting a wireless bridge.

Wireless User Group A term used within TCS that denotes a group of Bluetooth devices that support TCS. A WUG is made up of a WUG master and WUG slaves.

WLAN   Wireless Local Area Network.

WUG   Wireless User Group; see *Wireless User Group*.

WWW   World Wide Web. The embodiment of users on the Internet that are using HTTP to exchange information.

XOFF   Transmission Off.

XON   Transmission On.

References

Bluetooth Special Interest Group, "Specification of the Bluetooth System: Core," Volume 1, Version 1.1, February 2001.

Bluetooth Special Interest Group, "Specification of the Bluetooth System: Profiles," Volume 2, Version 1.1, February 2001.

Bluetooth Special Interest Group, "Bluetooth Assigned Numbers," Version 1.1, February 2001.

Bluetooth Special Interest Group, "Personal Area Networking Profile," Version 0.95a, June 2001.

Bluetooth Special Interest Group, "Bluetooth Network Encapsulation Protocol Specification," Version 0.95a, June 2001.

Bluetooth Special Interest Group, "Hands-Free Profile," Version 0.96, October 2001.

Bluetooth Special Interest Group, "Phone Access Profile," Version 0.51, August 2001.

Bluetooth Special Interest Group, "SIM Access Profile: Interoperability Specification," Version 0.70, September 2001.

Bluetooth Special Interest Group, "Bluetooth Extended Service Discovery Profile for Universal Plug and Play," Version 0.95b, March 2001.

Bluetooth Special Interest Group, "Bluetooth Device Identification," Version 0.95, November 2000.

Bluetooth Special Interest Group, "Basic Printing Profile: Interoperability Specification," Version 0.95a, October 2001.

Bluetooth Special Interest Group, "Basic Imaging Profile: Interoperability Specification," Version 0.95, September 2001.

Bluetooth Special Interest Group, "Bluetooth Personal Area Networking: Marketing Requirements Document," Version 0.9, July 2001.

Bluetooth Special Interest Group, "Bluetooth Imaging: Market and Technology Requirements Document: Phase One," Version 1.0, circa June 2000.

Bluetooth Special Interest Group, "Bluetooth Car: Marketing Requirements Document," Version 1.0, December 2000.

Bluetooth Special Interest Group, "Bluetooth Printing: Marketing Requirements Document," Version 1.2, July 2000.

Bluetooth Special Interest Group, "Qualification Program Reference Document (PRD)," Version 0.9, August 2000.

Blunk, L. and Vollbrecht, J., "PPP Extensible Authentication Protocol (EAP)," RFC 2284, Merit Network Inc., March 1998.

Bray, J. and Sturman, C. F., *Bluetooth 1.1: Connect Without Cables, Second Edition*, Prentice Hall PTR, New Jersey, USA, 2002.

Case, J., Fedor, M., Schoffstall, M. and Davin, J., "A Simple Network Management Protocol," RFC 1157, SNMP Research, Performance Systems International & MIT Laboratory for Computer Science, December 1995.

Cobb, S., "PPP Internet Protocol Control Protocol Extensions for Name Server Addresses," RFC 1877, Microsoft, December 1995.

European Telecommunications Standards Institute (ETSI), "Digital cellular telecommunications system (Phase 2+); Terminal Equipment to Mobile Station (TE-MS) multiplexer protocol (GSM 07.10 version 6.3.0)," 1999.

European Telecommunications Standards Institute (ETSI), "Digital cellular telecommunications system (Phase 2+); AT command set for GSM Mobile Equipment (ME) (GSM 07.07 version 5.6)," 1998.

McGregor, G., "The PPP Internet Protocol Control Protocol (IPCP)," RFC 1332, Merit, May 1992.

Megowan, P., Suvak, D. and Kogan, D., "IrDA Object Exchange Protocol OBEX™," Infrared Data Association, Version 1.2, March 1999.

Mettala, R., Editor, Bluetooth Special Interest Group, "Bluetooth Protocol Architecture," Version 1.0, August 1999.

Mettala, R., Editor, Bluetooth Special Interest Group, "Bluetooth PC Card Transport Layer," Version 1.0, August 1999.

Miller, B. A. and Bisdikian, C., *Bluetooth Revealed*, Prentice Hall PTR, New Jersey, USA, 2001.

Postel, J. "Transmission Control Protocol: DARPA Internet Program Protocol Specification," RFC793, Information Sciences Institute, September 1981.

Postel, J., "Internet Protocol: DARPA Internet Program Protocol Specification," RFC791, Information Sciences Institute, September 1981.

Simpson, W., Editor, "The Point-to-Point Protocol (PPP)", STD 50, RFC 1661, Daydreamer, July 1994.

Simpson, W., Editor, "PPP in HDLC Framing," STD 51, RFC 1662, Daydreamer, July 1994.

Simpson, W., "PPP Challenge Handshake Authentication Protocol (CHAP)," RFC 1994, Daydreamer, August 1996.

Suvak, D. et al., "Specifications for Infrared Mobile Communications (IrMC)," Infrared Data Association, Version 1.1, March 1999.

The Internet Mail Consortium, "vCalendar: The Electronic Calendaring and Scheduling Exchange Format," Version 1.0, September 1996.

The Internet Mail Consortium, "vCard: The Electronic Business Card," Version 1.0, September 1996.

The Universal Plug and Play Forum (www.upnp.org) "Universal Plug and Play Architecture," Version 1.0, June 2000.

Zorn, G. and Cobb, S., "Microsoft PPP CHAP Extensions," RFC 2433, Microsoft Corporation, October 1998.

About the Author

Dean Anthony Gratton has worked within the software engineering arena for close to fifteen years. His interest in wireless technology led him to form his own consultancy in the late '90s, where he witnessed firsthand the evolution of Bluetooth technology. He has personally worked as a consultant for a number of leading organisations, including TDK Systems Europe, Alcatel Microelectronics, Plantronics and 3Com Europe, during which time he became editor of the LAN Access Profile and was an active member of the PAN Working Group. He is accredited as a contributor on the latest Specification of the Bluetooth System: Profiles v1.1, and his work on defining new aspects of the Bluetooth technology has been patented. Dean's outside areas of interest have led him to study for both a diploma in Counselling and a BSc (Hons) in Psychology. More recently, he was appointed Technical Director of Camden Publications Ltd., a company that produces a variety of consumer and business-to-business related magazines.

INDEX

C

F

H

S

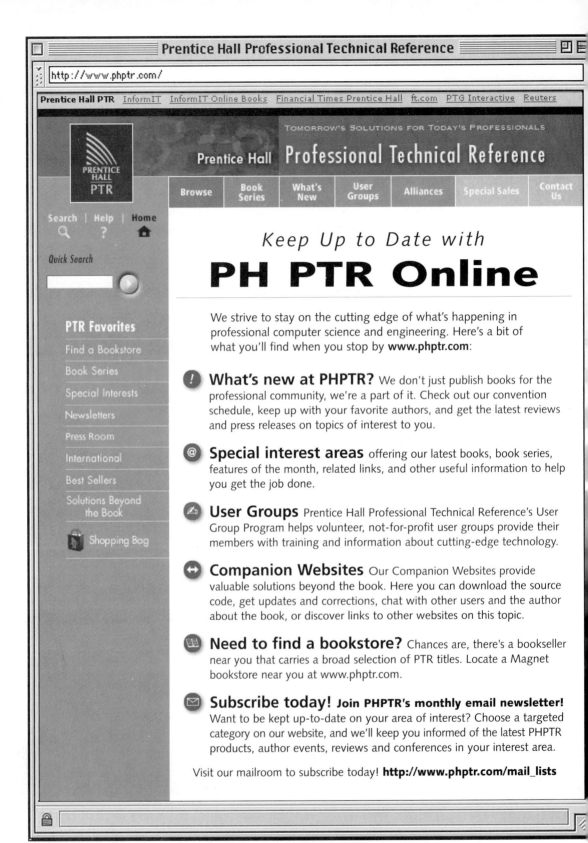